Contemporary Social Problems

SIXTH EDITION

Vincent N. Parrillo

William Paterson University

PEARSON

Boston ▪ New York ▪ San Francisco
Mexico City ▪ Montreal ▪ Toronto ▪ London ▪ Madrid ▪ Munich ▪ Paris
Hong Kong ▪ Singapore ▪ Tokyo ▪ Cape Town ▪ Sydney

To Beth,
for her support and understanding

Senior Editor: Jeff Lasser
Series Editorial Assistant: Sara Owen
Marketing Manager: Krista Groshong
Composition and Prepress Buyer: Linda Cox
Manufacturing Manager: JoAnne Sweeney
Cover Coordinator: Linda Knowles
Photo Researcher: Helane Manditch-Prottas
Editorial-Production Coordinator: Mary Beth Finch
Editorial-Production Service: The Book Company
Electronic Composition: Publisher's Design and Production Services, Inc.

For related titles and support materials, visit our online catalog at www.ablongman.com

Between the time Website information is gathered and then published, it is not unusual for some sites to have closed. Also, the transcription of URLs can result in unintended typographical errors. The publisher would appreciate notification where these errors occur so that they may be corrected in subsequent editions.

Library of Congress Cataloging-in-Publication Data

Parrillo, Vincent N.
    Contemporary social problems / Vincent N. Parrillo.—6th ed.
        p.   cm.
    Includes bibliographical reference and index.
    ISBN 0-205-42076-1
    1. Sociology.   2. Social problems.   3. United States—Social conditions—1980–   I. Title.

HM585 .P33   2005
361.1—dc22

                                                                        2004044292

Printed in the United States of America

10 9 8 7 6 5 4 3 2 1   09 08 07 06 05 04

List of Features

Contents

CHAPTER 2   The Individual in Modern Society / 29

CHAPTER 3   Population and the Environment / 55

CHAPTER 5 **Power, Work, and the Workplace / 119**

CHAPTER 7 **Gender Inequality and Heterosexism / 191**

CHAPTER 13   **Alcohol and Drug Abuse / 387**

Preface

In the three years since publication of the last edition of this book, unfolding events and social changes have redirected public thinking about some of our social problems. The death and destruction on 9/11 and our subsequent wars in Afghanistan and Iraq have heightened American anxiety about further terrorist attacks, leading to changed behaviors in air travel, city visits, and attendance at large public events. The 2003 Supreme Court decisions on affirmative action and on gay rights have pleased some and angered others. The weakened economy in recent years caused many forms of hardship, including lost jobs, erosion in the value of retirement accounts, and limited opportunities for new college graduates. Corrupt behavior in corporate giants like WorldCom and Enron ended their existence, costing stockholders many millions of dollars and workers their jobs. Health-care costs continue to skyrocket, and millions remain without insurance coverage, while many insured are denied important tests and treatment.

Other trends contribute to public misgivings. Megamergers and advances in technology and telecommunications encourage corporate downsizing, displacing skilled workers while generating new jobs that typically involve low pay and limited upward mobility. Governments at every level struggle to balance budgets without overburdening taxpayers. Meanwhile, crime, drugs, shortcomings in the educational system, environmental disasters, homelessness, population growth, poverty, racism, sexism, single-parent families, declining urban infrastructure, and violence all contribute to create major differences between the American ideal and American reality.

What's Unique About This Book

- Theory and content are interwoven in every chapter.

- Every chapter contains four perspectives: Functionalist, Conflict, Feminist, and Interactionist.

- Chapter 2 offers a macro perspective on modern society and its discontents stimulating the sociological imagination by illustrating the sociological process of connecting individual problems with social conditions.

- Every photograph—carefully selected for vivid impact—contains captions with thought-provoking questions to stimulate critical thinking skills.

- The Thinking About the Future sections in each chapter bring students "into" the topic, asking them a series of questions about what they envision for their future and what steps they would take to resolve a problem. As a reflective exercise while reading, a springboard for class discussion, or a vehicle for writing assignments, this unique feature stimulates the sociological imagination and also helps develop critical thinking skills.

- Each chapter has a Social Constructions of Social Problems feature revealing how problems may come into being, get recognized, become defined, and generate responses based on those definitions.

- Each chapter has a Globalization of Social Problems feature with cross-cultural comparisons to broaden the student's perspective and provide information about the similarities or dissimilarities of that problem.

- The book has a companion Web site offering directly relevant Internet readings and exercises on a chapter-by-chapter basis.

The Basic Approach

To establish a practical explanatory framework, in each chapter I apply sociological theoretical analysis to the factual content. Some other texts use only a Conflict perspective, but my approach is eclectic, offering Functionalist, Conflict, Feminist and Interactionist analyses, because I believe nonmajors should be acquainted with all viewpoints.

Instructors partial to one particular theoretical orientation can easily emphasize it in their classroom teaching while using this book as a source of supporting and contrasting ideas. Indeed, many past reviewers and adopters often have labeled the book's orientation as Functionalist, Conflict, or Interactionist, depending on their own predilections. No one should find the book antithetical to a particular theoretical view, yet the book does not indulge in amorphous sociological analyses. Readers will find more theoretical commentary and consistent application here than in most other texts.

Each chapter begins with a "facts" page of provocative data to pique reader interest, and a brief sociohistorical context section places each social problem in perspective. However, the primary focus is on present-day U.S. problems, their interrelationships, and the reasons they persist.

The text also stresses how social definitions of problems affect perceived causes and attempted cures. Integrating sociological theory and current knowledge draws the student into fuller understanding; for this purpose, boxed inserts illustrate or augment the topics under consideration.

I have a strong interest in stimulating each student's "sociological imagination." This term, coined by C. Wright Mills fifty years ago, refers to people's ability to see how their personal experiences and the changes within society are interrelated. Two unique features of this book—Chapter 2 and the Thinking About the Future sections in each chapter—employ what Mills called "the interplay of individuals and society, of biography and history, of self and world."

Chapter 2 looks at the individual in society and examines the problems of anomie and alienation caused by the modern world. Because individuals tend to define the troubles they endure in terms of blame and individual weakness, rather than in terms of historical and societal change, they need to see the impact of society on individuals' expectations about the quality of their lives. This chapter helps students gain sociological insights into the social arrangements and structural conditions that form people's self-images and self-evaluations and create life changes. Included is a discussion of the Postmodern orientation, which is a natural extension of the notion of the individual's "lostness" in modern society.

To maintain a flowing, readable style, I opted to run footnote citations at the back of the book instead of interrupting the text with parenthetical citations. Besides the boxed inserts mentioned previously, pedagogical aids include chapter summaries, annotated bibliographies, key terms, and an end-of-book glossary. An instructor's manual is available, with chapter overviews, chapter outlines, key terms, suggestions for class projects and activities, Internet exercises, and an annotated bibliography of relevant media materials. The manual also provides an objective test file and a set of essay/discussion questions for each chapter. Other instructional resources available with the text include: TestGen Computerized Testing Program; the Allyn & Bacon Social Problems Website (http://www.ablongman.com/socprobs) with practice test questions for this text; a Powerpoint presentation; Research Navigator Guide for Sociology; the Sociology Tutor Center; and a series of Allyn and Bacon/ABC News Sociology Videos (*Poverty and Stratification, Race and Ethnicity, Gender, Deviance,* and *Aging*). Ask your Allyn and Bacon/Longman representative for details.

New in the Sixth Edition

This new edition contains a number of changes.

First, all chapters contain new, detailed information from the 2000 census and subsequent government reports, the latest public opinion polls to reveal what people think about various societal issues, as well as the results of research published since the last edition.

Second, sufficient time has elapsed for us to evaluate the outcome of the 1996 welfare reform act and how the recent recession affected those living on the margins of society. A new section in the poverty chapter reports those findings and gives an assessment as to whether the liberals or conservatives were correct in their predictions about the consequences of this legislation.

Third, throughout the book, whenever recent events impacted on the subject matter in a particular chapter, relevant new informational and discussion material appears. Some of these subjects are terrorism; the Supreme Court's decisions on affirmative action, gay rights, and school vouchers; the crisis in the lack of health insurance coverage for millions; and increased use of club drugs, particularly ecstasy, and the consequences of their growing popularity.

Acknowledgments

First I want to acknowledge the role played by John and Ardyth Stimson, my co-authors in the first three editions, as well as by Mary Lou Mayo, who wrote the family chapter in those same editions. Although I have significantly revised those efforts at many levels, residuals of their ideas still remain.

As always, my association with the Allyn and Bacon editorial team has been a pleasant, cooperative, and productive experience. Thanks to Karen Hanson, Editor-in-Chief, whose strong support has made this edition a reality, and to Jeff Lasser, series editor, for signing the project. Thanks also to all the other Allyn and Bacon team members.

I also thank the past users of the book for their many helpful suggestions and comments. Special thanks goes to reviewers of this edition: Bart Grossman, University of California at Berkeley; Janice Joseph, Richard Stockton College of New Jersey; Cathy Loupy, Idaho State University; and Monte Rivera, SUNY Farmingdale. Also, I'd like to thank the reviewers of past editions: Lee Frank, Community College of Allegheny County; A. Levine, El Camino College; Keith Durkin, McNeese State University; Earl Schaeffer, Columbus State Community College; Mark Rubenfeld, Loyola University New Orleans; Angelika Hoeher, SUNY Agricultural and Technical College at Cobleskill; Lee D. Millar Bidwell, Longwood College; Anne R. Peterson, Columbus State Community College; Mary Jo Huth, University of Dayton; Lawrence S. Soloman, North Carolina State University; Robert H. Well, Florida State University; and Stuart A. Wright, Lamar University.

Vincent N. Parrillo
William Paterson University
Wayne, NJ 07470
E-mail: parrillov@wpunj.edu
http://www.wpunj.edu/cohss/sociology/parrillo

1

The Sociology of Social Problems

Facts About the Study of Social Problems

- People define social problems in terms of their values and perceptions.

- Solutions often follow ideas of what is right instead of scientific analysis.

- Interconnectivity makes solutions difficult; to fix one problem, we must alleviate others as well.

- The false belief that social problems are natural or inevitable is a strong deterrent to solving them.

- Sometimes we simply minimize social problems, ignoring real social conflict and damage.

- Scientific analysis helps us isolate and interpret facts of social life that we might otherwise miss.

Social problems affect everyone. Some of us encounter problems of unequal treatment and opportunity virtually every day as a result of our race, religion, gender, or low income. Others experience problems in their lives from chemical dependency, family dissolution and disorganization, technological change, or declining neighborhoods. Crime and violence affect many people directly, while others live fearfully in their shadow, threatened further by the possibility of terrorism.

Because so many actual and potential problems confront us, it is difficult to decide which one affects us most severely. Is it the direct threat of injury during a terrorist attack? Is it the indirect threat caused by industrial pollution that may poison us or destroy our physical environment? Or does quiet but viciously damaging gender, age, class, racial, or ethnic discrimination have the most far-reaching effect? Do the problems of cities affect us if we live in the suburbs? Do poorer nations' problems with overpopulation affect our quality of life?

Which of these problems can be solved? Do we have scientific evidence about their causes, or are we distracted by myths and traditional but unfounded explanations? Do we act with sufficient understanding?

Knowing specific data about the incidence of a problem is not enough. We need to probe beyond our assumptions about causes and effects to determine scientifically the underlying causes and the social costs of failing to remedy them. Reporting about social problems is journalism, and speculating over what to do about them is philosophy; but scientifically investigating and analyzing them is sociology—the "stuff" of this book.

Definitions and Solutions

Part of the challenge of studying social problems and trying to find ways to eliminate them lies in making sense of their conflicting definitions and solutions. Sometimes society changes its definitions about what is or is not a problem, even within a person's lifetime, requiring people to overcome their own socialization and adjust their behavior. And sometimes the "solution" to a problem creates new problems. Working with several social problems discussed in subsequent chapters, we'll look at some examples of the above points that may help us to understand them more fully.

Changing Definitions

Yesterday's rules about sexual expression and relationships no longer apply. As U.S. society evolves toward gender equality in the public and private spheres of life, the patterns of social interaction between men and women have changed. Only in this generation, for example, have "sexual harassment," "marital rape," and "date rape" come to be recognized and labeled as social problems. The "door-opening ceremony," once considered a male act of courtesy toward a female, now draws scorn from many women who view it as an act of masculine dominance. Men were once the initiators of romantic advances and sometimes persisted in their efforts, as recommended by the old saying, "Faint heart never won fair maiden." Now, such actions may be identified as "unwelcome advances" and thus a form of sexual harassment. Once admired for exhibiting a take-charge approach, men now gain greater esteem from women for demonstrating sensitivity and respect for women. Men now try to achieve a balance of behavior that is strong but not too strong, sensitive and caring but not ineffectual. Women now attempt to strike a balance between independence and being a desirable companion.

Only in this generation have gay rights activists succeeded in changing societal definitions of homosexuality. State and federal laws now protect individuals against discrimination resulting from their sexual preference. Same-sex couples can live together openly without suffering adverse consequences to their career opportunities, rights, or privileges as a result of their alternative lifestyle; they can also adopt children, if they wish. Although many religions still condemn homosexuality as immoral, some accept it among their clergy and congregations. All minorities, including homosexuals, now have the right to take action against a "hostile environment." For example, derogatory terms or comments—which once carried no legal accountability—can now draw correction under the law.

Conflicting Definitions

Perhaps no other social issue sparks more controversy than abortion. Antiabortion groups, with the vigorous backing of the Catholic Church and other religious organizations, oppose abortion on moral grounds; their efforts to repeal all pro-abortion laws have raised fundamental questions about the nature of human life. When does life begin—at the moment of conception, or when the fetus can live outside the womb? Is abortion murder, or is it a personal matter of a woman's right to control her own body? Does an unborn baby have rights? The question of whether abortion constitutes murder depends on what definition of life you accept. Clearly, this entire matter becomes intensely personal when an unexpected pregnancy forces a woman to make a difficult decision. All the classroom and courtroom arguments on abortion—once remote, abstract, and less meaningful—suddenly loom to the forefront if you personally must face this problem.

Similarly, if taking another person's life is wrong, what about physician-assisted suicides? In two separate rulings in 1997, the Supreme Court upheld the right of states to outlaw such assistance, but it also removed the last legal obstacle to enactment of Oregon's physician-assisted suicide law, although the Bush administration continues to seek ways to overturn the state law. Are a physician-conducted abortion and a physician-assisted suicide morally distinguishable? Again, you may have little direct interest in this issue until, perhaps, a terminally ill family member seeks this means of dying.

Conflicting Solutions

Even if we agree that, except in cases of self-defense, taking another life is wrong, how should we punish the offender? Should killers be executed? Is the death penalty a just punishment or is it a barbaric practice contradictory to a civilized society? Are some killings more cruel than others? Is there a fundamental difference between a robber who fatally shoots a police officer, a mother who drowns her two children in a car in a lake, and a teenager who asphyxiates her newborn baby and then returns to the dance floor at her high school prom? Arguably, the mother and the teenager acted with premeditation, whereas the robber killed spontaneously in reaction to an unexpected encounter. Certainly, murdering innocent, helpless children is horrific; but in these three real-life events, the mother and the teenager did not face the death penalty, while the robber did, having been convicted of murder in a state that mandates the death penalty for cop killers.

"Problem" Solutions

Sometimes the solution to a problem creates new problems through overzealous enforcement, as in the laws against sexual harassment. For example, in 1996 a school principal in North Carolina decided that a six-year-old boy who kissed a girl had committed sexual harassment and kept him from his classes for a day. That same year a New York City school principal suspended a seven-year-old boy for "sexual harassment" for kissing a girl and tearing a button from her skirt. While we might define these boys' behavior as "bad" and agree that school officials should warn them that such acts cannot be tolerated, perhaps sending a note home to the parents in the hopes of a reprimand, many of us might react with amusement or scorn to the application of a phrase describing adult misconduct to the actions of schoolchildren.

College speech codes, designed to eliminate hostile environments on campus, sometimes contained far-reaching provisions, such as a ban against "inappropriate laughter." More significantly, they violated First Amendment rights to freedom of speech. Indeed, until this and other fundamental principles were incorporated into the Constitution as the Bill of Rights (the first ten amendments), this document could not receive the necessary votes for ratification. Following a 1992 Supreme Court ruling declaring unconstitutional any governmental attempt to regulate expression based on hostility or favoritism, most colleges returned to general student conduct codes instead of specific ones dealing with speech issues.

Another example of a solution creating new problems was the 1996 Communications Decency Act. Concern over the ease with which minors could access pornography on the Internet prompted Congress to pass a law making it a crime to send or display indecent material online in a way that made the material available to minors. According to a 1997 Supreme Court ruling, this law, too, violated the First Amendment. In essence, the court concluded that the government could not solve the pornography problem in a way that violated a fundamental right of U.S. citizens.

These few examples show that defining social problems and finding satisfactory solutions to them are difficult tasks. The existing social structure and our values influence which social conditions we select and whether and how we define them as social problems. Varying interpretations lead to varying (and often conflicting) solution proposals, and sometimes efforts to resolve a problem create other problems. The complexity of social problems—with regard to their perception, actuality, and desired resolution—demands that people who would solve them bring more to the table than good intentions.

The Four Elements of a Social Problem

If you had to name the single most important social problem facing us today, what would you pick? Several candidates probably come quickly to mind, including terrorism, crime, drugs, poverty, and racism. However, identifying one as preeminent is difficult. Could any of us comfortably choose one problem as the target of all our society's immediate attention, to the exclusion of others? That's the concern of some people today who believe that the war on terrorism comes at the expense of other problem solutions. Before we proceed, we must be clear about what we mean by a social problem. We also must know that recognized social problems have the following four components:

1. They cause physical or mental damage to individuals or society.
2. They offend the values or standards of some powerful segment of society.
3. They persist for an extended period of time.
4. They generate competing proposed solutions because of varying evaluations from groups in different social positions within society, which then delays reaching consensus on how to attack the problem.

Let us examine each of these elements in greater detail.

Individual or Social Damage

City dwellers are often cynical about obtaining services from City Hall. One expression of this attitude is the saying, "The only way to get a street light installed at your busy intersection is to have a child hit by a car." Unfortunately, this is not always an unfounded attitude: government tends to respond only *after* significant damage occurs.

When assessing the damage that a problem causes to individuals, we must consider both present suffering and the loss of future opportunities. Ethnic, racial, or sexual discrimination, for example, hurts immediately through embarrassment, frustration, and lost income. But the ultimate damage is much greater. Exclusion from education and early job opportunities changes the course of entire lives. We must carefully consider these hidden costs when attempting to rank the most damaging problems.

Sociological analysis becomes an important tool for gauging social damage. We may learn that some seemingly severe problems are relatively unimportant, while other, less obvious problems have far-reaching effects. For example, a casual observer might view the cost of crime in city neighborhoods primarily in terms of, say, the number of older people who are mugged. But when we step back and sociologically analyze the overall effects, we find what may be an even greater problem: fear of assault. Older people don't leave their homes, they become lonely and isolated, and their community forgets they are there, so less help and protection are available, and their problems multiply.

Offense to a Powerful Group's Standards

All societies contain multiple strata, or layers, with varying degrees of power and prestige. In some places, as in fundamentalist Muslim countries such as Iran, religion is the basis of prestige and privilege, and the clergy hold positions of power. More often, however, stratification has an economic basis, and the dominant classes are closely identified with occupational prestige and the accumulation of wealth. Higher status typically translates into having the most power and influence in setting societal agendas, determining policy, and initiating social actions.

A social condition, whatever it may be, often does not become defined as a social problem unless members of some powerful group perceive it as a problem affecting them in some way—perhaps as a threat to their well-being. A subjective component of moral outrage thus sparks social problem definitions.

Members of a social class tend to see reality from their class's point of view and form a set of moral and lifestyle definitions about themselves and others that is unique to their stratum. Thus, what one group sees as important (such as welfare, social security, or tax loopholes), another may not consider valuable to society. People in positions of power tend to value stability, social order, and the preservation of the existing privilege structure. In contrast, people trying to gain power tend to be interested in new ideas, innovative policies, and challenges to the status quo. Sometimes age also influences these differences in perspective. People in power typically are older and try to maintain the structure that nurtured them, while those beginning their careers see many ways to improve the system.

Persistence

New social problems seem to surface continually: a new form of crime or pollution, or some new threat to the moral order of life. Although some new problems do indeed arise (e.g., computer crime is a new form of theft), most problems are old ones that keep returning in forms that seem brand new. The scenes of adolescent boy and girl prostitutes in New York or Los Angeles that shock us on the evening news are, after all, just a variation on the oldest profession, which has been viewed quite differently from time to time and place to place. Why have some social problems persisted for so long? We can isolate three forces that sustain them.

Persistence Due to Interconnectivity

When a social problem persists for as long as prostitution has, it is virtually built into society, almost as a natural part of everyday life. Excluding the moral issue, some sociologists suggest that prostitution serves positive societal functions—for example, as an outlet valve for sexual energies that might otherwise lead to more damaging forms of behavior. This male-oriented view suggests, for instance, that some marriages remain intact because men turn to prostitutes for sexual satisfaction lacking in relations with their wives or that the incidence of sexual assault remains lower when men have this means to satisfy their physical needs. These theorists thus see a high degree of interconnectivity between mutually supportive societal institutions; and successfully changing any single element would entail examining and changing many others.

Other sociologists, while acknowledging the reality of interconnectivity, reject the "positive functions" argument and insist that prostitution is a form of exploitation of women and is connected to social inequalities found in other institutions. As a result, eradicating prostitution would require first a thorough examination of the society's forms of dating and marriage, its gender roles and views of women, the sexism of seeing people only as sexual objects, and prevailing attitudes about morality and human dignity.

Does this angry public confrontation betray the presence of an underlying social problem? How is a social problem defined? Of the four elements of a social problem, which can be seen or inferred in this photo? What is involved in the process of identifying and addressing social problems?

Persistence Because Someone Is Profiting

One social group's loss can be another group's gain. Resistance to anti-pollution regulations, for example, is often rooted in producers' or workers' desires to avoid reducing profits or jobs. The benefits obtained by resisting new policies are not always monetary, though. Many proposed solutions encounter resistance because they threaten to upset society's traditional authority structure. The resistance to women in managerial authority is a recent example. The threat does not have to be direct or powerful or even real to cause a reaction. People resist change if it upsets how they think things should be. Every society's power structure of vested interest groups justifies itself by an ideology that seems to explain why some members "deserve" more power or privilege. It may respond to any solution that contradicts the ideological structure by dismissing the plan as nonsensical or too radical unless the solution enjoys strong enough proof and support to overcome the ideology.

Persistence Due to a Desire for Quick Cures

When John D. Rockefeller decided to put some of his many millions of dollars into major philanthropic works, he did so with his characteristic insistence on an immediate payoff. Rockefeller called together leading doctors and said he would put up the money to finance a large-scale health campaign if they could come up with a disease that could be totally wiped out, immediately. By a rare chance, it happened that, after many years of study, investigators had just found a cure for pellagra, a disease that caused much suffering in the southern United States. The doctors could therefore fulfill Rockefeller's demand for immediate results, but only because years of prior study had supplied the scientific underpinning.[1] Rockefeller's demand reflected a common attitude: the desire for quick cures. Many people give up if solutions do not demonstrate immediate curative powers.

Overabundance of Proposed Solutions

When a social problem persists, it generates considerable discussion and speculation. Some proposed causes and solutions are based on prejudice, cultural orientations, or rationalizations, not facts. Such sources often lead people to identify false causes and recommend misdirected interventions, as we will discuss shortly.

Holding the wrong causal interpretation causes much neglect and damage. We often cling most strongly to false beliefs in areas that threaten or disturb us the most. Because we so intensely feel the need to know, we often settle for plausible-sounding traditional myths rather than seeking a more objective understanding through time-consuming, deeper investigation.

Before we study social problems, then, we should bring some of these false cultural traditions and half-baked theories out into the open. This is similar to getting to know someone from another country or of another race. You should first examine and reject prejudices that might cloud your judgment and block acceptance of the things you are about to learn.

The Overabundance of Solutions Provided by Culture

A society's conception of what can and cannot be understood or solved is part of its culture. Like culture, though, this conception is not fixed or static; instead, it changes as frequently as do the rules about what is right and wrong. Furthermore, these ideas of why things happen and what must be done to correct damage, are sometimes no more rational or scientific than the morals and mores of that society. (**Mores** are rules of social living considered crucial for the survival of the society; and people who violate them incur strong sanctions.) The quickest way to demonstrate that our everyday culture sometimes provides contradictory and irrational suggestions about how to act is to quote common American proverbs:

"Look before you leap." . . . "He who hesitates is lost!"

"Out of sight, out of mind." . . . "Absence makes the heart grow fonder."

Which piece of advice should you follow? Neither! You should come to an independent conclusion after examining the specific facts of the case. But very few of us do. Instead, we make our decisions using guesses based on inadequate data and the prevalent cultural assumptions about why things happen.

Quasi-Theories

Every society develops ways of quickly smoothing things over, ways of explaining away disturbances so that people can get on with life's business. Sometimes these explanations are totally false, but in most situations their truth or falsity doesn't really matter. Their function is not to help us understand what's going on, but to calm the social situation by dissolving the fear, upset, or conflict that the problem caused. This is especially obvious in small social groups. If someone says something harshly critical to another, a third friend will immediately jump in to explain that "she's just like that," or "he's in a mood." Whatever the words, the message is: "I know the simple cause for the harsh words, but it's trivial, or will go away soon, so let's not examine it. Let's get on with our conversation." This type of quick cure is also evident in political life.[2]

We explain away real differences—and sometimes open conflicts—between groups by applying the **quasi-theory** of inadequate communication. "If people would just sit down quietly and discuss their differences, they would see that we are all basically the same." The problem is not real, this quasi-theory states, it is just a symptom of a failure to communicate. Sometimes this might be true; but frequently, fundamentally contradictory interests or competition for power divide conflicting groups.

The sweet-mystery-of-life quasi-theory says that love, birth, and death are areas of life that we will never understand. Mysterious forces beyond our comprehension control them. Therefore, this

In 1986, five million people formed a human chain that stretched 4,152 miles—from New York City's Battery Park to a pier in Long Beach, California. Hands Across America raised $20 million from corporations and individuals to fight hunger. Critics worried this hyped, mega-event would lull Americans into believing it would solve the problem. Indeed, public enthusiasm about fighting hunger waned afterwards. How does this experience illustrate concepts discussed under the persistence of social problems?

view implies social scientists are wasting their time seeking to understand those social phenomena. And yet, in the United States many marriages end in divorce, infants die at a higher rate than in many other countries, and young non-White males are far more likely to die violently than young White males. These and other aspects of love, birth, and death disrupt millions of lives; but we are making progress in understanding them, thanks to those who ignore this quasi-theory.

Another example is the Panglossian quasi-theory based on the notion that "time heals all wounds."[3] The argument usually runs like this: we live in a complicated society, with major changes underway; it is the best of all possible societies, but its problems will take a little while to work themselves out. The implication is that we should not interfere with the forces of globalization, urbanization, migration, assimilation, or economic downturns. We should just "grin and bear" their consequences.

Quasi-theories are damaging because they smooth over, neutralize, and de-emotionalize conflicts that we might otherwise resolve permanently and not just temporarily patch over.

The Fallacy of Inevitability

The scientific study of social problems is relatively new because, until recently, people did not feel any need for it. They resorted to other traditional or religious explanations for the conditions around them. For example, the notion of the "divine right of kings" once solved the problem of who should have power and privilege in society. A small group related by "royal blood" had the natural, God-given right to exercise the power of life and death over all other society members. Similarly, in the field of health, people accepted a high death rate during medical treatment as natural. The doctor was "doing the best he could."

The Role of the Social Scientist

Our views of social problems often intertwine with our personal prejudices, politics, and values. Each of us is a socialized creature imbued with certain values and perspectives, living in a value-laden social world. Developing an objective approach to social problems is thus a herculean task.

Value judgments are real; that is, they have real effects on what individuals and society decide to do. They are not simply emotional responses or irrational traditions that occur in a vacuum. People's moral judgments shape societal decisions about which problem is most serious, or which one should receive highest priority for solution. There is no scientific way to decide whether a high crime rate is "worse" than a high divorce rate, or whether robbery is "worse" than alcoholism.

But policy decisions on these and other issues should be based on objective evidence—on accurate statistics measuring the real extent of the problem and on reasonable estimates of the consequences of efforts to eliminate a given problem. It should be the job of social scientists to deal with questions of what is and what will occur if a particular policy is made. According to the traditional view, scientists' contributions lie in choosing the means to achieve solutions, not in choosing which problems should be attacked.

Research Thinking

Even when prejudices can be eliminated, everyday thinking about social problems is casual and disorganized. It tries to handle too many different things at once and often relies on little or no hard evidence. In contrast, researchers use hypotheses to structure their investigations. A **hypothesis** is a statement or prediction that can be compared with factual reality. For example, "If welfare payments are doubled for three years, fewer families will still need welfare at the end of the period than in a comparable group that receives normal payments." Notice that this hypothesis addresses only one small question within the whole arena of welfare issues. That is the price we pay for doing research: it must be limited in scope. Here is a list of considerations and guidelines for developing usable hypotheses that will help focus your thinking about social problems.

1. Hypotheses can be **deductive** or **inductive.** The goal of research is to build theory, to add one more tested statement to the theory to make it stronger. If we are interested in the sociology of education, for example, we might proceed deductively by first choosing the existing theory that seems most relevant to our concerns. We then search the theory for an interesting question that is as yet unanswered and state it in a way that can be tested in some specific schoolroom situation. If the evidence does not support the original theory, a revision of the theory may be in order.

This female field researcher, standing outside a mall, is collecting interview data on people's attitudes about some contemporary issues. Do you think that her choice of this locale will affect her findings? Why? What is the role of the social scientist in identifying and solving social problems? Why are sociological perspectives on social problems needed?

Alternatively, we may proceed inductively, starting from a concern with a particular problem that we have experienced—for example, a violent school. Studying facts about such schools may lead to a guess or hunch about why they are in trouble. This hunch can then be turned into a testable hypothesis for further research. It should not, however, be turned into a conclusion. Your guess is a good beginning, but it remains no more than an after-the-fact interpretation until it is tested.

2. Hypotheses must use **empirical referents,** not moral judgments or vague feelings. For example, you may hypothesize that "girls are attracted to bad boys." This is a dangerous way to state a hypothesis, however, because we all think we know what it means, but each of us may have a different interpretation. Does "bad" mean snarly, aggressive, prone to anti-social behavior, or something else?

3. Concepts in the hypothesis must be expressed clearly, using **operational definitions** whenever possible. "More education takes place in a co-educational classroom." What does "more" mean, and how do we measure it? Will we accept the judgments of trained observers? Will we use comparative test scores to assess learning? Or, will students' impressions of the experience be collected in postexperience interviews? Does a change in attitude qualify as education, or is education limited to factual learning? Answers to these questions will determine what part of "education" is being studied.

4. Conditions of the hypothesis-testing situation should be stated, and they should be *repeatable*. Science accepts only what a number of researchers can test. First, we guard against fakers and people with undisclosed personal biases by demanding that all conditions of the research be made public so that others can try to repeat it. Second, science progresses by accumulation. The next researcher may wish to do the study again, adding one new idea to the mix to extend the theory. Third, we usually state hypotheses within a context. For example: "In the United States, in a typical state college sociology classroom...more education takes place if it is coeducational."[4] In other words, specify the conditions surrounding the idea to be tested, including the location and the type of people involved.

Research Observation

The basic research tool is comparison. Emile Durkheim's *Suicide* provides the classic example of using available data to find relationships by comparing existing situations. He compared areas with high and low rates of suicide, ruling out possible causes when they failed to account for any of the difference. Religion stood the test of comparison: Protestant areas had higher rates of suicide no matter what other characteristics were involved. This fact led to his hypothesis that Protestants' lack of close guidance by a church led to anomic suicide.

Textbooks, other publications, and other media (such as television and movies) also provide data that are *not directly collected from individuals*. For example, a researcher could count the number of biased gender images presented in early and recent commercials to gauge the reduction of society's stereotypes. Observing available data eliminates the problems that arise from intruding into people's lives—in particular, the problem of disrupting the natural situation and therefore the subjects' natural behavior. It has the disadvantage that the researcher had no control over how the original data were collected.

Structured observation is an experiment in a controlled situation into which the researcher introduces a new element to judge its power to change the situation. We assess the amount of change by comparing it to another situation that is as nearly identical as possible in every way except that it does not receive the new input. This second, the control group, continues with normal life as it would have developed in the first group without the new input. If the first, the experimental group, develops differently, we can conclude that the new input was powerful. If the experiment is to be valid, all the other variables in the situation must be controlled: the researcher must ensure that both groups are equivalent at the start and that no other new element creeps in during the study period to contaminate the situation. Although this type of control can commonly be exercised in the laboratory, it is often impossible in sociological field experiments because social life is so complex. The disadvantage of controlling everything in the laboratory is that the resulting constructed, manipulated situation is often too unnatural to bear comparison to normal social life.

Survey research is familiar to anyone who has lived in the United States for even a few years. You might be surprised to learn, however, that professional surveys do not just use paper-and-pencil tests or quick collections of facts and multiple-choice answers to opinion questions. Researchers often use interviews to ensure proper interpretation of questions and to gauge the situation and the respondents' total reaction to each item. Paper-and-pencil anonymous surveys are reliable only when they have been elaborately pretested to ensure that the questions are clear and have the same meaning to different people. Guided conversation is a loosely structured form of interview that tries to eliminate the controlled research atmosphere in favor of a natural conversation in which new ideas and opinions may develop.

A basic flaw of paper-and-pencil questionnaires is that researchers can only ask about things that they already know exist. Frequently, guided conversation serves as a valuable technique in exploratory research before the dimensions of the problem are established. Accurate description of a problem—that is, finding how widespread it is and what social situations promote it—demands preliminary exploration of the situation to gain a clear idea of what really exists and to help researchers formulate relevant questions.

Direct observation of social life permits the recording of behaviors that fall only into strict preplanned categories. The researcher is on the scene only to make minimum interpretations to fit events into categories and count them. This is useful in testing a hypothesis. More frequently, researchers use observation to explore new situations. An anthropologist visiting a new culture is a familiar example. The key decision a researcher using participant observation must make is how much of a participant to become. A researcher who becomes significantly involved will eventually feel what members of the group feel, and this may lead to a better understanding of what is at work in the situation. Such involvement, however, can damage the detachment needed to get through the participants' feelings and beliefs to analyze the underlying social meaning of the situation (see Figure 1.1).

Figure 1.1   The Major Forms of Research Observation

Available Data	Historical/Comparative Studies Documents and Diaries Media/Publications (Content Analysis) Other Artifacts and Rituals Data Series and Census Reports	
Structured Observation (Experiment)	Laboratory (control of situation) Field (intrusion to gauge effect) Natural (comparing found situations)	
Surveys	Structured Questionnaires	Mail Telephone Personally Distributed
	Interviews	Structured Focused Guided "Conversation"
Naturalistic Observation	Case Study (one group studied intensively) Detached Observation (attempting objectivity, often combined with strict description) Participant Observation (involvement for understanding beyond description)	

The Importance of Theories

We are surrounded by a multitude of events. Those we notice stand out because we have been sensitized to their importance. Footsteps behind you at night are arresting, while the same noises in daylight would not even be heard. Loud behavior by a member of a disliked ethnic group is "proof" of your biased opinion, while the same behavior by a member of your own ethnic group is just "having fun." "Facts" thus exist only after we select and interpret portions of reality.

These same processes occur in science. Theories of society are not direct pictures of the social world. Scientists must first recognize an event as important and then classify it according to some set of meanings—some orientation to reality—before it can become part of scientific knowledge.

Sociological Perspectives

Sociologists approach social problems in several ways. Each approach contains broad assumptions about how society works and a preferred direction to take in looking for the causes of social problems. Think of them as different lenses, each offering a unique portrait of the same reality. A wide-angle lens, for example, reveals more in scope than a regular camera lens, while a telephoto lens offers greater detail. Yet all focus on the same subject and accurately depict the scene. Similarly, macrosocial and microsocial orientations provide different valid means of analyzing the same social problem.

We will refer to most of these orientations in every chapter. They will sometimes suggest contradictory ideas about what elements of a problem are important because they draw our attention to different aspects of society. You should see these disagreements as provocative—that is, as stimuli for thinking about which orientation is most useful in studying each social problem. You should not think that the lack of one dominant orientation renders any competing orientation less important. They all make significant contributions.

The Functionalist Viewpoint

Functionalism has been called the core tradition of sociology.[5] It sees sociology as the science of social order, focusing on the social structures that hold a society together over time. Society is a structure of beliefs and traditional ways of doing things. A society contains **values** (competition, honesty, success), **status positions** (occupational, class structure, gender roles), and **institutions** (family, education, religion, economics, and governance). Each of these parts plays a role in maintaining the operation of the whole society. When one part changes too quickly, it disrupts all parts connected to it. Herbert Spencer first described this idea of *society as an integrated system* in the nineteenth century. He compared society to a biological organism, with each class or institution playing a direct part in preserving the whole body. If the system can be kept in *dynamic equilibrium,* evolving slowly without disruption, all members profit. Spencer saw individuals in a direct "survival of the fittest" competition that led to slow evolutionary improvement of society. The limits to this competition were social contracts that people made to limit disruption and maximize gain. Social order, therefore, was the product of human rationality. The more rational a society became, the more it could progress.

Many sociologists consider Emile Durkheim the founder of the **Functionalist orientation,** as well as of modern sociology. He thought Spencer's solution to the problem of order was oversimplified. If pure rationality were the basis of society, it would lead to competition unlimited by feelings of relationship or common bond. Instead, Durkheim saw an abundance of common sentiments among people, and Spencer's ideas did not explain their importance. Durkheim felt that some precontractual solidarity is necessary to permit humans to trust each other enough to enter into contracts with a reasonable expectation that they will be upheld. There must be a *collective consciousness* of beliefs and feelings held in common as a basis for any contracts or other devices used to maintain social order.

Some critics attack Durkheim's view that consensus of belief and similarity form the crucial basis of solidarity and social order as too conservative. His position, they argue, leads too easily to the view that new ideas or subgroups with different lifestyles introduce deviance or disruption rather than neutral or positive innovations.

Functionalist Method

Robert Merton uses the assumption of a common American value of material success in his famous analysis of the sources of **deviance**. Why are some laws violated more than others? Why do some types of people violate rules more than others? And most important, what is it about society that creates nonconformists and deviants? Merton's theory of differential access to the means of achievement is the most influential example of a societal fault that leads to individual deviance.[6] Merton assumes that all members of U.S. society value achievement leading to success. Most of us take the approved route of educational and occupational striving. Some Americans, however, do not have access to this means of achieving success because of discrimination against their racial, ethnic, or class backgrounds. Discouraged from taking legitimate paths of preparation for success, they must invent and take illegitimate means. That is why, historically, members of the lower class—no matter who they are—disproportionately fill the jails. It is not a matter of "character"; it is the combination of a discriminatory environment and the socialization of strong success motivations forced on them by the majority culture.

Merton formalized the Functionalist method of looking at any social institution to determine the contribution it makes to upholding social order.[7] He felt that you could understand any social arrangement by isolating the function it plays in keeping society stable. If a social arrangement is disruptive, it is *dysfunctional*. These labels help us to understand why some incongruous behaviors (prostitution is cited most often) persist for so long: because they fill a need in society.

Merton's greatest contribution was to distinguish **manifest functions** from **latent functions**. Social changes usually have intended purposes. Often, however, these manifest functions do not materialize because the change has an unexpected side effect. For example, until recently many cities required police to use only .38 caliber weapons because these were less dangerous to bystanders. This is definitely a good safety feature. The unexpected consequence was that more police officers and bystanders were killed because criminals' automatic weapons overpowered situations. This idea of latent function will be important throughout our study of social problems. It guides us to look through society's accepted interpretation of a social event or arrangement to try to identify or anticipate other changes that might arise as an unintended result.

The basic flaw in Functionalist thought is that consensus is not society-wide; it is local. If we follow Merton's advice and look at each organization or social group for the function it performs, we soon see that each separate social unit maintains not the whole society, but its own special needs. Government agencies, families, friendship groups, and unions or professional groups each have something special to maintain; and these special interests often conflict.

The Conflict Viewpoint

Structural specialization and differentiation weaken the order and rules of society. Only a few hundred years ago, when most of our ancestors lived in small farming communities, there were only five important occupations: serf, landowner, craftsman, soldier, and priest. Each had its own firmly established rights and privileges. Although few of us would claim that this was the best of all possible worlds, it had the virtue of being simple and orderly. People knew who they were and what they were "allowed" to do. Industrialization, scientific and social invention, and political revolution have so radically transformed society that it seems impossible to count the number of occupations or to identify all the separate subgroups that exist in modern society. Some people find themselves in coalitions with members of other subgroups, uniting to achieve the same values or goals; but many find themselves contending against others for social or economic opportunities. For example, who has the more pressing social problem: farmers who have remained on the land but are in danger of losing their farms or exfarmers who have already been forced off the land and can't find jobs in the cities? The people involved have similar backgrounds, but their different statuses place them in direct competition for society's help and support.

In addition to experiencing economic or interest-group rivalry, subgroups may be divided by conflicting traditional values. The **Conflict orientation** sees most social problems as arising from disorganization due to group differences. The more specialized we become through differentiation, the more disagreements we have. A social problem arises when one group feels that its values or expectations are being violated. We find a solution either by reestablishing consensus through compromise, or by having one group exercise its power unilaterally to change the system to suit its own design. In a society as differentiated as the United States, the large number of value disagreements is hardly surprising; disputes over abortion, prayer in the schools, and affirmative action are obvious examples.

The central fact of society is that the prevailing social structure gives some individuals more power and privileges than others. These people control the unequal distribution of limited economic resources and rewards, and they wield the power associated with such control. Those who have more attempt to maintain or increase their advantages and to pass them on to future generations; those who have less attempt to equalize or reverse the structural inequality. For Conflict theorists, until the unequal social structure changes, problems such as crime, poverty, pollution, poor health care, and economic exploitation cannot be eradicated.

False Values

Conflict theorists—from Karl Marx to present-day advocates—see other theoretical emphases as little more than apologies for the present system, deflecting attention and blame away from the controlling, established group of elites, and instead blaming social problems either on victims or on the "bureaucrats." For example, Conflict theorists say that neither value conflicts nor inadequate socialization creates problems; rather, the dominant importance of the system's competition and success values is responsible. As a result, the common values that other socio-

In a materialistic society, people's "lust for property" finds expression in the acquisition of status symbols, those outward signs designed to impress others with one's social rank. Besides the Hummer pictured above, what would you identify as today's clearest symbols of social status? Why might conflict theorists label the desire for these objects as examples of false values?

logical emphases call the societal consensus, Conflict theorists call **false values** and see as the underlying destructive force. They argue that the primary American value of "lust for property" stimulates crime. Violent crime becomes legitimated when the ruling elite uses violence and naked power as instruments of social control to maintain the privilege structure.

Since the predominant values are repugnant to innate notions of virtue and human dignity, people become alienated. Alienation is thus a product of a defective society's social structure, and only progress toward a new society that allows true equality and individual dignity can overcome it. Because of their underlying faith in the perfectability of society, Conflict theorists are generally optimistic about social changes or new lifestyles. They view these not as expressions of deviance in need of social control, or of nonconformity in need of resocialization, but as attempts to protest against or to reorganize the faulty system. Hence, for example, many crimes are "natural" acts of an oppressed people, according to some adherents of this orientation.

Whose Problems? Whose Profit?

Even if you do not accept the somewhat radical version of Conflict orientation just presented, the Conflict emphasis offers practical guidelines for analyzing social problems. One of the first questions we should ask is: "Whose problem is it?" That is, who is being hurt or deprived? Each problem is identified with some specific group or layer of society. Knowing the relative power or social status of the problem sufferers helps us understand the type of social action that might aid them. The next question is: "Could some group be profiting from the problem?" For example, some factory owners do not discourage illegal immigration if they can hire undocumented aliens at poverty-level wages. Finally, if we help one problem group, what other groups might we be depriving in the competition for scarce resources or limited power?

The Interactionist Viewpoint

The social psychological emphasis known as the **Interactionist orientation** concentrates on how people perceive and define the events that influence their lives. Symbolic Interaction—which provides the theoretical background for this approach—deemphasizes the idea that society is an overpowering, consensual structure of rules and values in favor of an image of society as the sum total of individuals' interrelationships in everyday life. It sees society's operating rules not as a fixed set of commandments, but as millions of separate interpretations made by individuals facing problems together (see the box on the next page).

Symbolic Interactionists see the production of society as an ongoing process of negotiation among social actors, in the countless momentary situational encounters of human performers with one another. People in society must constantly coordinate their actions to reach common understandings, but these meanings do not just evolve out of one-on-one interactions. *Entrepreneurs of meaning* deal in reality construction: the media emphasize events and influence our reactions to them; organizations create attractive images through advertising; other organizations create repellant images (in their anti-smoking campaigns and other social protest crusades); and subcultures sometimes promote counterproductive ideas (excelling in school as a racial minority constitutes "acting White"). These all-powerful meanings are created from special points of view. We carry on day-to-day interactions within such meanings, and individuals must learn to interpret them in each unique context.

Production of Reality

Rather than seeing social life from the "official" societal position, Interactionists use the insider's approach. In instances of deviance, the violated standards are not natural or fixed, but socially and politically negotiated—often temporary and subject to local interpretation. Specific groups define who is deviant. Howard Becker uses the term **moral entrepreneur** to describe people who take an interest in creating or enforcing such definitions, to remind us that they have careers to protect and extend during the deviant-making process. Interactionists therefore take an "underdog slant."[8]

For example, sociologists who study crime using this emphasis might concentrate on the thought processes of the police officer who first arrives at the scene at a disturbance. How does he or she choose to see it? Is the man with a gun in his hand a murderer leaving the scene of a crime? Is he a neighbor trying to protect his home? Is he just distraught, or very dangerous? Persons' lives could be changed or ended by the way the officer defines that one moment.

Labeling theory states that frequently an individual's own behavior is not responsible for the outcome of being treated as a "deviant," "delinquent," or as "crazy." A delinquent career

Social Constructions of Social Problems

The Production of Reality

Why do some social conditions get defined as social problems while others do not? How does an "issue" become defined as a social problem? Why do such definitions often change over time? Elsewhere in this book are some possible explanations: the situation offends a powerful group's standards; some group profits from the situation; or entrepreneurs of meaning such as the media emphasize situations and influence our reactions to them. These and other interpretations, though different in their analyses, share in common the idea that "reality"—our sense of how the world works and why things are the way they are—is socially created.

Probably the most influential book on this subject has been *The Social Construction of Reality* (1966) by Peter Berger and Thomas Luckman. Social order, they explained, is a human product, both in its genesis (past human activity) and in its present existence (as the habitualization of social interactions continually reinforces it). This social creation process begins when humans create a social and cultural environment (such as relationships, conflicts, and exploitations) and then *externalize* what they believe is happening to describe such interactions. Subsequent encounters reinforce the first interaction, prompting their *"objective"* definition as undeniable "facts." We then *internalize* that new objective reality, even though it may have little basis in fact, because it corresponds with our experience and we act accordingly. In the process of cultural transmission from one generation to the next, this objectivity "thickens" and "hardens" and becomes firmly embedded in consciousness.

We thus "know" the world only as we perceive it, and we acquire those perceptions or interpretations through the social learning that comes from interaction with others. The "real conditions" of our existence have causes, meaning, value, and significance within the context of that social construction. Our sense of our-selves, our identity, and our goals also evolve out of that framework.

Interestingly, the social construction of reality results in several paradoxes. While the habitualization of social interactions bolsters that reality, it is also true that our selves, our institutions, even our societies, continually change through interaction. Moreover, because socialization occurs differently among the subcultures of a society, multiple realities exist, for not everyone sees things the same way. For example, the poor see the reason for their poverty rather differently than do the nonpoor. Every social problem or social conflict involves a clash of at least two contending realities, that of the mainstream group and that of the affected group. The "official" societal position (the view held by the mainstream group—those with economic, political, and social power) is only one view of that reality, but it is usually the one that dictates what corrective measures, if any, will be taken. Conflict theorists examine this reality aspect of social problems, while Interactionist and Feminist theorists prefer to explain reality by using the insider's or underdog's perspective.

The social constructions of social problems also explain why some social problems are emphasized over others. A common fear among Americans, for example, is street crime, and this area certainly attracts extensive media coverage as well as regular FBI reporting. Yet Americans pay far less attention to corporate white-collar crimes (including environmental crimes), which actually cost our nation more per year than street crime and often victimize far more people. Only in unusual cases is there much media coverage, and guilty verdicts, when they occur, often result in comparatively light punishment.

Social problems, then, get defined, addressed, or ignored as a result of socially interpreted realities. This awareness will guide our study of social problems in the following chapters.

develops through a long social process. Many of us participate in some form of rulebreaking or even lawbreaking when we are young. Something serious begins to happen only if we are caught and singled out through a process of official "tagging, defining, identifying, segregating, describing, and emphasizing."[9] If the labeling experience is powerful enough, individuals may come to accept the definition that society forces on them. Society's reaction may convince these individuals that they are "that type of person." A grammar-school student may be inattentive or distracted for any number of reasons (problems at home, poor teaching, hunger, etc.). If the school authorities notice and define him or her as a "bad student," it can lead to a self-definition as one of "those bad kids" who is just waiting to get old enough to leave school. Labeling theorists, therefore, study not deviants, but the ways in which society transforms people into deviants. Why do some individuals and not others get singled out? How can we interrupt the process of defining a person as a delinquent? And, how can we undo it, once society has destroyed a person's self-image?

The Feminist Viewpoint

Feminist sociologists suggest the need for different methodology—the **Feminist orientation**—that gives women a voice too long denied in the male-oriented perspective that dominated the development of social science. Traditional quantitative experimental science, they argue, reflects the male point of view: it tends to be objective, logical, task-oriented, and instrumental. This approach comports well with the typical male emphasis on individual competition, on domination and control of the environment, and on the hard facts and forces that act on the world. However, it also fails to note much of what really happens.[10]

The male-dominated approach can yield sexist research findings, as well, because it uses males as a point of reference, assumes traditional gender roles, and overgeneralizes from the experience of men to that of all people, regardless of gender. For example, medical researchers often tested medicines on males and then prescribed them for females after FDA approval, ignoring hormonal and weight differences. In social research, traditionalists use the term "unwed mother" but not the parallel term "unwed father." They consider a family in which the adult male cannot find steady work to have a serious problem, but they view a family in which the adult female cannot find work as having a less severe problem.

Empathetic Connections

In contrast to male preferences for objectivity, logic, and quantitative measurement, women tend to emphasize subjective, empathetic, process-oriented, and inclusive sides of social life. They see the social world as an interconnected web of human relations, full of people linked to one another by feelings of trust and mutual obligation. Women thus emphasize accommodation and gradually developing bonds.

In keeping with this female view of the world, Feminist researchers urge rejection of sexism in the assumptions, concepts, and questions forming the basis of investigation. Rather than espousing an "objectivity" that actually reflects the male viewpoint, they advocate incorporation of female values and perspectives into the research process. Researchers should assimilate their own personal feelings and experiences, creating responsive connections between them and those they study. Such an approach recognizes the dimensions of mutual dependence in the human experience.

Action-Oriented Research

Maintaining sensitivity to how gender and power relations permeate all spheres of social life, Feminist researchers challenge traditional restrictions and urge flexibility in choosing research techniques and crossing boundaries between academic fields. This approach is necessary because patriarchal stereotypes and methods biased most past sociological work. Moreover, such an approach empowers researchers to get at social truths unconstrained by the traditional boundaries that might otherwise limit their understanding of what really happens.

Another traditional viewpoint attacked by the Feminist orientation is that of objective neutrality in research and analysis, which asserts that, though you may seek to prove a hypothesis and analyze your findings, making use of those findings in social policy and action is the role of nonresearchers. To the contrary, many Feminist sociologists strongly believe in action-oriented research that seeks to advance Feminist values and to facilitate personal and societal change. Only through such efforts, they believe, can generations of male bias and false assumptions be corrected.

The Postmodernist Viewpoint

The **Postmodernist orientation** is a controversial approach to studying society. It suggests that the era we live in represents such a sharp break with all past epochs, that it is an age dominated by confusion; as such, it demands new theories and methods for understanding our social world. Postmodernists insist that the change is so great that a more complex and far less hopeful world has supplanted the modern one we thought we lived in.

Modernism began with the Enlightenment and promised a world of progress due to scientific investigation. It replaced the old faiths, which saw the world as an unchanging, predesigned product of divine creation. Modernism promised that society would inevitably evolve toward more humanistic treatment of individuals as science was applied to human arrangements. Modernists believed they could prove that it was rational for people to be good to each other, and that society would pass through ever more developed stages. Recently, some observers have seriously questioned this promise. For all our scientific and technological advances, we have not reached a stage that is significantly less violent, more benevolent, or more integrated than its predecessors, either ethnically or in terms of social classes. Science may not be the way to the future.

Postmodernism sees two main products of scientific thinking. First, technology has produced both mass consumerism and a computerized communications network that will destroy the borders and special worlds of traditional societies. Second, the belief in rational science has reinforced the current class and gender power structure by erecting a massive bureaucracy of belief and social organizations. Traditional knowledge, intuitions, and alternative interpretations of social life have been truncated and submerged among the many disenfranchised groups.

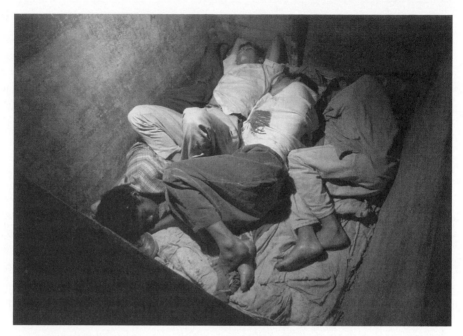

These children are homeless and destitute, have no family to take responsibility for them, and live in a society where the government does not take responsibility for them. They face hunger, sexual exploitation, disease, incarceration, and death. How might child abandonment be viewed as a social problem from each of the five different sociological perspectives discussed in this chapter?

Like the Feminist orientation, the Postmodernist approach challenges traditional thinking and practices. Unlike the Feminist viewpoint, however, which rejects objectivity in favor of subjectivity, Postmodernists say objectivity is impossible. We develop in a context of local knowledge that shapes our world view. Consequently, we can only understand so-called objective scientific writings by seeing how the researchers' social backgrounds led to their construction.

Guiding Principles for Thinking About the Future

Sociological orientations help us understand the origins of social problems and the social forces that reinforce their persistence. They also help us judge which problems will be most damaging in the future. The 1960s and 1970s were times of experimentation and protest in U.S. social life, and high hopes motivated movements to "make war on poverty" and give "power directly to the people." But we imperfectly anticipated the results of our actions, and we suffered notable failures as a result. Now, in the twenty-first century, we recognize that we must give much more time and study to a policy before we inaugurate it. Anticipating possible alternative futures is the main element of such thorough planning.

We face many critical choices on difficult problems: drugs, crime, and violence; poverty and welfare; struggling cities, developing nations, and the impact of the global economy; migration and racial/ethnic prejudice; environmental pollution; political domination by elites; family breakdown; inadequate urban schools; and so on. As a result, many people now doubt the inevitability of progress, having seen matters get worse instead of better. We must make choices, though, and their usefulness depends on our ability to estimate what will probably happen in the near future. Here are some guiding principles for examining our future.

We Can't Always Predict the Future, But We Do Invent It

Today's decisions are tomorrow's realities. We are living out the decisions of preceding generations. For example, the change in public preference from urban to suburban living owes much to federal legislation in the late 1940s and 1950s that provided low-cost builder and buyer loans, as well as to a massive highway-building program that made living away from city jobs and activities easier. (We will examine this subject in Chapter 4.) That growth in middle-class suburban housing, and the subsequent exodus of many businesses to suburban campuses or shopping malls, eroded the cities' economic vitality and tax base, which in turn worsened the quality of urban schools and the quality of life for many city dwellers.

One role of the sociologist is to try to isolate all the possible consequences of a proposed social change. As you read this book, you will discover that government policies and attitudes have had some unexpected—and often unwanted—side effects. For example, our commitment of billions of tax dollars to create a massive highway system subsidized the automobile, trucking, and oil industries. This decision helped establish our dependence on gasoline, weakened mass transit, significantly increased traffic and pollution, and promoted suburbanization.

Robert Merton's distinction between manifest and latent functions is a basic tool for anticipating consequences. Manifest effects are obvious and expected. We intend to help immigrants when we tell them to assimilate, drop their old-world ways, and participate in the American Dream. But we do not intend the latent effects of destroying their ethnic identity and leaving them isolated between heritages. Looking for all the alternative futures means paying special attention to latent consequences hidden inside the developing problem or the proposed solution.

"Plan or be planned for" was a motto found on the wall of a grass-roots community organization in the heart of a western Philadelphia ghetto area.[11] Without question, planning is an important element in our society, whether it is done by government agencies at the local, regional, state, or federal level, or by others in the private sector. Sometimes, as in the case of too many urban renewal projects in the 1960s and 1970s, the planners ignore social factors in their physical designs, leading to disastrous results, as we will also discuss in Chapter 4.[12] One job of the sociologist is to keep official planners thinking of innovative alternative solutions *and* of the human factor, to avoid latent consequences that sociological insight may anticipate.

Our society usually obtains estimates of what will happen in the future by consulting an authority—what is called a "talking head" (a term coined from the close-up shots on television)—and listening to him or her just as the ancient Greeks listened to an oracle. There are, however, much more scientific alternatives. We can learn to be our own experts in analyzing the important problems that will affect our lives.

Visualizing Alternative Scenarios

Willard Waller warned that our thinking about social policy tends to stay within the boundaries of our taken-for-granted assumptions.[13] We hardly ever look at all the potential alternatives, only at the ones that do not disturb our current values or ideas of what is correct. It took Americans many generations to act against monopolies and robber barons because the idea of free competition was so deeply entrenched in their view of economic life. Real criticism of present society must be done with the mind wide open, looking for all possible future solutions. We may have to upset traditional values or adapt accepted social institutions to solve our problems. In this endeavor, the tools and working attitudes of futurism can help us. By systematically considering scenarios that depict alternative futures, we can learn to shed our socially conditioned inflexibility.

We all use informal scenarios in everyday life. They usually begin, "What if . . ." or "Suppose I . . ."; "If I took that job in Hawaii . . ."; "If I married Bobbie next year instead of next month . . ." What we are doing is laying out alternative futures, like a pile of different movie scripts, or **scenarios,** so that we can choose future roles we want to play or avoid. The most interesting are the provocative, "surprise sensitive" forecasts. "If I inherited all the money in the world, or became President, what would be the first thing I would do?" Such daydreams and speculations often have a useful purpose: we get to "play with" deciding what we really want out of life.

Sociologists and futurists also compose scenarios for large-scale societal alternatives, following social forecasting techniques. Throughout this book, as part of each chapter's critical thinking activity, you will have opportunities to develop your own scenarios. You will discover proposed and piloted solutions to a particular problem, which you will evaluate and selectively include in your scenario. In forming your own hypotheses, debating the merits of these solutions, and supporting certain predictions, keep in mind the points mentioned in the paragraphs above, as summarized in Figure 1.2.

Figure 1.2   Guiding Principles for Thinking About the Future

1. Be aware that we invent the future.
   Today's decisions are tomorrow's realities.

   2. What you don't know CAN hurt you.
      Decisions have latent side effects.

      3. Plan or be planned for.
         Choose plans that take social factors into account.

         4. Examine your values and assumptions.
            Don't take social policies for granted.

            5. Visualize alternative futures.
               Choose positive solutions that can work.

SUMMARY

1. Social problems are not obvious. Different people have disagreed about whether the same condition was a problem or not and have given such conditions many social definitions throughout history. Sexual expression, homosexuality, abortion, physician-assisted suicide, and capital punishment are but a few examples.

2. Most recognized social problems have four attributes: they cause significant damage; they offend the values of some powerful segment of society; they persist; and they elicit a number of proposed solutions.

3. Values and standards of judgment about the severity of particular problems can change markedly over time. People also tend to evaluate problems from within the ideology of their own social class positions. Politics and group interest strongly influence how problems are defined.

4. Problems persist due to lack of knowledge, as a result of interconnectedness with other problems or cherished institutions, or because someone is profiting from them.

5. Cultural mores and contradictions, as well as quasi-theories, often make recognizing social problems more difficult.

6. Social scientists contribute to society's understanding of problems by avoiding value judgments and objectively studying the problems, using the scientific method. To replace emotional reactions and cultural biases, they develop sociological theories of social problems.

7. Research thinking uses hypotheses to focus on specific questions that are theory-relevant. We derive hypotheses deductively or inductively, using empirical referents and operational definitions. We must describe all the conditions present during hypothesis testing so that others can repeat the test.

8. Research observation uses available data, structured observation (experiments), surveys, and naturalistic observations.

9. The Functionalist orientation in sociology emphasizes the breakdown of the "organism" of society. When structural differentiation and change destroy the functional balance of society, individuals cannot find secure social positions.

10. The Conflict orientation concentrates on the alienation caused by misplaced belief in the profit motive and by society's unequal power structure.

11. The Interactionist orientation tells us that problems are often distorted—or even created—by how we socially define them. Labeling individuals as deviants is a complex and often inaccurate process.

12. The Feminist orientation rejects previous sociological methods involving intervention in and manipulation of social life, arguing that these are founded on the male habit of dominating. It aims at a comprehensive understanding that includes emotion, cooperation, and the reality of social bonds.

13. The Postmodernist orientation sees our time as an age of exceptional confusion. The old rules, and the hopes for the future they supported, no longer apply. Objectivity is impossible, and the only way to learn from past so-called objective scientific writings is to see how the researchers' social backgrounds contributed to their problems, to search for latent effects of inventions before implementing them, and not to allow others to plan our lives for us.

KEY TERMS

Conflict orientation	Latent functions
Deductive hypothesis	Manifest functions
Deviance	Moral entrepreneur
Empirical referent	Mores
False values	Operational definition
Feminist orientation	Postmodernist orientation
Functionalist orientation	Quasi-theory
Hypothesis	Scenario
Inductive hypothesis	Status position
Institution	Structured observation
Interactionist orientation	Survey research
Labeling theory	Values

INTERNET RESOURCES

At this book's Web site with Allyn & Bacon, you will find numerous links pertaining to the different sociological perspectives on social problems. To explore these resources, go first to the author's page (**http://www.ablongman.com/parrillo**). Next, select this edition of *Contemporary Social Problems* and then select **Internet Readings and Exercises**. Then select **Chapter 1**, where you will find both a variety of sites to investigate and some questions that pertain to those sites.

SUGGESTED READINGS

Berger, Peter. *Invitation to Sociology*. New York: Doubleday, 1963. The classic description of "Sociology as a Form of Consciousness" is very helpful in seeing through apparent problems and recognizing real social problems and their causes.

Collins, Randall. *Sociological Insight: An Introduction to Non-Obvious Sociology*, 2nd ed. New York: Oxford University Press, 1992. The social importance of nonrationality and unanticipated interrelationships is demonstrated in analyses of religion, power, love, crime, and property.

Collins, Randall. *Four Sociological Traditions*. New York: Oxford University Press, 1994. A recent regrouping and clear statement of the development of sociological thought.

Gergen, Kenneth. *An Invitation to Social Construction*. Thousand Oaks, Calif.: Sage, 1999. Offers a personable explanation and commentary on social constructionism, everyday metaphor, deconstructionism, relational selves, and Postmodern culture.

Katzer, Jeffrey; Kenneth Cook; and Wayne Crouch. *Evaluating Information, A Guide for Users of Social Science Research*, 4th ed. New York: McGraw Hill, 1997. How to read and understand research reports and determine how much belief you can safely invest in them. Excellent sections on assumptions, bias, noise, and rival explanations in research.

O'Brien, Jodi, and Peter Kollock. *The Production of Reality*, 2nd ed. Walnut Creek, Calif.: Altamira Press, 1997. Essays and readings applying the Symbolic Interactionist orientation, with many social problems as examples.

Tanur, Judith, et al. (eds.). *Statistics: A Guide to the Unknown*, 4th ed. Belmont CA: Duxberry Press, 2005. Studies specially collected to introduce the policy importance of statistics to "beginners."

Terkel, Studs. *American Dreams: Lost and Found*. New York: New Press, 1980. Interviews with hundreds of people who describe our problems and dissatisfactions from all possible social perspectives.

2

The Individual in Modern Society

Facts About the Individual in Society

- Individuals face twice as many significant life transitions now as in the recent past.

- The meaninglessness of repetitive work has followed us into the Information Age.

- Too often we package ourselves as commodities to sell to others.

- Two-thirds of Americans cannot name their congressional representative.

- Four in ten Americans cannot name the vice president, and a third do not know whether he is a Democrat or a Republican.

- More people die from suicide than from homicide in the United States.

- Suicide among teens and young adults has more than tripled since the mid-1950s.

Is life itself a social problem? Does modern society create alienation, a loss of community, and a sense of meaninglessness? Do we feel lost, disenchanted, or overwhelmed by the complexities of our secular world? Before we can fruitfully examine specific problems, we must first understand the impact of society on individuals and their expectations regarding quality of life. In Chapter 2 we look at these concerns, with particular emphasis on society's power in shaping roles, relationships, expectations. If we can grasp the contradiction of our disillusionment with modern life and our simultaneous discarding of the past, we will have gained valuable insight into people's reality perceptions about those life conditions called social problems.

Another focus of this chapter is to acquaint you further with some of the sociological orientations used throughout this book. By seeing the different approaches they take to the relationship between individuals and society, you should gain further insight into their different solutions to problems you have experienced.

The study of individual happiness is a fairly new interest in the United States. It marks a turning point in the way we evaluate and understand life in society. In the past, we judged how well society was *providing* for its members; we were concerned only with the *quantities* of necessities or luxuries available. The new trend toward concern with the **quality of life** alerts us to the need to understand and improve the full range of noneconomic societal institutions, each capable of limiting or lowering our health, freedom, or happiness.

Overconcern with economic productivity narrowed policymakers' views of social life. For decades, federal taxes have financed the collection of data on thousands of economic indicators, but study of the social indicators related to individuals' levels of satisfaction or happiness began relatively recently. Sociologists make two contributions to this new understanding of society's power to affect individuals' lives:

1. What appear to be microlevel individual problems often result from macrostructured societal problems. Sociologists emphasize that society causes many of our day-to-day difficulties in relating to each other (anomie) and confusions over how we define and feel about ourselves (alienation).

2. Sociologists demonstrate the side effects, or latent functions, of society's cherished values. By placing modern life in a historical context, we can see that overemphasis on materialism is not the sole cause of our value confusions. Our valued goals of individualism, rationalism, and technological progress have contributed heavily to our modern problems.

As we apply sociological perspectives to place individual problems within the larger societal context, you will explore aspects of being human that you may not have thought of before and so develop what C. Wright Mills called your **sociological imagination**.[1] This concept rests on the distinction made between "personal troubles" and "public issues," that is, between private matters about which a person is directly aware and events outside one's control that impact on daily life. The sociological imagination allows us to step back from our familiar world, observe it more objectively, and seek patterns and insights into the social forces shaping our lives. The sociological imagination enables us to distinguish between those realities about us resulting from our own actions and those explained by our place in society. Thus, the sociological imagination—in developing an understanding of these distinctions—helps us avoid needless self-blame for all our troubles and promotes realistic suggestions for a change in our lives and in society itself.

Functionalists: Social Situations Create Individuals' Problems

Emile Durkheim's *Suicide* became the classic sociological research study because it demonstrated that social forces contributed to even the most personal and seemingly psychological decision: the choice of whether to take one's own life. Through careful empirical study, Durkheim ruled out poverty, the natural environment, and other popular theories of the causes of suicide.

How might the nineteenth-century sociologist Emile Durkheim refer to the situation in this photograph? To what social forces might Durkheim have attributed the person's social isolation? On the basis of your knowledge of modern society, what other social forces might you add? What are some other functionalist explanations of the problems of individuals in modern societies? How might a Conflict theorist explain the situation in the photograph differently?

He demonstrated that social rhythms correlated highly with changes in the suicide rates. Durkheim's important theoretical contribution was the concept of **anomie**—the condition in which weakened social bonds and a lack of rules contribute to an increase in suicides.[2] His major finding was that change, not misery or even severe poverty, prompted suicides to increase. For example, rapid economic change, whether boom or bust, caused social disruption that shattered individuals' normal goals and rules, causing more to turn to suicide.

Durkheim isolated egoism as the second major social influence on increased suicide rates. In a nation whose values were strongly centered on group organization—as in Ireland, where the Catholic Church wielded influence—even terrible economic privation did not increase the suicide rate. In Protestant Germany, where individuals were supposed to work out their own relationships with God, suicides occurred more frequently, even during times of comparative economic plenty. Durkheim attributed this to the egoistic-individualistic values of Protestantism, which made the individual feel alone and unsupported by society.

If you find it surprising that an event as personal as suicide is socially influenced, you are not alone. Philip G. Zimbardo found that even professionals mistakenly think of isolation and shyness as personal problems.[3] When he discovered that about 5 percent of the student body at a college had visited the campus clinic complaining of loneliness, he asked how the therapist was dealing with the problem. Zimbardo learned that each patient was given some personalized treatment. Zimbardo then asked, "Suppose all 500 came to the clinic at the same time? . . . What would the diagnosis be, and where would you look for its causes?" The therapist readily replied that the clinic would call the dormitory office to find out what had caused such a mass reaction. But just because the students were presenting themselves one at a time, Zimbardo observed, it was no less irrational to continue to ask each of them "What's wrong with *you*?" instead of "What's wrong out there?" We pass sentence on individuals rather than on social situations. To avoid this error, social researchers examine the number of incidents of a problem among different segments of society to determine if it constitutes a larger concern.

The Loss of Community

In 1887, sociologist Ferdinand Tönnies made an important distinction between the traditional, all-encompassing, emotionally supportive **community** (*Gemeinschaft*) and the modern efficiency-based society (*Gesellschaft*). At the time, many commentators were extolling the freedom and wealth that would be available in the coming age, but Tönnies anticipated its social-psychological costs. His description of the horrors of *Gesellschaft*, "which for Tonnies meant the whole complex of impersonal, abstract, and anonymous relationships which characterized capitalism, nationalism, and all the forces of individualism, bureaucratization, and secularism which he could see eating away at the social fabric," was profoundly influential.[4]

Tönnies's distinction found its most influential expression in the Chicago School of Sociology's view of modern urban life as inherently undesirable and pathogenic. Many sociologists and social critics shared this assumption of the superiority of stable small communities, as exemplified by Robert MacIver's description of the "great emptiness":

> Back in the days when unremitting toil was the lot of all but the very few and leisure still a hopeless yearning, hard and painful as life was, it still felt real. People were in rapport with the small bit of reality allotted to them, the sense of the earth, the tang of the changing seasons, the consciousness of the eternal on-going of birth and death. Now, when so many have leisure, they become detached from themselves, not merely from the earth. From all the widened horizons of our greater world a thousand voices call us to come near, to understand, and to enjoy, but our ears are not trained to hear them. The leisure is ours but not the skill to use it. So leisure becomes a void, and from the ensuing restlessness men take refuge in delusive excitations or fictitious visions, returning to their own earth no more.[5]

In the mid-1980s, a group of social researchers reexamined U.S. values and in *Habits of the Heart* (1985) reported changes in U.S. social life that continue today. The researchers identified traditional communities in which individuals have permanent emotional bonds as "Communities of Memory." The distinguishing characteristic of such communities is that their members do not forget their history, their stories about people like themselves who embody the values of the group.[6] Ethnic, racial, and religious communities still have these living, resonant pasts. Their members grow up hearing the stories and participating in other "practices of commitment." Learning the community's hopes and fears, they come to share its goals.

American-style individualism, however, seems unlikely to allow such communities to continue much longer. The overarching demands of rational self-interest, which decrees that each value must pragmatically justify itself by showing immediate tangible benefits, destroy support

People with similar interests or appearances form lifestyle enclaves. These sorority "sisters" are showing what appears to be primary group solidarity, but their friendships will probably fade when their social situations change. Do your high school friendships still continue? Do our geographic mobility and life transitions result in a diminished sense of community and belonging than for previous generations?

for traditional values. Communities therefore degenerate into "lifestyle enclaves." People who grow tired of being isolated find groups with whom they share some social characteristic—being single for example, or older. These enclaves usually involve only a part of each individual; and they are often based on such superficial similarities as consumption style or leisure interest.[7]

The *Habits of the Heart* authors see this process as a definite diminishment of social life. Lifestyle enclaves, they argue, provide inadequate support for the individual for two reasons: they do not lessen or guide the modern obsession with maximizing self-interest; and they do not provide any valued goal or destination for the constant rational planning and social operating that make up modern life. Modern individuals are left with no fixed standards by which to measure their achievements. They can only compare their own material gains with those of their neighbors, to piece together some idea of "how they are doing."

On the other hand, U.S. society *does* offer many examples of social and community integration. Faith-based and community organizations, cultural support networks, and other activist groups all generate a sense of belonging and empowerment, ingroup solidarity, and opportunities to effect positive outcomes through social change.

Anomic Situations

Anomie is not an unfamiliar idea; people frequently discuss it using other names. We say that modern society is aimless, goalless, disorganized, fragmented, or in the process of dissolution. We hear that people are rootless, frustrated, and lacking in purpose. We will examine the historical roots of these feelings; but first let us look at some examples of how societal changes are related to these feelings.

Changing Lifestyles and Transitions

Not so long ago, we thought of ourselves as part of some larger unit, and only a few of us lived alone. Currently, 26 percent of the population lives alone, more than ever before. Most of these people are under forty-four and have chosen not to marry, for various reasons. Often the women in this group are the first females in their families to live alone.[8]

Significant changes in status cause emotional disruptions and necessitate difficult adaptations. Individuals today must face twice as many significant life transitions as did people in the recent past. The traditional phases of life used to be childhood, marriage, childbirth, childrearing, and finally, the dissolution of the marriage. Nowadays, you will also probably face: prolonged adolescence, a period of living away from your family before marriage, a longer time spent single, a four in ten chance of divorce, and remarriage (almost half of all marriages are now remarriages for at least one partner).[9] Each of these transitions is potentially disorienting, and the effects of such turbulent social relationships on children can be significant—a subject we will examine in Chapter 10.

Disenchantment

For more than a century, functionalists have warned that material progress cannot provide the structure and meaning that humans need.[10] Individuals, they maintain, are not strong enough to achieve or manage progress without social controls, which is why system disorganization is so serious. Durkheim said it this way:

> To achieve any result, the passions first must be limited. Only then can they be harmonized with the faculties and satisfied. But since the individual has no way of limiting them, this must be done by some force exterior to him.[11]

Today, material progress gives people longer and more comfortable lives, but many observers believe it provides no limits or sense of direction.

Modern life disillusions us, yet we have no patience with traditional solutions unless they work quickly. We modernize instead of valuing past explanations and techniques. In the process, we discard the meaning systems, spiritual or sacred justifications, and enchanting notions that made premodern life meaningful and orderly. Traditional solutions come to mean nothing.

This is usually called the **Weberian paradox**. German sociologist Max Weber made us aware that scientific efficiency demystifies our lives and threatens the very roots of our personalities: "Rationalization spreads at the cost of 'love, hatred, and all purely personal, irrational, and emotional elements which escape calculation.' "[12]

Sociologist William L. Thomas characterized modern life as a constant effort to define the vague: the inability to get a complete grip on a situation or the best of it. Premodern individuals did not constantly ask themselves, "Why do I do this, and why do I do this the way I do it?"[13] Instead of experiencing the past and its traditions as essential and useful reference points for present decisions, we see them as inadequate and irrelevant.

Progress and Problems

All of the foregoing discussion is not to suggest, however, that life is only a continual journey of disconnects and disenchantment. As functionalists readily point out, society also contains corrective mechanisms to advance social and community integration. We have made significant progress since the 1960s, for example, in empowering and improving the quality of life for disenfranchised groups. Moreover, subcultural groups living outside the mainstream benefit from their own cultural solidarity, finding strength and comfort in their group identity and social network. Although there is still much room for improvement, public and private efforts have produced positive outcomes, enriching the lives of individuals and upgrading our society. In that spirit, this chapter (and book) will look at other problem areas that need to be addressed, so that we can achieve further social progress.

Conflict Theorists: Powerlessness and Alienation

Freedom for self-actualization is the central concept of Karl Marx's view of the individual in society. True humanity emerges only after people overthrow the domination of "things." To liberate themselves, to develop all the capacities inherent in their generic essence, people must exercise conscious, rational control over their natural environment and over their own lives.[14] However, the demands of vast public and private bureaucracies, the impersonality of mass society, and the dictates of the workplace and of a complex, interdependent world leave individuals with little control over their lives and environment. The result, say Conflict theorists, is a sense of **alienation,** the sense of being a stranger within one's own social situations.

Powerlessness

Work plays a central role in the Marxian view of self-fulfillment. In the ideal situation, work becomes art, an expression of one's creativity and human talents; and each "job" grows naturally into its best result. No standardization, and certainly no assembly line, exists. Industrialization and capitalism, however, force the production of "things" that the worker feels no personal connection to. With labor disconnected from product identification, the process is too abstract to be personally satisfying.[15] This is the psychological importance of the famous Marxian phrase, the "loss of the tools of production." According to Marxists, capitalism demands that people become workers to be shifted from workplace to workplace as production needs change.

Increasing specialization of work, based on analyzing and breaking down the process of building of something such as an auto into smaller and simpler tasks, may be good engineering for production, but it destroys individuals' choices and skills. Robert Blauner offered the classic list of the effects of confining workers to oversimplified tasks:

- Powerlessness because of no control over work activities.
- Meaninglessness because of making only a small part of the final product.
- Social alienation because workers no longer belong to close work groups.
- Self-estrangement because work becomes only a means to a paycheck, and not an accomplishment worthy of pride.[16]

Only 13 percent of the U.S. labor force now works in manufacturing.[17] Most employed people are white-collar workers, who, like factory workers, face alienation as a result of meaningless jobs. Their "paper-pushing" work becomes just as routine and abstractly meaningless as blue-collar work:

> To get a white-collar job you must stay in school. Schooling is supposed to develop your internal powers, make you a person more powerful in relation to the productive order of the society. The move into white-collar work is in this way a consequence of your having become a more developed human being. Yet most of those flowing into white-collar work find the reality quite different—the content of the work in fact requires very little mind at all.[18]

The recent transition of our economy from one based primarily on manufacturing to one based on services, the so-called Information Society, might at first seem to do away with many of the problems of regimentation and meaninglessness at work. But on the other hand, it might be just a transition from "making things" to "making lists of things." If so, the transition represents a step backward from creative and self-fulfilling work toward becoming a society of clerks sitting at computer terminals (see the box on the next page for an insight into Russia's transition).

Political Alienation

In the 1960s a national survey about people's level of trust found that nearly two out of three Americans trusted others. In contrast, a 1996 national survey revealed that only one-third expressed a similar view. This dramatic rise in personal mistrust and alienation (paralleling a rise in the mistrust of government) occurred long before such television reality shows as *Survivor, Joe Millionaire,* and *The Apprentice* offered lying and backstabbing as strategy models for success.[19]

Researchers discovered that people who didn't trust other people also didn't trust government and didn't trust other institutions. Younger people were more mistrustful than older people. The most cynical were the eighteen- to twenty-four-year-olds, especially if their parents were divorced. They often told researchers that if they couldn't trust their parents, they couldn't trust anybody. An ABC News poll in 2002 identified only 38 percent of Americans who trusted the federal government on social issues, although 68 percent trusted it to handle national defense and the war on terrorism.

Robert Blendon, a co-director of the survey, argued that the source of mistrust is that people believe that government has failed to deliver the things that they care about: opportunities for their children to have a better life, solutions to violent crime, a way to prevent or recover from the breakup of families:

> They actually don't follow what goes on in government a lot, but they follow what goes on in their lives a lot, and they see government got bigger, their taxes went up, and the things that they most care about look like they either didn't get better, or got worse. So in their mind when people talk about new programs and solving problems and nothing happens. . . .
> I think people are just so discouraged about aspects of life not improving, they just don't trust the government every time you tell 'em you're going to spend more money or get larger, because they haven't seen things in their own personal experience change.[20]

By 2000, that mistrust had evolved to the point that another study found that nearly half of all Americans thought that the federal government threatened their personal rights and freedoms, with nearly one-fourth viewing this as a "major threat." However, Americans also felt less

The Globalization of Social Problems

Problems in a Changing Society

When any society goes through major social change, that transformation usually yields both positive and negative consequences. When the change disrupts the order of everyday life, its negative impact on individuals' lives can reach throughout society.

One such example is the Ik, a tribe of hunter-gatherers living in the mountains of northeastern Uganda. For generations the Ik lived in harmony with their physical environment, tracking game and taking from the land only when necessary. They were, according to anthropologist Colin Turnbull, a peaceful people whose social structure made few distinctions based on gender, power, or possessions. Then, in the 1960s, the government turned their traditional hunting ground, the Kidepo, into a national park. Expelling the Ik from that bountiful area and telling them not to "poach" game, the government relegated them to the less-productive mountains as subsistence farmers without cattle. Suffering constant drought, famine, and raids from neighboring tribes, the Ik changed from an open, friendly people to a society that displays weariness, mistrust, hunger, and fear toward the outside world. Richard V. Hoffman and other anthropologists reported that major changes in the tribe's lifestyle affected many aspects of their cultural and social structure.*

Another example is modern Russia. Since 1991, it has struggled in its efforts to build a democratic political system and market economy to replace the strict social, political, and economic controls of the communist period. In the process, the standard of living of the Russian people declined markedly, while corruption in privatization schemes produced new billionaires. In 2000, thousands of state workers were unpaid, pensioners were not receiving their pensions, and soldiers were begging in the streets of Moscow. Unemployment was widespread, and one-third of the population was below the poverty level.

This deprivation and instability in people's lives led to demographic trends of widespread public concern. The country is experiencing a dramatic annual population loss of about 800,000 people, caused by a decline in health care, precipitous drop in life expectancy, unusually high death rates from nonnatural causes (many related to alcoholism), and the unwillingness of people to have children. The Russian fertility rate has declined to among the world's lowest, while its abortion rate is the highest. As a result, for the first time in Russian history, the annual number of deaths exceeds the number of births.

Russians now consume more alcohol per person than any other country in the world and have one of the highest rates of alcoholism. Especially alarming is a growing number of teenagers under 14—now at 500,000—who suffer from alcoholism. Two thirds of Russian men die drunk and more than half of that number die in extreme stages of alcoholic intoxication. Growing alcohol consumption is not the only explanation of increased mortality, however. Deaths from violence, injuries, and nonnatural causes have contributed heavily to the latest rise. Russia's rates of homicide and suicide, often alcohol-related, are among the highest in the world.

Not surprisingly, Russia now has the lowest life expectancy for males in a developed country (fifty-eight years) and the largest disparity in the world between male and female life expectancy (thirteen and one-half years). Mortality rates for males between ages fifteen and sixty-four are about twice as high as they were a decade ago. Even more dire, mortality levels for men in their early thirties were twice as high in the 1990s as they were in the 1960s. Deaths of men in their early fifties are two and one-half times as high, while mortality rates for women older than twenty-five years are higher by half.

*To learn more about the Ik, go to this Web site: http://home1.gte.net/hoffmanr/

Sources: Nonna Chennyakova, "Russian Spirit Headed Down the Watch," *The Japan Times* (December 29, 2002), p. 1; Murray Feshbach, "Russia's Population Meltdown," *Wilson Quarterly* 25 (Winter 2001): 15–21.

alienated from their state and local governments. Believing they had more control over those governments, Americans generally placed greater trust in them.[21]

Political alienation results in lack of interest and thus lack of information. Two-thirds of the people interviewed in the 1996 survey could not name their congressional representative. Half of them didn't know whether their representative was a Republican or a Democrat. Four out of ten didn't know the name of the Vice President of the United States, and a third didn't know whether he was a Republican or a Democrat. Only 3.4 percent of the respondents said they had "a great deal" of confidence in Congress, and only 3.8 percent had a similar level of confidence in political organizations or parties.[22]

Without this sort of basic information, Americans "tune out politics and turn off to voting." People with low levels of information don't vote because they lack motivation and they don't know who to vote for. Registered voters make up only 64 percent of the voting-age population, but only 51 percent of that percentage voted in the 2000 presidential election (see Figure 2.1).[23] The United States now elects its president by only one-fourth of the voting-age public choosing that candidate!

What causes such *voter apathy?* Conservatives suggest that most people who do not vote are reasonably content with their lives and thus indifferent to policies. In contrast, liberals argue that most nonvoters are dissatisfied with societal conditions, but their political alienation prompts the belief that their vote does not matter and that the election results will bring no improvement to their lives. Since income significantly relates to voting (the lower one's income, the less likely it is that one votes), the liberal argument may be more accurate.

Figure 2 .1   Voting Participation: Registration and Voting Rates for U.S. Citizens Ages Eighteen and Older, by Educational Attainment, November 2000

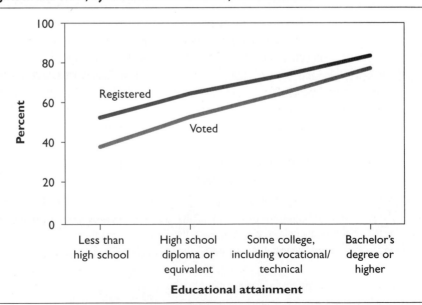

Source: U.S. Department of Education, *The Condition of Education 2003.*

This photo reflects the statistical profile of the majority of voters in the U.S. as older, white, and comparatively affluent. How might a Conflict theorist explain this profile? How might the situation be interpreted from a Feminist perspective? Voter apathy at all levels of government is a growing problem in the United States and has long been recognized as a threat to democracy. What are some specific causes and consequences of political alienation? What might be effective ways to address this social problem?

The United States is alone among democratic nations in its low level of voter turnout. How do we improve? One solution might be to follow Australia's lead: when faced with a voter turnout level less than 60 percent, the government instituted fines on those who fail to vote and increased voter turnout to over 90 percent. Another possible solution is to increase voters' choice through additional political parties. With only two major political parties and both seeking to appeal through the media to the greatest number of people, the candidates often sound more alike than different. Most other democracies have multiple parties and proportional representation, not a winner-take-all arrangement as in the United States. Indeed, in the United States, the highest percentages of voter turnout in presidential elections since 1968 were when a strong third-party candidate offered an alternative to "politics as usual" (Ross Perot in 1992 and George Wallace in 1968).

Consumption and the Human Commodity

Two coincidental changes in the societal role of individuals, forced by the maturing of industrial capitalism, have created even greater self-estrangement: the change from producer to consumer and the change from entrepreneur to **commodity-self** (the evaluation of oneself in terms of salability to others).

In the early days of factory-based capitalism, individuals were simply workers producing as much as possible, as cheaply and as quickly as possible. Producers soon realized that an economy based on mass production could not continue to grow without an endless demand for new goods. A plan to "civilize" the masses replaced the earlier goal of merely satisfying their basic material needs. Advertising began an "uninterrupted fabrication of pseudo-needs" to educate the "masses into an unappeasable appetite not only for goods but for new experiences and personal fulfillment."[24] Conflict theorists treat this personal growth through stimulation of consumption as one of the most dubious and distracting of our false values.

C. Wright Mills tried to alert Americans to the personal dangers involved in the change from small-business competition to the age of corporate bureaucracies.[25] No longer do we compete to produce a more salable product; now we sell our own personalities. We compete through our abilities to shape ourselves into the most attractive and effective tools for pleasing superiors in the system. This promotes the **stewardess syndrome:** we smile warmly at strangers we have just met, as if sharing some deep intimacy.[26] Even these commodity-emotions are not our own ideas. We are creating them in a conscious repackaging of the self into an "organization person."

Competition and the cold-blooded sale of our remade personalities have spread from the economic marketplace and now pervade our personal-emotional interactions. We have already outlived the era of passive conformity. Today, we no longer just give up our individuality to the organization; we become active predators, using our outer selves to attract opportunities to score career points against each other. This overriding **narcissism** is the ultimate alienation nightmare. False consumption values make us compete behind masks of voluntarily created false selves, and we are unable to see ourselves, or others, as real or valuable.[27]

Interactionists: Searching for Meaningful Identities

Symbolic Interactionists do not see individuals as controlled or dominated by the social structure. First, Interactionists acknowledge the need for stable reference standards so that everything need not be freshly created repeatedly. They do, however, see our interpersonal rules as changing constantly to adapt to new situations. This is an optimistic view. Inside even the most oppressive social structure persists the possibility of forming new agreements on how to live together within it or how to modify it. The self can survive.

The second disagreement that Interactionists have with the previous outlooks concerns "phoniness" or prearranged role-playing. Acting is constant and typical. Almost all of us preplan and present the best appearance and nicest personality we can. Most of us manage information and downplay what we consider to be our weaknesses. This is a normal adjustment to others' expectations, not a recent development caused by a particular societal situation. Interactionists acknowledge our problems but suggest that they are less overwhelmingly monolithic than other sociological orientations would have us believe. Our individual problems are exaggerations of the normal interpersonal processes and can be modified without changing the entire social structure.

Individual Negotiation and Social Change

Interactionists concentrate on the ways we select specific guidelines from cultural rules and how we continuously redefine those rules. We tend to adapt or modify ourselves in two ways: through role distance and through impression management.

Detachment from the current situation need not take the extreme form of total escape found in cults or in Eastern mysticism. We all sometimes feel "outside" the roles we play.[28] We want to feel that we are above certain roles, and we often want others to know we feel that way. The business executive who dresses like a college teacher (and vice versa) is making an overt statement, distancing himself or herself from the situation. The classic example is the parent who punishes a child and says, "I'm only doing this for your own good." In effect the parent is disavowing individual or personal responsibility for the spanking; rather, the parenting role has forced him or her to punish.

We often play social roles from a distance, without any personal commitment. Our use of **impression management** when we do so has two very different implications. The first is optimistic: we do not necessarily have to fit ourselves into the roles the structure attempts to force on us. We can reflect on them critically and take steps to avoid some of the worst restrictions or obligations. When we adopt a new status, such as a job or parenthood, we may find ourselves unable to feel everything we should. Supposedly, we "grow into" the role, eventually feeling the emotions people expect us to feel. This means both that insincere interaction allows the system to operate smoothly and that individuals can hide from the system while trying to change it.

The second implication is pessimistic: honesty is not a prerequisite of effective role performance. Indeed, insincere interaction is frequent and manipulative, as may be illustrated by two false poses that commonly occur in romantic relationships. In one pose, a partner frequently "plays hard to get" by managing to look uninterested when he or she actually is attracted to the other.[29] In another, a female partner "plays dumb," and hides her intelligence or capabilities in order to conform to the stereotypical expectations of a sexist society.[30]

Loss of Individualism: Society Packages Your New Identity

Our contemporary idea of individuality is that it comprises the sum of our differences from those with whom we have daily contact. We can only see ourselves clearly by seeing the ways we are not full members of the groups we attend. This separates us from our family and friends. To be individuals, we have to be different and do the new thing before our friends do. Therefore, routine becomes our enemy. If nothing new happens, instead of feeling safe in a stable social group, we feel "out of it." We look for new sports, interests, and beliefs, as we look for new clothing styles. But modern society can co-opt and subvert even these creations:

> No sooner has a new road to the true self been encountered than it is boxed and packaged for sale in the escape-attempts supermarket, no sooner has a new vocabulary of meaning been articulated than it is raided for concepts and slogans by calendar makers and record producers, no sooner have we begun acting in an entirely novel way than we see coming over the horizon a mass of others mimicking our every action.[31]

We think we have found a new direction only to discover that in no time it becomes routinized and overcrowded. It is difficult to be satisfied when society places such immense value on individuality based on ever-changing differences from those close to us. The complaint of Mick Jagger and the Rolling Stones that they "can't get no satisfaction" is something many understand (see the box on the next page).

▲ Social Constructions of Social Problems

Social Identity

Today's mass society—with its bewildering array of choices, rapid social change, and preference for the latest fashion or fad—presents enormous challenges for anyone attempting to build a personal identity. No one path looms as the "right" one. No "wise" counsel eliminates the confusion. Uncertain of what life decisions to make about their academic majors, careers, lifestyles, relationships, or residences, people make choices as best they can, then change them later in search of their "real" selves. In their sequential transformation of themselves, they shift from one identity to another. Such conversions occur among adults of all ages, partly generated by (1) the social diversity and changes in society, (2) the newest definition of the "good life," and (3) a vague sense of being trapped in an everyday life that is, as Max Weber (1864–1920) put it, "an iron cage."

It's not just in our life changes that we lack consistency in our social identity. Even our daily routines bring a measure of divergence. Our society values personal flexibility and sensitivity to others and so we become, as David Riesman (1909–2002) describes, "other-directed." But this widespread relativism results in a fluidity in our identities, giving us an inconsistency and superficiality in our varying role behaviors in different social settings. Erving Goffman (1922–1982) speaks of this as our assuming different "social selves" in our "performances" on the "stage of life." As useful as this chameleon-like behavior is, though, which of our social selves, if any, is the real us?

Charles Horton Cooley (1864–1929) conceptualized the "looking-glass self" to explain that other people represent a mirror in which we see ourselves. We develop a self-image based on what we believe others think of us. If we think others believe we are boring or unattractive, we will conceive of ourselves that way as well. George Herbert Mead (1863–1931) was more emphatic, saying that there is no self without society. As creative beings we initiate actions (the I

phase of self) in *anticipation* of how others will respond to us (the me phase of self). We thus become objects to ourselves and try to package ourselves in such a way as to be liked and respected. What then of the oft-quoted Shakespearean adage, "To thine own self be true"? How can we be true to ourselves when we continually act to secure the approval of others and the social surroundings in which we interact keep changing?

Some of us seek to construct our social identity through a desire to be "with it," up-to-date, and admired, often using role models in that quest. We imitate celebrities in their hair or clothing styles. We acquire things to define us and present a certain image to others: car; house, condo, or apartment; jewelry. Or, if we want to be nonconformists, we stress our "uniqueness" perhaps with a nontraditional, even bizarre, physical appearance in hair color and style, clothing, and bodily adornment in tattoos and piercings. Yet even this nonconformity has a uniformity (even conformity) to it. Once you have seen a biker or punk, for example, you thereafter can recognize such group members because of similarity in physical appearance within each group.

For some, religion offers the path to a secure self-identity. Numerous people are members of a religious subculture, such as the Amish or Hasidic Jews, in which tradition provides the foundation for developing a satisfying personal identity. Many mainstream Americans also have a strong religious faith to give meaning and purpose to their lives, endowing them with a sense of confidence about themselves. Others, lacking that anchor, change religions or join cults or New Age movements in search of their elusive "true self." Still others, feeling adrift without any spiritual support, lack certainty and security about who and what they are. But does this mean that religion is an essential component for a firm sense of self? Are there many nonreligious people whose self-identities are strong and stable?

These youths are confirming their social identity as Baptists and as members of a precision drill team. Note the second line of their banner. How might this scene be interpreted from an interactionist perspective? Would functionalists or conflict theorists view it differently? Do you think all three perspectives could contribute to understanding a social problem? Why or why not?

Secularization and the Search for Meaning

In the past, religion was a powerful and pervasive society-wide institution. It regulated both thought and action. "The world as defined by the religious institution . . . *was the world* . . . to step outside the world as religiously defined was to step into a chaotic darkness, into anomie, possibly into madness."[32]

Secularization is the process of removing both social-structural and symbolic elements of individuals' lives from religious control. Society has experienced not only a separation of church and state, but also a secularization of consciousness. As sociologist Peter Berger observes, "The modern West has produced an increasing number of individuals who look upon the world and their own lives without the benefit of religious interpretations."[33]

Berger notes that many people fail to notice the completeness of this shift; culture lag exists between secularization of the economy and of the family and state. Religious symbols survive in the statehouse and in politicians' rhetoric, and they remain part of the meanings attached to family formation. However, religious meaning no longer permeates the everyday life of the individual—especially economic activities and their related evaluations of self-worth. The plausibility of the religious definition of reality has collapsed for many people, taking with it the one common standard previously used to judge activities as legitimate. Individuals now face a wide variety of explanations, none of which has the power to coerce nor the traditional foundation to convince fully.

In the midst of these competing justifications for behavior in an increasingly secular society, many individuals seek meaning in their lives either by returning to fundamentalist beliefs or by joining a cult that offers both a sense of belonging and the promise of a better life.

Fundamentalism: The Return to Traditional Meanings

Religious dissent and the creation of new religious forms were part of the original foundation of American values. We have many churches, sects, denominations, and cults, but the recent growth in new cults has been extraordinary even by U.S. standards. Since 1965, over 1,000 new religious groups have been formed in the United States.[34] Many of these groups attempt to return to traditional forms of Christianity; many others are adaptations of Eastern mysticism.

How do we explain the resurgence of fundamentalism in the United States? Many social observers see it as a reaction against an alienating modern society. Irving Horowitz views this religious trend as part of a worldwide reaction to advancing modernity.[35] In the Middle East, especially in Iran, religious fundamentalists have made a powerful and dominating response to the industrial/scientific values of development. Widespread returns to fundamentalist Catholic, Protestant, or Islamic sects have occurred around the world.

Will religious revivalism become a stable element in U.S. society or merely a "cyclical event" or reactionary movement? Only time will tell, but Horowitz cautions against regarding it as an unimportant phase:

> What we are witnessing is not simply a challenge to modernity but an assault upon complexity, especially against scientific findings and formulas. The religious mood of exaltation and fervor, even if it remains confined to a statistical minority, is a relatively painless way to knowledge. In place of many books is The Good Book; in place of relativism is moral certainty; in place of a series of questions begetting more questions is a series of answers stimulated by the rhetoric of certainty.[36]

Altruistic Escape

Many people willingly surrender to what outsiders see as harsh discipline in order to be part of a rigid but meaningful order. The joiners do seem drawn from a special group of people constantly searching for a place in the world. Many join cults at a time of personal crisis or loneliness in their lives. Weak ties to the parents' religion as a teenager correlates strongly with young adults seeking nonconventional religions.[37]

To understand this phenomenon of willingly giving oneself fully to a group, we must once again call on Durkheim's analysis of the interrelationship between social integration and suicide. He described very tightly knit groups as promoting altruistic suicide, or **altruistic escape,** whenever the group's welfare took over primary importance in each member's mind. We frequently find this orientation in its extreme form in militaristic cultures. Kamikaze pilots sacrificed themselves by the thousands in an attempt to delay the invasion of the Japanese homeland. A nineteenth-century Prussian army officer would commit suicide to avoid bringing disgrace to

When traditional values fail, some people seek answers to life's meaning and their own social identity by adopting beliefs and lifestyles at variance with societal norms. Cults offer a means of altruistic escape, by surrendering one's individuality and finding fulfillment in contributing to the welfare of the group. Hare Krishna, brought to the United States in the 1960s, still attracts some Americans. Do you think Americans are more or less tolerant of such groups compared to earlier decades? Why?

his unit or family. Entire units of the army of the nineteenth-century Zulu chieftain Shaka would march over a cliff at his command rather than show disobedience.

These are only a few of the many historical examples of groups causing individuals to devalue and even forfeit their individual selves. In the current situation, however, the push to surrender does not arise from a monolithic, overly integrated society overwhelming the individual, but from social change and the disintegration of traditional values driving lost individuals to seek out new, small groups in which to submerge themselves.

Both the Hare Krishna movement and the Unification Church—the latter founded by Sun Myung Moon, a Korean industrialist—typify groups that demand conformity from their members, including renunciation of all property and rigid adherence to the group's doctrines. More extreme are cults whose beliefs lead them to murder-suicides, such as the People's Temple in Jonestown, Guyana (914 dead in 1978); the Solar Temple in Canada and Europe (74 dead in 1994–1997); and Heaven's Gate in Rancho Santa Fe, California (39 dead in 1997). An example of the submergence of individualism to the group was found in the list of member offenses posted by Heaven's Gate on its Web site. These offenses included:

- Taking any action without using my check partner.
- Trusting my own judgment—or using my own mind.
- Staying in my own head, having private thoughts.

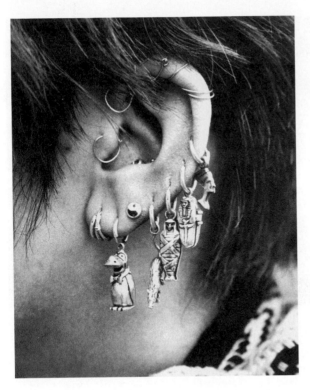

This teen sports symbols of her "coolness" and her membership in a popular cult. These symbols exaggerate her self-defined "deviance," identify her to other insiders as well as to outsiders, and reinforce group solidarity. Her behavior is emblematic of some of the factors involved in the causes of social problems and solutions to them. How might you apply to this example each of the sociological perspectives discussed in this chapter?

- Putting myself first, wanting my own way, rebelliousness—selfishness.
- Having likes or dislikes.
- Desiring attention or approval—wanting to be seen as good.

Marshall Applewhite, the leader of this cult—like Jim Jones of the People's Temple and David Koresh of the Branch Davidians (who died along with 79 followers in Waco, Texas, after a 51-day siege and government raid in 1993)—typifies the strong, charismatic cult leader, who often assumes the role of paternalistic superfather or divine representative. For its part, Heaven's Gate typifies the new authoritarian cult, which emphasizes intolerance of doubt or deviation among followers.

Whether we seek altruistic escape through a group or individually seek our own contentment, our emphasis on the self creates an "awareness trap." Concern with our personal meaningfulness and fulfillment can distract us from seeking societal causes of our unhappiness. Edwin Schur alerted us to our preoccupation with individual happiness and growth, and the danger of its exaggerating many of our social problems.[38] In our search for our "real" selves and "meaningful relationships," we lose sight of the structured, institutionalized sources of inequality and disintegration in the larger society.[39] Thus, again, we tend to blame ourselves and each other for problems solvable only by changing the social structure that provides our values and constraints.

Postmodernism: A Break with the Past

Postmodernists see individuals as being caught in the confusions of modern times. In some ways their views parallel those of the Functionalists, since both emphasize dysfunctions in society wrought by social change, particularly in technology, the workplace, and family life. Meanwhile, their concern about expanding mass consumerism resembles the Conflict theorists' interest in the false value of personal growth through stimulation of consumption. Also equivalent to the Conflict position is the Postmodernist stress on greed motivating exploitation of the environment. And their attention to the increase in artificial realities recalls the Interactionists' concerns about identity and meaning.

However, Postmodernists break with these orientations in many ways. They see all past conceptions of society as meaningless. To them, change is disruptive, not evolutionary. They reject the notions of objectivity and scientific analysis. Furthermore, the new technologies render present-day political boundaries and social arrangements obsolete. In the future, humans will have less and less individuality, free choice, and intimacy because the postindustrial age of high technology will dictate much of the realities and activities of life.

Postmodernism also rejects the "grand narratives" or stories that all belief systems and ideologies have. In U.S. culture, that might be that democracy is the most enlightened, rational form of government and will lead to universal human happiness. A Marxist culture might hold the idea that capitalism will implode and a utopian socialist world will evolve. In contrast, Postmodernism favors "mini-narratives," stories that explain small practices and local events rather than large-scale universal or global concepts.

Mary Klages says the rejection of this Postmodern movement toward fragmentation and provisionality has led to the rise of political conservatism and religious fundamentalism. On the other hand, the Postmodern affirmation of fragmentation and multiplicity attracts liberals and feminists. Furthermore, she states:

On another level, however, Postmodernism seems to offer some alternatives to joining the global culture of consumption, where commodities and forms of knowledge are offered by forces far beyond any individual's control. These alternatives focus on thinking of any and all action (or social struggle) as necessarily local, limited, and partial—but nonetheless effective. By discarding "grand narratives" (like the liberation of the entire working class) and focusing on specific local goals (such as improved day-care centers for working mothers in your own community), Postmodernist politics offers a way to theorize local situations as fluid and unpredictable, though influenced by global trends. Hence the motto for Postmodern politics might well be "think globally, act locally"—and don't worry about any grand scheme or master plan.[40]

Table 2.1 summarizes Modernism's assumptions of the present and future, together with Postmodernism's criticisms and alternative analyses. Though this orientation is still developing, the chart included here is the most complete Postmodernist statement to date of the confusions produced in modern times. It is here to make you think about several issues.

Table 2.1   Contrasting Tendencies of Modernism and Postmodernism

Modernism	Postmodernism
Scientific method: study of objective evidence.	Objectivity is impossible. We each develop in a context of local knowledge that shapes our world view. They are little more than linguistic constructions, the products of our particular time, place, and culture.
Scientific assumptions: the world is organized and structured by cause and effect. By studying scientifically, we can understand its essential balance and equilibrium.	The world is extremely complex and chaotic. Change is not regular or evolutionary, but disruptive. Equilibrium has never and will never be achieved.
Societal assumptions: as in the physical world, societies' norms and values will evolve toward an equilibrium in which individuals will find their proper places.	Hierarchies of privilege and divisions by ethnicity will persist. Norms and values exist in social contexts and can only be judged or understood in those contexts. Furthermore, so-called objective scientific writings are to be understood by seeing how the author's social background led to their construction.
Nature is to be rationally exploited to create an environment for humans.	The environment has been used for greed in shortsighted overdevelopment. Technology is now developing on a path of its own with little direction. Internet has put traditional nations and laws in jeopardy. Current social arrangements are obsolete.
Intimacy and mutual support will be enhanced through progress. Technology will allow more time for people to perfect their families and intimate arrangements.	Postindustrial occupations have taken both parents out of the home. Technology allows the simulation of intimacy as "real-time" intimacy. Symbols, celebrities, and their images will replace "reality" and further develop mass consumerism as a way of life.
Offers a master narrative of progress through science and technology.	Offers skepticism of progress, antitechnology reactions; new age religions.
Gives a sense of unified, center self; "individualism," unified identity.	Sees a sense of fragmentation and decentered self; multiple, conflicting identities.
Idea of "the family" is the central unit of social order: model of the middle-class, nuclear family.	New realities are alternative family units, alternatives to middle-class marriage model, multiple identities for couplings and childraising.
Hierarchy, order, centralized control are structural assets.	Subverted order, loss of centralized control, fragmentation are the new realities.
Maintains faith and personal investment in big politics (Nation-State, party).	Maintains trust and investment in micropolitics, identifies politics, local politics, institutional power struggles.

1. What is the position of the individual in our complex society?

2. How do you feel being a part of a major transition?

3. Are you optimistic, or have you become a victim of Postmodern pessimism?

Adolescent and Young Adult Suicide

Earlier we discussed Durkheim's study of suicide and his conclusion that weakened social bonds and a lack of rules contributed to an increase in suicides. Then we discussed the Conflict theorists' emphasis on alienation and powerlessness, the Interactionists' views about the search for meaning, and the Postmodernists' thoughts about the reduction of "real" intimacy and the obsolescence of current social arrangements. All of these viewpoints offer insights into the tragedy of suicide, helping us to understand the various social forces behind this seemingly personal action.

In the United States, the number of suicides is 70 percent greater than the number of homicide. On an average day, 84 people die by suicide and over 1,800 attempt suicide. Males are four times more likely to die by committing suicide than females, although females are more likely to attempt suicide. White males account for almost three-fourths of all suicides; and the suicide rates are generally higher than the national average in the western states and lower in the eastern and midwestern states.[41]

Especially disheartening is the high suicide rate among persons aged fifteen to twenty-four years, which has tripled since 1952 in this age group. Suicide rates among young men aged fifteen to twenty-four years remain twice as high as the overall average in the United States. Although suicide rates for blacks are lower than for whites, the rate for Black males aged fifteen to nineteen years increased 105 percent since 1980. Persons under twenty-five years commit 15 percent of all suicides. Among young people fifteen to twenty-four years old, suicide is the third leading cause of death, behind unintentional injury and homicide. More teenagers and young adults die from suicide than die from cancer, heart disease, AIDS, birth defects, stroke, pneumonia, influenza, and chronic lung disease *combined*.[42]

Motivations for Suicide

In 2001, the Division of Adolescent and School Health at the National Center for Chronic Disease Prevention commissioned a survey that questioned over 13,000 high school students across the country. The results were startling. Almost one-fifth (19 percent) of the students interviewed said they had seriously considered attempting suicide in the previous year; 15 percent had made a specific plan; and 9 percent (one in eleven students) had attempted suicide.[43]

Why would teenagers and young adults—with so much of their lives ahead of them and such a wide range of possibilities as well—kill themselves? No one really knows, but Alex Crosby, M.D., an epidemiologist at the Centers for Disease Control and Prevention (CDC), suggests that

> perhaps the risk factors—a history of substance abuse, a history of psychiatric disorders, exposure to suicide, disruption of the family, and exposure to violence—have changed, increased, or intensified in some way. For instance, researchers now believe children who witness violence in the home may be more likely to commit suicide. Other experts wonder if children's coping skills simply aren't adjusting to the fast-paced demands of the modern world. Kids are expected to grow up faster, take more responsibility, and excel in what they're doing, often with scant support from their main support system—the family.[44]

Applying the various sociological orientations to Dr. Crosby's comments, we easily find references to anomie and alienation. Self-estrangement, dysfunctional families, and an impersonal, rapidly changing technological society—either separately or in some combination—create a loss of community, disaffection, and a sense of meaninglessness. For many individuals, life itself becomes a social problem. They feel lost, disenchanted, and overwhelmed by the complexities of an uncaring world. Depressed young people often experiment with drugs and alcohol. Unfortunately, both are central nervous system depressants and can deepen a depression, exacerbating the impulse to attempt suicide.

Media Influences

The media also contributes to this problem, often portraying suicide as romantic, heroic, the answer to a problem, or simply inevitable. Movies such as *The Virgin Suicides, Dead Poets Society* and *Thelma and Louise* contain suicidal acts or threats without any discussion about the consequences. Newspaper and magazine articles often compare suicide victims to fictional romantic or heroic characters. Music, particularly in the death metal or speed metal subgenre of heavy metal, often contains lyrics about suicide, and many groups that sing about being young and dissatisfied give themselves names such as the Suicide Machine, Altruistic Suicide, Suburban Suicide, the Suicide Kings, Algebra Suicide, and Suicide Commando.

Two recent studies investigated the relationship between preference of high school students for heavy metal music and their vulnerability to suicide. Scheel and Westefeld found in 1999 that heavy metal fans expressed less-strong reasons for living (especially male fans) and had more thoughts of suicide (especially female fans). For a large majority, listening to music (all types) had a positive effect on mood. Overall, the results indicate that preference for heavy metal music among adolescents may be a "red flag" for increased suicidal vulnerability, but also suggest that the source of the problem may lie more in personal and familial characteristics than in any direct effects of the music.[45] The 2001 study by Lacourse, Claes, and Villeneuve supported that conclusion in finding that music preference, even to the point of music worship, was not significantly related to suicidal risk when controlling for other risk factors. In fact, the use of music was inversely related to suicidal risks for girls.[46]

Whatever role music and other media play, many teens and young adults find themselves in so desperate a situation that they see self-destruction as the only solution. The need to identify troubled young people is obvious. In 1991, the Centers for Disease Control and Prevention invited youth suicide prevention experts from around the country to present ideas on how to curb youth suicide. Two promising programs emerged out of that conference: The Gate Keeper, using adults from the school and community, and The Peer Support Program, using high school students. Both programs train people to identify young people at risk and steer them into an appropriate referral. Perhaps such intervention programs can reduce the often impulsive act of suicide among young people by reconnecting them with themselves and society.

▲ Thinking About the Future

The electronic revolution and the intensifying global economy are fundamentally altering our way of life, emphasizing technology, large managerial organizations, and the Information Society. It will take many chapters in this book to describe all the implications of this shift. In this chapter, our concern is with the effect it has on the average individual's image of society, relationships, and happiness.

We explored such topics as the loss of community, anomie, disillusionment, powerlessness, personal and political alienation, searching for meaningful identities, loss of individuality, altruistic escape into cults, Postmodern fragmentation, youth suicide, and media manipulation. What steps should we take now to reduce, even eliminate, these social problems? Will some of these current patterns worsen, improve, or remain the same? Which ones? What scenarios do you envision for the future, and what arguments can you make to support your predictions?

What Are the Solutions?

How can we get people more "connected" so they do not experience social isolation? Some suggest that technology, particularly telecommunications, already facilitates interactive communities with its instantaneous contact and wide choice of common-interest groups irrespective of distance, transportation needs, weather, or physical ability. What we need, these advocates suggest, is to get everyone "wired." Others say nothing beats face-to-face interaction, and we must facilitate this through more organized activities for all age groups, with designated places for them to come together and the means for them to get there. Some social planners speak to the need for more integrated physical designs of housing and neighborhoods that provide greater opportunities for chance meetings and social interaction.

What are our options, if any, for eliminating the fragmentation in people's lives? What steps can we take to optimize each individual's sense of self-worth, purpose, and fulfillment? Obviously, we cannot find simple or sweeping answers because our society is too large, complex, and diverse. Still, a few possible solutions present themselves. Religion in all its forms already offers solace to many, but many churches, clergy, and congregations could do more, for there are too many religious and semi-religious people needing help. What of the nonreligious? Perhaps part of the public schools' mission in preparing tomorrow's citizens should be instilling values and attitudes, as well as providing individual guidance, that bolster self-esteem and offer direction to one's life beyond college and career choices. Also, working to eliminate poverty and inequity resulting from discrimination would substantially improve the quality of life for many, bringing them to a level of personal happiness as yet unknown.

How do we keep our individuality in the face of a society demanding conformity? How do we resist media manipulation? The Social Constructions of Social Problems box (on p. 42) addressed some of the problems regarding social identity. Perhaps we need to encourage aspects in the socialization process to lessen other-directed tendencies and to promote more inner-directed tendencies. Education could play a greater role in developing critical-thinking skills to enable everyone to be more discerning in what the media presents, rather than allowing oneself to be easily persuaded to act or react in a certain way.

How do we overcome voter apathy? Proposed solutions include (1) negative sanctions (such as the Australian approach mentioned earlier); (2) easier registration and voting methods (such as using a computer at school, work, or home to increase people's participation in elections); (3) creating an interactive democracy (such as through weekly computerized inputs to the elected representatives from their constituents that would bind those officials' votes on legislation to the majority viewpoint in their districts). Each proposal has its dangers, but shouldn't something be done to get more people involved in the process of who governs them?

How do we combat the high levels of adolescent and young adult suicide? Compelling evidence indicates that adequate prevention and treatment of depression and alcohol and substance abuse can reduce suicide rates. So, too, do school-based interventions involving crisis management, self-esteem enhancement, and the development of coping skills and healthy decision making. Also effective are strategies involving restriction of access to common methods of suicide. Yet, as effective as these intervention strategies have been, the problem remains acute. Clearly, more needs to be done. But what? Should our approach be more of the same or something new, such as adopting approaches involving other levels of intervention and activities, such as crisis centers? Others point to countries such as Germany, which bans the airing of songs or particular groups deemed racist, and suggest similar censorship over any music or media form that glamorizes suicide. What do you think?

Considering Future Scenarios

Now it is time for you to consider what sort of life awaits each individual ten or twenty years from now. Recall the first chapter's statement, "Today's decisions are tomorrow's realities." Which of the current solution attempts should we continue, discontinue, or change? Can you think of other solutions not mentioned here? What future scenario do you envision? Which sociological orientation—Functionalist, Conflict, Interactionist, Feminist, Postmodernist—is most helpful to you in laying out this scenario? It's time for you to consider the material in this chapter, use your sociological imagination, and offer some possibilities.

What positive or negative impact will advances in telecommunications and computers, as well as their increased use by more and more people, have on our individual lives and personal identities? On our sense of belonging or community? On our social interactions? On our privacy? On our voting patterns? What of individuality versus social conformity?

Will work be more or less meaningful and fulfilling? Will we have more or less control over our work in where and when we do it? Will there be more or less structure to our lives? More or less stress? What about leisure time? What changes, if any, do you visualize in individuals' quest for personal fulfillment and in teen and young adult suicide rates? Should music and media be censored or otherwise controlled to prevent further glorification of suicide as something "romantic"?

What societal solutions do you recommend to make individuals' lives less problematic and more satisfying? What arguments can you make in support of your proposed solutions and scenario to convince your classmates?

SUMMARY

1. Concern for the quality of individuals' lives is recent. We once judged a society only by how well it provided for people's material needs, but now we think about how well individuals are integrated into society, and whether it makes them happy.

2. Society's values are the primary cause of what seem to be individual aberrations, such as suicide and shyness.

3. Anomie, the feeling of directionlessness and doubt about what is right or wrong, results from the destruction of communities of memory—close-knit groups with common histories—as

well as from social isolation, too many transitions from one status to another, an inability to define success, disillusionment with "the system," and the overall vagueness of modern life.

4. Conflict theorists see individuals' problems as being dominated by powerlessness and meaninglessness. Alienation from society, and from one's self, is caused by the false values of profit and competition, which force us to become human commodities that we sell to each other in the social marketplace. Our growing mistrust of one another parallels the growing mistrust of government. Many people take little interest in government, not even knowing who their elected representatives are, which results in low voter turnouts on election day.

5. Symbolic Interactionists view society as being more malleable than do adherents of the other emphases. Individuals remake society through everyday microinteractions. This optimistic attitude presupposes that adaptation and change are possible and that social problems are not rigidly fixed in the social structure. But individuals still have many problems. Their interactions consist of exercises in impression management and personality selling, and it is easy for people to lose their sense of self unless they understand this constant role-playing.

6. The secularization of society has complicated the search for meaning in life, causing some people to return to fundamentalist religious practices and others to seek altruistic escape through submission to the dictates of a cult.

7. Postmodernism sees our era as a new age of confusion. The old rules—and the hopes for the future they supported—no longer apply. Relying on objective science to solve our problems has led to a dead end, creating a technology that now generates its own undirected growth. The individual is lost in techno-electronic chaos.

8. The tripling of the suicide rate among teens and young adults since the mid-1950s poses a serious social problem. The various sociological orientations each offer some insight into motivations underlying this act of self-destruction. The media contribute to the problem by frequently portraying suicide as romantic, heroic, the answer to a problem, or inevitable.

KEY TERMS

Alienation	Narcissism
Altruistic escape	Quality of life
Anomie	Secularization
Commodity-self	Sociological imagination
Community	Stewardess syndrome
Impression management	Weberian paradox

At this book's Web site with Allyn & Bacon, you will find numerous links pertaining to the problems for the individual in society. To explore these resources, go first to the author's page (**http://www.ablongman.com/parrillo**). Next, select this edition of *Contemporary Social*

Problems and then select **Internet Readings and Exercises**. Then select **Chapter 2**, where you will find both a variety of sites to investigate and some questions that pertain to those sites.

SUGGESTED READINGS

Bellah, Robert N.; Richard Madsen; William M. Sullivan; Ann Swider; and Steven M. Tipton, *Habits of the Heart: Individualism and Commitment in American Life*, rev. ed. Los Angeles: University of California Press, 1996. An extensive examination of U.S. values and how the loss of traditional communities has prompted people to seek out lifestyle enclaves as lesser substitutes to overcome social isolation.

Berger, Peter; Brigette Berger; and Hansfried Kellner. *The Homeless Mind: Modernization and Consciousness*. New York: Vintage, 1973. A description of the effects of modernization on the individual's consciousness and the limits of attempts at demodernization.

Cohen, Stanley, and Laurie Taylor. *Escape Attempts: The Theory and Practice of Resistance to Everyday Life*, rev. ed. New York: Routledge, 1992. How we get through our days by mental management, identity shifts, and transformation of the banal, trivial, and repetitious.

Gergen, Kenneth J. *The Saturated Self: Dilemmas of Identity in Contemporary Life*. New York: Basic Books, reprinted 2000. A Postmodern classic detailing the consequences of the new technology on society and the formation of individual identity.

Goffman, Erving. *Interaction Ritual: Essays on Face-to-Face Behavior*. Garden City, N.Y.: Doubleday/Anchor, 1982. Individual problems traced in detail within their determining social fabrics. The sections on "Alienation from Interaction" and "Embarrassment and Social Organization" are pertinent classics.

Huxley, Aldous. *Brave New World Revisited*, reprint ed., New York: Harper/Perennial, 2000. The creator of one of the most famous fictional futures prophetically describes our current troubles with propaganda, the arts of selling, chemical persuasion, and overorganization.

Lasch, Christopher. *Culture of Narcissism: American Life in an Age of Diminishing Expectations*, rev. ed. New York: W.W. Norton & Company, 1991. A passionate, well-written indictment of U.S. society and penetrating analysis of our contemporary culture.

Pawley, Martin. *The Private Future*. New York: Pocket Books, 1977. The causes and consequences of community collapse in the Western world, including the retreat to secondary, created, private reality and the triumph of "sensation divorced from action."

Sayer, Derek. *Capitalism and Modernity: An Excursus on Marx and Weber*. New York: Routledge, 1991. An examination of the limits of Modernity and the prospects for Postmodernity through a review of the concepts of two of sociology's classic theorists.

Smith, Adam. *Powers of Mind*. New York: rev. ed. Simon & Shuster, 1982. "Every mind trip under the sun" is interestingly described: all the alternative escapes and self-improvement movements of the 1970s explained in a popular discussion.

3

Population and the Environment

Facts About Population and Ecology

- Each day the sun sets on 200,000 more human beings in the world, 97 percent of them in developing nations.[1]

- The world's population reached 6 billion in 1999 and will reach 7 billion by 2013.

- A football-sized field of rain forest is destroyed every second of every day.

- Every 3.6 seconds, someone dies of hunger.

- It will take decades, perhaps centuries, for U.S. lakes to recover from acid rain.

- Over 1 billion people lack access to clean drinking water.

- One in four Americans lives within 4 miles of a toxic waste dump.

The end of the human race will be that it will eventually die of civilization.
—Ralph Waldo Emerson

Population in Sociohistorical Context

The twentieth century surpassed all others in world population growth. The century began with fewer than 2 billion people and ended with more than 6 billion (see Figure 3.1 on the next page). For most of the 2 million years of human existence, population growth was relatively small, steadily maintaining perhaps about a 0.002 percent annual increase. High death rates from epidemics, famines, and war mostly offset the then-prevalent high birth rates. In 1804, the world's population reached 1 billion, at an annual growth rate of 0.5 percent. Better hygiene and public sanitation in more developed countries in the nineteenth century, plus expanded commerce bringing in more food supplies, led to longer life expectancies and a doubling of the population to 2 billion by 1927. In 1963, the annual population growth rate peaked at 2.19 percent, but since then it has slowed steadily, reaching 1.4 in 2000, or nearly 15,000 new births every hour.[2] However, even though the world's fertility rate is falling, it is not enough to halt population growth. Demographers expect the world population to reach 7 billion by 2013 and 8 billion by 2028[3] (see Figure 3.1).

For 200 years scientists have worried about the impact of uncontrolled population growth on the environment. Of the many attempts to address this social problem, two differing concepts now dominate present-day thinking.

Malthusian Pessimism

Thomas R. Malthus authored one of the most pessimistic statements ever made about the world's future. Until then, the spirit of political reform, together with scientific discoveries and inventions from the then-ending Age of Enlightenment, filled the public mind with hope that anything was possible. In 1798, Malthus's publication of *An Essay on the Principle of Population* dimmed that hope, and gave him the dubious honor of earning economics the nickname "the dismal science." Malthus argued that population was growing at a much faster rate than the food supply, and he asserted that this high birth rate would continue until the natural checks of disease and starvation or the artificial check of war raised the death rate and reduced

Figure 3.1   World Population Growth by Billions

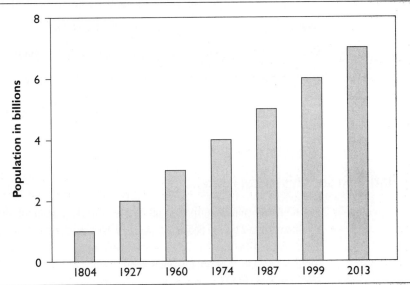

This night mosaic photographed from space reveals the urban concentrations of people in the United States and parts of Canada and Mexico. The swaths of light define the locations of cities and trace around nonurban areas. What are the impacts of population on environment in North America?

the population to a sustainable level. Progress, said Malthus, could not overcome this exponential population growth and therein lay the seeds of eventual disaster.

We can quickly grasp the power of **exponential growth** to generate immense numbers through the illustration of an old Persian legend:

> A clever courtier presented a beautiful chessboard to his king and requested that the king give him in return one grain of rice for the first square on the board, two grains for the second, four grains for the third and so forth. The king readily agreed and ordered rice to be brought from his stores. The fourth square of the chessboard required eight grains, the tenth took 512 grains, the fifteenth required 16,834 and the twenty-first gave the courtier more than a million grains of rice. By the fortieth square a million million rice grains had to be brought from the storerooms. The king's entire rice supply was exhausted long before he reached the sixty-fourth square.[4]

The seeming inevitability of Malthus's doctrine made it especially upsetting. It was called, "That black and terrible demon that is always ready to stifle the hopes of humanity."[5] The first implication seemed to be that nothing could be done to help the situation. If the food supply were increased by some technological invention, the population would simply increase until it ate up the progress. Moreover, people would continue to have more children in the expectation of further progress in food-supply productivity until some devastation killed off enough to rebalance the ratio of people to resources. Malthus's only solution was "moral restraint"—"the postponement of marriage until a man is able to support a wife and at least six children in conjunction with total pre-marital sexual abstinence."[6] In Malthus's time, of course, most birth-control methods were unknown, but he did not believe in birth control anyway because he thought that people were unreformedly indolent and that, unless given the burden of having to support a family, they would do nothing.

Criticisms of Malthus

We should not blame Malthus for his failure to anticipate the later stages of the Industrial Revolution and the popularity of birth-control devices. But we must deny Malthus's claim that the sex drive is so strong that, without enormous moral restraint, births will be uncontrollable. Birth control, in some form or other, occurs everywhere in the world, and usually not because all-powerful biological or environmental forces act on a population at its numerical maximum under subsistence conditions. We now know that changes in social values regarding how and when it is proper to have children can powerfully affect couples' desired family sizes. Not long ago in the United States, many wives said they would like to have "as many children as God would allow," and specified family sizes of five to seven were common. But a major shift in family attitudes occurred, and Americans now typically have two children—a number Malthus could hardly have criticized.

Was Malthus right? Critics of Malthus argue that advances in agriculture (the green revolution) have produced high-yield varieties of crops, notably wheat and rice, that dramatically increased the global food supply in relation to population growth. Moreover, biotechnological advances (use of growth hormones in animals and genetically altered microorganisms to protect plants against disease, frost, and insects) can also reduce global food shortages. However, both high-yield crops (requiring fertilizers, irrigation systems, and pesticides) and biotechnological innovations (requiring chemicals and drugs) are costly, making them unavailable to poor, developing nations most in need of greater food supplies. Furthermore, these approaches pose health hazards in runoffs from fertilizers and pesticides polluting the water and in the possible dangers to humans eating genetically altered foods or hormones. In fact, several European nations have banned any altered U.S. food or meat products for their potential health hazards.

Neo-Malthusians

Those agreeing with Malthus are called *neo-Malthusians* and use such expressions as the "population bomb" and "population explosion."[7] They continue to echo the concerns of Malthus about world population and an inadequate food supply, pointing out that in the last two decades of the twentieth century agricultural production slowed considerably. Although Asia and Latin America benefited somewhat from greater crop yields, Africa did not.[8] Neo-Malthusians argue that our environmental problems—global warming, destruction of the rain forests, growth of deserts in many developing countries, famine, and epidemics—result in large part from rapid population growth.

India's annual population growth of nearly 16 million leads the world. This scene of people packed into a crowded local train in Bombay vividly depicts the population density found in all this country's cities. What factors contribute to the high rate of population growth in developing countries such as India? What is the Malthusian view of population pressure as a social problem? How is the new-Malthusian view different? According to the demographic transition theory, where are cities like Bombay headed?

Demographic Transition Theory

The second model of population change—the **demographic transition theory**—is more hopeful. It postulates that people will spontaneously change to a desire for smaller families when their countries become economically and scientifically developed. If this is true, our political course is clear: we should do all that is possible to help nations develop.

Hope for decreased population growth in undeveloped countries rests on the histories of the Western world and of Japan, both of which went through a three-phase transition. Until about 1700, birth and death rates were very high and largely canceled each other out, causing little growth. Then sanitation and medical improvements enabled many more infants to survive and increased the average life span. This second phase is happening in much of the non-Western world today. A sharp lowering of the death rate yields rapid population growth. The third phase began around 1850 in Europe and spread to North America. The birth rate receded and approached the already lowered death rate. Except for the "baby boom" after World War II in the United States, a steady birth-rate downtrend continues today and could cause population growth to reach equilibrium early in the next century.

The theory of the demographic transition assumes that this three-phase change reflected modernization, industrialization, and increased standards of living.[9] The theory projects that when people leave farming for industrial jobs, they will come to realize that children are not

Social Constructions of Social Problems

Western Views on Population and Environment

Western tradition contains several prominent elements that strongly promote unlimited population growth and ecosystem exploitation. Three of the most powerful are the *dominant Western world view*, encouraging us to conquer nature; the *business ethic*, biasing our values in favor of accelerated growth; and the *motherhood mandate*, which creates a biased social position for women, forcing them to become mothers to achieve social acceptability.

Challenges from inside and outside Western culture to the centuries-old **Western world view** in recent years reflect growing concern about numerous ecological problems worsening the quality of life. This dominant view promotes an anthropocentric and overly optimistic view of our relationship to nature. **Anthropocentrism** is the belief that people fundamentally differ from all other creatures and that we are Earth's natural rulers. As the central product of creation/evolutionary progress, it is our right and even duty to impose our will on the rest of the planet because we are "the highest form of life" and the whole world revolves around us. Even more deeply entrenched is our optimism, which rests on three beliefs:

1. People are masters of their destiny; they can choose their goals and learn to do whatever is necessary to achieve them.

2. The world is effectively infinite, and thus provides unlimited opportunities.

3. The history of humanity is a record of progress; every problem has a solution, and thus progress need never cease.

Currently exemplifying this view is a group that other futurists call the "technological optimists." They believe that, as soon as a problem "gets bad enough," government attention and investment capital directed toward its solution will unleash technology to solve it. Many other observers disagree and say that industrialization aided by technology has *created,* not solved our problems.

The **business ethic** values rapid growth above all else. Unfortunately, this view keeps our entire economy geared to growing population and monumental waste. We are so in love with newness and change that we purchase products with built-in guarantees of obsolescence so that we can buy new ones sooner than we need to. Just as a business's profits must increase every year for the business to be deemed successful, so individuals measure personal success by continuous movement. "Getting ahead" only stops with forced retirement. In effect, we become programmed by our own momentum.

One powerful force that maintains population growth is the cultural norm mandating that a woman have at least two children (historically as many as possible and preferably sons) and that she raises them "well." Unlike past generations, today's society expects women to work outside the home, and "the pill" and other devices give them some control over their reproductive decisions. But the **motherhood mandate** remains strong, as society expects even a "working wife" to place "someday having children" uppermost in her concerns. This status requirement remains so deeply embedded in our culture that it is a dominant **unconscious ideology**. As one consequence, there is currently a mini baby boom among women in their thirties who feel they are "catching up" with the "family responsibilities."

needed to tend the fields or to inherit and work the farm when the parents are too old and must be supported. Consequently, people will voluntarily reduce their number of children. This attitude transition should naturally occur in all countries, according to the theory, solving the population problem as a by-product of industrialization.

Criticisms of the demographic transition theory center on the fallacy of Western ethnocentrism (see the box on page 60). The theory assumes that the only road possible to development is the one that Europe took in the nineteenth century. But development in new nations takes many forms and often happens much more rapidly than in the past. Studies show that rapid economic development does not necessarily bring smaller families. In fact, in many countries the first appearance of a higher standard of living increases the desire for children because it is easier to support them. On a hopeful note, though, demographic transition theory failed to predict the recent downturns in fertility in some developing nations. The belief that a country must be lifted out of poverty to bring down fertility turned out to be a Eurocentric myth. Fertility reduction occurs in developing countries whose governments make a strong commitment to population stability and promote easily accessible contraceptives.

In fact, the United Nations Population Division reports that fertility is now declining in all regions of the world. In the past twenty-five years, the number of children per couple has fallen from 6.6 to 5.2 in Africa, from 5.1 to 2.6 in Asia, and from 5.0 to 2.7 in Latin America and the Caribbean.[10] In some cases the decline has been dramatic. While it took the United States two hundred years to go from 7 babies per family to 2, Bangladesh has nearly done that in twenty years. In China, Japan, South Korea, Taiwan, and Thailand, the **total fertility rate** or TFR (the number of children a woman has during her lifetime) is less than the 2.1 break-even rate needed to achieve population stability.[11] Demographers call this TFR threshold **zero population growth**. If a country can sustain this 2.1 TFR for several generations, its population stabilizes and its percentage of young people are comparable to those who are older, creating a rectangular-looking graph of its population distribution as seen for more developed countries (MDCs) in Figure 3.2 on the next page. Otherwise, higher fertility rates mean ever-increasing numbers of young people, as illustrated by the broad base of the age-sex pyramid for less-developed countries (LDCs) also shown in Figure 3.2.

Population Pressure on the World

Three trends are causing substantial changes in our world environment. Each is the direct result of the human population explosion. First, even the most optimistic forecasts see population growth continuing. Second, people are depleting the ecological resources they need to support themselves—especially rain forests and groundwater supplies. Third, undernourishment is chronic in many developing countries.

Continuing Growth

Despite the worldwide drop in fertility rates, population is increasing, with the world adding 73 million more people every year—the population of France, Greece, and Sweden combined—or

Figure 3.2   Population by Age and Sex in More Developed and Less Developed Countries, 2002

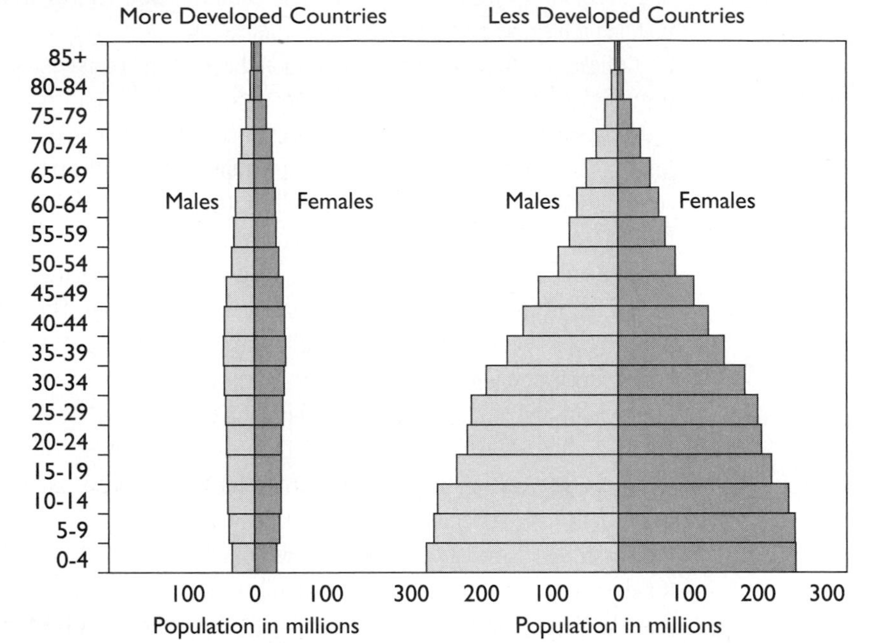

Source: United Nations Population Division.

the equivalent of a city the size of San Francisco every three days![12] On a daily basis the volume of population growth is astounding. Each day there are about 352,000 births and 152,000 deaths, resulting in a net gain of 200,000 humans added to the planet (see Figure 3.3).[13] These demographic changes have serious implications, whether countries are experiencing population reduction or growth.

Contrasts in Population Growth

Fertility rates in many of the MDCs have dropped so low that they face population decline. The United Nations estimates suggest that Italy will shrink 22 percent by 2050, Japan by 14 percent, Greece by 10 percent, Spain by 8 percent, and Germany by 4 percent.[14] Accompanying the dropping numbers in these and other countries is an aging population and an increase in the ratio of active to retired workers. Unless these countries make adjustments, their reduced labor force and intensified strain on the pension system and health-care system will generate some serious social problems.[15]

Concerned countries—Sweden, Hungary, and more recently Japan—have implemented policies to encourage childbearing and aid childrearing. An early experimenter in pronatalist programs, Sweden had the world's most generous family welfare benefits in the 1990s. Women could obtain fifteen months of maternity leave at 90 percent of their salary and be guaranteed

Figure 3.3 World Population Clock, 2000

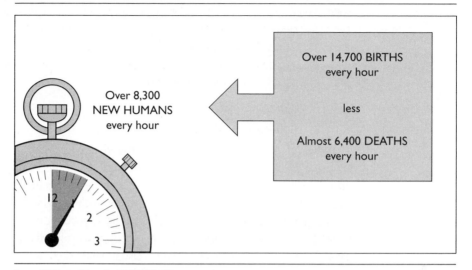

Over 8,300
NEW HUMANS
every hour

Over 14,700 BIRTHS
every hour

less

Almost 6,400 DEATHS
every hour

Source: U.S. Census Bureau, International Data Base.

a job (usually in government) when they returned to work. Swedish fathers were the first to have legal rights to paternity leave, parents could take extra leave days to attend their children's school events, and local governments expanded day-care centers and preschools. Sweden's total fertility rate rose from 1.7 around 1980 to 2.1 by 1990. However, when economic conditions worsened and a new conservative government scaled back many family benefits as cost-cutting measures, the fertility rate fell back to 1.5 by the turn of the century. Although it is difficult to measure which factors have the greatest effect in fertility rates, a clear influence on Sweden's fertility rate over the past twenty-five years has been resources available to families.[16]

In contrast, 96 percent of the world population increase now occurs in the LDCs, and this percentage will increase during the next quarter century.[17] Countries already lacking adequate resources will face even greater challenges in meeting needs for water, food, shelter, and energy as the already poor quality of life deteriorates even further.[18] Regions with the highest prevalence of malnutrition today are those most likely to undergo the greatest population increases in the foreseeable future. Although countries such as Bangladesh, India, and Pakistan decline significantly in fertility rates, they still remain well above the replacement level, and their populations will markedly increase by 2050: Bangladesh by 88 million, India by 546 million, and Pakistan by 197 million. Even with the ravaging AIDS epidemic in Africa, many countries will increase sharply in numbers. The Democratic Republic of Congo will triple in population with an 111 million increase, and the following countries will double in population: Kenya (22 million more), Mozambique (24 million more), Nigeria (138 million more), and Rwanda (10 million more). In the Western Hemisphere, continued high fertility rates will minimally double the populations in the following countries: Bolivia (9 million more), Guatemala (17 million more), Haiti (7 million more), Peru (18 million more), and Venezuela (19 million more).[19]

The different growth patterns in MDCs and LDCs means a changing distribution of the world's population. As Table 3.1 below shows, by 2050 the population share of Europe will decline to 7 percent, less than one-third its peak level, while Africa will more than double to 20 percent, Asia will stabilize at 59 percent, and Latin America will nearly double to 9 percent. In 1900, the population of Europe was three times that of Africa, but in 2050, the population of Africa will be nearly three times that of Europe.

Contrasts in Resource Use

Population growth and resource use are so intertwined with technological developments and the invasion of wild habitats for human exploitation that it is sometimes difficult to disentangle the resulting social problems to find the root cause. Let us be clear from the outset: the enormous number of people on Earth causes our problems. The gasoline engine, for example, is not a bad machine; but because there are so many of them, they degrade the quality of our air and water. In the "good old days," the warmth from wood or coal fires polluted the air and horse-powered transportation polluted the roads, while raw sewage polluted our streams and rivers. Modern technology, though it created new pollutions, reduced these old pollution sources. Unfortunately, today's populations are so large in many places that even these advances cannot yet control environmental degradation.[20]

The following formula illustrates why developed countries abuse the environment much more than do the faster-growing developing countries:

$$I = P \times CL \times T$$

In words, Environmental Impact equals Population multiplied by Consumption Level multiplied by Technology.

Each person in a developed country can take resources from and return waste to the environment at a rate expanded by the buying power of a credit card-based economy and further multiplied by the productive capacity of industries geared to a consumer-based society (see the accompanying box).[21]

Table 3.1 World Population, 1750–2050, by Percent

Major Area	1750	1800	1850	1900	1950	2000	2050
World	100	100	100	100	100	100	100
Africa	13.4	10.9	8.8	8.1	8.8	12.7	20.3
Asia	63.5	64.9	64.1	57.4	55.6	60.8	58.9
Europe	20.6	20.8	21.9	24.7	21.7	12.4	7.1
Latin American & the Caribbean	2.0	2.5	3.0	4.5	6.6	8.5	8.7
North America	0.3	0.7	2.1	5.0	6.8	5.2	5.0

Source: United Nations Population Division.

The Globalization of Social Problems

Population Impact on the Environment

At any level of development, human impact on the environment is a function of population size, per capita consumption and the environmental damage caused by the technology used to produce what is consumed. Currently, people living in developed countries have the greatest impact on the global environment. But as standards of living rise in developing countries, the environmental consequences of population growth in these countries will be amplified. With ever-increasing numbers of people aspiring, justifiably, to "live better," the potential for damage to the environment—beyond what we are already witnessing—also increases.

The most obvious environmental impacts are usually local, such as the disappearance of forests and associated watersheds, soil erosion or desertification or the brown haze hovering over cities like Los Angeles or Chengdu. Less obvious are phenomena such as the buildup of carbon dioxide in the atmosphere, the decline of fish catches around the world, dying coral reefs, melting glaciers, or the pollution of land and water resources with chemicals and other hazardous materials.

Each year, an estimated 12.5 to 17.5 million acres of agricultural lands are lost to erosion and an additional 3.75 million acres are lost because of waterlogging, salinization, or alkalinization. In recent decades, poor land and water management practices have resulted in the degradation of 4 billion acres of land—an area the size of China and India combined, that represents 11 percent of Earth's vegetated surface. Another 40 to 50 million acres of tropical forests and woodlands are also lost each year.

As the world's population increases, the amount of water per person decreases. The United Nations Educational, Scientific and Cultural Organization

(UNESCO) estimates that the amount of fresh water available per person has shrunk from more than 1.2 million cubic feet per year in 1850 to only 300,000 cubic feet today. In Florida and the U.S. Southwest, population growth is placing a strain on the **aquifers,** or underground water reservoirs, which cannot sustain unlimited pumping. Worldwide overpumping of aquifers—occurring mostly in China, India, North Africa, the Middle East, and the United States—exceeds 160 billion tons of water per year. Spreading water shortages threaten to reduce the global food supply by more than 10 percent. Although irrigation problems such as waterlogging, salting, and silting go back several thousand years, aquifer depletion is new, confined largely to the last half century, when powerful diesel and electric pumps made it possible to extract underground water far faster than the natural recharge from rain and snow.

The pollution and increasing scarcity of renewable fresh water supplies also threaten human health and welfare. A quarter of the world's people, living mainly in developing countries, lack access to safe water supplies, and around 3 million people lack sewage-treatment facilities. In Asia, for example, more than 1 billion people depend on groundwater for household use, yet these groundwater reserves are threatened by contamination from intensive agriculture needed to keep food production in pace with population growth. More than 3 million children die annually of water-related diseases such as diarrhea and fecal-oral infections, the world's greatest source of infant mortality.

Sources: Based on data from the Population Reference Bureau, United Nations Population Division, World Commission on Water, and Worldwatch Institute.

To illustrate, the 15 percent of the world's population living in MDCs account for 56 percent of the world's total consumption, while the poorest 40 percent in LDCs account for only 11 percent of consumption. While most people are consuming more today—with the expansion of the world's economy in the 1990s and rising living standards in many countries—consumption for the average African household is 20 percent less than it was 25 years ago. Here's a specific example: per capita consumption of fossil fuels remains highest in MDCs, where people consumed up to 6.4 tons of oil equivalent per year, ten times the consumption in developing countries.[22]

The world's 1.2 billion poorest people also do much environmental damage. Poverty compels them, as we will discuss shortly, to misuse their environment and ravage its resources, while lack of access to better technologies, credit, education, health care, and family planning condemns them to subsistence patterns that leave little concern about their environment. However, it is the richest 1.3 billion people who exploit and consume disproportionate amounts of resources and generate disproportionate quantities of waste. Each American, for example, uses an average of fifty-five barrels of oil each year, compared with an average of three barrels by a Bangladeshi. Even more, the slower growing U.S. population increases its energy consumption six or seven times faster annually than does the more rapidly growing Bangladeshi population.[23]

The Loss of Forests, Plants, and Animals

The decline of forests is not a modern phenomenon, as illustrated, for example, by the history of Easter Island and England. The remarkable circumstances today are the rapid rate and extent of deforestation worldwide. The twentieth century began with 40 percent of Earth covered by forests, and it ended with forest cover down to 27 percent, a loss of about one-third of its area. However, in developing countries the loss is nearer one-half because population pressures have spurred extensive clearing of forests for agricultural purposes and for fuel harvesting. (Over 2 billion people depend on wood for heating and cooking.)[24] In sub-Saharan Africa, for example, that dependency includes 93 percent of all Ethiopians, 74 percent of Ghanians, 70 percent of Kenyans, 80 percent of Malagasies, 82 percent of Nigerians, and 90 percent of Somalians. Because approximately 1.3 billion people are consuming wood faster than forest growth can replace it, some fear these and other countries might one day be like Haiti, which has none of its original primary forest remaining.[25]

Although deforestation rates are greatest in developing countries, developed countries consume over half of all harvested wood. The United States alone consumes over one-third of the world's total paper supply, the majority of which goes for packaging and advertising. The construction industry also consumes huge amounts of wood. One notable element here is that Americans now live in homes almost twice the size of fifty years ago and now occupy two and one-half times the residential space per person.[26]

Such destruction results in numerous environmental problems. Deforestation leads to soil erosion and increases sediment in rivers, making once navigable waterways less so. Silt carried downstream clogs hydroelectric dams and causes electricity shortages. Without trees to hold the soil and absorb the rainfall, increased flooding occurs. Experts link major floods in Bangladesh and India with deforestation in the Himalayan Mountains, where many of the subcontinent's rivers begin. Recent disastrous floods in China, Honduras, Mexico, and Venezuela also followed considerable forest loss.

Forest destruction has serious global implications also. Rain forests contain vast reserves of carbon in their vegetation, so that when they are burned, or the trees are cut and left to decay, the carbon is released into the atmosphere as carbon dioxide. Since a football field-sized piece of rain forest is destroyed every second of every day, or 500,000 trees every hour, the amount of gas released is considerable.[27] In fact, deforestation is second only to burning of fossil fuels as contributing to the **greenhouse effect**. As a consequence, temperatures increase around the world causes ice caps to melt and sea levels to rise, thus endangering coastal homes and causing major flooding. Furthermore, many plant and animal species face extinction because of the loss of their natural habitat. In subsequent sections, we will discuss both global warming and plant/animal extinction more fully.

Tropical Rain Forests

While the destruction of forests—whether boreal, temperate, or tropical—causes serious environmental problems, the eradication of the tropical rain forests carries additional consequences. Located near the equator, tropical rain forests receive over eighty inches of rainfall annually. The heavy vegetation forms a continuous canopy, which blocks the rainfall. The water reaches the forest floor through a falling fine spray or by rolling down tree branches and trunks. Rain forests are also distinctive in that they have no "seasonality"—no dry or cold season of slower growth. Once tropical rain forests covered more than 14 percent of Earth's land area, but now they occupy less than 6 percent. Yet this small portion is home to more than half of the world's plant and animal species.[28]

Certainly the Amazon region contains the world's largest tropical rain forest. However, nearly one-third of the world's tropical forests are in Africa, Asia, and other parts of Latin America. Even the United States has tropical forests—in Puerto Rico, Hawaii, Guam, American Samoa, and the U.S. Virgin Islands. No matter where they are, tropical rain forests play an important role in our everyday lives. They are an essential factor in regulating rainfall worldwide, which in turn affects global climate. Furthermore, they are an important source of food, herbs, and pharmaceuticals that may offer potential cures for diseases such as cancer and AIDS.

Worldwide, the tropical rain forests are diminishing at an alarming rate. The National Academy of Science estimates that at least 50 million acres—an area the size of England, Scotland, and Wales combined—are lost each year. Bangladesh, Haiti, India, and Sri Lanka have completely lost their primary rain forests, and the Ivory Coast has nearly logged away all of its rain forests. Both the Philippines and Thailand have lost more than half of theirs.[29] If current trends continue, most tropical forests will be destroyed or damaged beyond recovery. A rain forest that is chopped down can grow back over time, but it will never have the same variety of plants and animals it once did. Some species simply become extinct. Of the seventy-six countries that presently contain tropical rain forests, only four—Brazil, Guyana, Papua New Guinea, and Zaire—are likely to retain major undamaged tracts ten years from now, say the experts.[30] The chief causes of this emerging catastrophe are logging, farming, and ranching.

Once part of the Amazonian rain forest, this area has been destroyed by logging, slash-and-burn agricultural practices, and overgrazing. What are the implications of rain forest destruction for soil and water conservation, for biodiversity and resource management, and for global climatic change? What are some other ecosystem problems of the world today?

Logging, as already stated, occurs on a massive scale, both for fuel in LDCs and for other consumption uses in MDCs. In the latter, wood such as balsa, ebony, mahogany, rosewood, sandalwood, and teak is harvested as raw material to build houses, make furniture or household products (such as salad bowls), or provide pulp for newspapers and magazines.

Farming is another factor, as population pressures continue in the rain forest countries. Because the farmers are often poor and can't afford to buy land, they clear rain forest land to grow their crops. However, despite their lush vegetation, tropical forests contain only a thin layer of fertile soil; most of the land underneath is low in nutrients. A rain forest is a self-contained system that supports itself. The trees are fed by their own dying vegetation falling to the ground and temporarily enriching the soil. Deforestation leads either to rapid soil depletion from farming or to soil erosion from rainfall. Since it takes one hundred years to create an inch of soil, the land becomes barren very quickly.[31] Rain forest destruction has a number of deleterious—and as yet incompletely understood—consequences to the world, as the following sections reveal.

Ranching is the third contributor to tropical deforestation, especially in Central America, because of its use of former rain forest land as pastures to raise cattle for meat exports, mostly to the United States. As with use of tropical wood products, this is another example of the role of U.S. consumers in the deforestation of tropical rain forests. Consumers do not associate their fast-food consumption with deforestation in Central America, yet this is from where about 200 million pounds of meat is exported to the United States each year. Cheaper to produce than domestic beef, it is used in processed beef products, such as hamburgers sold at fast-food outlets, luncheon meats, pet food, baby food, sausage, and frozen dinners. Of all the areas being threatened by deforestation, Central America represents the most severe loss of biological diversity. After five to ten years of cattle grazing, a tropical pasture becomes useless. The ranchers must clear and move onto other areas, leaving behind an area with virtually no nutrients remaining; thus it will not naturally regenerate as forest. Two-thirds of Central American rain forest have been cleared since 1950, and it is estimated that within twenty years the remaining forest will disappear.[32]

Extinction of Plants and Animals

Plants provide us with food and medicines, many of them important in the treatment of cancer and AIDS. For example, of all plants identified by the National Cancer Institute as useful in the treatment of cancer, 70 percent come from the rain forests. Drugs from the tropical forests greatly increase the survival rate of children with leukemia, and at least 1,400 types of plants contain ingredients active against cancer.[33]

Over-the-counter drugs (analgesics, laxatives, tranquilizers, etc.) derived from tropical forests are a $20-billion-a-year industry. Important pharmaceuticals made at least partly from tropical forest products include birth control pills, steroids, and medications to treat arthritis, heart disease, high blood pressure, Hodgkin's disease, malaria, pain, pneumonia, and other health problems. Clearly, rain forest plants are a valuable asset for almost everyone and could prove to be even more advantageous. Fewer than 1 percent of tropical forest species have been thoroughly examined for their chemical compounds, as many await testing to determine their medicinal benefits. Moreover, many rain forest plants have not been identified. Scientists estimate that at least 30,000 plants remain undiscovered, most of them rain forest species.[34]

The 1 in 120 plants that scientists have found medically beneficial so far contribute about $40 billion to the world's economy and help save lives and make people well. However, destruction of the rain forest threatens Earth's **biodiversity** by imperiling about 25,000 plant species that grow only in those areas. If the same ratio holds for untested plants, we may lose an estimated two hundred beneficial plant species, cost the world $200 billion a year, and needlessly sacrifice countless human lives that could be saved by new drugs derived from these sources.[35]

The single greatest cause of species extinction in the next half century will be tropical deforestation. Scientists agree that roughly 5 to 10 percent of closed tropical forest species will become extinct *per decade* at current rates of tropical forest loss and disturbance. With more than 50 percent of species occurring in closed tropical forests and a total of roughly 10 million species on Earth, this amounts to the phenomenal extinction rate of more than one hundred species per day. Dozens of exotic birds and animals also face extinction in this massive destruction of their natural habitat. In addition, migratory birds—including various flycatchers and warblers—which spend the winter months in the tropics before flying north in the spring, are also threatened.[36]

World Hunger

In the last fifty years, almost 400 million people worldwide have died from hunger and poor sanitation. That's three times the number of people killed in all wars fought in the entire twentieth century.[37] Every day 24,000 people die from hunger or hunger-related causes; 75 percent are children under the age of five.[38] As terrible as that reality of famine and starvation is, the problem of chronic malnutrition is even more widespread. The tragic consequences of malnutrition include susceptibility to disease, death, disability, and stunted mental and physical growth. Worldwide, iodine deficiency is the greatest single preventable cause of brain damage and mental retardation, and vitamin A deficiency remains the single greatest preventable cause of needless childhood blindness.[39]

The Developing World

The United Nations Food and Agriculture Organization reports that 799 million people in the developing world were undernourished in 1998–2000. That number is 20 million less than in 1990–1992 and continues a downward trend since 1979–1981, when almost 920 million people, 30 percent of the developing world's population, went hungry. However, the progress is uneven. China alone reduced the number of undernourished people by 74 million in that period, while Indonesia, Vietnam, Thailand, Nigeria, Ghana, and Peru each achieved reductions of more than 3 million. In 47 other countries in the developing world, the number of undernourished people increased by over 80 million. The slowing pace of reducing world hunger means that the goal set at the 1996 World Food Summit will fall over 350 million short.[40]

In developing countries, 6 million children under the age of five die each year, mostly from hunger-related causes. In those countries one child in ten dies before his fifth birthday. Malnutrition can severely affect a child's intellectual development. The World Health Organization reports that children who have stunted growth due to malnutrition score significantly lower on math and language achievement tests than do healthy children.[41]

Malnutrition takes its heaviest toll on children, and the health damage can begin before birth. Pregnant women who receive inadequate nourishment are likely to have underweight babies, who are especially vulnerable to infections and parasites that can lead to early death. Children who survive but receive inadequate food in the first five years of life are susceptible to the permanent stunting of their physical growth. Incredibly, 60 percent of children in South Asia have stunted growth, as do 39 percent of children in sub-Saharan Africa, and 33 percent in East and Southeast Asia.[42]

Although hunger has declined in the past twenty years in the Asia-Pacific region because of economic growth and large-scale public investments in nutrition, health, and education, the region is home to most of the world's hungry people. Of its 508 million undernourished people, India alone has 233 million. With its neighbors added, the South Asian subregion contains about two-fifths of the world's total of undernourished people (315 million) and another 25 percent are located in Southeast and East Asia (204 million). An additional one-fourth lives in sub-Saharan Africa, particularly in the eastern half.[43]

In addition to absolute numbers, another important consideration is the proportion of a chronically hungry population in a country or region. West Africa, for example, has the largest total population of any of the African subregions, but the lowest percentage of undernourished people. In contrast, East Africa has twice as many undernourished people, but a slightly smaller population. Similarly, Central and Southern Africa are also proportionately higher than West Africa, but smaller in total populations. High prevalence rates also exist in Afghanistan, Bangladesh, Haiti, the Democratic People's Republic of Korea, Mongolia, and Yemen. Proportionately, the number of undernourished people in the MDCs is very low or extremely low, by United Nations guidelines. About 30 million people in countries in transition are undernourished. The greatest share of these, 26 million, live in Eastern Europe and the former Soviet Union.[44]

Causes of Hunger and Malnutrition

Problems of world hunger result from per capita shortages of basic food resources and the unfair distribution of food supplies. Available world cropland per capita declined 20 percent in the 1990s, partly because the burgeoning world population takes away agricultural land for roads, houses, and industries. Also, each year erosion by wind and water destroys nearly 25 million acres of cropland, and that erosion is intensifying worldwide, especially in developing countries where overgrazing is common. Irrigation is essential to agricultural productivity in arid areas, but irrigated cropland per capita declined 10 percent in the past decade. A good example of that impact is the major food group of grains, the mainstay of human diets, and about 80 to 90 percent of the world's food supply. Although there have been higher grain crop yields per acre since 1984, these harvests get divided among more people as the world's population grows. So the food availability per capita keeps declining steadily.[45]

The second problem is food distribution. The Food and Agriculture Organization of the United Nations has set the minimum requirement for caloric intake per person per day at 2,350. Worldwide, there are 2,720 calories available per person per day. Over fifty countries fall below that requirement; they do not produce enough food to feed their populations, nor are they able to afford to import the necessary commodities to make up the gap. Most of these countries are in sub-Saharan Africa.

Even in the United States, the richest nation in the world, chronic hunger is a problem for millions. Despite a booming economy in the late 1990s, hunger in the United States remained at the same level throughout that decade. The U.S. Department of Agriculture says about 3 percent of U.S. households—34 million people, including almost 13 million children—experience hunger; they must skip meals or eat less to make ends meet. Another 7 percent of all households are at risk of hunger because they have lower-quality diets or must resort to seeking emergency food because they cannot always afford the food they need. Thus, one in ten U.S. households experiences hunger or the risk of hunger.[46]

The Ecosystem

Arthur George Tansley, a British plant ecologist, coined the word **ecosystem** in 1935. He realized that in order to understand any plant, one also needed to know about the soil, the climate, and the animals around it: the plant's total environment. Since then, ecosystem thinking has emerged as a leading means of understanding our environmental problems.

Ecosystem Thinking

When we apply this concept to social problems, we think of human ecosystems and their psychological and sociocultural elements.[47] We must interpret problems holistically, treating the environment as a nondivisible whole when we study ecological problems. Holistic thinking may sound simple, but it is difficult for most Americans because they learn the scientific tradition of analytic thinking: break a problem down into parts with one variable each, and deal with the isolated variables, one at a time. Thus, farmers focus only on certain plant species. Their goal is to increase crop yields in the shortest amount of time. They define any plant that competes with the "crop" as a "weed" and get rid of it. Any animal or insect in the area is a "varmint" or pest that they must poison or trap. We do obtain high crop yields as a result, but we can also incur some devastating side effects to the land and to the water supply.

Farmers are by no means unique. Most of us share the same singlemindedness, believing that goal-oriented concentration on production is the key to success. But we are beginning to realize that we live in a context that has limits. Three aspects of this finite context are the critical elements of ecosystem thinking: interconnectivity, thresholds, and trigger effects (the latter two being manifestations of system overload).

Interconnectivity

Every part of an ecosystem, potentially at least, connects to every other part. Sometimes changes in one part can produce effects in other parts of the system far removed from the original action. A good example is hurricane Mitch, which in October 1998 became the fourth-strongest hurricane to enter the Caribbean in the twentieth century. That ferocious storm slammed into Central America and stalled for more than a week, causing horrendous mudslides that eradicated entire villages. About 10,000 people died. Honduras lost 95 percent of its crops, and half of its population lost their homes. Experts attributed that and other destructive storms to global warming. However, the major culprit was deforestation, for if the trees had been left to grip the soil on the hills, fewer villages would have been buried in mudslides.[48]

Overload: Thresholds and Triggers

The ecosystem can handle a good deal of pollution. Rivers can transform raw sewage into harmless chemicals, just as soil microorganisms can transform manure into fertilizer. At some point, however, a **threshold** is reached at which the system can no longer detoxify the effluent, and the organisms in the system begin to die. This happened to the Atlantic Ocean near New York City in the 1980s. Marine biologists found large ocean areas with no life at all, just green slime and an accumulation of the city's sewage sludge from years of dumping in the area. The frightening fact is that *we don't know what the thresholds are for most of our natural sys-*

tems. What we do know is that local ecosystems start to collapse when human demands on them become excessive.

Even the carefully watched forests of western Germany surprised their managers. The proportion of unhealthy trees soared from 8 percent to 54 percent in just two years, between 1982 and 1984. In the 1990s, Czech woodlands suffered extensive destruction. Obviously, something tipped the balance to trigger widespread decline within these and other forest systems in Europe. The culprit was acid rain—natural rainfall contaminated with so much acidic matter from the chemical emissions in factory smoke that it has the pH of lemon juice in some cases. When the acidity of rain crosses a tolerance threshold, trees and animals suddenly begin dying in large numbers.[49]

Trigger effects can be even more dramatic, since relatively small human inputs can totally upset the natural balance. This frequently happens when we import a new species into an ecosystem. When it has no controlling predators, it multiplies too rapidly, destroys the ecosystem's balance and takes over. Australians, for example, suffered greatly from a plague of imported rabbits and now must maintain "rabbit-proof" fencing across a good portion of their continent in order to contain them. Another "trigger" effect of gigantic proportions is the building of a dam. What sometimes happens is that the weight of the accumulated water becomes sufficient to make a geological fault line slip and cause an earthquake. This happened in 1967 in India, and the earthquake killed two hundred people. Similarly, after engineers created and filled Lake Mead in southern Nevada (1935–1939), hundreds of seismic events of significant magnitude were recorded.[50]

After the completion of the Aswan High Dam on the Nile in 1970, salinization and waterlogging adversely affected as much as 50 percent of Egypt's productive land. Up to 10 percent of Egypt's agricultural production may be lost because of deteriorating soil fertility. And with its annual floodwaters blocked before they reach the sea, the Nile no longer carries off excess sediment—the delta is sinking under its own weight. In Pakistan, meanwhile, a quarter of all arable soil is deteriorating due to salinity and waterlogging caused by indiscriminate construction of poorly engineered irrigation canals.[51]

Current Ecosystem Problems

In this section we will discuss how some ecological threats illustrate the three principles of interconnectivity, thresholds, and trigger effects just described.

Global Warming

Naturally occurring greenhouse gases (water vapor, carbon dioxide, methane, nitrous oxide, and ozone) trap some of the sun's warmth, much like the glass panels of a greenhouse. This natural "greenhouse effect" keeps Earth's average temperature at a hospitable sixty degrees Fahrenheit, allowing life to exist, as we know it. However, a combination of population growth, fossil fuel burning, and deforestation is affecting the mixture of gases in the atmosphere. Since the Industrial Revolution, atmospheric concentrations of carbon dioxide have increased nearly 30 percent from the

Solid waste disposal remains a problem in the United States despite mandatory and voluntary recycling programs and greater regulation of landfills and interstate waste management corporations. How can the persistence of problems with the disposal of hazardous waste and the cleanup of toxic dump sites be explained?

burning of fossil fuels, wood, or solid waste, and from deforestation. Methane concentrations (arising from oil and gas pipeline leaks, coal seams, landfill decomposition, raising of livestock, and rice paddies) have increased 145 percent. Nitrous oxide concentrations (arising during combustion of solid waste and fossil fuels and use of chemical fertilizers) have increased about 15 percent. These increases have resulted in more heat trapped in the atmosphere.[52]

The world's leading scientists agree that global warming is real and already occurring. The questions now are how fast will it occur and how bad it will be. The twentieth century's ten warmest years all occurred in its last fifteen years, part of a century-long warming trend. Signs of the melting are everywhere. The snow/ice pack in the Rockies, the Andes, the Alps, and the Himalayas is shrinking. The volume of the ice cap covering the Arctic Ocean has shrunk by more than 40 percent over the last thirty-five years (see Figure 3.4). In fact, the Arctic and Antarctic ice sheets are crumbling. The northern tundra has warmed so much that in some years it adds carbon to the atmosphere instead of soaking it up. Spring comes a week earlier to the Northern Hemisphere, where glaciers are the smallest they've been in a century.[53]

Because of the extensive melting of glaciers and polar ice, the sea levels are rising—nearly one foot in the twentieth century. If global warming continues at its present rate, the 2,000-plus scientists and technical experts from industry, government, and academia who make up the

Figure 3.4   Retreating Polar Ice

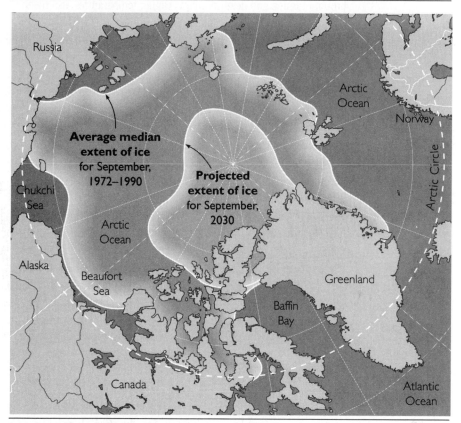

Source: Office of Naval Research, Naval Ice Center.

authoritative Intergovernmental Panel on Climate Change (IPCC) say that sea levels will rise another six to thirty-seven inches in this century. The Florida Keys would be obliterated, shore-front homes on all coasts would become driftwood, and inland subdivisions would become beachfront property.[54] Furthermore, fourteen of the world's fifteen largest cities are located on seacoasts, which means that they and many homes situated at sea level elevations could be submerged in the future.[55]

Our weather patterns are changing also. Extreme weather—heavy rains of more than two inches in twenty-four hours or extensive droughts—has increased in frequency. For example, the number of extreme precipitation events in North America has jumped 20 percent since 1900.[56] Some of the Western Hemisphere's extreme weather, say the experts, results from *El Nino*, the large mass of warm water that develops far out in the Pacific because of temperature changes due to deforestation and global warming.

Scientists tell us that global warming could make extreme weather the norm, that both floods and droughts could become more common and severe, with potentially devastating effects on agriculture around the world.[57] In recent years, droughts in sub-Saharan Africa brought famine and death to many. Higher temperatures also mean that insects and vermin that carry disease can now survive in places they couldn't before. In the summer of 2000, for example, vast amounts of Texas crops and fruit trees were destroyed by millions of grasshoppers, the most the state had seen since the 1930s.

What to do? Clearly, countries need to reduce their emissions of greenhouse gases. Development of alternative energy sources, such as cleaner-burning natural gas instead of coal, greater use of wind and solar power, and improved technologies to reduce emissions would be positive steps. As Eastern European nations like Poland and Hungary modernize their antiquated, coal-fired industries, they are significantly reducing their industrial emissions and hence their contribution to global warming. Much more needs to be done, however. The United States, with 4 percent of the world's population, contributes 23 percent of the total carbon dioxide to the atmosphere.[58]

> The most powerful argument for trying to mitigate climate change now is based on chemistry: carbon dioxide stays in the atmosphere for a century, on average; gas from the coal that kept President McKinley warm is still up there. As a result, the world would warm even if we stopped burning coal, oil and natural gas today. But if we wait to act until the greenhouse world is upon us, it will take decades to turn it around. Even stabilizing emissions doesn't stabilize climate; as long as the gases keep rising, even at current rates, so will the mercury.[59]

Acid Rain

Caused by air pollution, acid rain forms when sulfur dioxide and nitrogen oxides in the smoke and fumes from burning fossil fuels rise into the atmosphere and react with the moisture in the clouds. Sunlight increases the rate of most of these reactions to form a mild solution of sulfuric acid and nitric acid that falls to Earth as acid rain, not just as rainwater, but also as fog, snow, and other forms of precipitation. Some of the acidity in the atmosphere also falls to Earth through dry deposition as gases and particles, where they can then eat away at the things on which they settle, or they can wash away through rainstorms, resulting in a more acidic form than the falling rain alone.[60]

Power plants burn coal and oil to produce electricity and account for two-thirds of all sulfur dioxide emissions and one-fourth of all nitrogen oxide emissions in the United States. Other sources are the natural gas, oil, and coal burned to heat our homes and the gasoline to power cars, trucks, and airplanes.[61]

In some lakes and streams, acidification has completely eradicated fish species, such as the brook trout. Over 14,000 lakes in eastern Canada, 1,350 streams in the Mid-Atlantic Highlands (mid-Appalachia), and about 70 percent of Adirondack lakes are acidic. Through chemical reactions, acid rain is stripping away vital plant nutrients in forest soils, impairing tree growth, especially those at higher elevations, such as the red spruce along the Appalachian ridges from Maine to Georgia, including such areas as the Shenandoah and Great Smoky Mountain national parks.

Moreover, the dry sulfate particles in the air account for more than a 50 percent reduction in visibility in the eastern part of the United States, including those national parks just mentioned.[62]

Acid rain accelerates the erosion of automobiles, buildings, statues, and sculptures. It also increases the solubility of such metals as aluminum, copper, and lead, causing them to seep from water pipes into drinking water. In a dramatic example, in parts of Sweden, copper levels in water have reached high enough levels to turn hair green, as well as cause kidney and liver damage.[63]

Wind drift results in acid rain falling hundreds, even thousands, of miles away. For example, prevailing winds take the pollutants rising in the air in Great Britain, and they fall as acid rain on the once pristine lakes and forests of Scandinavia and beyond. The result has been severe damage to forests in Sweden and the contamination of fish in over 10,000 Swedish lakes, making them unfit for human consumption. Airborne muck from the industrial U.S. Midwest and central provinces of Canada falls back as acid rain on the much cleaner areas of southeast Canada and northeast United States. About half the sulfuric acid rain falling in Canada originated in the United States.[64] Taking an activist stance, New York State sued the owners of twelve coal-fired plants in the Midwest for failing to install federally mandated pollution controls.[65]

China, which depends on coal for 75 percent of its primary energy, is the second largest producer of greenhouse gases and could overtake the United States as early as 2010. China's six largest cities are among the world's most polluted. Acid rain destroys nearly one-third of that nation's crops, and then it drifts eastward to Japan and beyond. China has begun to take action, though. It now requires the use of unleaded gasoline in its major cities and has begun replacing its old coal-fired plants with newer and cleaner ones.[66] However, acidification in China remains a serious threat in the future, given the still-expected emissions, population density, and soil sensitivity. The threat is real in large portions of Africa, Asia, northern and central Europe, and South America, as well.[67]

The U.S. Congress amended the Clean Air Act in 1990, requiring polluters to reduce their emissions of sulfur dioxide. Since then, the lakes in many regions in the United States and Europe have become less acidic. The lakes are slowly regaining their normal water chemistry, which will eventually enable aquatic life to return to its normal level. Unfortunately, in four regions—the upper Midwest, south and central Ontario, and the Adirondack and Catskill Mountains—the lakes remain as acidic as ever. Surprised at first by their lack of recovery, scientists discovered that the lakes had lost their natural buffering capacity because prolonged exposure to heavy doses of acid rain leached large quantities of calcium and magnesium from the soil. Essentially, these chemicals work with nature in much the same way as antacids work in the stomach. Not only will it take decades, perhaps centuries, for the recovery of the soil and streamwater chemistry, but this realization also made us aware that scientists actually know very little about how ecosystems get damaged and what it takes to bring them back.[68]

Water Supply

Ironically, although the glaciers are melting and floods account for half of all deaths by natural catastrophes, the people on this planet face a water shortage. Although 70 percent of Earth's surface is covered by water, only 3 percent of the world's total water is fresh water, and two-thirds of that can't be used because it's frozen in polar ice caps or contaminated with wastes. Therefore only 1 percent of Earth's water is available for human use.[69]

Water is thus a finite resource. There is no more water on Earth now than there was 2,000 years ago when the world population was less than 3 percent of its current size. As the population increases, more people must share the available water, and human demand for water for agriculture (69 percent), industrial (23 percent), or personal use (8 percent) increases.[70] In the twentieth century, the population tripled while water withdrawals increased by over six times. Just between 1940 and 1990, the demand for fresh water quadrupled; the demand in many places now exceeds supply.[71] As Sandra L. Postel and Aaron T. Wolf warn:

> By 2015, nearly 3 billion people—40 percent of the projected world population—are expected to live in countries that find it difficult or impossible to mobilize enough water to satisfy the food, industrial, and domestic needs of their citizens.[72] This scarcity will translate into heightened competition for water between cities and farms, between neighboring states and provinces, and at times between nations.

As water becomes more scarce, conflict over water rights are inevitable. India and Bangladesh, for example, fought about water resources from the Ganges River for over fifty years until 1996, when they signed an agreement guaranteeing water to both countries during the dry season.

Water mining—the pumping of groundwater faster than it can be replenished—has caused water tables to drop in many locales. The water table under Beijing, for example, dropped nearly 200 feet between 1965 and 1999, as the country's aquifers were depleted.[73] An **aquifer** is a naturally stored, underground water supply. Overpumping in India, North Africa, the Middle East, and the United States also far exceeds aquifer recharge and cannot be sustained indefinitely.[74]

Other problems result from water mining. It can create huge sinkholes or, in coastal areas like Florida, cause the water table to drop below sea level, allowing salty ocean water to naturally seep in and contaminate the freshwater supply. Overpumping has caused rivers such as the Colorado in the western United States and the Huang He in China to dry up before they reach the ocean. Clearly, this harms the ecosystems found around the rivers. In addition, it prevents essential nutrients from rivers from entering the ocean, thereby eliminating food for the fisheries and, in turn, hurting the ocean's food chain. The end result of this is a loss in biodiversity.[75]

Water Pollution

Water quality is another concern. Domestic sewage and industrial waste, as well as runoffs from overfertilized farms, can pollute water resources. Even the use of water for industrial or power plant cooling processes can disrupt delicate river ecosystems as the water is returned hotter than when it was removed. Most serious is the threat to human health and welfare. Over 1 billion people lack access to clean drinking water and nearly 3 billion people lack access to sanitation services. Each year waterborne diseases infect about 250 million people, of whom about 10 million die.[76]

The 1972 Clean Water Act (amended in 1987) was a landmark piece of environmental legislation that dramatically improved the quality of U.S. waterways, but much work remains to be

The summer droughts of 2002 and 2003 were particularly devastating to U.S. farmers. This Illinois farmer, in danger of losing farmland his family has owned since the 1860s due to heavy financial losses, surveys a cornfield of shriveled crops from lack of water. Are droughts always natural phenomena? How might humans have a negative impact on rainfall and on water supply? Is there anything we can do to resolve this problem?

done.[77] Today we face several water contamination threats: eutrophication of our fresh water; disruption of the ocean's essential contribution to photosynthesis; and poisoning of our well-water supplies by agricultural chemicals.

Although water quality in the United States is generally good compared with global conditions, the problem of water pollution is steadily growing. The Sierra Club, an environmentalist activist organization, reports that each year U.S. rivers and streams absorb about 500 million pounds of toxic waste. The runoff from agricultural fertilizers and lawn chemicals, as well as intentional industrial dumping, are all contributors to this pollution.

Eutrophication results from overfertilization. Heavy applications of phosphate and nitrogen fertilizers by farmers lead to heavily contaminated water runoff into local streams, which accelerates the growth of algae in surrounding lakes. The algae population explosion uses up all the available dissolved oxygen, choking off other life. Dead plants, fish and algae foul the lakes. This is another case of an apparent benefit (powerful fertilizer) having unintended side effects. In developing countries where food is scarce, the increased harvest is very welcome until it is noticed that the fish catch has declined because of the deoxygenization of the water. Animal wastes are natural fertilizers, and the great feedlots that fatten animals for market in rural areas can produce almost as much eutrophication as do the outdated sewerage systems of our older cities.

Maryland's famed Chesapeake Bay—where thousands of fish died in 1997 from contamination of its tributaries through runoff of guano from chicken farms—still suffers extensive pollution from tens of millions of pounds of nitrogen and phosphorous from farm manure that wash annually into the bay.[78] Meanwhile, experts say, nitrogen-rich runoff from farmlands in the Midwest into the Mississippi River has created along the Louisiana Gulf Coast a "zone of dying water about the size of New Jersey," where aquatic life cannot exist.[79]

Photosynthesis—the process of plant growth using sunlight, water, and carbon dioxide—releases free oxygen that refreshes the planet's biosphere. Each large area of deforested land alters the world's balance of carbon dioxide to oxygen. We do not yet know the threshold of danger from deforestation, but we do know that another part of the process may be under severe stress itself. Most of our oxygen supply comes from ocean photosynthesis, and if the pollution reaches the threshold where the ocean's plant and blue-green algae populations are reduced, the entire biosphere will be jeopardized.

In 1979, the Food and Drug Administration (FDA) estimated that over a half-million substances were being dumped in the oceans.[80] Since then, ocean dumping laws and new technologies have had some effect; in 1992, for example, New York City stopped dumping its massive volumes of partially treated sewage sludge six miles offshore into the ocean.

International law now bans ocean dumping. The shutdown of beaches due to contaminated wastes from sewage-derived microorganisms, the closing of shellfish beds due to metal contamination, and infection of fish by lesion-causing parasites sparked the motivation for this ban. Nevertheless, coastal oceans, continually enriched by nutrients in waste products that run off the land, suffer from eutrophication, resulting in an increase in toxic algae blooms and decreased oxygen levels, both of which can kill fish populations. And massive dumpings of waste, including radioactive waste, into the ocean still occur. What the cumulative effect of all this poisoning of our oceans will be is of grave concern to environmentalists.

Chemical Explosions and Spills

In 1999, a chemical plant explosion in Lehigh County, Pennsylvania, killed five workers, injuring thirteen others, and sending up a billowing cloud of noxious smoke that left a white power covering nearby cars and homes. The National Environmental Law Center, a nonprofit litigation organization working to stop polluters through legal action, reports that, while such accidents are relatively uncommon, one in six Americans nevertheless faces the possibility of injury or death should a similar accident occur in their area. This is because 41 million people—1 in 6 Americans—live in zip codes that contain manufacturing companies using hazardous chemicals, with vulnerable zones that extend more than three miles away from the facility.[81] These vulnerable zones exist in nearly every county throughout the United States, but the greatest potential risk to the public lies in smaller, more densely populated industrial states such as Delaware, Maryland, and New Jersey.[82]

This public endangerment is not just material for alarmists. In a discomforting report, the U.S. Environmental Protection Agency (EPA) identified fifteen recent accidents in the United States in which the amount and toxicity of the chemicals released exceeded those released in the 1984 tragedy at Bhopal, India, when a deadly gas escaped a Union Carbide storage tank, killing more than 2,000 people. Only fortuitous circumstances, such as wind dispersal or rapid evacuation, prevented disastrous loss of life in the U.S. accidents.[83]

For the past two decades, chemical spills in the United States have declined in frequency. However, worldwide they remain a problem to the environment. Europe is one example. In January 2000, the dam of a mining lagoon in northwestern Romania broke, sending a twenty-five–mile sludge of cyanide and heavy metals down Hungary's Tisza River and into the Danube River. The mine waste, which poisoned river ecosystems in three countries, killed fish and fish-eating birds, contaminated drinking water wells, and left the Tisza River ecologically dead for as long as fifteen years. This spill was decried as Europe's worst environmental disaster since the 1986 Chernobyl nuclear accident.[84] Two years earlier, a similar ecological disaster affected the Guadiamar River and the Doñana wetlands in southern Spain, when millions of gallons of toxic sludge and acid waters spilled from the broken tailings of another mining lagoon. Significant pollution problems caused by leaks and spillages from toxic waste lagoons associated with metal mining also occurred in recent years in Italy, Portugal, Sweden, and the United Kingdom.

Toxic Dumps: Victimization Without Realization

Illegal dumping creates environmental disasters. Toxic and carcinogenic chemicals encrust the earth like old grounds in a coffeepot. Rain percolating through a landfill or illegal dump creates a polluted leachate. The EPA estimates that the average dumpsite of only seventeen acres can generate 4.6 million gallons of leachate each year.[85] The outflow of toxins can continue for up to one hundred years after the dump is closed, and the plume of contamination can extend for long distances, fouling or poisoning any subterranean water it contacts. About 80 percent of municipal water systems depend on aquifers: water that collects naturally in underground porous rocks, caverns, or sand beds. Aquifers are particularly important in the drier U.S. Southwest, where they may be the only sources of water. In such areas the draw on these resources has grown exponentially in the last decade. Once they become tainted, little can be done to restore their purity. People must either find a new source of water or move on.

The EPA estimates that one in four Americans—including 10 million children under the age of twelve—lives within four miles of a toxic waste dump. In fact, U.S. cities are littered with thousands of abandoned industrial sites, many of them containing hazardous wastes. Such dumps, along with sewage treatment plants and other pollution sources, are found more often in inner-city neighborhoods, rural villages, and Native American reservations rather than richer communities. The NIMBY (not in my back yard) response is more effective when people have power and influence to prevent landfill or dump sites in their neighborhoods.[86]

Sometimes polluters dump their toxic waste illegally. Not long ago in Florida, two children died because they inhaled a toxic chemical that had been dumped illegally near an open lot where they were playing. This is the greatest danger to all of us: unknown health hazards in buried toxic dumps. In the 1980s, the government had to relocate the entire communities of Love Canal, New York, and Times Beach, Missouri, because of high incidences of birth defects and cancer in these communities, which were built over toxic dump sites. For similar reasons the EPA decided in 1997 to move 358 families from the predominately black Escambia neighborhood of Pensacola, Florida, after scientists found dangerous levels of dioxin, arsenic, lead, and other toxic substances there, adjacent to an abandoned industrial plant.[87]

Evidently, some U.S. industries have forgotten or ignored the basic lesson that we learn in our first chemistry class: before you create a substance, think about what you are going to keep it in.

Sociological Perspectives

We can better understand the confusions that prevent experts from agreeing on an effective population policy by noting the many directions that proposed changes could take in different sociological emphases. Solutions to population problems focus on three central themes: the structures and values of society's institutions; the underlying conflicts caused by social inequality and the profit motive; or the social interpretation of fertility that individuals create.

The Functionalist Viewpoint

Sociologists who emphasize the structure of society see population growth and its resulting ecological problems as a vestigial, nonmodern behavior pattern that will fade away as societies reach full development. Large families are survivors of the agricultural age, when they served an economic function. Similarly, the drastic change in female role prescriptions mainly results from the automation of older, manual labor functions. This encourages women to seek outside employment and status in institutions other than the child-centered family. Smaller families appear to be the norm in all modernized societies. Therefore, Structural-Functionalist sociologists expect growth to achieve equilibrium, supplying fewer people because fewer are needed in a modern society.

Another group of sociologists and futurists believe that industrialization was central in forming our lifestyle, but that it is now outdated; thus, they conclude, a **new value consensus** is necessary for human survival. A commitment to voluntary simplicity attempts to reverse the prevailing values. In place of economic complexity, it would substitute appropriate technology in which each local area uses only the tools and methods it needs to become self-sufficient. All production would be scaled down. Elimination of desires for conspicuous consumption, material wealth, and technological gadgetry would relieve the pressure on resources. In *Small Is Beautiful*, Ernst Schumacher eloquently expressed the need for new values, entreating us to give up being "people of the forward stampede," and instead to become "homecomers." He observed that in "advanced" countries, where technology supposedly saves so much labor and time, people work much harder and have much less time for their homes and families than they do in undeveloped countries.[88]

Many sociologists respond, however, that—no matter how pressing the ecological need— you cannot forcibly change the consumption values of a society without changing many other institutions. For example, you would have to alter the current corporate structure and advertising methods before you could achieve any major economic value shifts.

With their focus on society as a social system of interdependent parts, Functionalists also analyze the interconnectivity of social institutions, technology, and environmental problems. Technological advances may generate higher agricultural yield and more comfortable lifestyles, but they also generate such dysfunctions as pollution of our air and water and serious overuse and depletion of our natural resources. They suggest solutions through educational and governmental social institutions by raising awareness about the limits to population growth and use of natural resources and by international cooperation and regulation on the use of these resources.

The Conflict Viewpoint

The Conflict orientation attributes population problems to social inequality and our lack of ecological concern to the central idea of the capitalist system: the profit motive.

Population pressure is not a high-priority problem for Conflict theorists. Unwanted fertility is a symptom of unequal opportunity and would soon diminish if ethnic injustice and class bigotry were eliminated. Following a redistribution of wealth, individuals could choose their own lifestyles and decisions about family size would be more effective.

Both Conflict theorists and ecological hawks feel that those who promote voluntary simplicity and rely on individual value changes to solve ecological problems are naive. For example, Barry Commoner presented evidence that pollution is profitable and will be extremely difficult to eliminate as long as the profit motive is the basis of the economic system.[89] Illegal dumping of radwaste, the radioactive tailings of nuclear energy or uranium mining, is encouraged because it represents such an attractive alternative to the expenses required for proper storage or treatment. More than fifty large radioactive waste dumpsites are known, including one within fifteen miles of Salt Lake City that holds a 4.3-billion-pound collection of uranium residues, which Utah Governor Scott Matheson once described as "the largest microwave oven in the West."[90]

Commoner has also identified a less obvious danger of the profit motive: the drive to create new technologies to generate high profits from a new, innovative chemical product (innovative firms enjoy about twice the rate of profit that noninnovative firms achieve, due to the temporary monopoly the firm that developed the materials enjoys). Without monitoring, these innovative firms proliferate, as they did after World War II and caused so many of today's dumpsite problems.

Though it seems irresponsible and ridiculous to wipe out your own industry's source of income, it is actually profitable for owners of whaling fleets to kill off all the whales. That is because a capitalist entrepreneur can use the temporary high rate of profit commanded by the items growing scarcity to reinvest in some other business. It's "profitable" to kill the goose that lays the golden eggs, as long as the goose first provides sufficient eggs to pay for the purchase of a new goose. Commoner's point is that we can't rely on the present system to control pollution or ecological assaults so long as it is based on short-term profits.

The Feminist Viewpoint

One emphasis of Feminist analysis of population and environmental challenges is on the needs of more than 1.3 billion people living in absolute poverty. Without a higher standard of living, one-fifth of the world's people will continue to suffer malnutrition, disease, and illiteracy. Astonishingly, women make up two-thirds of the world's poorest people and are nearly twice as likely as men to be illiterate. They receive less education, less food, and have fewer legal rights.[91]

In most parts of the developing world, both urban and rural, women are primarily responsible for finding water and fuel and for preparing food for meals. Spending hours each day cooking over smoky fires made from wood or dried dung, they inhale smoke more dangerous to health than tobacco smoke.[92] In rural areas, women are often also responsible for the care of livestock and for tending the crops. However, rarely do these women possess any ownership rights in these resources with which they spend so much of their lives.

This worldwide phenomenon generated an approach known as **ecofeminism,** which identifies the values and practices of patriarchal societies as the fundamental causes of environmental problems. Just as patriarchy results in the domination of women, the mindset extends to the belief that nature is something to be possessed, dominated, and exploited, rather than treated as a partner.[93]

Feminists argue that intervention is necessary. Only the empowerment of women will bring resolution to the problems of environmental degradation and absolute poverty from which they suffer, because they are the ones most able to influence change. The empowerment and autonomy of women is a highly complex issue and may require varying solutions, according to the cultural context.

One key component, however, is access to education. Advocates recommend legislation that promotes education, as well as family assistance living, for the stabilization of the population. This would enable women to make their own decisions about the number and spacing of their

An old cliché is "knowledge is power." By learning how to use computers, these Jordanian women are taking an important step to increase their knowledge. Why does computer access accelerate the learning process for women in developing countries? In what ways do feminists suggest that education, both through the computer and in formal learning situations, will improve women's lives in these countries?

children. Equal access to education, credit, land, and the enforcement of legal rights will not only benefit women as individuals, it will also improve the economic and environmental well-being of their families. As we have seen in such countries as Bangladesh, Cote d'Ivoire, Guatemala, and Sri Lanka, when women have control over their resources (land, income, or credit), they are more likely than men to spend their earnings on food, clothing, and other basic needs.[94]

The Interactionist Viewpoint

Symbolic Interactionists remind us that cultural definitions of the situation influence each decision to have another child or to buy a gas-guzzler. However, sudden shifts can take place in people's values and tastes. Americans once loved owning the biggest cars they could buy. Then, for a time, these cars crowded dealers' lots, practically unsellable. Now they are becoming some-what popular again. The baby boom suddenly ended—just as today's belief that "two children is enough" could evaporate tomorrow. Similarly, the reasons why we target one ecological problem for action and ignore so many others seem to defy reason, at least on the surface.

To understand these seemingly irrational and random decision shifts, we must study the specific contexts in which individuals construct their behaviors. For example, decades ago Margaret Mead summarized the conclusions of an international conference on population policies by stating that nationwide birth-control programs would inevitably fail. We cannot set goals and standards for a whole country or design one service for all people. Individuals do not make choices in the rarified atmosphere of nation states; they react to their regional, or even village conditions and traditions.[95]

Interactionists believe that neither economic development nor technological advances such as "the pill" can solve our population problem. To have a positive impact, they must first be fitted into the sociocultural values guiding individuals' decisions. Despite all the obvious dangers of automobile pollution and the energy wastefulness of driving to work in a private car instead of using public transportation, only one in twenty Americans now uses buses or trains to get to work, a marked decrease from the one in eight who did so in 1960.[96] Interactionists remind us that policies that ignore social definitions of a situation are doomed to failure.

Thinking About the Future

What will be our future if population growth, water use, and fossil fuel burning continue unchanged? What lifestyle changes and what differences in environmental resources and climate do you envision? Remember, today's decisions affect tomorrow's realities, so what should we do now?

Should we stabilize population growth? If so, how? If people could safely and reliably choose the number and spacing of their children, population growth would significantly decrease. How do we achieve this in a culturally appropriate manner? Some suggest that what is necessary is the creation of an infrastructure to deliver reproductive and community health care, education, social and gender equality, and sustainable livelihoods. Is that the answer? If so, then how do we do this and who pays for it?

Delivering education services, for example, would require sensitivity to local culture and concerns. Parents in developing world countries often view their children as economic assets and keep them out of school to work. Girls, in particular, are kept home to do housework and/or care for younger siblings. How do we overcome this? Is providing meals for students a sufficient incentive to parents, or should the government pay a stipend to parents to keep their children in school? If you do not favor government intervention, what alternative plan would you suggest?

How do we protect our primary forests, including the rain forests? We have discussed how this destruction has many global implications and how population growth in the developing world drives this deforestation. We have also discussed how consumer demand in the developed world is a bigger factor; one child born in the developed world adds more to consumption and pollution levels in a lifetime than do thirty to fifty children born in developing countries. What can we do to curtail depletion of natural resources as the means to economic growth? How do we persuade people in the developed world to change their consumer patterns to lessen exploitation of the natural environment and its irreversible destruction? What is our future if we don't change?

Should we invest public funds in development of alternative energy sources to reduce the burning of fossil fuels and the greenhouse effect? If not, how do we get people to shift to solar-based energy, wind power, geothermal energy, or other sources? We can see previews of the new energy economy in the solar electric roofs of homes in Japan and Germany, the wind turbines dotting the Danish countryside, and the new wind farms in Spain and in the U.S. states of Iowa, Minnesota, and Texas. The potential of wind energy is enormous; just three U.S. states—North Dakota, South Dakota, and Texas—have enough harnessable energy to supply national energy needs.

Since the developed world consumes most of the world's resources in disproportion to their population, we must raise awareness through education of the undeniable link between population growth and water scarcity. We must convince people to change their living habits to conserve this natural resource through efficient personal water use (such as capturing and using rain water, recycling, using low-flow showers and toilets). How do we do that?

We could seek international agreement to stabilize water tables by eliminating the overpumping that is depleting the world's aquifers. However, since this overpumping supplies food to about 480 million people (about 1,000 tons of water produces 1 ton of grain), its elimination would drive grain prices sky high.[97] That would deny necessary food to millions, thereby worsening world hunger. How do we address this problem? The World Commission on Water argues that water is too cheap and "full pricing" would bring about conservation, stoppage of waste, private sector investment in expanded sewerage and access, and revamped technology for more efficient use.[98] Do you think this is a good solution?

It's time now for you to consider all of these questions and proposed solutions. What future do you envision if nothing is done? What solutions do you endorse or propose to address these population and environmental issues?

How can *you personally* help reduce world hunger, save the rain forests, and solve other issues of world population growth and the resulting impacts? These problems all seem so huge that individuals may think they can't do anything about them. In truth, individuals can make a difference. Go to this book's Web site (www.ablongman.com/parrillo) for Chapter 3 to find out what you can do *now*, even before you graduate.

SUMMARY

1. Malthus's pessimism was the original warning about the dangers of population pressure. He said that the population's geometric increase would always outrun the resources available to support it. A more optimistic view, the theory of the demographic transition, predicts that developing countries will follow the West's three-phase pattern according to which fertility comes into balance with mortality as its development progresses.

2. By 2013, the world's population will number 7 billion people. Although the rate of world population growth has slowed in recent years, population growth will continue into the foreseeable future and further tax the planet's limited resources. Differing birth rates in LDCs and MDCs mean changing distribution of the world's population.

3. Population pressures create major problems. Developing nations suffer chronic malnutrition and poverty, and the needs of their burgeoning population impedes their efforts to industrialize. The complacency of many people in developed nations allows them to be powerful polluters and prodigious wasters of resources. We face shortages of water and cropland, and the rapid extinction of plant and animal species because of rain forest destruction.

4. Chronic malnutrition, though less than in previous years, is still a reality for 799 million people, who are therefore more susceptible to disease, disability, and death. Per capita food shortages and inequitable food distribution are most problematic in East Africa, Bangladesh, Eastern Europe, Haiti, Mongolia, North Korea, the former Soviet Union, and Yemen. In the United States, one in ten households experiences hunger or the risk of hunger.

5. Ecosystem-based thinking means understanding the relationship among all elements in the environment. We cannot separate out the goals of humans; instead we must see them in their holistic interconnectivity. Ecosystems are fragile and can be destroyed either by becoming too homogeneous and simplified (which renders them susceptible to catastrophic change from a single source) or by triggering an overload of their normal waste-handling capacities. We are in danger of modifying our weather and atmospheric balance and polluting rain with acids, poisoning our aquifers, killing our lakes and streams. Illegal dumping of toxic and carcinogenic chemicals remains a hidden threat to everyone.

6. The Functionalists' system disorganization view adheres to demographic transition theory. High fertility represents a cultural lag in attitudes that will automatically disappear as family life catches up to economic life. Conflict theory emphasizes economic inequality and accords low priority to population problems. High fertility is merely another instance of people not being allowed to control their own destinies, and it would disappear with economic equality. Feminists recommend an end to environmental degradation and world poverty through empowerment of women in equal access to education, credit, land, and legal rights. Interactionists emphasize interpreting family life and the place of children as

viewed by the potential parents within their own surroundings. Policies or international efforts that ignore these cultural elements, no matter how technologically efficient they may be, are doomed to failure.

KEY TERMS

Anthropocentrism	Motherhood mandate
Aquifer	New value consensus
Biodiversity	Photosynthesis
Business ethic	Threshold
Demographic transition theory	Total fertility rate
Ecofeminism	Trigger effects
Ecosystem	Unconscious ideology
Eutrophication	Water mining
Exponential growth	Western world view
Greenhouse effect	Zero population growth (ZPG)

INTERNET RESOURCES

At this book's Web site with Allyn & Bacon, you will find numerous links pertaining to the problems about population and the environment. To explore these resources, go first to the author's page (**http://www.ablongman.com/parrillo**). Next, select this edition of *Contemporary Social Problems* and then select **Internet Readings and Exercises**. Then select **Chapter 3,** where you will find both a variety of sites to investigate and some questions that pertain to those sites.

SUGGESTED READINGS

Brown, Lester R., et al. *The State of the World, 200–*. New York: W.W. Norton & Company. An annual publication describing recent changes in all the major indicators of environmental degradation.

Cylke, F. Kurt, Jr. *The Environment*. New York: HarperCollins, 1993. A concise discussion of most environmental issues, concerns, policies, and practices.

De Villiers, Marq. *Water: The Fate of Our Most Precious Resource*. Boston: Houghton Mifflin, 2000. A compelling, lucid account of the worldwide importance of water and its availability, drawing from cultural, ecological, and historical perspectives.

Diamond, Irene, and Gloria Feman Orenstein. *Reweaving the World: The Emergence of Ecofeminism*. San Francisco: Sierra Club Books, 1990. An anthology of feminist thought that elaborates a pro-environmentalist ideology and attacks patriarchal anti-environmentalism.

Grant, Lindsey. *Juggernaut: Growth on a Finite Planet.* Santa Ana, Calif.: Seven Locks Press, 1996. Comprehensive explanation of the interconnectivity of population growth and environmental issues such as energy, food, pollution, and resource depletion.

Houghton, John T. *Global Warming: The Complete Briefing*, 2d ed. Cambridge, England: Cambridge University Press, 1997. An excellent comprehensive insight into this complex subject written with remarkable directness and clarity.

McGinn, Anne P. *Safeguarding the Health of Oceans.* Washington, D.C.: Worldwatch Institute, 1999. Explains the extent of human dependence on oceans and addresses the problems of over-fishing and oceanic pollution.

Population Reference Bureau, *Population Today.* A valuable newsletter published eleven times a year, summarizing demographic patterns and recent population studies.

United Nations, *Demographic Yearbook.* A basic resource, published annually, that provides population data and trends from all countries.

4

Housing and Urbanization

Facts About Cities

- Most Americans commute between suburbs, not between cities and suburbs.
- About 4.7 million American hourseholds are in public housing.
- Habitat for Humanity has built over 45,000 new homes in cities.
- Families account for 41 percent of the 800,000-person homeless population of the United States.
- About 75 percent of the U.S. homeless family population consists of children.
- One in five Americans lives in the BosWash megalopolis.
- Inner-ring suburbs have many of the same problems as cities.

Cities have always represented the best and worst of a society. Because of their large, concentrated, heterogeneous populations, cities frequently magnify the social problems existing within the entire society. At the same time, cities are the centers of economic, cultural, governmental, and religious influence; they are the centers of civilization. As beacons of opportunity, cities continually attract people seeking an end to their problems elsewhere.

The key to successful cities, past and present, lies in their mutual interdependence with surrounding regions. As long as each benefits from the other—enjoying a reciprocity of relationships—both cities and outlying regions prosper. Serious social problems result when this symbiotic exchange ends, when farmland can no longer sustain an urban population, or when a city becomes parasitic on surrounding areas due to loss of industry, population, or tax revenues.

Failure to maintain regional integration helps explain why U.S. cities are in trouble. No other developed country has allowed its urban centers to deteriorate and decline as we have. Like all decay, urban degeneration is not a sudden occurrence; it results from decades of government neglect, misguided policy decisions, and exploitation by individual property owners.

The social problems discussed throughout this book coalesce in acute forms in many of our nation's cities. Drugs, crime, gangs, violence, poverty, difficulties in race relations, lack of affordable housing and homelessness, poor-quality schools, dysfunctional families, inadequate health care, pollution, and a decaying **infrastructure** of bridges, roads, sidewalks, and water and waste disposal systems cause many affluent Americans to turn their backs on cities. Factor in a shrinking tax base and serious urban budgetary problems, and the older cities would appear to be in their death throes. Are they? In this chapter we will investigate that question.

U.S. Cities in Sociohistorical Context

For the first sixty years of the twentieth century, central cities contained the large majority of the U.S. population, expanding their influence to surrounding towns and villages. Cities contained the best jobs, schools, and stores and offered a wide range of leisure activities as well. While bedroom suburbs have existed throughout the twentieth century, the exodus from the cities truly began after World War II. To meet the housing shortage caused by returning GIs and the resulting "baby boom," Congress passed the Housing Act of 1949, which encouraged building on vacant land outside city boundaries. Affordable housing on these suburban development tracts, financed through government-insured mortgages from the Federal Housing Authority or the Veterans Administration, helped end the housing shortage and encouraged outward migration from the cities.

Other federal policies and programs contributed to this population shift as well. Urban renewal replaced older neighborhoods with commercial properties, forcing residents to move elsewhere—which usually meant the suburbs, since little new urban housing stock was being built. Building interstate highways and expressways made vacant land farther away more attractive to developers by bringing prospective new suburbanites within commuting distance to their city jobs.[1]

In the 1960s, a new phase of suburban development took place: shopping malls proliferated and eventually surpassed the traditional city downtown as North America's retail center. By the 1970s, suburban areas had reached *critical mass*, that point at which population base has grown large enough to support various economic, cultural, and social activities. Regional and national corporate headquarters began locating outside cities in suburbs, as did accounting and banking services, movie theaters, restaurants, legal and medical offices, hospitals, and even hotels. Office and light industrial parks set up on large tracts of land as the suburbanization of economic activity reached a probably irreversible level.[2]

Many cities once prospered because they had developed profitable specialties in the U.S. industrial economy. Detroit was the automobile manufacturing center; Akron, the city of rubber; Pittsburgh, the city of steel; Scranton and Wilkes-Barre, coal-mining cities; Grand Rapids, a furniture city; Bridgeport, a metalworking trades city; and Paterson, a textile-manufacturing city. All fell on lean times because of global economic competition; but in attempting to convert to a service-based economy, these and other cities fell victim to the telecommunications revolution, which has enabled companies to locate anywhere and still maintain an interactive network of information and services.

Urban Changes in the United States

The 1980s witnessed the evolution of cities into an entirely new form, one that Joel Garreau calls "edge cities."[3] An **edge city**, situated on the fringe of an older urban area, is a new, sprawling, middle-class, automobile-dependent urban center with distinct living, working, shopping, and leisure sections. It is the site of many good jobs; safety is a high priority within its boundaries; and racial integration with social class lines has become a reality.

Edge cities fall into three categories, according to Garreau. Least common is the **greenfield city**, which is a master-planned city by one developer on thousands of acres of farmland, such as Los Colinas, Texas, west of Dallas, or Irvine, California, southeast of Los Angeles. An **uptown city** is one built on top of a pre-automobile city, such as Pasadena, California, or White Plains, New York. A **boomer city**, the most common type of edge city, is usually situated at the intersection of two major highways, with a shopping mall forming its urban core; examples include Tyson's Corner, Virginia, just outside the Washington, D.C. Beltway, and King of Prussia, Pennsylvania, northwest of Philadelphia. Boomer cities were not originally planned as cities, so buildings do not relate to one another and traffic congestion is common. Because it has a history, an uptown city has more texture than does the relatively sterile boomer city. A greenfield city attempts to avert the chaotic layout of a boomer city through the developer's control over all aspects of traffic patterns and land usage.

Urban Sprawl

As metropolitan areas spread out and overlap one another, the result is a **megalopolis**, or unbroken high-population tract of interconnected cities and adjoining suburbs. The spread of an unrelenting megalopolis concerns many people. As Americans move farther from core cities and into outlying regions, so do all the trappings of urban life: stores, offices, factories, hospitals, crime, congestion, and pollution. Developers gobble up more and more open land as the population increases and disperses. One town looks like another, stores on the highways erect signs to shout out their wares to the fast-moving traffic going by, and every activity requires a separate trip by car.

We pay a high social price for urban sprawl. By spreading residences, medical and commercial offices, and industries throughout a region on large tracts of land, we increase residents' dependence on automobile transportation. Everything and everyone is too spread out to make public transportation economically feasible. With insufficient coordination of work sites and highways, traffic congestion results. Nor can everyone get around by car: a lifestyle that requires a car discriminates against poor families, the elderly, the disabled, and the young. Suburban

Cities and urban life have implications for social identity and social isolation. Cities also concentrate people, goods, cars, services, and the forces of mass consumerism. What urban development patterns, housing, and transportation trends do American cities increasingly reflect today?

teenagers, for instance, usually lack sufficient activities in their town but are unable to travel to locations where such diversions do exist. Suburban parents thus spend a large part of their time chauffeuring their children to stores, juvenile activities, and other events.

When a company—lured by tax incentives and/or utility subsidies—relocates to a suburban location, the city loses jobs, tax revenues, and business revenues for stores, restaurants, and services that previously depended on that company as a source of customers. Other problems occur in the new setting. Several studies show that the average employee trip to work increases by several miles after relocation, thereby raising traveling costs.[4] Low-income workers who don't have a car must depend on a car pool or look for another job, both risky ventures. The company incurs some higher costs, too: maintaining grounds and parking facilities, running a subsidized cafeteria, arranging messenger service to specialized support firms in corporate law, marketing, bond transactions, or similar services. Businesses then pass on the cost of providing utilities to an isolated site to the general public.

According to the nonprofit Regional Plan Association, if the office space needed for each 5 million increase in population were built on suburban campuses, it would cut a swath one-half mile wide and fifty-four miles long.[5] In a large city with skyscrapers, two hundred acres would fulfill the same need. Each 1 million square feet of suburban office space occupies, on average, eighty acres (twenty-five acres for parking lots) as compared to occupying 1 acre in a large city, half of that for an office plaza. In smaller cities, the same 1 million square feet takes up about six acres (twenty-five–story buildings with landscaping and parking lots).

Yet urban and suburban sprawl continues at an alarming pace. In Pennsylvania over the past fifty years, more than 4 million acres of farmland—an area larger than Connecticut and Rhode Island combined—fell into sprawl. One of the nation's fastest-growing cities, Phoenix, now covers over 600 square miles, an area larger than the state of Delaware. Experts predict that, over the next fifty years, sprawl will consume more than 3.5 million acres of one of the nation's prime agricultural regions, California's great Central Valley.[6]

Sprawl hurts cities in several ways. First, it erodes a city's tax base as it lures more people to the suburbs, forcing cities to raise taxes on remaining taxpayers to pay for city services. Second, it destroys downtown commerce by pulling shoppers from once-thriving locally owned stores and restaurants to large regional malls and highway megastores. Such changes in demographics and shopping patterns lead to an increase in urban unemployment and concentrations of poverty in central cities. The out-migration also robs cities of character as abandoned factories, boarded-up homes, and decaying retail centers dominate the landscape.[7]

Traffic Congestion

More than twice as many commuters in the United States today journey from suburb to suburb as travel from suburb to central city. Most Americans now commute between suburbs—areas ill-prepared in terms of public facilities, roads, bridges, and transit to handle the volume—and traffic jams have become a way of life. In fact, a majority of residents in suburban areas, increasingly frustrated by repeated traffic delays that cost them money and waste time, consider traffic congestion their most serious local problem.[8] And the amount of time commuters spend stalled in traffic in small and medium-sized cities has more than quadrupled since 1982, although the bigger cities increased the most in travel time.[9]

Traffic congestion is a nationwide problem, from suburban Gwinnet County, Georgia (one of the nation's fastest growing counties), to Los Angeles (the nation's most congested area). One annual study reveals that drivers in one-third of the sixty-eight U.S. cities studied spend at least half as much time stuck in traffic as they do on vacation each year. This delay is growing worse, increasing by at least 350 percent over the past sixteen years in half of the cities studied. The annual cost of traffic congestion in over one-third of these cities exceeds the statewide average of auto insurance for those cities.[10]

With most new jobs involving suburb-to-suburb commutes, mass transit has declined from a 6.3 percent market share in 1980 to 4 percent in 2000. However, in the more densely populated Northeast, about 11 percent still rely on mass transit. In contrast, the number of licensed drivers nationwide has increased 64 percent since 1970, while the number of vehicle miles traveled has gone up 131 percent (partly due to increased work distances due to sprawl).[11]

Only in eight major cities does public transportation play a significant role. And in seven of them (Chicago; Washington, D.C.; Boston; San Francisco–Oakland; Philadelphia; Honolulu; and Pittsburgh) the mass transit share is only between 10 and 16 percent. New York City tops the list at 30 percent.[12] In smaller metropolitan areas, public transit accounts for less than 2 percent of trips, a pattern unlikely to change. Atlanta, Boston, Chicago, Cleveland, New York, Oakland–San Francisco, Philadelphia, and Washington, D.C., have subway systems, which accounts for their relatively high number of mass transit commuters. At first glance, extending and improving rapid transit systems would appear to be an ideal solution to the overabundance of automobiles and resulting urban congestion. A rapid transit track can move 40,000 persons past a given point in an hour; at 1.8 persons per car, it would take a sixteen-lane highway to do the same job.[13] Mass transit thus moves the greatest number of people for the least expenditure of energy and use of space.

In most large U.S. cities, mass transit has been placed in an untenable mixed-definition position. The government owns and operates most lines and sees them as a "public service," but it also insists they should pay for themselves. Comfort—and even necessary maintenance—seldom receives adequate funding because politicians set artificially low fare structures that they think will please voters and increase ridership. If we could decide whether transit should be a private enterprise, a government-run business, or a public utility, better planning would be possible. In most European cities, rapid transit has gone the whole definitional route and is now considered a public utility. Transit is better there.

Mass transit has been failing financially for many years. The precipitous decline in ridership is not merely due to people leaving for the suburbs or to conditions deteriorating. It is part of a vicious cycle of loss of income–deterioration–loss of riders–loss of income. Political neglect intensifies the cycle. Back in 1980, the Boston transit system briefly shut down because no government body would take responsibility for its debts. A similar battle has raged for years in New York City over how much of the mass transit deficit should be assumed by the city, state, and federal budgets. Curtailment of mass transit subsidies from the federal government obviously

Traffic congestion in Jakarta, Indonesia, and in many other cities of the world, is even greater than in U.S. cities. To what social problems does traffic congestion contribute? What are some other transportation challenges of cities and how do they contribute to problems of urban life? Why has public transportation so far failed to solve the problem, and what other solutions are there?

hampers efforts to upgrade urban mass transit. Nevertheless, mass transit carries more than 9.3 billion passengers yearly, and its quality is important to the vitality of cities' economies.[14]

Housing Problems and Solutions

Many central cities lack sufficient middle-income housing to meet demand, and much low-income housing needs extensive improvement. Part of today's urban housing problem can be traced to policies and actions undertaken six decades ago. Beginning in the 1930s, the federal government began to subsidize the movement of Whites to the suburbs. Through the Federal Home Bank System (1932), the Home Owners Loan Corporation (1933), and the National Housing Act (1934), which set up the Federal Housing Authority (FHA), banking practices became more liberal, allowing people without much capital to buy homes. The Housing Act of 1949, together with FHA loans and GI benefits to World War II veterans, funded the building of homes on vacant land, launching the suburban boom of the 1950s and 1960s. Significantly, during this booming postwar construction period, the FHA maintained an official policy against underwriting construction in racially integrated areas, thereby contributing to building decay in those areas.

Redlining and Abandonment

Long after the FHA discontinued its discriminatory practice of refusing financial support in "undesirable" areas, banks and savings and loan associations continued it. **Redlining**—drawing a red line on a map around "bad risk" neighborhoods—marks areas where lending institutions refuse to furnish mortgages or home improvement loans. Consequently, the older housing in these areas deteriorates, attracting few buyers, and reinforcing the bankers' supposed wisdom. Although illegal today, redlining continues at a reduced level. Bankers defend their actions by claiming that this is a response to deteriorating housing, not its cause.[15]

Beset by rising fuel and maintenance costs, city demands for compliance with housing codes, higher taxes, rent control laws, and spreading urban blight, urban landlords find themselves in a no-win situation. Unable to charge higher rents, obtain improvement loans, or sell their property, many owners try to squeeze the last ounce of profits from rental properties by ignoring necessary repairs and tax payments. After that, they abandon the buildings to junkies, looters, and arsonists.

Once urban decline commences, it's hard to stop. Anyone who can move out does so. The poor and helpless are left behind to cope with degenerating city services and increasing crime. Back in the 1970s and 1980s, landlords abandoned about 150,000 buildings each year. In the 1990s, the numbers dropped considerably, thanks to the economic revitalization in many cities and the gentrification process. Still, at that time Detroit was tearing down about 1,500 housing units each year, and cities such as Akron, Chicago, Cleveland, Los Angeles, and New York also experienced significant abandonment.[16]

Urban Renewal

Launched by the Housing Act of 1949 with the lofty goal of improving city neighborhoods through planned redevelopment, **urban renewal** proved to be a remarkably destructive force.

First, slum clearance displaced the poor without any provision having been made for their relocation. This action destroyed local neighborhoods, shattering sentimental attachments to old residences, neighborhood cohesiveness, friendships, and a whole way of life. Second, the cities sold the cleared land to private developers, who chose to build the most profitable forms of housing—almost never low-income housing.

One study found that replacement construction was 36 percent for housing (mostly for the upper middle class), 27 percent for commercial and industrial, and 37 percent for institutional and public use.[17] Another study showed that, from 1949 to 1965, only 166,288 new housing units replaced the 311,197 units demolished through urban renewal.[18] At an expenditure of $3 billion, urban renewal substantially reduced available low-cost housing in U.S. cities.[19]

Undoubtedly, the most notorious instance of community destruction through urban renewal involved the West End of Boston. Because it was an area of old buildings, city planners slated this tight-knit Italian neighborhood—popularized by Herbert Gans in *The Urban Villagers*—for urban renewal.[20] Noted urban sociologist Jane Jacobs, fighting the decision, said of this proud, cohesive, and stable neighborhood, "If this is a slum, we should have more of them." Nevertheless, the old ethnic neighborhood was bulldozed into oblivion and its residents scattered, to be replaced by high-rise luxury apartments and office buildings.

Public Housing

Another ill-conceived plan, introduced by the Housing Act of 1937, was **public housing** for the poor. The problem here was that policymakers ignored fundamental social concepts about human needs and interaction. Old, dilapidated buildings alone do not constitute a slum; a slum is an environment in which personal disorganization, apathy, alienation, lack of community, frustration, despair, and lack of opportunity exist. By attempting a purely physical solution to the social problem of poverty, the government simply created new slums.

The architectural design of the "supertenements" or "federal ghettos," as they came to be called, actually intensified the isolation, alienation, and crime already prevalent in disorganized low-income areas. Living in such a starkly segregated place set aside for impoverished minorities stigmatized the residents, and the poor considered such projects as dwellings of last resort. Moreover, income limits meant that the upwardly mobile were evicted, further concentrating the very poor and providing few legitimate successful role models for children.

Today there are about 4.7 million public housing units, which account for about 4 percent of the nation's housing stock.[21] In major need of repairs and replacement, many units are in poor condition. Yet in the 1990s, the Chicago Housing Authority encountered opposition from residents when it proposed to raze six high-rise buildings in the huge 3,600-unit Cabrini-Green monolithic ghetto and replace them with smaller buildings built for a mix of welfare and working-class families. Nevertheless, a stunning metamorphosis is occurring on adjacent property. Changes include a rejuvenated Seward Park playground, the new Jenner Academy of the Arts, the Neapolitan condominiums with $1 million-plus penthouses, and new retail outlets such as Blockbuster and Starbucks. Another notable addition is North Town Village, a bold mixed-income development of 261 homes, with one-third of them occupied by residents from Cabrini-Green. That public housing site will eventually duplicate Chicago's widely praised Lake Parc project—a mixed-income public

Housing the poor in high-rise apartment buildings built in the 1960s and 1970s was a dismal failure. These places became so unsafe that the poor did not want to live there; many were torn down and replaced with low-rise buildings. In contrast, Co-op City in the Bronx, the largest city housing project in the United States, is a good place to live. Why is this mostly middle-class, diverse community a success when others were not?

housing development project with 282 apartments, where (since its opening in 1991) crime and graffiti have been virtually nonexistent.[22] Half of the 230 new units in the nearby Wards redevelopment project are being set aside for public housing residents from Cabrini-Green, as more high-rise complexes are razed.[23]

Housing Subsidies

When government leaders realized that public housing projects were not the answer, they tried offering direct subsidies to the poor to purchase homes or rent apartments of their choice. Greedy speculators, exploiting the government and the poor through criminal collusion, undermined this program (the Housing and Urban Redevelopment of Act of 1968). Typically, a real estate broker or speculator would either buy rundown ghetto housing at low prices or frighten White owners in transitional neighborhoods into selling at much higher prices. By bribing government appraisers, the speculators could then sell the property at a much higher price to low-income buyers who qualified for the federal subsidies. Their tenuous financial situation forced some low-income buyers to subsequently default on their mortgages. More often, they abandoned the property because cosmetic repairs made before the sale had not corrected very serious defects in heating, plumbing, or structural soundness. In either case, having guaranteed the bank its money, the FHA or VA found itself owning another house no one wanted. Despite criminal prosecutions and the termination of this program, the Department of Housing and Urban

Development (HUD) found itself stuck with 150,000 abandoned properties, and to this day it remains one of the nation's largest slumlords.

In 1974, after other futile attempts at direct housing subsidy programs, the government created the **Section 8** program, which enables tenants to find private-market housing and have HUD pay landlords two-thirds of the "fair rental value" directly. Unfortunately, in the 1980s, this program lost $8 billion through gross mismanagement and fraud. Its budget has grown from $2.5 billion in 1974 to $7.2 billion in 1980 to nearly $16 billion in 2000.[24] Nonetheless Section 8 housing is a step above public housing projects, and it is valued by the persons who live in such units.

Gentrification

Some older cities in the Snowbelt—Baltimore, Boston, Chicago, New York, Philadelphia, and Washington, D.C.—have experienced a renaissance of sorts, with middle-class families moving into dilapidated neighborhoods and restoring them. In most major European cities, **gentrification** has long been a significant movement, but only in recent years have affluent, young professionals in the United States reversed the outward migration trend and moved into areas previously inhabited by low-income persons. In some areas such as New York City's SoHo district, formerly commercial buildings—like warehouses and factories—were converted into loft apartments. Most rehabilitation, however, occurs in older residential neighborhoods of formerly depressed city areas.

Numerous factors contribute to this trend: the increased proportion of young adults in the population, the high level of professional jobs in the city, the high cost of suburban living, the low cost of much inner-city real estate, the desire to eliminate or reduce commuter time and costs, and accessibility to urban activities. Even though the older homes are in disrepair when purchased, renovation often costs less than buying or constructing a suburban home. Moreover, older buildings were built to standards not available today: hardwood floors, oak or mahogany doors and woodwork, brick, marble, or tile fireplaces, leaded glass windows, lath-and-plaster walls, and greater square footage.

While gentrification revitalizes city neighborhoods and returns the middle class to the cities, it also has negative aspects. The influx of affluent families, mostly White, leads to higher rents and property taxes, forcing poor and minority residents out of their neighborhoods and into less desirable ones or into new ghettos outside the city. Encouraging economic redevelopment thus creates a dilemma: how to protect the poor and prevent the spread of urban blight elsewhere.

Urban Homesteading

Begun in Wilmington, Delaware, in 1973, and a moderate success in other cities, **urban homesteading** offers one example of how gentrification works. Cities sell abandoned or foreclosed dwellings for a token price to people who agree to rehabilitate the home, usually within two years, and live there for at least three years. Through city efforts and federal support, the homesteaders receive low-interest bank loans for the renovations needed to meet housing code standards. Such costs put this type of housing program beyond the reach of the urban poor, although "sweat equity" projects for low-income people, such as the People's Development Corporation (PDC) in the South Bronx have successfully reclaimed abandoned tenements.

Although urban homesteading would appear to be a local housing solution for troubled neighborhoods, it remains a relatively small program. Most restoration efforts have been in occupied buildings, not abandoned ones that looters have stripped and vandals have harmed. Many abandoned buildings are often beyond an economically feasible point of rehabilitation. These "lost" buildings or cleared land often surround salvageable buildings. Unless an entire neighborhood can be improved, urban homesteading is not the answer, continuing the problems of urban blight, street crime and violence, limited shopping opportunities, poor schools and inadequate public services.

Another form of urban homesteading requiring sweat equity of incoming homeowners is Habitat for Humanity. Habitat is a nonprofit organization that uses volunteer labor and some donated materials from area churches and organizations to build new housing for low-income families. In the first seventeen years of its existence, Habitat built 10,000 new homes, mostly in areas of massive urban blight, ultimately transforming many places into attractive, stable neighborhoods. Now comprising over 1,500 local organizations, Habitat has built over 45,000 homes nationwide and over 150,000 homes worldwide. If it continues at this pace, Habitat will soon surpass public urban homesteading in the number of urban homes built or restored.

Habitat for Humanity is a nonprofit organization that builds new low-income family housing. It has built more than 150,000 homes around the world to date through church fundraising, volunteer labor, and donated materials, as seen here in Detroit, Michigan. How do urban homesteading projects, such as Habitat for Humanity, gentrification, and condominium conversion offer alternative solutions to problems of urban housing?

Condominium Conversions

The conversion of urban rental apartments into condominium units has been extensive in recent years, with more than 600,000 such units now converted. Caught in a squeeze between increasing operating costs and narrowing profit margins, owners find it advantageous to convert their buildings. Middle-class tenants gain both property ownership and the accompanying tax advantages; but their monthly payments for mortgage, taxes, and maintenance fees exceed their previous monthly rents. As the condo trend continues, the persons most adversely affected are the working poor, who cannot afford ownership financing and yet do not qualify for subsidized housing. Often they are forced out of their rented apartments when the building converts into condominium units.

Homelessness

Although nearly everyone agrees that homelessness (primarily existing in the nation's cities) is a problem, opinions vary as to what extent it is a problem. While estimates of the actual number of homeless people vary, the Urban Institute estimates that on any given day, at least 800,000 people in the United States are homeless.[25] And the numbers grow higher each year; the U.S. Conference of Mayors reported a steady increase in requests for emergency shelters since the 1990s, with a 19 percent increase from 2001 to 2002. This organization also reported that the average length of time a person remains homeless is five months.[26]

Who are the homeless? For about twenty years now, they have been a diverse group from different backgrounds. In a twenty-six–city survey in 2000, the U.S. Conference of Mayors reported this demographic profile of the homeless:[27]

- Families with children (41 percent), of which 63 percent are single parents;
- Single men (41 percent);
- Single women (13 percent);
- Unaccompanied minors (5 percent).

Within these totals, the following subgroups existed:

- Veterans, mainly from the Vietnam War (10 percent);
- Mentally ill (23 percent);
- Substance abusers (32 percent);

The racial/ethnic breakdown was:

- African American (50 percent);
- Asian American (1 percent);
- Hispanic American (12 percent);
- Native American (2 percent);
- White American (35 percent).

What caused **homelessness** to become such a major social problem? Ironically, social forces unleashed to improve other aspects of life contributed to a massive increase in homelessness. Efforts to revitalize cities resulted in new construction on the edges of the central business districts, or downtowns, destroying in the process 2.2 million low-rent housing units between 1973 and 1993. The loss of low-cost housing due to urban renewal or gentrification forced many other poor people out of their neighborhoods, thereby increasing demand on remaining low-income housing, which in turn raised rents beyond what many could afford. As median rental costs paid by low-income renters rose 21 percent in the late 1990s, the affordable housing gap for them grew by 1 million.[28] Yet another factor was the 1975 Supreme Court ruling in *O'Connor v. Donaldson,* which held that nondangerous mental patients cannot be confined against their will. The resulting deinstitutionalization of mental patients released tens of thousands of marginally autonomous people into the streets. Other contributing elements include the growing number of female-headed families and addiction to crack or other drugs.

Particularly disturbing is the fact that 75 percent of the homeless family population consists of children, the most vulnerable members of our society.[29] The average age of homeless children is six. Homeless children are nine times more likely to repeat a grade and four times more likely to drop out of school than nonhomeless children.[30] A recent survey of homeless parents in New York City revealed that 35 percent are named in open cases of child abuse or neglect with the Child Welfare Administration. Moreover, in comparison to the overall homeless population, these

One of New York City's homeless lives in a mail cart near the post office. One can find the street people in all U.S. cities, indeed in all of the world's cities. Living in poverty, struggling daily to survive, many without hope or direction in their lives, they evoke pity, contempt, or indifference from the nonpoor. What makes homelessness a social problem that affects all of us and not just an individual problem the homeless should resolve themselves?

Social Constructions of Social Problems

Attitudes toward the Homeless

For much of the twentieth century, the stereotype of the homeless in our cities was that of an older male—the skid-row wino. Several decades ago, a second image evolved, that of a bag lady scavenging through refuse and carrying all her accumulated "treasures" with her wherever she went. Often these unfortunate people were disoriented, disorganized individuals released from psychiatric hospitals as part of a deinstitutionalization practice designed to end the warehousing of mentally ill patients. Supposedly, psychoactive drugs and transitional community services would aid their adjustment to life outside the hospital. In reality, many stopped taking the drugs, did not know how to find assistance, or refused to comply with the conditions for such help. As a result, some ended up homeless, panhandling and surviving as best they could on the streets.

Another, more recent, version of the homeless is that of the substance abuser. Crack, a relatively cheap alternative to alcohol, accelerated the problem of substance abuse among the homeless, especially among younger Black and Hispanic men. In Philadelphia in the past two decades, for example, the Diagnostic and Rehabilitation Center (DRC) has detoxified tens of thousands of homeless adults. The vast majority were alcoholics, but, in recent years, most now have a primary diagnosis of crack addiction and are problem drinkers as well.

Public attitudes and reactions to the increased visibility of the homeless and stereotyped perceptions of their acute personal problems are often negative. Disdain and discomfort are common responses of pedestrians encountering a homeless person. Frustrated at the lack of progress in addressing the homeless problem and pressured by angry residents and merchants over the continued presence and more aggressive panhandling by many of the street dwellers, local leaders have turned to evicting the homeless. Through new laws and tighter restrictions on panhandling and sleeping in public places, in at least 234 cities in the 1990s, according to the National Law Center of Homeless and Poverty, the police forcibly removed the homeless from certain sections of their cities.

Such actions do not deal with the causes of homelessness. Nor do public stereotypes accurately fit many of the homeless population. As explained elsewhere in this text, the homeless include families, mothers in poverty, and vagrant teenagers, as well as the mentally ill and substance abusers. Ironically, the public is more sympathetic to alcoholics and drug abusers who are rich and famous than to those who tug on the sleeves of passersby for a handout. What people need to understand is that addicts living in the streets need just as much help as the celebrities treated at private, expensive clinics.

parents are 30 percent more likely to have a history of substance abuse, 50 percent more likely to have a history of domestic violence, and twice as likely to have a history of mental illness.[31]

Virtually every city is taking steps to combat homelessness, not just with shelters, but with supportive programs as well. Best results have been obtained by turning shelters into transitional housing, and addressing health and job problems directly. Homes for the Homeless, for example, offers comprehensive programs such as Crisis Nursery, Together in Emotional Strength

(TIES), and the Residential Educational Training (RET) Center to address the multifaceted problems at the core of homelessness: poor education, inadequate health care, domestic violence, substance abuse, and the need for job training.

Despite these promising signs, however, the root causes of homelessness—the lack of education, insufficient low-cost housing, and poverty—are unlikely to go away soon. Homelessness still remains a national social problem heavily concentrated in our cities (see the box on the previous page).

Political Fragmentation

Our political structure's inability to adapt to the needs of metropolitan regions explains much about the causes and continuation of many urban problems. Traditional political boundaries are irrelevant to the need for services in adjacent communities. Crime control, education, housing, pollution, solid waste disposal, transportation, and water supply require planning and control over an entire region not within single localities. Museums, libraries, sports arenas, convention halls, cultural centers, and parks attract many suburbanites, but the city bears the cost of staff, police, sanitation, and transportation services.

We function in metropolitan regions but are not governed that way. The existence of multiple small governing bodies within the metropolis results in inefficient duplication of services (departments and agencies of government, fire and public safety, roads, sanitation, and so forth). Each municipality pursues its own course, without coordination and often in competition with others for ratables, creating unnecessary conflict and waste.

Cities actually have little control over their own affairs. Subject to many state and federal regulations, dependent on other levels of government for funding and policy decisions, urban governments are impotent to deal with many of their problems with mass transit, poverty, pollution, and so on. Until the 1970s, cities lacked political power in the rural-dominated state and federal legislatures, despite their higher overall population. By the time the Supreme Court ruled in favor of one-person, one-vote–mandated reapportionment to balance legislative district representation, the majority of the population had shifted to the suburbs. Added to the rural-suburban bias against cities is the frequent political split between Democratic-controlled city governments and Republican-controlled state legislatures, further hindering efforts to solve urban problems.

Another aspect of **political fragmentation** is the presence of so many decision-making points in a large city, making overall coordination difficult. One consequence of the 1960s reform movement to eliminate political machines was the creation of dozens of new (albeit smaller) machines—semiautonomous city agencies and bureaucracies staffed by career professionals. These agencies shape important policies, but their leadership tends to be self-perpetuating and does not readily submit to a higher authority. A city mayor, never certain if the bureau chiefs and career commissioners will look beyond their vested interests at the larger picture, serves more as a mediator between conflicting interest groups than as a chief executive in control of the city's operations.

Table 4.1   Largest U.S. Cities, 2000

1. New York	8,008,278	5. Philadelphia	1,517,550	8. Dallas	1,188,580
2. Los Angeles	3,694,280	6. Phoenix	1,321,045	9. San Antonio	1,144,646
3. Chicago	2,896,016	7. San Diego	1,223,400	10. Detroit	951,270
4. Houston	1,953,631				

Source: U.S. Bureau of the Census.

Can Snowbelt Cities Compete with Sunbelt Cities?

Updates from the Census Bureau continually reaffirm the continuing growth of Sunbelt cities and the concomitant decline in population of most Snowbelt cities. The South and West now claim over half the U.S. population and six of the ten largest cities (see Table 4.1 above). Of the ten fastest-growing metropolitan areas since 1990, seven were in Florida, two in Texas, and one in New Mexico. Cities experiencing the largest percentages of population loss in the same period were Hartford, Connecticut; St. Louis, Missouri; Gary, Indiana; Baltimore, Maryland; Flint, Michigan; and Buffalo, New York.[32] The 1990s also saw a large exodus of business and industry from the older central cities away from high taxes, energy costs, congestion, outmoded plants, and organized labor. The cumulative loss of people and manufacturing jobs led some observers to sound the death knell for the older cities.

Are the older, Snowbelt cities dying? Some experts predict economic disaster for them because of the loss of jobs to suburban or Sunbelt locations. A closer look, however, reveals a more balanced picture. For example, Columbus, Ohio, New York City, and Stamford gained in population, while such Sunbelt cities as Birmingham, Jackson, New Orleans, Norfolk, Richmond, and Savannah lost population.[33] Moreover, in 1998, office vacancy rates were higher in Atlanta, Dallas, Denver, and Orlando than they were in Detroit, New York, Philadelphia, and Washington, D.C.[34]

Sunbelt cities face many problems confronting the Snowbelt cities. Rapid population growth in the South and West brought urban sprawl, traffic congestion, air pollution, environmental deterioration, depletion of limited groundwater reserves, and strained water supply and sewer systems. Crime is another serious problem shared equally in Sunbelt and Snowbelt cities. In 2001, for example, the ten cities with the highest crime rates were St. Louis, Missouri, Atlanta, Kansas City, Missouri, Tampa, Memphis, Tucson, Columbus, Ohio, Baltimore, Miami, and Detroit.[35] In yet another area, economic problems can beset the Sunbelt as well as the Snowbelt. Unemployment rates in California, Florida, and Texas in recent years have exceeded the national average. The poverty rate in the South remains higher than in other parts of the country (see Chapter 6)—as it has for decades.

The BosWash Megalopolis

In a densely populated area that extends from the foothills of southern New Hampshire to the red-clay hills of northern Virginia, lie the cities of Boston, New York City, Philadelphia, Baltimore, and Washington, D.C.,—a region that French geographer Jean Gottman identified in 1961 as the first U.S. megalopolis.[36] Here, some measure of the strength of the Snowbelt can be illustrated.

Over 56 million people, one in every five Americans, lives in the BosWash megalopolis. This 22 percent of the nation's population produces more than its share (27 percent) of the nation's Gross Domestic Product (GDP); in comparison, the South and West, which contain 58 percent of the total U.S. population, produce 57 percent of the nation's GDP.[37] In 2000, banks in the Northeast held assets of $2.1 trillion, accounting for 33 percent of the nation's total bank assets.[38] The more assets banks have, the more venture capital they can lend; consequently, many corporations elsewhere in the nation—including movie studios—rely on the financial strength of the BosWash megalopolis for their activities.

Why does this region continue to attract job-creating investments? From interviews with employers and state secretaries of commerce, Rushworth Kidder identified the following factors[39]:

1. *Market concentration.* The region is the most concentrated market in the nation (one-fifth the population on one-twentieth the land mass). A centrally located manufacturer in the BosWash corridor can reach more than half of all U.S. and Canadian manufacturing firms and retail sales outlets within twenty-four hours by truck. The corridor states are also closer, by air and by sea, to the 376 million people in the European Union countries.

2. *Education.* The eleven-state region has the highest concentration of centers of higher education, sending about 3 million students annually to 875 colleges and universities. Proximity to top colleges influences the location choice of high-technology firms. Massachusetts's famous Route 128 (now called "America's Technology Highway") is near MIT and Harvard. New Jersey, with only 3 percent of the nation's population, has laboratories (many near Princeton University) that do 9 percent of America's research and development work.

3. *Infrastructure.* Although in need of repairs, the region's infrastructure—roads, bridges, and water systems—is already in place. Many fast-growth cities have not yet developed adequate systems, and the cost of doing so (including obtaining the necessary lands) is rising rapidly.

4. *Quality of life.* Many people consider the region to be the artistic and cultural center of the country. Access to the seacoast, lakes, and mountains brings a rich mix of city and country, work and leisure opportunities.

Each of the cities in BosWash is beset by problems of poverty and homelessness, drugs, crime, violence, teenage pregnancies, low-quality public education, and a decaying infrastructure. Within the megalopolis, the larger cities are undergoing a renaissance while smaller cities show less resiliency. Amid the mixed signs of rejuvenation and decline, this region reflects both the power and the perils of urban America.

Urban-Suburban Interdependence

Although the United States has been an urban society for over 100 years, we are redefining what it means to be an urban people. It is less a matter of place than a way of life. Distinctions between metropolitan and nonmetropolitan people blur as their occupations, consumer habits, and degree of sophistication become undistinguishable. Yet even as we blend into an interdependent urban system where local boundaries are meaningless, we often fail to recognize that problems in one area (the cities) adversely affect other areas (the suburbs).

The Central Cities

To offset loss of their manufacturing base, many cities evolved service-based economies, emerging as centers of sophisticated services in advertising, corporate management, finance, and government. This change eliminated many entry-level jobs traditionally held by the poorly educated urban poor, but it increased the need for computer-literate workers with verbal and quantitative skills. The result is a **skills mismatch** between people and jobs.[40] The skilled labor pool that companies require, therefore, tends to come from outside the cities, and many urban poor find fewer jobs available to them. As the job-generating power of cities weakens, their reduced independence places a heavier burden on suburbs for tax-supported relief.

The Outer-Ring Suburbs

The suburbs, seeking a broader tax base to relieve the burden on individual property owners, compete with cities for service-sector companies. They are often successful, as the lure of tax incentives, the freedom of telecommunications-based linkage, and the availability of desired workers make relocation practical. Furthermore, the concentration of social problems in our cities—crime, drugs, guns, gang violence, the inner-city AIDS epidemic, and racial problems—places cities at a disadvantage against the more positive suburban image. Each loss of a company to an edge city is an economic blow to the central city, further eroding its economic vitality and tax base. Meanwhile, each addition to the outer-ring further urbanizes that region.

The Inner-Ring Suburbs

The development of edge cities on the fringe of metropolitan regions has brought into usage the term **inner-ring suburbs** to refer to older suburbs directly adjacent to central cities. Over the past two decades, these inner-ring suburbs, like cities, have lost jobs and higher-income families while attracting lower-income residents fleeing inner-city chaos. Although one-fourth of the Black population now lives in the suburbs, they are mostly located in inner-ring suburbs, some of which are now predominantly Black. Consequently, economic and racial realities have drawn the political interests of inner-ring suburbs closer to those of central cities.

Thinking Regionally

At the beginning of this chapter we observed that the key to successful cities lies in their mutual interdependence with their surrounding region. It works the other way, too. Research shows that suburbs suffer if they let their central cities deteriorate. In *Cities Without Suburbs* (1993), former Albuquerque mayor David Rusk reasons that "elastic cities"—those that capture suburban

The Globalization of Social Problems

Cities in an International Context

Worldwide, people have flocked to cities for thousands of years, but within the next few years, for the first time in history, more people on Earth will live in and around cities than in rural areas. Explosive population growth and extensive migration from the countryside are creating huge concentrations of people. By 2015 the world will contain twenty-three **megacities**—metropolitan areas with populations of 10 million or more.[43] Most of these megacities will be in developing countries, including some of the poorest nations in the world (see Table 4.2 on the next page).

Since 1980, the number of megacities in less-developed regions has increased from three to fifteen. U.N. population growth projections for some cities are simply staggering: 10 million more people for Dhaka and 9 million more people for Delhi between 2000 and 2015. Accompanying this massive growth are many problems. Can these and other of the world's poorest megacities effectively absorb the millions of additional residents anticipated in the near future?

Despite any economic progress such rapid growth to enormous size brings, the strain on the infrastructure intensifies problems. An inadequate water supply and poor sanitation invite infections and disease. One report estimates that more than half of the 300 million urban poor in LDCs subsist in a permanently weakened condition because they carry one or more parasites. Other health problems result from high levels of pollution and fatalities from motor vehicles, illicit drug use, and widespread sexually transmitted infections such as HIV/AIDS. Furthermore, studies show that such cities have higher mortality rates than rural areas.[44]

As megacities grow, so do environmental concerns. Recall our discussion in the previous chapter about global warming. Imagine now the extensive energy demands, not just of modern urban systems, but of these megacities. Then consider the consequent emissions of carbon dioxide and nitrogen oxides from fossil fuel combustion that trap excess heat and contribute to climate change, rising sea levels, and changes in vegetation. Also, these rapidly growing cities create expanded demand for food, wood, building materials, and furniture, leading in turn to problems of soil depletion and deforestation. And this doesn't occur only in the immediate vicinity. For example, the decimation of Borneo's forests is due in large measure to the lumber needs of Japanese cities. Clearly, there exists an extensive interconnectivity between urbanization (particularly the rapid growth of megacities), environmental issues, and quality of life.

growth within their boundaries—generate more jobs and exhibit less racial segregation.[41] In *Citistates* (1993), Neal Peirce and his colleagues argue that only metropolitan areas that create flexible governance structures will succeed in the global marketplace.[42]

For decades, organizations such as the Regional Plan Association based in New York have encouraged cities and suburbs to eliminate wasteful duplication by consolidating and sharing school districts, mental health centers, sewage treatment, solid-waste disposal, and emergency services. State court decisions regarding urban school funding and public pressure to reduce taxes and government spending have forced many municipalities to take such steps. It remains to be seen whether similar cooperative efforts will extend into other areas.

**Table 4.2 Population of Metropolitan Areas with 10 Million Inhabitants
or More, 1975, 2000 and 2015 (in millions)**

1975		2000		2015	
City	**Population**	**City**	**Population**	**City**	**Population**
1 Tokyo	19.8	1 Tokyo	26.4	1 Tokyo	27.2
2 New York	15.9	2 Mexico City	18.1	2 Dhaka	22.8
3 Shanghai	11.4	3 Bombay	18.1	3 Bombay	22.6
4 Mexico City	11.2	4 São Paolo	17.8	4 São Paolo	21.2
5 São Paolo	10.0	5 New York	16.6	5 Delhi	20.9
		6 Lagos	13.4	6 Mexico City	20.4
		7 Los Angeles	13.1	7 New York	17.9
		8 Calcutta	12.9	8 Jakarta	17.3
		9 Shanghai	12.9	9 Calcutta	16.7
		10 Buenos Aires	12.6	10 Karachi	16.2
		11 Dhaka	12.3	11 Lagos	16.2
		12 Karachi	11.8	12 Los Angeles	14.5
		13 Delhi	11.7	13 Shanghai	13.6
		14 Jakarta	11.0	14 Buenos Aires	13.2
		15 Osaka	11.0	15 Metro Manila	12.6
		16 Metro Manila	10.9	16 Beijing	11.7
		17 Beijing	10.8	17 Rio de Janeiro	11.5
		18 Rio de Janeiro	10.6	18 Cairo	11.5
		19 Cairo	10.6	19 Istanbul	11.4
				20 Osaka	11.0
				21 Tianjin	10.3

Note: Metropolitan area estimates vary widely, depending on definitions and recency of census data.

Source: United Nations Population Division.

Living with Terrorism

All of us have become sensitized to the vulnerability of cities to terrorist attacks. In Tokyo in 1995 thousands fell victim to chemical terrorism with the use of the toxic gas sarin on defenseless civilians that killed 12 in a subway tunnel. The 2001 attacks on the Pentagon in Washington, D.C., and on the twin towers of the World Trade Center in New York City, with their horrific losses of 3,000 people and mass destruction, still reverberate in the minds of hundreds of millions of people worldwide. In 2002, Chechnyan terrorists took over 700 people hostage in a Moscow music theater resulting in the deaths of nearly 200 rebels and hostages, mostly by gas used during a rescue attempt.

These and other incidents remind us all too often that urban centers attract terrorists. The large concentrations of people—as well as the tall buildings, symbolic monuments, and infrastructure of bridges and tunnels—are all tempting targets to those intent on inflicting maximum damage and deaths. People once avoided cities for fear of becoming a victim of a violent crime. Now many fear, not just being in major cities, but even living near one in the event of biological, chemical, or nuclear attack.

Seeing concrete barricades at many important locations and undergoing bag searches at concerts, sporting events, and airports are part of our new reality. For some, living or working in tall buildings, or viewing the cityscape from high-perched observation decks, holds little appeal. Others, refusing to allow their lives to be ruled by fear, continue their daily urban routines and lifestyles.

Whether they respond by avoidance or defiance, however, urbanites recognize that their world is a different one than that which existed before September 11th, 2002. That realization is a new element in considering social problems that affect our cities.

Sociological Perspectives

Sociological analysis provides a means of interpreting the numerous changes and intensifying problems experienced by cities from more than a superficial viewpoint. Depending on the theoretical orientation used, however, definitions of the underlying problems and their proposed solutions vary.

The Functionalist Viewpoint

Functionalists blame rapid urbanization for disrupting the social organization of society. First, large masses of rural residents and immigrants came to U.S. cities, creating intolerable living conditions. Unprepared to assimilate the newcomers—who themselves were ill-equipped for urban living—the cities experienced increasing pathologies of sickness, disease, death, crime, and social disorganization. Before the urban system could regain its equilibrium, it suffered another jolt as the exodus to the suburbs began. Factories, stores, and offices followed the former urbanites, leaving the city core unable to assist the non-White minorities replacing them.

Much of this social change was functional. Modern manufacturing technology required horizontal plant expansion that cities could not provide but suburbs could. Suburban expansion created many job opportunities for the building, automotive, and transport industries. It also took population pressure off cities, reducing their density. Businesses and industries benefited from lower taxes and greater ease in shipping products. Workers gained the satisfaction of home ownership and travel flexibility by automobile. Yet many dysfunctions flowed from these social changes as well. Cities lost tax revenues, became disproportionately inhabited by the poor, and lacked employment opportunities and sufficient resources to provide adequately for them. Housing and schools deteriorated, demands for services increased, and the inner city declined into a near-comatose state.

To restore stability and equity to the system, Functionalists assert adjustments must occur. Since our communities have merged with each other in all ways but politically, perhaps reorganization along more realistic lines would return the governing and financial balance needed. Regional planning and coordination would ensure more rational land use and a greater sense of mutual interdependence. Problems that know no geographic boundary—water supply, pollution, traffic—could be addressed more effectively. We might resolve problems of employment and housing more easily if we redefined our community in terms of a metropolitan governing body to coordinate services, business locations, housing, and transportation.

Another possibility for restoring the social system's balance may be a further strengthening of the economic functions of the central cities to make companies want to stay or return there. We need to encourage further the processes already occurring—gentrification, new office building construction, and revitalized downtowns. Reduced density and numerous vacant lots provide the physical opportunity to rebuild a city, improving its aesthetic beauty while providing new opportunities for its poor. Urban enterprise zones offering tax incentives to industry, together with job-training programs, could bring jobs to the people who need them. Cities do not exist in isolation; their welfare hinges on taking steps to place them on an equal economic footing with other regions.

The Conflict Viewpoint

Conflict theorists view the problems in cities as being the uneven outcome of competition among various interest groups for limited resources. This struggle takes many forms, often pitting more powerful groups with little concern for particular urban problems against less powerful, but directly affected groups. The conflict often occurs among groups within the city; at other times it involves city dwellers and suburbanites.

Urban heterogeneity makes potential conflict among different groups quite likely. Should a city's limited funds be used to improve the downtown shopping district, build low-cost housing for the poor, construct recreation centers, improve the schools, or expand public transportation? All cannot be accomplished at once, yet all needs are immediate. Merchants and representatives of different citizen constituencies thus vie with one another, pressing for their own interests. Stirring up this oft-seething cauldron of conflict further are the vested interests of civic bureaucrats, seeking higher salaries, improved working conditions, or simply the preservation of their domain. As unresolved issues continue, the likelihood of organized protest—demonstrations, protest meetings, noisy confrontations, rent strikes, union job actions, or violence—increases.

Within the city lies another focal point for Conflict analysis: economic exploitation. When cities were manufacturing centers, powerful industrialists often maximized their profits by exploiting the available cheap labor; their one-sided gains led to widespread poverty and neighborhood deterioration for large sections of the city. Similarly, slumlords seeking maximum profits through "rent gouging" and/or minimal maintenance accelerated the decline. Forced eviction of low-rent tenants to upgrade a building into a middle-income rental facility and engineered condemnation of an area to build more lucrative structures are but two instances of how real estate entrepreneurs have garnered profits at others' expense. Political machines and crooked politicians often bilked cities of millions of dollars to the detriment of the public welfare.

In recent years a new urban sociology evolved—the political economy approach—that recommends examining cities in the context of their economic and political systems. Manuel Castells, for example, maintains that the fiscal crisis of cities is an inevitable consequence of a capitalistic economic system. Seeking ever-greater profits, corporations influenced federal approval of government-insured mortgages and subsidized expressways so that they and their executives could move to suburbs where property costs and taxes were lower.[45] On a global scale, cities in LDCs grow rapidly and become dependent links in the world system, serving as control centers in a web designed to exploit the rural sectors.[46]

The Feminist Viewpoint

As stated previously, female-headed households exist below the poverty line and among the homeless population in large numbers. Feminists point to a body of evidence showing that single-parent females and elderly females often suffer in the housing market because of landlord discrimination, limited fixed incomes, and inadequate public assistance. Thus female-headed households are more dependent on subsidized housing than other groups. However, the government makes existing subsidy mechanisms available primarily for construction or rehabilitation of single-family houses affordable only to two—wage-earner households. Some Feminists, citing the Tenant Interim Lease program in New York City as a model, suggest a more widespread creation of low-income tenant cooperatives, ones in which a system of women's values and relationships becomes an essential component of the co-op process.[47]

Another major factor of Feminist urban studies is the extent to which cities use space to meet the needs of women. For example, how does the city environment support the needs of today's working women? The emergence of a wide variety of specialized services (child care, household cleaning, shopping assistance, take-out restaurants, pick-up and delivery services) is one answer. Hot food delis and salad bars in supermarkets, mini-malls, large merchandising stores for one-stop shopping efficiently minimize time spent going from store to store.[48]

Feminist urban researchers also examine the allocation of public leisure space, which is often gendered, since it typically favors male-oriented activities such as sports, giving little consideration to the needs of women. Feminists argue that spatial arrangements should not segregate the sexes, thereby reinforcing traditional ideas about gender, but it should allocate space to help all individuals' lives. Moreover, more attention should be given to creating safe environments to protect children at play, providing less-constrained places for women to walk or jog, and creating housing that promotes more contact with neighbors, especially for children.[49] Judith DeSena suggests that women's greater movement in urban space allows them to control information/events and to create networks, making them more likely then men to recognize problems and develop community strategies to transform urban spaces and/or create new ones. Through this feminization of communities, women can thus be power brokers in directing and shaping social-physical space.[50]

The Interactionist Viewpoint

Focusing on how people subjectively define reality, interactionists examine how values, shared expectations, and perceptions apply to social problems in cities. Traditional American values have always stressed the small town ideal, with its personal cohesiveness and sense of community. Warnings against the corrupting influence of cities, while common throughout world history, have been especially pronounced in the U.S. experience. People living in the once-predominant rural regions of the United States mistrusted the cities. Later the influx of millions of culturally distinct European immigrants, followed by African Americans and then Hispanics triggered responses of prejudice and avoidance. Acclimation to suburban living similarly provoked disdain for urban lifestyles. Perceiving the city as a place inhabited by "lesser types" thus removes any sense of social responsibility to improve the situation.

Anti-city value orientations prompt the response that cities bring on their own problems, rather than the recognition that they intensely reflect broader and deeper societal problems. Media coverage—whether films or television shows about depressed urban areas or news reports of urban crime or racial tensions—further convey a rather pessimistic image of the nation's cities. These portrayals feed an already existing anti-city bias that has been a centuries-old component of U.S. culture. The resulting social construction of reality stereotypes most city dwellers as downtrodden, even dangerous, even though most urbanites live completely different lifestyles. Still, this false perception has negative consequences.

Because cities house large concentrations of poor people, nonurbanites often stereotype cities as being almost exclusively urban war zones and slum neighborhoods. While sections of cities do match that perception, other areas are safe, cohesive, and beautiful. Even in poor sections, problems of overcrowding, substandard housing, crime, and health are less severe than they were two generations ago. They remain matters of concern, however, because they still contrast with more favorable conditions elsewhere. The rise in living standards and expectations (car, TV, hot water, and other necessities once thought luxuries) cause the poor to feel deprived compared to the nonpoor who possess such items.

Another common interaction difficulty involves relations between poverty-stricken urban minorities and the police and city government agencies. Beginning with their treatment of the Irish in the mid-nineteenth century and continuing to the present day, officials responsible for maintaining formal social control mechanisms of the city often view minority groups as the enemy. The latter's physical and cultural differences, the pathologies flowing out of their poverty, and the ethnocentric attitudes of the privileged middle class all serve to reinforce this perception. Mutual antagonisms develop and a vicious circle of attitudes, actions, and reactions follows. By the time the minority achieves economic and political power, another group has replaced it at the bottom of the ladder, and the cycle begins anew. Currently, Blacks and Hispanics are gaining stronger representation in elected and appointive positions, suggesting that improved social policy reinterpretations and actions for their constituents may be on the way.

▲ Thinking About the Future

Our cities today offer both encouraging and disheartening signs. We appear to be going in two directions at the same time. On the one hand, we see an influx of middle-class, refurbished neighborhoods and new office buildings, as well as much cultural and economic activity. Yet, we also see decay and decline, congestion and pollution, crime and poverty, and suburbanites continuing to shun the city. Which trend will prevail?

What do we do about sprawling edge cities, malls, office and industrial parks, all with huge parking lots? At the present time, suburban growth gobbles up more and more land, as towns sprawl into each other. Every place is beginning to look like anyplace, giving fewer towns a unique sense of identity or community. Suburbs become more urbanized, suburban traffic congestion increases, and cities find it harder and harder to compete with cinema complexes, malls, and megastores out on the highway. What future do you envision for your community if the current growth and development patterns continue?

Should we keep letting local communities compete with one another and develop as they please regardless of their impact on the environment and neighboring towns? How can we promote greater urban-suburban cooperation and interdependence? Or shouldn't we? Do you favor some type of regional planning and control, perhaps at a county level, to contain growth, minimize traffic congestion, and protect the environment? Should we do more to encourage greater use of mass transit, such as through new light-rail systems (where feasible) that perhaps parallel our highways along the center islands? What are the implications and problems in these solutions?

What about housing? We are simply not building enough affordable housing, and the gentrification of some existing housing raises rents beyond the means of many former residents of those neighborhoods. What future do you see if these trends continue? How do we improve the quality of life in our urban communities presently suffering from substandard housing and lack of jobs, stores, and public amenities and services? How do we solve the problem of homelessness?

Give some thought to all these questions. What answers come to mind? Which of these proposed solutions seem practical in terms of cost and feasibility? Which do not? Can you think of others? Can you envision two futures, one if nothing is done and one if something is done? What *is* that something? How is that future different?

How can you *personally* help the homeless? There are a great many ways in which you can make an important difference in their lives *now*, even before you graduate. One instant way is just a mouse-click at a computer. Others involve advocacy actions, contributions (clothing, household items, "survival" kits, food certificates, etc.), and volunteer activities. To learn more go to Chapter 4 of this book's Web site (www.ablongman.com/parrillo) and be part of the solution.

SUMMARY

1. Cities are no longer the major places of residence or manufacturing in the United States. Since 1960, suburbs have evolved into independent urban entities. Many metropolitan areas overlap and interpenetrate each other, forming megalopolises. This urban sprawl uses up large tracts of land, increasing residents' dependency on automobiles, and raising the cost of living. Now edge cities are evolving on the fringes of older urban areas, forming greenfield, uptown, or boomer cities for the middle class.

2. The flight of jobs to the suburbs results in traffic congestion on interstate highways and within the suburbs themselves. Mass transit helps reduce urban congestion, but some people feel that it should be self-paying, not a public utility. Consequently, mass transit in the United States is not as good as elsewhere in the industrialized world.

3. Redlining remains an institutional contributor to housing deterioration, although it is not practiced as extensively today as in the past. A cycle of abandonment by landlords caught in an increasing costs–declining income syndrome spreads urban blight. Urban renewal was a disastrous public program, destroying neighborhoods and reducing available low-cost housing. High-rise public housing projects ignored human needs, inviting stigma, alienation, vandalism, and crime. Housing subsidies have had mixed results and are skyrocketing in cost.

4. Positive housing steps include gentrification, urban homesteading, low-interest city mortgages, and condominium conversions. The persons who benefit least from these measures—and often are displaced by them—are the poor. The homeless, numbering about 800,000 in the United States, are a mixture of different kinds of people, over one-third of them families. About 75 percent of the homeless family population consists of children, who are four times more likely to drop out of school than nonhomeless children.

5. Although a functional interdependence exists between cities and suburbs, each municipality governs itself independently, which usually results in unnecessary conflict and waste. Fragmentation of political authority prevents cities from controlling their own affairs and forces them to depend on state and federal bodies that are often biased against them. Competing civic bureaucracies within a city also impede coordinated efforts, since they seek their own narrow objectives.

6. Since 1980, population declines occurred in some Sunbelt cities and in most Snowbelt cities except Hartford, New York City, and Stamford. Sunbelt cities are beset with problems of crime, congestion, pollution, infrastructure needs, and economic concerns. The BosWash megalopolis is home to one in five Americans; generates 27 percent of the nation's GDP; and possesses a high concentration of consumers and educated workers, an established infrastructure, and many world-class cultural attractions.

7. Nonmetropolitan and metropolitan people are converging in their occupations, consumer habits, and sophistication. Inner-ring suburbs have similar problems to central cities, while outer-ring suburbs attract higher-income people and industries, creating edge cities. Regionalization of school districts and services is becoming more common among municipalities.

8. Within a few years, more people worldwide will live in or near a city than in rural areas. Urban growth, especially among megacities in developing countries, poses serious problems of environmental degradation.

9. Recent terrorist attacks in Tokyo, New York City, Washington, D.C., and Moscow have made us aware of the attraction of urban centers to such people. Avoidance and defiance are common responses, but everyone realizes the new social problem that cities now face.

10. Both urbanization and suburbanization were functional for society, according to Functionalists, but certain dysfunctions require adjustments: new political boundaries, new financing structures, or further evolution of cities as transactional centers. Conflict theorists point to competing urban constituencies, profiteering exploiters, outside political powers, and the competitive capitalistic system worldwide as causes of urban problems. Feminists emphasize the need for inclusion of women's values in the co-op process to meet critical housing needs for female-headed households and for greater equity in the allocation of public space. Interactionists stress value-biased perceptions, relative definitions of deprivation, and cultural differentiation as important to our understanding of interaction patterns.

KEY TERMS

Boomer city	Political fragmentation
Edge city	Public housing
Gentrification	Redlining
Greenfield city	Section 8
Homelessness	Skills mismatch
Infrastructure	Uptown city
Inner-ring suburbs	Urban homesteading
Megacities	Urban renewal
Megalopolis	

INTERNET RESOURCES

At this book's Web site with Allyn & Bacon, you will find numerous links pertaining to the problems about housing and urbanization. To explore these resources, go first to the author's page (**http://www.ablongman.com/parrillo**). Next, select this edition of *Contemporary Social Problems* and then select **Internet Readings and Exercises**. Then select **Chapter 4**, where you will find both a variety of sites to investigate and some questions that pertain to those sites.

SUGGESTED READINGS

Blau, Joel. *The Visible Poor: Homelessness in the United States*. New York: Oxford University Press, 1993. Debunks current myths about the homeless, thoughtfully discusses issues on America's poor, and attacks government policies as pointless, quick-fix solutions that don't deal with the underlying causes.

Fowler, Edmund P. *Building Cities that Work,* 11th ed. Montreal: McGill-Queens University Press, 1994. A thought-provoking critique of costly U.S. urban development programs that have had little positive impact.

Gans, Herbert J. *The Urban Villagers,* expanded ed. New York: Free Press, 1983. A classic case study of life in a tight-knit, working-class White ethnic community that was destroyed by urban renewal.

Garreau, Joel. *Edge City: Life on the New Frontier.* New York: Doubleday, 1992. Highly readable, informative analysis of geographic, economic, and sociological forces shaping our new downtowns and urban environments.

Jacobs, Jane. *The Death and Life of Great American Cities.* New York: Random House, 1961/1993. Still pertinent and provocative, an indictment of urban planning and urban renewal, with specific alternatives given.

Macionis, John J., and Vincent N. Parrillo. *Cities and Urban Life,* 3d ed. Upper Saddle River, N.J.: Prentice-Hall, 2004. A multidisciplinary approach, with a sociological emphasis on urban growth, life, and problems, including cross-cultural discussion and city case studies.

Pastor, Manuel, Jr., et al. *Regions That Work: How Cities and Suburbs Can Grow Together.* Minneapolis: University of Minnesota Press, 2000. Offering a new vision of community-based regionalism with a detailed study of three successful regions and a provocative call for new policies and new politics.

Phillips, E. Barbara. *City Lights: Urban-Suburban Life in a Global Society,* 2d ed. New York: Oxford University Press, 1996. An examination of the issues and problems facing U.S. cities, including the telecommunications revolution and cultural pluralism.

Rusk, David. *Cities Without Suburbs.* Baltimore: Woodrow Wilson Center Press, 1993. A former mayor of Albuquerque suggests that political restructuring through annexation solves economic problems and reduces racial segregation.

Sawers, Larry, and William K. Tabb (eds.). *Sunbelt/Snowbelt: Urban Development and Regional Restructuring.* New York: Oxford University Press, 1988. A collection of articles examining the social forces that change the structure and economy of metropolitan areas.

Squires, Gregory D. (ed.). *Urban Sprawl: Causes, Consequences, and Policy Responses.* Washington, D.C.: Urban Institute Press, 2002. Leading scholars in the field offer multiple perspectives on urban sprawl and the concerns facing citizens and communities across the country.

5 | Power, Work, and the Workplace

Facts About Work and the Workplace

- The top five U.S. companies have sales greater than the GNP of all but six countries.
- The top 1 percent of U.S. families possess nearly 40 percent of the nation's wealth.
- Multinational corporations constitute the world's second largest economy, trailing only the United States.
- The greater a person's education, the less likely that person is to be unemployed.
- Four of five new jobs are low-pay, low-prestige, dead-end jobs.
- Temporary jobs doubled to 3.6 million between 1994 and 2002.
- An employer's chances are one in sixty-five of a site inspection for unsafe or hazardous working conditions.

Traditional American values—democracy, freedom, equality, individualism, achievement, humanitarianism—foster contradictory beliefs in people. For example, we believe in local autonomy and control, but we want the federal government to intervene to correct social problems. We think government should help people, yet we don't want it to interfere in people's lives. We believe in the free enterprise system, but we want government to regulate big business. We distrust both big business and big government, yet we regard them as necessities.

How do we reconcile these conflicts? How do we encourage greater business productivity and government protection without impinging on individual rights? With the continuing growth of conglomerates and lobbies, does the government represent the public interest or special interests? Who really runs the United States?

In the near future, you will begin spending the greater part of your life as a full-time worker in U.S. society—most likely as an employee of someone else, perhaps a large corporation. No matter what career you pursue, however, work will provide you (as it does everyone) with more than just earnings for living a particular lifestyle. Work will also give you a social identity and a purpose. For some people, work is more personally fulfilling than it is for others. Yet because the social organization of work can also be alienating, dehumanizing, exploitative, and physically harmful, it is the source of many social problems.

This chapter examines some of the social forces that affect the U.S. consumer and the U.S. worker. First we look at the growing concentration of corporate power and its impact on individuals; then we examine the changing workplace in the midst of the electronic revolution. Finally, we will study the problems of unemployment, worker satisfaction, and health hazards in the workplace.

Work in Sociohistorical Context

Industrialization brought changes to U.S. society. Life became more complex, jobs more specialized, and each of us more dependent on others to obtain needed goods and services. Individual economic self-reliance gave way to dependence on large factories and natural resource producers for our livelihoods and material needs. The process was difficult. Exploitation of the land and of workers, abuse of power, and labor strife were ongoing realities.

In their battles for a greater share of the marketplace, competing companies expanded by absorbing smaller companies or simply eliminating their competitors. As they grew in size and power, a few large companies in each industry became monopolies, effectively controlling that market and manipulating prices to their own advantage. What began as a system of economic competition to meet market demand turned into economic dominance by gigantic corporations that controlled market supply. By the second half of the twentieth century, many large corporations had become global entities, with substantial foreign assets and sales, making their power even greater.

As economic institutions became bureaucratized and centralized, so did political institutions. In large cities and industrial states, and especially at the national level, cumbersome government bureaucracies evolved to handle ever-broadening responsibilities. Within the labyrinth of big government operations, lobbyists for special-interest groups work hard to obtain favorable decisions on new laws, regulations, and government policies. Using their enormous wealth, large corporations make sizable campaign contributions or hold out the promise of a future job to influence legislators or regulatory agency administrators.

Corporate Power

When a few producers dominate an industry, the economic arrangement is termed an **oligopoly**—the division of wealth and power among very few competitors. Oligopolies frequently engage in **price leadership**; that is, they adopt coordinated pricing or parallel pricing to avoid price competition. Thus, when one major auto, oil, or steel company raises its prices, the others quickly do the same. Obviously they gain far more in this way through added revenues than they lose by making their products too expensive for some would-be buyers. Sometimes such increases are justified, but many instances of artificially inflated prices also occur. One example is when Enron bought California electric energy at cheap, capped prices and routed it outside the state, then sold it back into California at vastly inflated prices. This manipulation of energy markets between 1998 and 2001 resulted in Enron's chief energy trader pleading guilty to federal charges.

Price fixing remains a serious problem and affects us in many areas, from buying gas to vitamins to carpets. When retail gas prices in the Midwest spiked as high as $2.50 a gallon in June 2000, the Federal Trade Commission subpoenaed the big-seven oil companies to determine whether price fixing pushed up these prices: prices then dropped dramatically within a week.[1] In 1999, Hoffmann-La Roche paid a $500 million fine levied by the U.S. Department of Justice, and four other pharmaceutical firms paid millions of dollars in criminal fines for illegally controlling vitamin prices.[2] In July 2000, generic drug maker Mylan Laboratories agreed to pay $135 million in fines to settle federal, state, and private lawsuits charging it with fixing the prices of two medications commonly used to treat anxiety and hypertension among the elderly.[3] And in August 2000, two carpet makers, Mohawk Industries and Shaw Industries, agreed to pay $41 million to settle a class-action lawsuit that alleged price fixing in the 1990s.[4]

The extent of big business dominance of the economy is revealed by the fact that the top 500 U.S. corporations employed about 22 million people in 2001, more than 10 percent of the U.S. workforce. They amassed nearly half of the nation's total profits and generated about three-fourths of the nation's GNP, more than the combined GNPs of Japan and Germany.[5] Even more astounding, the top five corporations—General Motors, Wal-Mart Stores, Exxon Mobil, Ford Motor Company, and General Electric—generated sales greater than the GNP of all but six countries: United States, Japan, Germany, France, Italy, United Kingdom (see the box on p. 123).[6]

Who Owns the Corporations?

Clearly, a small number of corporations play a major role in our nation's welfare; but who owns the corporations themselves? The answer lies hidden in three main areas: complex layers of interwoven corporate ownership of stock in other corporations; corporate investors acting on behalf of private investors; and concealed trust funds. Numerous analyses reveal that a small wealthy elite of Americans are the ultimate owners of most corporate stock. Millions of private investors may be involved in the stock market, but the bulk of the stock is controlled by a relative few.

The Wealthy Elite

Data about rich Americans are astounding. The top 20 percent of all U.S. families receives nearly half of all income earned and owns approximately 80 percent of the nation's wealth.[7] The "super rich," the top 1 percent of households, has doubled its share of the national wealth since the mid-1970s. In fact, this top 1 percent now has more wealth than the entire bottom 95 percent! This wealthy elite controls 40 percent of the nation's wealth, owns 71 percent of all tax-exempt municipal bonds, 42 percent of all real estate purchased as investments, and 62 percent of all stocks in private hands.[8] If we focus only on financial wealth (net worth minus equity in owner-occupied housing), the top 1 percent controls nearly half of that.[9]

Microsoft chief executive officer (CEO) Bill Gates owns more wealth than the bottom 45 percent of American households. His wealth exceeds the GNP of all but 58 countries.

Interlocking directorates

Besides corporate investment, another effective means of exercising economic control is **interlocking directorates**. This occurs when executives or directors from one corporation sit on the board of directors of another corporation. Such linkage can either be *direct* (one person on the board of directors of two companies) or *indirect* (two companies each having someone on the board of directors of a third company). Either way this tight, interlocking network of business executives concentrates economic or fiscal control in the hands of a few people who can effectively chart production and investment in one of several industries without outside interference. As C. Wright Mills said, "*Interlocking Directorate* is no mere phrase: it points to a solid feature of the facts of business life, and to a sociological anchor of the community of interest, the unification of outlooks and policy, that prevails among the propertied class."[10]

Interlocking directorates—both direct and indirect—are extremely common in business. One study of the thirteen largest corporations (which together possess one-eighth of the country's corporate assets), found that each had an average of 5 direct links and 123 indirect links to the other twelve.[11] Numerous other studies give evidence of the control of major banks and corporations through widespread use of interlocking directorates.[12]

Interlocks are created by both inside and outside directors. A firm's *inside directors,* especially its leading officers, often sit on the boards of other firms. A study of 456 Fortune 500 manufacturing firms revealed that more than 70 percent had at least one officer who sat on the board of a financial institution. This does not include cases in which a firm's officers sat on the boards of nonfinancial corporations. The sum of the affiliations of a firm's *outside directors* typically constitute the majority of its interlocks, comprising about three-fourths of all ties with financial institutions among the 456 firms in the aforementioned study.[13]

When competition becomes virtually nonexistent, when a few corporate giants have great concentrations of wealth and power, and when these corporations—controlled by a small wealthy elite—have little outside accountability or regulation, the free enterprise system ceases to function. Interlocking directorates are not illegal as long as direct competitors do not sit on each other's boards or on the boards of suppliers and customers. Nevertheless, the practice guarantees a privileged position of power to huge corporations and no protection to consumers.

Engulf and Devour

In recent decades, a number of monolithic **conglomerates** has arisen through mergers and acquisitions. This trend toward conglomerates—large firms that own businesses in highly diversified fields—increases the probability of corporate oligopolies and their greater influence on government policy. In recent years, more than 7,000 mergers occurred annually, with many in banking, oil and gas, brokerage and investment businesses, utilities, and telecommunications.[14]

The value of mergers and acquisitions soared to $9 trillion in the 1990s. Some of the biggest in recent years include the merger of Internet and media companies America Online and Time

The Globalization of Social Problems

The International Impact of Multinational Corporations

Since the middle of the last century some corporate giants have concentrated so much power and wealth in their hands that they have become prominent forces in the world economy. These **multinational corporations** operate across national boundaries, with plants and investments in many countries. Not under the sole regulatory authority of any one nation or international organization, these gigantic business enterprises conduct business across many national borders in the pursuit of profits. Yet their decisions, perhaps made in a boardroom thousands of miles away, affect nations' domestic and foreign policies, as well as their economies.

The multinationals, most of which are registered as U.S. companies, cumulatively constitute the world's second largest economy, after the economy of the United States, and account for more than one-fourth of economic production worldwide. Some of these global companies—General Motors, Ford, IBM, and the major petroleum companies—have annual sales that exceed the GNPs of all Developing World countries and of several industrialized countries including South Africa and Switzerland. Aggregate annual foreign sales of the top one hundred U.S. multinationals exceed $700 billion. Exxon, which does business in almost one hundred countries, has a tanker fleet equal in size to the entire British navy.

Driven by the goal of profit maximization, multinational corporations locate their manufacturing and production facilities in underdeveloped countries where labor costs are low. This causes a loss of jobs and increased importation of foreign goods in industrialized nations without, as analysts note, improving conditions for workers in the poor countries. Several sociologists have found that after an initial gain in the host nation's wealth, economic inequality actually increases, since only the upper and middle classes substantially benefit from economic expansion. The workers remain in subsistence-level jobs for long hours and barely meet living expenses.

Many impoverished countries encourage foreign investment in hopes of becoming more developed societies. Such countries, lacking the financial resources of the wealthier multinationals, often come to depend on tax revenues from the corporations for a sizable portion of their government income. As a result, they find it almost impossible to pursue regulatory policies that conflict with the multinationals' interests, since the companies' departure would devastate the nations' economy.

Warner ($182 billion); the merger of oil companies Chevron and Texaco ($97 billion) and of Exxon and Mobil ($80 billion); the merger of telecommunication companies Bell Atlantic and Nynex ($21.3 billion); the acquisition of aerospace manufacturers McDonnell Douglas Corporation by Boeing ($14 billion); and the merger of investment firms Morgan Stanley Group and Dean Witter, Discover & Company ($10.2 billion). Analysts call these actions—in which a multi–billion-dollar company acquires another company with assets valued at $1 billion or more—**megamergers**. Interestingly, one consulting firm's analysis revealed that most mergers fail and, in 2002, one-third of the largest international deals were being "unwound" in "demergers." Apparently, bigger is not always better.[15]

The presence of multinational corporations is visible in nearly all parts of the world, including by this rice paddy in Vietnam. What are the impacts of these global enterprises on developing countries? How have national economies, labor markets, and consumers in other countries been affected by multinationals such as Coca Cola, Dairy Queen, McDonalds, and Nike?

As recently as the mid-1970s, no respectable corporation or its investment banking advisors would consider undertaking a hostile raid on another company. Since then, tumultuous takeovers have dominated the business scene, prompting television commentator Bill Moyers to label the spectacle as one of "cannibals gorging on one another."[16] Analysts predict that the economic conditions are right for many more corporate takeovers, particularly among commercial banks, electric utilities, pharmaceutical and telecommunications industries on both a national and global level.[17] Experts expect these corporate takeovers to continue into the foreseeable future, particularly the absorption of companies ranked fourth or fifth in their field by their larger competitors.[18]

Corporate Technostructure

Impersonal corporate entities set the tone for today's economic environment, not identifiable power brokers like the Fords and Rockefellers of bygone eras. Occasionally a corporate leader becomes a media celebrity, such as Frank Perdue of Perdue Chickens or Dave Thomas of Wendy's. Still, behind the façade of their personal leadership lies an anonymous group of specialists who serve as the guiding intelligence in organizational decision making. Power may be concentrated in a strong and visible CEO, but modern corporations depend heavily on a faceless management team of talented and experienced experts for input and direction.

Economist John Kenneth Galbraith called this remote leadership group within an organization its "technostructure."[19] If oriented toward maximizing corporate profits, **technocrats** wield enormous power in decisions that affect national policy and quality of life.[20] The public may not know who these people are, but they act to produce profits for stockholders, with public welfare as (at best) a secondary consideration. For example, toxic waste disposal and air and water pollution become concerns for corporate planners only after government regulation and enforcement require them to respond.

Market Manipulation

Theoretically, our free market system of competition benefits consumers with better products at lower prices. In reality, corporations realized long ago that avoiding price competition was a far more profitable course of action.[21] Although price fixing is illegal, it is widespread, and a 1997 U.S. Supreme Court ruling may make it less subject to prosecution. In *Khan v. State Oil,* the court unanimously overturned a thirty-year legal precedent and ruled that manufacturers may cap prices retailers charge for their products. Although the intent may have been to protect consumers from price gouging, a coalition of thirty-three states argued the ruling will also make it more difficult to root out illegal pricing schemes.[22] Nevertheless, the decision still stands.

The illegal collusion of major companies to set uniformly high prices costs unknowing customers millions of dollars each year. These coordinated pricing actions become possible when a few producers dominate an industry. Only through the occasional lawsuits do we learn of the problem. In addition to the price-fixing cases mentioned a few pages earlier, the biggest settlement so far occurred in 1997 when thirty of Wall Street's biggest firms agreed to pay nearly $1 billion to settle a class-action lawsuit that they colluded to fix prices on the Nasdaq Stock Market.[23]

Price manipulation, whether in price fixing or in parallel pricing, is one way major corporations exploit consumers. Another way is by manipulating the market itself. An example was a court ruling that Toys 'R' Us used its market muscle to force major toymakers, including Mattel Inc. and Hasbro Inc., to sell their popular products (like Barbie, Mr. Potato Head, G.I. Joe, figures based on Disney's *Toy Story*) exclusively to Toys 'R' Us, shutting out its emerging chief competition, warehouse clubs like Price/Costco, BJ's, and Sam's Club.[24]

Probably the most far-reaching example of market manipulation involved the actions of General Motors in the first half of the twentieth century. After systematically acquiring locomotive companies and electric transportation systems, GM began reducing the supply of trains and trolleys in forty-five cities. Its goal was to sell buses, cars, and trucks instead, which would yield twenty-five to thirty-five times more profit than sales of train locomotives.[25] By 1955, the number of trolley cars operating in U.S. cities had dropped to 5,000, from 40,000 in 1936.[26]

In 1949, a federal grand jury in Chicago convicted GM of conspiring with Firestone Tires and Standard Oil of California to monopolize the sale of buses, gas, oil, and tires and to eliminate electric transportation. GM's fine was a paltry $5,000 and the GM executive responsible for the campaign paid a $1 fine, while the company's profits soared.[27] Half a century later, our legacy from this market manipulation includes continued dependence on the automobile and oil suppliers, crowded and congested streets, air pollution, and a rail system inferior to that of other industrialized nations.

This CEO and board room are symbols of corporate power. By what means have corporations gained their power? How does corporate power influence foreign governments and economies? In terms of personal wealth, this CEO, along with a growing number of other Americans, is a millionaire and could easily retire from work while still young. Does this prospect reflect a growing gap between haves and have-nots in the United States?

Consumer Manipulation

In an advanced industrial society that meets most people's primary needs of food, shelter, and clothing, corporations create artificial needs for new products through advertising. Two generations ago, Vance Packard warned in *The Hidden Persuaders* (1958) that advertisers deliberately exploit our psychological needs and desires to make us buy their products.[28] In 1974, Wilson Bryan Key called our attention to advertisers' successful use of *subliminal seduction*—the subtle use of images to appeal to our subconscious—to increase sales.[29] Today, advertisers no less effectively manipulate us to consume unnecessary products. More generally, the media has a strong influence in shaping social perceptions, even policy making. Since so much of the media is controlled by a relatively small number of large corporations, the result is the few affecting the many.

Advertisers play to our anxieties and insecurities. They sell us acceptance, affection, beauty, youth, sexual attractiveness, and the good life. You may think that commercials and print media advertisements do not influence you, but sales figures demonstrate how readily consumers succumb to their promise. Mass advertising encourages a philosophy of behavior that exerts an indirect influence on cultural value patterns in our personal desires and our daily activities.

Since little real difference exists between many products, corporations create imagined or artificial differences. Bayer may be "the most trusted name in aspirin," but all aspirin is alike, so we must credit advertising with propelling Bayer to the top. Similarly, Anacin may "contain the ingredient most doctors recommend," but that ingredient happens to be aspirin. And whether we fly "something special in the air" (American Airlines) or the "friendly skies" (United Airlines), we are really getting into the same type of plane and getting the same service. You may "taste the difference" in coffees, sodas, or beers, but your satisfaction with one product over another is mostly psychological not actual.

Deception and misrepresentation are fairly common in advertisements. The Federal Communications Commission (FCC) polices against deceptive product claims, but often an advertising campaign receives extensive play before the violator agrees to withdraw the offending ad. Jules Henry once observed that, to advertisers, "truth is what sells" and "truth is what is not legally false."[30] Although many people may not believe everything advertisements tell them, these ads nonetheless often convince them to buy products to achieve status, happiness, and the good life. After all, as one ad put it, "You only go around once in life, so go for the gusto."

The Military-Industrial Complex

Big business enjoyed close relationships with several U.S. presidential administrations in the more distant past, including those of McKinley and Taft, but its real partnership with government was forged in World War II. The immense demands of that global conflict prompted creation of the War Production Board, which coordinated all industrial efforts to meet wartime needs. When the war ended, the federal government expanded its own economic activities to promote full employment, low inflation, and sustained economic growth. Successful business executives provided a pool of skilled administrators to head cabinet departments and agencies. Long-range planning and business incentives (research subsidies, tax allowances) linked the government and corporate giants more closely, as business executives realized that their best interests were served by maintaining a favorable climate of mutual cooperation with public officials.

One of the most closely studied and debated areas of government-corporate alliance involves military spending. By 1961, the relationship between defense industries and the military branch of the government had grown so intertwined that Dwight D. Eisenhower warned the nation about its dangers in his farewell presidential address to the nation:

> Until the latest world conflicts, the United States had no armaments industry. American makers of ploughshares could, with time and as required, make swords as well. But now we can no longer risk emergency improvisation on national defense: we have been compelled to create a permanent armaments industry of vast proportions. . . . This conjunction of an immense Military Establishment and a large arms industry is new to the American experience. The total influence—economic, political, even spiritual—is felt in every statehouse, every office of the Federal Government. We recognize the imperative need for this development. Yet we must not fail to comprehend its grave implications. Our toil, resources, and livelihood are all involved: so is the very structure of our society. In the councils of government we must guard against the unwarranted influence, whether sought or unsought, by the military-industrial complex. The potential for a disastrous rise of misplaced power exists and will persist.[31]

This oft-quoted but largely ignored admonition came from a man who had been a career army officer, Supreme Commander of Allied Forces in Europe during World War II, and a political conservative who had included corporate executives in his cabinet. Such a background made his words even more ominous; but in the years since that 1961 address, the interlocking cooperative relationship and informal influencing of governmental support for weapons systems has grown even more pronounced. As a result, the **military-industrial complex** is more firmly entrenched than ever in the U.S. economy.

The Department of Defense, located in the Pentagon—the world's largest office building—employs almost 672,000 civilians, about 25 percent of all federal civilian employees.[32] The Pentagon owns more property than any other corporation or organization in the world, with $372.1 billion in property assets.[33] With annual purchase contracts exceeding $154 billion in defense-oriented industries, the Pentagon exercises enormous influence on the economy.[34] After steady defense-spending cutbacks from 1987 to 2001, the war against terrorism conducted in Afghanistan and Iraq spiked significantly higher defense expenditures, reviving flagging local economies where defense contractors are located.

Debates continually rage over how much defense spending is really necessary. Pentagon lobbyists, on behalf of corporate defense contractors or the Defense Department itself, provide information to members of Congress about how crucial proposed budget expenditures are. Global reports of aggression, subversion, insurrection, and repression help shape public opinion regarding the necessity of greater military spending for our national survival. Yet critics charge that the pressures of contract-seeking corporations promote the arms buildup more than does real strategic need, thus raising the question of whose definitions of need determine policy decisions.

Wasteful Spending

Waste of taxpayers' dollars occurs for several reasons. First, the Department of Defense awards about 80 percent of all its defense contracts without competitive bidding—and usually at a higher profit rate than the general industry average. The nation's top one hundred corporations, which monopolize these contracts, often subcontract to smaller companies who produce the product for them more quickly and inexpensively, allowing the contract-holding corporation to resell the finished product to the government at a substantial profit. Although some elimination of fraudulent overcharges has occurred, the problems of serious overpricing still continues. For example, instead of paying less than a dollar each for aluminum washers, Navy officials paid $127 each. A gas bottle, available through the government's own supply system for $103, was instead purchased for $1,975 from a primary contractor.[35]

Another source of wasteful expenditures is the practice of permitting massive **cost overruns** beyond the contracted price. Supposedly the Pentagon allows these cost overruns because of unforeseen rising production costs over a multiyear project. However, the policy of offering checkbook guarantees regardless of the excess amount billed does not encourage greater economy and production efficiency by suppliers to hold down costs. Final costs to the government are never known at the time when the Defense Department adopts a new weapons system or aircraft model. When costs exceed projections, as they often do, the Pentagon must cut back on the quantity ordered, thus driving up the actual cost per weapon. For example, in 1997 Congress approved spending $37 billion for 438 F22 fighter planes. Because of serious cost overruns, the total quantity of planes manufactured will be only 225 aircraft at a cost of over $42 billion.[36]

Another important factor in wasteful spending lies in the cozy relationship between the military and industry. The Pentagon sometimes approves proposals without sufficient critical evaluation, does not demand repayment if the product fails to meet performance standards, and compensates companies when it cancels a contract due to the incompetence of the corporate supplier. Among dozens of examples of scrapped project payments are $1.5 billion for the B-70 aircraft, which was so poor that only two unused models were ever built; $679.8 million for the Navaho missile; $511.6 million for the nuclear ANP aircraft; $330.4 million for the Seamaster aircraft; and $215 million for the F-111 aircraft.

The Revolving Door

The **revolving door** interchange of personnel between corporations and the government military illustrates another aspect of the military-industrial complex. Presidents frequently recruit corporate executives as administrators. Eisenhower's Secretary of Defense was Charles F. Wilson, former president of General Motors (which also produces military hardware), who exclaimed at his appointment hearing, "What is good for General Motors is good for the country." Other examples include Robert McNamara, former president of Ford Motor Company, who served as Kennedy's and Johnson's secretary of defense; David Packard, founder and principal stockholder of the major defense contractor Hewlett-Packard Company, who served as Nixon's undersecretary of defense; Reagan's secretary of state George Schultz, former corporate executive at Bechtel, a multinational engineering construction firm; and George W. Bush's Secretary of Defense Donald Rumsfeld, former CEO of the electronics firm, General Instruments.

Depending on government contracts for much of their income, or concerned about the effects of regulatory legislation and enforcement on their industry, corporations frequently hire former military and government officials as influence peddlers. With their established contacts, these individuals enjoy informal access to and exercise significant influence over government officials in decision-making positions. In turn, the decision makers, whether in regulatory agencies or in the military, see a lucrative future for themselves in a similar role when they leave office. Indeed, some argue that the only way to get good people into government service is to allow them to reap financial rewards afterward by influencing the government.

Although there is a mandated one-year waiting period, former government officials almost immediately become lobbyists when they leave their positions in government. In March 2003, for example, the Center for Public Integrity revealed that 51 percent of former top officials of the Clinton administration lobbied the government or worked for companies that do. This ratio was about the same as for previous administrations.[37]

Washington's lobbying industry employs over 67,000 people, quadruple the number employed in the mid-1960s. That works out to 125 lobbyists per congressperson, not counting lobbyists based in neighboring suburban Virginia and Maryland.[38] Among their ranks are over one hundred former cabinet secretaries, White House aides, and congressional representatives. The total number of former Pentagon officials now working in defense-related industries is perhaps three or four times greater. This disproportionately high number of people occupying influential corporate positions raises important questions about the impact of this intimate relationship on government's pursuit of the public interest, national priorities, and the economy. Moreover, one unintended consequence of term limits for elected officials would be to concede greater familiarity with the legislative process and with means of protecting special interest groups to veteran lobbyists.

Work in the United States

Work is an important focus of our lives, consuming an enormous portion of our time and energy. Our social status rests primarily on our occupation, which also heavily influences our sense of self—who and what we are. In a society that emphasizes the work ethic, as ours does, work provides a feeling of usefulness, fulfillment, and self-respect. Through work we meet other people and form friendships. Many people's identity or self-image is wholly bound up in their work, and thus unemployment or retirement causes not only a loss of income but a loss of self-definition and of place in society as well.

Because work dominates so many aspects of an individual's life and is crucial to societal welfare, social problems related to work are of concern to us all. In this section we examine the three areas of concern: the changing work force, unemployment and underemployment, and job satisfaction.

Occupational Trends

Since the 1950s, the U.S. economy has experienced a major restructuring. Just as industrialization brought enormous changes a few generations ago, current trends dramatically affect how we make our living, who is working, and who is unemployed. Changing demographic patterns, high technology, and a global economy have major impacts on the composition and earnings of the workforce. Moreover, value shifts regarding the role of women have brought an unprecedented number of women into the workplace to fill jobs once predominantly male.

Rise of the Information Sector

In 1956 the United States became the first nation in which more than half of the labor force engaged in a service or **tertiary occupation** rather than in a primary industry (farming, fishing, forestry, mining) or secondary industry (manufacturing). Most tertiary jobs are white-collar positions—clerical, administrative, research, or professional—but the category also includes maintenance and repair trades. Since then, we have become what Daniel Bell called a "post-industrial society."[39]

The actual growth, extraction, and production of products now occupy less than one-fifth of the nation's labor force, leaving more than four-fifths of American workers employed in service industries. Even more significant, about 60 percent of the U.S. economy is concentrated in the information sector, and that proportion continues to increase each year.[40]

What employment trends in the present U.S. service-based economy does this photo illustrate? What are the other main occupational and employment trends in the United States today? What issues concerning job security and workplace health and safety must workers and companies address?

Information has always been the basis for human organization, but today we are becoming a particularly knowledge-rich society. Because information is easily transmitted, shared, and diffused, it expands with use. New industries exploit this reality by providing information services. Computer software firms, for example, make a contribution to the U.S. economy that is larger than that of computer hardware firms. Similarly, computer engineers and support specialists are the fastest-growing occupations.[41]

The industrial era typified human influence over things, including nature and material objects. The new information era emphasizes the increased ability of humans to think and to organize. Technology will continue to replace humans for routine and repetitive tasks. Tomorrow's jobs will require more and more brainwork and job skills, especially in people-to-people relations—something machines are useless at accomplishing.

Impact of High Technology

We live in the midst of rapid technological change, a time when electronic achievements continue to make many traditional methods of work obsolete. Computer technology directly affects all our lives, whether at the bank, the supermarket, the department store, at home, or at work. Some analysts compare these computer-caused changes in the way we communicate, live, play, and work to the major changes brought on by the Industrial Revolution.[42] The changes in the past two decades have already revolutionized our lives in many ways, but they represent only a small sample of what is to come. Computer models and programs become obsolete quickly, and we struggle to keep abreast of it all:

> We now have computer-operated microprinters capable of turning out 10,000 to 20,000 lines per minute—more than 200 times faster than anyone can read them, and this is still the slowest part of computer systems. In twenty years computer scientists have gone from speaking in terms of milliseconds (thousandths of a second) to nanoseconds (billionths of a second)—a compression of time almost beyond our powers to imagine. It is as though a person's entire working life of, say, 80,000 paid hours—2,000 hours per year for forty years—could be crunched into a mere 4.8 minutes.[43]

Although computerization increased productivity in the United States by 13 percent between 1997 and 2001, it contributed to a reduction in the percentage of Americans working in manufacturing from 16 percent in 1995 to 14 percent in 2001, reflecting the elimination of more than 1.5 million jobs over that period. The areas in which U.S. workers find employment continues to change. A major trend is toward the home office, either for a personal business or as an outsourced contractor for a large company.[44]

Whether they be banks, department stores, insurance companies, or small businesses, service and manufacturing industries continue to invest in computers and electronics to cut costs and improve efficiency. Computer literacy is now essential for most careers, from teaching and social work to sales and corporate management.

The computer age does not necessarily mean job satisfaction, however, as we will discuss shortly. Many jobs today require different skills but not necessarily any change in level of skill; many computer-jobs simply require a different kind of rote, but it is still rote. Many clerical computer jobs thus are low-paying, monotonous, and dead-end.

Increase of Women Workers

Motivated by economic need or the desire to find meaningful, well-paid work, women continue to enter the labor force in growing proportions, often choosing relatively lucrative positions in business and the professions. In 2001, 76 percent of adult women aged twenty-five to forty-four held jobs; by 2010, according to the Bureau of Labor Statistics, that figure will exceed 80 percent.[45]

The more education a woman has, the more likely she is to have a job. Approximately 81 percent of women with a college degree work, compared to about 71 percent of women with a high school education and 52 percent of women who did not complete high school.[46] The presence of more highly educated women in the labor force is improving both the ratio of women's wages to men's wages and women's representation in previously male-dominated occupations (see Chapter 7).

Unemployment and Underemployment

Joblessness is undoubtedly the most serious problem confronting any society's work structure. Economists study unemployment rates and analyze their impact on the economy in lost income, decreased productivity and consumerism, and cost to the government in benefits paid out. Sociologists examine the interrelationship of unemployment and group membership by age, race, sex, and occupation, as well as the effects of prolonged unemployment on people's behavior and sense of self-worth. Unemployment therefore does more than reflect economic downturns and the rate at which jobs become obsolete. It also reflects inequities in the social system that hit one population segment disproportionately hard, and it can cause many devastating social consequences.

U.S. society has never had full employment, but its economic vitality is in part revealed by its unemployment rate at any given time. A shift of 0.1 percent indicates either economic and social well-being or deprivation for more than 100,000 families, so it is a significant barometer. Why do people become unemployed? The reasons are many and varied, but we can suggest four major causes.

Demographic Victims

Sometimes people lose their jobs because of population trends. For example, substantial economic and population growth in the Sunbelt obliged many Snowbelt workers to move to that part of the country to make a living. They left behind not only idle factories and shrinking town populations, but a generally depressed economy among other businesses—including stores, bars, diners, restaurants, and recreational-entertainment facilities—that depended on the patronage of primary- and secondary-industry workers.

Declining birth rates, except in areas experiencing high immigration, adversely affect the availability of jobs in teaching, as well as in the manufacture and sale of children's toys, games, furniture, and clothing. Sometimes changes in an area's socioeconomic base can end people's jobs. Examples might include low-income people coming into a neighborhood and replacing an exiting middle class and middle-class yuppies displacing low-income people in an urban gentrification location. Businesses that depended on the buying habits and tastes of previous residents will not appeal to the newcomers and will soon be forced to close their doors.

Economic Victims

The emergence of three economic trends—the old industrial system giving way to a networked economy with information technology at its core, the continuing trend of megamergers, and the emergence of a global economy—set in motion a business pattern devastating to the middle class: corporate **downsizing**.

Driven by rapid technological change, fierce competition here and abroad, the ease of contracting out work, and pressure from profit-obsessed investors, companies are cutting their workforces to the bone—on the rationale that in the long run a leaner and meaner style will be more efficient and economical. Another way corporations cut their expenses is by hiring temps instead of permanent workers, and thereby avoiding the need to pay contributory social security, health, and pension benefits (see the box on page 135). Another effect of corporate takeovers is to make many middle and senior management positions in the swallowed-up company obsolete, forcing out competent people who had invested their entire careers in one company. These layoffs have severe impacts on families, and wide social effects on civic stability, voluntarism, and social resentment:

> It speaks volumes that the nation's largest employer, renting out 767,000 substitute workers each year, is Manpower Inc., not General Motors. A college education provides help but no sure protection. For the first time since the Great Depression, the well-educated, middle-managing, mostly white middle class is now experiencing the chronic job insecurity long familiar to the unskilled poor, and with many of the same psychological consequences: post-traumatic stress disorders, collapsed self-respect, free-floating anger, marriages broken under the strain and bewildered children. Shared affliction, though, has not made for common ground with the poor; quite the opposite, it has fed middle-class resentment that their tax dollars go for social programs benefiting the disadvantaged.[47]

The social costs of downsizing—the way it robs individuals of dignity, shatters families, devastates communities, poisons the chemistry of the workplace (even for survivors), and prompts a search for scapegoats (immigrants, welfare recipients, government, big business)—embroil our politics. Sociologists are documenting another latent consequence: the tough new labor market often makes the survivors too busy or tired to volunteer any longer, and the typical laid-off employee withdraws from civic life. Downsizing tears communities apart, Boy Scout troops lose their scoutmasters, and Rotary and Kiwanis Clubs and churches lose committed members. What de Tocqueville once identified as the underpinning of American democracy—a dense network of civic associations—is unraveling just when people need it most.[48]

On a different front, certain jobs are very vulnerable to very slight changes in the economy. When the demand for a product falls, production line workers—whose wages are treated as a "variable" expense in company accounting procedures, unlike the "fixed" (and therefore unscrutinized) expense of management salaries—become an immediate focus of management's cost-cutting measures. Similarly, all suppliers, distributors, and retailers become expendable, if their products suffer loss of income. In a tight or retracting economy with high interest rates, individuals and businesses are less inclined to build new homes, offices, or plants, so construction workers and their suppliers also find less work and income. In turn, people whose livelihood is based on leisure activities—for example, travel agents, theaters, beach or ski resorts, restaurants, and electronics stores—find fewer customers with enough extra money to afford what they offer. Bad economic times directly affect production workers, but the ripple effect causes service occupations to suffer as well.

Education Victims

Education or training beyond high school is essential to land an entry-level, decent-paying job. People who fail to continue their education after high school are engaging, to a large degree, in occupational suicide. Yet too many youngsters quit school—an alarming percentage of them poor minority group members (see Chapter 8). Unless they resume their education, their future is one of limited employment opportunities and earnings.

Even high school graduates face an uphill battle in finding work or maintaining job security. With increased demand in the job market for people with higher skills, more judgment, and

Social Constructions of Social Problems

Permatemps

Temporary agencies, such as Manpower and Kelly Services, provide young adults with an effective way to enter the workforce, and these agencies provide exposure to a variety of business settings. Businesses love to use "temps" as a way to meet short-term fluctuations in workload and to try out potential workers. Although the temporary work industry has existed for generations, its explosive growth in the 1990s created a social phenomenon still prevalent today and for the foreseeable future. The U.S. Bureau of Labor Statistics reported that between 1994 and 2002 the number of temporary agency jobs doubled to over 3.6 million jobs. These jobs are found in all sectors of the economy, from low-wage service jobs to high-tech, high-paying positions.

So prevalent is this practice that nearly one in six young adults will probably take a temporary job at some point in their lives before the age of thirty-five. The employment of temporary workers would not constitute a social problem if it were not for the unprecedented rise in the use of "permatemps." These are employees who, despite their "temporary" designation, are actually part of a company's permanent work force, but without all the benefits that permanent employees receive. In reality, they are employed by the temporary agency, not the company.

Companies quickly realized both the flexibility and economic value of using temporary workers. By paying a fee to the agency (which includes the workers' wages), the companies greatly reduce their net labor costs and liabilities. They save recruiting costs and do not have to contribute to social security, health, pension, and unemployment programs. Also, these workers do not fall under the company's benefit plans, pay scales, and collective-bargaining agreements. Moreover, companies do not consider temporary workers as their employees, since they are supplied and paid by the agency. An ambiguity thus arises as to who is liable if a temporary worker is injured, harassed, or discriminated against. The agency, not wishing to alienate its steady client (the company), is unlikely to aggressively pursue any complaints of its temps, and so labor standards that protect workers from abuse and ensure civil rights protection become ineffective.

More and more, young adults want a permanent job but instead can find only temporary ones that offer lower pay and fewer benefits. The increase in temporary work is an important contributing factor to the economic decline of young workers. The Bureau of the Census reports that young adults without a college degree (three-fourths of this age group) earned about 25 percent less in 2000 (after adjusting for inflation) than their counterparts did in 1973. The facts that (1) on any given day about 1 million young adults go to a temporary job, and (2) temporary workers age twenty to thirty-four earn about 16 percent less than their counterparts with permanent jobs, are important contributing factors. Young adults are increasingly losing their ability to raise families, buy a home, and support a standard of living that was once fairly typical. Furthermore, about 12 million workers age nineteen to twenty-nine have no health insurance.

Until recently, nearly 35 percent of Microsoft's U.S. workers were hired through temporary agencies. After successfully repelling legal challenges for years, Microsoft lost its case in 1999, and the U.S. Supreme Court refused to hear an appeal. The ruling that the company's "temps" were really permanent workers, could signal the beginning of real reform nationwide. In addition, organizations such as the National Alliance for Fair Employment (NAFFE) and the Communication Workers of America have joined the effort to gain equal pay and benefits for temporary workers on a prorated basis and to make client companies "joint employers" and thus liable for all working conditions.

more analytical ability, people who lack education or training past high school find many doors closed to them. The greater one's educational level, the less likely one is to be unemployed (see Table 5.1).

Technological Victims

The conditions that created jobs two hundred years ago—mass production and the large organization—are disappearing. Technology now enables companies to automate and customize the production line, where job holders once did their repetitive tasks. Big firms, where most of the good jobs used to be, are unbundling activities and farming them out to little firms, which have created or taken over profitable niches. The same forces of unyielding technology also allow giant corporations to process paperwork with far fewer middle managers.[49]

The new technologies—computers, lasers, fiber optics, robotics, biotechnology—are dramatically changing the workplace, creating new jobs and destroying old ones. In all fields—agricultural, industrial, and office—technology eliminates many jobs. The disappearing jobs are not just among semi-skilled, blue-collar workers. Technology has enabled many companies to streamline their office operations, thereby eliminating many middle-class jobs. For example, the Department of Labor projected the following decline in jobs between 2000 and 2010: processing clerks, 20 percent; loan interviewers, 28 percent; telephone operators, 35 percent; and railroad operators, 61 percent.[50] Displaced blue-collar and white-collar workers often find that new jobs in the economy, if they can qualify for them, pay considerably less.

As technology produces structural changes in the economy, the new jobs it creates fall into two distinct types. About 20 percent of all new jobs are promising opportunities for high pay and prestige. Unfortunately, almost 80 percent of new jobs are low-pay, low-prestige, dead-end employment offering monotonous work and little personal satisfaction. The existence of fewer midrange job positions translates into fewer promotions and opportunities for upward mobility. We may be moving toward a radically stratified labor market consisting of a small elite management or professional group and a mass of "worker bees" (up to four-fifths of the labor force) earning low to moderate wages.[51]

The global economy is in the midst of a transformation as significant as the Industrial Revolution. We are in the early stages of a shift from "mass labor" to highly skilled "elite labor" accompanied by increasing automation in the production of goods and in the delivery of ser-

Table 5.1 Unemployment Rate by Sex, Race, and Educational Attainment: 2001

Education		Men	Women	Whites	Blacks	Hispanics
High School:	1–3 years	6.5	8.5	5.7	11.9	7.5
	4 years	4.3	4.0	7.5	7.5	4.4
College:	1–3 years	3.4	3.6	3.2	5.1	3.8
	4 years	2.2	2.3	2.1	2.7	2.6

Source: National Center for Education Statistics, *Digest of Education Statistics, 2002,* Table 380.

vices. Sophisticated computers, robots, telecommunications, and other Information Age technologies are replacing human beings in nearly every sector. In the United States alone, as many as 90 million jobs may be vulnerable to displacement by automation.[52]

Underemployment is another consequence of the elimination of some jobs and the creation of new, low-paying ones. Many people have little choice but to take less-challenging, less financially rewarding positions than their education and experience would seem to qualify them for. College graduates become store clerks or customer service representatives; middle managers become sales representatives; factory foremen become repairmen; and so on. Such jobs pay the bills but they often fail to satisfy well-educated, highly motivated employees.

Effects of Long-Term Unemployment

Unemployment means far more than financial hardship for workers. Social and psychological consequences reverberate through the entire family from the resulting intense emotional turmoil. Separated from the companionship of their fellow workers and from an important part of their daily lives, the newly unemployed must cope with disruption and financial strain. Even when the circumstances surrounding plant shutdown or layoff are clearly beyond their control, people tend to blame themselves for their job loss. Feelings of helplessness, inadequacy, disorientation, and depression set in.

As the days without work stretch into weeks and then months, the individual's problems intensify. From earlier feelings of apathy, boredom, embarrassment, despair, and bad temper, the frustrated worker may lapse into heavy drinking, child or spouse abuse, or even attempted suicide. One study found that the prevalence of depression, anxiety, and physical illness was four to twenty times higher than among employed people at baseline. Moreover, these symptoms led to a 70 percent reduction in chances of obtaining a job.[53]

Human flotsam adrift in a sea of despair, the long-term unemployed are unable to find the safe harbor of employment. Society places a high value on work, as do they, but they cannot find any. The contradiction takes its toll as they find it difficult to face daily reminders of their situation, particularly among working-class males for whom being powerful is typically associated with, among other things, being male and employed. In a recent study of a group of long-term unemployed men in the English West Midlands, the men felt a sense of emasculation and disempowerment, but hid it in bravado talk among peers, leading to even greater loss of self-esteem.[54]

One researcher found that admissions to mental hospitals increased during economic downturns and decreased when the economy improved. Similarly, suicide studies show this inverse correlation with economic changes. Other studies have found disorientation common among jobless workers, including an avoidance of wearing watches because they had no reason to structure their time. Symptoms of psychiatric problems are very pronounced among involuntarily unemployed men by the fourth month, while their wives by that time exhibit depression, anxiety, and phobia.[55]

Most studies of the emotional and social effects of long-term unemployment are fairly consistent in research findings. Headaches, high blood pressure, overeating, and heavy drinking are common. Feelings of inadequacy, incompetence, worthlessness, and depression prevail. One study of unemployed white-collar and professional men, most of them college graduates and out of work for the first time in their lives, discerned a permanent change of attitude that remained after the men found new jobs. The men had lost much of their self-esteem while unemployed and felt alienated from society, feeling themselves to be insignificant, mere statistics, easily replaced even in their own families. When they returned to work, they did not fully recover their self-esteem and maintained a deep cynicism toward other people and toward the political system and other social institutions. Their trauma of unemployment triggered a social transformation that persisted long after the problem situation was objectively resolved.[56] Health is affected too. One study found that prolonged unemployment is likely to have a persisting effect because it inflicts long-term damage to future socioeconomic chances and health.[57]

Job Satisfaction

Three major contributors to early sociological theory—Emile Durkheim, Max Weber, and Karl Marx—all expressed concern about growing alienation among workers. Durkheim believed that the increased division of labor and consequent specialization brought to workers a state of **anomie**, or loss of direction, because their limited work responsibilities no longer offered personal fulfillment. Weber provided insight into the inherent characteristic of impersonality found in bureaucratic organizations. Marx detailed the **alienation** of workers—their sense of powerlessness, isolation, and meaninglessness—brought on by the restrictive demands of production and the commodification of their labor. In varying ways, each of these pioneers of sociological thought saw work becoming an enforced activity instead of a creative or satisfying one.

Attributes of Job Satisfaction

Psychologist Abraham Maslow observed that human needs exist in certain priority levels. When the most immediate need has been met, the next level of need becomes more keenly felt, until it too is fulfilled and the next unfulfilled need demands greater attention. Maslow identified this **hierarchy of needs** as first, the basic needs for food, clothing, and shelter; second, the need for safety and security; third, the need for companionship and affection; fourth, the need for self-esteem and the esteem of others; and fifth, the need for self-actualization.[58] Our affluent society enables most Americans to satisfy the first three needs, but its large-scale organizational structure often thwarts fulfillment of the fourth and fifth priorities. The inability of work to meet the higher needs of workers—except persons in prestigious occupational positions—in turn generates job dissatisfaction and a search elsewhere to gratify those needs (family, church, clubs, leisure).

Adopting a different focus, Frederick Herzberg reached a conclusion similar to Maslow's. Instead of a sequential needs hierarchy, Herzberg suggested that both **intrinsic** and **extrinsic** factors influence job satisfaction. Income, supervision, and working conditions exemplify extrinsic factors, while a sense of personal achievement, responsibility, and challenge are typical intrinsic factors.[59] If the inherent nature of our work prevents us from fulfilling our potential, then the extrinsic factors alone—no matter how good they appear to be—cannot eradicate dissatisfaction. A 2001 study of more than 2,600 employees supports Herzberg. While a competitive salary is an important consideration, it is far from the magic bullet for attracting and retaining talent, concluded the study. Being trusted to get the job done ranked first, followed by getting the opportunity to do the type of work you want. Job stability also ranked ahead of salary and stock options. Other considerations were flexibility in work schedules for a work/life balance, and the amount of vacation time.[60]

The Value of Flex Time

Recent studies suggest that white-collar job discontent reflects the changed work orientations of a new generation of better-educated workers who value individuality, independence, and leisure activity as much as, if not more than, the traditional benefits of work. Consequently, they identify less personally with their work and feel less loyalty to their employer, but are willing to remain in jobs they dislike if flexible or favorable work schedules permit them more personal freedom. Due to their greater education and higher expectations, professional workers place more value on fulfillment in work and are thus more sensitive to alienating conditions.

One social consequence of electronic automation was **flex time**, an arrangement that allows workers, within predetermined limits, to set their own working hours. Since information can be stored and retrieved at any time, it becomes less important for all employees to begin and end work at the same time. In 2001, over 28 million U.S. full-time employees had flexible work schedules.[61] Personalized work schedules give individuals greater freedom without disrupting the work of others. As a result, employers report higher productivity and reduced absenteeism.[62]

Occupational Health and Safety

Concern about health problems related to work is as old as the ancient Greeks and Romans, whose miners, metalworkers, and weavers of asbestos cloth suffered a high incidence of lung disease. Throughout the Renaissance and Enlightenment periods, physicians grappled with special illnesses found only among workers in certain crafts. The Industrial Revolution brought new occupational hazards—poor ventilation, exposed machinery gears that mangled hands and feet, toxic fumes and harmful particles—that labor unions fought to overcome.[63] In some areas progress occurred, but in others the picture remains grim, even today.

The National Safety Council reported that the number of fatal work injuries increased to over 47,000 in 2000, the highest in a decade. The number of workers disabled on the job was 10.5 million, exceeding the yearly totals in the 1960s, 1970s, and 1980s by more than a million for the twelfth consecutive year.[64] Simultaneously, the number of high-risk jobs declined greatly, meaning that the proportion of industrial workers seriously injured has increased.

Another serious work hazard concern, requiring preventive action instead of accident treatment, lies in the growing problems of work-related illnesses and long-term degenerative and fatal effects of exposure to suspected toxins and carcinogens (cancer-causing substances). While some substances have an adverse impact within a fairly short time, others may take years to manifest their deadly effects. Then arguments arise as to whether those chemicals were solely responsible or whether other factors of heredity, lifestyle, or life experience might have been contributing variables. Such was the case of Gulf War veterans exposed to toxic gas, Vietnam war veterans exposed to Agent Orange, and World War II veterans exposed to atomic bomb radiation, all of

An increasing number of white-collar jobs are unchallenging, meaningless, and routine, with limited opportunities for creative expression or upward mobility. What are some problems with the way we work and with workplaces like the one shown in this photo?

whom encountered difficulties over many years in convincing the federal government of the link between their wartime exposure to the hazardous substance and their subsequent high cancer rates and other health problems.

Government Regulation

Many job-caused illnesses—damaging lungs, blood chemistry, the nervous system, or other organs—occur only after years of continual exposure to hazardous substances. To prevent such exposure to hazardous substances, the government must conduct on-site inspections and analyses of chemical products used in the workplace. Only then can regulations for new chemical compounds be established or safety violations cited and penalized. Unfortunately, the sheer magnitude of this task makes both regulation and control difficult.

With over 100 million workers at more than 6.5 million work sites, the Occupational Safety and Health Administration (OSHA), with its limited financial and worker resources, was able to conduct only 37,500 job site inspections in 2001. At this pace the OSHA staff, operating out of sixty-seven regional offices, could only inspect every work site once every eighty years.[65] The states also conduct their own safety inspections, but they are too understaffed and underbudgeted to be completely effective. If you add the 55,000 inspections each year by state compliance officials to the 37,500 federal inspections, an employer's chances of being singled out for an inspection are only one in sixty-five.[66] Obviously, workers cannot rely too heavily on the federal or state governments to ensure they work in a safe environment.

Despite this seemingly insurmountable challenge, few dispute that OSHA has had a positive effect in its three decades of existence. Work-related fatalities have dropped 50 percent, trenching and excavation deaths 35 percent, and brown lung disease—caused by inhalation of cotton dust—has been virtually eliminated in the textile industry.[67] Although OSHA levies fines against a few companies violating health and safety standards, the industry often prefers to pay the relatively small fine for noncompliance rather than to pay the larger costs of new equipment or plant remodeling required to correct the problem. Some companies recently fined were: Mohawk Industries ($100,000), following a fatal accident at the carpetmaker's Rome, Georgia plant[68]; metal manufacturer Dover Parkersburg ($288,000) for twenty-three safety and health violations;[69] Hanover Foods Corporation, Delaware ($297,500), for eleven violations, including respiratory and fall protection deficiencies; and Celanese Chemicals, Alabama ($250,000), after an accident killed one worker and seriously injured another[70]; Lukens Steel ($237,500) after an explosion at its Houston, Pennsylvania plant injured a worker.[71] More often, however, the fines are practically insignificant, as in the 1997 fine levied against Newport News Shipbuilding. For failing to provide adequate training and thereby contributing to an accident that caused the deaths of three employees, OSHA fined the big Peninsula shipyard $6,300.[72]

Health Hazard Occupations

All occupations entail some measure of stress, risk, and work-related illness, even white-collar and professional ones. Blue-collar workers, however, face far greater health risks because of the prevalence of hazards in the mines, on the farms, and in the factories and mills. Many workplaces are cleaner today than in years past, but they also contain new hazardous substances.

Miners and Quarry Workers

With a death rate of 21 per 100,000 workers, this industry constitutes the nation's most dangerous occupation.[73] This statistic not only reflects immediate accidental deaths from cave-ins, explosions, and sudden flooding, but also long-term casualties from respiratory diseases due to environmental exposure during work. Coal mining is the most deadly occupation of all, with a death rate of 53 per 100,000, mostly from black lung disease, which kills 1,400 coal miners each year. This disease has been known since 1813 to be caused by years of breathing coal dust. This incurable lung ailment scars the lung tissue, rendering it useless; gradually the miner becomes unable to work, later gasps for breath, and ultimately dies from the disease. Ventilation technology for the control of coal dust has existed for years, according to the National Academy of Sciences. However, limited enforcement of regulations defining permissible coal dust levels set by the 1969 Coal Mine and Safety Act has prevented any significant improvement. Moreover, the Black Lungs Benefit Act of 1981 actually made proving the cause of the disease harder, as a prerequisite to getting health benefits. Most disturbingly, say health experts, black lung is preventable but coal companies ignore or subvert laws enacted to reduce dust levels down in the mines.[74]

Another common respiratory disease is silicosis, caused by exposure to silica dust in mines, quarries, and foundries, or during removal of paint or rust from buildings, bridges, tanks, and other surfaces, or during construction. Dust-control technology exists, but it is not applied in all situations where it could be effective. Many occupational health physicians have called for the banning of silica sand in abrasive blasting, for example—a step taken by Great Britain in 1949 and by the European Economic Community in 1966, but not yet undertaken by the United States.[75]

Silicosis continues to be a major health problem, as shown by the rising number of steel workers who succumb to the disease. Health officials are alarmed by the rapid rise of silicosis cases in the steel and sand manufacturing industries. The National Institute for Occupational Health and Safety (NIOSH) estimates that over one million workers in construction, mining, and other "dusty trades" are at high risk of silica dust overexposure. OSHA reports that each year more than two million workers are exposed to crystalline silica, resulting in about three hundred deaths annually.[76]

Farm Laborers

With a death rate of 21 per 100,000, agricultural workers—who represent less than 3 percent of the total workforce—account for 12 percent of the nation's occupational deaths. One major reason is the danger of developing Organic Dust Toxic Syndrome (ODTS), a respiratory and systemic illness that results from exposure to heavy concentrations of organic dusts contaminated with microorganisms, a common occurrence among agricultural workers.[77] Another culprit is the widespread spraying of herbicides and pesticides. Agricultural workers, 25 percent of whom are children, live in shacks or work in fields adjacent to those sprayed from the air. The chemical residue that settles on plants they come into contact with as they work in the sprayed fields—or that drifts into their surroundings through the air—causes itching, nosebleeds, nausea, and diarrhea. No one is certain about the long-range effects, but the life expectancy of agricultural workers is below the national average.

Illustrating this sad reality are the facts that farmers and farm workers are at greater risk than the general population for cancers of the stomach, brain, prostate, and skin, as well as for leukemia, and non-Hodgkins lymphoma. Higher death rates due to kidney, bladder, prostate, lymphoma, and intestinal cancers also exist among farmers. Although the only direct link found to date between exposures to an agricultural environment and cancer is skin cancer, exposure to pesticides, chemical solvents, engine exhausts, animal viruses, and other substances commonly found in an industrialized farm operation are suspects.[78]

Asbestos Workers

The health problems from asbestos were unknown for the first several decades of its widespread use. Manufacturers used its fireproof mineral fibers in various products, including firefighters' gloves, theater curtains, ceiling tiles, and pipe insulation. Now we know that inhaling these minute particles causes a rare form of lung cancer. Doctors expect that about one-fourth of the 1 million workers exposed to asbestos in the past will die from asbestos-related cancer within thirty years.[79] And not just workers are affected. Tiny particles falling from school ceilings or clinging to workers' clothes, then handled by wives and washed with other family clothes, spread the contact throughout families. Once the hazard became known, inspectors required asbestos ceilings

Toxic chemical dumpsites are a serious threat not just to the environment, but to human and animal life in those areas. Although they are in protective gear, these workers elicit little envy from the rest of us as they go about their hazardous task of dealing with a corroded metal tank filled with contaminants. How do the various sociological perspectives help us understand the reasons such sites were allowed to exist and are now viewed as places to be eliminated?

and pipe insulations to be ripped out of hundreds of thousands of buildings by workers wearing protective clothing against its carcinogenic effects.

Asbestos deaths are also serious problems elsewhere. Over 300,000 people in Great Britain have died since 1900 as a result of exposure to asbestos. Because the disease takes twenty to sixty years to develop, asbestos-caused deaths will continue for the foreseeable future. Great Britain's Health and Safety Executive expects another 175,000 to die from past exposure over the next twenty-five years.[80] Throughout Western Europe, 5,000 people died of asbestos-related diseases in 1998, and experts predict that number will almost double by 2018, with a total of 250,000 people dying in the next thirty-five years. This means 1 of every 150 Western European men born between 1945 and 1950 will die from asbestos-related diseases. Meanwhile, in the developing world, the uncontrolled use of asbestos is still very common.[81]

Chemical Workers

Synthetic products dominate life in virtually every category of consumption. The chemicals used to create such diverse products also create two serious social problems: toxic chemical dump sites (discussed in Chapter 3) and health hazards to the workers in processing plants. Government studies found unusually high rates of cancer malignancies among workers who produced and processed such carcinogenic chemicals as benzene, acrylonitrile, beryllium, ethylene oxide, and vinyl chloride. The current surge in synthetic organic chemicals—as yet unscreened by NIOSH and having unknown long-term effects—presents a potentially dangerous work environment to the health of millions of workers, as noted by numerous studies.[82]

Sociological Perspectives

Each theoretical orientation provides a framework for analyzing the world of corporate power and work. Often an orientation focuses on the impact of demographic and technological changes on the social organization of work, as well as the impact of ever-growing megacorporations and multinationals on society.

The Functionalist Viewpoint

From the Functionalist perspective, work is a key element in the social organization of a society. Under ideal conditions, an equilibrium of society exists whereby the supply of all the differently skilled workers evenly complements the available jobs, and steady, continuous economic growth absorbs the increasing population. In reality, an industrial society is particularly vulnerable to economic fluctuations, technological changes, and outside influences such as a sharp rise in oil prices or the loss of raw materials from other countries due to civic unrest. Sudden or unexpected changes usually cause dysfunctions in a nation's economy, producing a ripple effect throughout the social system (unemployment, bankruptcies, alienation, social unrest, and even violence). The social system's inability to adapt quickly to social changes causes such problems, according to this view.

Our current problems, functionalists maintain, are due to rapid economic and social changes that have thrown the system out of balance. The emergence of huge corporations and powerful labor unions, together with greater government involvement in the economy, radically altered the free enterprise system. Moreover, continuing rapid technological and economic changes create additional problems before the old ones can be resolved. As corporations grow larger and more powerful, exercising social control over them becomes more and more elusive.

Economic Dysfunctions

In the past one hundred years, the growth of large corporations was functional for society in providing investment capital and extensive expertise to sustain the massive economic development that occurred. At the same time, this corporate growth has been dysfunctional, leading to a situation where a small number of companies now dominate the national and world economies with little accountability to the public. The economic system fails to function smoothly because of a lack of coordination between the economic institutions and other social institutions. In addition, social control mechanisms have become inadequate to monitor and deter improper and illegal corporate actions.

The often-invoked American value of individualism is virtually lost as mammoth organizations shape and control people's lives. Similarly, the cherished value of equality is undermined when powerful groups with vast resources at their disposal can pursue goals as a bloc, while most individuals lack adequate resources to pursue theirs. When a society's basic values are incompatible with its social institutions, its normative integration—the social cement that binds it together—becomes seriously threatened and requires correction.

Demographic Dysfunctions

Studies in **demography** show that changes in the age structure of U.S. society have created work problems. For example, expansive child-oriented industries (clothing, toys, furniture, games, schools) were fine for the post–World War II baby boom, but as the boom ebbed and the birth rate began to decline sharply, widespread unemployment in these industries occurred. Many towns closed schools or consolidated school districts, and teaching vacancies virtually dried up. As the median age of the population edged upward, the growing proportion of retired workers (versus active workers) caused funding difficulties for social security and health-care benefits.

Technological Dysfunctions

In the long run, technological innovations like computers and robots create new job opportunities such as manufacture, maintenance, repair, programming, and support services. In the short run, however, they displace workers whose skills are obsolete, causing them much stress, anxiety, hardship, and deprivation. Unemployed workers in dying occupations must acquire new skills if they wish to make a decent living, and many must move to another region of the country to obtain those other jobs. Retail businesses that depend on these customers and all government levels that depend on their tax revenues experience problems as well.

In time, the self-regulating mechanisms of society restore a balance. One example is Nashua, New Hampshire, a town of 68,000 people whose textile mills moved south in the 1950s, causing widespread depression in the area for a quarter of a century. Today it has one of the largest and most diversified job markets in the region and a low unemployment rate. Yet the recovery took thirty years to achieve, and many workers suffered great hardship during that time.

The Conflict Viewpoint

The study of economic political power and competing interest groups provides fertile ground for Conflict theorists, since competition for limited resources is at the heart of this perspective. It sees in society numerous groups continually struggling to gain advantages over the others. Social problems arise when those who succeed in accumulating power then act to advance their own interests at the expense of the rest of society. For the Conflict theorist, the social and economic inequalities within society provide the basis for understanding social problems related to work. In a capitalist system, powerful corporate interests exert a profound influence on national policy and the economy. Since their major objective is profit, employers and management exercise their power and influence to that end, usually at the expense of weaker groups.

Economic Inequality

Large corporations and conglomerates in business and industry have achieved so much power that they dominate most aspects of the U.S. and world economies. When they work for their own selfish interests—particularly if they form a coalition of mutual interest groups—curtailing them is extremely difficult. As a result, the danger that they will abuse their power is very real. The corporate giants also create a false consciousness among the populace through extensive media campaigns orchestrated to shape public opinion. One example is the Health Insurance Association of America's "Harry and Louise" television ad campaign in 1994 designed to influence the outcome of health-care reform efforts through media manipulation. It effectively scuttled proposed legislation by creating fears about government bureaucracy and (conversely) minimizing fears about corporate control over health care.[83]

Exploitation of workers by employers, who either constitute or represent the elite, is a fundamental cause of economic problems, according to this perspective. Labor unions provide organized unity to protect workers in some areas, but management decisions to relocate plants to the nonunionized Sunbelt or to foreign countries with cheap labor—as well as union-busting tactics of companies that declare bankruptcy and then reorganize under a new name—continue the exploitation.

Conflict theorists consider it no mere coincidence that the less powerful are the ones most severely harmed in difficult economic times. The pursuit of personal profit in a capitalist system dooms the less powerful in the competition for scarce resources, such as jobs and income. Some even suggest that the affluent favor some degree of unemployment because it keeps down wage demands, grievances, and absenteeism while improving productivity among the employed.

Alienation

A conflict of interest between employers and workers serves as this perspective's explanation of the problems of alienation and worker dissatisfaction. Industrialization separated people from the products of their labor, replacing the meaningfulness of labor and the intrinsic satisfaction from one's craftsmanship with the interchangeability of work station occupants. The division of labor thus fragments work assignments into more anonymous and less satisfying pieces. Whether in a manufacturing plant or (more likely) in a white-collar job, the goals of employer and employee take different directions.

Denied intrinsic satisfaction in many of today's jobs, workers perform boring, repetitive, unsatisfying, and demeaning tasks, and as a result have difficulty finding fulfillment in their work. Hence, their full human potential is unrealized. Work becomes a social problem because some groups of workers do not feel they receive sufficient rewards from work. Instead, it is an enforced activity in which the profits from one person's labors go to someone else. Little creativity or satisfaction emanate from the work, since the worker has little to say in the decision-making process.

The Feminist Viewpoint

Compared to working conditions that U.S. industrial workers endured in the late nineteenth and early twentieth century, office work offered genteel entry for women into the labor force. Originally a male domain, the lower ranks of office work became feminized in the twentieth century. That metamorphosis led to the sustained low-status, low-pay of such positions, while the higher-pay, higher-status positions remained male dominated and developed more "perks." Furthermore, stereotyped expectations of "women's work" led to female office workers always being the ones asked or assigned such tasks as making coffee and serving it, gift shopping for the boss, cleaning conference tables, and so on. All this would change, first through consciousness raising, then activism, and finally an insistence that women develop their own modes of analysis to challenge gender-based oppression found throughout the workplace in its daily routine.

Feminist Organization

From 1900 through the 1960s, female office workers had little interest either in office unionism or feminism. That changed with the Women's Liberation Movement of the 1970s. Like the broader Feminist movement, the women's office-worker movement that sprung from it was not a single coherent entity. Some grassroots organizations begun in the early 1970s were Union WAGE (San Francisco); Women Employed (Chicago); Working Women (Cleveland); Women Office Workers (or WOW, New York); 9 to 5 (Boston). In 1977, the scattered local organizations combined into a national group based in Cleveland called Working Women, which renamed itself 9 to 5 in 1983.[84]

These new organizations emerged not just as an outgrowth of Feminist consciousness raising, but also in reaction to the restructuring of corporate offices into new forms of exploitation. Technological changes made office work synonymous with computer work, with the mostly female clerical staff placed into warrens of cubicles crowded together for efficient use of floor space. These cubicles, with their modular partitions, effectively isolated the mostly female clerical staff from visual or communicative contact with one another.[85]

Occupational Health

In the first few decades of their existence, the women's office-worker organizations addressed such issues as equal pay, pregnancy/family leave, and sexual discrimination. Recently, Feminist research and activism has focused on the quality of life in the office, particularly occupational health. Beneath the deceptive appearance of carpeted, air-conditioned, clean interiors lie, Feminists argue, workplaces often filled with stress and toxic dangers.

How does one measure stress? At first, NIOSH could not measure it, and its investigators suggested the problems might be psychosomatic from mass hysteria or mass psychogenic illness.[86] In 1975, though, NIOSH reported that office workers had the second highest incidence of stress-induced diseases of any occupational group, and in 1980, NIOSH said that workers at video display terminals had the highest stress levels ever noticed.[87] No longer could office work be dismissed as "a gendered psychological response to life stresses," as NIOSH once claimed.

One usually thinks of toxic dangers at chemical and other industrial plants, but they exist in the office as well. Some of these hazards include: emission of ozone, a deadly substance, from photocopy machines (especially dangerous in small, poorly ventilated areas); nitropyrene or TNF-trinitroflourenone in these machines' black powder toner, both of which are suspected mutagens; TCE or trichloroethylene in correction fluid (whiteout), which in large doses can affect the central nervous system, cause liver damage and lung dysfunction; and PCBs or polychlorinated byphenyls in typing ribbons and carbonless typing paper. PCBs are extremely toxic and are suspected carcinogens; they can cause severe liver damage, as well as an irritation to eyes, skin, nose, and throat.[88] Each of these occupational health hazards produces a slow, subtle, insidious effect over time, so their symptoms are long in developing, making their low-level multiple causes difficult to understand.

Feminists thus see an important array of women's concerns in the workplace that center around behavioral, economic, health and safety, and work environment issues.

The Interactionist Viewpoint

Our subjective interpretations about our work, its meaning in our lives, and the work situations of others constitute the focal point of this perspective. Changing times bring about different interpretations, as, for example, the arrival of high technology and increased leisure time caused a shift in value orientations about work as the central focus of our lives. The rise in the standard of living increased our life expectations and reshaped our view of what it took to satisfy us (as discussed in connection with Maslow's hierarchy of needs). People in different situations have different perceptions of work, and Interactionists attempt to analyze the conditions under which certain groups view work as a social problem.

Occupational Identity

Part of the problem with job dissatisfaction is that technological changes have forged numerous new jobs whose content does not provide people with a firm profile, an **occupational identity**. As Peter Berger has suggested, saying "I am a railroad man" can be a source of pride, but saying "I am an electroencephalograph technician" means nothing to most people.[89] His point is that many individuals are unable to enjoy a full sense of identity from their work because others do not understand what it entails and because the worker cannot obtain any self-identification from the occupation. In a society that assigns prestige and esteem based on occupation, a job's vagueness limits its value as a source of dignity and satisfaction.

Many white-collar and blue-collar workers face a redefinition of work. No longer the central focus of a person's life, from which self-respect and societal acceptance flow, work is often a neutral area tolerated for the opportunities it affords to enjoy the more important things of life.[90] This significant shift means more than a lessening of the work ethic; it alters the presentation of self in the workplace. People are more likely to play roles as workers, restricting their real or actual selves for family and close friends.

Employee Perceptions

The nature of organizations, with their hierarchy of authority and limited area of responsibility for each person, requires individuals to work for corporate goals if they wish to succeed within that company. The "culture" of a corporation pressures employees at all levels to develop attitudes and behaviors necessary to advance the interests of their company. The individual's promotion in or continuance with the firm depends on his or her contribution to the company's financial well-being. This overriding preoccupation with meeting organizational goals may oblige some workers to take actions that contradict their personal values and ethics.

Rationalization is a common means by which individuals resolve their role conflict between personal morality and corporate demands. If people believe that "everybody's doing it," the pervasiveness of unethical or illegal behavior becomes the excuse to act similarly. After all, "business is business." Another example is when the argument that too much government interference exists is used to justify ignoring certain laws or regulations. Perhaps a person might also think that certain actions are necessary to keep an industry stable or profitable. Whatever the rationale, the important effect is that employees become socialized to see things from the company's perspective, which encourages them to act in harmony with its interpretation of reality.

Public Perceptions

Before the rise of big corporations and big government, Americans felt more independent, more powerful, and in greater control of their destinies than many people do today. Whether they actually were so autonomous is less important than their belief that they were. By acting in accordance with their beliefs, they often succeeded in their self-directed goals—in effect, creating a self-fulfilling prophecy. Today's mammoth bureaucracies intimidate many people, inspiring feelings of impotency and dependency. If indifferent or fatalistic attitudes lead to inaction or passive compliance, people obviously lose control over most things that affect their lives.

Since Americans measure success through achievement, individual competitiveness in an organizational society can breed considerable anxiety, dissatisfaction, insecurity, and hostility. Attitudes of cynicism and mistrust of others are likely under such circumstances, even among individuals who are economically secure. Combating such negative factors are family and religious influences, the shaping of public opinion by corporations and government alike through the media, and various ego gratification activities outside the workplace (clubs, hobbies, and so on).

Thinking About the Future

Numerous professional and amateur futurists alike offer scenarios about the future of work.[91] Advances in computer technology, dramatic cost reductions in related products, and the seemingly endless number of microprocessor applications being developed create a potentially enormous impact. Sophisticated software programs and computerized information storage/retrieval systems increasingly affect office jobs. Industrial robots, which bear little resemblance to the creations of science fiction authors and screenplay writers, are rapidly revolutionizing the manufacturing world. Despite all the predictions about how and where the "techtronic age" will take us, little consensus exists on the subject. From a sociological perspective, let us project where our current social problems relating to work may lead through the prism of future technology.

Bureaucratic organizations, such as large corporations, perform many valuable roles for a complex society such as ours. They have the resources to support research and product development, maximize efficiency and quality in product production, and find effective delivery systems to get the product into the hands of consumers. The problem lies in power concentrated in the hands of a few. You've read in this chapter about the continuing mergers and takeovers, and the power of oligarchies. What are the dangers of so much power?

Is there too much power and wealth in the hands of too few people? Is this a bad thing? Should people like Bill Gates have some of their wealth taken from them through taxation? If so, where should that money go? To the government? If so, for what? To the poor? Should they just get that money because they are poor? Would that solution have a negative impact on the work ethic we want everyone to have? Is it fair to take money away from those who earned it to give it to people who didn't? Or is it right that the least in our society should share in the good fortune of those with the most? Isn't that a form of socialism? What actions do you suggest? Should we leave things as they are or do something? What is that something? What would be the positive and negative consequences of your solution to keep the status quo or change it?

Many Americans oppose government interference in their lives, often electing politicians who promise to "get the government off our backs." Does this include government regulation of big business? How do we reconcile this desire for less government control with the desire of the government to protect us from exploitation? Corporations make large corporate campaign contributions to politicians "friendly" to their interests. Where do we draw the line between being free from the government and the reliance on the government to serve our interests? What model do you envision to deal with corporate power? Would you advocate greater government effort, less, or what we have now? What are the implications of your position for a democratic society?

How about the growing use of permatemps, a trend that may well impact on your own job prospects? Should anything be done to protect temporary workers? If so, what? Or what of the ability of corporations to access massive data banks and instant retrieval systems to learn nearly all aspects of people's lives? Should anything be done to protect individuals from the many invasions of privacy that computer technology makes possible? Can you envision a scenario if these two trends not only continue, but expand?

Do you think the future will increase people's job satisfaction and sense of personal fulfillment or lessen it? Will the work environment be more pleasant or less? Will workers, using computers even more, find more meaning in their work, or less? What of their personal and leisure time? What do you think the world of work will be like for you personally in twenty years?

The same question about the extent of government regulation also comes into play when we consider the issues of occupational health and safety. As you have read, work hazards exist in the office, as well as at many individual sites. Should NIOSH receive greater funding to expand its staff and site inspections? Do you think work dangers will lessen or increase? Why?

Once again, there's much here to think about. What alternative futures could possibly await us when it comes to power, work, and the workplace?

SUMMARY

1. One result of the emergence of corporate giants is oligopolies—a few producers that control an entire market. Facing little competition, these companies can set artificially inflated prices.

2. The largest five hundred companies in the United States generate three-fourths of the nation's GDP. The top 1 percent of families control most of the nation's corporations and 40 percent of the nation's wealth.

3. Another threat to the free enterprise system is the shared decision network that exists through interlocking directorates. Friendly and hostile takeovers have created immensely powerful conglomerates, whose anonymous technocrats provide input and direction that affect national policy.

4. Fragmentation of tasks and responsibility in the pursuit of corporate profits enables individuals to rationalize their morality (or lack thereof) into role requirements. Thus fixing prices, manipulating consumers, and selling unsafe products all become activities to which no personal blame attaches.

5. Government has grown huge and in many ways has forged a partnership with big business. Two significant illustrations of this alliance are the cozy relationship of the military-industrial complex and the revolving door of executive position interchange between government and industry.

6. Multinational corporations currently submit to little regulation but have a significant impact on national economies. Many have annual sales exceeding most nations' gross national products. Though some countries encourage foreign investment, studies show that the economic inequality in those countries usually worsens afterward.

7. Technology is changing the structure of the labor force. Blue-collar jobs are disappearing, and new jobs—even outside the high-tech industries—require people with education, computer literacy, and social skills. Women are entering a wider array of occupations and commanding better salaries than ever before.

8. Unemployment hits hardest among the individuals who are most vulnerable to economic downturns—production workers, suppliers and distributors, people in leisure activity occupations, and minority workers. Long-term unemployment can have devastating social effects: depression, heavy drinking, violence, mental stress, and prolonged cynicism.

9. Job satisfaction rests on more than just earning a competitive salary. Recent findings have shown that alienation often results from a lack of self-actualization: work fails to offer a challenge, some measure of control, and a sense of personal achievement. Flex-time schedules adopted by one-fourth of the labor force are a new trend designed to meet the needs of the "new breed" of workers.

10. Occupational hazards are a dangerous problem affecting the health and safety of many workers, especially those in the mining, farming, and chemical industries. Limited staff and funds curtail the activities of government regulators seeking to conduct safety inspection visits or chemical compound analyses and restrictions. Mining and farming have the two highest occupational death rates.

11. Functionalists suggest that rapid societal changes and growth have thrown the social system out of balance, politically and economically. Conflict theorists point to worker exploitation, corporate domination, and political power resting under the control of an economic elite as causes of our social problems. Feminists focus on exploitation and oppression in

the workplace, not just on economic and work environment, but also on health hazards in the office. Interactionists emphasize the system's impact on people's attitudes, noting evidence of cynicism, fatalism, and rationalized compliance.

INTERNET RESOURCES

At this book's Web site with Allyn & Bacon, you will find numerous links pertaining to the problems about power, work, and the workplace. To explore these resources, go first to the author's page (**http://www.ablongman.com/parrillo**). Next, select this edition of *Contemporary Social Problems* and then select **Internet Readings and Exercises**. Then select **Chapter 5**, where you will find both a variety of sites to investigate and some questions that pertain to those sites.

KEY TERMS

Alienation	Megamergers
Anomie	Military-industrial complex
Conglomerates	Multinational corporations
Cost overruns	Occupational identity
Demography	Oligopoly
Downsizing	Price leadership
Extrinsic satisfaction	Revolving door
Flex time	Technocrats
Hierarchy of needs	Tertiary occupation
Interlocking directorates	Underemployment
Intrinsic satisfaction	

SUGGESTED READINGS

Danaher, Kevin (ed.). *Corporations Are Gonna Get Your Mama: Globalization and the Downsizing of the American Dream.* Monroe, ME: Common Courage Press, 1997. Great writings that critique corporate subversion of democracy, pollution of the environment, and creation of criminal chaos all under the guise of free-market "freedom."

Dye, Thomas R. *Who's Running America? The Bush Restoration,* 7th ed. Upper Saddle River, Englewood Cliffs, N.J.: Prentice-Hall, 1994. A Conflict perspective offering an overview of America's power elite.

Grieder, William. *Who Will Tell the People: The Betrayal of American Democracy.* New York: Simon & Schuster, 1992. An indictment of powerful corporations that exploit the government and the American taxpayer to maximize profits.

Harrison, Bennett, and Barry Bluestone. *The Great U-Turn: Corporate Restructuring and the Polarizing of America.* New York: Basic Books, 1988. A thorough and disturbing examination of the evolution of a two-tier labor force—a system within which most new jobs are less rewarding than old jobs.

Jones, Barry. *Sleepers Awake! Technology and the Future of Work.* New York: Oxford University Press, 1991. Informative insight into how advanced technology affects the social organization of work and job choices.

Mattera, Philip. *Prosperity Lost.* Reading, Mass.: Addison-Wesley, 1991. An analytical portrait of how many workers find their higher-paying jobs eliminated and only lesser-paying ones available.

Mokhiber, Russell, and Robert Weissman. *Corporate Predators: The Hunt for Mega-Profits and the Attack on Democracy.* Monroe, Me: Common Courage Press, 1999. Investigative journalists critique corporate power and abuses from a human perspective and offer numerous examples.

Parenti, Michael. *Democracy for the Few,* 6th ed. New York: St. Martin's Press, 2001. An important book detailing the extent and dangers of the concentration of corporate and individual power to the detriment of most Americans.

Ritzer, George. *The McDonaldization of Society,* 4th ed. 2004. Newbury Park, Calif.: Pine Forge Press, 1992. A fascinating extension of the rationally efficient routinism of the fast-food chain into other fields.

Shaiken, Harley. *Work Transformed.* Cambridge, Mass.: M.I.T. Press, 1986. An in-depth study of the conversion of American manufacturing into electronic control technologies and how these have altered the workplace forever.

Toffler, Alvin. *The Third Wave.* New York: Morrow, 1980. Projections of current trends into a future world of work and leisure, with evaluations of their social impact on family life and social interactions.

6

Poverty and Social Class

Facts about Poverty

- About 34.6 million people in our nation—one out of every eight Americans—live in poverty.

- Of Americans living in poverty, 46 percent are non-Hispanic Whites, 25 percent are Blacks, 25 percent are Hispanics, and 4 percent are Asians or Native Americans.

- One out of every ten Whites lives in poverty, as do one out of every four Blacks and one of every five Hispanics.

- More U.S. children live in poverty than in any other developed country.

- In the United States, 77 percent of the poor live outside central cities, in rural or suburban areas.

- The infant mortality rate among the poor is nearly twice that of other Americans.

Poverty is not a condition most readers of this book have experienced firsthand. In fact, as a college graduate, you are extremely unlikely to confront this problem personally in your entire life. So why should you be concerned about the misfortunes of others if, as the Bible says, "the poor you will always have with you"?[1] Is poverty a social problem (the responsibility of society), or is it an individual problem that the poor themselves must overcome?

Although many different opinions exist, most social scientists agree that we can only understand the poverty problem within the larger context of the social system, not just by focusing on the subculture of the poor. Poverty may be an economic reality, but its continuance—and the continuance of some related social problems (crime, drugs, substandard education, single-parent households, and violence)—suggests that improving the material living conditions of the poor is not enough to reduce all the correlates of poverty. If U.S. society intends to eliminate these by-products of poverty, it must do more than declare a war on poverty, because material deprivation is not the main cause of most social problems. Sociological analysis helps us understand the various factors that contribute to the degradation and suffering poverty brings to millions of Americans.

Poverty in Sociohistorical Context

Despite the accomplishments and affluence of many of its people, the United States has long had a significant poverty problem. In his 1937 inaugural address, Franklin D. Roosevelt identified "one-third of our nation [as] ill-housed, ill-clad, ill-nourished." Matters had changed little for the poor by 1964 when President Lyndon B. Johnson launched the War on Poverty, based on the premise that the intergenerational lessons in socialization taught in poor families perpetuated poverty. According to the Council of Economic Advisors:

> Poverty breeds poverty. . . . Poor parents cannot give their children the opportunities for better health and education needed to improve their lot. Lack of motivation, hope, and incentive is a more subtle but not less powerful barrier than lack of financial means. Thus the cruel legacy of poverty is passed from parents to children.[2]

Subsequent government programs attempted to counteract self-defeating aspects of the poverty subculture through early intervention programs of cultural enrichment for children (endeavors as varied as Operation Head Start, preschool centers, and *Sesame Street*). The resocialization of adults, through various training programs (Job Corps, Comprehensive and Employment Training Act [CETA], Volunteers in Service to America [VISTA], and Community Action programs), was intended to build self-confidence and to reorient adults' work attitudes, as well as to generate earning opportunities. Although a few programs met expectations completely (such as those for consumer advocacy and legal services) or in part (Head Start, Job Corps, VISTA), the War on Poverty ultimately achieved mixed results.

The limited success of the War on Poverty prompted Sen. Robert F. Kennedy, during his ill-fated campaign for the Democratic Party's presidential nomination in 1968, to remark that millions of Americans went to bed hungry every night. In the intervening years, the level of poverty fluctuated; today, the United States—the richest nation in the world—still contains tens of millions of impoverished citizens. Despite billions of dollars spent on anti-poverty and social welfare programs, one out of eight Americans still lives in poverty. In 2002, African and Hispanic Americans are near their lowest percentage so far of people living in poverty (see Table 6.1).

Blaming the Poor

Blaming the poor for their difficult circumstances has been a common American practice for at least 150 years, ever since large numbers of Irish immigrants settled in urban slums and struggled to overcome bigotry and achieve a better life. Because the United States has served for many

Table 6.1   Persons Below Poverty Level, by Percent

Year	Total	White	Black	Hispanic
1960	22.2%	17.8%	not available	not available
1970	12.6	9.9	33.5%	not available
1980	13.0	10.2	32.5	25.7
1990	13.5	10.7	31.9	26.2
2000	11.7	9.9	22.7	21.4
2002	12.1	10.2	23.9	21.8

Source: U.S. Bureau of the Census.

decades as the beacon light of economic opportunity to millions of impoverished immigrants, native-born Americans have long associated poverty with the cultural differences of the newly arrived minorities. Regardless of which minority group stood at the bottom of the socioeconomic ladder, their contemporaneous American hosts often believed the group's cultural values or innate abilities were at fault for its poverty (see the box on the next page).

How such thinking prevailed for so long is easy to understand. The U.S. belief system revolves around individualism and the existence of widespread economic opportunity. In this country, advocates maintain, you can "make it" if you work hard and compete with others whole-heartedly. Invoking various rags-to-riches examples to demonstrate the validity of this belief, many Americans have for generations attributed economic failure to laziness, incompetence, and other imagined character defects in disadvantaged individuals and groups. A 2001 national poll, for example, found about half the poor weren't doing enough to get out of poverty.[3]

Intelligence as an Explanation

Controversial analyses by social scientists have periodically contributed to this tendency to blame individuals for their poverty. In 1973, Richard Herrnstein argued that the poor have a lower intellectual capability than the nonpoor, and that they marry other people of low intelligence, thus producing children of low intellectual capacity.[4] With the 1994 publication of *The Bell Curve,* Herrnstein and Charles Murray renewed this genetic argument, linking low IQ to poverty, welfare dependence, illegitimacy, and crime.[5] This old, discredited argument echoed similar claims once made against poor immigrants from southern and eastern Europe.[6] Substantial evidence refutes such arguments, however.[7] As if by magic, changes in people's economic conditions produce changes in their "intelligence" test results. Moreover, many poor people have raised children who subsequently rose to prominence in different fields of endeavor.

The Culture of Poverty

Another explanation, more widely accepted by the public, is that the poor develop a **culture of poverty**, as a means of adapting to their situation. According to anthropologist Oscar Lewis[8]—

Social Constructions of Social Problems

Social Concepts of the Poor

How we define a problem is a major factor in what solutions we seek to it. For centuries the nonpoor in virtually every country have blamed the poor for their own condition, as discussed in these pages. Such thinking frees one of guilt or a sense of social obligation to do something.

If we label them as lazy, immoral, or undeserving, then U.S. society and its leaders need not formulate any policies or enact any programs to assist the poor, because they simply are not worthy of our help. The underlying presumption of this thinking is that there are many decent-paying jobs the poor could take, if they possessed a work ethic. Many others have risen out of poverty and become middle class, and so can the current poor if they would make a serious effort.

In point of fact, this perception does not match the reality. Most poor people want to be as middle class as everyone else and wish that their efforts enabled them to escape poverty. Even the minority of poor people whose behavior draws criticism share this desire: the school dropouts, the unemployed, unmarried mothers, street criminals, alcoholics, and drug addicts. Their situation primarily resulted from poverty-related reasons, emanating from a precipitous lack of resources and the stresses of coping with poverty.

Lazy? With downsizing and economic restructuring, the news media often feature stories about new thousands of middle-class unemployed. Yet no one ever suggests that the middle-class jobless—some of them long-term unemployed—are lazy.

Immoral? Crime is immoral no matter who commits it, the poor or Wall Street millionaires. Yet no research data exists that show the poor, as a class, are less moral than the middle or upper classes. Interestingly, numerous studies show that the poor, as a group, have a higher percentage with a strong religious faith, although that in itself does not mean they are more moral than other class groups.

Undeserving? First of all, that label does nothing to reduce poverty or poverty-related behavior. Scholarly and ideological debates continue about how the different cultural, economic, psychological, and social factors interplay and contribute to keeping people poor. The only consensus on the subject is that when the poor lose the struggle to escape poverty, they often give up on mainstream behavior. For example, the high rate of male unemployment makes poor men—of any color—bad marital risks, and consequently this becomes a major reason for the formation of single-parent households.

Ultimately, poverty itself is the real evil. Throughout the two hundred years of U.S. history, the same problems have existed among virtually all poor groups regardless of racial or ethnic background or length of U.S. residence. Still, if mainstream America had less bias against the poor and was more thoughtful in its choice of concepts about them, that would only help the situation a little. What must be realized is the potent message found in the simple fact that young, middle-class men do not mug people, but some poor men do. The only really effective solution to poverty-related behavior is the elimination of poverty itself.

Adapted from Herbert J. Gans, *War Against the Poor* (New York: Basic Books, 1995).

and others such as Edward Banfield[9]—continual reinforcement of the cycle of poverty occurs because children learn poverty-induced values and attitudes from their parents. The resulting set of beliefs and behaviors includes attitudes of apathy, resignation, and fatalism; a deemphasis on schooling; a tendency toward immediate gratification instead of thrift; early sexual experience and resulting unwanted pregnancies; an unstable family life (often authoritarian and female-centered); and a mistrust of authority, whether it takes the form of police, school, government, or social agencies. As the children mature into adults, Lewis argued, their negative orientation toward life and work makes them ill-equipped to enter the societal mainstream. Critics of Lewis's view, such as William Ryan and Charles A. Valentine, contended that poverty can only be eliminated if we first recognize its societal causes. To them, low-income people were the victims, not the offenders.

Ryan maintained that **blaming the victim** results in misdirected social programs: by ascribing the socially acquired stigma of poverty to a genetic character defect or to a faulty subcultural value system, we ignore the continuing effect of victimizing social forces. As a result, outside interventions attempt to help the "disorganized" Black family instead of overcoming racism, or they strive to develop "better" attitudes and skills in low-income children rather than revamping the poor-quality schools they attend.[10]

Valentine argued that many of Lewis's "class distinctive traits" of the poor were actually either "externally imposed conditions" (unemployment, crowded and deteriorated housing, lack of education) or "unavoidable matters of situational expediency" (hostility toward social institutions, low expectations, negative self-image).[11] The poor, suggested Valentine, possess many positive values and behavior patterns that resemble those held by the middle class, but their life situation obliges them to develop some distinctive subcultural traits in order to cope and survive. Only changing the resources available to the poor and reforming the social structure can bring about changes in any poverty subcultural traits.

This discussion of theories asserting that the fault for poverty rests in the poor individuals themselves should remind you of our consideration in Chapter 1 of the character-flaw fallacy and quasi-theories. Here, the poor are analyzed to determine how they differ from the rest of us because they suffer deprivation. These identified differences then become incorrectly defined as the cause of the social problem of poverty, prompting publicly funded programs to eradicate or lessen the differences. Such programs are doomed before they begin because they fail to get at the root causes of poverty.

The Nature of Poverty

At first thought, poverty may seem a simple enough concept to explain: anyone is poor who lacks enough money to afford the basic necessities of life—food, shelter, and clothing. But how much money is enough? What minimum standard enables a person to attain these necessities? For example, what minimum conditions should a person's dwelling satisfy to be above the poverty standards? Are people poor if they pay their own rent and wear nice clothing? Is a family poor if it does not own a television set and cannot afford to go to the movies? What about the fact that necessities cost more in some locales than in others, or the fact that rural people, unlike city dwellers, can at least partly live off the land?

A precise definition of poverty is actually difficult to formulate. Where does one draw the line between the poor and the not quite poor? Difficult though it may be, we must identify the poor if we are to help them. Many experts have grappled with this problem, and their proposals are generally based on one of two major approaches: absolute deprivation or relative deprivation.

Absolute Deprivation

To avoid the pitfalls of measuring poverty subjectively, the federal government and other official agencies use the **absolute deprivation** approach, which relies on income as the determinant. The assumption here is that a family requires a minimum amount of money to secure the basic necessities of life, and it is classified as poor if it fails to earn that minimum amount.

Since government research shows that poor families spend one-third of their income on food, and since the Department of Agriculture provides cost estimates of average food prices for a minimum nutritional diet, the Social Security Administration (SSA) uses these data to set the official poverty income line each year. The SSA triples the annual food cost figure, factors in changes in the overall cost of living (as shown in the Consumer Price Index), and then establishes different cutoff numbers for the poverty level depending on the family's size and its farm or nonfarm family status. For example, in 2002 the weighted average poverty threshold for a nonfarm family of four was $18,392.

Poverty Index Changes

In absolute terms, the number of impoverished Americans declined during the War on Poverty years, dropping from 39.9 million (22 percent) in 1960 to 25.4 million (12.6 percent) in 1970. Since then the numbers and percentages of those living in poverty have fluctuated up and down, influenced by economic downturns and upturns, as well as by structural unemployment caused by such factors as manufacturing job losses and corporate mergers or downsizing (see Figure 6.1). Of particular note is the fact that, although the 2002 poverty total of 34.6 million Americans exceeds the number in 1970, the 2002 total percentage (12.1) is lower. Comparatively, almost the same proportion of Americans is living in poverty today as over thirty years ago.[12]

Many economists, social scientists, and activists consider the government figures too low, however, arguing that many poor people are not counted at all because of their transitory or illegal alien status, their residence in illegally reconverted multifamily dwellings, or their inaccessibility in remote rural areas. Other critics argue that the official number of poor is too high because noncash benefits such as food stamps, housing subsidies, and health benefits are not included with cash income in gauging whether a person's finances exceed the poverty level.[13]

Arbitrary Indicator

Using family income levels to determine which families are living in poverty is a direct measurement approach; but it is also arbitrary, since the cost of living varies from one region to another.

Figure 6 .1   Number of Americans Living in Poverty, 1960–2001 (in Millions)

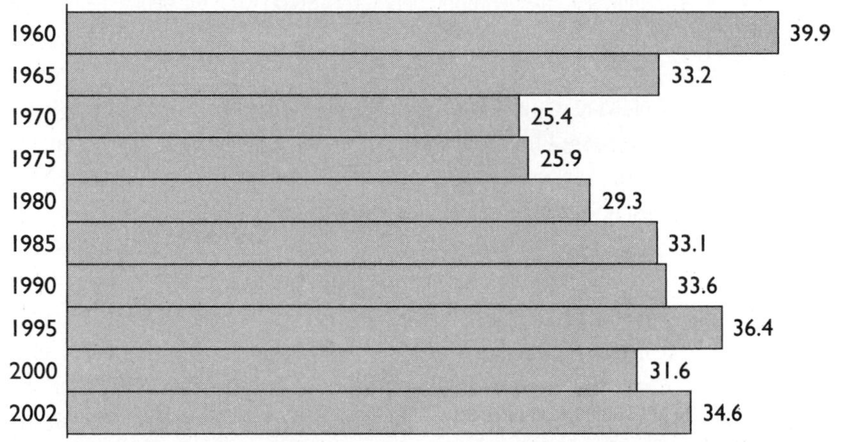

Year	Millions
1960	39.9
1965	33.2
1970	25.4
1975	25.9
1980	29.3
1985	33.1
1990	33.6
1995	36.4
2000	31.6
2002	34.6

Source: U.S. Bureau of the Census, *Current Population Reports,* Series P60–219. (Washington, D.C.: U.S. Government Printing Office, 2002).

Another important factor is that the federal experts who set the minimum food cost levels make assumptions about nutritional habits and consumer expertise among the poor that might not be warranted. Unlike the middle class, the poor cannot afford to stock up on food sale items; buy newspapers and magazines to clip food coupons; purchase larger, more economical, food packages; or avoid shopping in the usually higher-priced food and merchandise stores in their neighborhoods.[14]

One problem with relying on income alone to measure life among the poor is that it ignores in-kind aid. Food stamps, for example, provide on average about 16 percent of total family income to poor households with children. Other forms of support—such as free health care, rent subsidies, and school lunch programs—augment living conditions, too. Members of low-income households usually see doctors more often than do middle-class Americans.[15]

Another reality about income is that the poorest families often conceal money earned from odd jobs or received from friends or relatives so that they can remain eligible for welfare benefits or reduced tax liability. Economist Susan Mayer and sociologist Christopher Jencks argue that the consumption patterns and living conditions of low-income Americans offer a more realistic assessment of their material well-being among the poor than income does. Their research documents that, for more than a quarter of a century, the nation's poorest households have spent far more than their reported income. In fact, this gap has grown so large in recent decades that, in 1990, the poorest tenth of all households with children reportedly spent more than twice their reported income.[16]

Relative Deprivation

The absolute deprivation approach of considering the poor in terms of their needs may be the most commonly accepted; but other experts argue that the relationship of the poor to the nonpoor, or of the U.S. poor to the world poor, is far more significant. With the **relative deprivation** approach, the definition of poverty rests on what the people believe are their minimum needs.

In the United States, many of today's poor—especially if they have indoor plumbing, electricity, and a television set—are better off than the poor of yesteryear; but of course, the standard of living is higher now than in the past. The 1994 Mayer-Jencks study, for example, revealed that the poorest households were much more likely to have one room per person, a complete bathroom, air conditioning, central heating, telephone service, and a dishwasher than were the poorest households in the 1970s.[17]

The psychological dimensions of poverty encompass aspects of poverty that are usually disturbing the nonpoor: apathy, crime, deviance, poor educational performance, and social disorganization. For example, a neighborhood of old, dilapidated buildings is not necessarily a slum if a strong community cohesiveness exists; a slum is more accurately a state of mind of hopelessness, despair, and apathy, and thus it may be found in a modern high-rise housing project. If people feel so far removed from the average U.S. standard of living that they cannot identify with mainstream society, various lower-class pathologies will manifest themselves.[18]

Who Are the Poor?

Because most Americans do not come into direct contact with the poor, they rely on the media for their information about them. Unfortunately, the overemphasis on urban minorities distorts the reality of poverty in this country and fosters many popular misconceptions. In *The Other America,* an influential book of the 1960s that helped launch the War on Poverty, Michael Harrington spoke of the "invisibility" of the poor to most middle-class Americans.[19] The average person lives and works in areas containing few impoverished people, and this isolation is enhanced by zoning restrictions; highways that bypass poor neighborhoods; and heavily enforced local ordinances against peddling, panhandling, and the presence of "undesirables." When we examine what we do know about the nation's poor, however, the picture differs significantly from the stereotypes (see the box on p. 158).

Minority Status

Popular belief notwithstanding, far more of the poor in the United States are White than Black (15.2 million compared to 8.1 million in 2002). Within their group, 8 percent of those living in poverty were non-Hispanic White, 24 percent were Black, 22 percent were Hispanic, and 10 percent were Asian or Native American.[20] This information gives us an accurate overview of the U.S. poor, but a different perspective emerges when we examine the data more closely. Almost half of the total poor may be non-Hispanic Whites, but minority peoples are disproportionately represented within the totals. Blacks and Hispanics each make up 13 percent of the nation's population, but each group represents over one-fifth of the total poor. Put differently, about one out of ten Whites lives in poverty, but about almost one out of four Blacks and one out of five Hispanics are poor (see Figure 6.2).

Figure 6.2 **Who the Poor Are (in Millions): 2002**

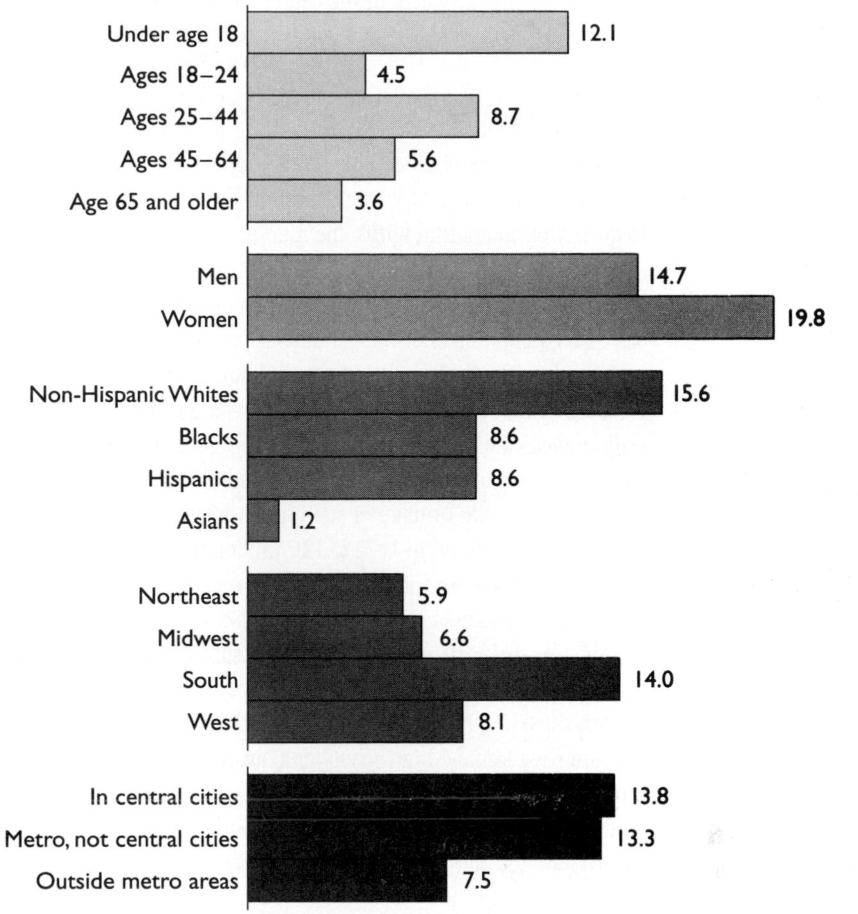

Under age 18	12.1
Ages 18–24	4.5
Ages 25–44	8.7
Ages 45–64	5.6
Age 65 and older	3.6
Men	14.7
Women	19.8
Non-Hispanic Whites	15.6
Blacks	8.6
Hispanics	8.6
Asians	1.2
Northeast	5.9
Midwest	6.6
South	14.0
West	8.1
In central cities	13.8
Metro, not central cities	13.3
Outside metro areas	7.5

Source: U.S. Department of Commerce, *Current Population Reports,* Series P60–222.

The overrepresentation of minorities in poverty occurs for several reasons. Since the Irish migration in the mid-nineteenth century, many poor people from other lands have come to this country to improve their economic situation. Although some achieved economic security rather quickly, most immigrants did not enter the American economic mainstream until the second or third generation. Part of the explanation for large numbers of minority poor, then, lies in the continuing arrival of impoverished immigrants from developing countries and the time required for them to move up the socioeconomic ladder.

Unfortunately, upward mobility can prove elusive to many minority people. For many decades racial discrimination denied equal educational and employment opportunities to African Americans. Poor non-White minorities today usually concentrate in decaying urban areas where both the quality of education for children and job opportunities for adults are limited. Whether they be Native Americans living on or near a reservation, Chicanos living in the Southwest, or Blacks or Latinos living anywhere in the country, their lack of educational attainment and occupational skills restricts their marketability and thus their income.

Family Structure

In 2002, 27 percent of all children under eighteen (22 percent White, 56 percent Black, and 29 percent Hispanic) lived in a single-parent home.[21] Because of the high divorce rate and the frequency of nonmarital births, the number of single-parent families with children under age eighteen rose from 6.2 million in 1980 to 9.7 million in 2000.[22] Since a household's composition has a direct relationship to the family's economic health, this statistic raises considerable concern. For example, in 2002 the annual median income for a married-couple family was $61,254 compared to $20,913 for a female-headed household.[23]

Women maintain five out of six single-parent families. The combination of limited job skills and education, poor work and earning opportunities, and the unavailability or excessive cost of childcare centers makes female-headed households more likely than others to live in poverty. In fact, the number of such families living in poverty almost doubled in twenty-five years, from 5.6 million in 1970 to 12.7 million in 2001.[24] Female-headed families thus constitute the largest segment of the population living in poverty. Today, 27 percent of children under age eighteen who are in female-headed families live below the government's official poverty line.[25]

This **feminization of poverty** corresponds to the high incidence of teenage and nonmarital births. As shown in Table 6.2, one out of every eight births is to a teenager, and one out of every three births is to unmarried mothers. One study found that 79 percent of children born to unmarried teenage high school dropouts lived in poverty.[26] On the U.S. mainland, certain groups are heavily overrepresented among single mothers: Blacks, Puerto Ricans, and Native Americans. Given the economic realities mentioned earlier, it is no coincidence that these same groups have the highest incidences of poverty.

Age

Children under age eighteen constitute 17 percent of the nation's poor—one of the two largest age categories. Most of these children live in single-parent families, with an average size of three persons (one adult and two children). Accounting for another 17 percent of the United States' poor are people in the eighteen–to–twenty-four age category. These young people are usually high school dropouts—unemployed, in low-paying jobs, or single mothers. Taken together, 34 percent of all poor people are twenty-four years or younger, and another 12 percent are found in the twenty-five–to–thirty-four age group. Persons sixty-five years old and older account for an additional 10 percent of the nation's poor.[27]

Locale

Most of us are familiar with urban poverty, thanks to extensive media coverage and the concentration of poor people in the central cities. However, 60 percent of the nation's poor live outside

Table 6.2 Births by Race and Hispanic Origin, 2000

Race and Hispanic Origin	No. of Births (in 1,000s)	Percentage of Births to Teenage Mothers	Percentage of Births to Unmarried Mothers
White	3,194	10.6	22.1
Black	623	19.7	68.5
Native American	42	19.7	58.4
Asian/Pacific Islander	201	4.5	14.8
Filipino	32	5.3	20.3
Chinese	34	0.9	7.6
Japanese	9	1.9	9.5
Hawaiian	7	17.4	50.0
Hispanic Origin	816	16.2	42.7
Mexican	582	17.0	40.7
Puerto Rican	58	20.0	59.6
Cuban	13	7.5	27.3
Central/South American	113	9.9	44.7
Total U.S.	4,059	11.8	33.2

Source: National Center for Health Statistics, *Births: Final Data for 2000* (February 2002).

This unmarried teenager looks competent and determined to raise her twin girls. According to sociological research, what challenges does she face? Why is she, along with her babies, more likely than not to become statistics in a portrait of poverty, American-style? How could the simple fact of poverty affect everything else in their lives?

These Eastern European farmers today live much like their peasant forebears. In parts of the U.S. and in many parts of the world, poverty is not an urban phenomenon, but a rural one. How does rural poverty differ from that found in inner-cities? What special social problems do rural communities face in the U.S. today?

central cities.[28] The rural poverty rate is higher than the national average partly because large, mechanized agribusiness farms have lessened the viability of small, independent farms and left many unskilled rural workers without means of support. Likewise, nonfarm rural people—such as those living in Appalachia, the Ozarks, the Southwest, and the Upper Great Lakes—also find only irregular or seasonal employment, if any, and face little prospect of improved opportunities.

A fairly high proportion of the rural population lives in the southern half of the United States. Not surprisingly, about 41 percent of the nation's poor live there, too, including large numbers of Haitian refugees, Mexican Americans, and migrant workers—three of the country's largest impoverished groups. Still, the majority of the rural poor are White.[29]

Repeating a centuries-old pattern, many of the rural poor migrate to urban areas to seek a better life. Instead, they find virtually no job openings, a higher cost of living, tenements to replace their shacks, unsafe streets, unhealthful and unsanitary living conditions, and the other urban problems encountered by the poor people already living there. Lacking education, job skills, and employment prospects, and unable to fish, raise vegetables, or trap small game as they once could in their rural areas, many rural migrants either resort to government welfare programs to secure the funds they need for survival or return to their rural roots.

The Impact of Poverty

The costs and consequences of poverty are detrimental not only to the poor themselves but also to the rest of society. As long as poverty remains extensive, American society loses a sizable and productive labor force whose tax payments and increased purchasing power would have stimulated the national economy further. Until we vanquish poverty, taxpayers must shoulder immense burdens in underwriting burgeoning social and welfare programs, slum clearance and urban renewal projects, and ongoing crime control activities. For the poor, lack of income has devastating and degrading effects on virtually every aspect of their lives.

Health

Research supported by the Public Health Service revealed that, in comparison to the nonpoor, the poor have four times higher an incidence of iron deficiency anemia and twice as many borderline cases. The poor also have twice the deficiency in vitamins A, C, and riboflavin. These dietary deficiencies are a significant cause of illness and death in newborns. Pregnant women who consume an inadequate diet are more likely to give birth prematurely and to rupture the amniotic sac before term—the two leading causes of death and illness in newborns.[30] Although stress, smoking, alcohol, and caffeine also have an effect, socioeconomic factors play a leading role in causing preterm deliveries.[31]

Infant mortality rates are thus higher in low-income families. Because racial minorities are disproportionately represented among the poor, their infant death rates are higher than Whites'. For example, although the death rate for African-American infants has been declining since 1989, it is nearly twice the White infant death rate—a ratio that has existed for several decades. In addition, poor women die in childbirth at a rate four times greater than nonpoor women do.[32]

Inadequate nutrition, substandard housing (particularly heating), poor sanitary conditions, air pollution, and inadequate medical attention render the poor susceptible to being sick more often. They also suffer acute or chronic ailments more frequently, and their average life span is seven years shorter than that of nonpoor people.[33]

On a positive note, the poor have greater access to health care now than in previous years. Medicaid mainly benefits poor children and the elderly, especially elderly residents of nursing homes. As a result, low-income children are just as likely to visit a doctor as high-income children.[34]

Housing

As the nation's rural population shrinks, its poor population becomes more concentrated. Almost twice as many people now live in concentrated urban poverty areas than did 30 years ago. In addition to such factors as immigration, housing costs, and lifestyle changes, federally funded, high-rise public housing projects also reinforced this concentration of poor people in blighted urban areas.[35]

When Americans think of the federal government's housing programs, they often think of the worst public housing projects in the urban United States. Fortunately, such units are decreasing. In recent years about 58,000 public-housing units have been demolished, with 85,000 more soon to follow. They are being replaced by low-rise, attractive town houses.[36]

Every two years, the American Housing Survey (AHS) collects information on housing conditions, including whether a family's housing unit has a complete bathroom, holes in the floors, cracks in the walls or ceiling, electrical outlets in every room, a leaky roof, peeling paint

Food stamp applicants in Austin, Texas, wait their turn at the local welfare office. Without this necessary means of support, many U.S. poor—children, adults, elderly—would suffer greatly. How is it possible that in this, the richest nation in the world, so many people are poor and lack sufficient food to eat? To what extent is it the role of government to ease the suffering of its people through social welfare programs?

or plaster, central heating, and signs of rats or mice. Since 1975, all of these housing conditions significantly improved for the poor, and most improved more for poor families than for middle-income families.[37]

Family Life

As social scientists consistently found among lower classes of all backgrounds and in all time periods, family instability is more common among the poor than elsewhere. Marriages and pregnancies occur at an earlier age; divorces and desertions happen at a higher rate; and incidents of family disputes and violence are more frequent. Since family life is an important factor in personality development, the greater possibility of experiencing stress and discord in the home, rather than a stable emotional support system, may serve as a causal factor of subsequent anti-social behavior.

Attitudinal Responses

Many nonpoor persons reject and even despise the poor, considering them lazy, incompetent, and immoral. A large number of employed inner-city African Americans share this attitude about unemployed ghetto residents. Sociologist William J. Wilson and a team of researchers interviewed more than 2,000 residents of inner-city Chicago neighborhoods and repeatedly heard harsh and scornful criticisms of neighbors and friends in connection with their attitudes about work, children, and marriage. Calling the unemployed "lazy" and questioning their diligence, working poor residents talked of the importance of individual character, preferring to "blame the victim" instead of "the system."[38] Clearly, they saw themselves as approaching life's difficulties in a more responsible manner.

Certainly, many poor people do struggle to survive and better themselves. Some, however, cannot find work to escape welfare assistance no matter how hard they try, causing feelings of hopelessness and apathy to set in. The resulting fatalistic attitude, encouraged by the person's inability to effect any change, can lead to a wide range of coping strategies for survival, from hostility and aggression (vandalism, theft, assault) to withdrawal and total apathy. Other people simply accommodate themselves to the situation, working as they can to survive. Yet another way of coping is escapism through religious fervor, drinking, or drugs.[39]

Education

Lack of education is both a cause and an effect of poverty. Among families living in poverty, one-fifth of all heads of household did not graduate from high school. Even more striking, that number increases among minorities (Black, 31 percent; Hispanic, 27 percent; Asian, 24 percent).[40] Their children are less likely than children of the nonpoor to graduate from high school or to enter college. Given little academic encouragement or assistance at home, and encountering the low expectations from their teachers that intensify their own low achievement, these students often drop out. As a result, they wind up in badly paying jobs, if any, and repeat the cycle of poverty. Low levels of educational attainment thus intimately intertwine with multigenerational poverty.

The poor who do not drop out often receive a substandard education. Formal schooling among the rural poor is often rudimentary or even nonexistent. The urban poor usually attend overcrowded schools with limited resources due to budget constraints. Negative environmental influences such as lack of parental involvement, peer pressure against achieving in school, poor discipline in the schools, and poor teaching undermine many students' learning potential. The result is young people who are unqualified as adults for most decent-paying jobs in our highly technological, postindustrial society. In Chapter 12, we will examine this problem more fully.

Work

Contrary to popular misconceptions, many poor people have jobs, and wages are a major source of income to poor families. About 20 percent of poor persons aged twenty-two to sixty-four work at least fifty weeks of the year; 10 percent work twenty-seven to forty-nine weeks; and 18 percent work twenty-six or fewer weeks. Thus, nearly half of all poor families received income from work-related activities.[41]

The majority of the poor are working poor, two-thirds of them in families with children with two or more adults present. White workers comprise about two-thirds of all working poor. Young workers typically experience the highest poverty rates, due in part to their lower earnings and higher rates of unemployment. Black and Hispanic young adults age eighteen to twenty-four are especially likely to be among the working poor.[42]

The working poor are poor simply because their earnings are not enough to keep them out of poverty. For example, in the 1990s, a person with a full-time minimum-wage job earned only about 70 percent of the money needed to reach the poverty threshold for a family of three.[43] Low-skill workers are also highly susceptible to downturns in the economy, finding themselves among the first to be laid off. Some find their jobs becoming scarcer because of technological obsolescence or the relocation of companies elsewhere. Working only part of the year or year-long at a low-paying job, the U.S. poor experience many of the same deprivations as the nonworking poor. Their health problems—ranging from frequent minor ills to stress-related heart disease—often entail loss of income when they miss work, since their jobs typically lack the sick-time benefits that others take for granted.

Work and Welfare

In the nineteenth century, Europeans and Americans operated workhouses to provide employment and industrial training for the poor. Today we no longer have workhouses, but the general public's attitude still holds that poverty could be eliminated if the poor were forced to work instead of being allowed to freeload. This attitude was the main impetus behind the welfare reform legislation known as the Personal Responsibility and Work Opportunity Act of 1996.

The Welfare Poor

Since the 1930s, **welfare**—public assistance programs for the poor—reallocated hundreds of billions of tax dollars and generated intense controversy, yet they failed to bring the problem of poverty under control. How could we have spent so much money for so many years, enacting dozens upon dozens of major social programs, and still have one out of every eight Americans living in poverty? Part of the answer lies in misdirected efforts: treating the symptoms rather than the structural causes, or (as in the case of the War on Poverty) emphasizing efforts to combat the "pathological" culture of poverty as the cause of the problem.

Another dimension is that a large and cumbersome bureaucracy, composed of over 9,000 federal and 529,000 state and local officials, administers the various public welfare programs in a nonsystematic, inconsistent manner.[44] Eligibility requirements and payment amounts vary considerably from one state to another. People who are eligible for certain forms of welfare assistance in some states are ineligible for these in others; maximum income requirements in a particular jurisdiction may be below or slightly above the poverty line.

A third factor is the attitude of some welfare agency personnel, whose paternalism discourages poor people who are dependent on them from extricating themselves from poverty. Finally, the stigma attached to welfare recipients disheartens many eligible poor, particularly the aged, from seeking assistance.

Public Welfare Programs

In common usage, *welfare* refers to public assistance programs for the poor. However, if we define welfare as any form of direct cash or in-kind government assistance to individuals and families, we discover that federal social spending programs are far more widespread. In fact, only one-fourth of federal social welfare payments go to the poor. Social assistance programs fall broadly into two categories: social insurance and **means-tested programs**, for which eligibility rests on income.

Social Insurance Programs

This form of public assistance is by far the largest (65 percent of the total) and most widely accepted. The largest portion (57 percent) provides social security and other income security payments to retired workers or, under certain conditions, their survivors. These plans have built-in cost-of-living increases. Even though many recipients receive more than they paid in through payroll deductions—including interest—within only a few years, the public attitude is that continued payments are their due for past years of work. The second largest portion (28 percent) is for Medicare, the health care plan for senior citizens that pays most expenses for prescription drugs, medical supplies, physician visits, and hospital care.[45]

Means-Tested Programs

Most programs in this category help sustain people who live in poverty, rather than helping them move out of poverty. Only about 10 percent of means-tested benefits provide education or training that could make recipients more self-sufficient. The rest cover such programs as Medicaid (10 percent of all public assistance), food stamps and commodity distribution programs (4 percent), Supplemental Security Income (SSI—3 percent), public and subsidized rental housing (3 percent), and the Earned Income Tax Credit (EITC—2 percent), which reduces the income tax for low-income taxpayers or gives them a refund if they don't owe taxes.

SSI provides monthly payments averaging $328 to about 6.6 million aged, blind, or disabled people deemed needy. Total expenditures of $32 billion in 2000, some $15 billion higher than in 1990, were primarily due to large numbers of newly arrived elderly immigrants joining family members already here who did not then assume responsibility for them.[46] This abuse and drain on the federal budget prompted Congress in 1996 to curtail the practice through welfare reform and hold family sponsors more responsible for their aged relatives' economic well-being. Whereas under the previous rules noncitizens could gain eligibility after residing in the United States for three years, today only citizens are eligible—and immigrants must reside in the country for five years to be eligible for citizenship.

In 1996, the Personal Responsibility and Work Opportunity Reconciliation Act replaced AFDC, as well as the Job Opportunities and Basic Skills (JOBS) and Emergency Assistance programs with the Temporary Assistance for Needy Families (TANF) block grant program. This law contains strong work requirements, comprehensive child support enforcement, and support for families moving from welfare to work. From a peak of 5 million AFDC families comprising 14.5 million recipients in 1994, TANF families dropped to less than 3 million families, comprising about 6 million recipients in 2000.[47] What is interesting is that under the former AFDC program its smaller proportional growth compared to that of female-headed families reveals that most single-parent families did not go on welfare, even before the tougher restrictions were enacted in 1996.

This worker no longer receives AFDC benefits. In the 1990s welfare reform eliminated or significantly reduced benefits to the poor. What groups were affected, and with what consequences? How has the balance shifted between federal and state power over the administration of public funds and availability of anti-poverty programs? How successful have workfare initiatives been so far? What are the implications of welfare reform for solving the problem of poverty in the long term?

Welfare as a Way of Life

Is welfare a trap, creating long-term dependency while discouraging its recipients from working? Or is it a short-term arrangement that enables recipients to overcome a crisis—such as death, disability, divorce, abandonment, or sudden unemployment—and to regain a stable situation? Although a few case studies and some "culture of poverty" writings created the popular notion of a persistently poor underclass, this is by no means a complete and accurate portrayal of the welfare poor.

In a major—and still continuing—longitudinal study begun in 1968, the University of Michigan Panel Study of Income Dynamics (PSID) each year follows the fortunes of over 7,000 representative families (altogether comprising over 50,000 individuals) who live in poverty throughout the United States. From this important database, researchers analyze the "dynamics" of poverty. In the mid-1980s, one important study reached the following conclusions:

1. Poverty is widespread but not usually persistent.

2. Only about one-sixth of all persons who ever live in poverty are trapped there for eight or more years in their lifetime.

3. The characteristics of the persistently poor do not conform to conventional wisdom.

4. The economic status of the poor does not appear to be caused by psychological dispositions.

5. More than one-half of persons *observed* to be poor at any given time have been so for eight or more years.

6. A weak link exists between the poverty or welfare status of parents and that of their children.

7. Substantial upward mobility exists among young adults from poor families.

8. Only one in five individuals who was at or near the poverty line as a child was at or near the poverty line as an adult.[48]

Does the last finding suggest that no correlation exists between parental poverty and children's later fortunes? Although only 4 percent of poor adults had experienced long-term welfare dependency when they were children, children from poor families are somewhat more likely than those from nonpoor families to be poor as adults. Other studies support these findings.[49]

The seeming inconsistency between findings 2 and 5 results from the fact that persons with long poverty spells are more likely observed than other sometimes-poor people at a moment when they are poor. Members of this fairly small group also are likely to receive the bulk of poverty program expenditures.[50]

More recently, other researchers analyzing the expanded PSID database found that chronic poverty was higher than previously identified—about 36 percent of all measured poverty. The most chronically poor group identified consisted of people living in families headed by African-American females without high-school diplomas, for whom chronic poverty is about twelve times more intense than in the entire U.S. population. This group's chronic poverty stays at about 69 percent, compared with about 36 percent for the longitudinal study population as a whole.[51]

Why did this latest study find more than twice as many people living in chronic poverty as the previous study had? Perhaps the expanded database tapped into more of the hidden poor, or

Homeless men sleep on the sidewalk, outside an upscale shop that sells furs. Not uncommonly, we see urban scenes like this one where ostentatious displays of wealth contrast with images of poverty. Matching this visual dichotomy is an attitudinal one, in which government programs for the affluent have no stigma, as do those for the poor. What are examples of government programs for the affluent? Why do people accept these but criticize those for the poor?

Figure 6.3   Distribution of Family Income in the United States, 2002

Percent share of 2002 total United States income

Top fifth ($84,017 and over)	49.7%
Second fifth ($53,163–$84,010)	23.3%
Third fifth ($33,378–$53,162)	14.8%
Fourth fifth ($17,917–$33,377)	8.8%
Bottom fifth (Less than $17,917)	3.5%

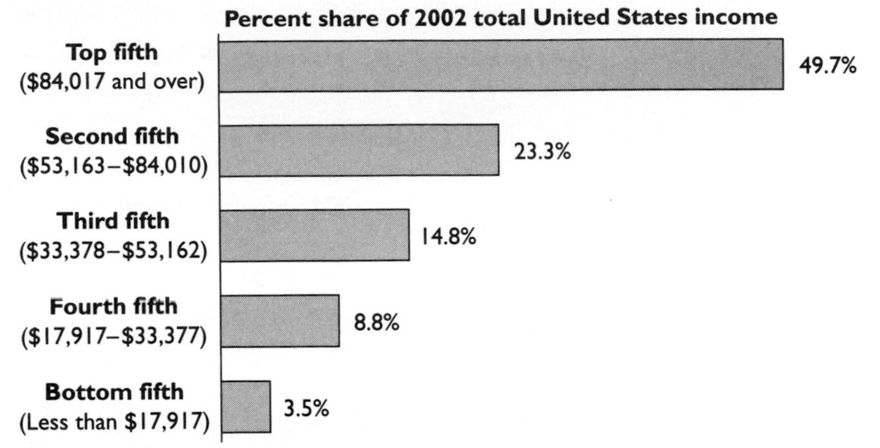

Source: U.S. Bureau of Census, *Income in the United States: 2002,* Series P60–221.

possibly people in the first study—not then classified as chronically poor—became so. Clearly, further research is needed to answer this question without speculation.

Income Distributions

The disparity between rich and poor is not simply a matter of difference in incomes (a normal fact in any competitive society), but in the proportionate share of total income each socioeconomic group possesses and in how each group's income situation changes from year to year. This information offers helpful insight into macrosocial factors relating to poverty.

If family income were distributed equally across the population, each **quintile**, or 20 percent segment, would receive one-fifth of the total. As Figure 6.3 above shows, in 2002 the top 20 percent of all U.S. families—those earning more than $84,017—earned 49.6 percent of all family income. That is as much as the remaining 80 percent of Americans combined. The top two-fifths earned almost three-fourths of all income, leaving the lowest 20 percent of families—those earning less than $17,917—drawing in only 3.4 percent.

Since 1968, the gap between the most affluent Americans and everyone else has been steadily widening; and by 1993, it reached its widest extent since the end of World War II in 1945.[52] It widened still further by 2002.[53]

Eliminating Poverty

The problem of poverty has concerned many people, yet poverty remains. What do we do now? As always, no shortage of suggestions exists. We will look at three approaches: "trickle down," "Robin Hood," and interventionist.

The "Trickle Down" Approach

The Reagan and both Bush Republican administrations addressed poverty and the nation's economic ills by adopting a supply-side policy sometimes termed **trickle-down economics**. Ironically using Democrat John F. Kennedy's metaphor, "A rising tide lifts all boats," conservatives sought to cut taxes and government spending, to eliminate cumbersome federal regulations and red tape that restrict the growth of business and industry, and to provide incentives for the private sector to expand and increase employment. Advocates argued that these controversial efforts would keep inflation in check and create a period of prosperity that trickled down to the lowest strata so that everyone would benefit. Critics contended that these policies would instead create a windfall for the wealthiest Americans, widen the gulf between the rich and poor, and do nothing for members of the poor—the aged, disabled, or unskilled—who gain nothing from others' improved economic situations but instead need direct assistance.[54] After enactment of the 1986 tax reform law, the federal deficit grew significantly, the income gap between the rich and poor widened, and the percentage of Americans living in poverty increased almost every year until 1993, when U.S. prosperity resulted in a federal surplus. However, a recession and increased expenditures for wars in Afghanistan and Iraq again increased the federal deficit as yet another tax cut followed in 2003.

The "Robin Hood" Approach

Advocates of the "Robin Hood" position seek a **redistribution of wealth**. Some recommend nationalizing large corporations and seizing large fortunes—proposals unlikely to gain much support in a society built on the principle of free enterprise. The only concept of equality Americans agree on is equality of opportunity. In contrast, European ideals emphasize equality of wealth and income, too; and most European countries have stringent tax laws with fewer loopholes than U.S. tax laws have, to lessen the net income disparity between quintiles.[55]

A more moderate, more popular (and less likely to be enacted) approach takes the form of a "soak the rich" attitude about taxes. Indeed, the 1986 tax reform law was written in part to eliminate loopholes involving tax shelters and estates, in an effort to have the wealthy pay a fairer share of the burdens of government. Despite elimination of some loop holes in recent years, tax cut initiatives offset them by favoring the affluent, while end runs around the tax code enable "financial engineers" to find new loopholes to avoid taxes.[56] So far, at least, efforts to require the richest Americans to pay more have achieved little success; but even if they become more successful, the congressional predisposition to reduce poverty does not include a positive attitude toward redistribution of wealth.

The Interventionist Approach

Yet another school of thought endorses bold and direct federal action, similar to that of the Roosevelt administration during the Great Depression, as the only solution to poverty. They advance various proposals, all involving the government.

Employment

Providing job training for unskilled workers was a major part of the War on Poverty, but one that had mixed results. Creating jobs for the unemployed worked during the Great Depression; however, this action is extremely expensive for taxpayers, and it fuels inflation—not a problem in the 1930s. Current federal policy is to stimulate the economy and provide tax incentives for the private sector to expand in depressed areas and to hire the unemployed. The Job Opportunities and Basic Skills training program for AFDC recipients, and the Job Corps, which provided education and training programs for over 60,000 persons between the ages of fourteen and twenty-one, were discontinued in 1996. With welfare responsibility now shifted to the states, any government interventionist approach will need to occur at that level.

Education

Since education often provides the means for upward mobility, and since lack of it tends to produce poverty, some commentators have argued for greater educational effort. Michael Harrington, for example, pressed for GI Bill–type legislation under which the federal government would pay for the poor to go to school for free and give them a living allowance if they had a family.[57] After World War II, such legislation was extremely effective in raising the educational levels and life opportunities of millions of war veterans. Similarly, a compensatory payment program for law enforcement personnel in the 1970s, also covering their education expenses, dramatically raised their educational achievement levels. Once again, however, education alone is not the answer; the poor need jobs once they complete their education.

Welfare Reform

For years, politicians, civic leaders, taxpayers, and welfare recipients themselves have disliked our welfare system's inefficient, ineffective, and inconsistent patchwork of federal, state, and local regulations and agencies. Treating symptoms, not causes, it discouraged many poor people from earning money because, when they did so, their benefits were immediately reduced or eliminated. In an influential 1984 book, *Losing Ground,* Charles Murray attacked the welfare system for prolonging poverty instead of eliminating it.[58] He argued that automatic welfare payments create a way of life, thereby removing any fiscal incentive for the poor to seek to escape their plight. As the public's conservative mood waxed (as reflected in congressional elections), Murray's book inspired numerous legislative proposals for welfare reform.

Eventually, Congress passed the Personal Responsibility and Work Opportunity Act of 1996, ending, President Clinton proclaimed, "welfare as we know it."

The 1996 Legislation

The welfare reform law of 1996, reversing sixty years of federal policy, ended an automatic legal entitlement to benefits by eliminating Aid to Families with Dependent Children (AFDC), creating the Temporary Assistance for Needy Families program (TANF), mandating that a large percentage of recipients work, and imposing a five-year time limit for receiving federally funded benefits.

The change has been dramatic. Between 1994 and 2000, the number of families receiving welfare assistance dropped by 60 percent to its lowest percentage level since 1960. Buoyed by the economic boom of the 1990s, this reduction in welfare caseload matched a decline in poverty itself, even among female-headed families with children.[59] Although critics of the welfare reform bill gave grim forecasts of its negative impact on the poor and near-poor, poverty rates went down among all groups, even those historically the most vulnerable: the elderly, children, women, and minorities.[60]

Although the percentage of single mothers on welfare decreased as more worked and gained higher incomes, these data do not tell the entire story. Fewer than half of these mothers are working regularly at full-time jobs. Studies in various states show most earn $6–$8 an hour (an average of $14,000 a year for full-time, full-year employment). Of course, this is not adequate for a woman with two children (about the average number of children for those leaving welfare).[61] But various government programs help make it pay for her to work. As Douglas Besharov explains:

> In 2001, a single mother with two children earning this salary would be entitled to about $3,800 from the EITC (Earned Income Tax Credit), up to $2,700 in food stamps, and about $1,200 in subsidized school meals for both children. After taxes, that comes to a total of almost $21,000. If she also receives subsidized housing, add another $3,000 or more. In addition, her children would remain eligible for Medicaid (an average of $2,428). Moreover, although by working she would have added costs, her biggest cost— child care—would generally be covered, and most states would also provide transportation assistance.[62]

Assessing the Impact of the Legislation

Do the results in welfare change prove the conservatives or liberals were correct? It appears each were both right and wrong. Conservatives proved that the welfare system itself encouraged dependence, because the new pro-work welfare system of limited, short-term assistance successfully pushed many mothers off welfare, showing that many welfare mothers could instead hold down jobs or rely on others for assistance. In addition, they take satisfaction in the fact that intensive investigations by liberal policy analysts and journalists have been unable to document any substantial increase in hardship. No social catastrophe happened.[63]

On the other hand, liberals were right about the difficulty of single mothers leaving welfare and becoming financially self-sufficient. There is instability in the caseload (about 50 percent higher than the historic rate) as single mothers cycle on and off welfare. They appear to be having a difficult time under welfare reform, and their numbers could easily increase if the economy continues to weaken. In 2001, for example, the national TANF caseload almost completely turned over, meaning that the number of families that entered welfare and left was almost equal to the total number of recipients. If exit rates decline or entry rates rise even a little, caseloads could rise quickly. Even now, some of these women, particularly those cycling on and off welfare, seem to be doing worse than before. Liberals also feel vindicated in their stressing the critical importance

The Globalization of Social Problems

Unemployment, Government Aid, and Child Poverty

Worldwide, more than 1 billion people live in poverty. While some live in developed countries, such as the 34.6 million poor Americans, most reside in developing countries. Among the poorest countries are Mozambique, Madagascar, Nepal, Tanzania, Uganda, and Ethiopia. Drawing international comparisons on poverty is extremely difficult, however, because differences in stage of development, living standards, and cost of living among countries are often too extensive to allow for meaningful contrasts. Thus, for example, poverty in the United States means something very different from poverty in Somalia, where it entails lacking even the barest essentials to survive.

One meaningful measure for comparison, however, is the unemployment rate in developed countries. Because many poor people in the United States work, employment is not a wholly satisfactory gauge of poverty; still, in an industrialized society unemploy-

ment is at least an indicator of poverty endangerment, if not of actual poverty. As Table 6.3 shows, the United States ranks sixteenth lowest among developed nations in its unemployment rate. In most cases, we can find a correlation between unemployment and poverty on a per capita basis. For example, we should expect to find less poverty in Switzerland, Luxembourg, Norway, Austria, and the Netherlands than in the United States, but far more poverty in Spain, Albania, Columbia, Slovakia, Poland, and Argentina. And indeed, the data show this. A notable exception is Mexico, with a low urban unemployment rate but high national poverty rate. Extensive rural poverty and low wages among the urban working poor explain this contradiction.

The United Nations Children's Fund reports that there is a close relationship between child poverty rates and the percentage of households with children in which there is no adult working. Sadly, 47 million

Table 6.3 Unemployment of Adults, Selected Countries (2002)

1.	Switzerland	1.9	12.	United Kingdom	5.1	25.	Italy	9.0
2.	Luxemburg	2.8	14.	Japan	5.4	26.	Finland	9.1
2.	Mexico	2.8	15.	Hungary	5.6	27.	Peru	9.7
2.	Netherlands	2.8	16.	United States	5.8	28.	Greece	9.9
5.	South Korea	3.3	17.	Australia	6.3	29.	Spain	11.3
6.	Norway	3.9	18.	Belgium	7.3	30.	Armenia	11.9
7.	Thailand	3.9	19.	Czech Republic	7.3	31.	Venezuela	15.2
8.	Austria	4.3	20.	Canada	7.7	32.	Albania	17.0
9.	Ireland	4.4	21.	El Salvador	8.0	33.	Colombia	17.0
10.	Denmark	4.5	21.	Russia	8.0	34.	Slovak Republic	18.6
11.	Sweden	4.9	23.	Germany	8.6	35.	Poland	19.9
12.	Portugal	5.1	24.	France	8.7	36.	Argentina	21.5

Source: Standardised Unemployment Rates (Paris: Organization for Economic Cooperation and Development, 2002; *Labour Overview: 2002* (London: International Labour Organisation, 2002).

The Globalization of Social Problems (continued)

children in the world's richest countries (one in six) live in poverty. In terms of *relative* poverty, the bottom four places are held by the United Kingdom, Italy, the United States, and Mexico. This study, *Child Poverty in Rich Nations* (2000) reported two interesting findings in connection with the international comparisons. First, a child's chances of living in poverty is, on average, four times greater in single-parent families. Second, the countries with the lowest child poverty rates allocate the highest proportions of their GNP to social expenditures. Such countries as Sweden, Luxembourg, France, Australia, and the United Kingdom—who have child poverty rates either higher or near that of the United States before government assistance—have lower child poverty rates after such aid (see Table 6.4).

Table 6.4   Child Poverty in Selected Developed Countries (1999)

Country	Percentage of Children in Poverty	
	Before Government Assistance	After Government Assistance
Sweden	23.4	2.8
Norway	15.9	3.9
Finland	16.4	4.3
Belgium	17.8	4.4
Luxembourg	22.2	4.5
Denmark	17.4	5.1
Netherlands	16.0	7.7
France	28.7	7.9
Hungary	38.1	10.3
Germany	16.8	10.7
Spain	21.4	12.3
Australia	28.1	12.4
Poland	44.4	15.4
Canada	24.0	15.5
United Kingdom	36.1	19.8
Italy	24.0	20.5
United States	26.7	22.4
Czech Republic	5.9	(NA)
Japan	12.2	(NA)
Greece	12.3	(NA)
Ireland	16.8	(NA)
Turkey	19.7	(NA)
Mexico	26.2	(NA)

Source: United Nations Children's Fund, *Child Poverty in Rich Nations* (Florence, Italy: Innocenti Research Centre, 2000).

of a strong economy, as the increase in entry-level jobs played a key role in the decline in case-loads. At issue is whether this impact was greater than that of welfare reform.

It is too soon to tell about the success of welfare reform. Caseload decline and the increase of working poor are certainly positive indicators, but only long-term, steady employment and income will produce self-sufficient, strong families. While hundreds of thousands of families are moving to that goal, they need more time and continued economic stability. Then, too, welfare reform is far from complete at the state level and complex challenges lie ahead.

Sociological Perspectives

Perhaps no other social issue has stirred as much controversy among political leaders, social scientists, and the public as the cause of poverty. Since correctly identifying the cause is critical to finding the solution, these differences of opinion affect how we as a society address the problem and paradox of poverty in this "land of opportunity."

The Functionalist Viewpoint

Using the Functionalist approach, we can understand poverty from two perspectives. One view is that the scope and nature of poverty are the results of rapid social change throughout the last century. Society's needs and demands were fundamentally altered by automation, high technology, the decline of low-skilled rural and urban labor opportunities, discrimination, and shifting residential patterns. Consequently, a large segment of the population found itself caught in the middle, vulnerable and untrained for this postindustrial society. Much as in the social upheaval that attended the Industrial Revolution, Americans of the late twentieth century experienced substantial economic changes that were not completely absorbed by the social system.

Another view is that, instead of representing a breakdown in social institutions, poverty functions as a necessary part of our social system. The threat of poverty motivates people to work; but if the work a person does is not highly regarded (picking crops, washing dishes, custodial work), the economic rewards it earns are low. Conversely, we give more money and prestige to individuals whose work we consider important, more difficult, or complex, and whose preparatory training is long and arduous.[64] While all work contributes to the functioning of the entire society, a hierarchy of rewards creates a system of social stratification within which the people at the bottom receive relatively little.

Negative Functions

Although poverty exists as a negative incentive to work or as a weak reward for low-valued work contributions, it becomes dysfunctional to the society as well. If poverty becomes too widespread, it can cause a serious drain on the economy, necessitating large public expenditures or fomenting violent disruptions within the society. In addition, if the pay incentives for the low-paying jobs are less than a person could receive in welfare benefits, a twofold problem arises: unfilled jobs and excessive unemployment. The Functionalist solution is to institute a more efficient economic system that effectively uses job training and educational programs and thereby meets the needs of agriculture, business, and industry.

Positive Functions

Poverty also persists because it directly benefits others, who therefore resist efforts to change the situation. Herbert Gans identified several positive functions the poor supply to the more powerful and affluent:

1. The poor offer a low-wage labor pool to do the "dirty work" that no one else wants to do and that subsidizes the economic activities of employers.

2. Their activities make life easier for the affluent, relieving them of tedious or labor-intensive daily chores by working as servants, gardeners, and so on.

3. Their poverty creates many jobs for the nonpoor: social workers, penologists, police, pawnshop owners, numbers racketeers, liquor store owners, drug sellers, loan sharks, and so forth.

4. Poor people subsidize merchants by purchasing second-hand, dilapidated products that others don't want (cars, housing, appliances, stale bread, fruits, and vegetables).

5. The poor make a convenient target for condemnation and punishment designed to reinforce the legitimacy of the traditional values of hard work, thrift, honesty, and morality.

6. The poor provide an opportunity for the nonpoor to feel good about themselves through altruistic or charitable activities, and they simultaneously serve as a reference point of favorable comparison.

7. The poor aid in the upward mobility of others, since they cannot compete for a good education and good jobs.

8. The poor are powerless and so can be made to absorb the cost of change in a society (getting displaced from their homes by urban renewal, expressways, or civic projects; being among the first victims of unemployment due to technological advances or inflation-fighting government actions to tighten the money supply).[65]

Although functional alternatives to poverty exist, Gans concludes, they would be dysfunctional to the affluent by imposing higher costs and demanding a forfeiture of some of the latter's wealth and power. Only when the existence of poverty becomes dysfunctional to the nonpoor or when the poor obtain enough power to change society will the situation change.

The Conflict Viewpoint

Gans's analysis of the positive functions of poverty actually merges into Conflict theory as well, since he examines the vested interest of the powerful in maintaining a poverty class. Perhaps no other social problem has elicited as much Conflict theoretical analysis as poverty. Economic inequality prompted Karl Marx more than a hundred years ago to argue that a capitalistic society promotes the interests of those owning the means of production and exploits those who do not. Sociologist Ralf Dahrendorf, considering the new forms of ownership in modern society (such as stocks and mutual funds), offered a neo-Marxian explanation that authority, rather than ownership, is the basis of class dominance and oppression of the poor.[66]

Blaming the System

Socialist Michael Harrington shared this view of capitalism as the root of all the problems facing the poor.[67] He argued that inadequate programs and misdirected priorities hampered efforts to solve this far from intractable problem. Only when a full national program—comparable to those of the democratic socialist countries of Western Europe—addresses the capitalist-induced class inequities in income, housing, public transportation, education, and medical and dental services will poverty be overcome.[68]

Conflict theorists reject the notion that the victims of poverty are to blame because of inadequate socialization or "improper" values. If anything, the system is at fault for fostering a false consciousness among the poor that they cannot achieve more than they have and must therefore depend on others. Alienated, robbed of human dignity, and filled with low self-esteem, the poor remain disorganized and apathetic. As long as they accept their plight, they remain in conceptual chains that negate their escape from poverty. Until poor people mobilize, take political action, and gain support from some of those in power, economic inequalities cannot be reduced much. Some evidence exists to support this contention of the Conflict theorists. Michael Betz, for example, found that the twenty-three cities torn by riots in 1965 and 1966 received a dramatic increase in welfare benefits thereafter compared to twenty similar cities that did not have riots.[69]

Frances Fox Piven and Richard A. Cloward also documented the expansion of welfare benefits in the late 1960s in response to the riots.[70] Noting that eligibility rules are more permissive in times of high unemployment and more restrictive in times of low unemployment, they concluded that welfare programs function as a safety measure to prevent disorder by absorbing and controlling the unemployed. Capitalism requires a pool of low-skilled workers from which to draw during times of economic growth, so it must also provide a place for laid-off workers to subsist when the economy declines; otherwise, political turmoil would be inevitable. Only when the poor become a threat does the government initiate or expand welfare relief to defuse social unrest, as demonstrated by the reduction and even elimination of ameliorative programs when conditions improve. Thus, efforts to aid the poor are situational responses to instances where society faces potential instability, rather than representing a genuine drive against poverty itself.

Guaranteed Annual Income

In a subsequent work Piven and Cloward advanced a radical strategy for ending poverty.[71] They called for a coalition of militant civil rights organizations, anti-poverty organizations, and the poor to generate a major political and economic crisis that would force Congress to enact a **guaranteed annual income** for everyone. Their plan was to conduct a massive recruitment drive of all eligible welfare recipients who were not already receiving benefits, which, they claimed, would double the number of people on the welfare rolls. Such a massive increase of recipients would cause such political and fiscal turmoil that Congress would have to act to end the poverty that lay behind the problem. This strategy might lead to class conflict and violence, the authors admitted, but so might a continuation of existing conditions. The hoped-for mobilization did not occur, however, and the redirection of welfare programs from the federal level to the state level further undermined the merits of such action. Although Piven and Cloward's proposal was more radical than most, the idea of a nationally guaranteed annual income is not new. The Scandinavian countries, for example, largely eradicated poverty through such a program of providing a minimum decent income for all.

The Feminist Viewpoint

The focus of all Feminist research is the condition of women in society: thus one major area of concentration is on income inequality and poverty. This is certainly understandable, given the growing number of female-headed households and the feminization of poverty, resulting in a growing proportion of the poverty population composed of women and their children.

Standpoint theory is a common Feminist research approach to overcome gender biases and the consequential neglect of women's perspectives and their daily lives. Feminist theorists argue that life experience structures a person's understanding of life, and so research must begin from concrete experience, rather than abstract concepts. Otherwise, we begin our analysis from an incorrect position.[72] One example would be the assumption that the female-headed family in and of itself is a cause of poverty and that such families occur more commonly among certain minority groups because of their "deviant" subcultural values. An examination of poverty from the perspective of the poor in such families would reveal another reality. Actually, substantial research has demonstrated that, historically, the Black female-headed family has often been a source of strength and resiliency against efforts at subjugation.[73] Feminists (and other social scientists as well) insist that we can only understand and resolve the problems associated with female-headed households if we examine how the inequalities of class, gender, and race intersect.[74]

Similarly, Feminist economic analysis challenges the claim that economic theory is wrapped in a value-free structure. Instead, from the Feminist viewpoint, the theoretical structure takes too much for granted, using methodologies, assumptions, and practices that contain systematic gender biases. Thus any findings based on this approach reinforce current power structures, inferior average outcomes for women, and policies based on these findings. What is needed is an emphasis placed on theories of collective action based on group membership, the social construction of interests, and the interlocking nature of constraints—including rules, norms, and preferences based on each of the structural power variables—that lead to greater real choices for some more than others.[75]

For example, many of the women swelling the ranks of the poor were not born into poverty, but were forced into it by such events as separation, divorce, desertion, parenthood, or widowhood. Longitudinal studies show that such events often have negative and prolonged consequences for women's economic well-being, unlike men, who often enjoy an improved economic standard of living following marital dissolution. Part of the problem is that the courts award child support payment only to about 56 percent of divorced mothers, and, of these, about 24 percent never actually receive a payment and another 24 percent receive only partial payments.[76] Feminists argue that unless women's work roles are reflected in social policy initiatives and men assume equal responsibility for children (within and out of marriage), economic opportunities for previously married women will remain limited.[77]

One example of such limitations is in the welfare reform legislation enacted in 1996. To receive welfare, women must participate in the workfare program. However, they often qualify only for low-paying jobs that do not provide enough income to meet transportation and childcare costs, in addition to basic needs, and so cannot continue in them. As a result, the strong economy, far more than these new policies, reduced unemployment for single mothers and raised families out of poverty.[78] Those with limited job skills and/or childcare needs remain either unemployed or vulnerable to economic downturns. Feminists insist on new social initiatives to address women's needs that the current legislation does not.

The Interactionist Orientation

The Interactionist perspective concentrates on the ways people perceive and define the events that influence their lives. Such perception and definition among the poor—the outgrowth of daily interaction with others—could reinforce the existence of poverty. For example, despite the popularity of some minority superstars in sports and entertainment, the main reference group for the poor are persons living in their neighborhood. If the area is an urban slum with high unemployment, serious crime, plentiful drugs, and alcohol abuse, as well as high absenteeism from school and a high dropout rate, then few positive role models exist. The model of "success" may be the clerk in a nearby store with a steady job, or the pimp, hustler, or numbers runner in the streets. Or a young person may fall victim to the pervasiveness of the dropout lifestyle with erratic, low-paying employment, early pregnancies, and crushing responsibilities.

Effects of Labeling

Another aspect of this view of poverty is the impact of societal **labeling** on concepts of self among poor people. How the poor respond to the "blaming the victim" approach we discussed earlier can help demonstrate how societal stereotypes help perpetuate poverty. If we define the poor as lazy, incompetent, immoral, apathetic, and lacking the necessary competitive determination to succeed, those individuals may well accept these definitions as accurate. This is especially probable if socialization sources, including family, friends, school, and the media continually apply such labels.[79] Recall, in this instance, Wilson's study of the views of employed Chicago ghetto residents, who repeatedly criticized unemployed neighbors and friends.

In the schools, low expectations can be devastating. If teachers have high achievement expectations for their students, their chances of realizing that level of accomplishment are high. Conversely, low expectations tend to produce low student motivation and minimal achievement.[80] Labeling a low-income child as a probable failure puts that child at a disadvantage and sets in motion a self-fulfilling prophecy: without encouragement and self-confidence, the child is indeed more likely to perform poorly and to quit school when old enough to do so.

Continuous Reinforcement

Not all low-income people internalize feelings of inferiority about themselves or conform to low expectations. Many adults attempt to emphasize the importance of a good education for their children, and many young people set their sights on lofty goals and work hard to achieve them. Still, members of each stratified tier of society share social class value orientations. Labeling theorists suggest that a long and continuous process of identifying the poor as inadequate often conditions them to believe that they are—a self-concept reinforced from inside and outside the poverty subculture.[81]

This perspective implies, therefore, that the ongoing interactions and interpretations in people's daily lives function to keep poor people at the bottom of the socioeconomic ladder. Poverty is a psychological trap as well as an economic one. The poor tend to define their social environment as being the result of their own shortcomings, because that is the prevailing view. This negative self-image induces a passive, fatalistic acceptance of the situation. Only through an interruption of the perpetual negative definition—encouraging a more positive redefining of themselves and their possibilities—can the poor overcome the economic hardships imposed on them. Such enrichment efforts to improve self-concept must be accompanied, however, by employment income opportunities.

Thinking About the Future

If we examine the course of poverty throughout the twentieth century, considering programs that have worked here and in other countries, we can project several possible future scenarios. Are you optimistic or pessimistic about the possibilities of eliminating poverty? Keep in mind that this is another social problem that involves not only varying social policy initiatives, but one that also depends on your political ideology and the prevailing political climate nationwide. In essence, should government play a major role in ending poverty or is the government's role already too big and too intrusive?

This is an age-old question that every democracy must confront. Over 2,300 years ago, Plato wrote in *Republic* that justice must be relative to the needs of the people who are served, not to the desires of those who serve them. To provide the greatest benefit to the least advantaged, society must eliminate social and economic inequalities that deny an equal opportunity to all. How is this done? Is it the role of government to create an environment where this ideal can be realized, or is it the role of government to be proactive, to take steps to ensure that equal opportunity? At what point do such steps cross the line and become interference and restrictions on our liberties? You will find politicians and leaders arguing for one position or the other, and the one that prevails determines how we do or do not address the problem of poverty. Which position do you favor? Should we launch major government initiatives to educate the uneducated, train the unskilled, and create jobs through work programs? The states are doing some of this now. Should we do more? Should we streamline the bureaucratic system to lessen the government payroll and redirect those savings directly to state programs?

Is the "Robin Hood" approach a viable option? Should we tax the corporations and rich more heavily to lessen the disparity of income distribution in this country? Or should we give them greater tax incentives to make charitable contributions and underwrite antipoverty programs? What other initiatives might we launch to combat this problem?

Do the various sociological perspectives give you any ideas on steps we might take? Welfare reform clearly has lowered the number of people who were receiving government aid. What do you think of the new welfare system and its workfare program? How do we address Feminist concerns that it hurts women who qualify only for low-paying jobs that do not provide enough income to meet transportation and childcare costs, plus basic daily needs? What scenario do you envision for this population segment if no changes are made?

In this chapter we discussed housing conditions, and in Chapter 4, on cities, we discussed the shortage of low-income housing and the problem of homelessness. Poverty is the common link they share. What solution can you propose to address these concerns? And what about single-parent families often caught up in this housing crisis? How do we help them, and is there anything we can do to stem the rising number of such families? Or shouldn't we meddle in people's personal lives?

Health, education, the quality of children's lives and their futures—all of these become negatives because of poverty. Its costs to individual lives and to society as a whole are enormous. It robs people of their dignity and self-esteem. It insidiously destroys lives, both in life span and in quality of life. Here, in the richest nation of the world, millions of people still go to bed hungry every night. What future for the poor do you envision in your lifetime? What solutions, if any, do you recommend?

SUMMARY

1. Poverty remains one of the most difficult social problems to resolve, despite the dozens of approaches attempted and the billions of dollars spent to eradicate it. More than 1 billion people worldwide live in poverty. Unemployment rates are not wholly satisfactory measures of poverty, but comparative statistics do offer some indication of the extent of poverty in industrialized nations. In 2002, the United States ranked sixteenth lowest in unemployment and indeed had lower poverty statistics than countries with much higher unemployment rates.

2. Blaming the poor for their plight typically focuses on assumptions of lower intelligence and a culture of poverty with a value system that negates responsibility and a work ethic. Critics of this tendency insist that the problems are systemic and require structural solutions, not individual-focused ones.

3. One way of measuring poverty is the absolute deprivation approach, wherein failure to earn a minimum amount of money (set by the government) to secure basic necessities constitutes being poor. A second approach is relative deprivation, wherein poverty is considered in comparison to the living standards of others. Poor people in the United States in the 1990s actually lived better than their counterparts did in the 1970s.

4. Although most U.S. poor are White, minorities are disproportionately represented. Female-headed families are the fastest-growing segment of the poor population, reflecting a "feminization of poverty." Among children under eighteen living in a female-headed family, 27 percent are poor. Some 60 percent of the nation's poor live outside central cities in rural or suburban areas.

5. Poverty has devastating and degrading effects on the poor. Inadequate nutrition causes a high incidence of premature births as well as of infant deaths. Only one in ten poor people lives in urban housing projects, but many endure unstable family environments. Most poor people do work, but their low-paying jobs are often vulnerable to downturns in the economy. Frequently they criticize their unemployed relatives and neighbors for not trying to get ahead. Unfortunately, the high dropout rates among the minority poor reduce their chances to extricate themselves from a lifetime of poverty.

6. Almost all poor people on welfare cannot work, since they are children, elderly, disabled, or mothers of young children. Most welfare programs (services and cash) treat the effects of poverty, not the causes. Insurance programs, such as social security, help the elderly poor and are widely accepted. Employment programs get to the underlying cause of poverty, but are not large enough. According to one study, only about one-sixth of those in poverty remain so for more than eight years; but a later study puts that figure at about one-third.

7. Almost two-thirds of all public welfare money is spent on the widely accepted social insurance programs of social security, Medicare, unemployment and workers' compensation, and veterans' benefits. Among means-tested programs, Medicaid accounts for 28 percent of total expenditures; other program areas are food stamps, Supplemental Security Income, housing assistance, the Earned Income Tax Credit, and Temporary Assistance for Needy Families. In recent years the income gap between rich and poor has widened, even though tax reform laws have eliminated many tax loopholes.

8. Some conservatives have suggested eliminating poverty by adopting a trickle-down approach that stimulates a healthy economy through tax incentives and encouraging the private sector to hire the unemployed. "Robin Hood" radicals urge nationalizing large corporations and seizing large personal fortunes, while more moderate proponents of wealth redistribution call for tax reform to create a more equal division of wealth. Interventionists recommend direct federal action in job training, job creation, education pay incentives, welfare reform, and income provisions.

9. The Personal Responsibility and Work Opportunity Reconciliation Act of 1996 fundamentally changed the federal government's relationship to low-income Americans, giving states more power over program rules. Changes included imposing a five-year lifetime limit on cash benefits for at least 80 percent of each state's welfare recipients, a two-year limit on able-bodied adults, a three-month limit within a three-year period for food stamp eligibility, and denial of benefits to noncitizens. As states seek to reduce expenditures, the Wisconsin model offers a promising option for reducing poverty.

10. Functionalists suggest that poverty results from system dysfunctions and argue that, ironically, it serves positive functions in society. Conflict theorists stress the exploitation of the poor, and some recommend implementing a guaranteed annual income to eliminate poverty. Feminists may use Standpoint theory to see reality from the viewpoint of women, which they contend is necessary to get past gender bias and formulate meaningful social initiatives. Interactionists emphasize the reinforcing power of stigmatic labeling, fostering conformity to those views by the persons so labeled.

KEY TERMS

Absolute deprivation

Blaming the victim

Culture of poverty

Feminization of poverty

Guaranteed annual income

Labeling

Means-tested programs

Quintile

Redistribution of wealth

Relative deprivation

Trickle-down economics

Welfare

INTERNET RESOURCES

At this book's Web site with Allyn & Bacon, you will find numerous links pertaining to the problem of poverty. To explore these resources, go first to the author's page (**http://www.ablongman.com/parrillo**). Next, select this edition of *Contemporary Social Problems* and then choose **Internet Readings and Exercises**. Then select **Chapter 6**, where you will find both a variety of sites to investigate and some questions that pertain to those sites.

SUGGESTED READINGS

Devine, Joel A., and James D. Wright. *The Greatest of Evils: Urban Poverty and the American Underclass.* New York: Aldine de Gruyter, 1993. A persuasive argument that the social and economic costs of poverty far exceed the costs of eliminating its causes.

Ellwood, David. *Poor Support: Poverty in the American Family.* New York: Basic Books, 1989. An influential summary of research, policy analysis, and underclass theory, with special emphasis on the working poor.

Hurst, Charles E. *Social Inequality: Forms, Causes, and Consequences,* 5th ed. Boston: Allyn & Bacon, 2003. A detailed examination of all aspects of U.S. poverty, covering many of the topics discussed in this chapter.

Jargowski, Paul A. *Poverty and Place: Ghettos, Barrios, and the American City.* New York: Russell Sage Foundation, 1997. A data-rich description and a conceptually innovative explanation of the spread of neighborhood poverty since 1970.

Jencks, Christopher. *Rethinking Social Policy: Race, Poverty, and the Underclass.* Cambridge, Mass.: Harvard University Press, 1993. A review of social science and social policy issues regarding affirmative action, crime, the urban poor, and welfare reform.

Lewis, Oscar. *La Vida*. New York: Random House, 1966. An introductory exposition of Lewis's "culture of poverty" hypothesis, followed by a detailed portrait of Puerto Rican families in New York City and San Juan illustrating the hypothesis.

Murray, Charles. *Losing Ground: American Social Policy, 1950–1980,* 2nd ed. New York: Basic Books, 1995. A provocative and influential conservative analysis of American anti-poverty programs, accusing the welfare system of contributing to the problem of poverty instead of helping to solve it.

Ryan, William. *Blaming the Victim,* rev. ed. New York: Vintage, 1976. A very effective analysis of how society incorrectly blames the poor for their poverty, with a systematic piercing of the myths supporting this type of thinking.

Schwartz, John E., and Thomas J. Volgy. *The Forgotten Americans.* New York: W. W. Norton, 1992. A penetrating examination of the breadth of poverty existing today among the U.S. working poor.

Sidel, Ruth. *Keeping Women and Children Last: America's War on the Poor,* rev. ed. New York: Penguin, 1998. A fine profile of the causes, conditions, and persistence of female poverty, and its impact on children.

Tilly, Charles. *Durable Inequality.* Berkeley: University of California Press, 1999. Award-winning and provocative book that offers a new way of looking at persistent social inequality by examining representative paired and unequal categories of people.

Wilson, William J. *When Work Disappears: The World of the New Urban Poor,* reprinted ed. New York: Vintage, 1997. Offers a detailed insight into the loss of city jobs and the creation of a culture indoctrinated in "ghetto-related behavior and attitudes" and creating a new generation of urbanites that have little hope of betterment.

7

Gender Inequality and Heterosexism

Facts About Gender Inequality

- A recent study identified 3 percent of males and 1 percent of females as active homosexuals.

- Today, six in ten Americans believe homosexual relations between consenting adults should be legal.

- Despite the practice's much longer existence, *sexual harassment* was an unknown term until the late 1970s.

- Today, 56 percent of all college degrees go to women.

- Today, 63 percent of all mothers in two-parent homes with children under age six work outside the home.

- Despite accounting for only 29 percent of the total U.S. population, White males hold 95 percent of all top management positions.

- Women make up 51 percent of the U.S. population, but only 14 percent of the Congress and 14 percent of the U.S. Senate.

- On average, women earn seventy-eight cents for every dollar a man earns for comparable work.

All societies prescribe certain behaviors and patterns of social interactions for their members. Within these cultural norms and role expectations lie the institutionalized standards for gender differentiation. Men and women differ physiologically, of course, but biological factors do not explain the stratified differences in power and privilege between the genders nor their impact on everyday life. Through societal determination, social learning, and social control mechanisms, a society sets into motion the system of social experiences, resources, and rewards for both genders.

Gender inequality occurs when the distribution of power, prestige, and property are arbitrarily assigned on the basis of sex, not on individual merit. **Sexism** includes both prejudicial attitudes and discriminatory behaviors based on gender. Out of sexism flow the stereotypes, social expectations, value-laden attributes and presumed abilities, social stratification, and unequal distribution of resources and rewards that constitute socially constructed gender inequality.

Gender inequality typically exists in patriarchal societies. A **patriarchy** is a social system in which men dominate women, with a higher value placed on anything deemed masculine over anything deemed feminine. Although patriarchy thus gives men an advantage over women, it does not favor all men, because sexual orientation is another component of this value system. A patriarchal society such as the United States endorses, even rewards heterosexuality while it stigmatizes, even punishes, homosexuality. Gay men and women face disadvantages and social problems for their sexual orientation, just as women do for their gender. Such a social condition—the privileging of heterosexuality over homosexuality—is called **heterosexism**. In this chapter we will examine gender inequality and heterosexism from sociohistorical and sociobiological perspectives, sexual harassment and discrimination, the women's and gay rights movements, and the arenas of change.

The Sociohistorical Context

Gender inequality and heterosexism are not new social phenomena in this or many other societies. Nor has there been universality in societal values and attitudes regarding homosexuality or the role of women. Before we discuss the current scene and future possibilities, a brief overview of the past will give us a wider frame of reference for understanding some of the origins and variations in these viewpoints and practices.

Sexism

The ideology that supports biased gender identification was invisible and largely accepted until recent decades. For example, supernatural justifications for male supremacy are easy to find in the sacred books of Judaism, Christianity, and Islam.[1] The morning prayer of the Orthodox Jew includes this line: "Blessed art Thou, oh Lord our God, King of the Universe, that I was not born a woman." In the New Testament, Saint Paul orders, "Let the woman learn in silence with all subjection. But I suffer not a woman to teach, nor to usurp authority over the man, but to be in silence." And the Koran states, "Men are superior to women on account of qualities in which God has given them preeminence."

A close relationship exists between Protestant religions in the United States and the acceptance of the passive, powerless place of women. The triumph of business and the popularity of competitive economic values secularized American life in the 1800s, effectively removing the Protestant clergy and women (who were their most ardent supporters) from many interactive aspects of everyday life. Confined to the moral-cultural realm of good manners, politeness, and sensitivity to

American and European women of the Victorian era ideally were supposed to devote themselves exclusively to husband and children, the home, and church. How did the roles and statuses of women change? What social forces are still at work reducing gender inequality?

the arts, they found themselves excluded from the "male" world of politics, fighting, brandy, cigars, and business.[2] In other words, only men did the "dirty work" of business and decision making. If a woman were to do anything in the "real" world, the exposure to the male realm might destroy her unassertive purity and her symbolic stature as a moral example.

As part of this nineteenth-century redirection of "appropriate" gender activities, society expected men, except Protestant ministers, to avoid cultural pursuits. It became "unmanly" to be interested in books, music, or anything else not associated with competition or money.

Homosexuality

History has recorded descriptive evidence of the existence of homosexuality for millennia. Most of our knowledge of the sexual behaviors and norms of past historical periods, however, comes by inference from the literature and public writings of the times. We do not really know how most people were behaving.

Homosexuality existed without sanctions among the ancient Babylonians and Egyptians. The ancient Greeks not only accepted it as a natural expression of sexual instinct, but praised it as more genuine and tender than heterosexual love. The word *pederasty* literally means the love of boys, and most homosexuality in ancient Greece was between men and adolescents—often between a well-born teacher or mentor and his student or apprentice—not between adult males.

Homosexuality among nonaristocratic ancient Greeks is less well documented. About the only evidence we have is the mention of freeborn male prostitutes.

The role and position of women and marriage in ancient Greece were very different from how they are in the modern United States. Marriages were arranged, and a woman remained under the authority of her father, never really becoming part of her husband's family. Women received no schooling and basically stayed isolated from the world. As a result, little companionship between the sexes was possible:

> To the bisexual Greek, women and boys were both defined as submissive nonmales. Many non-Western societies have similar attitudes and behavior patterns, and one finds this in highly diluted form in much of the Mediterranean world today. A man can have boys as well as women as long as he takes a clearly dominant role and "womanizes" partners of both genders.[3]

Throughout the Middle Ages and the Renaissance, European society viewed homosexuality and heterosexual sodomy as sins and crimes. Governments in most of Europe, from Sweden to England to Italy, executed individuals found guilty of such acts. In 1492, for example, Venetian officials ordered a nobleman and a priest to be publicly beheaded and burned for committing homosexual acts. In France, authorities in 1586 burned at the stake a former provost of the University of Paris for injuring a boy in the act of anal rape.[4] Such events indicate the stance of the Church and of society toward homosexuality, but not how prevalent such forbidden conduct was.

For many years social science researchers—influenced by societal norms that included religion-based condemnation and psychiatric labeling of homosexuality as an aberration signaling mental illness—focused on homosexuality as a social problem. In fact, much of what was written through the late 1980s came from a psychiatric or psychoanalytical perspective that assumed homosexuality was pathological and that homosexuals were "sick" or "perverted."[5] Nowadays—with homosexuality no longer labeled an illness, with an increasing body of research suggesting that sexual preference is a function of biology not choice,[6] with growing public acceptance, and with sexual preference protected under civil rights legislation—researchers emphasize discriminatory practices against homosexuals as a social problem instead.

The Biological Argument

False notions about biological differences determining social differences were once common among men of science. Charles Darwin thought that men were more intellectual and imaginative than women. Sigmund Freud and Erik Erikson both thought male genitalia made boys more aggressive and female genitalia made girls more limited. Perhaps though, the most biased pseudo-scientific statement came from an early French social-psychologist/sociologist:

> In 1879 Gustave LeBon . . . published what must be the most vicious attack upon women in modern scientific literature. . . . LeBon was no marginal hatemonger. He was a founder of Social Psychology and wrote a study of crowd behavior still cited and respected today. . . . "In the most intelligent races, as among the Parisians, there are a large number of women

whose brains are closer in size to those of gorillas than to the most developed male brains. This inferiority is so obvious that no one can contest it for a moment; only its degree is worth discussion. All psychologists who have studied the intelligence of women, as well as poets and novelists, recognize today that they represent the most inferior forms of human evolution and that they are closer to children and savages than to an adult, civilized man. They excel in fickleness, inconstancy, absence of thought and logic, and incapacity to reason. Without doubt there exist some distinguished women, very superior to the average man, but they are as exceptional as the birth of any monstrosity, as, for example, of a gorilla with two heads; consequently, we may neglect them entirely."[7]

Such thinking reflected a pervasive mindset and value orientation in male-dominated societies extending back to antiquity. It had little to do with science and more to do with a prevailing sexist ideology that did not face widespread attack until the last third of the twentieth century.

"Support" for the Biological Argument

Today scientists have no interest in biological arguments supporting sexism. However, continuing neurobiological discoveries inform us that sex differences include more than those involving genitalia, chromosomes, and hormones. Brain sex differences exist, and we are only beginning to learn what they mean in terms of male-female abilities.

British geneticist Anne Moir (*Brain Sex: The Real Difference Between Men and Women,* 1991) cited numerous studies that revealed sex-specific differences in the brain.[8] Such findings may not be politically correct, she argued, but they are nonetheless factual. For example, men have fewer fibers connecting the verbal and emotional areas of the brain, leading her to conclude that that is why men find it more difficult for them to express emotions. Because they have more fibers in the reasoning areas, however, they demonstrate a superior ability to understand abstract relationships, which may make them more naturally suited to disciplines such as mathematics and engineering.

Research shows a significant difference between men and women in how they perform certain spatial tasks. Evidence further suggests that this difference has a neurological basis.[9] Women's brains run hotter—that is, they employ more glucose—and for a given task, women use more of their brains.[10]

Men's brains are larger and, with age, shrink faster. Magnetic resonance imaging (MRI), which looks at brain anatomy, reveals that this aging is particularly visible in the frontal part of the brain, which is responsible for abstract reasoning, mental flexibility, and impulse control. The aging rate is so pronounced, in fact, that the frontal lobes on men's brains—which on average are larger and heavier than women's when both are young—become approximately the same size as women's by the time both reach their forties. The volume changes go hand-in-hand with reduced performance. Men lose verbal memory, spatial memory, general spatial abilities, and the ability to pay attention, whereas the difference correlations are not significant in women.[11]

The differences are most profound in the **limbic system**, the ring of structures that surround the brain stem and constitute the most primitive portions of the forebrain. Men display more activity in the oldest limbic structures, the ones that lie below the *corpus callosum* (the thick neural cable that connects the two brain hemispheres and permits them to communicate with each other). In contrast women's limbic activity is highest in the newer part of the brain cortex. As one researcher concluded, the logical conclusion is that men are emotionally more primitive and women "more evolved."[12]

Brain sex researchers continue to formulate explanations for the differences in abilities between males and females. Scientific evidence shows that sex differences may be attributed to the structure of the brain's lobes and to the exposure of fetuses to hormones in the womb.[13]

Weakness of the Biological Argument

Clearly, some biological differences between men and women have behavioral implications. But if anatomy were truly destiny, as Freud once argued, we should expect to see these inborn gender differences expressed in fairly similar statuses and roles of men and women in all cultures. We do not. Although we do find a strong pattern of male dominance in cross-cultural comparisons, we also find exceptions. Margaret Mead and other anthropologists reported on various societies where the women were more aggressive and the men more passive, or where virtually no role differences existed between them.[14] In many areas of Latin America, farming is considered men's work, but in sub-Saharan Africa, female farming systems predominate. In South Asia, women in public market roles lose respect; but in some African countries, women are active entrepreneurs in public markets.[15] Moreover, in industrialized societies, cultural values shape accepted male and female goals and activities differently. Unlike in the United States, for decades women were common as dentists in Denmark, as engineers in then–East Germany, and as doctors in Russia.

Biological differences explain general tendencies, not specific social behaviors. And even these tendencies refer to representative actions for men and women, not the full range of actions or their overlap between the sexes. Some men are far less aggressive than some women, for example, and some women are far less emotional than some men. Also, as the cross-cultural studies teach us, we learn our behavior. Because humans are not biologically programmed in this respect, males can learn to behave as we might expect females to behave, and females can learn to behave in stereotypically male fashion.[16] Nevertheless, to deny the possibility of any biological influence appears unreasonable.

Gay Genetics

Although people long argued that there was a biological explanation for homosexuality, not until the 1990s did several studies claim the discovery of such proof. One scientist, Simon LeVay, conducted postmortem examinations of brain tissues of nineteen homosexual males, sixteen heterosexual males, and six heterosexual females. In the anterior hypothalamus (a part of the brain scientists believe plays a part in sexual behavior), he found significant differences. In the homosexual males this region was about the same size as those found in women's brains, whereas those of the heterosexual males was three times larger.[17] Another study disclosed size differences in the anterior fissure (a cord of nerves scientists believe facilitates communication between the left and right hemispheres of the brain). This part of the brain was larger in homosexual men than in women or heterosexual men.[18] Other geneticists studied forty-four sets of gay male twins and found that 75 percent of them shared a unique part of the X chromosome, far greater than would occur by chance alone. Furthermore, they found that these men were significantly more likely to have gay male relatives on their mother's side. Since men receive the X chromosome from their mothers only, this finding would suggest a genetic link to sexual orientation.[19] However, no other scientist has been able to replicate this finding.[20]

All of these studies remain controversial, partly because there are so few of them and partly because their sample sizes were small, making it questionable that they can be applied to the general population. If these findings gain further support from other studies, they would still only show a biological component to homosexuality, not a cause and effect. Expression of a biological trait, such as left-handedness or temperament, depends not only on a great many social factors but also can be altered by them. At best, these studies on homosexuality suggest a partial biological explanation.

Homosexuality in the United States

Openness about being homosexual was uncommon in the United States prior to the 1960s, except in major cities, where strong subcultures thrived. George Chauncey described New York City's gay community from 1890 to 1940 as having its own traditions, gathering places, and cultural and social events that sustained and enhanced gay men's communal ties and group identity.[21] Although existing laws criminalized gay men's sexual behavior and even their nonsexual association with each other, these laws were indifferently enforced. As a result, gay men formed a large world of overlapping social networks with excellent support systems: emotional, social, and commercial. By the 1930s, popular fascination with gay culture led thousands of people to attend the city's drag balls, and newspapers published sketches of the most sensational gowns.

Stigma and Sanctions

A shift in public attitude about lifestyle experimentation—prompted perhaps by a coalescing of the conservative currents that underlay religious fundamentalism and Prohibitionism, and augmented by fears of social disintegration raised by the Depression, labor unrest, and the specter of Bolshevism—resulted in more stringent enforcement of all laws during the 1930s and 1940s, including the previously ignored ones against homosexuality, which society now labeled as deviant sexual behavior. During the Cold War of the 1950s, Communist hunter U.S. Senator Joseph McCarthy warned that homosexuals in the State Department were threatening national security. At that time being discovered or even suspected as a homosexual could severely disrupt a person's life in any occupation. Getting fired was quite possible; getting taunted was probable. Going into an area known to be frequented by homosexual men—or by lesbians—and beating them up was a popular teenage pastime. To most homosexuals, "passing," or carrying out their lives in such a way as to appear heterosexual, was crucial. As Chauncey observes, "The State built the closet and forced the homosexuals into it."[22]

Though not as severe as the laws in Britain (where, until 1861, anal intercourse was punishable by death), U.S. laws were still quite harsh toward homosexual men. Until recently, many sexual acts commonly practiced in the United States, such as oral-genital sex and anal sex, were considered "crimes against nature" and were illegal. Municipalities invoked these laws, usually lumped under sodomy statutes, primarily to prosecute homosexual men.

Tolerance and Backlash

The **homophobia** (an irrational fear of gay people) of the 1950s and the resulting stigma and harm that could result from an openness about their sexual preference led many homosexuals to adopt a low profile despite the efforts of activist organizers in several cities. To avoid exposure, many gays hid their true selves from the straight world and quietly sought companionship in their bathhouses and bars.[23] In 1969, at one such gay bar, the Stonewall Inn in New York City, an event occurred that marked a shift in the gay community from passive adaptive goals to active militancy. The police had routinely raided the bar in the past, but on this occasion, the customers fought back rather than retreating. The event galvanized the gay community to become more assertive and to publicly acknowledge their sexual identity. As other minorities had done earlier in the 1960s, gays and lesbians joined organizations and struggled to secure equal rights and opportunities.[24]

The 1970s and 1980s saw major gains in public tolerance, including the addition of "sexual orientation" to antidiscrimination policies and statutes at local, state, and national levels. Tolerance of gay people increased as the gay rights movement gained strength. More gays "came out of the closet" and annual Gay Pride parades became part of large city celebrations. But the AIDS epidemic of the 1980s devastated the gay community, bringing enormous personal loss and grief, but also a renewed outburst of prejudice, discrimination, and violence against homosexuals.[25] A dramatic increase in cases of arson, assault, and murder against homosexuals marked the 1990s.[26]

Religious and political conservatives launched campaigns in the 1990s to pass local ordinances condemning homosexuality and to prevent the inclusion of sexual orientation under the protection of state antidiscrimination laws.[27] They also objected, along with military leaders, when Bill Clinton attempted in 1993 to repeal the official ban on gays in the armed forces. The "don't ask, don't tell" compromise sidesteps the issue of equal rights for people of all sexual orientations, but it does allow gay men and women to serve in the military without surveillance or persecution provided they do not make their sexual preference known.[28]

Without question, a major advance in protecting gay rights occurred in 2003, when the Supreme Court reversed its own 1986 ruling with a sweeping declaration of constitutional rights for gay men and lesbians. In overturning a Texas law criminalizing homosexual behavior by a 6-to-3 vote, the court decreed that such laws were an unconstitutional violation of privacy rights. Gay rights activists called the decision historic, the equivalent of the 1954 *Brown v. Board of Education* desegregation ruling.

How Many Gays Are There?

How common is homosexuality in the United States? The exact population of homosexuals has always been difficult to determine. Until recently, the source most often cited was the 1948 research of Alfred Kinsey, which estimated that 10 percent of all Americans were homosexuals. However, although Kinsey used a large sample, it was not a **random sample,** an objective process that allows everyone the same chance of being selected. Instead, Kinsey settled for a **convenience sample,** which may differ from a truly representative cross-section of the American public in a number of (unknown) ways. This is because the precise ways a convenience sample differs from a random sample are unpredictable; as a result, most social scientists feel uncomfortable using it to make generalizations.

Recent studies from Britain, Canada, Denmark, France, and Norway have identified the number of homosexuals in these countries as being in the 1 to 4 percent range, significantly below Kinsey's findings of 10 percent in the United States. Gay rights activists argued that the European findings were flawed because sexual orientation is not just actual behavior but also feelings—how a person falls in love—which is not measurable. This issue of proportion has political overtones, since the accepted number could strengthen or weaken the impact of gays as a recognized constituency on lawmakers and other government officials.[29]

In 1994, a more definitive, scientific answer came from Robert T. Michael, John H. Gagnon, Edward O. Laumann, and Gina Kolata, who reported their findings from the largest study of sexual behavior ever conducted in the United States using a random sample.[30] The researchers used computers to select addresses at random; then they chose which members of households to interview, again at random. From interviewer training to question development, they conducted this study according to strict rules of scientific data collection. They found that 2.7 percent of the males and 1.3 percent of the females reported having had sex with someone of the same gender within the past year. The findings were higher when the time frame extended back to puberty: 7.3 percent for males and 3.8 percent for females. When asked if they were sexually attracted to others of the same gender, 6.2 percent of the males and 4.4 percent of the females said they were (see Figure 7.1).

The varying percentages suggest an important element about sexual behavior that Kinsey discovered in 1948. Sexual orientation is a continuum, not a simple classification of people into one of two distinct categories. Kinsey created a seven-point rating scale with exclusive homosexuality at one end and exclusive heterosexuality at the other—with desires, actions, and their frequency determining the five in-between stages. Whatever the criteria, however, the 1994 study suggests that the actively homosexual population is considerably smaller than Kinsey had estimated.

Public Attitudes About Homosexuality

Public opinion about homosexuality, including civil unions and gay adoptions, are steadily becoming more tolerant. For example, a 2003 Gallup poll showed six of ten Americans believing that homosexual relations between consenting adults should be legal. However, Americans were equally divided between those favoring and those opposing homosexual legal unions, while previous polls showed greater opposition.[31] Similarly, a 2002 ABC News poll identified 47 percent of those asked supportive of the right for gays and lesbians to adopt, with 42 percent opposed. In 1998, a similar poll found 57 percent opposed, and in a 1994 poll, there was 65 percent opposition.[32] Three states—Florida, Mississippi, and Utah—ban adoptions by gay adults, while twenty states and the District of Columbia expressly allow it. In other states gay adoptions often face obstacles

Figure 7.1   Homosexuality in the United States

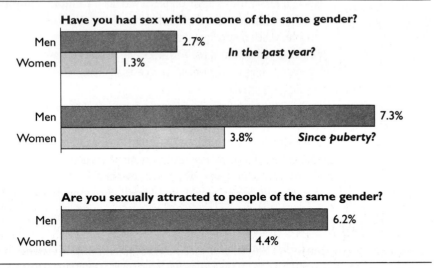

Have you had sex with someone of the same gender?

Men — 2.7%   *In the past year?*
Women — 1.3%

Men — 7.3%
Women — 3.8%   *Since puberty?*

Are you sexually attracted to people of the same gender?

Men — 6.2%
Women — 4.4%

Source: Sex in America: A Definitive Survey by Robert T. Michael, John H. Gagnon, Edward O. Laumann, and Gina Kolata (Boston: Little, Brown), 1994.

that typically rest on the erroneous belief that homosexual parents would "recruit" children to their lifestyle or would cause gender identity confusion or conflict in children. Researchers have found no evidence to support these fears.[33]

In a recent poll, a majority of Americans (53 percent) reported that they personally knew someone who was gay (a friend, relative, or co-worker). This is a dramatic increase from 1985, when pollsters routinely found that only 25 to 30 percent knew a homosexual. Significantly, persons who know a homosexual are more likely to have generally supportive attitudes toward gay rights—73 percent, as compared to 55 percent among respondents who do not know gay people.[34] Furthermore, 70 percent of all persons surveyed think society should allow gays and straights equal workplace opportunities.[35]

Homosexual relationships display wide diversity, as do heterosexual relationships. Similarly, public attitudes range from tolerant to intolerant, and practices range from fair to discriminatory. Although they apply radically different analyses, homosexuals and religious and political conservatives agree that serious social problems exist on the subject of homosexuality.

Some states have enacted legislation protecting the civil rights of gay men and lesbians, but others refuse to do so. Discrimination continues in many areas—marital rights (which include employment benefits such as health care, tax payments, pensions, annuities, survivor benefits) and parental rights (including child custody from a heterosexual marriage, visitation rights, foster parenting, and adoption). Gays also experience discrimination in housing, jobs, and medical care. Hate crime victimization is another serious concern. The FBI reported that in 2002, 17 percent of all hate crimes were due to sexual orientation bias. Although homosexuals get protection under hate crime and civil rights laws, their protection under the Constitution rests on a case-by-

Although homosexuals continue to be treated as pariahs by some U.S. population segments, the national government regards sexual preference as a matter of individual choice. Despite heterosexism, are homosexuals entitled to equal protection under the law? Can homosexuals marry? Can same-sex couples adopt and raise children? What does research show about the effects on children of having gay parents?

case judicial decision. A 1986 U.S. Supreme Court decision (*Bowers v. Hardwick*) said people do not have a constitutional protection to engage in private homosexual conduct. In other cases, the court has ruled in favor of gays, such as its 1996 negation of a Colorado referendum that banned all measures protecting homosexuals from discrimination. Experts view the 2003 decision as a significant step in securing constitutional protection for gays. The next battle, legalizing gay marriages, is now in full gear.

Socialization and Sexism

Sociologists characterize **gender identity** as an **ascribed status**—a label conferred on us at birth that determines how others define and treat us for our entire lives. Through major agents of socialization—the family, schools, and media—we learn the role behavior expected of us as males or females. Society shapes these gender identities by training us to internalize (that is, take on) that societally acceptable role as an integral part of ourselves. Through continual reinforcement, society also provides and justifies a self-evaluation that fits our gender position in society (see the box on the next page).

Family Influence

The gender role is already in place, waiting for the infant at birth, as the expectant parents create mental images of their new daughter or son. Studies show that parents' expectations shape

Social Constructions of Social Problems

Gender Differences and Gender Bias

Gender differences do exist—such as genitalia, brain activity, normal muscle development, lifting ability, height, weight, body hair, hip and shoulder width, fatty tissue, and voice depth. Do these biological differences explain behavioral and other social differences though? Basically, the answer is no, but it is incorrect also to suggest that gender bias is the sole determinant of differential outcomes.

Feminist Susan Douglas (*Where the Girls Are*, 1994), originally thought socialization alone explained behavior differences between men and women. As a parent, she discovered that her daughter, long before any exposure to television, engaged in "girl" rather than "boy" actions. She preferred dolls over trucks, built enclosures instead of towers with her blocks, and focused on interpersonal relationships when playing instead of throwing "missiles" into other objects. She recognized that although there was indeed an overlap of many traits between boys and girls, some gender differences existed. However, she also discovered that children's television programs typically ignored these overlaps and extensively reinforced and exaggerated the differences.

As products of their culture (and subculture), parents have gender-role expectations. As discussed elsewhere in this book, family socialization—through interaction patterns, choices of books, clothing, games, and toys—reinforce gender distinctions and gender stereotyping. Family, peer, school, and media socialization—reflecting a gender bias of what boys and girls should and should not be and do—affect their emotional and social development. Take just the simple statement, "She throws like a girl." Judith Lorber (*Paradoxes of Gender*, 1994) says we mean that "she throws like a female child, a carrier of XX chromosomes." In reality, she's had less opportunity from an early age to throw a ball. It's cultural *and* physical conditioning, not genetic. We know this because both boys and girls given tennis rackets at age three and encouraged to practice, tend to use their bodies similarly despite differences in shoulder and arm strength.

Another feminist, Robin Morgan (*Going Too Far*, 1978), found numerous examples of stereotyping leading to gender bias that she called "barbarous rituals." Here are a few:

- kicking strongly in your mother's womb, upon which she is told, "It must be a boy, if it's so active;
- being labeled a tomboy when all you wanted to do was climb that tree to look out and see a distance;
- seeing grown-ups chuckle when you say you want to be an engineer or doctor when you grow up—and learning to say you want to be a mommy or nurse, instead;
- liking math or history and getting hints that boys are turned off by smart girls;
- swinging down the street feeling good and smiling at people and being hassled like a piece of meat in return;
- being bugged by men in the office who assume you're a virginal prude if you don't flirt, and that you're an easy mark if you are halfway relaxed and pleasant.

When we construct a social reality based on a physical characteristic—whether it is gender, race, ethnicity, age, sexual orientation, or physical ability—we set a population segment apart from the rest. We tend to exaggerate differences, ignore similarities, and falsely attribute biological justifications for socially constructed inequalities.

behavior from the earliest moments. When asked to describe the behavior of babies, adults respond first to sexual cues. They attribute to the children characteristics they don't yet have. Presented with a group of babies wearing blue, pink, or yellow diapers, adults describe those in blue as active and loud and those in pink as quiet and sweet. The babies in yellow confuse the observers, who may even attempt to peek inside the diapers to find out the sex in order to know how to treat them. Parents typically play a bit rougher with their infant sons, which may encourage them to be more independent and aggressive than little girls.[36] Parents also tend to speak more explicitly to their sons, enhancing their cognitive development through greater verbal stimulation than they offer girls.[37]

Children also identify with their parents and learn by modeling their sex roles. This involves more than dressing up in Mommy's clothes. Children also assume the attitudes and evaluations of their gender. They can learn that Mommy is proud to be a "moron" about mechanical things, while Dad feels at home with them. Throughout childhood numerous verbal and physical cues continue the pattern—praise and reprimand, toys and games, books and clothing—all of which reinforce gender stereotypes.[38]

Media Influence

The mass media exert a powerful influence on gender role socialization. Advertisements, books, cartoons, movies, music, and television play major roles in this process, affecting how we think and act.

Many advertisements—particularly those for alcoholic beverages, cosmetics, jeans, and perfume—overtly exploit and reinforce gender stereotypes. Some magazine and newspaper advertisements are more subtle, implying male superiority by photographing the men in taller

Advertisers long ago discovered the effectiveness of using women as sex objects to get the viewer's attention and to sell a product. What is the overt message of this billboard? What is the covert message? What are some other examples of ways that mass media and advertising campaigns reinforce gender stereotypes.

or otherwise dominant positions, and frequently placing women lying down on sofas or beds, or sitting on the floor. Men display competence and authority, their eyes focused on the product, while women are often portrayed as submissive and supportive, their eyes focused on the men.[39] Authoritative voiceovers for commercials are usually done by men, while women most commonly serve as housewives, mothers, or sex objects, even for computer and machine tools.[40]

Movies and television have somewhat improved their depictions of women during the 1990s. Still, the old gender stereotypes prevail in Saturday morning television programming and in many children's movies. Little boy leads, adventures, and heroism abound in such movies as *Home Alone, The Karate Kid, Rookie of the Year, Free Willy,* and *Dennis the Menace,* while clever, gutsy, and enterprising girls remain unportrayed.[41] As Susan Douglas observed,

> When mothers cling to *The Little Mermaid* as one of the few positive representations of girls, we see how far we have not come. Ariel, the little mermaid in question, is indeed brave, curious, feisty, and defiant. She stands up to her father, saves Prince Eric from drowning, and stares down great white sharks as she hunts for sunken treasure. But her waist is the diameter of a chive, and her salvation comes through her marriage—at the age of sixteen, no less—to Eric. And the sadistic, consummately evil demon in the movie is, you guessed it, an older, overweight woman with too much purple eyeshadow and eyeliner, a female octopus who craves too much power. . . .[42]

Music also influences gender perceptions and attitudes. Despite the positive inspiration for women provided by such artists as Mary Chapin-Carpenter, Tracy Chapman, Jewel Kilcher, Queen Latifah, Natalie Merchant, and Alanis Morissette, much rap and rock music and many music videos still promote gender stereotypes of women as sex objects and little else. In *Where the Girls Are* (1994), Susan Douglas discusses the impact of such music on impressionable adolescents:

> MTV . . . switched . . . under the influence of market research, to one of the most relentless showcases of misogyny in America. If MTV is still around in ten years, and if its images don't change much, my daughter will see woman after woman tied up, strapped down, or on her knees in front of some strutting male hominid, begging to service him forever. These women are either garter-belt-clad nymphomaniacs or whip-wielding, castrating bitches: they all have long, red fingernails, huge breasts, buns of steel, and no brains; they adore sunken-chested, sickly looking boys with very big guitars. Worse, they either want to be or deserve to be violated. Anyone who doesn't think such representations matter hasn't read any headlines recently recounting the hostility with which all too many adolescent boys treat girls, or their eagerness to act on such hostilities, especially when they're in groups with names like Spur Posse. [Spur Posse was a mid-1990s group of California high school boys who devised a scoring system for keeping track of how many sexual conquests they had, treating females not as people but as points in a skirt.][43]

In many ways, the media contribute to **role entrapment,** the culturally defined imperative for girls and women to be "feminine," which often prevents them from doing things they might otherwise do to achieve success and self-realization as individuals.

Sexual Harassment

Since the dominant group determines the society's official language, the words we use in every-day interaction have an important relationship to power and sexism. Historically women in the United States often felt excluded from social discourse, sometimes lacking words to describe their experiences. For example, until the mid-1970s women could not easily describe why they felt uncomfortable and belittled by the behavior of men at work. Until 1976, women kept silent, perhaps imagining the experience to be an individual, personal problem and not realizing that it was part of a larger pattern connected to their subordination and vulnerability in the occupational structure. It took a 1976 survey by *Redbook* magazine to define the extent of the problem. Of the 9,000 self-selected women who volunteered answers, 90 percent said that at some time in their work lives they had been harassed.

By 1978, Lin Farley could describe the birth of a woman-centered concept:

The phrase *sexual harassment* is the first verbal description of women's feelings about this behavior, and it unstintingly conveys a negative perception of male aggression in the workplace. With this new awareness, sociologists, psychologists and management experts are now reexamining the matrix of male-female relations in the workplace. Our understanding of men, women and work will never be the same again.[44]

Next, a larger, more scientific study by the U.S. Merit System Protection Board revealed the shocking economic costs of sexual harassment. In the two years from 1978 until 1980, harassment caused the loss of $189 million in hiring, training, absenteeism, and job-turnover expenses. This estimate covered the federal government alone; the enormous additional costs in state and municipal governments and the private sector no doubt extended into the billions.[45] The personal costs were also severe. Using the same federal government survey, researchers conservatively estimated that 1 percent—or about 9,000 women—had been victims of attempted rape by supervisors or co-workers.

Motivations and the Context of Harassment

Sexual harassment is a power play committed by bosses against underlings, by professors against students, by more secure colleagues against weaker peers. Men do this, and more rarely so do women, but the powerless don't do it to the person in charge. Jarring this conventional wisdom, however, was a 1993 study in the *New England Journal of Medicine* reporting that 77 percent of the women doctors surveyed had been sexually harassed by their own (mostly male) patients, usually in their own offices. The reason, the researchers concluded, was that "Female doctors are treated primarily as women, not as physicians, by many of their male patients. The vulnerability inherent in their sex . . . override[s] their power as doctors."[46]

This finding reflects the fundamental underpinning of sexual harassment, which is the sexist stereotyping of women as sex objects. Typical excuses or cover-ups are that it was "only fun" or flattering to the woman; that such attention is only forced on women who "ask for it"; and that any woman who "really wants to" should know how to handle such situations on her own.

The boundary line between harassment and nonharassment is sometimes unclear. A man may think that his sexually aggressive action is only complimentary, or a woman may misinterpret an objectively innocent gesture as threatening or suggestive.[47] Usually, however, both parties recognize sexual harassment for what it is—an action based on an assumption of entitlement to sexual privileges:

> Sexual harassment by a boss or supervisor harkens back, in a way, to the medieval practice of *droit du seigneur,* which gave the feudal lord the right to sleep the first night with the bride of any of his vassals. Although feudalism ended many centuries ago, some people still feel that to be a boss is to be at least semi-divinely ordained—to have certain inalienable rights. . . . The idea of using a paycheck as a license for sex seems ludicrous, if not sick, but it happens all the time. Men who would never think, or at least never follow through on, the idea of pinching a woman's breast in a bus or on the street, feel free to subject their secretary to this humiliation as if it were a job-given right.[48]

Interpreting Sexual Harassment

Since 1980, U.S. courts have generally based their decisions in sexual harassment cases on guidelines set by the Equal Employment Opportunity Commission (EEOC) to protect employees from conduct deemed illegal under provisions of Title VII of the 1964 Civil Rights Act. These guidelines define **sexual harassment** as

> unwelcome sexual advances, requests for sexual favors, and other verbal or physical conduct of a sexual nature . . . when submission is made a condition of employment, or rejection of the advance is used as the basis for future employment decision, or interfering with the individual's performance or creating an intimidating, hostile, or offensive working environment.

In 1991, televised hearings held by the all-male U.S. Senate Judiciary Committee on sexual harassment charges by Anita Hill against Supreme Court nominee Clarence Thomas stunned the nation. The three days of testimony by Hill and others enlightened the public about how lewd and crude remarks constitute sexual harassment. Even though the Senate thereafter confirmed the nomination of Justice Thomas, the hearings galvanized public awareness, and formal complaints filed with the EEOC charging sexual harassment nearly doubled.[49]

In 1993, the Supreme Court ruled that a complainant need not prove that the offending behavior caused severe psychological damage or impaired the complainant's ability to do his or her job. Instead, it drew from the last phrase from Title VII quoted earlier and accepted as its standard whether a reasonable person would find the atmosphere so sexually tainted by abuse that it had become too hostile for the person to continue working there. Although this decision gives lower courts more freedom to decide in favor of plaintiffs who bring charges of abuse without evidence of medical damage, the precise meaning of the term *hostile atmosphere* remains unclear.[50] Local interpretation is given too wide a scope to decide how to distinguish a **hostile environment** from offensiveness and other abuses of power in the workplace.

Throughout the 1990s, sexual harassment in the military repeatedly attracted media attention. Beginning in 1991, with the Tailhook scandal involving male U.S. Navy combat aviators molesting female officers at a convention, all branches of the military have since faced serious accusations and embarrassments. Female sexual harassment, assault, and rape complaints by recruits against platoon sergeants, by cadets against classmates, by female pilots against male pilots, and by aides against superiors (including, in 1998, the U.S. Army's top noncommissioned officer) reveal continuing serious problems in the military in gender relations. In 1997, when the Air Force drummed out a female pilot for an adulterous affair, but sought to ignore the adulterous affair of a male candidate for chairman of the Joint Chiefs of Staff, a public uproar over the "double standard" forced the candidate to withdraw his name from consideration.

Sexual harassment remains a serious problem in the workplace too. Recent surveys conducted in Great Britain and the United States revealed that from 42 to 88 percent of women workers—regardless of their type of job—experienced sexual harassment at some point in their careers.[51] The International Labour Organisation recently conducted a survey in twenty-three countries that revealed what women already know: sexual harassment is a major problem.[52] In the United States, temporary workers—a growing portion of the workforce—are particularly vulnerable to sexual harassment. When complaints arise, employers prefer to handle the matter privately through mediation to avoid public notoriety.[53] However, studies show that the most successful means of lowering sexual harassment occurrences is when employers take a visible, proactive approach.[54]

Arenas of Change

Since the 1970s, women have substantially increased their participation in education and work. As a result, social definitions of women's family and reproductive roles have changed. Despite remarkable progress in a relatively short span of time, however, problems of gender inequality remain.

Education

The 1970s saw a sizable reduction, from 16 percent to only 7 percent, in the number of colleges that were not coeducational.[55] In 1996, another all-male bastion fell, when the Supreme Court ruled that the century-old, all-male admissions policy at Virginia Military Institute (VMI) violated the constitutional right of women to equal protection under the law, and ordered the school to admit women or give up its state funding. In one of the most important sex-discrimination cases in decades, the Court sounded the death knell for gender discrimination at schools where public funds are used.[56]

Single-Sex Classrooms

Yet even as progress occurred in this area of gender integration, another controversy arose over women seeking sex-segregated classes. The 1996 Supreme Court ruling in the VMI case apparently left women's colleges unaffected because it exempted places that "promote equal employment opportunity" and "address particular economic disabilities." The controversy arose not from them, but from efforts to create single-sex classes in elementary and secondary schools. In more than a dozen states, school districts experimented with sexual segregation, in the name of school reform, to eliminate distractions and gender biases. The intent of most of these programs was to boost girls' math and science scores following a 1992 report from the American Association of University Women, which argued that girls were being shortchanged in public-school classrooms—particularly in math and science.[57]

Dozens of studies found that an all-female education had positive effects. Graduates of girls' schools and women's colleges have more self-confidence, are more successful on the job, perform disproportionately well in math and science, and are more likely to pursue careers in those fields than female graduates of coed schools.[58] Noting such findings, some educators proposed all-girl classes in subjects such as math and science in coed public schools, which legal experts argued were legal as an alternative to but not as a replacement for coeducation.[59]

Critics of gender-segregated classes worry that such classes will set back the cause of gender equity just when girls are finally being integrated into all-male academies. The gender-equity researchers involved in the AAUW report say that they intended to help improve coeducation, not to dismantle it through single-sex classrooms.[60] Interestingly, one recent study measured the presence of sexism in specific curricular areas in eighty-six classrooms in twenty-one schools divided into three types of independent secondary schools—boys' schools, girls' schools, and coeducational schools. It found the severest form of sexism in boys' schools. Although girls' schools exhibited the most gender-equity events, they also perpetuated a pernicious form of sexism: the use of academic dependence and nonrigorous instruction to achieve self-worth. Schools with policies that actively promoted gender equity in enrollment, in the hiring of faculty, and in personal relations were the least likely sites of sexism.[61]

Although research shows that single-sex schools tend to produce girls with more confidence and higher grades, other studies measuring single-sex classrooms against coed schools claim this type of education is generally no better than mixed-sex education and that any school that sets high standards and has a rigorous academic program will give young women the skills they need to succed."[62]

College Enrollment and Majors

Positive signs for women abound at the college level. As late as the 1972–1973 academic year, 59 percent of college students were men. By 1980, women constituted 51 percent of the college population; and in 2002, 56 percent. Women's percentage of all college degrees awarded rose from 44 percent in 1975 to 51 percent in 1985 to 56 percent in 2002.[63] Since women comprise 51 percent of the total population, they now account for a disproportionate number of college enrollees and degree recipients.

Another area of significant change is in major fields of study formerly considered male domains. For example, between the years 1971 and 2002, women's share of degrees earned in business and management rose from 9 percent to 50 percent. Other areas experienced comparable changes: biological sciences, 29 to 59 percent; computer science, 14 to 28 percent; engineering, 1 to 18 percent; and law, 5 to a surprising 73 percent. The traditionally female-dominated areas of education, foreign languages, and health science remain heavily segregated.[64]

The Workplace

In the civilian labor force in the United States, women are approaching parity with men in participation ratios. In 2000, 74 percent of all women worked in wage-earning jobs, compared to 87 percent of all men.[65] Marital status is no longer as important a determinant of who works: 61 percent of married women worked, while 68 percent of single women worked.[66] Nor is the presence of preschool children any longer relevant to women working. In two-parent families, 63 percent of mothers with children under age 6 worked, compared to 45 percent in 1980.[67]

Just as the once mostly male college majors have opened up, so have occupational choices. Women continue to increase their rate of entry in occupations where they were once a rarity. They now fill nearly half the positions in all managerial and professional specialty occupations, with noticeable gains among college professors, lawyers, public officials and administrators, financial managers, and personnel managers.[68] Other occupations remain **pink-collar jobs,** stereotypically identified with women and therefore heavily female. In such occupations as nurse, dietitian, speech therapist, kindergarten teacher, dental hygienist, and secretary, women represent between 86 and 98 percent of all workers in the field (see Figure 7.2).[69]

The Fast Track and the Mommy Track

Despite the growing number of occupational opportunities available, women face subtle discrimination in hiring either because employers believe the gender-role stereotype that men are better at jobs requiring technical or managerial skills or because they worry that the woman's familial obligations will interfere with productivity and that the company will incur additional expenses for maternity leaves.[70] Certainly, women tend to assume more familial obligations than men in household tasks, child-rearing responsibilities, and ministering to sick relatives.[71]

Women in the United States face a difficult choice. The corporate **fast track**—which entails commitment to the management team to earn promotions over other candidates—requires 60-hour-plus work weeks, frequent travel, and weekend meetings, and occasionally presents the manager with "drop-everything" crises to resolve. To meet such demands, some women delay child-bearing or forgo motherhood entirely. Choosing motherhood usually forces women to lower their occupational goals and delay, if not eliminate, further promotions. Soon, women with children fall behind childless women in earnings, as the latter group passes them by up the corporate ladder. Women thus risk their career mobility by having children. Many women who took time off or cut back on their hours to raise their children have found it difficult to get back onto the corporate fast track later.[72]

Most women—particularly in their thirties—opt for the **mommy track**. Those trying to juggle both family and work require reliable childcare. Since most companies do not have on-site day-care centers, this need gets fulfilled through a relative or neighbor, or else through some nearby childcare center. Often, the cost of childcare is a major reason why women quit their jobs.[73]

Figure 7.2 Detailed Occupation Groups of the Employed Civilian Population by Sex: March 2000

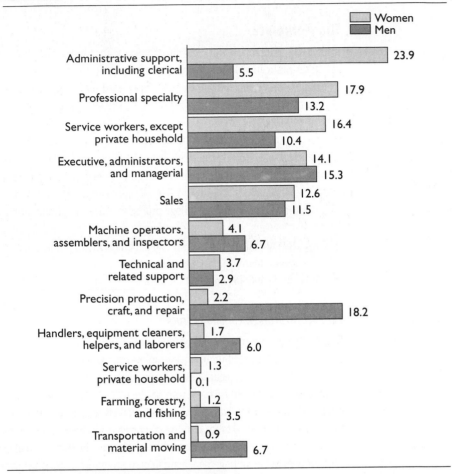

Source: U.S. Census Bureau, Current Population Survey, March 2000.

In addition, when women return home, they face a "second shift" of work in food shopping, cooking, cleaning, and childcare tasks. Their workload on the homefront consumes about twenty-six hours a week, compared to about seven hours a week for men on such chores as home repairs, yard work, and taking out the garbage.[74] The burden on working women is thus much heavier than on working men. As Arlie Hochschild puts it, "In the last forty years, many women have made a historic shift, into the economy. Now it is time for a whole generation of men to make a second historic shift—into work at home."[75]

The Glass Ceiling

For years feminists and social observers have spoken of a **glass ceiling**—a barrier preventing women from rising above middle management ranks—enforced by an "old-boy network"

One result of both the feminist movement and affirmative action has been the entry of women into top-level management positions, as typified by Carly Fiorina, CEO of Hewlett-Packard, shown here at a news conference introducing her company's new products. Is her position unique, or is she one of many female CEOs? Does the glass ceiling still exist? If so, what obstacles do women still face in climbing the corporate ladder?

among men at the highest corporate levels who support young men on their way up and exclude women. Critics blame a combination of tradition, gender stereotyping, and uneasiness about interacting with ambitious women for perpetuating this corporate-denied barrier.[76]

A 1995 report from the Glass Ceiling Commission, a bipartisan panel created by Congress, concluded that women remain blocked from top management positions (defined as those of vice president and above). Some small progress has occurred; the percentage of women among the United States' top executives rose from 8.7 percent in 1995 to 12.5 percent in 2000.[77] Despite constituting only 29 percent of the workforce, White men, however, hold 95 percent of senior management positions in industries across the nation. Women have had greater success in moving into the ranks of middle management (assistant vice presidents, office managers, and so on): White women hold close to 40 percent of those jobs, and African-American women about 5 percent. In contrast, African-American men fill about 4 percent of middle management positions.[78]

Some management consultant firms reject the pessimistic picture of the corporate woman banging her head against a glass ceiling. They note that, on average, corporate presidents took twenty-five years to reach the position of president and thirty years for CEO. Women have only been participating in the corporate workplace in large numbers for just about that length of time. A study of the ranks of most major companies below the top twenty people found that half of the managers at the next-highest level were female. Experts predict that over the next few years, these women—the first to have had unbroken, full-time management-track careers with twenty-five to thirty years of experience—will begin breaking through to the top positions. According to the nation's leading corporate consultants, many companies view the CEO's gender as a non-issue; competence is the issue.[79] The next few years will show which reading of the current situation is correct.

One frequently quoted statistic is the imbalance in comparative earnings of women and men. In 2002, women earned seventy-eight cents for every dollar that men earned, an all time high.[80] This ratio requires careful interpretation, however. Because it is an average, it includes many variables—education, skills, seniority, and continuous years on the job, among others. Many working women have low-paying jobs, not necessarily because they are women but because they lack the background of men for higher-paying jobs. What these figures generally do *not* mean is that employers cheat women by hiring them at three-fourths what they would pay a man. Essentially, the jobs pay the same salary, whether a man or a woman fills it. The primary reason for the average income differential between men and women is their differing qualifications and consequent job opportunities.

Political Representation

One of the most startling discrepancies between gender egalitarian expectations and actual results is in the limited number of women who hold positions of political power. Women outnumber men in total population, in registered voters, and in actual voters.[81] Yet among national office holders, women made up just 14 percent of the 108th Congress (2003–2005)—an all-time high. The numbers include 59 women members of the House of Representatives (out of 435) and 14 women Senators (out of 100).[82] In contrast, in 2000 women made up between 36 and 45 percent of the national legislators in Denmark, Finland, the Netherlands, Norway, and Sweden. Of 125 countries examined, the United States ranked fifty-ninth. The global average for women elected officials is 15 percent.[83]

In the United States, though women remain underrepresented in local, county, and state offices, they have made great strides forward in the past twenty years. Of the nearly 500,000 local and county elected offices in the nation, women hold 20 percent. About 22 percent of all state legislators are women, compared to 5 percent two decades earlier.[84]

Although the growing presence of women in political office increases the likelihood that female perspectives and interests will be heard in the formulation and implementation of social policies, women do not constitute a monolithic entity. Instead, women possess varied political ideologies—ranging from strict conservatism to ultra-liberalism—as well as different racial, social class, and ethnoreligious and regional backgrounds.

The Social Construction of Maleness

In social science research and in the public mind, males are no longer assumed to be "naturally" competitive or dominant or even sexist. Instead, we look to nonbiological sources for the origins and detrimental effects of stereotypically male behavior. The following discussion briefly examines three related findings: the development of aggression, racism, and sexism in "the dirty play of little boys"; men's inability to make emotional commitments; and men's confusions and anxieties when facing fatherhood (once viewed as the most naturally male of all behaviors).

"The Dirty Play of Little Boys," an observational study of Little League baseball teams, led Gary Fine to conclude that preadolescent boys were awful.[85] Their actions were unacceptable to just about anyone in the middle-class White society in which they were raised. Three types of behavior dominated interaction:

1. Aggressive pranks played on each other, especially any group member who was different, and violent behavior taken against outsiders.
2. Constant use of racist insults and ethnic slurs.
3. Sexual talk in which it was acceptable to admit sexual interest in a girl, but forbidden to like one.

Studying preadolescent development could reveal how negative stereotypes are reinforced. The need to develop personal status by differentiating their group from others leads boys to treat outsiders very roughly. However, these attitudes do not arise spontaneously. Mimicry of adult society is often a motivation for dirty play, but the behavior of preadolescent boys usually exaggerates and glorifies behaviors that even their parents regret passing along.

Inability to commit to relationships is a result of today's men living on "historically peculiar terrain where one of the main problems they face is that of being male."[86] Their commitments—to family, women, and work—have become ambiguous, and they do not yet understand the new goal of developing intimacy with an equal. Many men feel that this amounts to putting themselves under the control of a woman. When asked to explain their feelings and their actions, men feel that they are being held accountable; and the only model they have to understand accountability is in the context of work, where it means to be reporting to—and thus to be "working for"—someone.

But the main problem is **male anomie,** a lack of defining rules. Men no longer know where they fall on the wimp-macho scale. Baffled by this normlessness, men flee into compulsive work or sports, where the rules are more clearly defined.

The double-bind of fatherhood occurs when society increasingly expects men to be involved in pregnancy and birth, but gives them no way of handling the emotions those events inevitably arouse. Traditional men stayed out of the way, and examples from popular culture portrayed the expectant father who did try to help as a buffoon who got in the way and had to be calmed by his wife. Gender equality has raised expectations that birth should be a shared experience, but the man still cannot voice fears or confusions. Ironically, this gap in the rules has in some cases led to resurrection of traditional roles: men become the director or coach of the birthing drama, and women become the obedient subordinate. This is simply a new form of dominant role playing, not sharing or open intimacy.[87]

These three examples illustrate an entirely new phenomenon in human history: maleness as a subject of concern and scientific study. For millennia, maleness has been considered a privilege, and privileged people tend to think they naturally deserve their advantages; hence they rarely do studies to find out why they are "special." Like other class and ethnic privileges, maleness was taken for granted. Changing this attitude may be the most important arena of change in the struggle to overcome sexism.

Sociological Perspectives

As you might expect, the Feminist perspective on gender inequality is particularly important. In addition, however, the Functionalist, Conflict, and Interactionist approaches offer valuable insights.

The Functionalist Viewpoint

Functionalist sociologists see essential family needs as forming the basis of gender roles. For hundreds of generations human families needed both a long-term caretaker for the dependent children and a provider sufficiently mobile to hunt, gather, and fight far afield. In most societies gender divides these roles, and the persistence of this division of labor seems to argue for its naturalness.

Conditions changed, however, in the twentieth century. Prior to it, women had children throughout their fertile years and had an expected life span of forty-five years. In a modern industrialized society, women typically have two children within a five-year period during their twenties, and go on to live, on average, a total of seventy-nine years. Men no longer are warriors, and most do not use muscles or perceptual skills requiring special long-term training, as was once essential for the old hunter role.

Early Functionalists concentrated on the disruptions caused by these changes. They compared contemporaneous confusions with the supposedly stable past and worried about how functions fulfilled by traditional roles might be overlooked in a structure that incorporated more equal sex roles.

As late as the 1950s, an adapted form of Functionalism retained the view that basic role differentiation was necessary. The new arena had broadened beyond child-rearing and hunting, but the roles required were similar. Talcott Parsons suggested that every social group, particularly the family, still needed specialists to perform two functions:[88] an **instrumental leader** to guide decision making and task completion, and an **expressive leader** to hold the group together and guide emotions. Males usually fulfilled the instrumental role, and females the expressive. However, recent studies of interaction patterns in problem-solving groups found that, when these roles exist, they usually relate to the power structure rather than gender. That is, "the boss" is usually instrumental, making decisions and controlling interaction.

The Functionalist viewpoint offers a plausible picture of how early gender roles may have developed. But our complex society demands answers to questions the Functionalists do not address. Why do so many persons feel unfulfilled by their traditionally prescribed roles? Is child-rearing really a woman's function? Few contemporary sociologists would agree. They have moved on to questions such as, "Can a society that erects barriers to the full economic participation of half its members really be functional?"

The Conflict Viewpoint

Social scientists' assumptions, like everyone else's, can be biased. Most macrosocial theories assume that the family is the basic unit of social structure. Even in a time when traditional families represent a shrinking minority of all families, people tend to judge the social status of the family by the status of the main wage earner—the "head of the household." To Conflict theorists, gender inequality flows out of economic inequality. When men, whether in past or present societies, make a great economic contribution to the family, their status, power, and prestige rise accordingly. Logically then, if women increase their economic contribution to the family, gender inequality should lessen.[89]

Conflict theorists also examine the role of sexism, drawing from the Marxian concept of **false consciousness** (a subjective understanding of one's situation that does not correspond to the objective facts). Sexist ideology about women's emotionalism and inferiority justifies excluding them from positions of leadership and power, denying them other opportunities, subordinating them at home and in the workplace, paying them less, and subjecting them to manipulation and abuse (see international examples in the box on the next page).

Women as Property

The Conflict-oriented Realpolitik view demonstrates how women's lower status benefits men and supports the capitalist consumer economy.[90] Traditional sex roles are nothing but ideological justifications of men's power. Men see women as private property and encourage them to sell themselves on the marriage market and to concentrate on preparing for this sale by becoming attractive commodities in competition with other women.[91] Their long history in a subordinate status makes women more sensitive to the behavior of others. They do not inherently seek to please others more than men do, but they have had to learn indirect manipulation because men denied them equal or direct power. Unless actively counteracted, this system will continue as long as men continue to profit from it.[92] (See the Globalization box on the next page.)

Sexist Consumerism

Today, advertising attempts to prevent women's social position from changing, as it has since the early 1800s when industrialization created the first excess wealth and the need to find new markets to reabsorb the new products. Advertising encourages women—in their role as homemakers—to become voracious consumers and obsessive maintainers of spotless, well-furnished households. To accomplish this, advertising manipulates a woman's anxiety, seeking to convince her that this area of home life is entirely her responsibility. The comment of Gloria Steinem, editor of *Ms.* magazine, about a once-common detergent TV commercial highlights the ridiculous extent of this creation and manipulation of guilt. She wished that, just once, when the "ring around the collar" commercial came to the moment of discovery of the inculpatory dirt, the wife would turn to her husband and say, "Wash your neck," instead of cringing.

Christopher Lasch has provided a devastating analysis of the advertising industry's motivation in supposedly promoting women's liberation. He says that the need for even more consumption

The Globalization of Social Problems

Gender, Malnutrition, and Death

Gender inequality takes a horrendous turn in many developing countries, where women have lower survival rates, partly because of poverty and gender-biased cultural values. Shortened life expectancies for females, for example, result from differences in feeding girls and boys, as well as in the strong preference for sons in some countries. People in a few regions put a low value on women's lives, viewing them as disposable property, even to the point of killing them.

The World Health Organization (www.who.int/inf-fs/en/fact251.html) reported that women endure a disproportionate share of the burden of poverty, comprising 70 percent of the world's 1.2 billion poor people. The problem appears to be getting worse, as the numbers of poor rural women in forty-one developing countries increased about 17 percent more than the numbers of poor men. The poverty impacts negatively on their health. Half a million women die unnecessarily from pregnancy-related complications each year, the causes exacerbated by issues of poverty and remoteness. In Mozambique one in seven women die from pregnancy or childbirth complications because of inadequate health services, illegal abortions, and early pregnancies (often at age ten or eleven).

The death rate for females, Nancy E. Riley reported for the Population Reference Bureau (www.prb.org/pubs/population_bulletin/bu52-1/part3.htm), is much higher than for males in rural Bangladesh. Male preferential treatment explains this. By tradition, men and boys eat first, often leaving insufficient food for female family members. Girls thus get less protein, less food, and are undernourished. Also, although both boys and girls contract serious diseases at about the same rate, parents take their sons to the free health clinics more often than their daughters.

Elsewhere, the lower value and status of women compared to men affects their different survival rates.

In developed countries, girls and boys have similar survival rates through age five. However, in Algeria, Bangladesh, Egypt, Grenada, Guatemala, Jamaica, the Maldives, Pakistan, and Singapore, the death rates are much higher for girls than boys due to undernourishment and poorer health care.

Dramatic differences in birth statistics in several Asian countries reflect their cultural preferences for sons, although the average male-female birth ratio in any society is typically 106 boys for every 100 girls. In the 1990s the average sex ratio was 112 boys in India, 114 in Korea, and 118 in China. In China alone, this imbalanced sex ratio means that over a half-million infant girls are "missing" from the 1990s. Madhu Gurung reports that India tops the list in illegal abortions and female infanticide (www.hsph.harvard.edu/grhf/SAsia/forums/foeticide/articles/foeticide.html). Of the 15 million illegal abortions worldwide yearly, India accounts for 4 million, 90 percent of which were intended to eliminate the girl child. According to the UNICEF, 40 to 50 million girls have gone "missing" in India since 1901—missing because they were not allowed to be born, or if born, murdered immediately thereafter.

Even more disgusting are the bride burnings in India. From its traditional origin of the bride's family paying the husband a dowry as part of the wedding contract, as a gift and a form of female inheritance, the dowry evolved into a purely commercial transaction (and a cause among poor families for the selected abortion of female fetuses). Since the late 1970s, an epidemic of deaths among new brides has occurred, supposedly as a result of carelessness with cooking fires. In reality, the deaths mostly result from the bride's family's failure to comply with the dowry demands of the husband's family, prompted also by the low status of women in Hindu society. Shaguant, Reddy reported in 2002 that there are an estimated

The Globalization of Social Problems (continued)

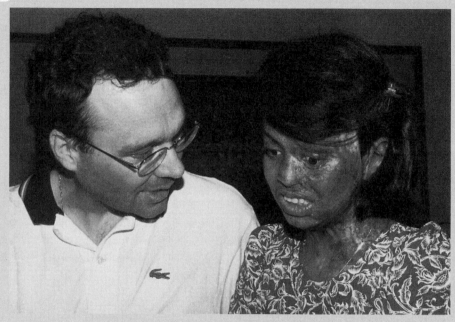

Acid burn victims, such as this young woman in Bangladesh, illustrate another vicious example of the problems of gender inequality. Usually attacked by boyfriends or husbands, the victims seek refuge at a rehabilitation center run by the Acid Survivors Foundation in Dhaka, where they await surgery, eight months of treatment, and get mentally ready to return to their villages. What are some other examples of gender inequality in the global community?

6,000–25,000 bride burnings each year in India due to disputes over dowries. (www.dfn.org/news/India/dowry.htm). Surprisingly, the rate of dowry death is higher in educated, well-to-do families, and lower among the poor, uneducated, so-called "backwards" classes.

motivated corporations to express enthusiasm for the nominal freeing of women to work for wages so that they would earn more and buy more. He added, "The logic of demand creation requires that women smoke and drink in public, move about freely, and assert their right to happiness instead of living for others . . . [thus] disguising freedom to consume as genuine autonomy."

The Interactionist Viewpoint

Interactionists see gender as a **master status**—the most important social position a person has in determining social identity and in affecting most aspects of life. For example, our earlier discussion about the sexual harassment of female doctors illustrated how their gender status superseded all their other statuses.[93] Since everyday interaction is organized around master statuses, changing biased definitions at this fundamental level can be difficult. For many people, it is easier to use consciously or unconsciously biased categories than to be uncertain about what to expect of others. Despite this problem, Interactionists emphasize that social expectations are not fixed or rigid, and that sexist definitions are products of self-other interactions. In other words, gender roles are cultural-verbal constructs that we use to understand each other. If we decide not to confirm them, however, or if we decide to use other constructs that better fit the current environment, they can and will change.

Situationality and Multiple Realities

Members of society share common master status definitions, but individuals usually see most situations through the specific subcultural definitions they learned through their own social statuses. When an Interactionist studies the sexes, the first points of focus are the differences between the social realities in which they live. Just as we now accept that many IQ tests are culturally biased because they only test knowledge of middle-class White reality, we must also accept that "male reality" is not the only reality. We will explore this point more fully in the Feminist viewpoint section.

Early Categorizations and Evaluations of Self

A person's concept of self emerges through internalization of the expectations and evaluations of others. Gender evaluations await the infant even before birth. The parents' immediate concern is the sex of the child. Studies show that new parents rate the characteristics of their newborn boys and girls differently even before they have any physical contact with them. Evaluations of "good" and "bad" depend on the child's choosing appropriately or inappropriately between "boy stuff" and "girl stuff." Girls internalize as desirable various socially approved images of themselves that—viewed outside the context of constant, indirect societal coercion—would seem to be irrationally limiting or subservient. This is not just a matter of adopting what is comfortable. Society dictates appropriate behaviors, ambitions, and even emotions; and because they start so early and are so widely accepted by those they define, these social definitions can erroneously appear to be "natural" differences.

The Consequences of Social Definitions

Although Interactionists see gender differences as being based on social definitions, they do not see them as trivial. William I. Thomas's oft-quoted theorem used a now-sexist noun for human beings, and that makes it even more socially true: "If men define situations as real, they are real in their consequences." Our definitions of the situation guide our behavior, and they can lead us down false paths to dangerous conclusions.

One example of the real costs to males of sexist gender images lies in differences in male-female longevity. Studies of male and female death rates attribute as much as 75 percent of the eight-year difference in life spans between men and women to differential socialization. Infant boys are more delicate than girls. They are more prone to some birth defects and illnesses, but we treat them as tougher than girls and sometimes withhold necessary protections. During later socialization the inculcation of the "macho" achievement-aggression orientation makes men vulnerable to stress-related diseases. One of the most obvious dangers is smoking, long a male behavior signifying toughness, but in reality related to anxiety. The male sex role is dangerous to men's health![94]

The Feminist Viewpoint

Feminist sociology draws from the Interactionist perspective in focusing on the social creation of gender and on the resulting social expectations. Although biology plays an important role in our lives, even affecting some personality and behavioral differences between men and women, this fact does not make one sex superior to the other, nor does it justify distributing society's resources and rewards unequally on the basis of gender.

Multiple Viewpoints

Feminist theorists adopt an advocacy position and seek to overcome sexist theorizing and research that distort reality. As yet, however, no unified Feminist theory exists in sociology. Feminism no longer accepts the idea of there being a single truth for all women, but it does embrace the concerted struggle for women's rights.[95] In fact, challenges to hegemonic White, heterosexual, affluent Feminism from Black women, lesbians, and working-class women have resulted in complex feminist endeavors and problematics within the movement.[96]

   Black Feminist bell hooks introduced an academic theoretical perspective by stating that the converging factors of race, class, and gender must be considered equally, for they emerge in combination as "immutable facets of human identity."[97] She explained that "racism is fundamentally a feminist issue because it is so interconnected with sexist oppression."[98] In light of the interlocking nature of all oppressions, she asserted, it is futile to argue about which oppression is primary. Instead, it is more fruitful to determine the links among oppressive systems and to understand their interactions.[99]

Feminist Standpoint Theory

An individual's standpoint—or social position in society—includes a level of awareness that brings certain features of reality into prominence and obscures others. **Standpoint theory** begins with the idea that the less powerful members of society experience a different reality as a result of their oppression. To survive, subordinate people must be dually sensitive: to the dominant perspective of society, and to their own perspective. As a result, members of subordinate groups have the potential to develop a broader view of social reality, employing multiple perspectives. This broader view, however, in no way negates the serious and debilitating consequences of oppression. On the contrary, members of oppressed groups must develop the view as a survival skill to cope with oppression.[100]

Murray Forman suggests that by grounding theory in the empirical daily routine and recognizing that informal interactions give people a sense of place and identity in society, we expose the taken for granted as a force shaping both individuals and communities. Furthermore, by working toward critically formulating a distinctive perspective on reality, advocates of standpoint theory may make the institutional mechanisms of patriarchal inequity and the social oppression of women more recognizable and, in turn, easier to confront.[101]

Mary Swigonski comments that, since life experience structures a person's understanding of life, research must begin from concrete experience, rather than abstract concepts. Otherwise, she says, we begin our analysis from an incorrect position:

> The life experiences of members of marginalized groups have been erroneously devalued as starting points for scientific research and as generators of evidence for or against knowledge claims. Beginning from life experiences grounded in cultural diversity can decrease the partialities and distortions in the picture of nature and social life. For example, beginning research from the lives of women has made visible issues such as childbirth, housework, wife abuse, incest, rape, sexual harassment, pornography, and prostitution. These concerns are simply not visible from the life experiences of most men.[102]

Nancy Hartsock suggests locating women's "standpoint" within historical materialism, since "each division of labour can be expected to have consequences for knowledge."[103] She says that focusing on the sexual division of labor and the resulting material conditions may reveal facets of experience that these conditions simultaneously obscure and reveal:

> Like the experience of the proletariat, women's experience and activity as a dominated group contain both negative and positive aspects. A feminist standpoint picks out and amplifies the liberatory possibilities contained in that experience.[104]

Feminists believe that standpoint theory allows new questions to be asked and new things to be learned about nature and social relations, not from the lives of those who control the ruling apparatus, but from the lives of those at the margin. This research approach furnishes a means to identify and control both individual and sociocultural assumptions and biases, thereby strengthening objectivity. With no group's insights excluded, each contributes distinctive knowledge emerging from its particular social situation and social structure. Furthermore, this theory insists that members of each group work to understand the standpoint of others, to construct views of our shared reality that are more impartial.[105]

◢◣ Thinking About the Future

In the past three decades the United States has taken great strides toward gender equality. Many people now recognize the inadequacy, waste, and unfairness inherent in the traditional male and female roles. Such roles are no longer accepted as the "natural order"; and evidence from surveys of sex-role attitudes indicates that men as well as women have substantially increased their acceptance of women in nontraditional roles. In fact, by 1978 men's attitudes on this subject resembled women's.[106] Technological changes have contributed to making sex-role changes seem necessary and inevitable.

The remaining questions are, "How long and how difficult will the period of transition be?" The political confrontation has not yet occurred in the legislatures or the boardrooms. Women account for the majority of voters, but most politicians are still men, and it is unclear how long this imbalance will persist. Women are forming networks to help each other secure jobs and powerful positions; these are called **new woman networks,** after the model of the "old boy" networks that for generations were so effective in placing the alumni of men's private schools into powerful positions. What happens when these networks collide?

One more element clouds the future: how entrenched are the male-macho individual-achievement-oriented competitive values that define the U.S. version of success? Will women bring or create a more rational, cooperative, humane, and moderate approach that eases the pressure and helps integrate work into life? Or will there be a long period during which everyone uses the old success values and gender equality simply accelerates competition?

Our society has not fully acknowledged the links between gender inequality and the many forms of impoverishment suffered by women. This is another example of the interconnectivity we discussed in Chapter 1. Poverty, particularly for women, is more than income deficiency. Women continue to lag behind men in control over the means of production such as cash, credit, and collateral: but they are also disadvantaged by other forms of impoverishment in areas such as literacy, education, skills, employment opportunities, mobility, political representation, and pressures on their available time and energy linked to role responsibilities. These factors diminish their human development capacity and affect their health status both directly and indirectly. For these reasons, women are often poorer relative to men of the same social group, both in the United States and in most other nations. This is a wide range of problem areas to address. Where do we begin? What social policies or program initiatives do you recommend?

No less important is discrimination against people for their sexual orientation. No constitutional amendment protects citizens against an infringement of their civil rights resulting from their sexual preference. Although the federal government and major corporations no longer ban homosexual employees, job discrimination—including promotions—remains a problem. Can we reduce the inequalities based on sexual preference? Many states and organizations oppose reversal of sodomy laws and legal recognition of same-sex marriages on moral grounds. They argue that to allow homosexuality, which undermines societal mores, to go unchallenged and unpunished could in time undermine other societal pillars regarding monogamous marital sex.[107] Others assert that the constitutional principles of equality protect gay men and lesbians just as they do all other minorities.[108] What do you think? Does it matter whether homosexuality is a matter of choice or biologically predetermined? Is society threatened if we do something or if we do nothing? Does the problem have a solution, or are the proposed solutions a bigger problem?

SUMMARY

1. Religious history and sacred books contain pejorative definitions of women's inherent abilities and moral capacities. The Protestant clergy in America joined in the "feminization" of

religion and, thereby, the further segregation of social life into the "women's world" of art, culture, and religion, and the "men's world" of power, money, and decision making.

2. Homosexuality existed in ancient civilizations without sanctions and was institutionalized among ancient Greeks as a natural expression of sexual instinct. During the Middle Ages and Renaissance, European society viewed homosexuality and heterosexual sodomy as sinful and criminal, with the guilty often executed. Twentieth-century social scientists changed from viewing homosexuality as a mental illness and social problem to emphasizing instead the discrimination against homosexuals as the social problem.

3. Many early social scientists thought women were biologically inferior to men. Research suggests that biological differences generate differing personality and behavioral patterns in males and females. Biological differences, however, explain general tendencies, not specific behavior patterns. Biology cannot explain the wide range of differences within each gender, nor the many cultural variations in male and female behavior.

4. A 1994 U.S. study identified 3 percent of males and 1 percent of females as active homosexuals. Although the public has grown more tolerant to sexual difference than in the past, and although antidiscrimination laws now exist, many of Americans still consider homosexuality as immoral; and only 60 percent approve of recognizing "legal partnerships" for homosexuals; and only 47 percent support the idea of allowing gays to adopt children.

5. The socialization of sexist gender roles starts so early and is supported by such a consistent and integrated structure of values, norms, and ideologies that people imagine that gender roles are natural instead of social. Both family and media play critical roles in gender socialization.

6. Pervasive in all countries is sexual harassment, an exploitation of women's gender identity. The 1991 Anita Hill–Clarence Thomas hearings made Americans more aware of the subject, and a 1993 Supreme Court ruling affirmed that the existence of a hostile environment provided sufficient grounds for legal redress.

7. Arenas of change toward gender equality include education, where controversy swirls over the implementation of single-sex classrooms. More women than men attend and graduate from college, and they major in a wider variety of fields than in previous decades. In the workplace, women face a difficult choice of the fast track or the mommy track. Some observers argue that the existence of a metaphorical glass ceiling prevents women from reaching senior management positions; others reject this claim, saying that women are now poised to move into such slots, after having put in the requisite twenty-five to thirty years of corporate service. Some women work in "pink-collar" jobs, ones identified as "female." Progress in the political arena has been steady but very slow. Social scientists now study maleness as a socially acquired behavior, not something natural and normal.

8. Functionalists see a continuing division of labor as necessary but note that disruptions from technological innovation make it difficult to find a workable new family structure. Conflict theorists see the traditional family model as merely an ideology for justifying continued

male domination. Interactionists see gender role definitions as flexible and believe that social concern about their unfairness will probably cause society members to change them in everyday life. Feminists prefer standpoint theory, using concrete experiences rather than abstract concepts to understand the perceptions and experiences of subordinate groups.

KEY TERMS

Ascribed status	Limbic system
Convenience sample	Male anomie
Expressive leader	Master status
False consciousness	Mommy track
Fast track	New woman networks
Gender identity	Patriarchy
Gender inequality	Pink-collar jobs
Glass ceiling	Random sample
Heterosexism	Role entrapment
Homophobia	Sexism
Hostile environment	Sexual harassment
Instrumental leader	Standpoint theory

INTERNET RESOURCES

At this book's Web site with Allyn & Bacon, you will find numerous links pertaining to the problems related to gender inequality and heterosexism. To explore these resources, go first to the author's page (**http://www.ablongman.com/parrillo**). Next, select this edition of *Contemporary Social Problems* and then choose **Internet Readings and Exercises**. Then select **Chapter 7,** where you will find both a variety of sites to investigate and some questions that pertain to those sites.

SUGGESTED READINGS

Baca Zinn, Maxine, and Bonnie Thorton Dill (eds.). *Women of Color in American Society*. Philadelphia: Temple University Press, 1994. An anthology of articles representing the new scholarship on the intersection of race, gender, and class and its social impact.

Chauncey, George. *Gay in New York: Gender, Urban Culture, and the Making of the Gay Male World: 1890–1940*. New York: Basic Books, 1995. A well-researched look at gay life in New York City before society built the closet.

Douglas, Ann. *The Feminization of American Culture*. New York: Farrar Straus & Giroux, 1998. How American women were segregated from the "dirty" parts of life (money and power) and into domesticity, sentimentality, and "culture."

Douglas, Susan J. *Where the Girls Are: Growing Up Female with the Mass Media.* New York: Random House, 1995. Delightful, insightful autobiographical commentary on the many media influences on young girls from the 1950s to the present.

Herdt, Gilbet H. *Same Sex, Different Cultures: Gays and Lesbians Across Cultures.* Boulder, Colo.: Westview Press, 1998. A cross-cultural examination of varying customs, norms, practices, and societal responses to homosexuality.

Hochschild, Arlie. *The Second Shift: Working Parents and the Revolution at Home,* reprint ed. New York: Avon, 2003. A case study approach and discussion of the strategies, strains, successes, and failures of working couples in dividing the tasks at home.

Lorber, Judith. *Paradoxes of Gender.* New Haven, Conn.: Yale University Press, 1995. A strong, detailed argument that examines gender as a major component of the social structure, whose social institutions promote and maintain inequality.

Reskin, Barbara E., and Irene Padavic. *Women and Men at Work.* Thousand Oaks, Calif.: Pine Forge Press, 1994. A comprehensive yet concise examination of the gender and work issues raised in this chapter, including work-family choices, wages, and pink-collar jobs.

Rotundo, E. Anthony. *American Manhood.* New York: Basic Books, 1994. The history of the transformations (not to say development) of masculinity since the Civil War period.

Schacht, Stephen P., and Doris W. Ewing, (eds.) *Feminism and Men: Reconstructing Gender Relations.* New York: New York University Press, 1998. This collection of essays argues for a cooperative, not combative, approach to achieve gender equity.

Tannen, Deborah. *You Just Don't Understand: Women and Men in Conversation.* New York: Ballantine Books, 2001. A captivating book about how different perceptions of everyday events lead to miscommunication and conflict between men and women.

Walker, Alice, and Pratibha Parmar. *Warrior Marks: Female Genital Mutilation and the Sexual Blinding of Women.* Collingdale, PA: DIANE Publishing, 1998. A powerful study of female genital mutilation in Africa, Middle Eastern societies, and Europe. Its effects and the justifications given for it are complex and thought provoking.

8

Race and Ethnic Relations

Facts About Race and Ethnic Relations

- The infant mortality rate among African Americans is nearly twice that among Whites.

- Black males are seven times more likely to be homicide victims than White males.

- Latinos are the fastest growing minority group and attend the most severely segregated schools.

- The school dropout rate for Hispanic Americans is more than nearly twice that for Blacks.

- Black unemployment is higher than for other minority groups, except Native Americans.

- Asian Americans have the highest educational attainment and median family income of any racial group in the United States.

- Each year over 1.3 million illegal aliens are caught, but an estimated 275,000 newcomers escape detection.

In recent decades, the United States has made remarkable strides in advancing the ideals of equality and opportunity for minority groups. Civil rights legislation in the 1960s and subsequent federal and state actions eliminated many overt forms of discrimination, dramatically improving the quality of life for millions of racial and ethnic minority people. The changes were sufficiently encouraging to prompt Benjamin Hooks, former executive director of the National Association for the Advancement of Colored People to declare, "I do not know of anywhere else in the world where minorities have advanced as fast as they have in this nation in such a short time."[1]

Serious problems remain, however. One out of every four African Americans and Hispanic Americans live in poverty; on some reservations, poverty encompasses almost everyone in entire tribes of Native Americans. Whether in a barrio, a ghetto, a slum, or a reservation, substandard housing and economic deprivation confront too many people. Compounding the problems of **intergroup relations** are heavy immigration and growing racial diversity, triggering an anti-immigrant backlash of vocal outcries, political reaction, ethnoviolence, and bias crimes.

The Sociohistorical Context

Racial minorities were long denied the same rights and privileges enjoyed by White Americans. Not until passage of the Fifteenth Amendment in 1870 did African Americans secure the right to vote. Native Americans only gained status as U.S. citizens in 1924, and for decades (ending only in the 1950s), Asian immigrants were legally prohibited from becoming citizens. Much of American history contains unconscionable patterns of racial enslavement, exploitation, and expulsion, and innumerable instances of prejudice, discrimination, and violence. That grim racist legacy still influences present-day interaction patterns, for Americans have never fully resolved their race relations problems nor achieved any significant degree of racial integration in close, primary social relationships.

Traditionally, poor minority groups have settled in residential clusters in the nation's cities, eliciting scorn, resentment, and avoidance by native-born Americans of higher **socioeconomic status** and different backgrounds. Nineteenth-century Irish Catholics, early-twentieth-century Italians and Jews, and late-twentieth-century Blacks and Latinos have each confronted the pathologies of crime, disease, disorganization, poor education, unemployment, and violence that attend urban poverty. One key difference today is that few low-skill jobs exist in a technologically advanced society, which reduces upward mobility opportunities for those on the lowest rung of the socioeconomic ladder.

Historically, whenever groups of immigrants entered the country, the American public and some of its leaders expressed alarm over the "threat" that the newcomers supposedly presented to societal cohesiveness. Today's fears about immigrants' "clannishness," race, culture, language retention, and values and about their maintenance of **ethnic subcultures** merely repeat concerns expressed by previous generations about earlier immigrant groups. As time passes, a succeeding generation of home-grown Americans hails those groups—previously feared and reviled as a danger to the "strength and purity of the American character"—as models of industry and **assimilation,** in contrast to some newly arriving group. The pattern has repeated itself many times since the nation's founding.[2] (See the accompanying box for international examples.)

Dimensions of the Problem

Numerous interconnected problems beset U.S. racial and ethnic minorities, making solutions difficult to find. Despite billions of dollars spent on antipoverty programs and some progress, disproportionately high numbers of African Americans, Hispanic Americans, and Native Americans

The Globalization of Social Problems

International Immigration Issues

Dramatic population changes in Europe are bringing increased diversity to the continent, as well as many problems. Accustomed for generations to seeing its people emigrating, many European countries evolved into immigrant receiving areas in the late 1960s. In recent years the pace of immigration increased dramatically, as has the number of illegal aliens. This influx is mostly from people outside the European Union (EU), a new alliance created to enhance political, economic and social cooperation, including use of a single currency and a free flow of workers and tourists across national borders.

Many of these European countries have low, even negative, birth rates. In fact, in 2000, the United Nations Population Division projected that the European Union's population, which in 1995 was about 100 million larger than the United States, will be 20 million smaller by 2050. With shrinking numbers comes a declining labor force and the need—particularly in industrial countries such as France, Germany, Italy, and the United Kingdom—for foreign workers. The European Union's fifteen member countries hosted 18.1 million immigrants in 1995, 80 percent of whom came from outside the EU. Germany ranked first with 7.2 million immigrants, followed by France (3.6 million), and the United Kingdom (2.2 million).

According to government figures, there were about 1.2 million foreigners in Italy, which has a total population of around 60 million. Of the total number of immigrants in Italy, 40 percent are from Europe (two-thirds of them from eastern Europe), 30 percent are North Africans, 16 percent Asians, and 14 percent from the Americas. Italy set a quota of 63,000 for legal immigration in 2000, but reached that total by midyear. Strong opposition to raising the cap forced

the government to abandon that plan. In addition, thousands of illegal immigrants reach Italy's long coastline every year, especially in summer, and the Italian navy succeeds in stopping only a small proportion of them. The Italian government estimates that a total number of 600,000 illegal immigrants are presently in Italy.

Not unlike many immigrants in the United States, the foreign-born residents in most European countries often live in distinct territorial neighborhoods or high-rise projects, with their children concentrated in nearby neighborhood schools. Compared to native-born workers, they have higher rates of unemployment, and most who do work receive less pay. They also face increasing hostility because of local perceptions that their presence places too great a burden on the nation's health, education, and social welfare programs. Moreover, many native-born residents fear a loss of their cultural identity because of the large influx of immigrants. In many instances, this has become a case of "we need you, but we don't like it that you're here."

That attitude often erupted into violent actions against minorities, not just in war-torn Bosnia and Kosovo in the 1990s, but throughout Europe. Thousands of violent attacks and dozens of killings—some by right-wing extremists and some by so-called ordinary people, often youth—occurred, and unfortunately the ethno-violence continues. National governments have taken various steps to (1) curtail illegal entries, hate group activities, and violence; (2) punish severely the perpetrators; and (3) improve the quality of life for its newcomers and long-established national minorities, but the European countries continue to experience many of the problems surrounding immigration, nativism, and prejudice that also exist in the United States.

still remain mired in poverty. They live in increasing social isolation in regions where high dropout rates from school, chronic unemployment, crime, disproportionate numbers of infant deaths, early deaths of adults, substandard housing, social disorganization, and violence are unfortunate norms.

Two sets of statistics pointedly reveal some of the disparities in the quality of life between Black and White Americans. Blacks have an infant mortality rate of 14 per 1,000 births, as compared to 5.7 for Whites.[3] The death rate from homicides for Blacks in 2000 was 20.5 per 100,000, versus 3.3 for Whites, making their death rate six times greater. Although the Black homicide victim rate has dropped in recent years, the odds of surviving infancy and dying a peaceful death in one's old age are far less for African Americans than for White Americans.[4]

Violence is a recurring reality for many minority Americans. In most cases the victim is of the same race as the perpetrator (except for Native Americans, against whom members of other races commit 71 percent of violent crimes). Incidents of violence against minorities occur by the thousands each year, according to the U.S. Commission on Civil Rights. They include baseball-bat beatings, home or store firebombings, shootings, vandalism, and riots such as those in Miami in 1989 and in Los Angeles in 1992. In multiethnic urban communities, fractious intergroup relations sometimes ignite into violent outbursts.[5]

Minorities tend to live in segregated residential areas, but settlement patterns vary. For example, in metropolitan areas receiving large numbers of Asian and Hispanic immigrants, the segregation of Blacks declined.[6] Housing patterns are one of several areas of institutionalized discrimination that resonate among racial/ethnic minorities, as the next section will detail.

Institutional Discrimination

Among the most difficult problems in race and ethnic relations is **institutional discrimination**—differential and unequal treatment of a group or groups that thoroughly infiltrates a society's customs and institutions (economic, educational, legal, and political).

Prejudice need not drive this differential treatment. Instead it may flow from the dominant group's assumptions about the abilities and role of a minority group. Because such practices are built into the structure of a society, the discrimination is subtle, informal, and (therefore) less obvious to the society's members. Because the actions may be neither deliberate nor caused by hatred, their discriminatory effects may be difficult to recognize. It all seems so normal and "natural."

For instance, a White child growing up in the South in the first half of the twentieth century did not need to be taught prejudice against African Americans. All that was necessary was to observe the situation. Blacks could not use the same parks, playgrounds, drinking fountains, restrooms, restaurants, waiting rooms, or railroad cars. They always rode in the back of the bus, attended different schools, and usually dropped out of school early. They lived in shanties, tenements, or substandard housing on the back streets. They worked only in low-status, low-paying jobs, and police arrested them frequently for drunkenness, brawling, or more serious crimes. When that White child grew into an adult, the status of African Americans as an "inferior" group probably struck him or her as unremarkable and incontestable. Few Whites then realized that

This minority father and his children appear to be enjoying a middle-class lifestyle. What is the traditional opportunity structure for upward social mobility for members of minority groups in the United States? In what ways and to what extent do individual and institutional discrimination influence social mobility? What are the sources of risk for downward social mobility that minorities may disproportionately share with other Americans?

Separate drinking fountains for Whites and "Colored" were once common throughout the U.S. South for the first two-thirds of the twentieth century. This was but one of many examples of institutional discrimination into which new generations were born and lived. How do such practices affect children's racial attitudes? As adults, would their attitudes change if such practices end, or would their end only impact on a new generation?

the social problems involving Southern Blacks were due to patterns of discrimination outside the Black community, not to weakness within it. Elimination of the state laws that created and upheld this racially stratified society, however, reshaped attitudes, behavior, and lifestyles.

We could easily redraw the preceding capsule portrait—with certain variations—and produce a realistic account of the experience of many other minority groups in the United States, past and present. People and times may change, but the patterns continue, and the blame usually falls on the victim rather than on the social structure that shapes the situation. Such false definitions of problems prevent their solution. In an analysis of four specific areas of institutional discrimination—education, employment, housing, and justice—we will discuss these points further.

Education

From the time Thomas Jefferson first advocated mass education for an enlightened citizenry to the present, America's approach toward education has differed from that of the rest of the world. Instead of reserving a high-quality education exclusively for members of the economic and/or intellectual elite, this country seeks to provide a full education for everyone. Although the nation has never fully realized that goal, the underlying idea remains deeply ingrained in U.S. culture. Americans place great faith in education as the route to upward mobility and a better socioeconomic status than members of the previous generation enjoyed.

Despite its importance as a social institution, however, the education system provides schooling of widely variable quality to different children. Social class and cultural biases are built into the schools. Middle-class values of order, discipline, self-control, and deferred gratification place at a disadvantage lower-class children whose family environment typically encourages freer emotional expression, less self-restraint, and immediate gratification. Most schools no longer consciously try to strip away ethnic identity, as was commonly done just two generations ago; and multicultural awareness is now an important component of teacher training. However, social class biases still often lead to schools' reproducing class-based inequalities.[7]

Busing as a Solution

Busing was once the most utilized solution to ending segregated schools. Its purpose was to improve the quality of education and the achievement of minority youngsters, thought to be at a disadvantage because they lacked positive peer role models and a "middle-class" school environment. Such considerations emerged from an extensive 1966 study, led by sociologist James S. Coleman, that gathered data on approximately 4,000 schools, 570,000 students, and 60,000 teachers.[8] The report's surprising conclusion, defying conventional wisdom, was that social class backgrounds, not differences in school or teacher resources, caused racial differences in educational achievement.

The Coleman Report implied that integrating lower-class minority students into middle-class majority schools would result in higher achievement for them without any negative impact on majority student achievement. This report profoundly influenced educational policy and provided the stimulus for desegregation through busing. Ever since the 1954 Supreme Court ruling in

Brown v. Board of Education of Topeka, Kansas, struck down the dual system of so-called separate-but-equal segregated schools, the courts and local, state, and federal governments have attempted—and failed—to end racially segregated schools. Today, almost one-third of all African American and Hispanic American students attend schools where racial minority students account for 90 percent or more of the student body. Since 1986, a high proportion of African American students have attended schools increasingly more segregated. Southern schools, once desegregating at a faster pace than elsewhere, rapidly resegregated in the 1990s. Latinos, the fastest growing minority group, attend the most severely segregated schools.[9]

Residential Patterning

Residential patterning helps explain the tenacity of school segregation. Many Whites moved from cities into the suburbs, leaving large concentrations of Blacks and Hispanics in steadily increasing, urban neighborhood clusters. By 2002, the minority share of central-city populations was 50 percent. Even among Blacks who move to the suburbs, the racial clustering continues, as Whites move farther away from cities, causing the inner suburbs to turn increasingly Black.[10] Racial segregation alone does not necessarily translate into poor schooling, however. For the suburban middle class, this is not a problem; and for lower-class urbanites, parental involvement and the positive climate fostered in urban parochial schools can overcome the social class negatives uncovered in the Coleman Report.[11]

Middle-class Blacks and Whites, driven by fear of drugs and violence in city streets and classrooms, seek the relative security of private schools or suburbs. As a result, urban public schools become repositories of (primarily) lower-class racial minority children, and inadequate funding often weakens their segregated education further. Moreover, urban public schools—unlike newer schools in affluent suburbs—are in many cases aging, decaying, and in need of major repairs. Critics argue that a deteriorating school environment makes children less likely to learn, due to its unpleasant atmosphere and its powerful suggestion of education's unimportance, given society's neglect of the physical condition of the school.[12]

For some students, schools are an alien world, in which they feel self-conscious and inadequate. If sensitive teachers do not take corrective action, the alienation of these students leads to their dropping out. This is an especially serious problem among lower-class minority youth (see Figure 8.1 on the next page). Those who remain in school often demonstrate lower scholastic achievement than other students, partly because of environmental influences and partly because their teachers' low expectations offer little motivation to do better. Concerted efforts increased the enrollment of racial and ethnic minorities in colleges in recent years, but as Figure 8.2 indicates, Blacks and Hispanics still trail behind Whites in educational attainment.

Continuing School Segregation

Until 1971, court desegregation plans focused mostly on the South and consisted of assigning children to nearby schools ("zoning"). Then, in *Swann v. Charlotte-Mecklenburg Board of Education,* the Supreme Court ruled that busing was "a normal and accepted tool of educational policy." For twenty years, the courts insisted on the implementation of "forced busing" (as

Figure 8.1   School Dropouts by Percent, 1980 and 2000

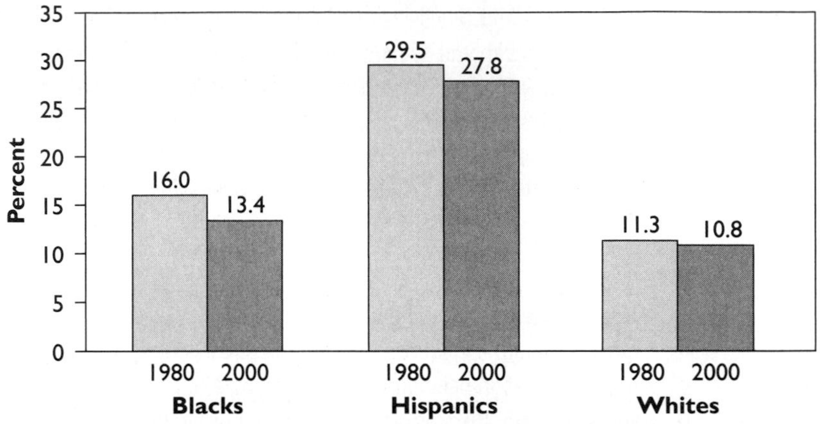

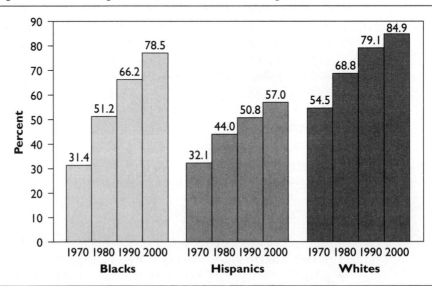

Source: U.S. Bureau of the Census.

opponents called it) in the North and West, across neighborhood school lines, in an effort to achieve racial balance. Usually minority children were the ones bused long distances to distant schools. As Charles Willie noted, in Milwaukee nine times as many Black children as White were bused to other schools, while in the Charlotte-Mecklenberg (North Carolina) district, their numbers were more nearly equal, but Black students were bused for four years, compared with two years for White students.[13]

Figure 8.2   Percentage of Adults with Four Years of High School or More

Source: U.S. Bureau of the Census.

Minority parents objected to the longer busing of their children, as angry, even violent, responses in places such as South Boston and Louisville created tensions within the newly integrated districts. In addition, White flight from affected areas undermined attempts at racial balance. Another Supreme Court ruling, *Milliken v. Bradley* (1974)—holding that desegregation efforts could not be imposed across school district lines to apply to an entire metropolitan area (in this case greater Detroit)—further encouraged White flight. In 1986, the Supreme Court allowed Norfolk, Virginia, to end busing "to stem white flight." Then in its 1991 decision in *Board of Education of Oklahoma City v. Dowell,* the Supreme Court reversed its previous position on busing as a remedy, releasing all segregated school systems from court-ordered busing-based methods of desegregation.

Research findings on the effects of busing are mixed. In desegregated schools, minority students' achievement did improve, especially if it occurred early in the children's education within a positive, multiethnic curriculum.[14] However, these positive findings relate to the consequences of desegregation and not to the means by which it is achieved. Other studies indicate that such factors as unequal socioeconomic status, widely divergent family backgrounds, racial tensions in the schools, and competitive classroom environments among academically mismatched students have worked against any significant gains.[15] Given the racial imbalance in our urban public schools, any effective busing plan would have to join inner cities and suburbs, and that simply is not politically viable in most cases.

For the past two decades, the emphasis in school reform has been away from outside desegregation efforts such as busing and toward parental choice. Two of the most popular approaches have been **charter schools** and **magnet schools**. Charter schools are autonomous public schools that, because they have some freedom from district and state regulations, can use innovative methods for teaching, spending, and hiring. However, they must meet student performance goals within a specified time, or lose their charter and be forced to close. Magnet schools are public schools with specialties in such areas as environmental science or fine and performing arts that draw students from an entire region, not just one school district, thus overcoming segregation based on residential patterning. Charlotte, Mecklenberg County, mentioned earlier, for example, changed course after the 1991 court ruling and opted for a voluntary system based on magnet schools, fulfilling the wishes of most White and some African-American parents.[16] We will discuss both charter schools and magnet schools more fully in Chapter 12 on education.

Employment

In its transformation from an industrial society to a postindustrial one, the U.S. economy moved from dominance by the manufacturing sector to dominance by the information and service sectors. Gone are many of the low-skill jobs that earlier minority workers—even those with little command of English—could fill to gain economic stability and a better quality of life. Even many entry-level jobs in the service sector require relatively strong educational backgrounds and skills such as computer literacy. Individuals who drop out of school or who newly arrive with weak educational backgrounds thus have fewer opportunities to earn a decent living. This relationship between a good education and meaningful employment explains much about statistics on income and unemployment.

The unemployment rate for African Americans, compared to the rate for Whites, has remained at about a 2:1 ratio since the 1950s. In 2001, the unemployment rates were Blacks 6.5 percent and Whites 3.1 percent; Hispanic unemployment was 5.5 percent (see Figure 8.3).[17]

The nature of a person's employment determines the level of his or her income. Not surprisingly, minority incomes lag behind White income. As shown in Table 8.1, median Black family income as a percentage of median White family income is at its highest level ever, and has also lessened in the actual gap. Hispanic median family income, still higher than Black, is now less so, the result of a continuing influx of Hispanic immigrants and the higher Hispanic dropout rate. In actual dollars, the income gap is higher than ever between Whites and both Blacks and Hispanics.

Another reflection of the employment and income picture for minorities is the poverty rate (see Figure 8.4). In 1959, 55.1 percent of all African Americans lived below the poverty line; in 2002, that figure was at 23.9 percent. White poverty percentages were 18.1 in 1959 and 8.0 in 2002. The Hispanic poverty of 21.8 percent in 2002 compares favorably with 30.7 in 1994.[18]

Affirmative Action

The controversy swirling around **affirmative action** programs began in 1964 when the Civil Rights Act mandated that prospective employers demonstrate equal opportunity hiring practices. If the percentage of their minority employees was significantly lower than that in the labor force, employers had to take steps to correct the imbalance in future hirings. Similarly, if minorities were significantly underrepresented in supervisory positions, employers had to act to correct existing disparities.

Figure 8.3   Percentage of Adult Unemployment, 2000

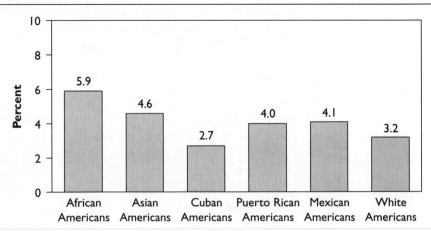

Source: U.S. Bureau of Labor Statistics.

Table 8.1 Median Income of Families

Year	White ($)	Black ($)	Hispanic ($)	Percentage of White Income Black	Percentage of White Income Hispanic	Income Gap ($) Black	Income Gap ($) Hispanic
1950	3,445	1,869	na	54.3	na	1,576	na
1960	5,835	3,233	na	55.4	na	2,602	na
1970	10,236	6,516	na	63.7	na	3,720	na
1980	21,904	12,674	14,716	57.9	67.2	8,061	7,188
1990	36,915	21,423	23,431	58.0	63.5	15,492	13,484
2000	53,256	34,192	35,054	64.2	65.8	19,064	18,202

Source: U.S. Bureau of the Census.

Conservative critics, such as Black economist Thomas Sowell, subsequently complained that the civil rights legislation was not intended to create a "numbers game" or quota system.[19] The interpretation requiring preferential treatment for certain minority groups, instead of ensuring equal rights in hiring, they argued, discriminated against White men and broke society into warring fragments. They called affirmative action unnecessary and a violation of Title VII of the 1964 Civil Rights Law, which bans preference based on race, ethnicity, gender, and religion in government and business.[20] Proponents of affirmative action insisted that such preference was necessary to create a "level playing field" to offset institutional discrimination.[21]

Earliest Court Decisions

The courts and government leaders agreed with the latter. An array of state and federal policy guidelines affected many aspects of business, education, and government practices. Federal

Figure 8.4 Percentage of Persons Below Poverty Level, 2002

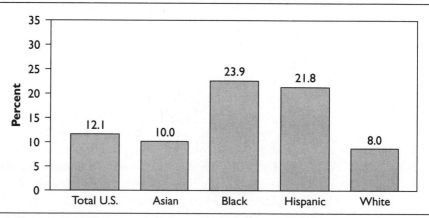

Source: U.S. Bureau of the Census.

legislation enacted in 1972 gave the courts power to enforce affirmative action standards. Preference programs became the norm in college and graduate school admissions, job hirings and promotions, and government set-aside contracts for minority-owned businesses.[22] In civil service fields, where mandated tests determined candidates' ranked eligibility for hirings and promotions, officials instituted "race norming," the use of statistical techniques to rework test scores. Either they gave minority candidates extra points, or put Black and White test takers in separate categories and then compared them by rank order rather than score. Whatever the technique, the results were the same: more minorities were hired or promoted, often ahead of Whites with higher scores.[23] Critics attacked this practice as unfair and discriminatory, and in 1991 Congress specifically banned race norming in the Civil Rights Restoration Act.

The controversy and resulting social tensions continued. Since 1989, a more conservative Supreme Court has shown growing reluctance to use "race-conscious remedies"—the practice of trying to overcome past discrimination by helping minorities—in affirmative action, school desegregation, and voting rights cases (see Table 8.2). A significant ruling came in 1995 in *Adarand Constructors v. Pena,* when the court decided that "strict scrutiny and evidence" of alleged past discrimination, not just a "general history of racial discrimination in the nation," must be provided prior to adoption of any system of preferential treatment.

The first salvo fired against affirmative action came in 1995, when the California Board of Regents banned its use in admissions, effective for professional schools in 1997 and for undergraduate freshmen entering in September 1998. Then in 1996, California voters overwhelmingly passed the California Civil Rights Initiative, which forbids the use of race, ethnicity, or gender "as a criterion for either discriminating against, or granting preferential treatment to, any individual or group," thereby dismantling state affirmative action programs. A sweeping ruling in 1996 by the U.S. 5th Circuit Court of Appeals in *Hopwood v. Texas* led the Texas Attorney General to interpret the opinion as banning affirmative action in admissions, scholarships, and outreach programs.

Without affirmative action, both California and Texas universities suffered minority enrollment drops in undergraduate and graduate enrollments in Fall, 1997. However, both states then implemented percentage plans as a viable alternative to achieve a racial ethnic balance in higher education without the stigma of set-asides and lowered admission standards. California guaranteed university admission to the top 4 percent of high school graduates, while Texas guaranteed the top 10 percent. When Florida ended its affirmative action program, it guaranteed college admission to the top 20 percent if students completed a minimum of two years of foreign language and other academic credits.

Percentage plans are not without their critics. The NAACP challenged the Florida plan in the courts. Mary Frances Berry, chairperson of the U.S. Commission on Civil Rights, called the California plan especially flawed because, unlike Texas and Florida where students are at least guaranteed a spot at the flagship university, the applicants will not be ensured admission to the campus of their choice. "As a result," she said, "the end of affirmative action in California has led to a two-tier system that keeps both Berkeley and UCLA largely free from the duty of educating Hispanic and African-American students. Those students are prevented from obtaining the educational and social benefits of attending a flagship campus, and are steered, or 'cascaded,' to lower-ranked state institutions." She added that those "less-prestigious" universities were forced to accept more

Table 8.2   Affirmative Action: Forty Years of Actions and Decisions

1964—The Civil Rights Act of 1964 established legal recourse against discrimination based on race, color, religion, sex, or national origin in public accommodations, transportation, public education, and federally assisted programs.

1972—Legislation gives the courts power to enforce affirmative action standards.

1978—In Bakke v. Regents of the University of California, the Supreme Court, by a five-to-four vote, ruled that racial quotas are illegal, but said that colleges and universities could consider race as one factor in admitting students.

1980—The court ruled that a federal public works program that set aside 10 percent of its spending for minority contractors was constitutional.

1981—The court ruled that the city of Hartford, Connecticut, could require that 15 percent of all workers on city-financed projects be women or minorities.

1987—For the first time, the Supreme Court upheld an affirmative-action plan for women, ruling that companies can give special preferences to hire and promote female employees to create a more balanced workforce.

1989—The court threw out a set-aside program in Richmond, Virginia, in which contractors on city building contracts were required to give at least 30 percent of the value of the project to firms that were at least one-half minority owned.

1990—The court upheld federal policies favoring women and minorities in granting broadcasting licenses.

1995—The court set a stricter standard on state programs or laws designed to help minorities. Only race-based preferences narrowly tailored to address identifiable past discrimination would be deemed constitutional.

1996—The court declined to hear an appeal of a 5th U.S. Circuit Court of Appeals ruling that "race itself cannot be taken into account" by the University of Texas in admitting students to its law school, which knocked down its affirmative action admissions plan.

1996—The court ordered the Virginia Military Institute to admit women or give up state funding. The decision also affected The Citadel, South Carolina's state-run military school.

1996—Californians voted to forbid any consideration of race, gender, or national origin in hiring or school admissions.

1997—The Supreme Court declined to hear a challenge to California's Proposition 209, the measure that banned race or gender from being a factor in state hiring or school admission.

1998—Washington state voters eliminated all preferential treatment based on race or gender in government hiring and school admissions.

2000—Florida ended the consideration of race in university admissions and state contracts, instead calling for more aid based on financial need.

2003—The court upheld an affirmative action program at the University of Michigan law school, but struck down the university's system that awarded extra points to minorities in its point-based admissions policy.

minority students without receiving more resources to serve them, creating an "unfortunate scenario" in which some campuses are far more diverse than others but without the means to ensure students' success.[24]

The Latest Court Decision

A major Supreme Court decision in 2002 preserved affirmative action in university admissions at the University of Michigan law school by a five-to-four vote, while at the same time striking down that university's undergraduate admissions program that used a point system based in part

Affirmative action sparks strong feelings on both sides of the issue. Here, hundreds of supporters demonstrate outside the U.S. Supreme Court in April 2003, as the court heard arguments about whether the University of Michigan's undergraduate college and law school should be allowed to use race as a factor in admissions. Is affirmative action a form of reverse discrimination or a necessary tool to end racial discrimination?

on race. In making a forceful endorsement of the role of racial diversity on campus in achieving a more equal society, the court's ruling was a broad one that applies to all admissions programs. Moreover, this ruling strengthened the solitary view of Justice Lewis Powell at the time of the Bakke decision that there was a "compelling state interest" in racial diversity. At the same time the court suggested a time limit on such programs, with Justice Sandra Day O'Connor writing in the majority opinion, "We expect that 25 years from now the use of racial preferences will no longer be necessary to further the interest approved today."[25]

Adding significance to this ruling is the fact that it also sends a strong signal to the nation's employers that they should continue their own affirmative action plans to hire more women and minorities. Perhaps demonstrating the commitment of business to affirmative action were the series of friend of the court briefs filed by sixty-five corporations (including General Motors and Microsoft) in support of the university.[26]

This ruling, however, is not the final word on affirmative action, because numerous groups still oppose it. With several Supreme Court justices about to end their careers on the bench, new challenges to a differently constituted court may result in different rulings.

Housing

Like all valued resources, high-quality housing is distributed very unequally. Not surprisingly, the worst housing is concentrated more among the poor and among minorities subject to discrimination—in short, among people who have "the least social choice." Their choice is reduced further by the steady decline in the number of low-rent housing units and the increase in the number of higher-rent housing units.

In 1998, the Center of Budget and Policy Priorities released the findings of a study that found some good news: the proportion of poor renters living in physically deficient housing fell from 22 percent in 1985 to 14 percent in 1995. However, the study also found that 55 percent of all poor renters living in physically deficient, overcrowded, or "doubled-up" housing spent at least half of their income for such housing, compared with 20 percent of renters with incomes between 100 percent and 200 percent of poverty levels. Many of these are working poor families with children, and these rents leave them with little money for other necessities.[27]

The basic economics of supply and demand help explain this situation. The loss of current low-rent units to urban gentrification and the failure to build sufficient new low-rent units has led to a shortage, which in turn has led to higher rents. By 1995, there were only 6.1 million low-rent units for the nation's 10.5 million low-income renter households, a shortage of 4.4 million units, the most severe deficiency ever recorded.[28]

Racial Segregation

As we discussed earlier, the problem of segregated schools is closely related to that of housing segregation. For the most part, American minorities remain highly concentrated—often isolated—in specific regions, neighborhoods, or blocks. Blacks and Hispanics often live in the cities, and Whites live increasingly in the suburbs. African Americans have been moving outward though, and those living in central cities dropped from about 78 percent in 1960 to about 52 percent in 2002.[29]

Yet even when minorities live in communities classified as suburbs, not all are part of the emerging Black or Hispanic middle class. Older, adjoining "suburbs" are often urban in character and may be inhabited mostly by low-income minorities. Such suburbs are typically the nation's poorest. An example is Robbins, Illinois, named by the U.S. Census Bureau as one of the nation's poorest suburbs. Founded in 1917, Robbins is the oldest all-Black community in the North. Its commercial development consists mostly of rundown liquor stores that open as early as 8 A.M., mom-and-pop convenience stores, and the underground bazaar of pimps, prostitutes, and drug dealers. The town's biggest employer is a nursing home with 105 employees. Between 1970 and 1990, Robbins lost a third of its population, and now numbers about 7,000. Over the years community leaders tried in vain to attract banks, drugstores, grocers, shopping malls, and factories. Hoping to entice health-care workers, the town built a medical clinic, but no one ever occupied the building and the town tore it down. Area bankers discouraged developers interested in building homes or opening businesses from doing so, say economists, historians, and elected officials. Area banks typically either refused to lend money for commercial projects in Robbins or redirected development to neighboring White communities.[30]

The United States displays an increasing pattern of residential segregation in which people of color are confined to the decaying urban core and adjoining older suburbs, surrounded by a ring of predominantly White, newer suburbs. With the growth of suburban office and industrial parks and shopping malls—as well as of social, cultural, and recreational facilities—fewer White suburbanites ever venture into the central cities. Racial isolation is becoming even more extreme than before.

Yesterday's Policies, Today's Problems

Today's racial housing patterns partly reflect federal legislation and policy decisions made almost fifty years ago. A serious housing crisis confronted the nation in the aftermath of World War II, caused by returning GIs, the baby boom, migration from rural areas to the cities, and the scarcity of new housing built during the Depression and war years. Passage of the Housing Act of 1949 emphasized building on vacant land, not rebuilding on already developed land (see Chapter 4). With government supporting private builders and providing low-cost mortgages to buyers, suburbia boomed, setting in motion the movement of stores, hospitals, churches, offices, industries, and other support services that soon followed. In the 1950s, the results were impressive: the housing crisis evaporated, and half of all Americans could afford to own a home.

This first instance of White flight, aided by the Federal Housing Administration's decision to approve mortgages only in neighborhoods with socially and racially homogeneous groups, created segregated urban/suburban residential patterns. Residents, realtors, bankers, and civic leaders quietly implemented this emerging value orientation in favor of preserving such homogeneous communities. In the 1960s and 1970s, towns increased the minimum lot sizes for new homes in an effort to restrict the number of families of school-age children, and thereby to control rapidly increasing school expenditures. As a result, the price of single-family houses spiraled upward, putting a first house out of reach for many renters, especially members of the working class and of minority groups.

Sometimes living in a racially segregated community is a conscious minority choice. Examples of affluent new Black suburbs attracting middle-class African Americans who prefer living and socializing within a racially homogeneous environment include Rolling Oaks near Miami; Brook Glen, Panola Mill, and Wyndham Park near Atlanta; and Black Jack, Jennings, Normandy, and University City near St. Louis. Similarly, many black residents in suburban Prince George's County, Maryland, where they make up 55 percent of the total population, live in affluent but predominantly Black communities or subdivisions.[31]

Certainly, the phenomenon of people choosing to live where they wish and finding contentment in that choice does not in itself constitute a social problem. The larger issue, though, is whether such patterns perpetuate problems in race relations by restricting interracial social interactions. What do you think?

Justice

Another form of institutionalized discrimination exists in the justice system. The blindfolded symbol of Justice holding balanced scales represents the U.S. ideal of equal treatment for all under the law. In reality, the legal system is flawed, because it is administered by human beings whose biases reflect those of the society. The police officer, acting as gatekeeper into the system; the jury members, who decide a defendant's fate; and the judge, who sentences the guilty, all attempt to be objective; but as many studies show, subjective factors influence their actions.[32]

Throughout U.S. history, minority groups at the bottom of the socioeconomic ladder have been disproportionately represented in arrests, convictions, and imprisonment. Irish, Chinese, Italians, Poles, Slovaks, Blacks, Native Americans, and Hispanics were or presently are caught in the inequality of administering justice. Like earlier minority groups, almost all members of today's minority groups are law-abiding citizens who feel as eager as dominant group members do about incarcerating criminals, since they themselves are most often the victims of street crime. They often get the chance, too, because their sizable proportion in major cities increases their likelihood of serving on juries. Nevertheless, disparities exist throughout the criminal justice system, and several reasons have been suggested as explanations for their existence:

1. The tendency of police to arrest minority group members disproportionately, even in discretionary cases

2. The tendency of judges to set high bail in cases involving minority defendants, using it punitively to detain them

3. The difficulty the poor have in paying bail, which may result in their languishing in jail for months before their trial

4. The lack of a jury of peers for minority defendants, since juries tend to be overrepresented by people of a higher social class and often of different racial and ethnic backgrounds as well

5. The poor quality of court-appointed legal defense

6. The disparities in sentences imposed on minority and dominant group members for the same crimes[33]

Inequality is glaringly evident in the racial and ethnic distributions of persons who are stopped by police, arrested, convicted, sentenced to prison, incarcerated, and executed. What explanations are offered for the disproportionate representation of minorities in the criminal justice system? What might be some solutions to the problem?

Like other social institutions, the justice system reflects the value orientations of the dominant middle class, which typically (and falsely) believes that low-income minority groups have a "characteristic" disrespect for the law. This negative stereotyping and suspicion lead to tighter surveillance, more frequent arrests, a higher rate of convictions, and the imposition of harsher punishments.[34] Even when mandated sentencing guidelines were imposed to take away the wide latitude judges had in determining the severity of punishment, studies show that Blacks and Hispanics still received longer sentences than Whites for comparable crimes.[35]

Moreover, African Americans and Hispanic Americans are disproportionately represented in prisons, just as earlier ethnic groups were. Although they constitute slightly less than 13 percent of the total U.S. population, Blacks account for 46 percent of all jail inmates. Hispanics, who make up 9 percent of the population, constitute 18 percent of all prisoners.[36] Why this disparity in the commission of violent and property crimes, as well as in arrests, convictions, and punishments, between minority group members and dominant group members? At one level, the answer may lie in the presence of bias within the criminal justice system, but this is part of a much larger problem. Given the interconnectivity of social problems, this form of institutional discrimination may be impossible to overcome until we first resolve its source problems in education and employment.

Minority Groups Today

A note of caution: within each of the following classifications of peoples of color, extensive diversity exists, due to cultural differences and economic variation among specific groups. Among the 483 officially recognized Native American cultures, for example, tribal well-being ranges from the successful Passamaquoddy, who run a multi-million-dollar commercial empire, to the destitute Rosebud Sioux, among whom unemployment stands at 90 percent. Black Americans include Caribbean and African immigrants as well as native-born African Americans; and viewed economically they comprise a growing middle class and an entrapped, impoverished lower class. Hispanic Americans encompass middle-class Cuban, Nicaraguan, and South American professionals, working-class Salvadorans and Colombians, and impoverished Puerto Ricans and Mexicans. Asian Americans comprise Chinese and Japanese businessmen and scientists, Korean entrepreneurs, Filipino health-care workers, and lower-class Indochinese laborers struggling to gain economic security. Even with such extensive intra-group diversity, however, socioeconomic disparities between White and non-White Americans offer a vivid insight into problems of race and ethnic relations.

Native Americans

Without question, Native Americans are the most disadvantaged minority group in the United States. They have the highest school dropout, unemployment, and poverty rates. Their average family income is about two-thirds the national average. Furthermore, their life expectancy on reservations, their infant mortality rates, and the adult death rates from alcoholism, diabetes, suicide, and tuberculosis are much higher than the national averages.[37]

Less than half of the 2.5 million Native Americans in the United States today live on or near their tribal lands. Most now live in urban areas, often in or near central cities. About one-third of all young adults living on reservations leave in search of better economic opportunities. According to recent federal reports, depression is a serious problem for Native American youth. The suicide rate is three times the national average. Also, teen pregnancy rates increased 15 percent in the 1990s, putting it at a recent high.[38]

About 19 percent of Native Americans are aged ten to nineteen, compared to 14 percent of the total U.S. population.[39] Fewer Native American than Black teens graduate from high school (65.6 to 76.0 percent), and fewer still graduate college (9.4 to 14.7 percent).[40] Lower educational attainment appears to result from less faith in the relevance of education to one's future, as well as feelings of alienation, despair, and frustration at a lifetime of poverty.[41]

Chronic unemployment is a serious problem on most of the 314 reservations. It presently hovers at about 37 percent nationally, with some reservations reporting over 70 percent. Those jobs that are available are mostly in the service industry with little chance of career growth.[42] Also, more Native Americans live in overcrowded housing than any other minority group. Although substantial progress has been made since 1985 in providing better housing, mostly single-family homes, one in five families lack indoor plumbing or adequate sewage facilities, permitting infectious diseases to spread more rapidly.[43]

One study of New Mexico Native Americans found their mortality rate from infectious diseases such as tuberculosis, influenza, pneumonia, kidney infection, meningitis, and parasitic diseases to be greater than the corresponding rates for other population groups.[44]

Black Americans

Among Black immigrants, Haitians experience the highest rates of unemployment and poverty. Jamaicans tend to find work in service occupations, particularly in health, while African immigrants are likely to be better educated and to enter middle-class occupations. Among native-born African Americans, two distinct worlds of reality exist. One, comprising nearly 80 percent of the Black population, consists of working- or middle-class people, who tend to earn about one-fourth less than non-Hispanic Whites with comparable educational backgrounds—a possible indicator of the persistence of racial discrimination.[45] The remainder consists of people who live in poverty. This proportion of poverty-stricken people is triple the percentage for White Americans, and that three-to-one ratio has remained fairly constant since the 1950s.

As discussed more fully in the chapters on poverty and the family, the majority of impoverished African American children and youth live in female-headed households. In 2002, 48 percent of all African American children under the age of eighteen were living in households headed by single mothers. About 35 percent of all female-headed households with children under eighteen fell below the poverty line. The usual reasons for their poverty are limited job skills and educational qualifications, which prevent them from earning enough money to get out of poverty, even if affordable day care were available for their children (see the box on the next page).

In recent decades the education gap between Blacks and Whites closed among adults aged twenty-five and older. Part of that is due to improvements in the school dropout rate. The Black dropout rate among persons sixteen to twenty-four years old declined from 16 percent in 1980

Social Constructions of Social Problems

The Debate about African-American Families

In the mid-1960s, Daniel Patrick Moynihan, then an assistant secretary of labor, ignited a firestorm by declaring that "the fundamental source of the weakness of the [Black] community" was "fatherless homes." When Moynihan, a sociologist and later a U.S. Senator from New York, made that statement, women headed one-fourth of all Black families. By 1998, a majority of Black families with children—62 percent—were headed by one parent, compared to 21 percent of White families. This expanding proportion prompted sociologist Andrew Cherlin to describe this social phenomenon as "an almost complete separation of marriage and childbearing among African Americans."

This disparity between Black and White marriage patterns was not only different before 1950, it was virtually nonexistent. However, from this remarkable similarity in the first half of the twentieth century, Black marriage rates dropped sharply in the second half. Back in the 1960s, the nation experienced the peak of the battle over civil rights. In this climate, Moynihan enraged Blacks with his comments, particularly in his describing a "tangle of pathology" capable of "perpetuating itself without assistance from the White world." Understandably, Blacks were unwilling to permit a public discussion that implied they were different, or less deserving, than Whites. The debate quickly turned bitter and polarized Black and White, liberal and conservative. White psychologist William Ryan responded to Moynihan's study as a case of "blaming the victim," which will lead to misdirected social programs. As a result, we focus on helping the "disorganized" Black family, he argued, instead of overcoming racism, or we strive to develop "better" attitudes and skills in low-income children, rather than revamping the poor quality schools they attend.

Since the 1980s, conservatives have insisted that family values and family structure are at the core of the problem. They argued that what Blacks needed were mainstream U.S. values (read: White). Basically, their position was "go to school, get a job, get married, and the family will be just fine." Firing back, sociologist William Julius Wilson, in *The Declining Significance of Race* (1978), maintained that the breakdown of the African-American family resulted from rising unemployment, not falling values. Overlooked, said the liberals, were such factors as jobs and discrimination and their impact on Black family structure. As the United States shifted from an industrial to a service base, the resulting economic dislocations and restructuring were particularly devastating to Black men, who had migrated north in vast numbers to manufacturing jobs.

Both Blacks and liberals also declare that any family structure is good as long as it is nurturing, and Black families have historically proven incredibly resilient in the face of adverse social conditions. What should be important to social observers and policymakers is the strategies by which Black families survive and endure in this context. Sociologist Andrew Billingsley (*Black Families in White America,* 1968/1988) adds that marriage *is* important in the Black community, just not the most important thing. It is thus not an imperative for Black people who can afford it.

The debate continues in the new century about family structure, values, jobs, and discrimination. Who's right? Both sides are too busy pointing the finger to find out. If the Black school dropout, unemployment, and poverty rates continue to drop as they did in much of the 1990s, perhaps we'll see a change in Black marriage patterns, as the jobs advocates suggested. What do you think?

to 10.9 percent in 2002, compared to dropout rates for Whites of 11.3 in 1980 and 7.3 in 2001. However, that Black dropout rate of 10.9 percent was the lowest ever in recorded history.[46] Still, in 2000, the Census Bureau could report that both races were comparable in the number of high school graduates with no college (35.7 percent for Blacks and 34.3 percent for Whites). However, differences remained in the category of high school graduate or more education, (79 percent Black and 89 percent White). About 17 percent of all Blacks in 2002 had a Bachelor's degree or more, while the percentage for Whites was 29 percent.[47] In 2000, about 64 percent of recent White high school graduates went on to college, up from 50 percent in 1980, while 56 percent of Blacks went on to college, up from 42 percent, in 1980, but a 6 percent drop from 1998.[48] This translates into a gap of 8 percent in 2000 compared to a gap of 8 percent in 1980.

The infant mortality rate among African Americans is nearly twice that among Whites. Surviving into one's teens, however, brings another grim reality. Although they constitute only about 13 percent of the population, African Americans account for about 45 percent of all homicide victims, especially between the ages of eighteen and twenty-four.[49] In fact, homicide is the leading cause of death among African American males, who are eight times more likely to be murdered than White males.[50]

Hispanic Americans

Hispanic Americans now constitute 13 percent of the total population. The Census Bureau says that they have now become the nation's largest minority group and that one in four Americans will be of Hispanic ancestry by 2050.[51] In our examination of social problems among the Latinos, we need not focus on Cuban Americans. Cubans today are the most affluent Hispanic group in the United States, maintaining high education and family income levels along with low rates of unemployment and poverty. In the remainder of this section, the observations refer mostly to Hispanic Americans with Puerto Rican, Mexican, and Central American roots. Keep in mind, however, that a great amount of fluctuation in socioeconomic variables exists even within these groups.

Education indicators are discouraging. The high school dropout rate in 2002 among Hispanic 16- to 24-year-olds was 27.0 percent, compared to 10.8 percent for Blacks and 7.3 percent for Whites.[52] By 2002, 16 percent of all Hispanic males aged twenty-five and older had not graduated from high school, compared to 13 percent of non-Hispanics.[53]

Hispanics fare worse than Blacks in poverty rates but exceed them in median family income. Against a White unemployment rate of 5.1 percent in 2002 and a non-White unemployment rate of 9.7 percent, the Hispanic rate was 8.1 percent. Their 21.8 percent of persons living in poverty in 2002 was higher than the 19.4 percent among non-Whites, and it was far higher than the 8.0 percent among Whites.[54]

About 53 percent of Hispanic Americans live in rented housing units, compared to 50 percent of non-Whites and 25 percent of non-Hispanic Whites.[55] Because they live mostly in residential clusters, their urban neighborhoods are similar to earlier European immigrant communities. While these provide the strength of ethnic solidarity, they also create social isolation and segregated schools, as discussed earlier.

Asian Americans

Constituting 4 percent of the U.S. population in 2002, Asian Americans may reach 9 percent by 2050, given current demographic patterns. Often referred to as a "model minority" because their educational attainment and earnings surpass all U.S. groups, including Whites, Asians appear more assimilated than other racial groups. Among adults aged twenty-five and older, 47 percent have a bachelor's degree or more, compared to 29 percent of Whites, 17 percent of Blacks, and 11 percent of Hispanics. Their work ethic and high representation in managerial and professional occupations has resulted in Asian Americans' achieving a median household income $5,000 higher than that of non-Hispanic White households, nearly double that of Black households, and one-third higher than Hispanic households.[56]

Beneath these favorable general statistics, however, lie some less positive facts. Several subgroups of Asians—Cambodians, Hmong, Laotians, and Vietnamese—are far less successful. Their median family income, especially among families with little command of English, is half that of Whites. Asians who own and operate small businesses in Black or Hispanic urban neighborhoods may encounter resentment against their presence, which sometimes escalates into interracial conflicts with community residents in the form of boycotts, vandalism, or worse. Even successful middle-class Asian Americans have difficulty gaining acceptance in suburbia, where they frequently remain socially segregated from and ostracized by other Americans.[57]

Part of the aversion to Asians experienced by some African Americans, Hispanic Americans, and White Americans may result from racism and/or Western and non-Western cultural differentiation. Another component could be the ethnic ingroup solidarity Asians display in the midst of a Black or White community. Racial and ethnic minority groups have always tended to be "clannish," finding comfort in interacting with their own people. However, they usually did so within their own territorial ethnic neighborhoods. Middle-class Asians bring a heretofore unknown ethnicity either as residents in previously homogeneous suburbia or as storeowners to urban ethnic neighborhoods, where it often provokes ethnocentric reactions.

High success rates among Asian Americans sometimes trigger envious negative responses. Poorer urban minorities may begrudge Asian economic achievement within their home territories. Non-Asian suburbanites may react adversely to what they perceive as the disproportionately many scholarships and other awards won by Asian Americans, thanks to the students' work ethic. Some universities have begun discriminating against Asian American college applicants to prevent their "overrepresentation" in the student population.

White Americans

Just as enormous diversity exists within the previously discussed categories of Native, African, Hispanic, and Asian Americans, so, too, does it lie within the White racial grouping. Within this category is "homogenized" Americans, those whose immigrant ancestors trace back so many generations that their ethnicity is so distilled or nonexistent that it is not visible in their everyday lives. Others are European Americans, those of mixed ancestry who are usually more keenly aware of their heritage than homogenized Americans, but for whom also ethnicity is not an active part of their daily lives. Still others are White ethnics, usually second- or third-generation Americans, often with older, immigrant relatives with memories of past discrimination against them, and whose ethnicity induces some elements of it in the newer generations. Yet others are immigrants, perhaps part of the 1.5 million Europeans who came since 1991 to put down roots in their adopted country. For them and other immigrants, ethnicity is an everyday reality in their efforts to acculturate and find economic security.

Economic well-being and social class status are important components of White society, as they are for all minority groups. White American standing does not in itself guarantee power or affluence, as indicated by the 23.5 million Whites living in poverty in 2002. Poor Whites—some derisively called "hillbillies," "rednecks," or "White trash"—often live in rural or mountainous regions and clearly live on the fringes of society despite their typical Anglo-Saxon Protestant backgrounds. For them, poverty, illiteracy, poor diet, and health problems are everyday realities. Other poor Whites and many White ethnics are either working poor, blue-collar, or working-class people. Stereotypes about "angry white males" reacting against diversity initiatives are usually portrayals of White ethnics or rednecks.

Ethnicity and social class are heavily intertwined, and for many Whites this is as true today as it is for people of color. Ethnic pride is an important element among these groups, as politicians know well. From the social class perspective, poverty and all its related problems affect a sizable proportion of White America as they do numerous minority groups. When it comes to these social problems, we are truly a color-free society.

Illegal Aliens

Although undocumented aliens come to the United States from about a hundred countries, most are from Mexico, where a rapidly growing population (from 101 million in 2002 to a projected 139 million by 2030) and economic deprivation impel many to seek better opportunities here. U.S. Immigration and Naturalization Service (INS) agents apprehend over 1.3 million illegal aliens every year, but an estimated 8 million undocumented immigrants now reside in the United States.[58]

The 1986 Immigration and Reform Act offered amnesty and citizenship opportunities for all illegal aliens who could document that they had entered the United States before 1982. Fewer than 3 million sought legal status, a far smaller number than officials had expected. Lacking receipts to prove their presence before 1982, illiterate and thus doubtful of passing required tests in civics and English within eighteen months, and fearful of deportation of other family members who arrived after 1982, many illegals chose to remain underground.[59] A limited amnesty program in 2000–2001 enabled over 500,000 illegal aliens to apply for a green card without leaving, provided they had a family sponsor.

The issue of illegal aliens riles Americans for several reasons. The most frequent complaint is that aliens do not pay taxes and yet exact a high cost to the taxpayer in education, health, and welfare expenses. This problem is especially acute in six populous states that receive about 80 percent of all foreign-born: California, Florida, Texas, New York, New Jersey, and Illinois. Critics complain that undocumented aliens depress the wage scale and displace low-skilled U.S. workers,

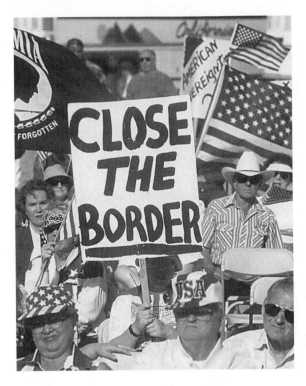

Anti-immigrant sentiment in the U.S. is strongest in border states, such as California and Texas. Many people fear that large-scale migrations of Mexicans and Central Americans to their states, legally or otherwise, will have a negative impact on their economy and system of social relations. Is anti-immigrant sentiment new in the U.S.? Are all immigrant groups seen as threats at all borders? Who are the new immigrants?

who are often other minorities. Other observers dismiss these charges, however, arguing that the illegals take jobs no one else wants; that they pay rent that goes in part to cover property taxes, which support the public schools; and that they help the economy through their consumerism.

Perhaps the most vivid recent example of public hostility was the 1994 approval of Proposition 187 by 59 percent of California voters. This measure denied government-funded education and health-care services to illegal aliens, although its constitutionality was immediately challenged. The basis for this action was a 1982 Supreme Court ruling that Texas must provide education for undocumented minors—the five-to-four decision was based upon the Fourteenth Amendment, which states "nor shall any state . . . deny to any person within its jurisdiction the equal protection of the laws." Opponents of this ruling claim that the Constitution's definition of "person" does not include noncitizens who deny that jurisdiction by willfully entering the state illegally. In 1997, the U.S. District Court disagreed, striking down Proposition 187 as unconstitutional.

Sociological Perspectives

Sociological analysis can provide helpful insights into the problems of intergroup relations. Functionalist and Conflict views examine the social factors that allow institutional discrimination to persist, thereby keeping some groups out of the mainstream. These macrosocial views also explain smoldering tensions and occasional outbreaks of violence, as does the Interactionist approach, which examines the consequences of social interpretations of outgroup members.

The Functionalist Viewpoint

Functionalist analysis begins with the premise that, in an ideally structured social system, all the parts interact smoothly. The social cement binding a society together is its **normative integration**—the mutual sharing of values and attitudes that allows people to live together equally and harmoniously. However, societies can also function smoothly in the presence of social inequality. Since the required tasks in a society demand varying levels of talent and expertise, they also yield unequal rewards (income and prestige). Social inequality can thus result from a functionally integrated society. Sometimes groups find themselves in lower stratification layers through a natural process of labor segmentation, such as unskilled immigrants becoming farm laborers.

Social equilibrium can be upset either by rapid social change or by dysfunctions occurring within certain groups that also affect the larger society. For example, system disorganization can occur if a society cannot quickly absorb into its culture the influx of a large number of culturally distinct immigrants. Even the continued presence of partially assimilated minority groups present problems. Both minority groups—the new and the old—retain enough differences to reduce the unity and cohesiveness of the society.

Unsuccessful efforts at integration can heighten intergroup tensions and conflict. This situation is dysfunctional to society because denying people full opportunities to make contributions wastes human resources. This system disorganization, if not corrected, becomes entrenched, resulting in some groups' being denied equal opportunity from one generation to the next. As a tradition of restricted opportunities and participation continues, problems of poor education, income, unemployment, housing, health and longevity, and crime and delinquency become a burden to society and to the minority people who endure them. The dysfunctions of discrimination to society are its costs in lost productivity and welfare assistance and its continued presence as a source of social unrest and reciprocal antagonism.

Functionalists stress that the most effective method of resolving these problems is to put the social system back into balance. Effective reform to eliminate discrimination must occur, eliminating the barriers to full social, political, and economic opportunities. If we make these adjustments and reorganize our social institutions, we build new relationships among people and foster mutual respect and cooperation. A fully integrated society would probably produce the fewest conflicts; but we can also attain unity in a pluralistic society, if all groups accept and respect the rights and subcultures of each other. If all work together in peaceful coexistence and cooperation, and if a common core exists with allegiance to U.S. society, differences need not be divisive.

The Conflict Viewpoint

Because people tend to become more hostile when their security is threatened, some social scientists closely examine how economic competition and conflict breed prejudice. U.S. history records many examples of rising ethnic antagonism in times of high unemployment and intense job competition. This pattern held true in the late nineteenth and early twentieth centuries for many different minority groups: Asians on the West Coast; Germans and Italians in the South; southern, central, and eastern Europeans in the industrial Northeast and North Central states; and (since the 1960s) African Americans and Hispanic Americans in many parts of the country.

Economic exploitation is a key cause of inequality. Employers often hire cheaper minority workers at the expense of nonminority wage earners. When the labor market splits this way along ethnic lines, ethnic prejudice, racism, and hostility arise and dominate the labor conflict.[60] Among the numerous examples are the efforts of Samuel Gompers and the American Federation of Labor in the late nineteenth century to bar Chinese workers from coming to America, the killings of Hungarian and Slavic miners in Pennsylvania in the 1890s, and the race riots in many U.S. cities in 1919 following the return of war veterans seeking jobs in competition with Blacks who had migrated to the North.

Factory sweatshops still exist and still exploit minority workers, whose limited English, lack of resources, or illegal alien status renders them helpless to object to low wages or dangerous working conditions. Whether in factories or on farms, illegal and legal alien workers also accept wages that are low by U.S. standards because they are still better than what they have previously known. This situation can depress the wage scale in that region, displace native-born U.S. workers, and set the stage for antagonism and confrontation. When manufacturers find labor costs rising because of the collective bargaining process, they often relocate to nonunion areas in the South or to such countries as Mexico, Sri Lanka, South Korea, or Taiwan, thereby generating ethnic prejudices among affected U.S. workers against those who have replaced them in foreign lands.

Conflict theorists examine both past and present minority problems by asking, "Who benefits?" Members of a society who occupy privileged positions strive to maintain their status and allow only a small number of newcomers to enter their circle. Acting to further their own self-interests, they exploit those with little power and create an ideology and value system to reinforce their dominance. As this belief system pervades society, a false consciousness evolves that deceives people into thinking that what they see is the "normal" state of affairs. Institutional discrimination thus reinforces the dominant group's misperception of the inferiority of the subordinate group(s).

The Interactionist Viewpoint

Interactionists concentrate on daily encounters between members of different groups. When the dominant and minority groups share similar values, appearance, and lifestyle, the interrelationship tends to be harmonious and assimilation occurs. The greater and more visible the cultural differences, however, the greater the probability of conflict and the more difficult the process of assimilation.[61] This perspective emphasizes ethnocentric factors influencing the definition of the situation, which can lead to misunderstandings and problems between members of unlike groups.

Many non–Hispanic Americans misinterpret the widespread use of Spanish as a threat to the unifying effect of English usage in American society. Claiming that earlier immigrants learned English quickly, they believe today's new arrivals are nonassimilationist in thought and deed. Interactionist analysis of past and present immigrants, however, reveals that second-generation Asian and Hispanic Americans do use English as their primary language, learning it even more quickly than earlier immigrants because of the influence of the mass media.[62] Moreover, non–Western immigrants become naturalized American citizens at a far higher rate than Westerners, one sign of their desire to join—not keep separate from—the American collectivity. The ingroup solidarity and social isolation among first-generation Americans is a normal pattern that changes over the generations, unless deterred by racial barriers.

Racial, religious, and other cultural differentiation can create social distance, suspicion, and tensions between groups. Although their land has been ethnologically diverse from its colonial beginnings to the present, Americans seldom knew, or know now, how to handle diversity in social interaction. Race relations have a dismal history and an unresolved present. Religious bigotry may have existed with more sustained intensity in the past, but it continues to exist today in many forms. People still express ethnocentric disapproval of the attributes of various subcultures (appearance, food, customs, etc.).

Until changes occur in the structural conditions of inequality that promote and maintain prejudicial attitudes, Interactionists suggest two strategies to improve intergroup relations. First, public enlightenment through education and positive interaction opportunities could strengthen intergroup understanding, tolerance, and acceptance. Second, once public consciousness about intergroup dynamics is raised, the lessened appeal of ethnocentrism could generate an atmosphere of greater inclusiveness.

Thinking About the Future

Scars from past mistreatment of African Americans and Native Americans still mar U.S. society, but the same is not true of the descendants of past waves of European immigrants. Those previously maltreated White ethnic groups are now for the most part well-integrated, even though their retention of Catholicism or Judaism and certain other cultural attributes made the nation a more pluralistic one. Today's immigrants—many of them Asians or Hispanics—come to a far different country, raising concerns about whether past assimilation patterns are reliable indicators for the newcomers. Let us project some future possibilities based on current trends, understanding that unforeseen events may dramatically alter the picture in unexpected ways.

Demographic projections show that in your lifetime U.S. society will become far more diverse than it is today. Those changes include a far greater proportion of Asians, Blacks, and Hispanics, with a shrinking proportion of non-Hispanic Whites. As we become a more pluralistic and multiracial society, will we achieve greater intergroup harmony or will we be torn apart by dissension, distrust, and conflict? Will Whites, seeing their numerical majority disappearing, use their political power to reduce immigration? We have already seen attacks on affirmative action. What do you see as White initiatives/reactions to minority preferences in undergraduate and graduate admissions, hiring and promotion policies, as Whites decline in percentage of the total U.S. population? And, with Hispanics now passing Blacks as the nation's largest minority group, will we witness clashes between these two groups in fierce economic competition for jobs? And what of Asians with their growing power because of numbers, education, and higher income? Or of Native Americans off and on the reservations? Do you foresee greater strife among the different groups vying for their share of the American Dream, or do you envision a smoother evolution into a more diverse society? How does your future scenario change, if the economy worsens?

Another aspect of our future is the "social cement" that holds us together as a society. As immigrants continue to pour in from all over the globe, will we be able to sustain cultural integration and maintain a sense of community and unified national identity? Or will cultural separatism—with its emphasis on foreign language maintenance, nonassimilation, and adherence to the group's ways over those of society—unravel the societal fabric that for so long has made us a successful nation of immigrants?

What about today's minorities languishing in poverty, denied the life opportunities that the Declaration of Independence and the Constitution promise? This question interconnects with those in the chapters on cities, gender, and poverty, so those considerations resurface here. What do you think needs to be done to improve their situation? Should we just let things work themselves out, or do we need some sort of private or government initiative? What would that be? What exactly should we do to make the American ideal the American reality?

SUMMARY

1. The United States' long history includes many instances of exploitation and conflict involving both people of color and White ethnic groups. In recent years, Western Europe has experienced a large influx of immigrants, creating response patterns similar to those in the United States. While many successes have been achieved in the United States, serious problems remain, encompassing health, housing, education, employment, income, safety, and quality of life.

2. Americans' faith in education as the route to upward mobility overlooks biases in the system. For some minority children, schools are an alien world with an unfamiliar value orientation and frequent cultural insensitivity. Busing has yielded mixed results, but it has been a divisive program, and public school systems are now even more segregated than they were thirty years ago. Magnet schools have had limited success, but many frustrated minority parents now advocate minority-only schools.

3. Although minority workers have made some gains, they remain disproportionately unemployed and vulnerable to economic downturns. Median Black family income is less than two-thirds that of White families, and the Black poverty rate is more than twice that of Whites. Affirmative action programs are under attack, with California setting the tone for what may be a retrenchment nationwide. The next few years will witness further battles over this issue.

4. Housing segregation remains a serious problem, particularly among Blacks and Hispanics. In part, the situation is attributable to past government discriminatory policies, combined with migration patterns and employment realities. The criminal justice system also reveals serious inequalities in the overrepresentation and disproportionately severe treatment of minorities at all phases of the process—from arrests to imprisonment.

5. Native Americans have a proportionately larger age cohort aged ten to nineteen (with a lower level of educational attainment) than the rest of the U.S. population. Unemployment, poverty, substandard housing, and poor health remain common problems on most reservations.

6. One-fourth of all African Americans live in poverty; among this segment of the population, high infant mortality and homicide rates continue. More Blacks are getting a high school education, but their college enrollments are lagging.

7. Hispanic Americans, except those of Cuban descent, have high dropout and poverty rates.

8. Asian Americans, except some Indochinese refugees, are doing well on various statistical measures of educational and economic achievement, but they experience various negative responses from other Americans.

9. Illegal aliens spark anger and calls for action among native-born Americans, as in California's Proposition 187. Economic issues are a major factor in this ethnic antagonism.

10. Functionalists see the inability of society to absorb the large influx of immigrants as dysfunctional; in their view, a system imbalance has become entrenched, necessitating reform to eliminate the discrimination. Conflict theorists emphasize the economic exploitation of minorities and the efforts of the privileged class to maintain its own status. Interactionists focus on problems that arise because of misunderstandings and the lack of shared realities.

KEY TERMS

Affirmative action

Assimilation

Charter schools

Ethnic subculturs

Institutional discrimination

Intergroup relations

Magnet schools

Normative integration

Residential patterning

Socioeconomic status

INTERNET RESOURCES

At this book's Web site with Allyn & Bacon, you will find numerous links pertaining to the problems related to race and ethnic relations. To explore these resources, go first to the author's page (**http://www.ablongman.com/parrillo**). Next, select this edition of *Contemporary Social Problems* and then choose **Internet Readings and Exercises**. Then select **Chapter 8,** where you will find both a variety of sites to investigate and some questions that pertain to those sites.

SUGGESTED READINGS

Bouvier, Leon F. *Peaceful Invasions: Immigration and Changing America,* Lanham, Md.: University Press of America, 1992. A demographic analysis of the impact of immigration on population, with arguments for lowering the current legal limit.

Chavez, Leo. *Shadowed Lives: Undocumented Immigrants in American Society.* 2nd ed. Boston: International Thomson Publishing, 1997. Informative insight into skilled and unskilled Mexican aliens residing in the urban and rural United States.

Curry, George E., and Cornel West (eds.). *The Affirmative Action Debate.* New York: Perseus Press, 1996. An excellent collection of essays that gives all sides equal voice in discussing this highly controversial topic.

Hacker, Andrew. *Two Nations: Black and White, Separate, Hostile, Unequal.* New York: Scribners, 1992. A data-intensive comparison of social indicators and power that assesses the relative status of the two races.

Kitano, Harry H. L., and Roger Daniels. *Asian Americans: Emerging Minorities,* 3rd ed. Upper Saddle River, N.J.: Prentice-Hall, 2000. A thorough sociohistorical profile of the different Asian peoples who have migrated to the United States.

Lind, Michael. *The Next American Nation: The New Nationalism and the Fourth American Revolution* reprint ed. New York: Free Press, 1996. A wide-ranging, thought-provoking proposal for a coherent, unified national identity that seeks to merge the opposing forces of nationalism and the ideal of a transracial melting pot.

Lott, Bernice E., and Dianne Maluso (eds.). *The Social Psychology of Interpersonal Discrimination.* Guilford, Conn.: Guilford Press, 1995. Provides an overview of current research focusing on behavior rather than attitudes and beliefs, exploring how and why people discriminate against others in everyday life.

Moore, Joan W., and Harry Pachon. *Hispanics in the United States.* Englewood Cliffs, N.J.: Prentice-Hall, 1985. A fine sociological portrait of values, socioeconomic characteristics, and diversity among Hispanic groups.

Parrillo, Vincent N. *Diversity in America.* Thousand Oaks, Calif.: Pine Forge Press, 1996. Examination of past and present immigration and multiculturalism in the United States, to dispel misunderstandings and anxieties about our future.

————. *Strangers to These Shores,* 7th ed. Boston: Allyn & Bacon, 2003. A comprehensive examination of ethnoracial and religious groups and issues that confront American pluralism.

Snipp, C. Matthew. *American Indians: The First of This Land.* New York: Russell Sage Foundation, 1991. A demographic profile of Native Americans, with detailed reports on education, employment, and housing.

9

Crime and Violence

Facts About Crime

- A serious crime occurs in the United States every three seconds.

- Less than two-thirds of all violent crimes and only one-fifth of all property crimes result in an arrest.

- One-third of the U.S. population is afraid to walk at night in their own neighborhoods.

- Young Black males are eight times more likely to be murdered than young White males.

- The U.S. rape rate is triple that of England and Wales.

- U.S. organized crime is the twentieth richest organization in the world.

- Employee theft costs retail businesses over $15 billion each year.

- The number of prisoners in the United States now exceeds 2 million, the highest of any country.

Crime is an excellent example of the point made in the first chapter that people define social problems in terms of their values and perceptions. Certainly, crime, violence, and terrorism are all unfortunate realities, as the media continually inform us, so there is justifiable cause for concern. However, a person's age, ethnicity, race, place of residence, and social class heavily determine the probability of becoming a victim. Middle-class Whites, for example, are less likely to be crime victims than lower-class non-Whites. We will examine crime victimization more fully and also explore the widespread belief among Americans that crime is worse, even though statistics show a steadily declining crime rate. By examining the facts and gaining some sociological insights into the problem, you will be able to make an informed conclusion about the current situation.

Crime, Laws, and Prosecution

Is everyone equal under the law? The law as a type of formal social control comprises three main lines of force: explicit rules of conduct; planned use of sanctions to support the rules; and designated officials to interpret and enforce the rules.[1] The goal of these formally prescribed patterns is to ensure that every person is treated equally, so that, when a rule is violated, only the nature of the violation matters, not the identity of the violator. In actual practice, however, the values and norms of the groups in power play a significant role in determining which laws are enforced and which offenders are arrested. With some exceptions, the law also allows for a great deal of **judicial discretion** in the severity of the sanctions judges impose on wrongdoers for violating the same rule.

The mere existence of a law does not ensure that violators will be treated as criminals. An act is only a crime if it is treated as a crime. In many states, most forms of gambling are against the law. For example, if you run a weekly poker game, where the players bet real money and the winners keep their winnings, you are violating a law. Will you ever be arrested and prosecuted? That depends. Are you a middle-class person, well established in your community? Are the other players like you? Do you have a place where this game can take place "privately," away from the eyes of others? If so, you are unlikely ever to be charged with engaging in a criminal activity. But if you are a "street kid" organizing the same poker game, but in a more accessible place where people can see you, you may well be arrested.

Such differential arrest patterns are a problem in our society. Often, **police discretion** in determining whether to make an arrest reflects societal prejudices, leading to discriminatory behavior and/or preferential treatment. Studies show that police are more likely to make arrests in poor neighborhoods than in middle-class ones.[2] Or as William Ryan once put it, "If you are a poor black ghetto dweller, then the odds are about one out of five or six that you will be arrested during the next twelve months."[3] Quite possibly it will be for an activity that an affluent White person pursues completely unpenalized (see the accompanying box).

When the police make an arrest, the prosecutor must decide whether to drop the case, reduce the charges, seek an indictment, or petition for adjudication. Prosecuting all offenders would overburden the courts and quickly exhaust available financial resources, so **prosecutorial discretion** enables authorities to apportion their resources in a way that best serves their community. Another contributor to differential enforcement is that nonpoor defendants can hire lawyers who zealously pursue their client's best interests, while poor defendants get public defenders with heavy caseloads who often recommend a **plea bargain**—pleading guilty to a lesser charge to resolve the matter quickly without a time-consuming trial.

Social Constructions of Social Problems

Social Norms, Deviance, and Crime

Society defines all crime as deviance, but not all deviance as a crime. Some forms of inappropriate behavior (such as laughing loudly at a funeral or cheating on a test) may violate social norms and elicit disapproval, but society may not label them as "criminal." Crime is a legal category, and the law is forever changing—with new crimes added here, and old ones deleted there.

What you do freely today may have been a crime in the past or perhaps may be a crime in the future. In colonial New Jersey, a man could be fined for kissing his wife in public on a Sunday, although it was permissible during the week. For two-thirds of the twentieth century, a mostly Dutch municipality in New Jersey forbade washing one's car or hanging washed clothes outside on Sundays. Today these old laws may seem silly, but in those days officials emphatically enforced them. Just a few years ago, people smoked anywhere they wished, but now they no longer can. Sexual harassment, previously an ignored practice, is now a punishable offense.

As the groups wielding power and influence in society change, the laws often change. For example, today some groups seek to decriminalize certain drugs and, indeed, some states have modified their drug laws. This appears to be a mellowing on the part of society, until you consider that opium was once an active ingredient in various cough or health medicines, as was cocaine in cola sodas. With concerns about drug addiction and the pathological fallout, our drug laws have become much stricter, with mandated imprisonment terms.

These people are at an illegal cockfight, a traditional sport in their culture of origin. What determines if a certain activity will be defined as a crime? What are some other examples of the criminalization or decriminalization of behavior that illustrate how crime is socially constructed? What do you think would be some effects of decriminalizing marijuana?

(continued)

Social Constructions of Social Problems (continued)

Some laws that protect citizens from bodily harm (murder, assault, rape) or property loss (theft, vandalism) evoke universal agreement. Other laws may reflect religious or political values of only some groups and thus become contested. The controversy over abortion laws is a prime example of conflicting religious values. We can understand the political nature of some laws and their enforcement if we examine actions that challenge those in power. For example, the public and police response to property damage during a sports championship celebration or college-student drinking binges in Florida during spring break is usually less than during a protest demonstration against the establishment. Generally speaking, acts that threaten the political structure summon a stronger reaction than those that do not.

If we assume that criminal laws accurately reflect the cultural norms of virtually everyone in society, we would not be correct. In a complex society such as ours, many diverse groups live together with differing values and norms within their subcultures. People, therefore,

could hold cherished values not reflected in law, and some laws may conflict with those values.

For example, first-generation Americans may find some of their transplanted cultural beliefs and practices in violation of U.S. laws. Recent examples in the news include: (1) the practice among some Africans and Middle Easterners of surgically removing a young woman's clitoris, (2) the pastime among some Hispanics of holding rooster fights, (3) aspects of the Caribbean religion Santería that involve animal sacrifices, and (4) the custom of some Arabs and Gypsies of arranging marriages of minors with adults. An older example was the adoption of the Eighteenth Amendment to the U.S. Constitution in 1919 that made it a crime for anyone to manufacture, buy, sell, or transport alcoholic beverages. Until repealed in 1933, that law was more often violated than observed, allowing organized crime to profit greatly in its illegal activities.

Still, laws enable a society to maintain some measure of cohesiveness and stability. We need to recognize, though, that they are social constructs, not neutral, universal entities.

Measuring the Extent of Crime

Accurate crime statistics are important for measuring changes in the crime rate and the effectiveness of crime prevention programs, as well as for evaluating the applicability of crime causation theories. The main sources of such information in the United States are two annual reports: the *Uniform Crime Report (UCR)* and the *National Crime Victimization Survey (NCVS)*.

Index Crimes and the *Uniform Crime Report*

The *Uniform Crime Report (UCR)* acts as a common standard for local, county, and state law enforcement agencies to use in defining and tabulating criminal offenses, and then reporting them to the Federal Bureau of Investigation (FBI). Concentrating on the most frequent and serious crimes likely to come to the attention of the police, the *UCR* maintains a **crime index** for eight categories of crime. These are further classified as *crimes against the person* (murder, rape, aggravated assault, and robbery) and *crimes against property* (burglary, larceny, motor vehicle theft, and arson). As Figure 9.1 shows, an Index crime was committed, on average, every three seconds in 2002. The slight increase in the violent crime rate of 2001 dropped in 2002, as the volume of violent crime fell in all geographic regions.[4]

From this compilation of data, the *UCR* tabulates total crimes in each category for that year, thereby providing a basis for comparing statistics for different years. Another important statistic is the **crime rate** (the number of crimes committed per 100,000 people), which permits comparisons of crime frequency in different cities or regions.

Critics—particularly Conflict theorists—charge that the *UCR* ignores white-collar crimes, corporate criminal behavior, and organized crime, all of which have a strong impact on society, annually costing over $300 billion.[5] Limiting the focus to street crimes, which are more often committed by poor minorities, promotes the false impression that criminal behavior is mostly confined to that segment of the population. Furthermore, the *UCR* only keeps track of crimes reported to the police, and victims do not always report the crime to police, as findings in the *National Crime Victimization Survey* strikingly illustrate.

Figure 9.1   Crime Clock: 2001

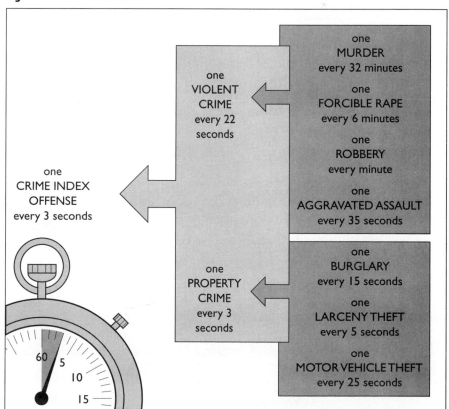

Source: U.S. Department of Justice, "Crime in the United States, 2002:" *Uniform Crime Reports.* Washington, D.C.: U.S. Government Printing Office, 2003.

Victims and the *National Crime Victimization Survey*

The *__National Crime Victimization Survey,__* begun in 1972, offers an enlightening alternative to official statistics as reported in the *UCR*. By interviewing a representative national sample of about 44,000 households, government researchers learn more about unreported crimes and their victims. The dramatic contrast in statistics between the *UCR* and the *NCVS* reveals significant underreporting of crime. For example, only 40 percent of all crimes were reported to the police in 2001. This figure breaks down into the reporting of 49 percent of all violent crimes (excluding murder) and 37 percent of all property crimes.[6]

Obviously, the nonreporting of 60 percent of crimes means no police investigation, no filing of charges, and no prosecution in those cases. Since only 46 percent of all reported violent crimes and 16 percent of all reported property crimes lead to an arrest,[7] only one in five property crime cases and three in fifty violent crime cases result in charges being filed against a suspect. These are hardly encouraging statistics about society's ability to maintain law and order. Another discouraging statistic is the percentage of crimes cleared by an arrest (see Figure 9.2). Police investigators are unable to solve most property crimes, as well as many violent crimes.

Why aren't all crimes reported? Perhaps the offender is a friend or relative whom the victim does not want to harm or embarrass, or perhaps the victim finds the offense (such as blackmail or rape) potentially embarrassing. Other people may fear reprisals from their assailants, or the crime may seem too trivial to justify the time and effort involved in reporting it. In some places, a "what's the use" attitude develops, with low expectations of the offender getting convicted and

Figure 9.2 Crimes Cleared by Arrest: 2002

Crimes of violence

	Cleared	Not cleared
Murder	64%	36%
Aggravated assault	57%	43%
Forcible rape	45%	55%
Robbery	26%	74%

Crimes against property

	Cleared	Not cleared
Larceny-theft	18%	82%
Motor vehicle theft	14%	86%
Burglary	13%	87%

☐ Cleared ▨ Not cleared

Source: U.S. Department of Justice, "Crime in the United States 2002:" *Uniform Crime Reports,* Washington, D.C.: U.S. Department of Justice, Federal Bureau of Investigation, 2003, Table 25, p. 223.

imprisoned; in others, the public generally opposes enforcing certain laws, such as underage drinking, gambling, or drug sales. Finally, the victim may be reluctant to have any contact with the police, either because of previous unfair or harsh police treatment or out of fear that his or her own illegal activities might be revealed, since people who operate outside the law constantly victimize each other.

Figure 9.3   Violent Crime and Property Crime Rates: 1973–2002

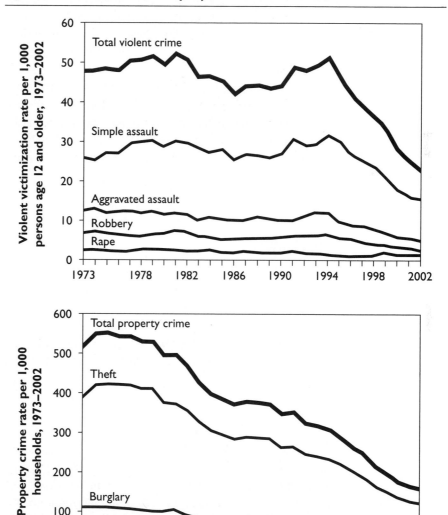

Source: National Crime Victimization Survey, 2002.

How Much Crime Really Exists?

Property crimes account for almost 90 percent of all crime, and Figure 9.3 on page 261 shows their steady decline in U.S. households between 1973 and 2001. Officials consider entire households, not individuals, as victims of these crimes, and calculate property crime rates accordingly. These crimes include about 13.5 million thefts, 3.1 million household burglaries, and 989,000 motor vehicle thefts annually.[8] About one in four households falls victim to crime annually.

Experts took encouragement from news that violent crimes' rates dropped sharply since 1994, reaching the lowest level since the Bureau of Justice Statistics started measuring them in 1973.[9] Tempering this news was an increase in the homicide rate in 2001, while rates for forcible rape, aggravated or simple assault, and robbery declined. Violent crimes include about 3.6 million simple assaults, 990,000 aggravated assaults, 512,000 robberies, and 248,000 rapes or other types of sexual assault annually.

Teenagers and young adults are twice as likely to be victims of violent crime as adults aged twenty-five to forty-nine and about five times more likely than people aged fifty or older. Most victimized by violent crime are the young, Blacks, Hispanics, males, and the poor. People in households earning less than $25,000 annually were twice as likely to be raped, sexually assaulted, robbed, or the victims of aggravated assault as people living in households with incomes over $50,000.

Violence in the United States

Americans hold contradictory attitudes toward violence. We deplore violent crime, enter war with great reluctance, and find violent solutions to be least satisfactory in all situations. Yet we flock to movies where heroes played by Jean-Claude Van Damme, Sylvester Stallone, Clint Eastwood, Bruce Willis, and Jackie Chan shoot, beat, torture, and blow up criminals in the name of justice. These movies usually make a huge profit, so people must find them interesting, if not admirable heroes. Part of the reason for our often contradictory fascination with, and horror of, violence, may lie in our own history.

Violence in a Sociohistorical Context

Vigilantism, the use of violent force to protect community values, is a big part of U.S. history. From 1767 until about 1900, extralegal (not sanctioned by law) vigilante activity was an almost constant factor in U.S. life.[10] The groups were not just the well-known lynch mobs of the Western frontier towns or the Ku Klux Klan of the South. Vigilantism occurred at least as often in the eastern half of the United States as in the western half, justified as a necessary response to the absence of effective law and order in many newly settled regions. Lacking an orderly, stable social structure (churches, schools, cohesive communities, and effective systems of law and order), groups of citizens banded together to create or preserve the way of life they felt was right:

A Vigilante roundup of ne'er-do-wells and outlaws, followed by flogging, expulsion or killing, not only solved the problem of disorder but had crucial symbolic value as well. Vigilante action was a clear warning to disorderly inhabitants that the newness of the settlement would provide no opportunity for eroding the established values of civilization.[11]

Innocent people often suffer from cruel and ugly acts committed in the name of preserving community values. In the beginning, vigilantism may appear to be the only available solution to the absence of a legal system of social control, but it easily turns into a form of terrorist control by any group that has the power to enforce its will violently. For evidence, one need look only at the 1995 Oklahoma City bombing or violent acts committed by extremist militia groups acting in the name of "American" values through means totally rejected by most of our society.

Recent Forms of Social Violence

One increasingly common form of violent behavior is **road rage,** aggressive driving by an impatient or angry driver trying to intimidate, injure, or even kill others after some type of traffic confrontation. A 1997 report by the American Automobile Association on the most extreme forms of road rage found a 51 percent increase in such incidents since 1990. In 37 percent of these cases, offenders used firearms against other drivers; another 28 percent used other weapons; and 35 percent used their cars. The U.S. Department of Transportation estimates that two-thirds of all traffic fatalities are at least partly due to aggressive driving, and the American Automobile Association (AAA) attributes over 12,000 injuries annually to enraged drivers. Road rage also finds expression in angry gestures, tailgating, cutting cars off, sudden braking, and bumping. As roads get more congested and road rage becomes more prevalent, some states—including Delaware, New Jersey, and Pennsylvania—have initiated special highway patrols that target aggressive drivers.[12]

Another threat comes from **citizens' militias**—paramilitary groups that cloak themselves in the Constitution even though they acknowledge no laws or authority. This movement began in the 1980s as a reaction to a radical right-wing perception that a corrupt federal government would soon try to confiscate the weapons of free-thinking American patriots. Confrontations with armed government agents and the deaths of innocent people at Ruby Ridge in 1992 and Waco in 1993 supplied rallying cries for the budding movement, which gained further impetus from passage of the Brady Law (requiring gun owners to register their firearms) and the assault weapons ban. Militia leaders heightened the paranoia of followers by claiming that the impending confiscation of weapons was merely a prelude to the advent of a socialist one-world government, or "New World Order."

Avoiding the mainstream media, they popularized their movement through booths at gun shows, newsletters, computer bulletin boards, the Internet, fax machines, and shortwave radio. Media publicity after the Oklahoma City bombing increased their visibility and attracted others with similar beliefs, so that by mid-1996 citizens' militia groups existed in all 50 states.[13]

The very existence of such groups implies the use of raw force rather than the power of ideas to achieve one's goals. Even though most militia groups claim to operate in a purely defensive capacity, the high levels of paranoia most such groups exhibit leads them to suppose they are acting justifiably when they are not. Every month brings new reports of violent attacks and arrests concerning militia groups, but most of the groups content themselves with stockpiling weapons for an eventual confrontation, which could lead to a self-fulfilling prophecy of violence.

Violent Crime

Only one in ten reported crimes is a violent crime, yet ordinary citizens consider few things as terrifying as the prospect of becoming such a victim. The fear of being mugged, robbed, assaulted, raped, or murdered is part of the lives of almost all Americans. Yet a change in attitude is occurring among Americans as the crime rate drops. In 1989, 84 percent of respondents in a Gallup Poll thought crime was worse than the year before. In 2002, 62 percent thought there was more crime than the year before. Though varying by a few percentage points, this majority viewpoint held constant when controlled for gender, race, age, education, income, community, region, or politics.[14] This persistent attitude, despite official statistics, reveals a sociological insight that, in many aspects of life, there is often a difference between perception and reality.

Strong differences also exist in American's perceptions of the crime problem nationally in comparison to their perceptions of crime in their own local area. Although 62 percent of Americans perceive crime as increasing in the United States, only 37 percent think that it has increased in their community (43 percent think so in urban areas). These highly significant differences are reflective of the same type of national versus local distinction that pollsters have found for years relating to such topics as health care, education, and Congress. Americans in general tend to see problems as more severe on the national level than at their own local level, and perceptions of crime appear to be no different.

Still, a 2000 Gallup poll revealed that, on average, one-third of Americans are afraid to walk alone at night in places within a mile of their homes, a percentage that has remained relatively unchanged for thirty-five years. Not surprisingly, residents of urban areas are more likely to perceive dangerous areas nearby (48 percent) than are those who live in suburban (32 percent) and rural (21 percent) areas. Women are also more likely to feel that there is an area in their neighborhood in which they would be afraid to walk alone at night—43 percent of women feel this way compared to 25 percent of men. Also, 41 percent of young Americans between the ages of eighteen and twenty-nine say there is an area close to them that they would be scared to walk in at night, compared to 33 percent of those over the age of 50.[15] Residents living in the South and Midwest were as likely to express concern over crime as those living in the East and West.[16]

The mass media may not affect all people the same way, but it does appear to influence the general public's perceptions and attitudes in direct proportion to its coverage of crime.[17] For example, a *Los Angeles Times* poll of its readers in 1994 that found only 21 percent named personal experience—compared to 61 percent naming the media—as the source of information for their attitudes about crime.[18]

We can partly understand these concerns with the realization that sharp declines in the violent crime rate do not translate into a vanquishing of the problem. Elsewhere in this book we examine the problems of family violence and hate crimes. In the following section, we direct our attention to two index crimes of violence: murder and rape.

Homicide

Although some murderers have criminal records, most do not. Furthermore, they do not fit any recognizable stereotype nor do their actions often conform neatly to simplistic explanations. Still, certain geographic and social patterns offer insights into the U.S. experience.[19]

Geographical Demographics

More murders occur in the South, and fewer in the Northeast, than in other regions of the country. Together, the South and West account for 58 percent of the U.S. population but 66 percent of its murders. What makes the South and West, with their greater expanses of rural land, more prone to homicides? Perhaps the answer lies in both regions' cultural history condoning weapons possession and vigilante justice. Not coincidentally, nearly two-thirds of all homicides involve firearms, but gun control advocates encounter fierce resistance from the National Rifle Association and many individual citizens in the South and West whenever they propose restrictive legislation.

Though the homicide rate is higher in large metropolitan areas than in small cities and suburbs, those murders tend to occur in certain well-defined areas of large cities. Most city neighborhoods, in fact, are just as safe as the suburbs. Since 1995, as small cities, suburbs, and rural areas all experienced declines in violent crime, cities with populations greater than 1 million experienced even more dramatic declines.

Unlike most Western nations, the United States allows individual gun ownership and we exceed by far all other countries in violent deaths from firearms. Like other social issues, this one generates protests on both sides, as shown here with the Second Amendment Sisters rallying against gun control. Would gun control limit the number of violent deaths or only leave criminals with guns as critics argue?

Social Demographics

Most murderers are males under age thirty, and most victims are males under age thirty-five. Males eighteen and older commit 89 percent of all murders and account for 78 percent of the murder victims. Nine times out of ten, both killer and victim are of the same race. Why so many males? Males are more likely to use guns (the most common murder weapon) for hunting, military purposes, or protection, and their socialization encourages more violent behavior.

Statistics on the relationship between murderer and victim are also revealing. Husbands or boyfriends kill 30 percent of all female murder victims, whereas wives or girlfriends kill 6 percent of all male murder victims. Often a connection between drinking, depression, frustration, and/or rage exists. Helpful insights into family homicides came from a detailed 1995 report of murder cases handled by courts in the seventy-five largest U.S. urban counties, where over 50 percent of the nation's murders occurred during the previous year out of the 3,000-plus total number of counties. Of those who murdered a family member, 7 percent killed a spouse: 41 percent of these involved wives killing their husbands, and 59 percent involved husbands killing their wives. The murderers ranged in age from eighteen to eighty-seven, with a median age of thirty-nine. Parents committed 57 percent of all murders of children under age twelve.[20]

As Figure 9.4 shows, young Black females aged eighteen to twenty-four are four times more likely to die violently than White females. Young Black males are eight times more likely to be

Figure 9.4 Homicide Rates Per 100,000 by Race and Sex of Victims Aged Eighteen to Twenty-Four

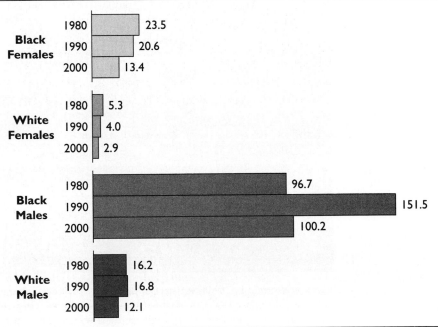

Source: Bureau of Justice Statistics.

murdered than White males. As the author of a homicide study for the Centers for Disease Control observed, "In some areas of the country, it is now more likely for a black male between his 15th and 24th birthdays to die from homicide than it was for a U.S. soldier to be killed in a tour of duty in Vietnam."[21]

Almost one-third of all murders occur because of an argument, either between two people who know each other well or between strangers involved in a sudden, unexpected altercation. Typically, both the attacker and the victim are male, and drinking is often a factor. Another one-sixth of murders are typically unpremeditated adjuncts of other crimes, resulting when something goes wrong during such felonies as robbery and arson.

Capital Punishment

In recent years sentiment in favor of capital punishment has increased in the United States. The ninety-eight executions that occurred in 1999 represented the highest number since 1951. In 2002, fifty-three Whites (including two women) and eighteen Blacks were executed. Over 3,500 prisoners are in prison under sentence of death.[22] Numerous polls conducted during the past decade have consistently found that more than 70 percent of Americans favor the death penalty.[23] Some people favor the death penalty as a deterrent to future crime, but available data do not support this view; states with relatively high numbers of executions continue to experience persistently high murder rates.[24] Another argument is "therapeutic vengeance," quelling the rage and helplessness felt by the victim's loved ones to gain them peace of mind and bring closure to the tragedy. Death-penalty opponents argue that such personal retribution is barbaric and that a system of justice should function on laws and objectivity, not on emotions. Supporters maintain that providing solace through execution is a legitimate and powerful form of restitution.[25]

Rape

Some people misclassify rape as a crime of passion. It is not. Rape is an assaultive crime based on anger, frustration, a need for power, or (possibly) other complex social-psychological disturbances. Despite the common image of rape occurring in the dark in parks, parking lots, or deserted streets and alleyways of a large city, the reality is somewhat different. About two-thirds of all rapes do indeed take place between 6 P.M. and 6 A.M., but almost 60 percent of them occur in the victim's home or at the home of a friend, relative, or neighbor. Moreover, in almost three-fourths of all rape cases, the victim and offender know each other, and almost half of these incidents involve so-called date rape.[26]

Perhaps the most disturbing statistics relate to age. About 15 percent of all rapes involve victims under age twelve, while 29 percent involve victims between the ages of twelve and eighteen. Thus over four in ten rapes happen to victims who have not reached age eighteen. The largest number of rape victims are between sixteen and nineteen years old, but the largest number of rapists are between twenty-five and forty-four, an older age group than commits most other major crimes.[27]

Although women living in large metropolitan areas are more likely to be raped than those living in small cities, size alone is not the only factor. For example, the nation's largest city—New

York—has one-third the rape rate of Columbus, Ohio, or Colorado Springs. Moreover, only metropolitan areas experienced a 14 percent rate decline throughout the 1990s; cities outside metropolitan areas and rural countries experienced increases of 32 and 10 percent, respectively, over the same ten-year period. Rape also varies significantly by geographical area, with the highest rate and number of rapes in the Midwest and the lowest number and rate in the Northeast.[28]

Prosecuting and convicting rapists has long been difficult because of lack of evidence (bruises, torn clothing, witnesses), and the victim's embarrassment and reluctance to press charges for fear of hostile court proceedings or retaliation by the rapist. Today, sensitized police, medical, and counseling units help victims deal with the trauma, and DNA test matching provides a powerful evidentiary tool for confirming the rapist's identity. These positive steps may encourage more women to press charges, but rape remains highly underreported; with only 39 percent of rapes reported to the police.[29]

Date Rape

Date rape, sometimes called acquaintance rape, comprises more than half of all cases of rape, and its occurrence on college campuses in recent years has been cause for concern.[30] One study found that 28 percent of female college students identified themselves as a victim of rape or attempted rape. Sixteen percent of college male students admitted to committing acts that meet the legal definition of sexual assault, and about 33 percent admitted that they continue to make sexual advances even after a woman says no.[31]

Objectively, date rape differs little from rape by a stranger. The legal definition of rape turns on force and nonconsent, not on the relationship between the accuser and the accused. A man should take "no" for an answer, regardless of where he and his companion are or what he may have spent on their date. If a man does not accept "no" and overpowers the woman, he cannot evade culpability by manufacturing such rationales as "she asked for it by coming into my room for a drink."[32] However, men and women often bring different attitudes and expectations into a dating situation and may not accurately interpret each other's cues.[33] As a result, researchers find that the ambiguity of the situation makes outsiders less sympathetic to the woman's plight than when a stranger sexually assaults her.[34]

Preventing Rape

Successful rape prevention is extremely difficult to implement. The first and most obvious strategy involves teaching individual women to avoid rape by attending workshops on self-defense tactics and learning other rape avoidance techniques. Another approach is to change socialization patterns for boys and girls so that no one views rape as a phenomenon at the extreme end of a continuum associating male sexuality with aggressiveness. Rape Shield state laws now limit the admissibility of evidence of victims' prior sexual conduct with persons other than the offender; this makes it more difficult for rapists to pursue a "she asked for it" defense of arguing that the victim was so promiscuous, she couldn't have been raped. The 1996 national law requiring community notification when a sex offender moves into the neighborhood serves as a warning measure, as does the Crime Control Act of 1994, which requires states to set up registers of sex offenders.

Another deterrent is the longer prison time convicted sex offenders now serve. Many experts attribute the dramatic drop in rapes in 1995 (and maintained since then) to a combination of these measures.

International Comparisons

A 2002 United Nations report revealed that women in the United States run a much higher risk of being raped than women in Europe, even allowing for some difference in the rate of reporting. The U.S. rate of 32 rapes per 100,000 women was nearly three times higher than England and Wales, second at 16 rapes per 100,000 women. France and Spain were next (14), followed by Norway (12); Finland (11); the Netherlands (10); Denmark (9); Bulgaria (7); Hungary, Poland, Switzerland (6); Czech Republic (5); Italy, Latvia, Portugal (4); and Slovakia (3). The U.S. rate was 2.5 times greater than that for Mexico (13) but far below that for Canada (78) and Australia (81).[35]

Differences in reporting and record keeping prevent these comparisons from being more than suggestive. Nevertheless, the findings support the notion that the violence endemic in American culture makes rape a more serious problem here than in other nations.

Fourteen Latin American countries have laws that exonerate rapists who marry their victims, and often family pressures and threats by the rapist leave the woman little choice. In these countries—Argentina, Brazil, Chile, Colombia, Costa Rica, the Dominican Republic, Ecuador, Guatemala, Honduras, Nicaragua, Panama, Paraguay, Peru, and Venezuela—the couple need not stay married; and indeed, the rapists usually abandon their wives after a few months. In Peru (with a rape rate of 10 per 100,000) all co-defendants in a gang rape case are absolved if one of them marries the victim. Feminists have so far been unsuccessful in trying to get the law repealed, but most Peruvians support it. Feminists argue that the law sends a message to society condoning rape and reveals a fundamental misunderstanding of what rape is.[36]

Organized Crime

As its name implies, organized crime is a system with a hierarchy of authority, defined division of labor, and elaborate rules of behavior governing its day-to-day functioning. These elements, as in any bureaucracy, run on the profit motive, enable it to function efficiently and to make money effectively. The several hundred-billion-dollar earnings of U.S. organized crime makes it the twentieth richest organization in the world.[37] These crime syndicates engage in such illegal activities as drug trafficking, loansharking, pornography, and prostitution. Their recently expanded activities include motor fuel excise tax evasion schemes, insurance, health-care fraud and insurance fraud, as well as food stamp fraud, telemarketing fraud, stock market manipulation, and financial institution fraud. They usually employ extortion, bribery, corruption, and violence or the threat of violence to achieve their objectives. Another activity is **labor racketeering**—infiltrating labor unions to gain access to pension funds and to extort money from management to avoid labor disputes. Often it infiltrates legitimate businesses to launder money or to coerce companies to buy supplies from companies it controls.

The Globalization of Social Problems

International Organized Crime

Once viewed as a local or at most a regional threat, organized crime has become a highly sophisticated transnational activity. So serious is this growing menace that national governments are working together through the United Nations and law enforcement agencies to combat the problem. They seek to curb such criminal activity as the illegal trafficking of drugs, firearms, and persons (women and children forced into prostitution and the smuggling of migrants).

The problem is everywhere. Organized criminals in Mexico run large-scale drug trafficking rings, a criminal arena once monopolized by Colombian cartels in the past. According to a 1999 study by the U.S. Drug Enforcement Administration (DEA), about 29 percent of the heroin consumed here filters into the country through the hands of Mexican organized criminals.

Economic, political, and social changes occurring in Eastern Europe and in the former Soviet Union gave great opportunities for organized criminals. Crumbling state control was an open invitation for organized crime to step in and reap profits from struggling democracies and other countries with shaky or nonexistent laws, ill-equipped police, and uncertain market forces. The number of known criminal groups in Russia increased in the 1990s from 785 to an incredible 9,000, with a combined membership of more than 100,000, according to the country's Interior Ministry. The Ministry estimates that organized crime controls over 40,000 Russian businesses—including banks and law firms. Throughout Central Europe organized crime makes vast profits in guns, prostitution, extortion, car theft, black market oil, and smuggled, tax-free cigarettes.

Both Latin American and European criminal groups have expanded their activities beyond their continents. Drugs are flowing into Eastern Europe and the former Soviet Union. Elsewhere, the Hong Kong–based Triads and the Japanese Yakuza market synthetic drugs and traffic in women and children for sexual slavery on a global scale. The United Nations labels the Yakuza—which also engages in gun smuggling and specializes in corruption in addition to its drug sales and prostitution rings—as one of the "most powerful criminal organizations in the world."

Even worse than their international activities is that these criminal organizations have created multinational alliances. Colombia's National Police reports that its powerful drug cartels "deal" with the Russian mafia and Eastern European crime groups. Several Russian/Eurasian organized crime groups and criminal enterprises operate in the United States, and they often work closely with other non-Russian/non-Eurasian organized crime groups.

Despite some local successes in fighting crime—most notably in Bolivia, Columbia, and Italy—no country on its own can cope successfully with the growth of international crime. These transnational criminals continue to extend their tentacles worldwide, foiling law enforcement by hiding out in "safe" countries or changing trafficking routes from one nation to another when the trail gets hot. National governments thus realize the need to work cooperatively.

International treaties are in force against drug trafficking and money laundering, and the U.N. General Assembly adopted new strategies in 1998 to reduce both the supply of and the demand for illicit drugs. In December 2000, 120 countries signed a new treaty to close the major loopholes that allow organized crime to flourish and that block international efforts to combat it. Known as "The United Nations Convention against Transnational Organized Crime," the treaty is intended to serve as a blueprint for countries to improve their systems to shut down international criminal organizations, eliminate "safe havens", protect witnesses, and block money laundering. It is the first legally binding UN instrument in the field of crime.

Although the Mafia gets the most attention for its organized crime activities, other racial and ethnic groups also have highly organized crime organizations in the United States. Most of these function like legitimate corporations. Organized crime remains a highly profitable enterprise because of high public demand for its products and services, and because of its ability to use force when necessary and to bribe police and other public officials to ignore them (see the box on the previous page).

White-Collar Crime

Edwin H. Sutherland introduced the concept of **white-collar crime** in 1940.[38] He originally defined it as violations of law by persons of the upper socioeconomic class, committed as part of their normal business activity and not as part of some individual pathology. Such activities include any gain by deception: insider trading, tax evasion, embezzlement, false advertising, fraud, price-fixing, restraint of trade, or knowingly manufacturing unsafe products. A notorious recent corporate example is Enron (see Chapter 3). Doctors and lawyers can commit occupational crimes through Medicare/Medicaid fraud, false testimony in accident cases, fee-splitting, undisclosed conflict of interest, and other deceptive practices. The daily electronic transfer of millions of dollars enables computer hackers—a relatively new category of white-collar criminal—unlawfully to access and manipulate confidential data or to remove funds from accounts. Employee theft remains the largest contributor to retail losses, costing businesses $15.1 billion dollars each year in lost inventory, compared to $9.7 billion in shoplifting losses. Such losses mean the average family of four spends more than $440 a year in higher prices because of inventory theft.[39]

Property Crime

Index crimes listed as property crimes include burglary, larceny-theft, motor vehicle theft, and arson. Nonindex property crimes include check forgery, shoplifting, and vandalism. Many offenders in the latter group of crimes are otherwise law-abiding citizens acting on impulse and opportunity. Both criminals who systematically commit index crimes for a living and nonprofessionals who act sporadically for momentary gain usually act alone. Juveniles under age eighteen commit a greater proportion of serious property crimes than any other age group. Arrest-based *UCR* statistics reveal that youthful offenders in 2002 accounted for 31 percent of all burglaries, 30 percent of all larceny-thefts, 33 percent of all motor vehicle thefts, and 50 percent of all arson cases.[40]

Juvenile Delinquency

Societies from Socrates' time onward have frequently criticized the "rampant misconduct of youth." In seventeenth-century France, pupils frequently beat their teachers. U.S. writers in the 1800s lamented that no one could safely walk San Francisco's streets without encountering "hoodlums," a term coined then to describe members of teenage gangs.[41] For centuries, most societies treated children as miniature adults. Slowly, the notion developed that childhood was a special time and that children should be protected, nurtured, and disciplined in specific ways. Such thinking led to the concept of **juvenile delinquency**—the idea that a crime committed by a "child" should not be viewed in the same way as an adult's criminal action and should not be similarly punished.

What Is Juvenile Delinquency?

Juvenile delinquency is a *legal* category. A young person committing a violation of the **Juvenile Justice Code** comes under the jurisdiction of a special judicial system set up specifically to deal with young offenders. The maximum age of persons who fall within the juvenile court's jurisdiction varies from state to state, and in some cases it differs for boys and girls within the same state, but eighteen is the usual dividing line.

Juvenile courts were an innovation of the early 1900s. Before that time, young offenders were subject to the same legal process (and the same punitive treatment) as any adult. The courts exempted only children under seven from responsibility for their acts, defining them as lacking the capacity to form a criminal intent. In dealing with offenders between the ages of seven and fourteen, judges sometimes gave special weight to the circumstances surrounding the act. After fourteen, however, a person was legally an adult, and thus subject to the same range of penalties as any other adult, including whipping, imprisonment, and hanging.[42]

The Crips, the Bloods, the Hisp Florencias (pictured here), and others are notorious gangs with nationwide membership and spreading influence. Who is in these gangs? What perks do gangs offer that attract low-income, at-risk urban youths? What social factors have encouraged the extension of gang activities to affluent suburbs?

As the twentieth century dawned, social reformers sought to control children instead of punishing them. Accepting the prevailing belief that children naturally inclined to be bad, they argued that the job of society was to force obedience. Subsequently, numerous activities were classified as special juvenile "crimes"—what we now call **status offenses**—requiring court intervention. Today, status offenses constitute about 20 percent of all juvenile court referrals. They include such misdeeds as cutting school, violating curfew, running away, disobeying parents, possessing or consuming alcohol, and exhibiting uncontrollable behavior.

Although commonly imagined to be primarily a lower-class phenomenon, juvenile delinquency exists in all social classes.[43] The strongest and most consistent class-crime associations do exist between continuing lower-class status and sustained involvement in street crimes.[44] Many researchers have found no significant differences in self-reported acts of delinquency along class lines, however, and one national study found that middle-class dropouts are more likely to engage in delinquency after dropping out than are lower-class dropouts.[45]

Gangs

Some young criminals act individually, but most belong to gangs. A good definition of a gang is "a group whose members meet together with some regularity, over time, on the basis of some group-determined criteria for membership and group-determined organizational structure, usually with some sense of territoriality."[46]

Lately, the age structure of gang membership has been changing. Adolescents remain in the majority, but gangs recruit even preteens now. Exploited, and encouraged or forced to commit criminal acts for their "boss," the youngsters identify older criminal gang members as role models of success. More and more individuals remain in gangs after their teen years, too, as the phenomenon known as "maturing out" (leaving the gang after one's teenage years are over) weakens.[47] For persons who lack the skills and/or motivation to join the larger economy, the gang provides both purpose and (often illegal) economic opportunity. Because relatively few good jobs are available to poor, minority young men, gang membership often continues into adulthood, with older members assuming leadership roles. As a result, gang involvement in profitable criminal activities has become sophisticated and extensive. Simultaneously, law-abiding adults in the community have lower prestige and less influence.[48]

Today, delinquent gangs exist in virtually every state. Several North Central mountain states and a few Northeastern states have little gang activity; but in most states, gang activity has increased and worsened significantly in the past decade. Two California gangs, the Crips and the Bloods, now have chapters in other states as well. And one New Jersey county prosecutor estimates that 99 major youth gangs exist in just seven towns. Members of these gangs commit crimes ranging from carjacking to drug distribution to sexual assault.

A study of twenty-seven youth gangs in St. Louis identified their ten most common activities, which experts suggest represent gang activities throughout the urban United States: fighting/practicing intimidation; committing assaults; committing drive-by shootings; tagging property with graffiti; selling drugs; using profits on drugs, guns, or cars; committing robbery/burglary; stealing or vandalizing cars; practicing extortion; and fencing or bartering stolen goods.[49] Increasingly, the public mind associates gangs with drugs and the attendant violence they generate.

Rethinking Juvenile Crime

Beginning with the crack epidemic in the mid-1980s, the nation's streets became increasingly dangerous as competing drug gangs engaged in shootouts with one another. Soon juveniles were freely using guns instead of fists to obtain gold chains, to settle disputes over real or imagined slights, or simply to prove their manhood. Between 1985 and 1995, the total number of arrested murder suspects aged ten to seventeen years old leapt by 75 percent.[50] As violent youth crime soared, anti-crime hardliners urged that laws be changed to make it easier to try juvenile suspects as adults, so they could receive harsher punishments. Victims of adolescent felons demanded changes in the juvenile justice system, challenging the long-standing belief that youngsters who kill, rob and rape should be treated differently from adult criminals.[51] Since 1995, the percentage of murder suspects under age eighteen has dropped 60 percent.[52]

As the public lost faith in the effectiveness of rehabilitation for serious and violent juvenile criminals, states enacted legislation or administrative guidelines mandating the length of confinement for the most violent and chronic juvenile offenders. Since 1992, nearly every state has passed laws making it easier to prosecute juveniles as adults. While judges in the juvenile system have always had the authority to send particularly brutal or chronic young offenders into the adult system, the new state laws make it easier for less-serious wrongdoers to meet the same fate. In fifteen states, prosecutors now have sole discretion to make such decisions for certain offenses, not only violent crimes, but some property and drug crimes as well. In fact, about one-third of the juveniles prosecuted as adults are charged with property offenses such as burglary and theft, or drug or public nuisance offenses. Many states allow children fourteen and older to be prosecuted as adults, while Kansas and Vermont have set the minimum age at ten.[53]

What have been the results? Nearly 8,000 juveniles, double the number in 1985, are now held in adult prisons, in many cases mixed in with adult criminals. That amounts to one in ten juveniles, on any given day, incarcerated in an adult jail or prison.[54] And what of juvenile crime? Since 1994, offending rates for teens have declined but still remain higher than levels prior to the mid-1980s. However, it is not clear whether changes in juvenile offender laws or demographic and economic factors played an important role in this decline. Moreover, two recent studies, one of Florida youth and the other of youth in New York and New Jersey, found that individuals tried as adults instead of juveniles were more likely to be arrested again, often for more serious offenses.[55] In a survey of attitudes toward proposed juvenile justice system reforms, American Correctional Association members rejected any procedural rule that would automatically certify youths to adult status for certain offenses or that would impose mandatory sentencing of young offenders. Instead, more than 80 percent supported the prevention and control of juvenile gangs and 99 percent said that intervention programs require collaborations among education, social, health services, and the criminal justice system.[56]

The Criminal Justice System

Two elements within the social structure that are supposed to resolve problems of crime and violence are the police (created to serve and protect the public) and the prisons (created to incapacitate and rehabilitate offenders and deter them from further criminal activities). Many people, however, believe that these institutions are part of the problem, not part of the solution.

The Police

As gatekeepers to the criminal justice system, police officers are its most visible and strategic element. They are the legal authorities whom the community encounters most often, as well as being the first contact for persons who violate the law, and the decision makers of what action to take in most on-the-ground situations. Since more than 708,000 full-time state and local police work in the United States on various assignments in departments of varying sizes in different types of communities, it is difficult to comment generally about their role.[57] However, they do share a few similarities. Most police officers come from working-class backgrounds and have at least a high school education; about one in four is a college graduate. They tend to have a conservative outlook, are committed to the status quo, and reflect the prejudices of the larger society.

Charges of police insensitivity, corruption, or brutality are all too common, particularly in urban areas with high concentrations of minorities. Occasionally, a notorious case such as the 1992 police beating of Rodney King in Los Angeles or the 1997 police stick sodomy torture of Abner Louima in New York City draws public outrage. More often, however, unpublicized daily encounters breed an atmosphere of suspicion and hostility between minorities and police that feeds on itself. Both groups develop an ingroup solidarity based in part on a shared negative judgment of the other, as well as on resenting the larger community that does not understand them.

One of the more encouraging approaches to the problem is the now-dominant emphasis on **community policing**. This strategy creates a strong working relationship between the police and the community to control crime. Police establish an enhanced presence in the community through foot patrols and sometimes even residence in that same neighborhood. Through neighborhood watch units, community-based response teams, newsletters, and police contact facilities, police and neighbors forge a partnership.

Another successful approach is **strategic policing,** an aggressive tactic intended to reduce street crime by conducting computer analyses of the most frequent crime locales, and then directing increased patrols, decoys, and sting operations in those areas. This approach in New York City, coupled with a crackdown on quality-of-life offenses (drinking in public, fare-beating in the subways, public urination), resulted in a dramatic drop in the city's crime rate—to its lowest level since 1980—and it became a model for other major cities.[58]

The Prisons

By the end of 2002, inmates in federal and state prisons numbered over 1.3 million (the highest number in the nation's history), up 26 percent since 1995. Our national incarceration rate of 701 prison and jail inmates per 100,000 inhabitants, up from 601 per 100,000 in 1995, is the highest in the world. If we add to this number the 665,000 locked up in local and county jails, the total number of U.S. prison and jail inmates exceeds an astounding 2 million persons, or one in every 143 U.S. residents.[59]

The United States has the world's highest incarceration rate. Why? Would dropping manadatory minimum sentences for minor drug offenses significantly affect the incarceration rate? What problem of a high incarceration rate does this photo illustrate? This problem makes rehabilitating criminals difficult, and periodic court orders to eliminate overcrowding necessitate the early release of violent offenders. What have been some consequences of early release, and how have communities attempted to cope with these consequences?

Most inmates, 1.2 million, are in state prisons; and California and Texas together hold one in every four prisoners in the nation. State prisoners have the following crime profile: 49 percent are serving time for a violent offense, 12 percent for a property offense, and 20 percent for a drug offense. Of the nation's approximately 129,000 federal prisoners, about 49 percent are serving a sentence for a drug offense.[60]

The sharp increase in prisoners is largely due to longer time served, which has several causes. First, several national and state laws of the past decade set mandatory minimum sentences for various drug offenses. Second, "truth-in-sentencing" provisions requiring jail time to approximate more closely the actual sentences imposed rather than an earlier release following parole board recommendation. Third, rates of release are themselves declining. And fourth, the courts are sending more people to prison, mostly for drug-related crimes.

Consequences of Overcrowding

Despite massive spending on prison construction, the Federal Bureau of Prisons and state governments have been unable to keep pace with the growing prison population. At the end of 2002, twenty-five states and the federal prison system reported operating at 100 percent or more of their highest capacity.[61] Some states, under court orders to ease prison overcrowding, routinely release other criminals, even violent ones, to make room for incoming drug offenders who have been sentenced to receive mandatory-length jail terms. Because many violent offenders do not receive statutorily defined minimum sentences, they become candidates for early release.

Overcrowding contributes to another serious problem: lack of professional staff to provide counseling or job-training services. Only one in ten inmates receives any job training at all. Nor are there enough guards to protect inmates from each other. Violence and drugs proliferate, opportunities for rehabilitation are skimpy, and exchange of tips on criminal techniques is a major pastime. As one inmate said, "Many of us come in here ignorant, and we won't come out able to cope with society any better because we can't even deal with our own problems."[62]

Disproportionate Prison Compositions

Closer examination of the prison population reveals some disturbing facts. About 41 percent of all prison inmates aged twenty to twenty-nine were high school dropouts, compared to 11 percent of the U.S. population. Most prisoners were unemployed prior to their arrest, and the median income of all inmates was below the poverty level during the year before their arrest. Since minority group members are more likely than Whites to fit these criteria, they are predictably over-represented in the prison population. According to the Bureau of Justice Statistics, at current levels of incarceration, a Black male has greater than a one in four chance of going to prison during his lifetime, and a Hispanic male has a one in six chance, compared to a one in twenty-two chance for White males.[63]

Black Americans account for 13 percent of the U.S. population but 49 percent of all state and federal prisoners. Hispanic Americans make up 13 percent of the U.S. population but 17 percent of the prison population. Part of the Hispanic prisoner increase is due to noncitizens, whose proportion is also increasing. About 25 percent of federal prisoners are noncitizens, and almost half of these are serving sentences for drug offenses.[64]

Alternative Prison Programs

Addressing the problems of overcrowded prisons, inadequate prison job training, and ineffective rehabilitation efforts, most large jail jurisdictions offer special alternatives to incarceration. At least thirty-five states run military-style boot camps. Proponents say the strict rules and discipline, rigorous physical activity, and indoctrination will turn criminals into productive citizens. Using the model of turning citizens into soldiers, these programs work on the theory that learned discipline will transfer into strength under stress. Studies show that program "graduates" commit new crimes at the same rate as do those who went to prison, but camp education and drug treatment are more successful.[65]

Community-based corrections for persons on probation appear more effective in lowering **recidivism,** or relapse into crime.[66] The most common form is the daily work release, which allows an inmate to work in the community unsupervised by correctional staff during the day, but return to a halfway house after the work shift. This program seeks to encourage productivity and self-esteem while restricting free-time activities, so inmates experience both punishment and a sense of purpose.

Day reporting, now practiced in at least twenty-two states, requires daily check-ins enroute to work or to counseling and drug and alcohol testing sessions. Electronic monitoring affects a minuscule fraction of probationers, who wear an electronic signaling device so that officials can track their whereabouts and keep them within a particular geographical area, away from others whom they might threaten.[67]

Provide Work for Prisoners

Former Chief Justice Warren Burger once proposed that we transform our prisons from "warehouses" into factories with fences around them. This would help in two ways. First, prisoners could develop useful job skills that they could use on the outside. Second, the work of prisoners could help pay the great cost of keeping them in prison, a total estimated to be as high as $25,000 per prisoner per year.

Whether it involves job training in prison or job training while on probation, this approach shows some promise of improving the recidivism rate by providing a means of reentry into society. Each year, U.S. prisons release more than 400,000 criminal offenders back to their communities. Most of those released do not remain crime-free, and national statistics show that about half return to prison or jail within a few years.[68] That is a pattern in need of improvement.

Terrorism

Terrorism is the use of intimidation, coercion, threats, and violent attacks to achieve the objectives of an individual or of a group. Terrorism always implies violence and destruction or the threat of violence and destruction. Terrorist acts physically harm individuals and destroy property.

Governments sometimes use terrorist tactics to control their citizens. For example, during the 1970s and 1980s, certain Latin American rulers used **repressive terrorism** that included sending death squads out to round up "enemies of the government" and secretly execute them. The same actions become **revolutionary terrorism** when taken by groups not in power. **Criminal terrorism** is simply another form of violent crime, in which the perpetrator's motive is to make a profit. Sometimes the persons who commit terrorist acts defend their conduct as "justified revolutionary terrorism," but the majority of society defines it as violent crime. In short, we define and treat terrorist tactics within the situation in which they occur.

Most acts of terrorism have a political motive. Domestic terrorists practice revolutionary terrorism, intent on destroying the federal government and its employees. Foreign revolutionary terrorists view the United States as an enemy, often because it supports a government that they oppose in or near their homeland. By bringing terrorist violence to the United States, they believe, they enhance their own power and prestige and publicize their cause.

Domestic Terrorism

On Wednesday, April 19, 1995, about 600 office workers and an estimated 250 visitors were inside the Alfred Murrah Federal Building in Oklahoma City. At the day-care center in the building, at nine o'clock that morning, preschool children played, laughed, talked excitedly, and busied them-

hijacked and crashed four U.S. commercial jets, two into the World Trade Center in New York City, one into the Pentagon near Washington, D.C., and a fourth—thanks to the heroic efforts of passengers on board—crashed into a field in Shanksville, Pennsylvania, instead of another Washington, D.C. target. The combined attacks resulted in almost 3,000 deaths.

Today's terrorists, whether domestic or foreign, claim the right to kill anyone or everyone. They accept the principle that "the end justifies the means," according to which nothing can be morally wrong if it is done for the right reason. Modern terrorists thus justify killing as "necessary." There are no innocent people.

Dealing with Terrorists

Dealing with political terrorists is a difficult issue. Should any bargaining occur at all? Some governments refuse to negotiate with terrorists, believing that it only encourages others to try the same tactics. Terrorism was an extremely rare event in once-Communist European countries; it still is in Cuba, China, and North Korea because terrorists know that these governments are unlikely to make concessions to them. Other governments, usually ones that place a great value on individual human life, say that protecting innocent people from harm is the most important consideration in all situations.

The counterterrorist strategy of the United States stresses four guiding principles. First, make no concessions to terrorists and strike no deals. Second, bring terrorists to justice for their crimes. Third, isolate and apply pressure on states that sponsor terrorism to force them to change their behavior. Fourth, bolster the counterterrorism capabilities of those countries that work with the United States and require assistance.[72]

After 9-11, U.S. policy regarding terrorism changed from a reactive stance to a proactive one to prevent it. The first phase directed attention to the leadership and training bases of Al-Qa'ida, which were under the protection of the Taliban rulers in Afghanistan. A massive military campaign, involving forces from fifty-five countries, ended Taliban rule, eliminating an important power base for Al-Qa'ida. This successful military action sent out a message that the United States would act decisively to pursue and eliminate terrorism.

U.S. initiatives in its war on terrorism took an unprecedented direction with the war against Iraq in 2003. For the first time in U.S. history, the country launched a preemptive attack against a country it accused of supporting terrorism. Undaunted by criticism within the country and around the world, the new "Bush Doctrine" declared that the United States did not need the approval of anyone else to take action against any organization, even a country, that it saw as a threat. Although the Iraqi war eliminated the regime of Iraqi dictator Saddam Hussein, at this writing stability in that country—particularly in the form of a democratic government—has yet to be realized. While another government supportive of terrorism has been eliminated, our military action also motivated other Islamic extremists into taking action against Americans when they can.

How Effective Is Terrorism?

To determine the effectiveness of terrorism, we must first identify the goals of terrorist activity. Three goals seem paramount: to call attention to the existence, importance, and power of the group; to discredit the regime currently in power by demonstrating its inability to protect the people; and to force the government in power to use such repressive retaliatory measures that previously uncommitted people will turn against the government and rebel.

The effectiveness of a terrorist act depends entirely on governmental and public reaction to it. Terrorist acts seem to be most effective in calling attention to the group. Some experts, in fact, call terrorism primarily an "advertising" activity. The Russian anarchist Pyotr Alekseevitch Kropotkin noted the "conversion" effects of such acts, saying, "Through the terrorist deeds which attract general attention, a new idea insinuates itself into people's heads and makes converts. Such an act does more propagandizing in a few days than do thousands of pamphlets."[73]

Does this actually happen? Both domestic and international terrorists have repeatedly succeeded in their first goal. Americans are aware of causes, issues, and groups whose actual political settings are thousands of miles away, and likewise they have learned about previously unknown militia groups. However, terrorists have failed to achieve their second and third goals in the United States. They have won few converts through violence, and their terrorist acts have failed to discredit the government.

However, few would argue that American lives were changed after 9-11. The creation of a Department of Homeland Security—with its color-coded levels of alert against terrorist attacks occasionally changing—keep the public aware of the threat. As some refuse to give in to vague terrorism fears, others are uneasy. Some avoid cities altogether now, fearful of increased vulnerability in densely crowded urban areas. Others avoid not just traveling abroad, but air travel itself,

Among the grim reminders of our post-9-11 reality is the presence of armed troops and a greater police presence at airports, bridges, tunnels, and other public places. In what ways have our lives changed since the terrorist attacks in New York City and Washington? What makes this social problem so difficult to overcome?

even to domestic destinations. Those who do fly experience heightened security measures, as do those going to any public gathering in sports, entertainment, or other special events. To the degree that Americans live in fear or stereotype all Muslim Americans as a threat, or to the degree that foreigners turn against the United States because of our proactive stance, then the terrorism can be effective in reaching its goals. This serious social problem will be with us for many years to come.

Sociological Perspectives

Most early nonsociological attempts to explain crime emphasized the faults and inadequacies of the criminals themselves. These explanations included physical appearance, heredity, and personality and character flaws. Such thinking left people with little hope that criminals could be rehabilitated. In contrast, sociological analysis seeks insights so that solutions can be found.

The Functionalist Viewpoint

Robert Merton noted that American culture places great emphasis on success but that the social structure does not provide the means for each person to gain the status and lifestyle everyone seeks.[74] The cause of deviant behavior is the unequal distribution of the resources needed to follow acceptable paths to success. Age, gender, ethnic, racial, or social class discrimination may block a person's ability to pursue certain desirable goals legitimately; and the divergence between goals and means causes anomie, a state of norm confusion. When a society is anomic and contains people blocked from advancement by institutional obstacles, the odds increase that many will try to achieve socially approved goals by socially unacceptable means. This not only explains high crime rates among lower-class youths and minorities, but also offers insight into middle-class, white-collar crime. If wealth and success are prized in themselves, it follows that more is better and a person can never have enough.

Another approach involves bonding, control, and drift theories, which posit a weakened relationship between the conventional moral order and the criminal as the cause of crime. This weakened bonding occurs either because society's social control agencies have become weak or disorganized, or because the individual is for some reason unaffected by the control these agencies try to exert. Social control agencies comprise both informal groups (family, neighborhood, and friends), and formal organizations (churches, schools, and the criminal justice system).

Social Control theorists believe that the socialization process forms an important bond between the individual and the society, resulting in conformity. This bond involves four major elements:

1. Attachments, especially to the family, with parents serving as important role models.

2. Commitment to the acceptable goals of the society, such as wanting and seeking a good education to get a good-paying job later. (A person with this commitment would not risk the future by participating in criminal behavior.)

3. Involvement in the society, through participation in conventional activities that can lead to socially valued success and higher status.

4. Belief in the rules of society and acceptance of the moral values of society.[75]

When all elements of the bond are strong, they insulate the individual from the temptation to commit crimes.

Functionalists also stress that violence reflects underlying social maladies. Dysfunctions within the social structure create conflicts between social groups, such as between Blacks and Whites or between the government and its citizens. Social conditions foster a climate of frustration and anger that prompts violent actions.

The Conflict Viewpoint

Interestingly, Conflict theorists converge with functionalists on the starting point for analyzing crime and violence: the disparity between means and goals identified by Merton. They immediately part company, however, by focusing on power relationships, rather than on innovative criminal actions by the have-nots. The people in power write the laws defining what is and is not criminal. Laws are thus simply an instrument whereby one group exercises control over others; and accordingly, the criminal justice system operates to the benefit of the dominant group.[76] For this reason, say Conflict theorists, the *Crime Index* emphasizes street crimes, which members of the lower class are more likely to commit, and not embezzlement or corporate crimes, which are more the province of the affluent and powerful. A burglary that yields a few thousand dollars is punishable by several years in prison, but polluting a stream or fixing prices, which endangers public health or costs the public millions of dollars in artificially inflated costs, often draw a fine and no prison time.

Conflict theorists thus emphasize how the preferences, predispositions, and vested interests of powerful groups define the social problem of crime.[77] The powerful determine the amount of resources to devote to controlling particular types of crime. They set the agenda for the police to enforce the laws against some crimes while ignoring others. Thus, "normal" people without power to control the criminalization process may find their actions—acceptable within their subculture—defined as criminally deviant in the larger society.

For the Conflict theorist, violence is the natural and inevitable consequence of inequality and repression in society. Individual, national, and international violence can only be dealt with by eliminating oppression. The unfair distribution of resources and opportunities within society forces people into violent crime. The resulting stress and despair lead to violent acts. Violence is merely an extreme means of resolving social conflict. To understand violence, one must understand how power is distributed and exercised within the society.

Conflict theorists believe that society and most sociologists focus too narrowly on individual and criminal violence, with dangerous consequences. They think we frequently use our concerns about violence as excuses for repression and for maintaining overly powerful police and military establishments. How can we champion nonviolent social solutions, they argue, when the government uses execution as a punishment and extends its international influence through covert and overt uses of force?

Society's values and institutions encourage individual violence. The excessive emphasis on competition, profit, and winning at all costs all promotes the adoption of violent solutions. We are inconsistent in our definition of violent actions: only when carried out by an enemy are actions defined as violent.

The Feminist Viewpoint

Not too many years ago, definitions of crime, as well as police behavior and the judicial process, reflected little sensitivity to a woman's situation and gave scant attention to her rights and status in society. That changed, in large part, because of the important influence Feminists had on the criminal justice system.

Through gender-bias studies, researchers showed that the police, juries, and judges shared gender-based traditional attitudes, biases, and myths about women. Empirical studies by legal scholars and social scientists also confirmed that male judges tended to adhere to traditional values and beliefs about the "nature" of and proper roles for men and women, and preferred conformity to traditional roles and familiar institutions. Although some judges were less influenced by such attitudes, they remained embedded in the law itself.

Redefining violence against women, protecting women against sexual predators, and reforming the criminal justice system became central goals of the Feminist movement.[78] Their efforts, enhanced by research findings, led to a recognition of the gendered nature of a considerable amount of crime (such as domestic violence) and the deconstruction of many myths and assumptions (such as a woman's past as a factor in a current rape case). New police procedures in questioning rape victims, special training to handle domestic violence cases and authorization to make discretionary arrests in wife-beating cases even without the wife's complaint, and new guidelines in court proceedings for rape cases were a few of the important changes that followed. Previously, when women were followed constantly, the police were powerless to do anything until after threats or physical assault occurred, often at the cost of the women's lives. Passage of stalking laws now protect women from living in constant fear. Recognition of the battered wives' syndrome brought Standpoint theory into medical recognition and provided a basis for legal defense for women accused of killing abusive spouses. These and other changes in crime definition, prosecution, and adjudication of cases reflect the prevalence of the Feminist movement.

Today, Feminist criminologists may be liberal, radical, Marxist, and even Postmodernist. Often their work involves critiques about how women offenders have been ignored or else misrepresented or stereotyped within traditional criminology. In any examination of gender and crime, one common emphasis is the "gender ratio" problem (why women are less likely, and men more likely, to commit crimes). Another area of study is the generalization problem (whether traditional male theories can be modified to explain female criminal actions).

The Interactionist Viewpoint

Instead of adopting the Functionalist and Conflict emphases on how the structure or the values of the larger society spawn criminal behavior, Interactionists seek to understand how and why some similarly situated people resort to crime while others do not. One of the most influential theories on how a person becomes a criminal is **differential association,** formulated by Edwin Sutherland.[79] People who associate with others engaged in criminal or delinquent behavior learn the methods and techniques used in committing such acts. They also learn a rationale for these actions and eventually learn to value them above conventional behavior. Contact alone does not produce criminals and delinquents, however. The extent, intensity, and continuity of those contacts—and the emotional ties that connect the individual with those criminals or delinquents—determine whether that person becomes one, too.

Another important Interactionist emphasis is **labeling theory,** which examines the process by which society labels someone a deviant.[80] Most people occasionally violate norms, but they do so secretly and seldom face any adverse public consequences. Individuals who are caught or even falsely accused, however, go from primary deviance (random, secret norm violations) to secondary deviance (persistent behavior in response to others' reaction to the primary deviance).[81] The "offender," once in the hands of law enforcement officials, is branded and becomes an outcast. Membership in a deviant subculture with norms and standards that support lawbreaking may be the final step in the process. Changes in self-concept, as well as in social concepts, because of labeling increase the likelihood of a deviant career because the individual has fewer choices and the deviance becomes part of his or her social identity.[82]

An extremely popular explanation for violent behavior has been the **violence subculture** hypothesis, which asserts that a person behaves violently because he or she was taught proviolent values and attitudes. Proponents of this still unverified theory say this subculture of violence exists worldwide and within many cultures. In this subculture, violence is the only appropriate response to a perceived challenge or insult. To react in any other way is to lose face. A study of inmates of a Michigan prison, however, found no value differences in a comparison of violent and nonviolent offenders. In a study of violence in hockey, however, players who fought more and received more major penalties had more pro-violent value-attitude patterns than did nonviolent players.

People perceive the world differently and thus learn different value orientations. To the terrorist, detonating a bomb in a crowded public place is not an attack on "innocent victims," but a blow against members of the oppressor group in the name of freedom or truth. In all violent conflicts, combatants typically form contrasting conceptions of each other. Definitions of others as "enemies" thus makes otherwise intolerable atrocities feasible. "Offing a pig" is quite different from coldly murdering a young man just doing his job. "Keeping the peace" is quite different from brutally beating an anti-war protester. Interactionists thus believe we cannot understand or explain a violent act without understanding how the aggressor defines that act.

▲ Thinking About the Future

As stated at the beginning of this chapter, crime and violence remain important concerns among Americans even though the violent crime rate has steadily dropped. Will this trend continue, or will it reverse if economic conditions change? Also, homicide rates by teens and young adults have declined, but they remain higher than levels prior to the mid-1980s, and this age cohort is increasing in numbers. What does this imply for the future? What interconnections, if any, do you see between crime and immigration or poverty? Whether you do or don't see a connection, what unfolding scenario can you foresee if current patterns continue? What changes would you suggest to alter that scenario?

What role will further technological advances play in crime and crime prevention? Will we become less afraid of violent crime and more fearful of becoming a computer crime victim from hackers into our bank accounts and other personal records? Will better security systems and "firewalls" protect us from such tampering? Will law enforcement be more effective as the technology links all agencies on a common network with complete profiles of criminals and criminal activity? Organized crime also uses the new technology for its purposes. Do you foresee the activities and influence of these groups growing or declining because of improved technology?

Will the current greater emphasis in treating more juvenile offenders as adults lessen juvenile crime or create a new group of adult criminals? What treatment of juvenile offenders do you endorse? What do we do about the growing presence, even in suburban towns, of such violent gangs as the Bloods and Crips? Do you expect youth gangs to continue to expand elsewhere or will they diminish in time? Should we do anything to prevent the former and hasten the latter? What?

What of our prisons? We have built more to lessen overcrowding, but we have more prisoners than ever before, the most of any country in the world. Many prisons thus remain at or above capacity. We still warehouse criminals, not rehabilitate them, although such community corrections programs as day reporting offer some promise. Recidivism rates decline among those prisoners raising their levels of education, so perhaps we should do more in prison education programs. What do you think? What proposals can you offer to improve this facet of the criminal justice system? How do we pay for your suggested programs or projects?

Today we worry about both domestic and international terrorism and rightly so. Where are we headed? Do you think we will evolve into a more fortresslike defense mentality or can you visualize a more positive scenario when it comes to the threat of terrorism? How so?

SUMMARY

1. Crime is a relative concept. What you freely do today may have been a crime in the past, or perhaps it may be a crime in the future.

2. Despite assumptions that criminal law reflects the social norms of most people, in a complex society like the United States this is not always true. Often the law does not reflect the cherished values of many people, and it may even go against strongly held values of others.

3. We learn of reported crimes from the FBI *Crime Index,* which measures eight serious offenses: murder, forcible rape, burglary, robbery, aggravated assault, larceny, motor vehicle theft, and arson. The *National Crime Victimization Survey,* compiled from about 44,000 national sample interviews conducted annually, reveals that only 40 percent of all crimes get reported to the police.

4. People do not report crimes because they fear embarrassment or reprisal, they believe the crime's triviality does not justify the time and effort it would take to report it, they believe that the effort would be futile, they are unwilling to ask the government to enforce some laws, or

they are reluctant to have any contact with the police because of past mistreatment or their own illegal activities.

5. Property crimes, which constitute 90 percent all crime, have been steadily dropping since 1973. Violent crime surged in the late 1980s and early 1990s, but it has dropped since the mid-1990s. The people most victimized by violent crime are Blacks, males, the young, and the poor.

6. Americans hold ambivalent attitudes toward violence. We deplore violence, yet we glorify those who use it "in the name of the law." The use of violent force (particularly vigilantism) to protect community values is part of American history. Two recent forms of social violence are road rage and the anti-government attacks of citizens' militia group members.

7. Despite the recent drop in violent crime and its low proportion to all crimes committed, it remains the greatest fear among Americans. Most murderers and their victims are young males of the same race. Black females are four times more likely than White females to be a murder victim, and Black males are eight times more likely than White males to die violently. Most Americans favor capital punishment and the number of executions has increased in recent years. Supporters and opponents continue to argue of its merits as a deterrent or its justification as therapeutic vengeance.

8. Young women under age eighteen represent 44 percent of all rape victims. Acquaintance or date rape accounts for more than half of all rape cases. The rapist and the victim usually share the same race, age group, neighborhood, and socioeconomic status.

9. Organized crime is big business, earning hundreds of billions annually. White-collar crime includes corporate crimes such as fraud, price-fixing, and unsafe product manufacture; professional crimes such as embezzlement and fraud; and employee theft, which cost employers more than $15 billion annually. Juveniles commit the greatest proportion of serious property crimes.

10. Juvenile delinquency is a legal category that places minors—usually seventeen or younger—under the protection of the Juvenile Justice Code. Gangs now recruit younger members and keep older ones longer; their activities typically involve drugs, as well as property and violent crimes. Increased juvenile violence led almost every state since 1992 to pass laws making it easier to try juveniles as adults to mete out harsher punishments.

11. Community policing and strategic policing are effective methods of reducing street crime. Prison overcrowding and the high incarceration rate result from mandatory sentencing for drug crimes, longer time served (truth-in-sentencing), and reduced release rates. Blacks and Hispanics account for a highly disproportionate number of prisoners. Boot camps—if coupled with education and drug treatment—and work release programs are hopeful prison alternatives.

12. Terrorism, as demonstrated by the World Trade Center and Pentagon attacks in 2001, has become a greater threat than ever. Terrorists view no one, not even children, as innocents; and they tend to favor acts of massive destruction over attacks on smaller targets.

13. Functionalists and Conflict theorists employ a macrosocial analysis of the social structure, value system, and social control mechanisms to explain crime, delinquency, and violence. Feminists gender-bias studies helped change laws about domestic violence, testimony about a rape victim's past, and stalking. Interactionists utilize a microsocial analysis to study how and why some people commit crime and violence while others do not.

KEY TERMS

Citizens' militias

Community policing

Crime index

Crime rate

Criminal terrorism

Date rape

Differential association

Judicial discretion

Juvenile delinquency

Juvenile Justice Code

Labeling theory

Labor racketeering

National Crime Victimization Survey

Plea bargain

Police discretion

Prosecutorial discretion

Recidivism

Repressive terrorism

Revolutionary terrorism

Road rage

Status offenses

Strategic policing

Terrorism

Uniform Crime Report

Vigilantism

Violence subculture

White-collar crime

INTERNET RESOURCES

At this book's Web site with Allyn & Bacon, you will find numerous links related to the problems pertaining to crime and violence. To explore these resources, go first to the author's page (**http://www.ablongman.com/parrillo**). Next, select this edition of *Contemporary Social Problems* and then choose **Internet Readings and Exercises**. Then select **Chapter 9,** where you will find both a variety of sites to investigate and some questions that pertain to those sites.

SUGGESTED READINGS

Athens, Lonnie H. *The Creation of Dangerous Violent Criminals,* reprint ed. Champaign: University of Illinois Press, 1992. Through in-depth interviews with imprisoned violent offenders, the author employs Interactionist theory to explain the evolution of dangerous criminals.

Bernard, Thomas J. *The Cycle of Juvenile Justice.* New York: Oxford University Press, 1997. A helpful historical overview of legal cases and policy changes in juvenile justice.

Coleman, James W. *The Criminal Elite,* 5th ed. New York: W.H. Freeman, 2001. An informative and detailed analysis of white-collar crime, including at the top levels of society.

Cox, Steven M. *Police: Practices, Perspectives, Problems.* Boston: Allyn & Bacon, 1997. A comprehensive historical and social look at police issues, including discussions of current problems and potential solutions in the context of change.

Cummings, Scott, and Daniel J. Monti (eds.). *The Origins and Impact of Youth Gangs in the United States.* Albany: State University of New York Press, 1993. A series of excellent articles providing vivid descriptions of and insights into the motivations, activities, and behaviors of gang members.

Gaines, Donna. *Teenage Wasteland: Suburbia's Dead End Kids.* New York: HarperCollins, 1992. From a case study of four New Jersey teens who succeeded in their suicide pact, this study expands into an analysis of the fascination with deviance among all troubled youth.

Lesser, Ian O. (ed.). *Countering the New Terrorism.* Washington, D.C.: Rand Corporation, 1999. Featuring the works of world-renowned experts, this book traces the recent evolution of international terrorism against civilian and U.S. military targets, looks ahead to where terrorism is going, and assesses how it might be contained.

Mann, Coramae Richey. *Unequal Justice: A Question of Color.* Bloomington: Indiana University Press, 1994. An indictment of the U.S. criminal justice system for its treatment of people of color, based on extensive research and analysis of their treatment.

Matza, David. *Becoming Deviant.* Englewood Cliffs, N.J.: Prentice-Hall, 1969. An excellent review of the weaknesses of the "pathology" and "correction" perspectives, and a theoretical reorientation of the delinquency field.

Monti, Daniel J. *Wannabe: Gangs in Suburbs and Schools.* New York: Blackwell, 1994. Offers a comprehensive look at suburban gangs from the perspective of kids who live the life and those who only observe, revealing the complexity of gangs in suburbs.

Quinney, Richard. *The Social Reality of Crime,* Somerset, N.J.: Transaction Publishers, 2001. Comprehensive review of the history of American crime and the emergence of the many views that make up American criminology.

Reiman, Jeffrey H. *The Rich Get Richer and the Poor Get Prison: Ideology, Class, and Criminal Justice,* 6th ed. New York: Allyn & Bacon, 2000. A Conflict analysis of the disparity in the criminal justice system for the wealthy and for the poor.

Zimring, Franklin E. *American Youth Violence.* New York: Oxford University Press, 1998. This book is devoted to the most important juvenile question facing policy makers: what is the appropriate sanction for young people who commit violent acts?

10

The Family

Facts About the Family

- Unmarried couples living together in the United States now total 5.5 million.

- Approximately 50 percent of first marriages end in divorce.

- About 40 to 50 percent of all children will reach age eighteen without having lived continuously with both biological parents.

- Only one-half of American children who are granted child support payments by court orders actually receive them.

- One-third of all U.S. births occur among unmarried women.

- Over 2 million wives are beaten annually.

- Every day three children in the United States die from child abuse.

- One in six females is a victim of incest.

The most compelling question about the family today is how to define it. Swept by the currents of change, the family exists in innumerable forms and appears to be best characterized as "in transition." Most families have someone in their midst who is divorced. Many people know individuals who are living together and are not legally married. Among these may be gay men or women who consider themselves "domestic partners"—in effect, same-sex married couples. Some observers have noted the disappointment of would-be grandparents when their married but career-oriented children decide not to have children themselves. In the circle of the family, we hear these and other changes discussed. The assessments range from the opinion that family life is better now (since individuals are no longer locked into traditional marital and parental roles, but instead can make a choice) to the view that families are falling apart and that the disorganization is bringing society to the brink of ruin.

Family in Sociohistorical Context

To grasp what changes are occurring in family life, we must first have a clear sense of how the family looked and functioned historically. Television reruns on cable channels have portrayed the golden age of the family as consisting of several children and a harmoniously married mother and father, all working together, sometimes aided by live-in grandparents. Lines of authority and respect were based on age, and a strong work ethic and spiritual values were passed on to the children. The elusiveness of this reality, however, is reflected in *The Way We Never Were: American Families and the Nostalgia Trap* (1992, 2000), by Stephanie Coontz.[1] In the past, few extended families existed, due to high death rates. The higher death rates also meant that parents often suffered the loss of infant children; children lost siblings; and marriages ended abruptly. In short, death disrupted the family then as divorce does today. Each historical era of the family, in fact, if judged by today's standards, had major shortcomings. Our desire to produce children

In what ways has the classic American family changed since this photo was taken? Why might the social history of any institution or situation be important in understanding social problems pertinent to that institution or situation?

steeped in the work ethic, for example, would nonetheless lead few of us to condone the practices common during the latter half of the nineteenth century of requiring many children to work twelve or more hours per day under abysmal factory conditions.

Idealization of the past also leads us to posit the prevalence of one type of family, ignoring the multiplicity of class, race, and ethnic differences in any era. The struggle for subsistence of poor families, for instance, must be contrasted with the lifestyles of the middle class and of the elite.

In general, however, families in the last two hundred years, responding to urbanization and industrialization, have become smaller, with fewer children; kinship has become less important; and a growing emphasis on individual rights has led to the redefinition of marriage as a source of personal fulfillment rather than as a social obligation or an economically rewarding partnership—and to higher divorce rates. Women have moved into the paid labor force outside the home more rapidly than men have assumed domestic roles. Some of the resulting changes have created problems for society (see the box on the next page).

Table 10.1 reveals some prominent changes that occurred in families from 1970 to 2000: the decrease in the proportion of married-couple households with children under eighteen; the concomitant increase in single-parent families, especially female householders with children; the

Table 10.1 Household Composition by Presence of Own Children Under 18: 2000, 1990, 1980, and 1970 (Numbers in Thousands)

Type of Household	2000		1990		1980		1970	
	Number	Percent	Number	Percent	Number	Percent	Number	Percent
ALL HOUSEHOLDS	104,705	100.0	93,347	100.0	80,776	100.0	63,401	100.0
Family households	72,025	68.7	66,090	70.8	59,550	73.7	51,456	81.2
No own children under 18	37,420	35.7	33,801	36.2	28,528	35.3	22,725	35.8
With own children under 18	34,605	33.0	32,289	34.6	31,022	38.4	28,732	45.3
Married-couple family	55,311	52.8	52,317	56.0	49,112	60.8	44,728	70.5
No own children under 18	30,062	27.7	27,780	29.8	24,151	29.9	19,196	30.3
With own children under 18	25,248	24.1	24,537	26.3	24,961	30.9	25,532	40.3
Other family, male householder	4,028	5.8	2,884	3.1	1,733	2.1	1,228	1.9
No own children under 18	2,242	2.1	1,731	1.9	1,117	1.4	887	1.4
With own children under 18	1,786	1.7	1,153	1.2	616	0.8	341	0.5
Other family, female householder	12,687	12.1	10,890	11.7	8,705	10.8	5,500	8.7
No own children under 18	5,116	4.9	4,290	4.6	3,261	4.0	2,642	4.2
With own children under 18	7,571	7.2	6,599	7.1	5,445	6.7	2,858	4.5
Nonfamily households	32,680	31.2	27,257	29.2	21,226	26.3	11,945	18.8
Living alone	26,724	25.5	22,999	24.6	18,296	22.7	10,851	17.1
Male householder	14,641	14.0	11,606	12.4	8,807	10.9	4,063	6.4
Living alone	11,181	10.7	9,049	9.7	6,966	8.6	3,532	5.6
Female householder	18,039	17.2	15,651	16.8	12,419	15.4	7,882	12.4
Living alone	15,543	14.8	13,950	14.9	11,330	14.0	7,319	11.5

Source: U.S. Bureau of the Census, *Current Population Reports,* series P20–537, "Household and Family Characteristics: March 2000" (Washington D.C.: U.S. Gov't Printing Office, 2002).

Social Constructions of Social Problems

What Is Marriage? What Is Family?

For most of the twentieth century, Americans defined marriage as a lifelong, legally and morally sanctioned relationship, in which a heterosexual couple became an economically cooperative unit in which they lived together, had sexual relations, and raised children. Only in this form was that unit considered a family—one that had a working husband, a homemaker wife, and their children. Society viewed any variance from that singular vision—such as casual sex, divorce, heterosexual or homosexual cohabiting, unwed mothers, and their "illegitimate" children—as sinful, shameful, and deviant. Criticized and condemned, defined as abnormal, people falling into any of these categories found themselves ostracized and treated with contempt by the "good folk." Seen as a social problem, they frequently encountered negative reactions and so often masked their real selves if they could.

By the end of the twentieth century, no social institution had changed so dramatically as that of the family, both in structure and in gender roles. To illustrate, in 1960, about 90 percent of family households had two parents present, and about 28 percent of married women with children worked outside the home. By 2002, about 77 percent of family households had two parents present and about 71 percent of married women with children worked outside the home. No longer is the woman simply a gender-defined "keeper of home and hearth." More than three of four work outside the home, and many fathers now share in household and child-rearing duties once the sole province of the woman. Dual-career families are more the norm, and many women now work in professions and occupations once male bastions, making important economic contributions to the family's economic well-being.

This 13 percent drop in two-parent families and the 43 percent increase in working mothers are only part of the social changes in the family. Changed even is the definition of what constitutes a "family," for only one in four households now fits the old cultural ideal of a married couple with one or more children under age eighteen. Another 29 percent of family households are married couples without children, while 16 percent are single-parent families. Then there are what the Census Bureau calls "nonfamily" households, people who live alone, now comprising 31 percent of all households. These are a mixture of young singles as well as middle-aged or elderly adults who are divorced, never married, or widowed.

In 2003, the Massachusetts Supreme Court upheld same-sex marriages, Vermont allows civil unions, and some cities (including New York City and San Francisco) and some states—led by Hawaii—now extend limited marital benefits (including inheritance, medical insurance, and state pension rights) to gay couples. Gay parenting is another recently gained legal right, and over 1 million gay couples in the United States are currently raising children. These children are either offspring from a previous heterosexual union or else adopted children. Clearly, gay parenting challenges some traditional concepts about families, but it also reveals that people of all sexual orientations hold "traditional family values" when it comes to rearing children.

The many changes in family structure and roles has brought great diversity to the definition of "family," and with it new challenges and problems. Not everyone accepts these changes. Some politicians criticize single-parent families, and some religious groups condemn gay couples and gay parenting. Indeed, in a few widely publicized cases, courts have removed children from gay couples as in "the best interests" of the children. The definition of "family" may have changed, but so have the defined social problems.

Source: Drawn from the U.S. Bureau of the Census, *Current Population Reports*, P20-547 (June 2003).

Figure 10.1   Median Age at First Marriage of the Population 15 Years and Over by Sex: Selected Years, 1970 to 2000

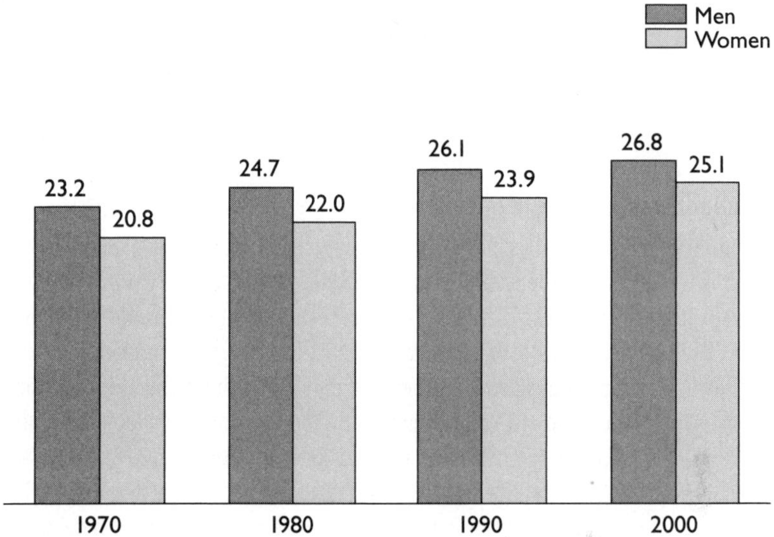

Source: U.S. Census Bureau, Current Population Survey, March Supplements: 1970–2000.

increase in households where persons live alone. Figure 10.1 above shows the overall decline in the percentage of married adults. This reflects both the increase in the percentage of divorced persons and the large increase in the "never married" category.

The Scope of Family Problems

On the most general level, the family suffers from existing within a society that is largely anti-family. The United States lags behind other industrialized nations in the level of support given to families in the form of child allowances, good-quality childcare and medical attention, and paternity and maternity leaves. Not until 1993 did the United States create a Family Leave Act that requires employers to allow their workers to take leave to care for family members without jeopardizing their jobs.

Workplaces have been slow to add childcare facilities; corporations have established "mommy tracks" for women who combine careers with family, retarding their advancement and training; and evidently they have even created a similar "daddy track" for men who perform a significant share of their family's childcare.[2]

The vast majority of women who have a paying job and have children do most of the family's housework; this amounts to a second shift when they return home, making their lives very stressful.[3] We don't know the cost to society of overworked women, but adverse health consequences and increased employee absences are probable. As yet, this issue of stress continues to be individualized rather than being defined as a collective problem.

Many other family concerns today fall into this individualized realm as well, such as the ambiguity provoked when adult children return home to live, the phenomenon of "sandwich generation" adults caring for both young and old family members, and the new intensive role of some grandparents as primary care providers for their grandchildren in situations where their own children are unable to perform the role because of drug abuse, unemployment, or other social problems.

Many people find certain changes in the family—such as **cohabitation**—morally objectionable despite their having as yet had no measurable negative impact upon the society. Cohabiting couples (individuals living together without legal marriage) now number about 5.5 million (11 percent same-sex couples).[4] One negative scenario based on this phenomenon is the suggestion that, if cohabitation were to become so common that few people bothered to get married, and if this depressed the birth rate, society might see a reduction in economic production levels because of the decline in native-born recruits available from the new generation of workers. Basically, when other institutions in society begin to feel adverse consequences from ongoing changes in the family, these patterns are redefined as social problems.

Three family-related social problems are addressed here: the high incidence of divorce, the increase in single-parent families, and the significant levels of family violence.

Divorce

For the first half of the twentieth century, the divorce rate in the United States was relatively stable. A downward fluctuation occurred during the Depression, when people could not afford to pay for a divorce or to maintain two households. An upward surge followed World War II, due in part to unstable marriages hastily contracted before or during the war and in part to changes wrought by the effects of separation. Between 1965 and 1979, however, the divorce rate more than doubled, from 2.5 to 5.4 divorces per 1,000 population. The incidence of divorce peaked in 1981, and has dropped since then, reaching 4.0 in 2002.[5] Possible explanations include the rising age of persons at first marriage, the increase in numbers remaining single, a lower rate of remarriage (from 75 to 80 percent in the 1980s to 42 percent of divorced women and 45 percent of divorced men), and economic slowdowns, which tend to depress the divorce rate. Despite the moderating pattern of the 1980s and early 1990s, the number of divorces remains high; about half of all marriages end in divorce.[6] Interestingly, cohabiting couples who marry have a higher rate of divorce than couples who did not live together before marriage.[7]

Factors Contributing to the High Rate of Divorce

The phrases in marriage vows express a lifelong commitment—"until death do us part" and "as long as you both shall live"—and once meant just that to most married couples. Today many of us have experienced divorce firsthand or have divorced relatives or close friends. The scariest thing about marriage may not be the big level of commitment it entails, but the concern that, as right as the step may seem at the moment it is taken, it might one day prove to be one of the half of all marriages that fail. Aside from the personal factors that break up a marriage, three social forces are contributors.

Changing Roles of Women

In examining the social factors associated with a high divorce rate, we must acknowledge the change in women's roles. Women in the past often depended on men for financial support and so might have hesitated to terminate even a miserable marriage; but now many have the ability to become self-supporting. Likewise, the option may be more attractive to men, who are less likely to be saddled with alimony payments to their working wives. Research shows that women in higher-status, better-paying occupations are less likely to experience marriage disruption.[8]

Attitudes, Laws, and Demographic Factors

Societal attitudes toward divorce have changed as it has grown more common. Today there is less discrimination, more tolerance, and greater acceptance of the divorced. Beliefs about divorce have also changed—in particular, regarding the proposition that it is better for unhappy partners to stay together for the sake of children. Liberalized divorce laws, beginning with California's implementation in 1970 of **no-fault divorce,** made divorces easier to obtain. (*No-fault* means that neither party is blamed for the divorce; the decision is a mutual one.) Now all but two states have no-fault provisions. Furthermore, in the 1970s, the rise in the divorce rate was affected by the end of the Vietnam War and by a sheer demographic fact: divorce for women most often occurs between the ages of twenty and twenty-four and, for men, between twenty-five and twenty-nine.[9] In the 1970s large numbers of individuals fell into these age categories as the baby boom generation grew into young adulthood. In subsequent years, fewer people fell in these age categories reflecting the lower birthrate of the 1960s and 1970s. And finally, the average age of divorce today has shifted upward as people marry later.

Changing Expectations for Marriage

Even more fundamental to explaining the high divorce rate, however, is the change in people's expectations for marriage: the underpinnings of marriage today are largely psychological. Individuals seek self-fulfillment through a union with another person, and if their emotional needs are unmet, the basis of the contract no longer exists. Ann Swidler describes the emerging love ethic today as one that emphasizes the rebellious, free, individualistic side of love, endorsing flexibility and avoiding permanence.[10] In the past, the "success" of a marriage was often gauged on the basis of how well individuals fulfilled their social roles (the man as a good provider and the woman as a skilled housewife and good mother). Because it is easier to become an experienced baker or to make more money for the family than to become a day-to-day expert in interpersonal relations, marriage has become much more risky.

The Impact of Divorce on Adults

A high rate of divorce raises societal concerns about the long- and short-term effects of such break-ups on the individuals involved. The two major costs of divorce are economic and physical/emotional. Several studies have confirmed that men improve their economic status after a divorce, but that women average a 30 percent drop in income that typically lasts for several years.[11] Although they may eventually return to their income level prior to the divorce, they do not do as well as women who remain in stable, married families. Many divorced women recover financially only through remarriage. The differential economic impact is partly an outcome of no-fault divorce laws, which assume independence and equality between husbands and wives, but ignore gender inequities in pay. It is also due to the fact that women most often have custody of children, and that many fathers are remiss in their court-ordered child support payments.

Divorce has both long- and short-term consequences for mental and physical well-being. Three types of people—the newly divorced, those who divorce more than once, and women—are especially susceptible to depression as a result of divorce. For divorced men, who typically remarry sooner than divorced women, remaining unmarried for more than six years correlates with increased rates of car accidents, alcoholism, drug abuse, depression, and anxiety. For divorced women, the most serious long-term health effects come from the stresses of poverty, continued conflicts with former husbands, and problems in child rearing.[12]

Paul Bohannan described divorce as a multistage process of separation: the emotional divorce, the legal separation, the economic divorce, the custodial divorce (regarding care of children), the community divorce (when family and friends must be informed), and the psychic divorce (when individuals must crystallize a new, partnerless identity for themselves).[13]

Robert Weiss categorized various stages of marital separation in which individuals experience separation distress, anxiety, panic, and depression as the object of attachment becomes detached. Each such stage may be followed by a sense of euphoria that one no longer needs the former partner and then by periods of intense loneliness.[14] The bonds of attachment last much longer than most divorcing partners expect, even if they both wanted the divorce. Recovery usually comes from remarriage or through the formation of new intimate relationships.[15]

The Impact of Divorce on Children

Experts predict that 40 to 50 percent of children today will reach age eighteen without having lived continuously with both biological parents. The greatest odds face African-American children; fewer than 20 percent of them may spend their entire childhood with both biological parents.[16] The disruption could stem from divorce, separation, or abandonment; from having parents who never married; or from placement with neither parent. In the 1990s, the average number of children per divorce decree has fallen, due to an increase in childless divorcing couples or lower birth rates among those divorcing. Still, one in ten U.S. children under age eighteen lives with a divorced single parent.[17]

Research Findings

We know that divorce affects men, women, and children differently. The impact on children varies with their age when the divorce occurred, the level of parental conflict, the nature and degree of subsequent contact with the noncustodial parent, and the stepfamily (if any) arrangement. Research findings do not always agree, but a review of ninety-two studies by Paul Amato and Bruce Keith drew several general conclusions. First, compared to children who grew up in intact families, children of divorced parents are less likely to graduate from high school, are more likely to have lower earnings, are more likely to become dependent on welfare, and are more likely to marry at an early age. Daughters of divorced parents are more likely to have a child out of wedlock, and to be divorced themselves.[18] Other studies noted a higher rate of delinquency, problems in peer relations, and in school performance among postdivorce children. Boys tend to display more explicit and immediate behavioral symptoms—such as aggression and acting-out—than girls. By adolescence, girls in divorced families often have trouble managing sexuality and making emotional commitments.[19] Finally, researchers have found that divorce correlates with an increase in children's reported illnesses.[20]

In a longitudinal study over a twenty-five-year period, Judith Wallerstein found that, while children do learn to cope with divorce, its effect are nonetheless long lasting. As adults, the sons and daughters of divorced parents battle their own demons when embarking on their own romantic relationships. Then, pain plays out in their relationships, their work lives, and their confidence about their own parenting abilities. Wallerstein argues that although the situation is dire, through good counseling and healing, the long-term outcomes can be positive, as they come to terms with their past and build satisfying relationships.[21]

About half of all U.S. marriages end in divorce. Normally, mothers get custody of the children but they do not necessarily get child support, even when awarded by the courts. What are the short-term and long-term consequences of divorce on adults? How different are these effects on women compared to men? What is the impact of divorce on children? What variables affect these results?

Today sociologists recognize that the happiness and adjustment of divorced children are superior to those of children in intact conflict-ridden homes but lower than those of children in happy homes with both parents. Moreover, divorce may have a wide range of impacts on children. Let us direct our attention to factors that reduce these adverse consequences.

Child Support

The most significant impact of divorce on children is the reduction in standard of living that many suffer. This happens because custody is most often awarded to the mother, whose children then share in her downward mobility. Economic hardship can result in moving to less desirable neighborhoods, attending inferior schools, and receiving poorer nutrition and health care. Older children may feel stigmatized among peers when they cannot afford material status symbols.

A major contributing factor to children's economic problems is the failure of noncustodial fathers to support their children financially. Frank Furstenberg noted a bifurcation among fathers today into good dads and bad dads.[22] The good dad is a full partner in parenting, is emotionally involved with his children, and adopts egalitarian norms within the family. The bad dads shirk their paternal obligations (or even deny paternity). Nationwide, less than half of all families with judicially decreed child support orders receive the full amount owed to them, and 1.8 million get nothing. Keeping track of parents who move from state to state is one of the most difficult tasks involved in collecting child support, officials say. More than 25 percent of the 14 million child support cases nationwide involve parents who do not live in the same state as their children.[23]

Lack of support often occurs even when the father has the ability to pay. Failure to support children seems to be linked to the quality of the relationship between the former spouses and the degree of contact the father has with the children. Fathers who visit their children contribute more regularly. However, nearly one-half of all children of divorce have not seen their fathers for more than a year, and one-sixth have seen him only once or twice in the past year. The frequency of contacts drops off sharply as the length of time since the separation increases. Fathers who remarry tend to disengage themselves even further from the children of their earlier marriage.[24]

Enforcing child support obligations entered a new era in 1997, when the federal government began operating a computerized directory that lists every person newly hired by every employer in the country, enabling federal and state investigators to track down parents who owe money to their children. States use the directory to locate parents and dun them, typically by securing court orders requiring employers to deduct child support payments from the parents' wages and salaries. Even so, the improvement in collecting awarded child support payments from deadbeat parents remain limited.

Changes in Family Structure

The institution of marriage and family structure in general have changed considerably since the end of World War II. Social trends, legal reforms, and the increased proportion of women in the workplace have contributed to higher rates of divorce and nonmarital childbearing. Women's increased economic independence, the advent of modern contraception, and other societal shifts have led Americans to evaluate marriage outside traditional constraints. People are also waiting longer to get married (see Figure 10.2 on page 304). The once-typical family structure of a married couple with children now exists in just over one in four U.S. households (see Table 10.2). The many variations on this important social institution affect family life and sometimes serve as contributing factors in social problems involving the family.

Remarriages and Blended Families

Although the number of married people who divorce remains high, the percentage who remarry is also high, indicating that the disillusionment is with an individual partner rather than with the institution. The remarriage rate—about 42 percent for women and 45 percent for men—has fallen slightly in recent years, especially among educated women.[25] Remarriage among divorced parents creates a **blended family,** consisting of a husband, a wife, children of previous marriages, and any children from the new marital union.

African American women have a lower rate of remarriage than White or Hispanic-American women. In general, remarried couples report themselves to be as happy as currently married, never-divorced couples and happier than the divorced people who do not remarry. Their probability of divorce a second time is higher than the probability of a divorce among all first-time married couples, however, especially when adolescent children from a previous marriage are present.[26]

For children, remarriage may ease the economic hardships they may be experiencing, but it also requires new family and kin adjustments that may be acutely stressful. One of the main problems is that remarriage remains "an incomplete institution" within which roles and boundaries are ambiguous.[27] The authority of the stepmother is particularly lacking in clarity, but so are the responsibilities and rights of stepfathers and the various sets of grandparents. The ambiguities seem related to the greater risk of physical and sexual abuse posed to children in stepfamily settings. The majority of stepfamilies are nonviolent; overall, however, children are more likely to be abused by a stepparent than a biological parent.[28]

Table 10.2   U.S. Household Composition in 2000 by Percent

Family households		68.7%
Married couple with children under 18	24.1%	
Married couple, no children under 18	28.7%	
Other, with children under 18	8.9%	
Other, without children under 18	7.0%	
Nonfamily households		31.2%
Men living alone	10.7%	
Women living alone	14.8%	
Other	5.7%	

Source: U.S. Bureau of the Census, P20–515, 2002, Table A.

Marriage, divorce, and remarriage statistics point to greater numbers of mixed-race families and blended families in which children from multiple previous marriages are recombined in a new family. At the same time, proportionally more individuals are choosing to remain single, and more couples are choosing not to have children. What do these trends signify?

The research on the impact of divorce confirms the need for a stronger societal response in the form of counseling and other services to ease people through a series of difficult transitions. On average, children in family types other than those with both biological parents, are more likely to achieve lower levels of education, to become teen parents, to experience health, behavior, and mental health problems, and to be poor. Although the likelihood is greater, most children not growing up with both biological parents do not have serious problems.[29]

Single-Parent Families

The high incidence of divorce is associated with the large increase in **single-parent families** in the United States. Since women overwhelmingly obtain custody of children, the vast majority of these families are female-headed. In 2000, as indicated in Table 10.3 on the next page, 21 percent of White children, 55 percent of African American children, and 28 percent of Hispanic-origin children under eighteen lived with their mothers only. However, the route to the single-parent family differs among these groups: White female-headed families typically result most often from divorce; African American ones most often arise from never-married mothers; and Hispanic-origin ones in substantial part from divorce, never-married parents, and married but absent parents (Figure 10.2). A decade ago, a child in a single-parent situation was almost twice as likely to be living with a divorced parent as with a never-married parent; but today such a child is less likely to be living with a divorced parent than with a never-married parent.[30]

While female-headed households may provide necessary levels of emotional support for children's development, a major societal concern is in the number of these families who are poor:

Table 10.3 Family Groups with Children under Eighteen Years Old by Race and Hispanic Origin: 1980 to 2000

Household	1980		1990		2000	
	Number	Percent	Number	Percent	Number	Percent
ALL RACES, TOTAL*	32,150	100.0	34,670	100.0	37,496	100.0
Two-parent family groups	25,231	78.5	24,921	71.9	25,771	68.7
One-parent family groups	6,920	21.5	9,749	28.1	11,725	31.3
Maintained by mother	6,230	19.4	8,398	24.2	9,681	25.8
Maintained by father	690	2.1	1,351	3.9	2,044	5.5
WHITE, TOTAL	27,294	100.0	28,294	100.0	30,079	100.0
Two-parent family groups	22,628	82.9	21,905	77.4	22,241	73.9
One-parent family groups	4,664	17.1	6,389	22.6	7,838	26.1
Maintained by mother	4,122	15.1	5,310	18.8	6,216	20.7
Maintained by father	542	2.0	1,079	3.8	1,622	5.4
BLACK, TOTAL	4,074	100.0	5,087	100.0	5,530	100.0
Two-parent family groups	1,961	48.1	2,006	39.4	2,135	38.6
One-parent family groups	2,114	51.9	3,081	60.6	3,396	61.4
Maintained by mother	1,984	48.7	2,860	56.2	3,060	55.3
Maintained by father	129	3.2	221	4.4	335	6.1
HISPANIC, TOTAL**	2,194	100.0	3,429	100.0	5,503	100.0
Two-parent family groups	1,626	74.1	2,289	66.8	3,625	65.9
One-parent family groups	568	25.9	1,140	33.2	1,877	34.1
Maintained by mother	526	24.0	1,003	29.3	1,565	28.4
Maintained by father	42	1.9	138	3.9	313	5.7

* Includes other races, not shown separately.

**Hispanic persons may be of any race.

Source: U.S. Bureau of the Census, *Statistical Abstract of the United States: 2002* (Washington, D.C.: U.S. Government Printing Office, 2002), Table 54, p. 51.

about one of four White and two of five African American and Hispanic-origin female householder families without a husband present live in poverty.[31] The most significant factor, however, seems to be their experience of poverty rather than of single parenthood per se. African American children, for example, frequently have strong informal support networks of kin.[32]

We have already seen that divorce may disadvantage women financially, especially when the father's child support payments are inadequate; for children of never-married mothers, the route to poverty is linked to the low rate of marriage. The marriage rate in turn is directly related to both an absence of males (who have unusually high death rates and incarceration rates) and to joblessness and the attendant inability to play the role of provider in the family. The high levels of

Figure 10.2 Marital Status by Race and Hispanic Origin, 1980 and 2000 (Persons 18 Years and Older)

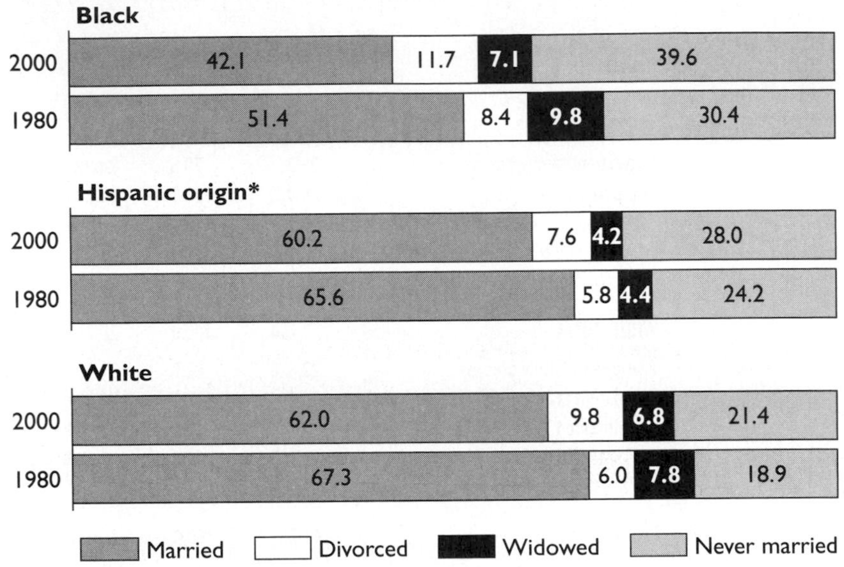

Black

	Married	Divorced	Widowed	Never married
2000	42.1	11.7	7.1	39.6
1980	51.4	8.4	9.8	30.4

Hispanic origin*

	Married	Divorced	Widowed	Never married
2000	60.2	7.6	4.2	28.0
1980	65.6	5.8	4.4	24.2

White

	Married	Divorced	Widowed	Never married
2000	62.0	9.8	6.8	21.4
1980	67.3	6.0	7.8	18.9

☐ Married   ☐ Divorced   ■ Widowed   ☐ Never married

*Persons of Hispanic origin may be of any race.

Source: U.S. Bureau of the Census, *Current Population Reports,* Series P20–537. (Washington , D.C.: U.S. Government Printing Office, 2002).

unemployment for African American and Hispanic-origin males are associated with two broad structural changes in our society: loss of manufacturing jobs as these jobs either disappear altogether or shift to other localities; and residential racial segregation that ghettoizes African Americans, restricts them to inferior schools, and limits them to low-paying, unskilled occupations.[33]

Long-term economic strategies are necessary to address these problems. In the short term, society might more wisely focus on the women heading the families, ensuring that any "workfare" arrangement provides them with meaningful work with potential for advancement, as well as adequate childcare and health benefits and a reduction in discriminatory pay scales. Recent welfare reform did not adequately address these issues.

Births to Unmarried Women

Births occurring to unmarried women now account for one-third of the total, compared to 4 percent in 1950. The proportions vary significantly among subgroups: non-Hispanic White, approximately 22 percent; non-Hispanic Black, about 69 percent; Hispanic, about 43 percent. However, the birth rates among unmarried Black and Hispanic women dropped steadily throughout the 1990s and, by the end of the decade, Blacks reached their lowest level ever for births to unmarried women while Hispanics attained their lowest level since 1990.[34]

Birth rates to unmarried women are highest among those aged eighteen to nineteen and twenty to twenty-four, followed by women aged twenty-five to twenty-nine (see Figure 10.3). The good news is that births among unmarried teenagers aged fifteen to nineteen years dropped 22 percent in the 1990s. Previously, they had increased 24 percent between 1986 and 1991 to a record high. The declines in birth rates were steepest for non-Hispanic black teenagers.[35]

Although the proportion of unmarried women having children may have decreased in recent years, the actual number of such births is at an all-time high, over 1.3 million in 2000.[36] How can we explain this seeming contradiction? The greatest number of these births results from the rise in the number of unmarried women in the child-bearing ages. A smaller proportion of a larger number produces a greater total. Given the increased total of births to unmarried women, we must consider the negative ramifications, particularly with regard to teenagers and to the dangers of unmarried mothers with limited earnings potential living in poverty.

Some negative consequences of teenage pregnancy are that young women are more likely to drop out of school, have low-paying jobs, or be unemployed. Additionally, infants of adolescent mothers are at higher risk for health problems and are more likely than women in their early 20s to give birth to underweight, premature, and small babies; to risk congenital malformations in their newborns; and infant mortality.[37]

Figure 10.3   Birth Rate of U.S. Unmarried Women, 1980 and 2000

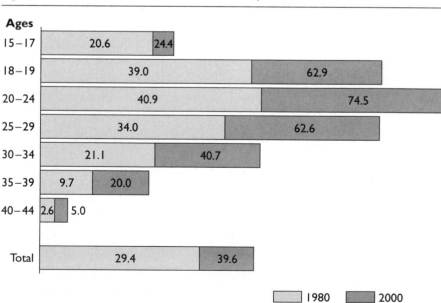

NOTE: Birth rates are live births per 1,000 unmarried women.

Source: National Center for Health Statistics.

Violence and Abuse

In 1994, in a case that stunned the nation, a young South Carolina mother admitted that she had deliberately rolled her car into a lake, drowning her two small children who were strapped into the back seat. Although many people wondered how a sweet-looking person could do that to her own children, the U.S. Department of Justice reports that each year about six hundred mothers kill their children.[38] That covers only the murders; the nonlethal physical violence in the family is much more prevalent. Indeed, an epidemic of family violence rages in the United States. Far from being an idyllic retreat from the pressures of everyday life, many families are a battlefield and a training school for future violence. Although abuse has always existed, no one publicly identified the problem of battered children until 1962.[39] Spouse abuse—specifically, wife beating—did not emerge as a serious concern until the mid-1970s; and abuse of elderly parents surfaced even more recently. The term **abuse** in a broad sense includes both physical and psychological harm; more narrowly, it often refers to the former alone, as substantiated by the empirical evidence of police records.

Incidence of Family Violence

As more and more facts about family violence become known, they reveal that other family members besides children and wives experience mistreatment. The web of family violence entangles husbands abused by wives, parents abused by children, and brothers and sisters abused by each other (see Table 10.4 on the next page). A special study drawn from the National Incident-Based Reporting System (NIBRS) revealed that 27 percent of all violence in 1998 occurred in a family setting, over 90 percent of these incidents were some type of assault.[40]

A recent study examining almost 7,000 couples who participated in the National Survey of Families and Households, found that men and women engage in similar patterns of physical violence during marital fights. Approximately 5 percent of women and 6 percent of men reported that marital disagreements sometimes led to physical violence; and they were equally likely to report that their spouse had hit, shoved, or thrown something at them. Also, 45 percent of men and 40 percent of women reporting physically violent arguments reported that both partners were violent. Urban residents, younger couples, lower-income couples, and less-educated couples were more likely to report physical violence. Black respondents were 58 percent more likely to report violence than Whites. By contrast, Hispanics were half as likely as Whites to report violence.[41]

Experts now recognize marital violence as a serious social problem. Each year, according to recent surveys, one out of eight husbands is physically aggressive at least once toward his wife, and nearly 2 million men assault their female partners. Counting acts by both partners, 8.7 million American couples (nearly one out of six) experience violence each year, and 3.4 million experience severe violence.[42]

That severe violence results in 15 percent of all homicide victims comprising spouses or family members.[43] Furthermore, a connection also exists between marital violence and many psychological problems, including depression, alcohol abuse, and post-traumatic stress disorder. Marital violence often spills over into child abuse, and it may psychologically harm the children even

Table 10.4   Number and Percent of Family Violence by Relationship, 1998

Relationship	Number	Percent
Spouse	49,089	35.1
Common-law spouse	10,544	7.6
Parent	11,100	7.9
Sibling	11,726	8.4
Child	12,570	9.0
Grandparent	573	0.4
Grandchild	762	0.6
In-law	3,411	2.4
Stepparent	1,957	1.4
Stepchild	2,981	2.1
Stepsibling	630	0.4
Other family member	10,038	7.3
Offender*	24,360	17.4
Total	139,731	100.0

*Cases where a participant in the incident is a victim and offender, such as bar fights or family disputes where both husband and wife are charged with assault.

Source: Federal Bureau of Investigation, *Special Report on Family Violence.*

when it does not physically harm them. Male violence is more serious, partly because of men's greater size and strength; it causes more injury, ill health, stress, and psychosomatic symptoms than women's aggression.

Violence Between Spouses

The statistics on family violence are staggering. Every fifteen seconds a woman in this country is battered, adding up to almost 2 million women severely assaulted every year. As discussed in Chapter 9, one-fourth of female homicide victims are killed by a husband or partner. Spousal abuse occurs in families of every racial, ethnic, and economic group. In a recent study at the University of Rhode Island, for example, nearly 2 percent of women with family incomes over $40,000 reported being victims of severe violence.[44]

Part of the problem in identifying and helping battered women is that they often do not disclose their suffering, due to notions of privacy and secrecy in a couple's relationship. In addition to this, shame and the social stigma of abuse prevent women from seeking outside help. Such an attitude results in their estrangement from society and increases their battering by men.[45]

Moreover, spouse abuse—tragic enough in isolation—produces subsequent violence-connected problems. Children who witness violence may suffer permanent psychological and emotional damage. Surveys in some cities show that 10 percent of young children witnessed an assault and up to 90 percent witnessed some kind of violent interaction. Children who witness domestic violence may suffer even more because their parents cannot comfort them. Such children may grow up to believe that violence is an acceptable way of dealing with problems. Boys may become abusers and girls may seek out abusive relationships; or they may resort to alcohol or drugs to relieve their anxiety.[46]

Child Abuse

Last year more than 1 million teens ran away from home. Most left, not for the excitement of the streets or to be grown-up, but to escape beatings, sexual abuse, and worse at home. Over 900,000 cases of child abuse and neglect occur each year; and every day, on average, three children die from abuse, according to the U.S. Department of Health and Human Services. Half of all child abuse victims are White, one-fourth Black, one-sixth Hispanic, and the remainder Native American or Asian-Pacific Islander.[47]

Furthermore, corporal punishment in adolescence may lead to approval of violence against a spouse, depression, and heightened levels of marital conflict in adult life. Witnessing violence between parents as a child is also linked to increased physical violence against a spouse subse-

The high incidence of family violence-whether the physical abuse of children, spouses, or seniors-tells us that this social problem is more than just a series of clashes resulting from individual personality disorders or other family situations. In what ways do the different sociological perspectives help us understand what are the problems facing today's families?

quently. Eliminating corporal punishment correlates with a lower incidence of marital violence and depression later.[48]

Abuse of the Elderly

In the late 1970s, public concern arose over the issue of elder abuse, or what Jean Renvoize called "granny bashing."[49] After several surveys offered findings that suggested there were possibly as many as 1 million abused elders, Congress requested the Department of Health and Human Services to conduct a national study.[50] In 1998, the National Center on Elder Abuse issued its results from this first-ever National Elder Abuse Incidence Study. It shed new light on this significant problem by reporting approximately 450,000 elderly persons, aged sixty and over, experience abuse and/or neglect in domestic settings each year, and that for every reported incident of elder abuse, neglect or self-neglect, approximately five go unreported. Our oldest elders (eighty years and over) are abused and neglected at two to three times their proportion of the elderly population. In almost 90 percent of the elder abuse and neglect incidents with a known perpetrator, the perpetrator is a family member, and two-thirds of the perpetrators are adult children or spouses.[51] According to the National Aging Resource Center on Elder Abuse, almost one-third of this maltreatment is by adult children of the elderly, and includes physical, financial, psychological, and emotional abuse.[52]

As individuals live longer, some (especially widows) may be welcomed by adult children only to have the relationship go sour under daily rounds of demands, complaints, and conflicts. Often adult children take in their elderly parents reluctantly in the first place, and the abuse may be an expression of resentment. For others, abuse of the elderly parent may be a further display of the violent responses already exhibited in the family.

The elders most vulnerable to abuse are women over eighty suffering from dementia and other diseases, who may have communication difficulties, hearing loss, immobility, and incontinence. Some elder abuse is actually spouse abuse. In many situations, however, the abuser is a caregiving child who is financially dependent on the elder.[53]

Unlike caring for children, where the pleasures of watching the child develop moderate the child's constant demands, caring for an older person may involve coping with permanent disabilities and may raise the level of stress within the family. Now that awareness of abuse of the elderly exists, much work remains to be done to alleviate the problem. Needs include hotlines, support groups, day-care centers for the aged, and temporary residential shelters where the elderly relative can be left while the remainder of the family enjoys a weekend or vacation.

Social Factors Linked to Violence

A strong link connects domestic violence to stress, especially when brought on by male unemployment or part-time employment, pregnancy, single-parent family status, or financial problems. A greater risk of physical abuse also occurs among families that are more socially isolated and less tied into a network of kin, neighbors, or friends who might lend support or intervene.

Factors related to violence toward children include larger-than-average family size, low birth weight or premature children (who presumably require more attention), and lack of attachment between mother and child. Victims are most likely to be infants, young children, or older adolescents. Members of these groups are either unable or uninclined to "listen to reason." Women are more likely to abuse their children since they spend so much time with the child and since motherhood is so essential an element in their identity. Handicapped, retarded, or "different" children are at greater risk, too.

The studies on wife abuse found it more common when both husband and wife report the male as experiencing low job satisfaction, when the husband has no religious affiliation, and when alcohol problems exist. Alcohol often plays a major role in domestic violence, but experts are not clear whether it is a cause or simply an associated factor.[54]

Socioeconomic Status

Although the media pays more attention to instances of violence among married couples in the middle or upper classes (the attention focused on O. J. Simpson, for example), more known cases of abuse occur among members of the lower class. This is partly because lower-income people more often use hospital emergency rooms and clinics and because they receive different treatment from the police, making their abuse more visible. Still, although family violence certainly occurs at all socioeconomic levels of society, denying the greater incidence in the lower class ignores the social basis of family violence. If all classes had the same levels of violence, abuse could be explained as an individual psychopathology—a sickness needing psychiatric treatment without societal response. The very real differences in class behavior, however, force us to acknowledge that society itself contributes to the behavior. As Murray Straus stated:

> Rather than psychological factors being anywhere nearly equal in importance to the social causes of family violence, I am now convinced that they account for only a minuscule proportion of the violence which occurs in families—at the outside 10 percent. In short, at least 90 percent of the violence which takes place in American families grows out of the very nature of the family and of the larger society, rather than out of individual aberrations.[55]

Recent Findings

Murray Straus and Christine Smith identified five social factors related to high rates of family violence: intrafamily conflict, male dominance, cultural norms, socialization, and the pervasiveness of violence in society.[56]

In the setting of intense intimacy that a small **nuclear family** creates, a mere handful of individuals must rely on each other's pooled physical and emotional resources to meet the family's needs. Within that setting, individuals are vulnerable to the remarks of others, thus sparking more easily a conflict and subsequent violence. In contrast, the **extended family** setting—which includes perhaps grandparents, aunts, and uncles—is better situated to defuse or disperse emotional conflicts, thereby restoring family stability. Straus and Smith suggest further that, as a throwback to traditional patriarchal society, the nuclear family may adopt force as the chief way for males to assert authority and resolve conflicts.

Violence pervades the institutions of American society: force by the police and by the military, widespread ownership of guns and other weapons, violence on the television and in films, and

Globalization of Social Problems

The Family in an International Context

Family life is in flux all over the world, as the forces of urbanization, industrialization, and modernization buffet even developing countries. These changes tend to weaken kinship, thus "freeing" the individual to make choices. One result has been widespread contraceptive use and a consequent reduction in family size, as traditional societies adopt the industrialized economic viewpoint that children are not economic assets. The pattern is not uniform, however. Families in Ethiopia, for example, still have an average of six children, as do families in other countries in sub-Saharan Africa. Whether it is Africa, Asia, or Latin America, the degree of control women exercise over their lives and the alternatives provided are key factors in family-size reduction.

In developed nations, women focus on equal rights in workplace advancement. Women with opportunities choose more often than others to avoid marriage, to have fewer or no children, and to divorce. At the same time, many other women struggle with the burdens of work, housework, and childcare. In another change, more women are heads of households. What seems to be similar in all parts of the world, however, is the devastating effect of poverty on family life and the potentially violent consequences of gender inequality.

Numerous cross-cultural studies of both developing and developed countries show many similarities in family violence, with wife-beating and the physical punishment of children its two most common forms. Wife-beating occurs in societies where husbands hold the economic and ultimate decision-making power in the household, and where adults often resolve conflicts with other adults by fighting one another. Physical punishment of children tends to be a routine part of child rearing in societies with relatively complex social, economic, and political systems.

Violence is not, however, an inevitable consequence of family life, for it is virtually nonexistent in some societies. Those societies that allow men to control women's lives and accept violent conflict resolution as legitimate have the highest level, while those characterized by cooperation, sharing, and equality typically have the lowest incidents of family violence.

Sweden, for example, has attained perhaps the greatest degree of equality between men and women. For years it has had the highest labor force participation rates of women, including mothers with young children, and women have the highest ratio of salary to males, over 90 percent. More men take paternity leaves to care for newborns than in any other society, although more women than men remain involved in the care of children and the home.

Sweden also has the lowest marriage rate in the industrialized world and the highest rate of cohabitation. So institutionalized is cohabitation, that virtually no couple marries who has not previously lived together. However, the dissolution rate among couples is also the highest in Europe, resulting in about one-fifth of all households with children being single-parent families. These families do not suffer the same level of deprivation as do similar U.S. households, thanks to guaranteed maintenance by the Swedish government. High rates of taxation provide money for childcare, health care, and education. Despite the high rates of cohabitation and divorce, researchers find that commitment to family life is strong and that most people desire to live as couples and to have children.

Sources: Drawn from Resource Centre for Access to Data on Europe, *Eurostat,* available at: http://europa.eu.int/eurostat.html; Ann-Zofie E. Duvander, "The Transition from Cohabilitation to Marriage: A Longitudinal Study of the Propensity to Marry in Sweden in the Early 1990s," *Journal of Family Issues* 20 (September 1999): 698–717.

so forth. Not surprisingly, the ubiquity of violence in society spills over into family life. Some cultural norms even permit family violence; for example, many adults in the United States approve of spanking children as a form of discipline, and most people do not define siblings' hitting each other as family violence.

Violence tends to run in families whose members are socialized into it as a mode of response. (See the box on the previous page for an international example.) Abused children are more likely to grow up to become child and spouse abusers than individuals who experienced little or no violence as children. Authorities estimate that abused children are 30 percent more likely than nonabused children to become abusive parents.

Sexual Violence and Victimization in the Family

Out of the dark closets of families comes the disturbing reality of sexual victimization of spouses and children. Such actions can be violent or nonviolent, taking form in marital rape or instances of incest.

Marital Rape

The issue of spousal rape briefly came to the forefront of public attention in 1993 when Lorena Bobbitt was accused of mutilating her husband after he allegedly raped her. Following a torrent of sensationalistic media coverage, both were eventually acquitted—he of sexual assault, and she of malicious wounding. At the time, many experts noted that spousal rape was notoriously difficult to prove and that convictions for the charge were extremely rare. Yet in 1994, the reopening of a notorious Michigan case, in which the husband steadfastly maintained his innocence before and after his conviction, revealed another difficulty with marital rape cases. Convicted on "dubious circumstantial evidence" with "testimony manipulated for political purposes," the man finally had his conviction overturned after serving nine years in prison.[57]

Marital rape occurs more frequently than most people realize. In several studies, 10–14 percent of wives, one in every seven to ten women, reported either a completed or attempted rape by a husband/ex-husband.[58] Marital rape occurs most often when a marriage is breaking up or during separation. Almost half of the cases involved battering rape, with pain deliberately inflicted to punish the wife or to retaliate against her. In either case, the lingering effects of the rape experience have led many victimized women to experience depression, eating or sleeping disorders, self-esteem problems, sexual dysfunctions, and problems in establishing relationships.[59]

Part of the difficulty in dealing with marital rape lies in prevailing attitudes that support nonenforcement. As is often true in cases of wife-beating, many women do not recognize or define their forced sexual compliance as deviant. They accept that they are the sexual property of their husbands and assume that denying them sexual intercourse on demand is a sign of their own sexual frigidity or failure as a wife; thus, they conclude they deserve punishment—the blaming-the-victim perspective.

Traditional Native American families and first-generation immigrant families often live in extended-family households with one or more parents; children; grandparents; other relatives, such as siblings, aunts, uncles, nieces, nephews, and cousins; and close non-kin, such as a godparent, co-worker, or friend. How can the size and compositon of family households both contribute to and alleviate social problems? What particular problems do first families and immigrant families face?

In a recent study of college undergraduates, both male and female students tended to minimize the seriousness of rape perpetrated by a husband as against rape committed by a stranger. Even though the females considered rape a more damaging event than did the males, sex-role expectations influenced their perception of marital rape. These rape-excusing beliefs are consistent with similar research on date rape.[60]

As recently as 1976, no state had a law against marital rape; but since 1993, all states have removed the exception formerly built into rape laws to cover actions between spouses. However, experts argue that more needs to be done to ensure that rape laws protect married women. Educational efforts should include challenging the myths that wives' bodies are the property of their husbands and that consent to sexual contact is a perpetual duty in marriage. At the same time, prosecutors, judges, and juries need to be educated so that spousal rape laws do not place excessive power in the hands of vindictive wives. Marital rape is a serious problem, but the charge can encompass the same ambiguities as child molestation: both often come down to one person's word against another, and both may be used as weapons in divorce or child custody battles.[61]

Child Sexual Abuse

Because so much goes unreported and definitions vary, it is difficult to give accurate estimates about the prevalence of child sexual abuse. Through surveys and interviews, researchers have attempted to find out, though. Based on that research, experts suggest that perhaps as many as one in five girls and one in six boys is sexually abused by the age of eighteen.[62] In one study of almost eight hundred college students, David Finkelhor found that about 19 percent of the women and 9 percent of the men had been sexually victimized as children. In over half of these cases, coercion forced their compliance.[63]

The term **sexual victimization** indicates that a child is victimized because of age, naiveté, and relationship to the older person rather than because of aggressive intent. Females are two to three times more likely to be victims of sexual abuse as well as **incest**—sexual relations between siblings or other relatives, as well as parent-child relations. The narrower category of incest appears to occur among more than 17 percent of all girls (one in six), with almost 5 percent of these victims sexually abused by their fathers.[64] Researchers also discovered that about half of all substance abusers enrolled in treatment centers had histories as incest victims.[65]

A Traumatic Experience

Judith Herman's studies of victims of father-daughter incest found that sexual contact with an adult, especially a trusted relative, causes significant trauma. Long-lasting deleterious effects frequently reported include various problems later in life—notably repeated victimization by men. Herman found that about one-third of victims ran away from home and nearly half became pregnant, hoping to escape. Interestingly enough, many of them idealized men and hated women, the latter animosity evidently stemming from their own self-contempt and guilt and from their anger toward their mothers who failed to intervene. Women with a history of father-daughter incest also often report difficulty in parenting their own children.[66]

Social Factors Related to Incest

One structural family characteristic that increases the chances of incest seems to be a **patriarchal unit**, where fathers assume they have the right to use female members of the family as they see fit—first wives, and then daughters. Typically, mothers in incestuous families are weak, incompetent, subservient, alcoholic, or largely absent and unable to protect their daughters. Many are unresponsive when informed of the situation.[67] They themselves are emotionally debilitated victims of patriarchy. If they depend economically on their husbands and have few alternatives, they may fear jeopardizing the marriage by confronting the husband. Therefore, one of the main thrusts of treating a victim is to build the mother's confidence and to improve the mother-daughter relationship.

Institutional clarification of the roles of stepfathers and stepsiblings would be useful, too. Reconstituted families have a much higher risk of sexual victimization. Such families often lack defined relationships, which may often enable a stepfather or stepbrother to feel freer to take advantage of a vulnerable, accessible family victim.[68] Such a predisposition by some may be due in part to media portrayals of young girls as little Lolitas, seducing their adult victims rather than realistically depicting the power of the relative over the unprotected child. Similarly, advertising often uses young girls in settings suggestive of soft-core pornography to sell products by exploiting their emergent sexuality.

The Need for Societal Intervention

Awakened social awareness and revelations about the large numbers of people abused within their families have prompted calls for immediate intervention to protect victims.

Services for Battered Wives

In Great Britain, Erin Pizzey's book *Scream Quietly or the Neighbours Will Hear* led to the founding of Women's Aid of Chiswick, a house that became a model for battered women's shelters around the world. Such shelters not only provide food and lodging but offer individual and group counseling to begin building self-esteem. Other shelter services include job referrals and advice on training for work, since a major problem many battered wives face is their financial dependence on the abusive husband. A 1994 federal law, the Violence Against Women Act, provides funding for battered women's shelters and programs, mandates harsh penalties for batterers, and makes crossing state lines to pursue a partner a federal offense.

Intervention in Child Abuse

For children, intervention generally means being placed in a foster home while charges of abuse are investigated. Since doctors and counselors are required to report abuse cases in the United States, expansion of social service efforts in this area is desperately needed. Currently, resources are poorly allocated in light of the large number of child abuse cases. Too often, an intervention response to a crisis situation is delayed, followed by temporary placement of the child in another home, and then reinstatement in the unchanged, abusing home. Meanwhile, the foster-care arrangements may create further psychological confusion for the child. Most children do not want to be separated from their parents and usually interpret a government-ordered removal as being "their fault." We need more extensive follow-ups on families instead of short-term monitoring. Again, resources are the bottom line: society, through leaders and public pressure, must decide that social goals be treated as a priority.

The Police

In the past, the usual response of police and the courts to family violence—especially battered wives—was part of the problem. Police, unwilling to intervene, tended to dismiss instances of domestic violence as conflicts for the parties to work out privately. Today, however, police receive training in domestic intervention. Nonetheless, in many states, police cannot make an arrest in a spouse abuse case unless the wife files a criminal complaint; and many do not. Moreover, many of those who do later drop the charges. As a result, many states have adopted laws mandating the arrest of batterers, which allows the prosecutor's office to file charges without the wife's permission. Since 1990, all states have approved stalking laws, as well, prohibiting ex-partners from following or otherwise threatening their former mates, which enables law enforcement officials to address this related problem.

Prevention of Family Violence

Beyond the need for greater resource allocation to support intervention is the more fundamental need to prevent family violence. Here research points the direction for social and economic change in the society. First, changes calculated to reduce stress in families need attention: reduced unemployment and poverty; increased family planning to lower the number of unwanted children; more day-care centers for children; and more hot-line services for adults. Second, parenting training would benefit many adults, since abusive parents often have unrealistic expectations of their children. Third, measures that promote sexual equality may, in the long run, alleviate the problem of violence, because emphasizing male dominance over wives and children seems in past years to have encouraged abuse. Ultimately, an egalitarian family structure will discourage abuse, as will changes in cultural norms that encourage violence.[69] Accomplishing this would entail restricting the portrayal of violence on television and in video games. Sweden, for example, banned the children's television show *Power Rangers* and passed a law making spanking illegal.

Sociological Perspectives

In the past, divorced families were treated as deviant. With divorce so prevalent today, such treatment is far less common, although we still hear the phrase, "broken families." Black and Hispanic families with a high incidence of single parenthood and out-of-wedlock births are commonly stigmatized.

In the area of abuse, the explanation of individual faults is commonplace. Abusers are seen as "sick"—as psychopaths with serious personality disorders. Likewise, child abusers are analyzed as being unable to delay gratification and as individuals whose emotional needs went unmet in their own childhood, leading them to seek satisfaction from their own children—even from infants—who of course are not capable of filling such emotional voids. Finally, parents or other relatives who sexually victimize young family members are treated as "perverts."

Sociologists, while acknowledging that both "sick" individuals and selfish, self-centered ones do exist, look for broader social patterns to gain insights into the problems facing the family.

The Functionalist Viewpoint

The Functionalist viewpoint views the family as one institution within a societal system for which it performs essential functions. According to William Ogburn, colonial families served at least seven functions:

1. The economic function, wherein the family acted as a production unit supplying its own food, clothing, and shelter.

2. Education, since the family passed on to children the knowledge and skills necessary for participation and survival in the society.

3. Protection, especially in the figure of the father who protected members from outside physical harm without relying on a police force; additionally, the family protected its members by caring for them in old age and during illness.

4. Recreation, which occurred within the home in the form of family activities such as singing and dancing.

5. Religion, as beliefs were taught by family elders and worship took place within the home.

6. Status placement, which determined the status and prestige of family members.

7. Reproduction and affection among members.[70]

When we analyze the family today, we find that outside agencies perform many of these functions, such as the schools, police, nursing homes, insurance agencies, and so on. Industrialization removed the production function from the family; and as other social and economic changes occurred, most of the remaining functions were stripped away. Left with few tasks to perform, the family becomes a fragile unit. The disturbing question posed by Robert Nisbet is whether a unit stripped of functions can remain a source of psychological identification for its members.[71] Divorce and its attendant negative consequences for society stem from the weakened family, which is no longer perceived as essential for individual survival.

On the other hand, some theorists (notably Talcott Parsons) see the contemporary family as being free to specialize in a small number of tasks. The family, linked to the impersonal world of bureaucracies, specializes in providing affection and supplying emotional gratification to its members, thereby performing an essential function for both society and the individual. Feminists attack Parsons's ideas, however, because women are expected to create the emotional refuge for family members while many of their own needs go unmet. It is also questionable how adequately the family today performs this function.

Following the Functionalist line of thought, we would describe the economy today as consumer-oriented, based increasingly on the growth of the service sector. The family's adaptation to such change is reflected in declining birth rates and in the increased number of women working in society. Having a two-income household allows the family to consume more. At the same time, consumer standards have risen, and parents expect to provide each child with more goods, more lessons, and so on. Except perhaps among the wealthy (who can afford more children) and the very poor (who have little control), having two or fewer children is now the norm.

The consumer family is still expected to meet its members' emotional needs, however. Since the number of people in the family is smaller, and since more women are now working, family members may have little time or energy left over to meet the psychological demands of others within the home. A high rate of divorce is not surprising when so much is expected from one, two, or three other people.

We can conclude, then, that the Functionalist perspective would view the family as disorganized in response to changes in the larger society. Until a new stabilized system or a new equilibrium is attained, we can continue to expect family-related social problems. A partial explanation for some abuse by husbands is that men resist the democratic family structure that increasingly promotes both the family's and society's survival. Instead, they seek to maintain the roles and values of an older, patriarchal, industrialized social system.

The Conflict and Feminist Viewpoints

Rejecting the idealistic Functionalist view of the family as a mutually beneficial entity for all its members, most Conflict and Feminist analysts see it instead as a source of social inequality. That inequality manifests itself both within and outside the family unit in conflicts over goals, functions, values, shared power and access to resources.[72]

The Inequality of Women

An early depiction of the family from the framework of inequality was Friedrich Engels's classic work, *The Origin of the Family, Private Property, and the State* (1884), wherein he claimed that the family was the source of female oppression.[73] In fact, the only difference between a wife and a prostitute, Engels said, was that the former had sold herself for life! He attributed the subjection of women to the capitalistic system with its fundamental belief in the preeminence of private property. Industrialization took men out of the home and enslaved some children as well, leaving women economically dependent on men.

Today Conflict theorists direct our attention to the power relationships within the family. We observe that women who return to work gain a measure of power. Following the Marxian line of thought, women—made aware of their economic oppression—are engaged in pitched battles with their male oppressors. They wage the struggle in the home as well as in the marketplace; and for many women, divorce represents a release from inequity. Some of the violence in the home also derives directly from the changing balance of power, as men—no longer socially and economically supreme—resort to force to keep women "in their place."

Feminists, while agreeing with Conflict analysts about economic oppression and domestic violence, contend that male domination of women was not an outgrowth of the capitalist system and a belief in the preeminence of private property. Rather, they argue such exploitation predates capitalism and lies rooted in a centuries-old patriarchal social system.[74] Today, as in years past, men undervalue and underpay women's labor, whether in the home or in the workplace. Such attitudes and practices enable men to control women in terms of status, rights, independence, and decision making within the family.[75]

Conflict with External Organizations

On the macrosocial level, the family unit, rather than being interdependent with and adapting to the other institutions of society as Functionalists maintain, is pressured by external organizations. Economic organizations pursue profit-making activities and expect families to conform to bureaucratic schedules. With more women working, two members of the family are now under workplace pressures, while children must meet the demands of educational and recreational organizations. The family tries to maintain the ideology that it is a safe haven from such pressures, but individuals find it difficult to compartmentalize their public and private lives. Unfortunately, many people blame themselves for personal failures in marriage when, in fact, the major contributing factor may be the unrelenting stress created by extrafamilial organizations. The outside organizations of society are often unsympathetic to and in conflict with the values held most important in family life, frequently resulting in family role strain.[76]

The Class Structure

Finally, the perspective of inequality directs our attention to the higher incidence of many family-related problems, such as divorce and violence, in the lower classes. Inequalities of the social structure result in scarce resources, forcing poorer families to struggle to keep the unit intact. Ill health, unemployment, and larger family size are among the stresses linked to poverty, contributing to the instability of family life.

For those at the bottom of the class structure, the deprivation intersects with gender and racial inequality, resulting in a high incidence of poverty and family instability in African American and Hispanic American female-headed households. With nearly one-sixth of all children growing up in poverty, we have strong reason to doubt the level of our society's commitment to families, notwithstanding the many references by politicians to "family values."

The Interactionist Viewpoint

Throughout our discussion, we have returned to the theme that the reinterpretation of family roles is a basic process occurring today. As noted previously, the meaning given to marriage itself has changed, with gratification of emotional needs assuming primary importance. This has made the marriage contract more precarious, which goes far toward explaining the high divorce rate. Furthermore, society has reinterpreted the nature of the contract itself, transforming it from a sacred to a civil to a personal bond between two people. Accompanying this change in the definition of marriage has been a reinterpretation of divorce. More and more people do not blame their divorce on personal failure but rather assess it as a stage in their ongoing personal development—as a relationship that "did not work out." Divorce no longer carries much social stigma, and so many people view sequential marriages as "normal."

Shifting Family Roles

Interactionist analysis directs our attention to the changing expectations for family roles. The clash over shifting interpretations of what properly constitutes the husband's, wife's, parent's, or child's role results in power struggles as each tries to impose his or her own definition. Men who beat their wives or children or sexually victimize their daughters offer a prominent example of a dominant group trying to retain the traditional definition of the man's role. Increasingly, the two adult partners define their marital roles, custom-made to their particular situation and lifestyles. They may allocate tasks in the home, for example, on the basis of who has the time or preference, rather than according to some stereotyped division of labor. Since society less often defines marital roles, the couple may need to undergo lengthy processes of negotiation before they can come to an equitable agreement on the expectations each has for the other. Still burdened by traditional definitions of the female role, women do most of the housework; and in the job market, they earn only about three-fourths of men's incomes.

With the higher divorce rate has come remarriage and stepparenting roles. Obligations and rights in this area are poorly defined and have few legal underpinnings. Consequently, children in stepfamilies are at higher risk for abuse.

Change in the Meaning of Childhood

In the case of child abuse, the Symbolic Interactionist looks at the changing meanings given to childhood: from historical periods, when society regarded children as miniature adults and economic assets, to modern times, when children—now economic liabilities—are conceived for emotional gratification.[77] Nowadays society imposes higher standards for childcare, with performance judged by experts—nutritionists, psychologists, and educators. The pressures on parents to meet these new performance levels has intensified and has been accompanied by a meteoric rise in costs. Of concern to some social observers is "the disappearance of childhood," as children learn from television at an early age many of the "secrets" withheld from them until adolescence or young adulthood in previous generations; today, programs reveal as a matter of course the problems, concerns, and weaknesses of the adult world.[78] Violence, politics, and sexual matters are vividly present in the media, laying bare much of adult mystery. At the same time, the new generation of young people in many cases surpasses the technological knowledge of its predecessors, particularly in computer usage. The definitions, redefinitions, and attendant confusion in role expectations are part of the general pool of stress-related elements suffered by families today.

Defining Family Matters as Social Problems

Finally, many of the concerns we have discussed in this chapter only recently emerged as societally defined problems. Child abuse and wife beating entered the public arena only within the last thirty years, although their occurrence goes back to ancient times. When they were defined as "family matters," the police and courts only reluctantly intervened. But with recognition of their social basis has come societal acknowledgment of its responsibility and the need to redefine its role.

Thinking About the Future

What do the current trends tell us about the future of the family? Couples wait longer to get married and have children. Half of all marriages end in divorce. From 40 to 50 percent of all children live in a single-parent home before the age of eighteen. The proportion of married couples is declining as other household forms increase. More and more people live together without benefit of marriage. Are we headed toward a similar fate as Sweden, where virtually everyone cohabits before getting married? Will marriage remain a mainstream choice? What do you think?

Will the family survive? A wide array of people—including politicians, religious groups, and some sociologists, such as David Popenoe (*Life Without Father: Compelling New Evidence That Fatherhood and Marriage Are Indispensable for the Good of Children and Society,* 1996)—believe a return to traditional family values is necessary to preserve this important social institution and to stabilize society itself. If this is the solution, how do we do this?

Other sociologists, such as Lillian Rubin (*Families on the Fault Line,* 1994) argue that holding up the traditional image of families as an ideal is hollow because we fail to provide tax-supported childcare facilities. Also, she says, because both parents must work to make ends meet, "family life has become impoverished for want of time, adding another threat to the already fragile bonds that hold families together" (pp. 244–245). Time has become a precious commodity and there is little of it nowadays to nurture relationships between husband and wife, between parents and child, and to provide time for oneself. If this is the problem, how do we fix it? What role, if any, should government and employers play in providing affordable, high-quality childcare and in making it available to people whose jobs require weekend or shift work past the usual 5 P.M. quitting time?

Domestic violence, marital rape, child sexual abuse, and elder abuse are important social concerns today. Some of the social factors linked to this violence are stress, economics, and patriarchal power. Which of the previously discussed steps to prevent family violence do you think are practical for immediate implementation? How do we change our cultural norms about violence in the media and in video games? How do we move toward a more egalitarian family structure to curb domestic violence and abuse? Do you foresee the problem lessening soon? Why?

Are you optimistic or pessimistic about the future of the family? Does your view of the future simply see more of the same: more single adults, late marriages, fewer children, high divorce rates, high remarriage rates, continued stress and fragility for families? Or do you think families will be more egalitarian, more stable both economically and socially, with greater social awareness from the business community and government about the needs of children?

SUMMARY

1. Families, responding to urbanization and industrialization, have undergone significant changes in the last two hundred years. They have become smaller, with weaker kinship ties and a growing emphasis on individual rights. Many observers fall into the trap of viewing these changes against the standard of some idealized family of the past.

2. Specific recent changes in families have included a decrease in the number of married-couple households with children under eighteen; an increase in single-parent families, especially female-headed with children; an increase in households in which persons live alone; and increases in the percentages of persons divorced and of persons never married. The previously rapid rate of change has slowed in recent years, but the number of female-headed households continues to increase.

3. The United States lags behind other industrialized nations in the level of support its government offers families. Many stresses and problems of family life remain individualized and are not treated as public issues.

4. The impact of divorce on children varies by the child's age, the level of parental conflict, the nature and degree of the child's contact with the noncustodial parent, and the nature of the stepfamily arrangements. In general, divorce has negative economic and emotional consequences for children. One of the most severe of these is the reduction in their standard of living, due to the failure of many noncustodial fathers to pay child support.

5. The large number of remarriages eases some of the negative consequences of divorce, but they also require new family and kin adjustments that may be stressful. Because stepfamily roles are not clearly defined, stepchildren are at greater risk for abuse.

6. The United States has experienced a sharp rise in the number of single-parent families, most of them headed by women. In addition to divorce, a major contributor is out-of-wedlock births, which account for an increasing proportion of all births. This is especially true among African Americans, whose marriage rate has declined due to a lack of jobs for males in a shifting economy. The consequences are a greatly increased likelihood of poverty and a higher health risk to infants.

7. Violence between spouses and abuse of children are widespread. Abuse of elderly family members has been more recently uncovered. Social factors linked to a higher incidence of abuse are the nuclear family structure, male dominance, cultural norms condoning family and societal violence, an experience of abuse in one's own background, lower-class status, stress, and social isolation.

8. Forms of sexual victimization within the family include marital rape and child sexual abuse. Both have lingering deleterious effects on women and are linked to male supremacy.

9. Given the high incidence of family violence, a need exists for more shelters and counseling services for battered wives, more extensive intervention in child abuse cases, and police training for domestic situations. Preventive efforts should aim to alleviate family stress, train people in the parent role, promote sexual equality, and reduce the overall level of violence in society at large.

10. Family-related social problems are inadequately explained by theories that attribute them simply to selfish individuals (divorce) or to sick personalities (abuse). Functionalist sociological explanations view the family as disorganized, having lost its traditional functions in the society, and as under stress, trying to specialize in the emotional gratification of its members. Conflict and Feminist analysts see family problems as being a function of a shifting balance of power between men and women, as being engendered by conflicts with external organizations, and as being linked to the inequities of the class structure. Finally, according to the Interactionists, new definitions of marriage, family roles, and childhood lead to confusion and greater stress in families today.

KEY TERMS

Abuse

Blended family

Cohabitation

Extended family

Incest

No-fault divorce

Nuclear family

Patriarchal unit

Sexual victimization

Single-parent families

INTERNET RESOURCES

At this book's Web site with Allyn & Bacon, you will find numerous links related to the problems pertaining to the family. To explore these resources, go first to the author's page (**http://www.ablongman.com/parrillo**). Next, select this edition of *Contemporary Social Problems* and then choose **Internet Readings and Exercises**. Then select **Chapter 10,** where you will find both a variety of sites to investigate and some questions that pertain to those sites.

SUGGESTED READINGS

Allan, Joyce. *Because I Love You: The Silent Shadow of Child Sexual Abuse.* VHF Press, 2002. A compelling, sensitve memoir enhanced by a professional report on the beliefs, values, and behavior patterns of victims, family, and friends.

Coontz, Stephanie. *The Way We Never Were: American Families and the Nostalgia Trap,* reprint ed. New York: Basic Books, 1998. An informative book that punctures myths about families of the past and assesses contrived fears about families of the present.

Finkelor, David, and Kersti Yllo. *License to Rape: Sexual Violence Against Wives,* reprint ed. New York: Free Press, 1987. A study of fifty wives who admit to being victims of marital rape, clarifying the types of violence and describing the lingering effects.

Gelles, Richard J., and Donileen Loseke. *Current Controversies on Family Violence.* Newbury Park, Calif.: Sage Publications, 1993. A collection of articles presenting various theoretical explanations for family violence and examining current controversies in the literature.

Russell, Diana E. *The Secret Trauma: Incest in the Lives of Girls and Women,* rev. ed. New York: Basic Books, 1999. A detailed picture of the experiences of 152 women abused by relatives before age eighteen, drawn from a major study of 930 women in San Francisco.

Skolnick, Arlene S., and Jerome H. Skolnick. *Family in Transition,* 12th ed. Reading, Mass.: Allyn & Bacon, 2002. A collection of 36 articles, including theoretical discussions and empirical research, that focus attention on major issues confronting the family today.

Summers, Randal W., and Allan M. Hoffman, *Domestic Violence: A Global View.* Westport, Conn.: Greenwood Publishing, 2002. Compares and contrasts how thirteen countries view and handle domestic violence.

Tepperman, Lorne, and Susannah J. Wilson (eds.). *Next of Kin: An International Reader on Changing Families.* Englewood Cliffs, N.J.: Prentice Hall, 1993. A reader on the changes occurring in families around the world, including a focus on problems stemming from the rapid pace of change.

Wallerstein, Judith S., Julia M. Lewis, Sandra Blakeslee, and Julie Lewis. *The Unexpected Legacy of Divorce*. New York: Hyperion Books, 2000. Working from a thirty-year longitudinal study and other research, the authors conclude that divorce hurts children and it hurts them even later when they are adults.

11 Health Care

Facts About Health Care

- In 2003, the United States ranked twentieth highest worldwide in lowest infant mortality rate.

- Studies show that hundreds of thousands of operations performed each year are unnecessary.

- The cost of hospital care more than tripled between 1985 and 2000.

- Approximately 41 million Americans have little or no health coverage.

- Over 1.3 million legal abortions occur each year in the United States.

- More than 468,000 Americans suffering from AIDS have died.

- Surveys indicate that 61 percent of Americans favor legalizing physician-assisted suicide.

- One in five Americans experiences some form of mental illness.

Good health is one of our most highly prized personal possessions, something closely associated with our satisfaction with life. Such health is easy to take for granted, especially when you are young and feel that the world lies before you. Only when serious illness or injury besets us, do we recognize how important health is. Worry, fear, depression, torment, disability, loss of self-sufficiency, and heavy financial burdens can then dominate and change the focus of our daily lives.

Health and sickness are, however, much more than the sum of personal, physiological, and psychological effects. Sociocultural factors can cause many health problems. For example, fewer people in the United States today die from diphtheria, typhoid, cholera, tuberculosis, influenza, pneumonia, and other contagious diseases than do in preindustrial societies in other parts of the world. On the other hand, our lifestyle—alcohol drinking, smoking, polluted air and water, food additives, fatty foods, little exercise, recreational sex—cause other health problems such as heart disease, cancer, and herpes that are less common in preindustrial societies. Bad health is also a matter of societal concern because it means lost worker productivity, wasted potential in children denied the right to become adults contributing to society, high costs of institutional care, and strain on the social commitment to provide everyone—regardless of income—with adequate medical care to prevent needless pain and suffering.

Health care in the United States displays many paradoxes. This nation spends more money on health care than any other country in the world—about one-seventh of all national expenditures, a sum that now exceeds $1.3 trillion.[1] Yet we are the only industrialized society today that has no national health insurance program or universal health-care system. Despite our vast expenditures, health-care services are unequally distributed, with poor-quality care or none at all available to rural and small-town America and to the urban poor. In 2002, despite our vast expenditures, we ranked a dismal twentieth in infant mortality rate, compared to 1950 when we ranked fifth (see Table 11.1). Life expectancy in the United States is only twenty-first best worldwide.[2] (See the accompanying box.)

Health Care in Sociohistorical Context

As a society, we have come a long way in our health achievements. Americans born in 1776 had a life expectancy of thirty-five years, compared to the seventy-seven years of today's newborn child. We conquered most contagious diseases that had previously claimed many lives—smallpox, diphtheria, whooping cough (pertussis), typhoid, cholera, scarlet fever, and polio. Yet medical care had far less to do with these dramatic health gains than did scientific discoveries and improved living conditions (better nutrition, sanitation, education, and economic well-being). Still, our technological and scientific advances enabled U.S. medicine to save many lives, reduce pain and suffering, and allow people to live normal lives longer. Unfortunately, our

Table 11.1   Comparative Infant Mortality Rate (per 1,000 Births) of Countries with a Population of 5 Million or More, 2002

1. Sweden	3.44	9. Germany	4.65	17. Hong Kong S.A.R.	5.73
2. Finland	3.76	10. Spain	4.85	18. Portugal	5.84
3. Japan	3.84	11. Australia	4.9	19. Greece	6.25
4. Netherlands	4.31	12. Canada	4.95	20. United States	6.69
5. Austria	4.39	13. Denmark	4.97	21. Taiwan	6.8
6. France	4.41	14. United Kingdom	5.45	22. Cuba	7.27
7. Switzerland	4.42	15. Czech Republic	5.46	23. Israel	7.55
8. Belgium	4.64	16. Italy	5.76	24. Korea	7.58

Source: U.S. Bureau of the Census, International Data Base, 2003.

The Globalization of Social Problems

Health Care in an International Context

Although health care in the United States is, in many ways, among the best in the world, it is not equally available to all Americans, nor is it available at a price everyone can afford. To understand the shortcomings of the U.S. health-care delivery system, we need to compare it with that of other developed countries, all members of the Organization for Economic Cooperation and Development (OECD) and with costs of living comparable to those of the United States. The key difference among the nations shown in Figure 11.1 is that only the United States lacks a national health plan that controls both costs and services.

In Figure 11.1, PPP refers to purchases of goods and services by consumers and government, as well as to gross domestic investments and net exports of goods and services. As in previous years, the United States continued to top the OECD ranking for overall health-care spending at about $4,900 per capita in 2001—more than twice the OECD average of $2,100. Not shown is that, in the United States, health expenditures constitute 13.9 percent of the GDP compared to an average 8.4 percent in other OECD countries.

Even more striking in Figure 11.1 are the differences among countries in the proportion of public

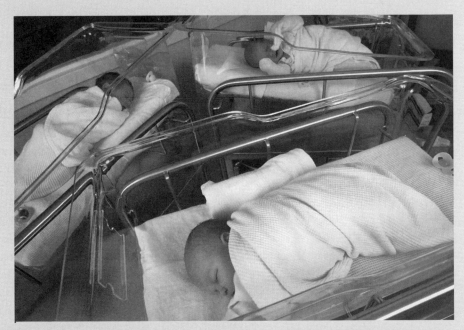

If these babies were born in Sweden, they likely would survive infancy, as Sweden has the lowest infant mortality rate in the world. What factors contribute to statistics such as infant mortality and longevity in a society? What social problems can interfere with the distribution and delivery of health care?

(continued)

The Globalization of Social Problems (continued)

health (or government-funded) expenditures. In the United States, public health spending is only 44 percent, compared to the OECD average of 72 percent and over 80 percent in the Nordic countries. These data suggest that U.S. citizens shoulder a much greater amount of health costs—in personal payments, insurance premiums, and tax dollars.

Despite these high expenditures, as mentioned earlier, Table 11.1 shows the U.S. infant mortality rate exceeding that of other large, developed countries. Since these other nations are the same ones that have national health plans, they would appear to have better and more cost-effective health-care delivery systems.

This apparently is also the case in providing health care for the elderly, as most of these countries also have a growing proportion of elderly citizens, some of them (Belgium, France, Germany, Greece, Italy, Japan, Spain) with about a 50 percent greater proportion of citizens over age sixty-five.

How did we reach this situation? Why are health costs soaring faster than any other part of the economy? Why do Americans fare more poorly than many other peoples in adequate health care and life expectancy? Why do we pay more but get less? Why are we unable to provide everyone with equal health care? Is managed health care the answer?

advances also created problems as they reshaped our values and attitudes, altered the structure of the health-care system, and changed the quality of personal care.

As medical science advanced in the twentieth century, personalized medical care declined. The nostalgic and sentimental image of the old-fashioned family doctor who made house calls and maintained a personal interest in the well-being of patients dates from a period when specialization in medicine was rather limited. Beginning early in the twentieth century, but accelerating dramatically after World War II, due to the massive growth of medical knowledge and technological capabilities, medical specialization became the norm. Keeping abreast of all developments in all areas of human illness was simply unrealistic. General practitioners lost prestige and popularity; more and more new medical school graduates opted for a specialization.

At first the advent of specialized medicine spurred a greater reliance on hospital care and treatment rather than home care and doctor's visits. And since specialized medicine necessitates advanced training and scientific expertise, medical schools, research-oriented medical centers, and major teaching hospitals grew into medical empires. Bolstered by extensive federal funding—but with little public accountability—they achieved many medical breakthroughs, trained a new medical elite, and replaced the small, independent hospitals as the primary medical care unit.

One significant change is that the sick rarely have a doctor come to them. Instead they travel to laboratories for tests, to doctors' offices for examinations, and to clinics or hospitals for treatment. Because health care is so fragmented by specialization, people frequently see several physicians for the same health problem, thus increasing their medical bills. This arrangement also depersonalized the practice of medicine, with physicians viewing patients as objects instead of as human beings, and with patients seldom feeling a close rapport with their doctors. The growth in medical office partnerships and managed health-care facilities has further intensified this pattern.

This growth of large institutional medical care and training spawned hundreds of corporations ready to profit from the medical business. Most of these ancillary firms sell diagnostic and

Figure 11.1   Health Expenditure per Capita, U.S.$ PPP*, 2001

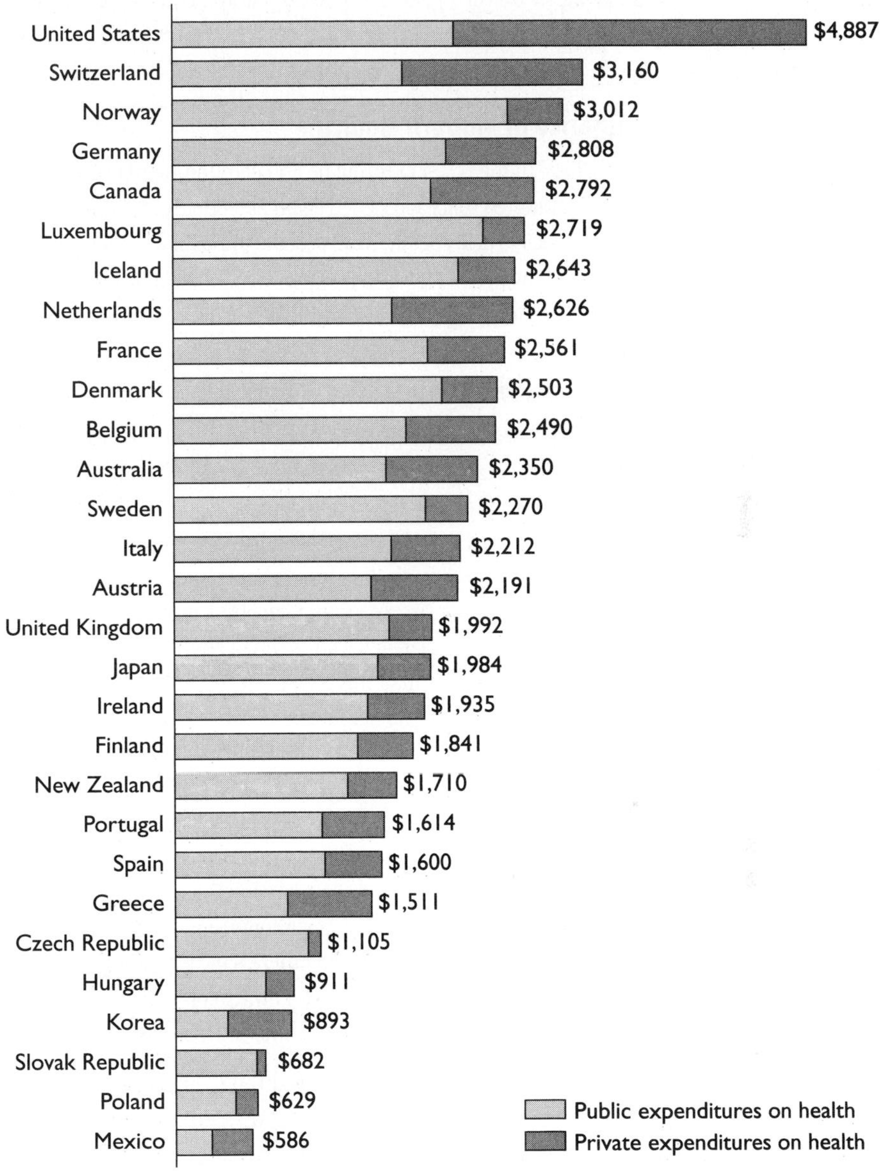

United States	$4,887
Switzerland	$3,160
Norway	$3,012
Germany	$2,808
Canada	$2,792
Luxembourg	$2,719
Iceland	$2,643
Netherlands	$2,626
France	$2,561
Denmark	$2,503
Belgium	$2,490
Australia	$2,350
Sweden	$2,270
Italy	$2,212
Austria	$2,191
United Kingdom	$1,992
Japan	$1,984
Ireland	$1,935
Finland	$1,841
New Zealand	$1,710
Portugal	$1,614
Spain	$1,600
Greece	$1,511
Czech Republic	$1,105
Hungary	$911
Korea	$893
Slovak Republic	$682
Poland	$629
Mexico	$586

Public expenditures on health
Private expenditures on health

Notes: Australia, Japan, Korea, Luxemborg and Switzerland: 2000.

*Purchasing power parities (PPPs) provide a means of comparing spending between countries on a common base. PPPs are the rates of currency conversion that equalize the cost of a given "basket" of goods and services in different countries.

Source: OECD Health Data 2003.

therapeutic equipment to the hospitals, whose staffs are fascinated by the latest gadgetry. The result is higher overhead costs—sometimes from acquiring equipment whose limited use does not justify its purchase—as well as increased personnel costs for technicians and support staff.

Dominance of Modern Medicine

People believe in the power of medicine and demand more from it than did earlier generations. People one hundred years ago viewed death as something natural and inevitable; today, in contrast, many seek to delay death. We expect the impossible, and if a doctor loses a patient, the first thought of many surviving relatives is to sue for medical malpractice. Often physicians employ heroic methods to prolong life, at considerable expense, even though no hope for recovery exists.

Overmedicalization

What has happened in the United States, critics maintain, is the **overmedicalization** of life—due to a medical establishment that exercises too much control over people's lives and a society that has become far too dependent on medical care. Ivan Illich, one of the health-care system's harsher critics, claims in being "overmedicalized" we have been stripped of our rights regarding sickness and death.[3] The medical profession achieved a "mystification" of knowledge and expertise beyond the average person's grasp; now physicians exclusively determine what constitutes sickness, what medicines to treat it with, when to admit patients to the hospital, and when to discharge them. One outgrowth of this is that expensive institutional care has replaced personalized home care. Most people no longer consider it "proper" to have babies at home, to convalesce there from a serious illness, or to die in that familiar setting.

Medicine can do little about the major causes of death today. Chronological age, lifestyle, genetic weaknesses, and environmental pollutants bring about accidents, arteriosclerosis, cancer, cirrhosis of the liver, diabetes, heart attacks, and strokes. Little benefit comes to patients with these conditions from the elaborate and expensive treatments given in hospitals. Clinical medicine is effective in some areas, such as polio, pneumonia, and venereal disease. Advances in microsurgery allow severed limbs to be restored; and progress in heart surgery enables infants to live normal lives or adults to live longer, active lives following corrective repairs. Yet some people believe that we have paid a heavy price for these and other miraculous achievements:

> Medicine undermines health not only through direct aggression against individuals but also through the impact of its organization on the total milieu. . . . It obtains when medical bureaucracy creates ill-health by increasing stress, by multiplying disabling dependence, by generating new painful needs, by lowering the levels of tolerance for discomfort or pain, by reducing the leeway that people are wont to concede to an individual when he suffers, and by abolishing even the right to self-care. [It] is at work when health care is turned into a standardized item, a staple; when all suffering is "hospitalized" and homes become inhospitable to birth, sickness, and death; when the language in which people could experience their bodies is turned into bureaucratic gobbledegook; or when suffering, mourning, and healing outside the patient role are labeled a form of deviance.[4]

The Health-Care Delivery System

The previous section described some of the unfortunate consequences in the evolution of health care in the United States, but by far the biggest social problem in medicine is the unequal health-care delivery system. Although the U.S. health care is probably the best in the world for those who can afford it, not everyone can. Over 44 million Americans, more than one in six non-elderly persons, do not have health insurance, and these are mostly working-class people. Only one-fourth of the uninsured come from families with incomes below the poverty level. The greater proportion (74 percent) comes from families with at least one full-time worker, most working in year-round positions.[5]

Other factors affect both access to health care and its quality. These include social class, race and ethnicity, and geographic locale.

Why Don't All Americans Have Health Insurance?

Because the United States is the only industrialized country without a national health plan, coverage is essentially job based. That is, most non-elderly Americans receive health insurance as a benefit through their employers. However, employers are not obligated to provide health insurance. Companies that are older, have two hundred or more employees, are incorporated, or are in an industry where workers tend to be unionized are more likely to sponsor health insurance. In contrast, less than two-thirds of small firms offer health coverage. Workers in construction, agriculture, or the service sector are less likely to have health coverage. Moreover, these types of business tend to employ more part-time or temporary workers to whom they do not offer coverage. Since they also pay less, employees have difficulty affording their contributory part of the payment even when offered health benefits.[6]

Ironically, those individuals who leave welfare and move into the workplace lose health coverage. This occurs because they lose Medicaid coverage because they typically take low-wage positions, where health benefits are less likely to be offered or affordable.

Consequences

Uninsured Americans are less likely to seek medical help until their illness has progressed to a serious state. For example, they are twice as likely as those with health insurance to be hospitalized for avoidable complications of conditions such as diabetes and hypertension—problems that could be managed in a doctor's office. In diseases where early detection is critical, such as cancer, they are more likely to be diagnosed at a more advanced stage of cancer (late-stage breast or prostate cancer, or melanoma). Such poor access and delayed care has dire results. As just one example, uninsured women are 40 to 50 percent more likely to die from breast cancer than insured women.[7]

Costs to Society

Lack of health insurance affects society as well as the uninsured individuals. Hospitals, clinics, and doctors cannot absorb uncompensated costs, especially since managed care contracts of the insured have become more competitive with lower remuneration rates. When the uninsured go to a public hospital, clinic, or physician for care and are unable to pay the full cost, some of that bill is passed on to those who do pay—through higher insurance premiums and in taxes that support the public insurance programs. All of us, in one form or another, pay indirectly for our growing uninsured population.[8]

Social Class

Lack of access to good medical care had been a key factor affecting the health of the poor, resulting in higher rates of illness and death. Positive change occurred with the advent of Medicaid in 1965, funded almost equally by federal and state governments. This program enabled over 30 million poor people to avail themselves of medical services they otherwise would not have obtained because of affordability. However, the 1996 welfare reform act reduced federal funding for this program, resulting in many poor people getting significantly less medical care in decades.[9] This decline is alarming, since the lower class has a higher rate of illness, partly due to poor nutrition as well as congested and/or polluted living conditions. Not surprisingly, the poor also have higher mortality rates for most disease.[10]

Race and Ethnicity

Non-Whites and immigrants are disproportionately represented in the ranks of low-income or temporary workers, often uncovered by health-care insurance, so they are at high risk of receiving inadequate health care. One study of U.S. hospitals revealed that, while 70 percent of seriously sick White and poor Medicare patients were placed in intensive-care units, only 47 percent of similarly sick Black, poor patients were so placed.[11] The list of disparities between Black and White health begins with higher infant mortality and ends with a lower life expectancy. Blacks are twice as likely to have diabetes as Whites and are 9.5 times more likely to get AIDS. Death rates from cancer, strokes, and heart disease are also higher among Blacks, all of which leads to a life expectancy for Black men at least a decade less than that for other men.[12]

Geographic Locale

Physician availability fluctuates by region and type of locale. An oversupply of doctors exists in suburbs and in affluent urban neighborhoods, particularly those near teaching and research-oriented hospitals (see Table 11.2). Few doctors locate in low-income neighborhoods or rural communities, although some foreign-born doctors have done so. The number of doctors per person in metropolitan counties is estimated to be triple that in rural counties.[13] The United States' ranking below other countries in infant mortality rate and life expectancy is partly due to this inequity of medical care access.

Several socioeconomic factors influence this uneven distribution of physicians. Like other educated, upper-middle-class professionals, physicians prefer the lifestyle, cultural, and recreational opportunities available in metropolitan areas. Small-town and rural America cannot provide the expensive, sophisticated equipment and technical support personnel that many of today's physicians prefer, and they don't comprise enough patients to justify these high capital

Table 11.2   Physician Rate per 100,000 Persons, 2000

Highest Proportion		Lowest Proportion	
1. Massachusetts	417	1. Idaho	154
2. New York	380	2. Mississippi	164
3. Maryland	373	3. Oklahoma	164
4. Connecticut	351	4. Wyoming	171
5. Rhode Island	328	5. Nevada	172
6. Vermont	327	6. Iowa	174

Source: American Medical Association, *Physician Characteristics and Distribution in the U.S.,* annual.

costs. Finally, physicians can earn much greater incomes in affluent, more densely populated areas than in poor and/or more sparsely inhabited regions.

Health Care for Profit

Despite its professed purpose of serving humanity, the health-care system is a business designed to make profits. As recently as 1968, for example, the president of the AMA publicly argued that health care should be available only to those able to pay.

The AMA still forbids doctors to advertise, and a highly effective informal network uses peer pressure to keep fees comparable among physicians. This price-fixing monopoly prevents economic competition. In addition, doctors remain relatively unconcerned about how their bills affect patients because so many patients are subsidized by third-party insurers or the government. Even so, the public pays a high price through higher taxes and insurance premiums.

Private medical practice is the most lucrative small business in the country: the average physician earns seven times as much as the average American wage earner. The average *net* income for all physicians exceeds $200,000 (for surgeons, the average is over $275,000). The argument usually used to justify high doctors' fees is that doctors invest more time and money in their training than do other professionals, work longer hours, and incur heavy expenses, including malpractice insurance. Physicians do work an average of fifty-three hours a week (sixty-one hours in obstetrics/gynecology); and they pay, on average, $16,800 in annual liability premiums ($22,800 for surgeons).[14] Furthermore, the rise in physicians' incomes has slowed in recent years as managed care has forced them to accept lower fees for their services, and the median debt of recent graduates from medical school has soared to $80,000.[15]

Needless Operations

Surgeons earn their incomes by performing surgery; the more they operate, the more they make. Such a system lends itself to abuse. A series of recent Rand Corporation studies led to the conclusion that one-third or more of all U.S. surgical procedures were of questionable benefit.[16]

Another insight lies in data from the 1970s, when the U.S. population grew by 10 percent, while the number of operations increased by 23 percent. Since then, the proliferation of managed-care companies (which earn no extra money from member patients having surgical procedures) and medical insurance company requirements often mandating a second opinion before approving surgery, have helped reduce the total number of operations—from 108.6 per 1,000 persons in 1980 to 83.6 by 2000.[17]

Still, many operations occur unnecessarily, such as cesarean sections, which account for about one-fifth of all births. That proportion is lower than just a decade ago, but significantly higher than the 12–14 percent that experts say is medicaly justified.[18] A major reason for the unnecessary procedure is doctors' fear of litigation, prompting them to resort to a cesarean section at the first sign of trouble. Thus they also use expensive technology to give early alarms, such as the routine use of electronic fetal monitoring, originally designed for high-risk births only.[19]

Numerous studies reveal that hundreds of thousands of operations remain unnecessary.[20] A Rand Corporation study found as unnecessary surgery: 50 percent of all cesarean sections, 27 percent of all hysterectomies, 20 percent of all pacemaker implants, 17 percent of carpal tunnel syndrome operations, 16 percent of tonsillectomies, and 14 percent of laminectomies (the most common back surgery).[21] A government study found twice as many surgeries conducted by fee for-service surgeons as by surgeons employed by health-maintenance organizations (HMOs), which do not profit—and indeed may lose money—from such operations.[22]

Unnecessary operations put patients at risk. Jeffrey Reiman estimates that perhaps 20,000 patients die each year under the scalpel, far more than the total number murdered with cutting or stabbing instruments.[23] Another study found that women who had hysterectomies to remove benign ovarian cysts incurred five times the number of complications experienced by women who have the same diagnosis but no hysterectomy.[24]

The Hospital Industry

Most hospitals were once locally controlled, nonprofit places of refuge for the sick and dying, but that has been changing since the mid-1960s. Today about 30 percent of all hospitals are owned privately, usually as part of for-profit chains.[25] Small hospitals continue to merge with hospital chains to stay afloat, while others forge links with each other to systematize their purchases and procedures and thus to reduce expenses.[26]

The cost of hospital care is rising at an alarming rate, more than tripling between 1985 and 2000.[27] The reasons for this increase, which is considerably steeper than the increase in the cost of other goods and services, do not stop with the acquisition of needed expensive equipment and hospital workers' higher wages. To offset government restrictions on the length of hospital stays and fixed-fee hospital reimbursement plans, hospitals have raised their prices to meet overhead expenses. In addition, they need to subsidize the cost of caring for indigent patients. Medical technology, however, places a heavy financial burden on hospitals, accounting for about one-third of increased hospital costs.[28]

Hospitals compete with each other over which has the most prestigious or fashionable high-cost equipment. Acquiring some of this expensive (though perhaps seldom-used) equipment adds to a hospital's fixed operating expenses—a cost that is passed along in part to all patients. For

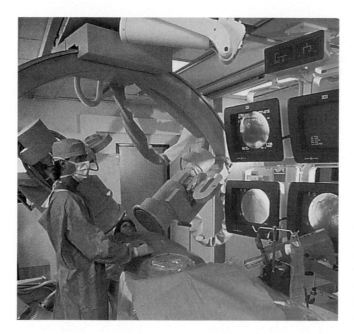

Expensive diagnostic equipment increases a hospital's fixed operating expenses, often by as much as a third, and owning such equipment is prestigious. Who pays for the cost of hospitals' capital equipment expenses? What role does medical equipment play in a "medical-industrial complex"? How has the medical insurance industry attempted to restrict patient access to expensive diagnostic equipment, and with what results?

example, magnetic resonance imaging (MRI) is a "prestige" technique, capable of detecting tumors in the brain, lungs, respiratory tract, and liver that are undetectable even by such sophisticated means as computerized axial tomography (CAT scans). While MRI devices can be an immense help in certain cases, their price tag ($2 million apiece) suggests that a multiple-hospital shared purchase and utilization arrangement might make more sense than individual hospitals' buying their own. To offset overhead costs, using expensive high technology equipment becomes established procedure, further driving up health-care costs. Nationwide, for example, MRI scans doubled and CAT scans quadrupled over a twelve-year period.[29]

To understand fully how these capital expenditures accelerate hospital costs, you must realize that hospitals are seldom filled to capacity. When hospitals operate below capacity, the cost per patient increases because fewer persons help pay fixed operating expenses. One consequence, therefore, of shorter hospital stays, as mandated by Medicare reform and managed care payment plans, has been fewer persons to help pay fixed operating expenses. As a result, hundreds of hospitals are in serious financial difficulty. In fact, there are 500 fewer hospitals nationwide today than in 1995.[30]

Medical Insurance

Until the Great Depression of the 1930s impoverished so many Americans, patients once paid almost all their medical bills directly to doctors and hospitals. Thereafter, medical insurance programs emerged—particularly when labor unions successfully negotiated to have them included as a fringe benefit, during the 1940s and 1950s. As stated earlier, over 44 million Americans (14 percent of them non-Hispanic Whites)—including many rural residents and nonunion, seasonal, or temporary workers—have little or no health coverage.[31] In addition, millions of other workers have medical insurance only as long as they continue to work; if they are fired or laid off, they and their families lose their medical coverage. And finally, people who are covered by health insurance still pay one-third of their medical costs out-of-pocket because of deductibles on their coverage or services not covered (such as office visits, routine examinations, and inoculations).

The "Blues"

When the Great Depression created widespread destitution, many people could not pay their hospital bills. To protect themselves against this loss of income in future years, U.S. hospitals created Blue Cross, a nonprofit organization, to collect individual insurance premiums in advance to pay for eventual hospitalization expenses (or at least a substantial portion of them). Later came Blue Shield to pay medical and surgical doctors' fees incurred in hospitals. Both "Blues" programs are overseen by state or regional executive boards dominated by hospital doctors and other medical professionals. Today, the national network of Blue Cross and Blue Shield plans, intimately linked with the hospitals, provides about 35 percent of the nation's private patient coverage.

Medicare and Medicaid

Despite strenuous lobbying by the AMA in the 1960s, Congress created the **Medicare** and **Medicaid** health assistance programs as part of its War on Poverty. Medicare is funded from federal taxes and pays for some medical services for people over sixty-five. Medicaid is funded from federal and state taxes and assists the poor, blind, and disabled. Because Medicaid is administered by the states, its eligibility requirements and benefits vary considerably from state to state. Medicare, on the other hand, is fairly uniform throughout the country. Both programs, however, require patients to pay part of the initial treatment costs and have a coinsurance provision that requires patients to pay part of all additional costs.

These well-intentioned programs of medical payment assistance to the elderly and the poor created a new social problem. When the AMA realized it could not prevent passage of Medicare and Medicaid, it changed its tactics to ensure that fees for services rendered through the programs would be set by the doctors and hospitals. Within two years, these programs raised physicians' income by an average of $7,000, even though virtually no increase in the amount or quality of health care provided had occurred. Not surprisingly, the attitude of physicians changed from only 38 percent in favor of the legislation at the time of its passage to 92 percent in favor by 1970.[32]

With little accountability or control—just unchallenged forms for reimbursement—doctors and hospitals had no incentive to keep costs down; and so expenses skyrocketed. "Medicaid mills" came into existence: storefront clinics in low-income neighborhoods that indiscriminately provided unnecessary tests and treatment to as many people as possible to gain six-figure incomes for the owners. Besides such fraudulent abuse, however, legitimate medical establishments used Medicare and Medicaid to reap whatever profits they could.

The New System

A revolution in hospital care, slowly phased in during the 1980s, attempted to slow the rise in health costs, streamline some treatments, and shorten hospital stays. The key change was that the federal government no longer reimbursed hospitals for the actual costs of treating Medicare patients. Instead, it paid a set fee based on costs for 467 "diagnostic related groups," or DRGs.

Under this system, which remains in effect today, hospitals that exceed their dollar limit must cover the extra expenses themselves, but hospitals that maintain lower charges can pocket the difference—an incentive to reduce costs. Unable to bill patients for over-limit charges and no longer reimbursed for itemized daily charges, hospital administrators now place greater pressure on doctors to prescribe only necessary care and to avoid nonessential tests. State governments also require fixed-fee hospital reimbursement plans that cut hospital revenues and reduce support personnel.

Although health leaders and consumers applauded this purse-tightening approach, new problems emerged. Reduced revenues placed hundreds of hospitals in financial trouble, causing more than five hundred of them to close. Moreover, critics charged that patients were being discharged "quicker and sicker," without community support.[33] The elderly now find themselves deemed not sick enough to stay but not well enough to take care of themselves. A booming growth in home-care health services in most communities occurred, but many patients found that their insurance did not provide coverage for at-home care.

Rise of Managed-Care Programs

One of the most significant recent developments in the health-care industry has been the rapid nationwide rise of managed-care programs and facilities. Designed to keep costs down through shifting the medical emphasis from treatment to prevention, **health maintenance organizations (HMOs)** emerged as a major force in health care, covering nearly 80 million members by 2002.[34] Over 60 percent of Americans now belong to managed care plans, and that number is expected to rise to 70 percent in the next ten years.[35] For a fixed, prepaid monthly or annual fee, almost four-fifths of all Americans (and their dependents) insured through their employers are in an HMO plan. Since their only source of income is members' fees, HMOs strive for treatment efficiency and place a premium on keeping members healthy. They emphasize regular checkups and inoculations, early detection and treatment, use of generic drugs, and ambulatory care instead of hospitalization. Corporations, eager to reduce their health-insurance premiums for employee coverage, find such prepaid group health care attractive for cost savings.[36]

Initial public reaction was that the managed care revolution brought many positive changes to our health-care system. It shifted the emphasis from treatment to prevention, eliminated many unnecessary hospital stays, and limited the use of very expensive technology, thereby squeezing billions of dollars of inefficiencies from the system. In addition to corporate America, politicians also embraced managed care, as it gave the government some short-term relief from exploding costs in the Medicare and Medicaid programs. In essence, managed care gave those paying the bills exactly what they wanted—more controlled health-care costs.

By the late 1990s, though, managed care came under heavy fire. In paring costs and making health care more efficient, the public raised serious questions about nonmedical "bean counters" sacrificing quality care to make a profit. For example, the HMOs claim to cut unnecessary treatment by requiring a visit to a primary-care physician, who then determines what should be done. HMOs thus become "agents of rationing" medical services, giving doctors discretionary powers as to treatment. The major problem is that HMO doctors receive financial incentives to keep costs down, resulting in fewer referrals to specialists and fewer diagnostic tests, and they can lose their affiliation if their referral costs run too high. In some cases, patients may be denied expensive drugs, tests, or treatments, as a means of reducing costs.

Less than 60 percent of consumers are highly satisfied with their HMO, according to a recent survey of 130,000 HMO enrollees. And many feel if they were seriously ill, they would not get the care they needed from their HMO.[37] Assailing "the corporate takeover of medicine," hospitals, physicians, nurses, and consumers criticize managed care for making it harder for providers to offer their patients the kind of care medical practitioners deem best.

As a result, the provider community is actively seeking to regain their lost power, such as by forming physician practice management companies (PPMs), which put the physician in a better negotiating position. Also, experts expect the rapid growth of provider-sponsored organizations (PSOs), which are groups of physicians and hospitals that resemble HMOs, but without the involvement of an insurance company. This new health-care form is a result of the Balanced Budget Act of 1997, which allows physicians and hospitals to assume the risk normally taken by the insurance company or the HMO, but without putting up a large reserve of money. In this continuing battle between controlled health-care costs and the best health care possible, it remains to be seen whether consumers will get both, one, or neither of these.

Bioethics: Life and Death Decisions

Our medical advances enable us to save prematurely born babies weighing under two pounds and other "distressed" newborns with genetic defects (including serious heart problems), who just a few years ago would have died. Conversely, just as we can save a new life we would have previously lost, we can prevent a new life through abortion if the mother does not want to have that baby. Furthermore, doctors now have drugs and machinery capable of prolonging the lives of the terminally ill and the hopelessly injured. We have it in our power, at a cost of over $1,800 a day to maintain on life support systems a life that can't be saved. These are the concerns of **bioethics.**

A common question connects all these instances: what should we do? The issue of abortion pits medicine against religion. Is abortion an act of murder? Are a woman's rights over her body paramount, or does society's interest in the developing life of her unborn child prevail at some point? Can parents be charged as criminals for refusing medical treatment to their children, even on religious grounds? Is prolonging life among the dying a duty, a humanitarian act, or an unnecessary extension of suffering? The toughest ethical dilemma in ending treatment involves patients who cannot express their wishes because of infancy or incapacity.

Nurses sometimes let their charges die. For example, they may respond slowly if a terminally ill patient takes a turn for the worse or increase a morphine dosage slightly to a child with terminal cancer, not only dulling the pain but also suppressing respiration and hastening death. One study found that one in five intensive-care nurses admitted hastening the deaths of terminally ill people, sometimes without the knowledge of doctors, families, or the patients themselves.[38]

Abortion

Since the 1973 U.S. Supreme Court ruling in *Roe v. Wade* that abortions were legal during the early months of pregnancy, they have become one of the most common surgical procedures in the United States, as about 1.3 million legal abortions occur each year. The ratio for non-White women is triple that for White women. About 81 percent of all women who have abortions are unmarried, about 42 percent are childless, and one-third are between twenty and twenty-four.[39] Although some abortions occur to prevent the birth of babies with serious genetic defects such as severe mental retardation, cystic fibrosis, or Down's syndrome, most are simply the result of pregnancies unwanted for reasons of age of the woman, social stigma, or economic hardship.

Many doctors will not perform abortions, but physicians' groups such as the AMA and American College of Obstetricians and Gynecologists, oppose government restrictions. Medical considerations aside, other questions remain. On the one hand, can we justify compulsory pregnancy? Is it moral to force a woman to have a child she does not want? On the other hand, doesn't the unborn child have a right to live? When does a fetus become a human being?

The dilemma exists because people cannot agree about when human life begins. Pro-life advocates maintain that human life begins at conception and that terminating a fetus's existence is murder. One medical researcher argues that life, like death, should be defined by the existence of brain activity—usually eight weeks after conception. Others argue that a fetus unable

Abortion is a perennial emotional issue in the United States. In this scene, pro-choice demonstrators in Chicago outnumber the lone pro-life activist. In what ways have anti-abortion activists become more militant in recent years, and with what consequences? How is abortion a subject of debate on the basis of bioethics? What other bioethical issues are at the forefront of health care in the U.S. today? For instance, what issues cloud the future of persons who are mentally ill?

to live independently from the mother outside the womb (a technology-dependent variable, it would seem) does not yet possess human life.[40]

Emotion-charged debate continues. Pro-choice advocates argue that making government-subsidized abortions illegal discriminates against the poor, who are unable to pay a private physician or travel out of state to secure a legal abortion. A return to dangerous self-induced or back-street abortions is likely if abortions are banned. These methods often cause death, serious injury, or sterility to the women who use them. Pro-life advocates, meanwhile, argue that a fetus is a living and growing human life form, entitled to the same protection and rights of other living persons.

Recent Supreme Court decisions have restricted women's reproductive freedom beyond the original "moment of viability" limits imposed in *Roe v. Wade*. States may refuse to use welfare or Medicaid funds to pay for abortions for poor women, and they may require minors to inform their parents before having an abortion. States may also require all women seeking abortions to see a presentation on fetal development and may subsequently require a twenty-four-hour waiting period before the abortion can occur.

However, the U.S. Supreme Court's 1992 decision in *Planned Parenthood v. Casey* reaffirmed the protection of a woman's right to choose first accorded in 1973 with *Roe v. Wade*. And, in September 2000, the Food and Drug Administration approved the marketing of an abortion-inducing pill, the first alternative to surgical abortion, an action that reshaped the abortion debate. The battle lines remain intense. Angry demonstrations, counterdemonstrations, confrontations, even acts of violence sporadically occur. Public opinion polls consistently find a good majority of Americans take a pro-choice stance, with Catholics—defying the official position of their church—holding no less a pro-choice stance than Protestants.[41]

Keeping the Dying Alive

A slowly dying 86-year-old woman in a hospital bed goes into cardiac arrest. Quickly the medical staff takes emergency measures—including cardiopulmonary resuscitation (CPR), cardiac injections, and possibly defibrilation—and the woman returns to life. In the next two weeks this situation occurs three more times before the woman dies. This actual series of events, with slightly varying particulars, is common in hospitals nationwide. Should doctors let that woman, and others like her, die without such "heroic efforts"? In other hospital beds lie patients whose bodies are wasted by cancer and whose pain is lessened by frequent, mind-numbing doses of morphine. Some of these patients would already be dead, if not for short-term life-prolonging drugs and surgery. Yet they lie in their beds, with no possibility of recovery, and suffer. Still other patients lie comatose, hooked up to expensive machines that perform essential life-supporting functions, without which they would probably die.

Euthanasia, also called **mercy killing,** is the act of deliberately causing or allowing the death of someone who has a serious illness. Most religions and governments forbid it. But is deliberately withholding life-sustaining efforts to permit the dying to succumb to the natural progression of their disease a wrongful act? Since state laws hold the physician responsible for maintaining life, most hospital doctors do not terminate life-preserving measures unless the patient has made a living-will declaration against "heroic measures" or unless the family gives "no code" instructions—that is, instructions to take no "heroic measures" to prolong life. The Patient Self-Determination Act, passed in 1991, requires hospitals to inform incoming patients about "living wills" and to offer them assistance in completing one.

A 1999 Gallup Poll showed that 61 percent of the respondents believed that physician-assisted suicide should be legally available to the terminally ill.[42] In Oregon, where a 1994 voter referendum approved an aid-in-dying measure, the National Right to Life Committee used legal challenges to block its implementation, but in separate decisions in June and October 1997, the U.S. Supreme Court upheld Oregon's statute.

As with abortion, advocates on both sides of the euthanasia debate continue to argue their cause. Interestingly, in 1957, the conservative Pope Pius XII decreed that the primary duty of a physician is to relieve pain in hopeless cases, even if that means taking action inconsistent with prolonging life. Today, many hospitals use a staff committee of experts (often including a medical ethicist) to make appropriate decisions in such cases. rather than placing this heavy burden on one doctor.

The AIDS Epidemic

Of all contagious diseases and conditions causing death, AIDS (acquired immune deficiency syndrome) is perhaps the most frightening. A virus known as HIV (human immunodeficiency virus) causes AIDS by attacking the body's immune system and rendering it incapable of resisting other infections and diseases. Different strains of the HIV virus exist, some more aggressive than others, so some HIV-infected people can develop AIDS quickly or may experience a latency period for many years.

HIV-infected individuals who show no physical symptoms can still transmit the virus to other persons. Infection with HIV may occur through direct exchange of the infected person's blood, semen, or vaginal secretions into another person's bloodstream. Sexual activity involving torn membranes in the mouth, vagina, or rectum; sharing of hypodermic needles; or infected mothers sharing blood with their unborn children or breast-feeding their newborns are the known means of transmitting the virus. Handshakes; hugs; sneezes; coughs; shared utensils, beds, or toilets; and any casual contact do not lead to infection.

Scope of the Problem

In the United States, more than 468,000 Americans with AIDS have died (see Figure 11.2). The HIV/AIDS epidemic is having a particularly dramatic impact on minority Americans. African Americans, who constitute about 13 percent of the U.S. population, account for about 38 percent of all AIDS cases. Their AIDS incidence rate per 100,000 is 58.1, compared to 22.5 for Hispanics and 6.6 for Whites. About 58 percent of all U.S. women reported with AIDS are African American. Researchers estimate that about 1 in 50 African American men and 1 in 160 African American women are infected with HIV. AIDS is now the leading killer of African Americans between the ages of twenty-five and forty-four. Hispanics represent about 13 percent of the U.S. population (including residents of Puerto Rico), but account for 19 percent of the total number of new U.S. AIDS cases.[43]

Figure 11.2   Who Gets AIDS, by Percentage of Total, 2001

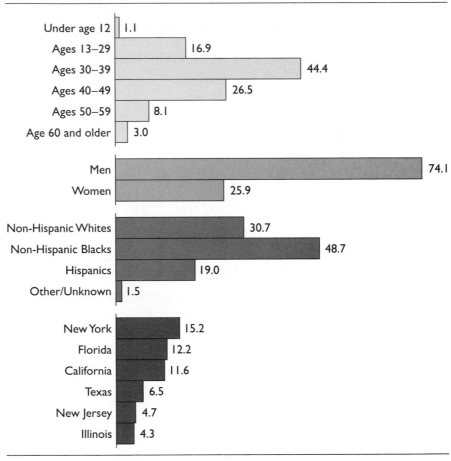

Source: U.S. Centers for Disease Control and Prevention.

Over 42 million people worldwide are HIV infected. The great majority, nearly 30 million, live in sub-Saharan Africa, with one in five in the southern core of the continent. The second greatest concentration of HIV-infected cases is in South and Southeast Asia, where the United Nations identifies 6 million cases. India has the highest number of infected people of all Asian countries, almost 4 million cases.[44] In 2003, no cure for AIDS yet existed, so experts everywhere placed great emphasis on behavior modification to prevent spreading the disease, including safer-sex practices (including condom use), safer intravenous drug use (no sharing of needles), or abstinence from sex or drug use entirely.

For those who are infected, early treatment is the most promising option. While no cure yet exists, scientists in recent years have developed effective treatments that center on inhibiting HIV's ability to replicate. Usually taken in combination with other drugs, these inhibitors, first introduced in the mid-1990s, have been effective in lowering the viral amounts to undetectable levels.

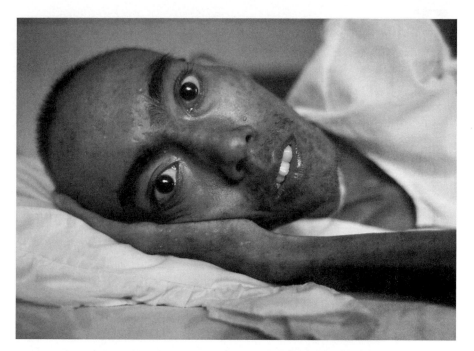

This is one of the tens of thousands of AIDS patients in Thailand, a country so overwhelmed that it lacks the resources to care for all of them or even keep them alive. In many cases, whole villages of men, women, and children are infected with HIV. What areas have the fastest annual rates of growth in AIDS cases? What are the long-term consequences of the AIDS epidemic for world health and health care systems? What solutions are being explored?

Unfortunately, the most effective treatments for AIDS are extremely expensive. Consequently, poor people, whether in the United States or elsewhere, have not benefited as widely from these drugs as have the nonpoor. For that reason, the best hope remains an effective educational campaign to prevent the further spread of this deadly disease.

Impact on Health Care

Aside from the wrenching personal tragedy of every AIDS case, the epidemic places a severe burden on the health-care system in beds, professional care, and costs. Treatment for each AIDS patient totals about $20,000 a year, and drug therapy for HIV patients is also costly.[45] As the number of patients increases, so does the strain on the health-care system, on health-care insurance premiums, and on hospital costs, as hospitals pass on their expenses from indigent AIDS patients to their paying patients.

Mental Health

Although people often use the words *mental disorder* and *mental illness* interchangeably, a *mental disorder* refers to a condition making it difficult for someone to cope with everyday life,

Social Constructions of Social Problems

The Social Construction of Mental Illness

No consensus exists among mental health experts about how to classify or diagnose mental disorders; neither is there any consistent public perception. Moses received instructions from God on a mountaintop; Joan of Arc heard supernatural "voices"; Mormon leader Joseph Smith conversed with an archangel; and Mohammed heeded the voice of Allah. They all became political/religious leaders, not patients in an asylum. In modern times, a person who attempts to communicate directly to God through prayer, either silently or aloud, is considered normal; but a person who talks to the spirits of nature or to the deceased is considered, at the very least, "strange." A person can "get away" with unique behavior more easily in a city than in a small town—or if affluent, not poor. Even court psychiatrists examining the same defendant often disagree about the sanity of that person.

A generation ago, psychiatrist D. L. Rosenhan fueled the debate on defining mental illness when he published the results of an experiment in which he fooled twelve mental hospitals in five states on the West and East Coasts (including some of the most prestigious) into admitting people who had no history of mental illness. In the admissions interview his volunteers pretended to have heard a voice say a word such as "thud," "hollow," or "empty." Otherwise, they gave correct life histories except for their names and occupations. Diagnosed as schizophrenic, each volunteer was admitted.

Thereafter, the pseudo-patients acted normally, no longer claiming to hear voices. All the staff, however, reacted to them on the basis of the prior diagnosis, not their current behavior. One humorous example occurred when one of the staff witnessed a pseudo-patient taking notes of what was happening, viewed this as a pathological symptom, and wrote down that the "patient engages in note-taking behavior," which apparently was fine for the staff member to do, but not the patient.

Interestingly, the real mental patients almost immediately detected the normality of the pseudo-patients, and insisted they were either academics or journalists who were "checking up on the place." No one on staff ever found out, though. The pseudo-patients remained hospitalized anywhere from seven to fifty-two days, averaging nineteen days each. Even then, they were released because their schizophrenia was "in remission."

After publication of this study, officials at another mental hospital scoffed at the findings and said they could always detect a phony patient. Rosenhan accepted the challenge and said he would send them phony patients. The hospital, its staff alerted, identified forty-one impostors sent by Rosenhan over the next three months. Actually, he had sent no one, and all forty-one cases had been genuine. Once again, he had demonstrated the subjective nature and difficulty of diagnosing mental disorders. In the intervening years since this study, the difficulty of recognizing mental disorders—whether by other family members or by professionals—remains.

How we treat the mentally ill is another example of a socially constructed problem. **Deinstitutionalization,** conceived as a solution to the warehousing of mentally ill patients in large, prisonlike hospitals in violation of their civil rights, created new problems. Released into the community, many patients—particularly schizophrenics with no private insurance or Medicare coverage—cannot or will not get the medications and treatment they need. Often they end up homeless or in jail by committing petty, even serious, crimes. Today, in our desire not to infringe on the personal rights of the mentally ill, we abandon and ignore those unable to handle their own affairs unless we deem certain individuals' actions dangerous to the rest of us.

whereas a *mental illness* refers to a condition requiring treatment such as medication, psychotherapy, and possibly hospitalization. Mental illness qualifies as a social problem because it affects so many people and because disagreement exists on how to define, identify, and treat it (see the box on the previous page).

Maladies ranging from mild depression to paranoid schizophrenia affect one in five Americans from all social and economic strata in any given year. In the United States, major depression is the leading cause of disability; an estimated 10 percent of persons have some recent disability from a diagnosable mental illness (e.g., schizophrenia, phobias, depression, and anxiety disorders). Also near the top of these rankings are manic-depressive illness, schizophrenia, and obsessive-compulsive disorder. Mental disorders also are tragic contributors to mortality, with suicide perennially representing one of the leading preventable causes of death in the United States and worldwide.[46]

Grim as they are, such statistics do not capture fully the costs of mental illness. Mental disorders often strike early in life, during childhood, adolescence, or early adulthood. Because mental disorders may have severe symptoms and often run a chronic or recurrent course, they are profoundly destructive, not only to life and productivity, but to the well-being of families, causing immeasurable suffering to affected individuals and their loved ones.

Mental disorders can take many forms, ranging from personality disorders or **neuroses** (including deep anxiety or depressive states, hypochondria, phobias, compulsive behaviors, and psychosomatic illness) to more severe disorders or **psychoses** (including paranoia, schizophrenia, manic depression [bipolar illness], and melancholia brought on by a physiological life change such as menopause or physical decline). From a sociological viewpoint, our interest centers on variations in social definitions of the problem and the resulting social reaction and treatment.

Socioeconomic Factors

Numerous investigators have examined the relationship between the prevalence of mental disorders and various socioeconomic factors. Their findings, while allowing some generalized conclusions, also require interpretive caution. First, we must take into account the problem of how reliable the psychiatric diagnosis is, since mental illness is much harder to identify correctly than physical illness; even psychiatrists frequently disagree with each other on a diagnosis. In addition, not everyone who requires treatment actually undergoes treatment; and relatively affluent and educated people may distort their group's incidence rate by seeking mental health care for even the most minor problems. A third consideration is that obtaining statistical information about persons treated in private practice is far more difficult than obtaining similar data about those treated in mental hospitals, clinics, or outpatient facilities. Fourth, changes in social conditions—war, depression, rapid social change—can intensify rates of mental disorders.

Despite these significant considerations, social scientists have reached several conclusions that have remained fairly consistent over fifty years of investigation. Of the hundreds of studies conducted, three major studies dominate, reinforced by the findings of many others. In 1939, scientists investigating patients at public and private mental hospitals in Chicago revealed that mental disorders followed a pattern, not a random distribution among the population.[47] In 1958, researchers in New Haven, Connecticut, examined patients in private, clinical, and hospital treatment and found significant differences when they controlled for social class.[48] Another team of investigators did a midtown Manhattan study in 1954, with a follow-up study in 1974, interviewing a cross section of adults to determine whether they had ever had mental problems, obtained treatment, or displayed neurotic symptoms.[49] Again, the findings revealed patterns found in earlier studies, subsequently reinforced in recent studies, all of which are summarized in the following sections.

Social Class

An inverse correlation exists between social class and mental disorders.[50] Members of the lower classes have higher rates of mental disorder and people of higher socioeconomic status have lower rates. The poor and deprived are much more likely to suffer psychosis, particularly schizophrenia. On the other hand, neuroses were far more common among people of high socioeconomic status and income than among the lower classes.

Treatment also varies considerably according to social class. Lower-class people are less likely to receive treatment; but their rate of hospitalization is much higher, and their stay in those mental hospitals is much longer. Probable explanations for this pattern are that the poor cannot be protected or supported by their family, must turn to public facilities that tend to institution-

Deep depression is one of the more common forms of mental illness, unlike the images of raving madmen in the public mind. These mental patients, depressed and withdrawn, sit impassively, alone in their own private world. Even so, they receive the professional help that so many other mentally ill Americans do not. What socioeconomic factors impact on the diagnosis and treatment of mental illness?

alize them, and have more contact with social workers, welfare agencies, and the courts, all of which make referrals about recommended hospitalization. In contrast, middle- and upper-class Americans are more likely to use outpatient or expensive private facilities; and if institutionalized, they tend to remain in the facility for a relatively brief period. Psychotherapy is the most common treatment for the more affluent, whereas drug treatment or electroshock therapy are more common treatments for lower-class patients.

Race

Neither the prevalence of mental illness nor the proportion of persons with resulting disabilities (concentration, social functioning, ability to work) differs significantly for Blacks and for Whites. Both the prevalence of a severe mental illness (SMI) and the resulting disability, however, are clearly related to lower educational attainment and poverty status. SMI was twice more likely among adults in poverty than among the nonpoor.[51]

Since a disproportionate number of African Americans are poor, it is not surprising that their hospitalization rate for mental disorders is about 33 percent higher than that of Whites. Their higher incidence of psychosis is comparable to that of low-income Whites, meaning that this high rate of incidence appears to be a social-class variable, not a racial one. As previously mentioned, people of lower social status are more likely to be hospitalized than to receive private therapy, and they tend to have greater contact with social agencies, including mental health officials.

Gender and Marital Status

In the United States, nearly twice as many women (12 percent) as men (7 percent) experience a depressive disorder each year. Research shows that before adolescence and late in life, females and males experience depression with the same frequency. Because the gender difference in depression is not seen until after puberty and disappears following menopause, scientists hypothesize that hormonal factors are involved in women's greater vulnerability to depression. Stress due to psychosocial factors, such as multiple roles in the home and at work and the increased likelihood of women being poor, at risk for violence and abuse, and raising children alone, also plays a role in the development of depression and other mental disorders.[52]

Men experience a much higher hospitalization rate for mental disorders in all marital status groups. The admission rate for males aged fourteen years and older is about twice that of females. Women are more likely to be diagnosed with neuroses (emotional disorders) and to receive outpatient care, while men are more likely to be diagnosed with psychoses (personality disorders) and to be hospitalized. Women are more often treated for depression and alcoholism, especially when their traditional motherly role lessens as their children grow up and leave home.[53]

Marital status appears to be an important factor in mental disorder cases. Married people have much lower rates of treatment and hospitalization. Both men and women who never married have considerably higher rates; but separation, divorce, and death of a spouse are other important variables in mental health.[54]

Sociological Perspectives

The concepts of physical and mental health have deep roots in sociocultural as well as organic explanations. Sociologists offer various analyses to enhance our understanding of the social problems that surround public expectations, incidence of illness, actual health care, and recovery.

The Functionalist Viewpoint

From the Functionalist perspective, problems in health care result from rapid social change and altered public attitudes. Advances in medical technology have shifted the focus of medical practice from the family doctor to specialists and large hospitals. Despite its high financial cost to patients, the hospital-based system is highly functional in providing income for physicians, hospitals, pharmaceutical companies, and medical suppliers. The U.S. concept of free enterprise and the fee-based medical system encouraged unregulated, unplanned rapid growth of a medical industry, as well as an uneven health-care delivery system.

One consequence of the patchwork growth of group or corporate medicine has been its depersonalization. No longer the well-known patient of a family doctor, an individual seeking health care is now "the third patient" sitting in the waiting room, "the pregnancy" in hospital room 254, or "the broken leg" in the emergency room. Another dysfunction involves the growth of third-party payments that have raised medical costs to pay for bill padding or nonessential expenditures instead of actual health-care needs. Still another dysfunction is the imbalanced doctor-patient ratio in different parts of the country. Finally, a cultural lag exists between the public's belief in private, personalized professional care and the reality of a diversified, large-scale medical industry. Functionalists would argue that the system is correcting itself through the evolution of lower-cost outpatient clinics, managed care plans, and cost controls on third-party payments.

More than 50 years ago, Talcott Parsons identified **interdependent functioning** as a process wherein the sick person assumes a mostly passive behavioral stance.[55] In the sick role, the ill person is not held responsible for the sickness and is exempted from normal role obligations; however, the sick person's cooperation in seeking expert help and in wanting to get well is necessary. Otherwise, the individual is considered lazy or malingering, and others will no longer excuse that person's absence from normal role obligations. Through the social control mechanism, society regulates both illness and the behavior that accompanies it. This analysis, while helpful, explains neither ethnic behavioral variations in avoidance of doctors for minor ailments nor diseases for which the victims are blamed.

The Conflict and Feminist Viewpoints

Conflict theorists view the problems surrounding the health-care delivery system as being the result of the domination of the rich and powerful. Because physicians want to maximize their incomes, their offices and superior private medical facilities are disproportionately located in urban and suburban areas where the affluent and influential live, not in rural or ghetto areas. Additionally, rates of infant mortality and disease are higher among low-income people, while life expectancy is lower, because the poor have less access to medical services than the affluent. Health care is not only a profit-making industry, but a monopoly that totally controls prices, maintains high demand by limiting the number of new physicians, and effectively opposes efforts at outside regulation.

Of the many health industry groups that lobby intensively in their own self-interest, the AMA offers Conflict theorists a prime example of a quasi-official body wielding political and economic power not in the public interest. The AMA has successfully fought off many attempts over the past fifty years to create a national health-insurance system. Although such a system exists in every other industrialized nation and would help people in this country cope with runaway medical costs, the medical profession fears it would impair their ability to set their own fees and would undermine their independence from outside regulation. Consequently, the AMA has in the past branded such proposals as "socialized medicine" or "Marxist medicine." Besides successfully lobbying to defeat such proposals, the AMA has donated millions of dollars to opponents of congressional advocates of national health-insurance plans, helping to defeat many of them. Congressional fear of the AMA lobby and respect for its continuing campaign contributions to legislative "friends" demonstrate how a powerful special-interest group can thwart the public good.

Besides being accused of exploiting illness for financial gain, the health-care industry comes under attack from Conflict theorists for its treatment of the mentally disturbed. Persons who can afford private care receive it, while those who cannot are ignored until they create a problem. Then they are put in mental hospitals, where they receive inadequate attention because of deficient funding and mediocre professional staff.

Conflict theorists also emphasize the stress and anxiety produced by our economic system as a source of mental illness. The constant competitive struggle to achieve breeds tension and intense pressure, setting the stage for some form of psychological breakdown. The economically exploited, who feel alienated and powerless to change the conditions in which they live, develop a frustration that often leads to serious mental problems. The high incidence of psychoses among low-income peoples—this perspective holds—is due to economic, political, and social exploitation.

Since Feminist theoretical analysis focuses on the impact of oppression and the politics of domination, its approach to health care is one that minimizes hierarchy and situates the individual's experience in its societal context. Managed care would seem to meet Feminist goals in its creation of an integrated system of health care that promotes wellness at less expense than the traditional fee-for-service structures of health-care delivery. However, it still is a profit-making enterprise. Therefore, Feminists view it as simply another form of power and control, with corporate cost-cutting decisions sometimes denying needed care. Feminists thus question basic assumptions that HMOs sometimes make in denying coverage and treatment and seek an empowering response to managed care. Feminists also are leery of diagnoses of mental disorders that are not informed by an understanding of oppression and abuse that women experience and the reluctance of HMOs to provide treatment. Thus they seek to interest HMOs in less costly alternatives to traditional psychiatric treatment—such as crisis phone lines, psychoeducational groups for survivors who dissociate or injure themselves, and peer networks and supports—as a means of maximizing individual treatment within the constraints of the economics of managed care.[56]

The Interactionist Viewpoint

Some aspects of the Interactionist perspective have already been mentioned in this chapter: impersonal doctor-patient relationships engendered by specialization and hospital-based health care, and the effects of labeling on physically or mentally sick persons. In examining problems of health care, Interactionist theorists emphasize the means by which people communicate, define, and alter the social reality of illness. Whether a person is considered healthy or ill depends on how others define that person and the person's resulting self-concept. Two further examples will demonstrate how social interaction patterns help explain mental illness.

According to psychiatrist Thomas Szasz, mental disorders are not illnesses but an unconscious excuse to avoid an unpleasant reality.[57] Some social factor—an unbearable personal and emotional situation, say, or an unresolved problem in living—causes the person unable to deal with the problem to adopt a defensive strategy to escape one role and assume another. Since the psychiatrist makes a value judgment based on his or her behavioral norms, identified mental illness is often a "myth" that penalizes people with involuntary treatment, thereby depriving them of their freedom and the opportunity to face responsibility.

About a quarter of a century ago, sociologist Erving Goffman worked for a year as a hospital aide at a mental hospital, where he had complete access to the patients and took notes of his impressions. The resulting important work led to a change in the discharge rates. Goffman found that a lengthy stay in a **total institution** was counterproductive. Cut off from the rest of society, the inmates led an enclosed, formally administered life.[58] They had no choice but to forsake their former, self-determining roles and assume that of an inmate, totally dependent on the institution for all physical needs. The staff tended to treat the patients in terms of the institution's expectations, ignoring normal behavior but recording all aspects of abnormal behavior. Anyone who challenged the system was considered a problem. Some patients thus went into withdrawal, while still others passively conformed to the rules.

Goffman found that the atmosphere of a mental institution worsened people's mental problems; and because they adapted to their sick role more and more, their chances of being released grew smaller the longer they were confined. Today most experts recognize the adverse long-term effects of such institutionalized interaction, and mental health professionals now strive to release new patients within a few months, before they lose their ability to assume personal responsibility for their actions.

▲ Thinking About the Future

Medical advances and genetic research promise to revolutionize health care even more. We now have a complete map of all the human genes and one day should be able to cure many diseases by altering genes. New developments in spare-parts medicine—replacing damaged body parts with artificial and natural substitutes—will prolong life. Identifying the hundreds of neurotransmitters (or chemical messengers) in the brain will enable doctors to use specific drugs to combat mental disorders such as depression, schizophrenia, and senility. Many present-day operations will become obsolete through advances in laser technology, drug therapy, and other new techniques.

Our future concerns do not focus on technological progress, though. At the beginning of this chapter, we discussed how the quality of health care had not improved despite the medical achievements of the past few decades. As long as social inequalities remain with society, no health-care system will be able to solve the problems created by poverty, prejudice, and discrimination. This interconnectivity is an important facet to addressing the issues of access, care, cost, and recovery in the field of health care.

Do you think a national health plan is the solution of our uneven health-care delivery system? Before you answer too quickly, consider how HMOs were once viewed as the solution to sky-rocketing costs and the dominance of doctors, hospitals, and insurance companies. Although they improved health care in many ways, especially with an emphasis on preventive medicine, they came under attack for their cost-cutting policies that sometimes denied necessary diagnostic tests and treatment. How do we overcome this problem and still keep costs down? Foes of big government oppose additional bureaucracy controlling health care. Is there another approach? Is there any way to adapt today's managed care programs into a national plan? And even if we do implement a national health plan, how do we persuade doctors to locate in small-town and rural America where a shortage of doctors exists?

FDA approval of the abortion pill has reshaped the fierce controversy on this subject, as women now have a nonsurgical means to terminate pregnancies. Do you foresee a lessening of the demonstrations and arguments of recent decades between pro-life and pro-choice advocates as aborting fetuses becomes a private action, without need of procedures in clinics and hospitals? Or will the battleground shift to doctors' offices and pharmacies? Will some states act to ban the sales of the abortion pill, and is such action constitutional? Does society have a responsibility to protect the rights of the unborn, or should it give women the right to choose what happens to their bodies?

Do you think other states will join Oregon in approving physician-approved suicide? Does a person have the right to decide when to die once one's quality of life deteriorates? What is society's responsibility in such cases? Should there be a national policy on this? A state policy?

AIDS continues to decimate populations in many parts of the world. In the United States, it is especially devastating among Blacks and growing numbers of Hispanics. No longer confined to homosexuals and drug users who share needles, HIV/AIDS now affects a greater proportion of the drug-free, heterosexual world. Some of this results from cultural attitudes rejecting safe-sex practices. What additional educational programs or other approaches do you suggest to combat this problem? How do we change attitudes and behavior? Is AIDS with us forever?

We attempted to solve the problem of the involuntary, long-term commitment of mentally ill people through deinstitutionalization, resulting in many patients essentially "dumped in the streets" and homeless. We have welfare agencies, community health clinics, and homeless shelters, but many do not seek their help. What do we do about the mentally ill? In a culture that values personal freedom, what is our society's responsibility to these individuals who have no supportive families and who are unable to handle their own affairs?

SUMMARY

1. The United States has made many advances in medicine, spending more money on health care than any other nation. Paradoxically, the quality and equity of our health-care delivery system is out of balance, and our health statistics are not as strong as those of many other countries.

2. Advances in medical science engendered the medicalization of life, wherein people submit to the dominance of the health-care practitioner. Increased specialization and the growth of institutions led to impersonalized medical care and hospital-based treatment. Although modern medicine cannot do much about the major causes of death, critics charge that it strips patients of their rights and can even be a threat to health because of errors in diagnosis, drug therapy, or surgery.

3. Because the medical profession is based on a fee-for-service model, the distribution of physicians and medical facilities is uneven, with affluent suburbs and urban areas oversupplied and small towns and low-income neighborhoods underrepresented. Private medical practice is extremely lucrative, but too many surgeons now exist; and as a result, many unnecessary operations occur. Doctors increasingly practice defensive medicine as a safeguard against malpractice suits.

4. Both for-profit and nonprofit hospitals benefit from extended patient stays. Until recently, hospitals had complete control over determining costs from diagnosis, treatment, and patient care, which third-party payers unquestioningly reimbursed. Costs skyrocketed, caused by hospitals' securing expensive new equipment and running extensive (and often irrelevant) tests. Despite new government restrictions, unnecessarily prolonged hospitalization still occurs.

5. Medical insurance brings some coverage to some people. Whether employer-employee supported or government-supported (Medicaid and Medicare), preset fee payment has now replaced the former blank check payment. The rise of health maintenance organization (HMO) programs is a private-sector response to high health costs; HMOs now enroll about four-fifths of all Americans insured through their employers. However, concern exists that necessary tests and services are sometimes denied in managed care to keep costs low. HMOs are now under fire for inadequate health care and physicians and hospitals are now forming alternative organizations known as physician practice management companies (PPMs) and provider sponsored organizations (PSOs).

6. Of the 1.3 million abortions that annually occur in the United States, 81 percent involve unmarried women. Heated debate continues over the "right" and "wrong" of this practice. Another difficult choice area involves the use of heroic efforts to keep terminally ill patients alive.

7. AIDS is the leading cause of death among African-American men aged twenty-four to forty-four. Over 468,000 Americans have died from this disease, and Blacks and Hispanics are disproportionately represented, with non-Hispanic Blacks (49 percent) the largest single group affected. Worldwide, 42 million known cases existed in 2003, about 30 million of them in sub-Saharan Africa, and another 6 million in South and Southeast Asia.

8. Mental health problems affect one in five Americans, and many of these illnesses require professional help. Social scientists find significant correlations between the incidence and treatment of mental disorders and such variables as social class, race, sex, marital status, and age.

9. The Functionalist view examines the functional advantages of the health-care system to health practitioners and suppliers, as well as the dysfunctional problems of depersonalization, high costs, cultural lag, and uneven quality care. Conflict and Feminist theorists emphasize the exploitation of the rest of society by the medical elite and related special-interest groups and point out how the system generates many health problems. Interactionists focus on the many ways social interpretations of illness and behavior affect diagnosis and treatment.

KEY TERMS

Bioethics

Deinstitutionalization

Euthanasia (mercy killing)

Health maintenance organization (HMO)

Interdependent functioning

Medicaid

Medicare

Neuroses

Overmedicalization

Psychoses

Total institution

INTERNET RESOURCES

At this book's Web site with Allyn & Bacon, you will find numerous links pertaining to health care. To explore these resources, go first to the author's page (**http://www.ablongman.com/parrillo**). Next, select this edition of *Contemporary Social Problems* and then choose **Internet Readings and Exercises.** Then select **Chapter 11,** where you will find both a variety of sites to investigate and some questions that pertain to those sites.

SUGGESTED READINGS

Birenbaum, Arnold. *Putting Health Care on the National Agenda.* Westport, Conn.: Frederick Praeger, 1995. Fine overview of the American health-care system and its problems, particularly rising costs, with discussion of various reform proposals.

Braithwaite, Ronald L. and Sandra E. Taylor. *Health Issues in the Black Community.* San Francisco: Jossey-Bass, 2nd ed. 2001. Examines such health concerns as AIDS, heart disease, substance abuse, and violence that disproportionately affect the black community.

Colombotos, John, and Corinne Kirchner. *Physicians and Social Change.* New York: Oxford University Press, 1997. A fine analysis of the role of socialization in developing values and attitudes among physicians.

Conrad, Peter, and Joseph W. Schneider. *Deviance and Medicalization: From Badness to Sickness,* 2d ed. Philadelphia: Temple University Press, 1992. An excellent sociohistorical analysis of how society redefined its social problems in medical terms and the implications of these changed values and attitudes on American life.

Court, Jamie, and Smith, Francis. *Making a Killing: HMOs and the Threat to Your Health.* Monroe, ME: Common Courage Press, 1999. Exposes appalling practices of HMOs, the corrupt world of managed care, the profit motive behind patients' misery, and the collusion with Congress and state legislatures to block any serious reforms.

Goffman, Erving. *Asylums: Essays on the Social Situation of Mental Patients and Other Inmates.* Garden City, N.Y.: Doubleday, 1961. This classic participant-observer study still offers fine insight into how daily interaction patterns in a mental hospital can be counterproductive to patients' well-being.

Illich, Ivan. *Medical Nemesis: The Expropriation of Health.* London: Marion Boyars Publishers, 2001. A carefully documented attack on modern medicine's inability to cure disease despite expensive procedures. Not only is faith in medicine unjustified, the author argues, but health care is often harmful instead of helpful.

Mechanic, David. *Inescapable Decisions: The Imperatives of Health Reform.* New Brunswick, N.J.: Transaction, 1994. A leading medical sociologist offers an extensive portrait of the U.S. health-care system and argues for basic changes in our national priorities.

Nuland, Sherwin. *How We Die.* New York: Alfred A. Knopf, 1995. An unsparing look at death in all its forms by a surgeon who wants doctors to regain their pastoral function of ministering to the dying, not staving off death at any cost.

Sherwin, Susan. *No Longer Patient: Feminist Ethics and Health Care.* Philadelphia: Temple University Press, 1993. An examination of the ethical issues in medicine, which the author insists must be resolved in a Feminist context.

Starr, Paul. *The Social Transformation of American Medicine,* reprint ed. New York: Basic Books, 1984. A comprehensive study of the social and economic development of medicine in the United States throughout the nation's history, with an analysis of why we are now confronted with problems of poor-quality health care, corporate medicine, and physician dominance.

Waitzin, Howard, *The Second Sickness: Contradictions of Capitalist Health Care.* 2d ed. Lanham, MD: Rowman and Littlefield, 2000. A scathing critique of the U.S. health-care system from the Conflict perspective.

12

Education for the Masses

Facts About Education

- Today's SAT verbal scores average 33 points lower than those in 1970.

- U.S. students finish in the middle in math and science test scores when compared to other industrialized countries.

- Hispanics aged sixteen to twenty-four had a dropout rate of 27 percent in 2001, compared to 11 percent for Blacks and 7 percent for Whites.

- Twenty-nine percent of all college freshmen need to take at least one remedial course.

- Nearly half of the nation's adult population is functionally illiterate.

- Some suburban public school districts spend up to nine times more per pupil than inner-city public school districts.

- Alternative charter schools now exceed 2,700 in number.

- Over 29 percent of urban students and 18 percent of suburban students report the presence of street gangs at their schools.

The public places great faith in education as a social institution capable of solving personal and societal problems, including alcohol and drug abuse, teenage pregnancies, reckless driving, crime, poverty, and prejudice. People tend to view schools as the great equalizers, the pathway to success, and the transmitters and preservers of all that is good about the United States—the work ethic, a belief in democracy and free enterprise, and a sense of responsibility to one's family and community. Such lofty goals identify education as a means to an end, rather than as an end in itself. Basic skills are taught, of course; but for many, the greater emphasis is neither on such skills nor on the value of intellectual growth or learning for its own sake. Rather, through education a person gets to be something, to get somewhere else, to become successful.

Ironically, the greater demands on U.S. education have a negative correlation with the status of educators, who are held in lower esteem here than in African, Asian, or European countries. Because so much is expected from the educational system, it makes an easy target for criticism from all directions. Liberals, conservatives, and radicals all find fault, as do Feminists, minorities, parents, teachers, and students. Others lambaste education for helping to maintain inequality instead of eliminating it. Problems of school discipline, integration, and financing also draw fire from many sides.

Resolving educational problems is not simple, because they are heavily intertwined with those of poverty, race and ethnic relations, and urban and rural economies.

Education in Sociohistorical Context

Ever since Thomas Jefferson first advocated mass education to produce an enlightened citizenry to sustain democracy, Americans have looked on the educational system as the springboard for individual achievement and national well-being. Not until the mid-nineteenth century, however, did free public education for all become the norm. In the early twentieth century, native-born Americans relied heavily on the public schools to Americanize the large numbers of people of diverse ethnicities coming from southern and eastern Europe.

Social Promotions

Until the 1960s, children would be "left back" and required to repeat a grade if they were unable to meet the minimum requirements at that level. Then the prevailing attitude changed, and educators recommended moving children through grades with their age peers regardless of their actual learning achievement. The new operative philosophy was that those who were not promoted were stigmatized, suffered a loss of self-esteem, and became less motivated. **Social promotions** became the standard practice to avoid introducing any impediments to learning because of poor self-image and social interaction networks. Whatever merit this practice had, it produced graduates deluded into thinking they had received an education when, in reality, many lacked even basic skills.

Another consequence of social promotions was a watering-down of course content because of the gradual but steady lowering of general class ability. At the college level, remedial courses in basic skills became both necessary and commonplace. Many professors stopped assigning term papers or giving essay exams because of large course enrollments and because so many students wrote so badly. For many students, reading and writing skills were not essential for getting a high school diploma or even, in some cases, a college degree. All a student had to do was listen in class to what the instructor emphasized, and then find the same phrase—or guess at the multiple-choice answers—on the exams.

Americans have long relied on education as the best means to achieve upward social mobility and to improve living standards. How has the widespread abandonment of affirmative action policies and programs affected these goals? In what ways do educational systems in the U.S. tend to maintain social and economic inequality? How do you think education reforms that focus on accountability for test scores affect students' learning? What problem in education does debate over the MCAS test highlight?

Grade Inflation

During the unpopular Vietnam War, male college students dismissed for low scholarship lost their draft deferment. Whether as a protest against the war or out of guilt at being partly responsible for sending someone to possible maiming or death in combat, professors became more liberal in their grading practices. Whereas a C grade had once been both average and respectable, higher grades became far more commonplace, with an A or B grade often accounting for at least half the total grades given out. This **grade inflation** distorted the picture of what students really learned.

Grade inflation extended down into the elementary and secondary schools, too. Teachers frequently interpreted giving high grades as evidence of their effectiveness and as a means of opening the high school academic track or college opportunities to youngsters who might otherwise have a less promising future. Grades were defined, like education itself, as a means to an end rather than as a measure of scholastic achievement. The problem continues. In 1996, 15 percent of college freshmen had an A average in high school; in 2001, it was 44 percent. Embarrassed by reports in 2002 that almost all its seniors graduated with honors, in 2003 Harvard awarded far fewer top grades.[1]

Curriculum Change

In the 1920s, U.S. high schools offered about 175 distinct academic courses. Between the 1930s and the 1970s, the proportion of academic course taken by students fell steadily as the number of distinct course offerings rose to more than 2,100. Many of these additions came in the 1960s, when educators initiated changes on the premise that the traditional curriculum was too restrictive and not relevant to the needs of a changing society. Tracked away from both academic and vocational courses, students enrolled in less rigorous, nonacademic, "personal service" elective courses. By the late 1970s, concern over high school graduates' being less well-prepared than in the past for jobs or higher education prompted a reversal in the decline in academic course-taking.[2] As we will discuss shortly, that trend gained momentum in the 1980s with the influential 1983 report by the National Commission on Excellence in Education.

The School as a Bureaucracy

Ideally, schools stimulate intellectual curiosity, encourage creativity and individualism, help students develop critical thinking, and provide an opportunity for students to reach their potential. In practice, schools often fail to do these things altogether or reflect institutional biases that favor certain categories of students over others. Part of the reason for this lies in social class differences, which we will discuss in the next section. In addition, however, each school system is a complex organization, with structural difficulties similar to those found in other forms of bureaucracy: an emphasis on efficiency; elaborate rules and regulations; regimentation and conformity; and weakness in handling nonroutine situations.

Critics frequently compare schools to factories or prisons. Alvin Toffler suggests that assembling large masses of students (raw material) to be processed by teachers (workers) in a centrally located school (factory) under discipline and regimentation was an acceptable system to the assembly-line age.[3] The prison analogy offers a warden (principal), guards (teachers), prisoners (students) forced to be there, a repressive atmosphere (hall passes and monitors, quick punishment for rule infractions), and demands for total silence, straight lines, and movement only with permission.[4]

Conformity and Obedience

Traditionally, the schools geared themselves toward teaching large groups of learners, requiring them to fit into the bureaucratic framework rather than structuring the school to meet individual needs. The resulting authoritarian system demanded submissive acceptance of an elaborate set of rules and regulations designed to maintain order and maximize efficiency. In *Crisis in the Classroom,* a highly influential book that redirected educational aims in the 1970s, Charles Silberman, warned that high schools—which were even more repressive than elementary schools—unintentionally transmitted the values of "docility, passivity, conformity, and lack of trust."[5]

In some school districts, progressive educators have succeeded in creating an open, diversified classroom environment that encourages creativity, curiosity, and an individualized pace of learning. Lessening the rigidly controlled approach toward collective uniformity of learning is a positive shift in educators' focus, but unfortunately, many schools remain preoccupied with regimentation and discipline. Obedience to time modules, lesson plans, dress and hairstyle codes, approved reading lists, emphasis on silence and straight lines, and conformity to teacher performance expectations instead of individual inquiry and pursuit of study remain the norm in many schools. The result is a student body with a slave mentality, where individuals sacrifice their real feelings and intuition, lose their growth potential for self-reliance and self-motivation, and instead become apathetic, conforming, and obedient drones.[6]

Hierarchy of Authority

Because schools are bureaucracies, they function through multiple strata of personnel, with the limits of authority clearly set at each level and with specific procedures delineated for various situations. Teachers especially find themselves enmeshed in a quagmire of paperwork (grading papers, composing lesson plans, authoring reports, writing recommendations, putting together evaluation studies, etc.). They must cover specific content material, use specific textbooks, and keep classrooms quiet and orderly. Administrators pressure teachers to report "tardy" students, to patrol restrooms for smoking or drug use, and to serve as cafeteria, hallway, or study hall watchdogs or general detention monitors. Teachers do not set policy, but they must implement it. Their job performance evaluations depend heavily on their ability to command respect and maintain order.

In a rather cynical observation, Christopher Jencks suggested that the hierarchy of school authority rests on the premise of distrust: "The school board has no faith in the central administration, the central administration has no faith in the principals, the principals have no faith in the teachers, and the teachers have no faith in the students."[7] Obviously, situations vary from one school district to another. But the emphasis on conformity promoted by bureaucratic structures everywhere could produce increasingly rigid personalities among those in the hierarchy, thus tending to stifle creativity and innovation.

Education and Social Class

Our insistence on universal public education opens the schools to young people from all social classes. Citizens have long believed that formal education can decrease social inequalities and provide the means for lower-class youth to achieve a higher socioeconomic status than their parents. For the past thirty years, though, research findings have offered contrary evidence. Although some low-income individuals do succeed through education, most youngsters' educational achievement correlates strongly with their socioeconomic background.

Dominance of Middle-Class Values

As we observed earlier, schools reflect the prevailing values and attitudes of society; and in the postindustrial United States, this means middle-class values and attitudes. To provide a standard education for all, schools stress certain value orientations and behavior patterns. In early grades, teachers emphasize cleanliness, neatness, quiet, orderliness, maintaining straight lines in going to and from recess or fire drills, punctuality, and conformity. In later grades, teachers often replace the earlier thrill of discovery and success in learning how to do things (self-realization) with a focus on simply learning subject matter, with grade competition and deferred gratification (good grades for college for good jobs) as the primary motivating factors.

As part of their teacher preparation, educators learn to recognize individual differences among their students in the classroom. Unfortunately, the orientation usually stresses supposed intellectual differences, with little or no education about class or cultural differences—such as language, family and peer influences, and teacher expectations—that may affect perceived intellectual differences. Consequently, many teachers evaluate classroom performance as it conforms to middle-class expectations.

Language

In all countries, the "correct" grammar and pronunciation are those used by the ruling class. Consider the basic premise in George Bernard Shaw's *Pygmalion* or its musical version, *My Fair Lady:* acceptance comes when a person overcomes a lower-class dialect. Students who speak Black English or a lower-class White dialect, which both differ from standard American English—and students of immigrant families who have a limited ability to speak any English—are at a disadvantage in school. They have difficulty understanding what they read and hear, and they get lower grades for their test answers and essays due to grammatical errors in what they write. Many students entering school never overcome the initial language barrier because they fall behind their classmates, become discouraged, and set lower educational goals for themselves.

Family and Peer Influence

Family and peers are the two most influential agents of socialization during a person's formative years. Consequently, their attitudes about high school and college play a major role in an individual's motivations about education. In the past, for example, the value orientation in most Italian and Polish immigrant families favored entering the workforce after high school, whereas Armenian, Greek, Japanese, and Jewish immigrant families stressed a college education.[8] Today, other groups show similarly distinct preferences. Family expectations among the middle and upper classes assume academic success and a college education, which is less often the case among lower- and working-class families, whether native-born or immigrant.

Learning potential also increases in middle- and upper-income families because they possess more books and educational toys; can take trips to zoos, theaters, museums, planetariums, and other cultural centers; and emphasize long-term goals (deferred gratification). The plans and actions of a person's school or neighborhood friends also affect a student's aspirations, regardless of teachers' efforts to motivate the individual.

Teacher Expectations

Teacher expectations often serve as a positive or negative motivating factor in student conformity. If a teacher believes that a student can achieve highly, he or she may use various forms

Students' backgrounds are important in determining the effectiveness of instruction, but even more critical is the learning environment. What aspects of the educational environment affect learning? How do teachers' expectations of student behavior and achievement affect learning? How do ability grouping and tracking affect learning? What might be benefits to all students of the type of learning experience shown in this photo?

of encouragement in attitude, comments, allowing more time to respond, or offering second chances to promote better performance. Conversely, if the teacher does not have high hopes for an individual, the teacher's attitude and behavior convey to the student a distinct message of low expectations that may well discourage further effort.

In a provocative and controversial experiment, Robert Rosenthal and Lenore Jacobson administered intelligence tests in a San Francisco elementary school and then randomly identified 20 percent of the students tested as "spurters"—ones whom teachers were asked to watch.[9] Eight months later, when all were retested, the "spurters" scored significantly higher and their teachers evaluated them as happier, better adjusted, and more appealing, interesting, and curious than their classmates. Actually, the only real difference was in teacher expectations in the arbitrarily chosen "spurters," suggesting that the change in the teachers' attitudes affected the students' progress. Subsequent similar experiments had mixed results, however, indicating that we need more research to identify precisely how the self-fulfilling prophecy works in the classroom.[10]

Standardized Testing

IQ tests are widely used as a basis for ability grouping because most people associate educational achievement with intelligence. A number of difficulties, however, surround the use of IQ tests to measure intelligence. Psychologists disagree significantly about what these tests actually measure and how valid the scores are in predicting achievement. One major argument surrounds the tests' evident cultural bias, since they use language, concepts, and basic information much more familiar to White middle-class Americans than to other Americans.[11] Critics argue that IQ tests do not measure innate abilities exclusively, but reflect environmental influences as well. Moreover, these tests appraise only certain intellectual aptitudes: language, mathematical reasoning, and spatial and symbolic relationships. Not measured are such intellectual capacities as artistic aptitude, creativity, imagination, and intuition and such social skills as persuasiveness, perseverance, cleverness, and charm—all of which can help a person do well in life.

The heredity and environment, or nature versus nurture, argument is generations old, but the touchstone of the modern debate was an article in the 1969 *Harvard Educational Review* in which psychologist Arthur Jensen argued that environment played only a minor role in test scores.[12] To support his contention Jensen pointed out that lower-class youth score equally to middle-class youth in tasks requiring memorization or rote learning but consistently lower in problem solving, seeing relationships, and abstract reasoning; the difference in conceptual performance, he argued, is attributable to genetic factors, not testing bias.[13] Others, such as William Shockley, Richard Herrnstein, and Charles Murray, have similarly asserted that genetic differences, not environmental opportunities, are the basic determinants of success or failure.[14]

Of all the criticisms leveled at this position, two of the most compelling came from Lee J. Cronbach and Thomas Sowell. Cronbach's position is that the differences in conceptual scores do not reflect lesser innate ability but lack of training in conceptual skills.[15] Indeed, considerable empirical evidence has demonstrated that lower-class children, after initially scoring lower than middle-class children in conceptual ability tests, can score higher than the middle-class children after receiving brief training in conceptual skill development.[16] Economist Thomas Sowell observed that all lower-class newcomers—including immigrants from southern and eastern Europe in the early twentieth century—have historically scored lower in the abstract portions of intelligence tests.[17] After they experience upward mobility, however, their IQ scores also rise; this suggests that—whatever the precise nature of the cognitive abilities or tendencies that IQ tests actually measure may be—test performance varies in response to environmental influences. Moreover, persons able to afford test prep training courses can raise their scores significantly, leading to further discrepancies between affluent and poor students' scores.

Despite all the controversy, use of standardized tests such as the Stanford Achievement Test and the California Achievement Tests (CAT) as placement tools is widespread. Although they may accurately measure certain forms of intellectual ability at a particular point, they also produce differential groupings for instructional purposes, within which teacher expectations and student self-image may stifle further growth in intellectual capacity. In the late 1970s, a California state court partly supported this position, ruling that using standardized test scores to assign children to different tracks violated the principle of equal educational opportunity.[18] (See the accompanying box.)

Education Problem Areas

As we have already discussed, our educational system is beset by many problems. Three of the most serious areas of concern are the high number of dropouts, illiterate adults, and school financing.

Social Constructions of Social Problems

The Effects of Tracking and Labeling

The basic premise of **ability grouping** in the public schools appears sound. Instead of assembling a class that contains students of varying abilities—where high achievers may not be sufficiently challenged, and low achievers may feel intimidated or overwhelmed—why not group students of similar ability in separate classes to provide a common level of instruction for everyone? Such a system does indeed have merit, but it simultaneously creates behavioral patterns that work to the detriment of many students.

Ability grouping often begins as early as first grade, with students assigned to reading groups on the basis of comparable ability. From that moment forward, students receive different challenges and assignments, with curriculum material oriented to their perceived ability to comprehend it. The benefits of these differential educational "fits" between capabilities/needs and instruction are real, but they often remain fixed instead of flexibly pursuing a long-term goal of greater challenge to intellectual growth potential. Too frequently, this process of labeling students as above average, average, or below average sets in motion a cumulative set of teacher expectations and student conformity to those expectations.

Students quickly realize how they are grouped, and this affects their self-image and motivation. Those in the upper track often develop a smug attitude of superiority, while those in the lower track may have a negative self-image or sense of inferiority. Assignment to the lowest track carries a stigma. These students, seeing how educators and other students identify and relate to them, lose much of their self-esteem and desire to learn and excel in school.

Significantly, a highly disproportionate number of students in the lowest track come from low-income families; students from upper-middle-income families are disproportionately represented in the upper, college-bound track. The tracking system thus reflects and reinforces the U.S. social class structure. A sifting and sorting process occurs in the schools to fit each individual into a place in society. The combination of social class bias and tracking affects teachers' treatment and students' attitudes, motivation, self-image, curriculum choice, career goals, dropout and further education decisions, and subsequent earning power. Conflict theorists argue further that the schools thereby deny equality of educational opportunity.

Before I became a professor of sociology, I was a high school teacher for four years, and I saw firsthand that smugness and negative self-image among students in different tracks. I have a particularly haunting memory of three, junior-level male students in a lowest-track section coming up to me after a wonderfully successful class. It had been a nontraditional, interactive lesson that included music, stories, demonstrations, and role playing. After all three complimented me on how enjoyable and educational they found the class, one of them asked, "Why did you bother?"

Stunned, I asked what he meant.

"Why did you go to so much trouble?" he asked. "Don't you know we're the losers? We ain't never gonna amount to anything. Why don't you save all that stuff for those in the other class, the ones going to college?" The others nodded their agreement. I responded as I hope any teacher would, with positive comments about them, their potential, and almost limitless future choices, and how they were well worth my effort, just like anyone else. They thanked me, but I could tell they remained unconvinced. My rapport with them and the others in that class remained strong throughout the year, and all did graduate.

I moved away and took a new position at William Paterson University, where I am still. Over the years, though, I have wondered what became of those seventeen- and eighteen-year-olds who were so certain they were losers, an attitude that I believe was heavily reinforced by tracking.

School Dropouts

Although nationwide the school dropout rate decreased from 14.1 percent in 1980 to 10.7 percent in 2001, it remains unusually high among urban minorities and the rural poor (see Figure 12.1).[19] The stereotype of disruptive boys and pregnant girls constituting most dropouts is inaccurate, although they do account for 40 percent of the total. Both sexes tend to drop out for reasons associated with poverty, urban settings, families with parents who lack diplomas, and minority status.[20]

Why do poverty and minority status increase a person's likelihood of dropping out? According to the National Coalition of Advocates for Students, a child who is poor, Black, or Hispanic is much more likely to be physically disciplined, suspended, expelled, or made to repeat a grade. These practices in turn increase the likelihood that a child will drop out of school. A minority child is also three times more likely to wind up in vocational education or in classes for the mildly mentally retarded. Hispanics aged sixteen to twenty-four had a dropout rate of 27.0 percent in 2001, compared to rates of 10.9 percent for Blacks and 7.3 percent for Whites.[21]

If education is the pathway into the societal mainstream, lack of education is a road to nowhere. Today's dropouts are tomorrow's unemployed and poverty-stricken adults. All of society, not just the individual victims, suffer economically when the schools and the young abandon each other.

Figure 12.1   Dropout Rates of Sixteen-to Twenty-Four-Year-Olds by Race/Ethnicity, October 1972–2001

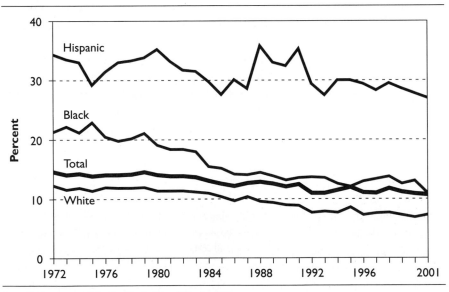

Source: U.S. Department of Education, *The Condition of Education,* 2003.

Adult Illiteracy

Literacy is a fundamental tool necessary for successful economic performance in an industrialized society. No longer simply defined as a basic threshold of reading ability, literacy today means the ability to understand and use written and printed information in daily activities at home, at work, and in the community. As society becomes more complex and as low-skill jobs continue to disappear, concern about adults' ability to use written information to function in society increases. Compared to most other industrialized countries assessed in 1995, the United States had a greater concentration of adults who scored at the lowest levels across the prose, document, and quantitative literacy domains.[22]

In 1986, the U.S. Department of Education conducted the first comprehensive study of illiteracy by administering to a national sample a test of twenty-six multiple-choice questions designed to measure understanding of simple words and phrases. The study identified 13 percent of the population—about 21 million persons—as illiterate. Most of the adult illiterates, the study found, were under age 50 and lived in cities. The illiteracy rate was 9 percent among native-born Americans, the majority of them high school dropouts. Among adults who spoke a different language at home, the English illiteracy rate was 48 percent.

In 1993, the Department of Education revealed an even more appalling portrait of Americans' deficiencies with words and numbers. This new, even more comprehensive study found that some 90 million persons—47 percent of the total U.S. adult population—were functionally illiterate. This greater number reflects, in part, the newer definition of literacy mentioned at the beginning of this section. Now, instead of just measuring reading skills in decoding words, the study measured practical literacy, such as the ability to fill out a bank deposit slip, compute the cost of carpeting a room, or read a bus schedule (see Figure 12.2). Half the individuals who scored in the lowest 20 percent on this test had graduated from high school, disturbing proof that a high school diploma doesn't necessarily signify mastery of fundamentals important in everyday life.[23] It is hoped that a follow-up study in 2003, with results to be released in 2004, will show an improvement.

In today's information society, workers need to possess these interpretive abilities if American business is to remain competitive with other countries. By some estimates, employers are spending about $50 billion in an attempt to eliminate this practical illiteracy.[24] Illiterate adults can be an additional drag on the national economy, since they are more likely to require welfare assistance than to hold a decent job and contribute to the economy.

School Funding

Perhaps the most significant educational problem the United States faces today involves finances, since these affect all other aspects of the quality and effectiveness of the learning environment. Tax dollars pay for public education, but the federal government provides only about 8 percent of needed school revenues; as a result, budget allocations at the state and local levels provide most funds. Because states and communities within states vary greatly in their ability to generate revenues, the wealthier ones can afford to spend more per student than the poorer ones. As Table 12.1 shows, the contrasts in average expenditures per pupil in such neighboring states

Figure 12.2   Measuring Adult Literacy

The 1993 Department of Education study found many adults couldn't execute common daily tasks, as reading a bus schedule. Some questions below:

Question 1
What is the gross pay for this year to date?

HOURS					PERIOD ENDING					
REGULAR	XXX SHIFT	OVERTIME	TOTAL		3/15/92	REGULAR	OVERTIME	GROSS	XXX	NET PAY
5.00			5.00		CURRENT	625 00		625 00		459 68
					YEAR TO DATE			4268 85		

TAX DEDUCTIONS					
	FED	STATE	CITY	FICA	
CURRENT	108 94	13 75		38 31	
YEAR TO DATE	734 98	82 50		261 67	

NON-NEGOTIABLE

OTHER DEDUCTIONS				
CR UNION	UNITED FD	PERS XX	MISC	MISC CODE

OTHER DEDUCTIONS					
CODE	TYPE	AMOUNT	CODE	TYPE	AMOUNT
07	DEN	4 12			

Question 2
Here is a social-security card. Sign your name on the line that reads "signature."

SOCIAL SECURITY

301-02-0304

THIS NUMBER HAS BEEN ESTABLISHED FOR

_____

SIGNATURE

Question 3
On Saturday afternoon, if you miss the 2:35 bus leaving Hancock and Buena Ventura going to Flintridge and Academy, how long will you have to wait for the next bus?

CASH	$		00
LIST CHECKS BY BANK NO.	ENDORSE WITH NAME & ACCOUNT NUMBER		
		557	19
		75	00
TOTAL			

Question 4
You wish to use the automatic teller machine at your bank to make a deposit. Figure the total amount of the two checks being deposited. Enter the amount on the form in the space next to total.

OUTBOUND
from Terminal

	Leave Downtown Terminal	Leave Hancock and Buena Ventura	Leave Canada	Leave Russia House	Leave North Carolina and One Bianco	Arrive Flintridge and Academy
A	6:20	6:35	6:45	6:50	7:03	7:15
	6:50	7:05	7:15	7:20	7:33	7:45
	7:20	7:35	7:45	7:50	8:03	8:15
	7:50	8:05	8:15	8:20	8:33	8:45
	8:20	8:35	8:45	8:50	9:03	9:15
	8:50	9:05	9:15	9:20	9:33	9:45
	9:20	9:35	9:45	9:50	10:03	10:15
M	10:20	10:35	10:45	10:50	11:03	11:15
	11:20	11:35	11:45	11:50	12:03	12:15
	12:20	12:35	12:45	12:50	1:03	1:15
	1:20	1:35	1:45	1:50	2:03	2:15
	2:20	2:35	2:45	2:50	3:03	3:15
PM	2:50	3:05	3:15	3:20	3:33	3:45
	3:20	3:35	3:45	3:50	4:03	4:15
	3:50	4:05	4:15	4:20	4:33	4:45
	4:20	4:35	4:45	4:50	5:03	5:15
	4:50	5:05	5:15	5:20	5:33	5:45
	5:20	5:35	5:45	5:50	6:03	6:15
	5:50	6:05	6:15	6:20	6:33	6:45
	6:20	6:35	6:45	6:50	7:03	7:15

Question 5
The price of one ticket and bus for "Sleuth" costs how much less than the price of one ticket and bus for "On the Town"? A charter bus will leave from the bus stop at 4 p.m. giving you plenty of time for dinner in New York. Return trip will start from W. 45th St. directly following the plays. Both theaters are on W. 45th St. Allow 1 1/2 hours for the return.

Time: 4 p.m., Saturday, Nov. 20

Price: "On the Town"   Ticket and Bus $11.00
          "Sleuth"   Ticket and Bus $8.50

ANSWERS

1. $4,268.85
2. Sign your name
3. 30 minutes
4. $632.19
5. $2.50

as Alabama and South Carolina, Kansas and Missouri, Utah and Wyoming, and Idaho and Oregon demonstrate a wide range of state funding even in the same geographic areas.

Because substantial funding comes from property taxes, local communities with a strong tax base can spend more per student (while costing taxpayers proportionately less), than poorer communities where the needs are greatest. In some affluent school districts, per-pupil spending is nine times greater than in inner-city school districts.[25] The effects of tighter, urban budgets are obvious. Cities, large and small, struggle with schools in disrepair that contain too few teachers and too many students who lack sufficient textbooks and supplies.

Schools in just six states—California, Texas, Florida, New York, New Jersey, and Illinois—are especially hit hard because they receive over 80 percent of all immigrants. Most of these newcomers settle in cities or older, adjacent suburbs, their numbers overburdening the schools and straining their budgets and tax support systems.

Since minorities are overrepresented in poorer school districts, the lack of resources denies these students the same opportunities as students in affluent districts to work with microscopes, computers, or other modern technological equipment. When good-quality public education comes only to children of a higher socioeconomic background, the educational system fosters inequalities in society rather than helping to ensure equal opportunities in life for all Americans.

At present we have a decidedly mixed situation. While some states have attempted to provide everyone with equal access to a high-quality education, other states have not. Discrepancies

Table 12.1   State Spending on Public Education, K-to-12 Average per Pupil, 2002

1. District of Columbia	$15,281	18. Indiana	$ 8,555	35. California	$ 7,324
2. New York	$11,472	19. New Hampshire	$ 8,432	36. Iowa	$ 7,212
3. New Jersey	$11,458	20. Georgia	$ 8,395	37. Louisiana	$ 7,055
4. Connecticut	$11,431	21. Kansas	$ 8,262	38. North Carolina	$ 6,970
5. Alaska	$11,103	22. Maryland	$ 8,164	39. South Dakota	$ 6,911
6. Massachusetts	$11,079	23. Minnesota	$ 8,139	40. Idaho	$ 6,884
7. Vermont	$10,531	24. Hawaii	$ 7,969	41. Virginia	$ 6,792
8. Delaware	$10,166	25. Montana	$ 7,901	42. Oklahoma	$ 6,681
9. Rhode Island	$10,118	26. Ohio	$ 7,881	43. Florida	$ 6,592
10. Illinois	$ 9,788	27. Kentucky	$ 7,763	44. Nevada	$ 6,507
11. Wisconsin	$ 9,539	28. Washington	$ 7,501	45. Tennessee	$ 6,367
12. Maine	$ 9,529	29. Colorado	$ 7,453	46. Arkansas	$ 6,025
13. Wyoming	$ 9,478	30. New Mexico	$ 7,450	47. Mississippi	$ 5,828
14. West Virginia	$ 9,056	31. Missouri	$ 7,395	48. Alabama	$ 5,419
15. Michigan	$ 8,987	32. South Carolina	$ 7,381	49. Arizona	$ 5,353
16. Oregon	$ 8,910	33. Texas	$ 7,374	50. Utah	$ 4,989
17. Pennsylvania	$ 8,771	34. Nebraska	$ 7,336	51. North Dakota	$ 4,851

Sources: NEA Research, *Rankings and Estimates,* Washington, D.C.: U.S. National Education Association, 2003, Table H16, p. 58.

remain among the states and among school districts within many states. Until a more equitable distribution of educational funding occurs, equal opportunity will remain an American myth.

A Question of Quality

Even though the average number of years of schooling completed in the United States rose year after year, numerous experts questioned the quality of education students were receiving. In 1983, an important turning point occurred when the National Commission on Excellence in Education issued a scathing report of its findings after an eighteen-month study. In *A Nation at Risk,* the commission asserted that "a rising tide of mediocrity" had devastated all aspects of public education: teacher competency, curriculum, and achievement. So inadequate was the quality of education, maintained the commission, that the nation was actually reversing a long trend of intergenerational educational progress:

> Each generation of Americans has outstripped its parents in education, in literacy and in economic attainment. For the first time in the history of our country, the educational skills of one generation will not surpass, will not equal, will not even approach, those of their parents.[26]

Following the Commission's report that the nation had "in effect, been committing an act of unthinking, unilateral educational disarmament," many state and local school districts initiated reforms. Despite some progress, however, recent reports suggest that problems remain.

- A 2003 report revealed that the average reading literacy score for fourth-grade students was above the international average, though lower than eight countries.[27]
- That same report reported the average reading literacy score for fifteen-year-olds was comparable to the international average, though lower than thirteen countries.[28]
- A 2002 report disclosed that eighth-graders exceeded the international average of thirty-eight countries in math and science, but performed lower than fourteen countries.[29]
- A 2001 report stated that little change occurred in the reading performance of seventeen-year-olds since 1971.[30]
- In 2001, average SAT verbal scores were 33 points lower than they were in 1970.[31]
- In 2002, 29 percent of all college students needed to take at least one remedial course.[32]

What is the problem? Why does the United States (which spends more money per student than do most countries whose students outperform ours) produce graduates with, on average, less knowledge and competency? Let us examine the three primary areas identified in *A Nation at Risk*—curriculum offerings, academic standards, and teaching competency—as the 1983 report found them and as they are today.

Subject Matter

The commission reported that a smorgasbord of electives had subverted academic standards and undercut efforts to emphasize the challenging courses necessary to prepare students for advanced study in scientific and technological fields. Since 1969, the proportion of allotted classroom time devoted to academic subjects had fallen from 70 percent to 62 percent, while the time devoted to nontraditional subjects like driver's education and consumer living had grown from 8 to 13 percent.[33] In thirty-five states, only one year each of math and science was required, and no state mandated taking a foreign language. The result, said the commission, was a "cafeteria-style curriculum in which the appetizers and desserts can easily be mistaken for the main course." By permitting students to drift away from academic subjects, the schools had undermined the traditional purpose of education and placed the United States at a disadvantage in comparison to other industrialized nations.[34]

In 2003, the U.S. Department of Education could report some positive developments. High school graduates increasingly graduate with more academic units and fewer units of vocational/personal subjects than graduates in 1982. Moreover, the percentage of graduates who complete the recommended minimum units in English, mathematics, social studies, and science increased dramatically from 2 percent in 1982 to 31 percent by 2000.[35] Of course, this still left two-thirds of all U.S. high school graduates going to college without the right courses, which no doubt is a key reason so many students must take remedial courses there. (See the accompanying box for international comparisons.)

Academic Standards

Declining academic standards were a by-product of the drive to provide everyone with the credentials of a high school diploma or college degree, as educators all too often graduated functionally illiterate students (reading below the sixth-grade level). This problem area may be disappearing, as the demand for school accountability and student responsibility has spawned a "back-to-basics" movement across the country. Many school systems now stress fundamental reading, writing, and math skills. Almost all states now mandate student testing standards, requiring students to achieve minimum scores in these fundamental areas as a precondition for earning a high school diploma.

This **minimum competency test** (MCT) measures the level of proficiency a student has achieved in basic skills, but critics argue that it is not an accurate indicator of the student's ability and that it encourages teachers to prepare students to pass the test without truly learning anything. Others stress its positiveness in restoring credibility to the high school diploma. Many colleges also now require an MCT or basic skills test for first-year placement in freshman math and English classes or third-year entry into the major. In a credential-oriented society, a passing MCT score is now another necessary credential.

Assessment testing at various age levels shows mixed results in elementary school achievement in math and science. Average proficiency in both subjects improved between 1978 and 2000 for all age groups, with the largest improvements occurring among nine- and thirteen-year-olds. However, the overall pattern of reading achievement changed minimally over the assessment years from 1971 to 2000. For both Blacks and Hispanics, average performance scores have increased but remain significantly lower than those of Whites. After a lessening of the gap from the early 1970s to the mid-1980s, no further reductions have occurred except between Hispanics and Whites in mathematics scores among seventeen-year-olds.[36]

The Globalization of Social Problems

Education in an International Context

For years students in other nations have surpassed young Americans in their academic knowledge, even though the United State spends more money per student than other nations. For example, in the math and science test series administered by the International Association for Evaluation of Educational Attainment, the Associated Press reported that U.S. twelfth-graders scored behind nineteen other nations, outperforming only Cyprus and South Africa. A comparison of the high-school elite—those who took physics and advanced math—showed Americans tied for the bottom, and in physics they had sole possession of last place. Students from Asian nations, who usually do very well, did not take the test this time—so U.S. students trailed a pack of also-rans.

While many U.S. schools appear to avoid solid academic training in favor of "self-esteem" training, this must be working since, in the latest round of international tests, U.S. students led the world in one area: "self-esteem." As in previous international tests, U.S. students had the highest perception of how well they had done. Seventy percent said they thought they had done well. This would be comic if it were not so tragic.

While the U.S. education system is falling behind academically, it is also leading the world in excuses. One of these excuses is that more of our students reach the twelfth grade, so we are comparing our average with the elite from other nations. While this may be true for a few nations, there are many others with as high a percentage of students finishing secondary school as we do, and some have a higher percentage completion rate. Both categories of nations beat our students. Another excuse is our population has so many disadvantaged minorities that this drags down our average. But when you compare our best with those of other countries, our best students still get clobbered.

Why do other nations have more effective schooling? The reasons include longer school calendars, greater emphasis on academic subjects, and pressure to test well in the twelfth grade in order to be allowed to attend a university. A *U.S. News & World Report* study showed that students in France, Germany, and Japan spend 100 percent more hours studying math, science, and history than U.S. students. Most studies show that students' achievement scores rise as time they spend on homework increases, so it is hardly surprising that students in other countries outscore U.S. students on various achievement tests. Experts also agree that many other countries do a much better job of teaching virtually all subjects, including the grammar of the students' own language.

One indicator of the depth of foreign student subject mastery is that a full 50 percent of all students take advanced examinations, compared to only 6.6 percent of the students in the United States. Not only do more foreign students take advanced exams, but the same data show that their passing rate is eight times higher than among U.S. students (33 percent to 4 percent). The contrast paints a terrible picture for successful U.S. competition in a global economy. (It is as if our football team has 3 good players against the competition with 165 good players.) U.S. Secretary of Education Richard Riley responded to the sad results from these international tests by calling them "unacceptable."

Source: Michael Hodges and Bill Mechlenburg, *Grandfather International Education Report.* Available at http://mwhodges. home.att.net/education. Accessed March 3, 2004.

SAT scores do not yet reflect any learning improvement. As already mentioned, the average SAT verbal score in 2002 was 33 points lower than in 1970. Some educators suggested that this decline was due to the larger percentage of minority students taking the SAT. To bolster their argument they point to verbal mean score differences, which in 2002 were 504; Blacks, 427; Hispanics, 460; Whites, 530.[37]

In 1995, the College Board raised average SAT scores to 500, the midpoint on its 200-to-800 scale. The average verbal score thus rose from 424 to 500, while the average math score increased from 478 to 500. The College Board denied charges of nationwide score inflation, saying the SATs weren't weakened, only "recentered," because percentile rankings remained unaffected. Critics contend that the changes "sanction mediocrity" in the high schools by hiding lower scores and obscuring the crucial fact that reading skills have deteriorated significantly since 1966.[38]

Teacher Competency

Although nine out of ten teachers perform adequately, increasing cases of incompetence came to public attention in the early 1980s. Frequent complaints included teachers' using poor grammar, misspelling words, having poor communication skills, lacking sufficient knowledge of their subjects, and possessing low mental ability.[39] Among the reasons for the existence of some poor teachers were the noncompetitive levels of teachers' salaries, which discouraged the brightest college students from becoming teachers; the inadequate academic preparation provided by teacher training programs; and the lack of a national standard examination for entrance into the profession.[40]

Recommendations

In 1986, the Carnegie Forum on Education and the Economy issued its *Report on Teaching as a Profession,* offering reform proposals designed to upgrade the profession.[41] Prepared by a panel of educators, including presidents of both major teachers' unions, as well as business and political leaders, it subsequently received endorsements at conventions of both the American Federation of Teachers and the National Education Association. The report went to the core of the problem: the need for proper training, professionalism, and a positive working environment. Among the document's recommendations were the following:

1. More energetic minority recruitment
2. A bachelor's degree requirement in arts and sciences as a prerequisite to studying teaching at the graduate level
3. Creation of a national standards board to set high criteria for entrance into teaching and to certify applicants who meet those levels
4. A rigorous national proficiency exam for board-certified teachers, similar to the bar exam for lawyers
5. A greater voice for teachers in school administrative decisions, and instructor incentives tied to schoolwide student performance

6. A new twelve-month position, titled "lead teacher," for teachers who hold advanced certificates, plus higher salaries tied to job functions and certification, with lead teachers earning as much as $72,000

Results

Since that report was issued, some progress has occurred. Public school teachers are more ethnically diverse, increasing from 9 percent of the total teaching force to 14 percent.[42] College course-taking patterns of new teachers are now similar to those for all bachelor's degrees, and public school teachers today are more likely to have an advanced degree than they were ten or twenty years ago.[43] Almost all states now require new teachers to take precertification competency tests, and several states mandate competency tests of experienced teachers.

Many colleges delay declaration of a major in education until sophomore year and mandate a minimum GPA to enter. Other schools offer five-year programs of study, with professional training provided in graduate courses during the final year. A number of states require elementary education majors to have an academic major, believing that a liberal arts background gives teachers a stronger knowledge base. Some school districts have also established mentor programs, in which experienced teachers offer guidance and support to new teachers.

The effectiveness of education involves many factors, including students' backgrounds, the learning environment, and teachers' expectations. How does each of these elements affect an individual's motivation and academic achievement? Why do we say that teachers, particularly in elementary school, have an enormous amount of power in the classroom?

Attracting and retaining quality teachers are growing concerns among education officials and the public. This is especially true for beginning teachers, as school districts compete with each other and with other industries for additional teaching personnel to cope with growing enrollments and an aging workforce of experienced teachers nearing retirement. Increased salaries potentially provide a means of attracting and retaining the increased numbers of high-quality young teachers who will be needed in the years ahead. However, since 1989 there has been little change in average median salaries (adjusted for inflation) to lessen the disparity in pay with other occupations. Since their income is based on a ten-month contract, we might expect teachers to receive lower salaries than most other white-collar professionals. Still, teachers' salaries are much lower. In New York City in 2000, for example, the average teacher earned less than a city garbage collector![44]

Although teaching attracts many people for nonmonetary reasons (working with young people, personal satisfaction), higher salaries in other fields undoubtedly lure away some bright young people who would make fine teachers. Teachers still have relatively little influence over school policies; but as a result of improvement in other areas, they report being happier about their choice of a profession than in the early 1980s, and attrition is now only 6 percent in all fields, including mathematics and science, compared to 20 percent of beginning teachers' leaving the profession after just one year during the 1970s.[45]

How Else Can We Improve Education?

Some problems in education are more manageable than others. All, however, necessitate bureaucratic changes and greater accountability from the educational system regarding effectiveness and efficiency. Main areas of focus these days include equitable school districts, voucher plans, charter schools, and school violence.

Equitable School Districts

Despite the good intentions of government officials and educators, the nation's public schools do not provide equal educational opportunity. Residential patterns frequently cause racial and socioeconomic imbalances among school populations. Urban, rural, and even small-town school districts lack the revenue base of affluent suburbs in financial support of school needs. Busing to achieve minority integration, though of limited success in a few urban areas, often hastened White flight; and now government officials, the courts and many minority leaders no longer see this approach as viable.[46] Some states have tried to equalize school expenditures per student by setting budget caps for school districts, but nationwide great disparities remain. Several alternative proposals—some already tried in certain areas—offer promise but also controversy.

Redistricting

Redrawing the boundary lines within a community to determine which school each student will attend preserves the neighborhood school concept, yet creates a better balance in student enrollment. White Plains, New York, was among the first to adopt an integration program of this kind, declaring that no school would have less than 10 percent nor more than 30 percent Black enrollment. Today in White Plains, through redrawn boundary lines and integrated housing, some children walk to a neighborhood school, while others are bused.

Another **redistricting** approach establishes equitable revenue bases and integrated schools by creating school districts independent of municipal boundaries. This may work in Los Angeles, for example, where the county rather than the city provides other services, such as firefighters and ambulance paramedics. In the Northeast, however, local resistance to this type of solution is quite strong because of the longer presence of traditional local boundaries and the "home rule" philosophy of local control.

Magnet Schools

Another effort at achieving school desegregation involves magnet schools, whose number has quadrupled in the past ten years. **Magnet schools,** mentioned in Chapter 8, are rigorously academic and teach a specialized curriculum with a focus such as math and science, the arts, or computer science. These advanced programs attract talented students from beyond traditional neighborhood boundaries, thereby overcoming residential segregation patterns to create a more diversified student population. Over half of the nation's 1,700 magnets serve low socioeconomic districts.[47] However, about 21 percent are partial-site magnet schools—the result (except for Milwaukee) of court-ordered desegregation plans since the 1980s. At these schools, the buildings are desegregated, but the classrooms remain segregated along racial lines.[48]

Magnets began as an alternative to mandatory busing, but their success in raising students' scholastic achievement gained them even more popularity. Studies show that magnet school children perform better than those in comprehensive public high schools in math, science, reading, and social studies.[49] Since teachers have a greater say in running these schools, their motivation is higher and their absenteeism and attrition rates are lower than among peers teaching in regular schools. Unfortunately, magnet schools are much more expensive to operate than neighborhood schools and thus are impractical as the sole means of achieving high-quality schools.

On the other hand, critics charge that magnet schools are elitist because they lavish resources on the best and the brightest while relegating the majority of students to the "mediocrity" of ordinary neighborhood schools. Moreover, the best teachers get lured away from ordinary schools to the magnet schools because the latter offer better students, greater resources, and higher professional prestige.[50] In addition, some critics think that magnet schools intensify the problems of tracking by creating a mentality of privilege that alienates gifted students from the rest of the school community, thereby widening the gulf between them.[51] Thus, while magnet schools may offer a partial solution to the difficulty of establishing high-quality integrated schools, they may also create inequities for other public schools.

Voucher Plans

The most radical form of parental choice option for sending children to high-quality integrated schools is the **school voucher** approach. Under this system, parents receive a voucher equal to the state's share of the cost of educating a child (see Table 12.1 on page 367), which is sufficient to pay about 90 percent of an average private school's tuition. The idea is to let parents completely bypass the public school system at government expense and place their children in the private school of their choice. The program is limited at present because there are not enough private-school spaces to meet demand; usually a lottery determines who goes to choice schools in such cases.

Proponents of a fully operational voucher plan argue that parental choice puts schools in competition with each other, forcing them either to improve to attract students or to cease to exist. Opponents fear that the measure would destroy the public schools by siphoning off much-needed public education funding to put students in private schools with no accountability for program quality. They also argue that such programs violate the First Amendment separation of church and state in the case of parents' using vouchers to pay for parochial school education.[52]

Vermont has used such a system for over one hundred years to avoid building schools in sparsely populated areas. In 1990, Milwaukee initiated the first city-funded voucher plan, enabling parents to send their children to one of eleven private schools instead of to inner-city public schools. Indianapolis contracted with a private foundation to provide vouchers for almost 1,000 schoolchildren to attend the school of their choice, private or religious.[53] In 1996, Cleveland began the nation's first state-funded voucher program to give low-income students a genuine choice of schools, including religious ones. The program appeared to be a success. One year later, test scores of participating students—drawn from a true cross section of the population, not just the best students—were meaningfully higher and the students' parents were overwhelmingly satisfied.[54] Once the 2002 U.S. Supreme Court ruling upheld the constitutionality of the Cleveland voucher program, demand increased for more such programs elsewhere.[55]

Americans remain divided on the issue of school vouchers, according to several polls in 2002, although some experts see a coalition forming among free-marketers, inner-city minorities, and Catholics. The 2002 annual Phi Delta Kappa/Gallup poll found 52 percent opposed to school vouchers, with 46 percent in favor, up from just 34 percent support in 2001.[56] A 2002 poll by the Joint Center for Political and Economic Studies identified 43 percent of Americans in favor of school vouchers and 50 percent opposed.[57] Far stronger support, 63 percent, was found in a poll by the Center for Education Reform.[58] An Associated Press poll found 51 percent in favor and 40 percent opposed. However, when poll responders were asked if they still support the idea if it takes money from public schools, opposition to vouchers rose to 60 percent with 31 percent supporting (a 2-to-1 margin).[59]

A growing number of states are now considering tax-funded school vouchers to allow poor—and not-so-poor—families an opportunity to send their children to private schools for little or no money. Colorado was the first to do so after the Supreme Court decision. Earlier, Minnesota increased its state tax deduction for public or private education and instituted a tax credit that can be used for a variety of educational purposes, including private tutoring, textbooks, and transportation (but not for private-school tuition). Arizona passed a tax credit for citizens who want to contribute to a private scholarship fund. Conservatives argue that putting students into private and parochial schools at taxpayers' expense would help poor youths and spur public school reform. Liberal organizations such as the Urban Institute and the Annie C. Casey Foundation also support school vouchers. This approach has emerged as a popular solution effort for the problem of poor-quality education in the nation's urban schools.[60]

Charter Schools

Charter schools are a recent alternative to traditional public schools and, in cities where a voucher plan exists, a major beneficiary of such payments. Charters are publicly funded and operate with less state regulation so that teachers and administrators can try out new teaching strategies. Unlike public schools, however, they are held accountable for achieving educational results. If a school fails to meet the terms of its charter with the local school board or state, the charter can be revoked and the school closed. In essence, then, a charter school receives greater autonomy to operate in return for greater accountability for student performance. Over 2,700 charter schools now exist in thirty states, the District of Columbia, and Puerto Rico.

Public charter schools are more likely than regular public schools to be located in urban areas, to enroll a higher proportion of Black and Hispanic students, and to employ teachers with fewer years of teaching experience.[61] Small school size appears to be a principal reason for the high demand for charter schools. The median enrollment of charter schools in 2000–2001 was 264, compared with a median enrollment of 477 students in the regular public schools in the same states.[62] Smaller classes afford teachers the space to be more creative with curriculum and the time to provide more individualized instruction. Some charter schools have been founded with a particular type of student in mind. Whether for the arts-oriented or the at-risk student, these schools provide assistance to those who are otherwise underserved by the public school system.

Supporters of charter systems hope that local educators, ministers, parents, community members, school boards, and other sponsors will provide new models of schooling and exert competitive pressures on public schools that will improve the current system of public education.

The charter school these students are attending has a waiting list. The charter school movement in the United States, as well as the homeschool movement, reflect widespread dissatisfaction with public school systems. What are some of the sources of this dissatisfaction, and how do charter schools address them? What are some drawbacks of charter schools? Why are charter schools considered by others to be a threat to democratic values?

Others fear, however, that charter schools, at best, may be little more than escape valves that relieve pressure for genuine reform of the whole system and, at worst, may add to centrifugal forces that threaten to pull public education apart.

In fact, some charter schools are no better than their pubic school counterparts. Critics say that many have weak curricula and teaching, substandard buildings, and a surprising prevalence of financial abuses. Basic classroom supplies are often lacking, labs and libraries are rare, and staff turnover is high among the low-paid, inexperienced teachers. Also, the segregation of many charter schools along ethnic, racial, and religious lines has created church-state conflicts in conjunction with the voucher controversy.[63]

School Violence

Despite research showing a significant drop in incidences of school violence and in-school weapon violations, students and educators feel less safe within their own schools and more worried about attacks. One of the causes for this heightened sense of fear is the high-profile cases of recent years. The tragic school shootings in New Orleans (one killed, three wounded) in 2003; Santee, California (two killed, thirteen wounded) in 2001; Littleton, Colorado (fifteen killed, twenty-three wounded) and Conyers, Georgia (six wounded) in 1999; Jonesboro, Arkansas (five killed, ten wounded), Springfield, Oregon (two killed, twenty-two wounded), and Edinboro, Pennsylvania (one killed, two wounded) in 1998; West Paducah, Kentucky (three killed, five wounded) and Pearl, Mississippi (two killed, seven wounded) in 1997 are grim reminders that, despite progress in reducing crime and violence within schools, this fear is not unfounded. In addition to those tragic killings, each year at schools over 128,000 students aged twelve to eighteen and over 14,000 teachers are victims of serious violent crimes (rape, sexual assault, robbery, and aggravated assault).[64]

Not surprisingly, students feel less safe at school now than they did a few years ago. In fact, one in ten students ages twelve to nineteen recently reported that they avoid one or more places at school in fear for their safety, a fear no doubt partly fueled by the growing presence of street gangs on school property. The percentage of students in 2001 who reported that street gangs were present at their schools was 29 percent in urban schools and 18 percent in suburban schools.[65]

Just a few years ago, serious violence in school settings (see Figure 12.3) almost exclusively occurred in central city schools. That is no longer the case, as demonstrated by the above-mentioned shootings. Although the number of school-associated violent deaths has dropped in recent years, the specter of a school shooting or stabbing haunts parents and educators. While multiple-homicide deaths have captured headlines in recent years, there still exists a less than one in a million chance of suffering a school-associated violent death. Students are three times more likely to be victims of nonfatal serious violent crimes away from school than at school. Still, the fear of parents, educators, and students are real, and both urban and suburban schools often confront violence on school grounds.

To combat school violence, educators have launched a variety of preventive programs. The most successful ones are not separate, all-inclusive strategies, but rather programs that readily integrate into other activities to effectively address local needs in reducing substance abuse, antisocial and violent behavior, and problem behavior in general. The program at Abington Senior

Figure 12.3 Percentage of Students ages Twelve to Eighteen Who Reported Criminal Victimization at School According to Type of Victimization, by their Perception of Conditions at School, 1999

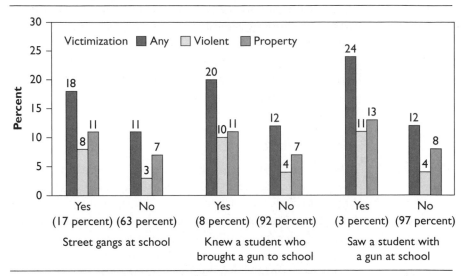

Source: U.S. Department of Education, *The Condition of Education 2003.*

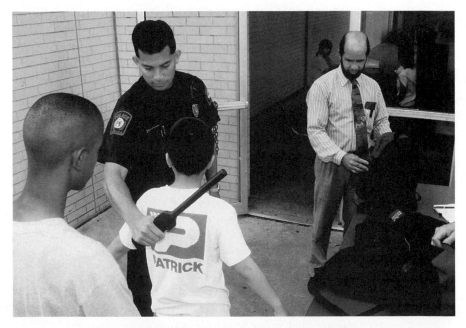

Violence is primarily an urban education problem, but some of the deadliest shootings in recent years were in suburban schools. The use of metal detectors at school entrances is now routine in some places, for learning cannot occur in an environment in which students do not feel safe. What other steps have been taken to ensure that they feel safe? What other steps do you think should be taken?

High School in Pennsylvania, for example, emphasizes early prevention. It includes programs that begin in the early elementary years, then continually builds on previous knowledge throughout all grade levels. Early programming builds a strong social skill foundation among students through a series of lessons on decision-making skills, resistance, and refusal skills. At higher-grade levels, these skills are infused with prevention education in multiple areas, including awareness of alcohol, tobacco, and violence issues. One key prevention component is the infusion of anti-drug and violence messages in the curriculum and instruction program in science, health, physical education, family, and consumer science courses. Coupled with effective discipline policies, Abington has seen its suspensions for fighting and substance abuse drop by more than half in four years.[66]

Sociological Perspectives

Throughout this chapter, various sociological considerations have intertwined with our discussion of educational concerns. Now we will focus more sharply on those sociological perspectives as they relate to the goals, practices, and problems of our educational system.

The Functionalist Viewpoint

All developed countries consider formal education critically important to the welfare of their societies. Schools have the dual responsibilities of transmitting the nation's culture from one generation to the next and of teaching young people the knowledge and skills necessary to function in a technologically advanced society. In the United States, we further expect the schools to help solve such social problems as alcohol and drug abuse, reckless driving, sexual promiscuity, prejudice, and poverty. Above all, the curriculum must be "relevant" and teaching methods must be adaptable to the varying abilities of the students. Functionalists maintain that educational problems are a consequence of system strain, because the schools simultaneously try to be too many things to too many people.

Even if schools simply taught traditional subjects and basic skills, they might not do those jobs well because the educational bureaucratic system is often disorganized and is subject to contradictory pressures from within the school and from the outside community. The probability of system dysfunction greatly increases, however, with the addition of other roles. One aspect of the social movement of the 1960s was a desire to make education relevant, leading to the introduction of a wide array of elective courses into the public schools. Often these courses reflected educators' personal preferences or courses in college they liked; previously exclusive college-level courses such as psychology, sociology, race and ethnic relations, and specialized humanities courses soon became common in many high schools.

Other competing courses in art and music—together with offerings in theater, computers, first aid, driver's education, personal health, shop, home economics, typing, stenography, accounting, and many other areas—made the traditional subjects less appealing to students. Excused class absences for athletic events, pep rallies, assemblies, play rehearsals, band competitions, field trips, and guidance sessions further intensified the clash of educational goals. All too often, the unintended consequences of these multipronged educational efforts were misdirected priorities, a deemphasis of mastering basic skills, and goals lacking any unified and coherent approach.

Through their schools, Americans seek to correct the inequities in society and fit individuals into various available adult slots. Sometimes this effort at **social engineering** interferes with the learning process—for example, in the case of the antagonisms generated by integration solutions. Curriculum changes intended to avoid discouraging weaker students may insufficiently challenge more able students. Placing students in academic tracks by ability grouping often creates latent dysfunctions of negative self-image and low expectation fulfillment among students in the lower tracks. When schools, in the interests of fairness and completeness, avoid school prayer but promote sex and health education, evolutionary theory, or provocative literature, they frequently come into conflict with other social institutions such as family and religion. The resulting value conflicts create difficult learning environments for parents, teachers, and students.

The Conflict Viewpoint

Conflict analysts reject the concept that public schools ever functioned as the great equalizer in U.S. society by providing opportunities for the poor to achieve upward mobility. To them, the schools reflect the inequities in society, favor the ruling class, and perpetuate both social and economic disparities. Class biases in the schools and socioeconomic differences among the school districts are their primary concerns.

Theoretically, schools sift and select students for higher educational attainment on the basis of each child's ability. In practice, an individual's educational success is linked closely to social class background, due in part to clashing values. Many studies confirm strong correlations between socioeconomic background and educational performance and level of attainment with low-income children, on average, receiving four years less schooling than higher-income children, even with similar IQ scores.[67]

Many factors having nothing to do with ability contribute to these differences in educational level. Poor children often have no choice but to drop out of school to help support their families. The tracking system "cools out" others, as do low expectations and motivation, and negative reinforcement. Because occupational opportunity and economic earnings rest heavily on educational attainment levels, schools tend to reinforce the social class ranking of the next generation in the same order as that of their parents.

Local school funding difficulties result in significant differences in the quality of school facilities, staff, and instruction. The poor primarily concentrate in poorly funded and poorly staffed schools, which continue to deteriorate in discipline and quality. From the Conflict perspective, the current system of economically segregated schools—with minorities disproportionately represented within the urban schools—operates to keep oppressed people in the lowest strata of society. The affluent and powerful make certain that they benefit from the educational system and resist efforts at change that would negatively affect the advantages they hold. Possessing the necessary resources for geographic mobility or for enrolling their children in private schools, the nonpoor can avoid any public school system they dislike. They also hold sufficient political clout to influence busing and redistricting decisions. Most Conflict theorists therefore believe that inequities in the educational system can be eliminated only by changes in society itself.

The Feminist Viewpoint

Early Feminist analysis showed how schools reinforced traditional sex role attitudes and behavior, thus perpetuating existing inequalities between the sexes. The educational system emphasized a sexual script that socially constructed women into gender-specific roles that narrowed their life choices. Furthermore, the early socialization of girls toward obedience and approval seeking predisposed them to accept more readily the school's demands of conformity to rules.

Feminist researchers showed how, at the elementary level, children's readers, social studies books, and even math textbooks were written within a social context that reinforced sex-role stereotypes. Other research revealed that teachers and guidance counselors in the secondary schools guided female students into curriculum choices leading to "feminine" occupations that tracked them into dull, dead-end careers. Feminists also conducted surveys of sex-role attitudes and classroom behavior of teachers that showed teachers differentiated ideal behavior by gender and acted out sex-role stereotypes in the classroom. Their research findings led Feminists to call for new educational environments designed to eliminate restrictive sex role training.[68]

Although they succeeded in removing sexist content from most children's books and school textbooks, more subtle manifestations of teacher sexism still remain. For example, Myra Sadker and David Sadker (1994) found that teachers' daily interactions with their students favored boys more by calling on them, allowing their interruptions, and giving them praise, criticism, or suggestions. The implied but unmistaken message was that boys were more important and warranted more time and attention.[69]

Today Feminist analysts continue to examine all facets of the educational setting for any lingering patriarchal manifestations of control or bias that could lead to gender inequalities within the school or in preparation for adulthood. Curriculum, textbooks, teacher-student interactions, student achievement and opportunities, teacher expectations and counseling, even female teacher working conditions and advancement opportunities, remain focal points of study.

The Interactionist Viewpoint

Education serves as an important part of the socialization process through which individuals develop their personalities and learn their culture. Through the formal structure of the schools and the informal structure of peer relationships, each student experiences many years of continuous interactions that help shape a concept of self. The impact of education on an individual extends far beyond the subject matter taught in the classrooms. For example, if you construct two lists of the first ten memories you recall from elementary school and from high school, your two lists will likely contain mostly emotion-charged events in your life that affected your self-esteem (being hurt, embarrassed, ridiculed, rejected, loved, honored, etc.). Shared interpretations of day-by-day interactions determine whether school is perceived as a positive or negative experience, and they also affect students' motivation and academic achievement.

Exposure to an ongoing system of rational discipline and work tasks helps many students develop goal orientations, a sense of responsibility, initiative, perseverance, and a work ethic. Immersed in a microcosmic world of rules and regulations with competing students, they become prepared to function more effectively in the outside world. Students learn how to develop social relationships, work together, and face challenges in a positive way. Some social psychologists therefore believe that most traditional schools are quite beneficial in helping children learn, develop, and function. Although no school can ever be perfect, these experts view the schools as capable of providing opportunities for personal growth and fulfillment.

Other behavioral scientists are less optimistic. Too many schools are authoritarian and demand unquestioning conformity to rules, procedures, and teachers' expectations. Such a repressive atmosphere, they say, stifles creativity and encourages passive compliance with authority in later life—a dangerous tendency in any democracy. Moreover, the schools' competitive structure and their use of the fear of failure as a motivation encourage feelings of anxiety, insecurity, and inadequacy among many students. Poor performance—or even expected poor performance, together with the tracking system—sets in motion a series of interpretations and reinterpretations that works against individuals and instills in them a negative self-image. Once labeled by themselves, their peers, and/or their teachers as below average, that definition becomes reinforced through subsequent interactions. From this perspective, the daily interactions and interpretations that arise in school can actually impede the ability of children to learn, to develop positive personality characteristics, and eventually to function effectively as adults in society.

Thinking About the Future

In the next several decades, education will become even more important to success in life, and further advances in technology may dramatically change the way we educate young people. Perhaps more formal learning will occur outside the classroom than inside, something we already see at the college level, with the growing number of on-line courses. Are we moving toward a "virtual university" where on-campus classes become the exception instead of the norm? Will this form of instruction soon trickle down, with Internet classes and distance learning replacing classrooms at the high school level? What happens to the development of social skills, relationships, and appreciation for diversity if we spend less time together in educational settings both within and outside the classroom?

Computers won't completely eliminate classrooms, though, especially at the elementary level. Teachers use a variety of teaching techniques to motivate and educate these youngsters. One of the best techniques is cooperative learning, where students are placed in small interdependent groups to learn from one another, rather than competing against each other for teacher recognition. But what of teacher bias and expectations, of the value of ability grouping and its harmful effects? How do we address these issues?

School dropout rates are decreasing, but remain much too high among minority students. What more can we do in this area? What about those adults not in school? How do we reach them? How do we reduce the high adult illiteracy rate? How do we motivate adults to become more literate? Do you recommend some type of aggressive literacy campaign or special programs?

School funding is still uneven and negatively affects the quality of education in our poorer districts and states. What solution do you propose to change this? Are school vouchers an answer by giving parents a choice of schools, or does such a plan further undermine our urban schools by taking away even more funding? Even in many nonpoor districts, students' academic knowledge is far less than in many other countries. What social policy initiatives would you recommend regarding curriculum, standards, and teacher competency to enable the United States to catch up to other nations? Like other countries, should we lengthen the school year to ten to eleven months? Should there be more required homework study? If you don't agree, what alternative solutions do you recommend?

What do we do about school violence? Is this a problem to be contained within the schools only, or should we look closely at music lyrics and videos, films, and television programming that glorify violence? What of the school's community? After all, is not school a part of a community, rather than an isolated entity breeding its own violence? What kind of preventive action program do you think is best to create a safe learning environment?

Ideally, an effective school achieves a balance between discipline and self-expression, treating students as mature, responsible persons in a cooperative, orderly, positive, and democratic atmosphere. You are a product of the elementary and secondary school systems. From your own experience as a student, what would you change and what would you keep in school practices to give all students equal educational opportunities and maximize individual development?

SUMMARY

1. Americans have long believed in education as the means to economic success and as the cure for society's problems. Deeply ingrained in the U.S. way of life is advocacy for universal educational opportunity and insistence on local community control. The problems of education intertwine with the problems of poverty, race and ethnic relations, and urban and rural economies.

2. Unlike the United States, most other industrialized nations have a meritocratic approach to education. A longer school calendar, more rigorous curriculum, and greater time spent on homework seem to explain why foreign students usually surpass U.S. students' performance on various achievement tests.

3. As a bureaucracy, the school system allows little flexibility through its hierarchy of authority. Curiosity, creativity, and individualism decline due to the institutional insistence on uniformity, obedience, and conformity to a structured approach.

4. Middle-class values dominate the schools, often at the expense of low-income students. Ability grouping and teacher expectations affect students' self-esteem, motivation, and achievement. Since a disproportionate number of low-income students are placed in the lowest track, schools tend to reinforce the social class structure rather than serving as the great equalizer.

5. Urban minorities (especially Hispanics) and rural poor have higher-than-average dropout rates; and dropping out seriously reduces a person's probable earning capacity. Nearly one-half of the nation's adult population was deemed functionally illiterate in a study conducted in 1993.

6. Local property taxes, supplemented by state funds, are the primary means of financing education. States and communities vary greatly in their ability to generate revenues.

Consequently, the quality of education an individual receives depends directly on the wealth of his or her parents and neighbors.

7. Following a national commission's blistering attack in 1983, U.S. education made some progress in improving teacher competency, academic standards, and student competency in verbal and math skills. Efforts continue to improve teaching and to reduce teachers' exodus by offering better pay and working conditions.

8. Educational reform efforts include attempts to create more equitable school districts through redistricting, magnet schools, charter schools, and voucher plans. Although schools are safer in recent years, serious problems of school violence remain, prompting educators to implement preventive programs.

9. Functionalists see educational problems as a result of system strain, resulting from excessive demands placed on the schools. Conflict analysts see the inequities of social class and school funding as major causes of poor academic achievement. Feminists examine various manifestations of gender inequality in the schools' programs and teacher interaction as problems to be addressed. Interactionists emphasize the positive and negative daily interactions in school settings as either stimulating or undermining the learning environment.

KEY TERMS

Ability grouping	Minimum competency test (MCT)
Charter schools	Redistricting
Grade inflation	School voucher
IQ tests	Social engineering
Literacy	Social promotions
Magnet schools	Teacher expectations

INTERNET RESOURCES

At this book's Web site with Allyn & Bacon, you will find numerous links pertaining to problems in education. To explore these resources, go first to the author's page (**http://www.ablongman. com/parrillo**). Next, select this edition of *Contemporary Social Problems* and then choose **Internet Readings and Exercises.** Then select **Chapter 12,** where you will find both a variety of sites to investigate and some questions that pertain to those sites.

SUGGESTED READINGS

Altenbaugh, Richard J., ed. *The Teacher's Voice: A Social History of Teaching in Twentieth-Century America.* Washington, D.C.: Palmer Press, 1992. A direct look at the classroom behavior of teachers and the resulting learning environment.

Cookson, Peter W. *Social Choice: The Struggle for the Soul of American Education.* New Haven, Conn.: Yale University Press, 1994. A comparative analysis of school choice plans and their potential effects on students, teachers, school systems, and communities.

Finn, Chester, E., Jr., Gregg Vanourek, and Bruno V. Manno. *Charter Schools in Action.* Princeton, N.J.: Princeton University Press, 2001. Excellent profile of charter schools, providing information about what they have done well and where they need to improve.

Hill, Paul T., and Mary Beth Celio. *Fixing Urban Schools.* Washington, D.C.: Brookings Institute, 1998. Identifies the essential elements of reform strategies that can transform school performance in big cities beset by poverty, social instability, and racial isolation.

Kozol, Jonathan. *Savage Inequalities: Children in America's Schools,* reprinted. New York: Perennial, 1992. A highly respected education analyst delineates the disparities in the quality of schools as determined by the economic strength of the sending district.

Oakes, Jeannie. *Keeping Track: How Schools Structure Inequality.* New Haven, Conn.: Yale University Press, 1986. How the attempt to provide homogeneous learning groups detrimentally affects self-image, achievement, and future success.

Ravitch, Diane. *Left Back: A Century of Failed School Reforms.* New York: Simon & Schuster, 2001. A detailed, informative account of the negative effects of progressive educational reforms over the past one hundred years by reducing the schools' ability to educate children.

Ravitch, Diane and Joseph Viteritti (eds.). *New Schools for a New Century: The Redesign of Urban Education.* New Haven, Conn.: Yale University Press, 1999. A fine collection of ten essays that examine educational reform, particularly urban public schools, from numerous perspectives.

Wheelock, Anne. *Crossing the Tracks: How Untracking Can Save America's Schools.* New York: New Press, 1993. An analytical commentary on ability-grouped classes and an argument for replacing them with more effective teaching techniques.

Wood, George H. *Schools That Work: America's Most Innovative Public Education Programs.* New York: Dutton, 1993. A hopeful book that describes a variety of innovative programs in U.S. public schools that enjoy a high success rate.

13

Alcohol and Drug Abuse

Facts About Alcohol and Drugs

- More than half of all Americans have experienced alcoholism in their families.

- Alcohol-related accidents are the leading cause of death among Americans aged fifteen to twenty-four.

- About 70 percent of eighth graders say it is easy for them to get alcohol.

- Cocaine is the most addictive drug, and cocaine addiction is the fastest-growing drug problem.

- Heroin and marijuana use is increasing, in part due to encouragement from the media and from musical groups.

- A lifelong smoker is as likely to die as a direct result of tobacco use as from all other potential causes of death combined.

- About three in every ten Americans will be involved in an alcohol-related crash at some time in their lives.

Alcohol and drug abuse is more than a personal problem that dramatically affects individuals' lives. It is a major social problem that affects society as a whole. Accidents, antisocial behavior, broken relationships, family instability, crime and violence, poverty, unsafe streets and highways, and worker absenteeism and nonproductivity often have drug-related causes.

Though most Americans agree that we have a drug problem in our society, attitudes about the nature of the problem vary. Is drug abuse a medical problem or a criminal problem? Tobacco causes more deaths than any other drug, but persons eighteen and older can legally consume it, whereas marijuana possession and use are illegal. Alcohol is another legal drug that Americans widely abuse, with dire consequences.

From a scientific and sociolegal perspective, a drug is any substance that chemically alters the functioning of the brain or nervous system. A **psychoactive drug** is a chemical substance that affects consciousness, mood, or perception. As just mentioned, society views some—but not all—psychoactive drugs as problematic; and the distinction between acceptable and unacceptable drugs clearly is not based on their injuriousness to users' health. For example, despite the scientific proof of its harmful qualities and habit-forming nature, society does not classify alcohol as a harmful drug. Similarly, only in recent years did the government take steps against tobacco advertising and sales to lessen the product's appeal and accessibility.

Why is U.S. society willing to spend billions of dollars to eliminate certain addictive drugs but not others? Is our "war on drugs" a mistake? Psychiatrist Thomas Szasz (1996) argues that our current approach does far more harm than good, contributing to a deterioration of everyone's lifestyle, user and nonuser alike.[1] In this section we will explore that notion and examine the societal realities surrounding all commonly used drugs, regardless of their social definition (see the accompanying box).

Alcohol

Taken in moderation (a maximum of two drinks daily for men and one drink for women), alcohol is rather harmless and may even be beneficial in relieving stress. As a mild sedative at the end of a workday or as a moderate social activity, drinking alcoholic beverages is both fashionable and fairly safe. The problem, of course, is excessive drinking. Currently, about 14 million Americans—one in every thirteen adults—abuse alcohol or are alcoholic.[2]

More than half of all adults have a family history of alcoholism or problem drinking. An estimated 9 million children under the age of eighteen years live in households with at least one alcoholic.[3]

Alcohol abuse creates staggering social problems: traffic accidents and fatalities, broken marriages, disorderly behavior, crime, ruined careers, poverty, and physical debilitation. Virtually all social scientists and medical experts agree that alcohol abuse is a serious drug problem in our society today. Each year alcohol claims about 100,000 lives, almost eight times the number of deaths resulting from all other drug-induced causes (excluding nicotine addiction) combined.[4]

Dangers

Alcohol is a **depressant** that acts on the central nervous system. Its effects vary with the amount consumed, its speed of consumption, and the tolerance level of each individual. It can reduce tension, loosen inhibitions, and therefore make the user feel relaxed and happy. It can also impair memory, judgment, coordination, stimulus response time, and motor skills (speech, walking, and hand and arm movements). Excessive drinking may produce a stupor, deep sleep, coma, or death (see Table 13.1).

Social Constructions of Social Problems

Changing Definitions and Societal Responses

Although most Americans express concern about substance abuse and its societal ramifications, that concern is not a united one. Some people see real dangers in drinking alcohol, ingesting cocaine, or smoking marijuana, for example, but others do not. Such conflicting definitions about what is or is not a problem go beyond individuals' values and practices. They also reflect a sociohistorical reality that no commonly shared "absolute truth" exists in society about drug use because cultural attitudes may change from one generation to another, or even within the same generation.

Throughout history, public attitudes toward a particular drug may change. For example, coffee, containing the drug stimulant caffeine, was under attack in seventeenth-century England. In 1674, a pamphlet called "The Women's Petition Against Coffee" claimed that men were becoming less sexually active because they were forsaking "good old" ale to drink "base, black, thick, nasty, bitter, stinking, nauseous" coffee. Yet by the eighteenth century, English coffee houses were a respectable social institution. A century ago people viewed smoking in mixed company as more offensive than drinking either ale or coffee. In contrast, for much of the twentieth century, cigarette smoking in public was an accepted and indeed commonplace practice, until public awareness of its health hazards prompted a shift in public attitude hostile to cigarette advertising and smoking in public areas.

In the mid-nineteenth century, the (anti-alcohol) temperance movement in Europe and America led to the adoption of opiates such as laudanum and morphine as alcohol substitutes in medicine. Many opium elixirs were available in stores and by mail order, including Brown's Teething Cordial for fretful babies. As these remedies proved highly addictive, cocaine became the preferred substitute: physicians valued its energy-producing, mood-elevating, alertness-improving abilities. By 1885, cocaine was a key ingredient in cigarettes,

inhalants (as the official remedy of the American Hay Fever Association), elixirs, ointments, soda drinks, sprays, syrups, teas, and wine. In the late 1800s, Bayer Pharmaceutical Company introduced heroin as a "sedative for coughs," supposedly naming the drug *heroin* to connote its heroic medicinal effects. Then, in 1914, when the dangers of cocaine and heroin became apparent, Congress passed the Harrison Narcotics Act. Soon thereafter, the street price of heroin, now an illegal drug, rose from $6.50 to $100 an ounce. Meanwhile, alcohol continued as the legal mood-altering drug of choice, until most states banned it (thirty-four did so between 1907 and 1919); finally, the Eighteenth Amendment (ratified in 1919) prohibited the manufacture, sale, or transportation of alcohol nationwide.

In summary, cultural values and group norms determine what forms of drug use are socially acceptable and what forms constitute a social problem. Definitions of drug use and abuse change through historical periods and may vary from one setting to another. Moreover, legal definitions may be at odds with public mores, as during Prohibition; and, legal and public definitions may be inconsistent within a society, as exemplified by recent state differences in the minimum drinking age and the decriminalization of marijuana use in some localities.

Another part of the difficulty in dealing with the problem of alcohol and drug abuse lies in societal responses, as influenced by those definitions. If society classifies drug use, say tobacco, as harmful but legal, then the police won't stop/arrest smokers. But if we characterize marijuana as harmful *and* illegal, then they will. What's important about that last point is that we *labeled* marijuana use as *criminal,* thereby socially constructing that framework for the problem and our response. Similarly, if we identify heroin use as a medical and not a criminal problem, then our attitudes and societal responses are different. Social constructions thus are key to problem solving.

Table 13.1 Effects of Alcohol

Amount of Distilled Spirits Consumed in 2 Hours (fl. oz.)	Percentage of Alcohol in Blood	Typical Effects
3	0.05%	Loosening of judgment, thought, and restraint, release of tension; carefree sensation
4.5	0.08%	Tensions and inhibitions of everyday life lessened.
6	0.10%	Voluntary motor action affected; hand and arm movements, walking, and speech clumsy
10	0.20%	Severe motor impairment; staggering, loud, incoherent speech; emotional instability (extreme drunkenness); 100 times greater traffic risk
14	0.30%	Deeper areas of brain affected; parts affecting stimulus response and understanding confused, stuporous
18	0.40%	Deep sleep; inability to take voluntary action (equivalent of surgical anesthesia)
22	0.50%	Coma; anesthesia of centers controlling breathing and heartbeat; death

Source: Adapted from information furnished by the National Clearinghouse for Alcohol Information.

Drinkers can become psychologically dependent on alcohol, needing it to feel at ease among people or to cope with a difficult situation. They may further become physically dependent, unable to abstain without experiencing severe withdrawal symptoms (rapid heartbeat, sweating, nausea, and tremors). Alcohol withdrawal also involves a greater probability of being fatal than narcotics withdrawal. Also potentially deadly is the combination of alcohol and other drugs, particularly barbiturates.

Alcohol can irreversibly damage the liver (cirrhosis of the liver is the fourth major cause of death among people aged twenty-five to fifty), brain cells, and other body tissue. Drinkers also run a significantly higher risk than nondrinkers of contracting cancer of the mouth or throat, and a fifteen times greater risk if they both smoke and drink. Alcoholics usually suffer from malnutrition, are more susceptible to heart disease, and are six times more likely to commit suicide.

Youth and Alcohol Consumption

Over 10 million Americans under the age of twenty-one had at least one drink last month. Of these, nearly 6.8 million were "binge" drinkers (consuming five or more drinks in a row on a single occasion), including 2.1 million heavy drinkers (consuming five or more drinks in a row on the same occasion at least five different days).[5] Although purchase and public possession of alcohol by people under the age of twenty-one is illegal in all fifty states, 95 percent of twelfth graders, 85 percent of tenth graders, and nearly 70 percent of eighth graders in a national survey in 2002 said it was "fairly easy" or "very easy" to get alcohol.[6]

Teenage Drinking

Boys usually begin using alcohol at around age eleven and girls at thirteen . By the time they are high school seniors, 81 percent of teens have used alcohol. Moreover, approximately 12 percent of the nation's eighth graders, 22 percent of tenth graders, and 39 percent of twelfth graders reported their heavy drinking (five drinks in a row) within the past two weeks. Junior/middle and senior high school students drink 35 percent of all wine coolers sold in the United States; they also consume 1.1 billion cans of beer a year. Despite such consumption, teenage knowledge of alcohol is limited; for example, 80 percent of the teenagers interviewed in a national survey did not know that a can of beer has the same amount of alcohol as a shot of whiskey or a glass of wine. Another study found that, among teenagers who binge-drink, 39 percent say they drink alone; 58 percent drink when they are upset; 30 percent drink when they are bored; and 37 percent drink to feel high.[7]

Another study revealed the impact of advertising on underage drinking. An astonishing 56 percent of students in grades five to twelve said that alcohol advertising encourages them to drink.[8] A second influence is peer pressure. In a study conducted by *The Weekly Reader,* 30 percent of children in grades four through six said that their classmates pressured them "a lot" to drink beer.[9] Clearly, alcohol consumption and alcohol abuse are more widespread among young people than many adults realize; and in view of the many negative consequences, such drinking patterns are cause for alarm.

College Drinking

For most students, drinking alcohol is part of college life. Studies show that, even though about 80 percent of students are under the legal drinking age, an average of four out of five drink each month. Columbia University's Center on Addiction and Substance Abuse reported that students in the Northeast drink the most—about twice as much as students in the western United States. Over 40 percent had had recent binges compared to about 33 percent of young adults their age outside college.[10] Among college students in one survey, rates of binge drinking were highest among Caucasians (43.3 percent for males and 24.4 percent for females); among African Americans the rates were 24.8 percent for males and 5.4 percent for females; and among Asians, 32 percent for males and 20 percent for females.[11]

Nationwide, drinking among college students decreases proportionally with credits earned: freshmen drink the most, and seniors the least. Also, a direct correlation exists between weekly alcohol consumption and grade point average: the more a student drinks, the lower his or her GPA.[12]

Research shows that male college students are far more likely than female college students to engage in offensive behavior after drinking—to get into a fight, have an automobile accident, or damage property. A gender convergence occurs for other negative consequences, with little difference between the sexes. Males and females have very similar records of academic problems, memory loss, unintended sex, harmed relationships, and injury to self.[13]

Gender and Alcohol Consumption

Males are more likely than females (34 percent to 23 percent in 2002) to be heavy drinkers, a differential that is steadily shrinking.[14] Moreover, research suggests that women—because of their different metabolism rate—may be at higher risk for developing alcohol-related problems

Statistics show that binge drinking among college-age and younger Americans is a growing problem. What are the social contexts of binge drinking? At what point does alcohol consumption become a social problem? What are some social consequences of alcohol abuse and other substance abuse such as smoking?

at lower levels of consumption than men.[15] Nearly 4 million U.S. women aged eighteen and older can be classified as alcoholics or problem drinkers, one-third the number of men. Of these women, 58 percent are between the ages of eighteen and twenty-nine.[16] Women make up about 30 percent of all individuals in treatment for alcoholism.[17] They constitute 35 percent of the Alcoholics Anonymous (AA) members, and 43 percent of AA members aged thirty and under.[18] A recent study linking victimization to alcohol problems found that almost 90 percent of alcoholic women were physically or sexually abused as children.[19]

Their pains are not confined to childhood, though; adult women experience a variety of alcohol-related problems. A national survey of women's drinking found sexual dysfunction to be the most consistent predictor of chronic problem drinking.[20] Moreover, three of every five college women with sexually transmitted diseases report having been drunk when infected; one in five students abandons safe-sex practices after drinking, running the risk of pregnancy or disease; and 95 percent of violent campus crime—as well as 90 percent of campus rapes—involve alcohol.[21] Among college women, a strong link exists between dieting and eating disorders and problem drinking.[22]

Excessive drinking exacts a heavy toll on family life. Of the estimated 19 million adult problem drinkers, about 8 million are alcoholics, almost half of them women. One out of every ten Americans, about 28 million people, is the child of an alcoholic, and 7 million of these children are under age 18 and live at home with an alcoholic parent. The combination of genetic and environmental factors makes sons of alcoholic fathers four times more likely to become alcoholics than sons of nonalcoholics. Daughters of alcoholic mothers are three times more likely to have the problem.[23] Finally, alcohol is present in more than one-half of all incidents of domestic violence, with women more likely to be battered when both partners have been drinking.[24]

Cocaine and Crack

Cocaine is a powerfully addictive drug. Its abusers range across all socioeconomic groups, and its use may vary from episodic or occasional use to repeated or compulsive use, with many different patterns between these extremes. Most clinicians estimate that approximately 10 percent of people who begin by using the drug "recreationally" go on to serious, heavy use. Once having tried cocaine, an individual cannot predict or control the extent to which he or she will continue to use the drug.[25]

The main ways of ingesting cocaine are sniffing or snorting, injecting, and smoking (including free-base and crack cocaine). "Crack" is the street name for cocaine that has been processed from cocaine hydrochloride with sodium bicarbonate (baking soda) or ammonia and water and then heated to remove the hydrochloride; the resulting form of cocaine is smokable. The term "crack" refers to the crackling sound a user hears when smoking the mixture; presumably this effect is due to heating of the sodium bicarbonate.

Use

The 2002 National Household Survey on Drug Abuse (NHSDA) identified the total number of current cocaine users of all ages in the United States at nearly 1.7 million, significantly higher than the 1.2 million in 2000, but still far below the 1985 peak of 5.7 million cocaine users (3 percent of the population).[26]

Current trends give mixed signals. The proportion of high school seniors who have used cocaine at least once in their lifetimes was 7.8 percent in 2002, down from 9.8 percent in 1999, and far below the peak of 17.3 percent in 1985. However, in 2002, 7.8 percent of tenth-graders had tried cocaine at least once, up from a low of 3.3 percent in 1992. The percentage of eighth-graders who had tried cocaine increased from a low of 2.3 percent in 1991 to 3.6 percent in 2002.[27] Overall, Hispanic and White high school students, both male and female, were at least four times more likely than Black students to report either current or lifetime cocaine use.[28]

The age group with the highest rate of current cocaine use is adults twenty-six or older (see Table 13.2). In this age range, African Americans are about twice as likely to be current users of cocaine than Whites and Hispanics. Except in New York and Miami where there has been a decrease, most other metropolitan areas (Baltimore, Boston, Chicago, Dallas, Denver, Los Angeles, Minneapolis-St. Paul, Philadelphia, Phoenix, San Francisco, and Washington, D.C.) reported an increase or stabilization in cocaine/crack indicators in the late 1990s. Overall, men have a higher rate of current cocaine use than do women.[29]

Table 13.2   Drug Use by Type of Drug and by Age Group, 2001

Type of Drug	Percentage of Youths (12–17 Years Old)		Percentage of Young Adults (18–25 Years Old)		Percentage of Adults (26 Years and Older)	
	Ever Used	**Current User**	**Ever Used**	**Current User**	**Ever Used**	**Current User**
Marijuana and Hashish	19.7%	8.0%	50.0%	16.0%	41.2%	4.5%
Inhalants	8.6%	1.0%	13.4%	0.6%	7.1%	0.1%
Hallucinogens	5.7%	1.2%	22.1%	2.7%	11.9%	0.1%
Cocaine	2.3%	0.4%	13.0%	1.9%	13.6%	0.6%
Heroin	0.3%	0.0%	1.6%	0.2%	1.5%	0.0%
Pain Relievers	9.4%	2.6%	18.2%	3.6%	8.4%	1.1%
Stimulants*	3.7%	0.7%	9.5%	1.3%	7.1%	0.3%
Sedatives*	0.7%	0.1%	1.9%	0.2%	3.9%	0.1%
Tranquilizers*	2.6%	0.5%	8.9%	1.3%	6.2%	0.5%
Alcohol	42.9%	17.3%	85.0%	58.8%	86.5%	50.8%
Cigarettes	33.6%	13.0%	69.0%	39.1%	71.5%	24.2%

*Nonmedical use, does not include over-the-counter drugs.

Source: U.S. Department of Health and Human Services, *2001 National Household Survey on Drug Abuse* (Washington, D.C.: U.S. Government Printing Office, 2002).

Cocaine and Public Policy

The U.S. experience with cocaine serves as an excellent example of manifest and latent functions, as discussed in Chapter 1. Here we can see well-intentioned actions, with praiseworthy goals, nonetheless creating unexpected and serious social problems.

Opening the Door for Cocaine Use

After passage of the Harrison Narcotics Act in 1914, cocaine use declined significantly, limited primarily to jazz musicians and others living on the margins of society.[30] Beginning in the late 1960s, though, two federal policy decisions prompted a return of cocaine from the underground to mainstream society.[31] First, Congress passed legislation reducing the legal production of amphetamine-type drugs and placing strict controls on Quaaludes and other abused sedatives. This get-tough policy did not lessen the demand for psychoactive drugs, but it did prompt a switch to cocaine as the "new" drug of choice. Second, the World Bank funded construction of the Pan American Highway, linking the remote coca-producing regions of South America with major cities and thus facilitating the flow of mass quantities of refined coca paste concentrate, which was eventually "cut" into street cocaine. The combination of these two factors ushered in the cocaine era.

Sentencing Disparities

In the 1980s, crack—much cheaper than powder cocaine and capable of producing a more intense "high"—became the street drug of choice. As its popularity increased, so did warfare among dealers, which led to soaring murder rates and street violence. Alarmed at the damage the drug was doing, and convinced that crack cocaine was more dangerous than powder cocaine, lawmakers in Washington racheted up the penalty first for selling crack and, in a subsequent bill, for possessing it. The laws set a one hundred-to-one equivalence between powder cocaine and crack in establishing mandatory minimum sentences. Selling as little as five grams of crack—barely a teaspoon—became punishable by a minimum of five years in prison, whereas selling an amount of cocaine powder (the more expensive kind preferred by most Whites) one hundred times greater was necessary to trigger a comparable sentence. At the time of their passage, the harsher penalty bills for crack were not debated in racial terms; and indeed, many members of the Congressional Black Caucus voted for them.[32]

By 1990, however, it became obvious that the anticrack laws were having a disproportionate effect on African Americans. In 1995, a news magazine reported that an astounding 80 percent of the individuals convicted of crack offenses in federal court under the new laws were Black, compared with 30 percent convicted of powdered-cocaine charges.[33] By 1997, the violence long associated with the crack trade had leveled off, and criticism by activists who claimed the laws were racist prodded government officials to seek a smaller gap in the sentences. Still insisting on more severe penalties for crack because of its continued association with greater violence, particularly among street-level dealers, the U.S. Sentencing Commission in 1995 proposed raising the 5-gram crack threshold to a level somewhere between 25 and 75 grams, while lowering the powder cocaine threshold from 500 grams to somewhere between 125 and 375 grams. Congress discarded the Commission's request and President Clinton signed the rejection into law. Thus, the crack/powder cocaine disparity remains.

Club Drugs

MDMA (ecstasy), Rohypnol, GHB, and ketamine are among the synthetic drugs that teens and young adults use, often at a nightclub, bar, rave, or trance scene. Raves and trance events are typically night-long dances, often held in warehouses. Many who attend do not use drugs, but those who do may be attracted to the generally low cost, seemingly increased stamina, and intoxicating highs that are said to deepen the rave or trance.[34]

Ecstasy is the most commonly used of the club drugs. Although it only recently reared its ugly head in the media, it is not a new drug. Its origin dates back to the early 1900s when the pharmaceutical company Merck developed and patented it, even though it was not put to any use at the time. In essence, the drug remained dormant until the 1970s when some psychotherapists began to use it, claiming that it enhanced communication in patient sessions. In the mid 1980s, MDMA emerged as the "party" or "club" drug for which it is now known.[35]

Dangers

MDMA is not a harmless, "fun" drug. It is neurotoxic, meaning it literally damages brain cells. It can produce increases in heart rate, blood pressure, and body temperature. This becomes dangerous because its stimulant properties enable users to dance for extended periods, and their dehydration can lead to muscle breakdown and kidney and cardiovascular system failure. The reality of the dangers are demonstrated in the notable increase in hospital emergency cases related to ecstasy, a total of 5,542 in 2001, compared to just 253 in 1994.[36]

The harm of this drug goes alarmingly further. Brain-imagining research has determined that MDMA causes long-term injury to those parts of the brain critical to thought and memory. One study, in primates, showed that exposure to MDMA for four days caused brain damage still evident six to seven years later. In addition to the brain imaging that illustrates impaired brain tissue from MDMA, studies using standardized tests of mental abilities have consistently shown an association between repeated MDMA exposure and significant impairments in visual and verbal memory. Furthermore, MDMA-related deaths are increasing each year.[37]

Use

MDMA use is increasing throughout the country, moving beyond the raves and into other social settings, such as college campuses, small parties, and on the street. In 2001, over 8.1 million Americans said they had tried ecstasy at some time, with 786,000 saying they had done so that

Raves are often the locale for the use of club drugs, particularly ecstasy, to seemingly increase stamina and create a high. Exceedingly dangerous in causing serious dehydration and long-term brain injury, the drug has become less popular in recent years. Why would hundreds of thousands of young people still use such a dangerous drug though? How can we further reduce its use?

year. The *2002 Monitoring the Future Study* revealed a decline from 2001 in use of this drug among students, going from 3.5 percent to 2.9 percent among eighth graders, from 6.2 percent to 4.9 percent among tenth graders, and from 9.2 percent to 7.4 percent among twelfth graders. Since the perceived availability of MDMA rose about a percentage point among all three grade levels, the lower usage rates may reflect increased awareness of the drug's harmful effects.[38]

Marijuana

The dried leaves of the hemp plant *Cannabis sativa* is marijuana; the plant's dried resin is hashish, which is six times more powerful than marijuana. Marijuana is the most widely misunderstood drug, despite extensive study by researchers and national commissions in Canada, Great Britain, and the United States. In 1972 Canada eliminated marijuana use from its list of criminal narcotics offenses and shortly thereafter reduced penalties for marijuana possession. In the same year the U.S. National Commission on Marijuana and Drug Use recommended similar action. Eleven states now have adopted mild penalties, but possessing marijuana in other states remains a criminal offense that carries potentially stiff jail sentences.

About two in of three all Americans over eighteen think the drug should remain illegal; but since 1991, the percentage of those who believe smoking marijuana is very harmful has dropped by about 10 percent.[39] Influencing this attitude change are humorous skits on such TV shows as *Saturday Night Live* and the lyrics and stage props of musical groups like Black Crowes, Cypress Hill, Faith No More, Nirvana, Guns 'N Roses, Metallica, Soundgarden, Spin Doctors, and rapper Dr. Dre. Pot fashioned in the form of clothing, jewelry, and even tattoos has blossomed into a multimillion-dollar business.

Dangers

Although users argue that marijuana use is natural, nonaddictive, and not associated with violence or domestic abuse as is alcohol and crack, the substance carries a few undisputed health risks. It contains much higher levels of carcinogenic tars and benzopyrenes than tobacco; and the level of THC, the drug's main psychoactive ingredient, is far higher today than in past years. Claims of genetic damage and reduced fertility are not supported by research, according to the National Institute on Drug Abuse (NIDA). However, the drug does impair motor coordination, thereby increasing the risk of automobile accidents.[40]

The "amotivational syndrome"—a lack of concentration on life-goal motivation among heavy marijuana users—does exist, but other variables such as personality and family environment may be causative factors as well. Among long-term users marijuana can be addictive, and it has withdrawal symptoms. Even more than tobacco, it can promote cancer of the lungs and other parts of the respiratory tract. Despite charges spanning several decades that marijuana serves as a **gateway drug** to use of other, more dangerous drugs, no such causal relationship has ever been established. Peer pressure is the greatest cause of multidrug use; and so far as marijuana is concerned, the two most likely additional drugs are alcohol and tobacco.[41]

Use

Marijuana remains the most commonly used illicit drug in the United States. According to the 2001 National Household Survey on Drug Abuse, more than 83 million Americans (37 percent) had tried marijuana at least once in their lifetimes, and 21.1 million (9 percent) had used marijuana within the past year.

Marijuana use among youth increased significantly in the 1990s, then leveled off. The NIDA's Monitoring the Future Study reported that the number of students who had smoked marijuana in 2002 was 15 percent among eighth graders, 30 percent among tenth graders, and 36 percent among twelfth graders. For eighth and tenth graders, these proportions are twice those in 1992 and two-thirds higher for seniors.

With increased use have come increased arrests. In 2001, the number of marijuana-related arrests in the United States (by state and local police) was 723,627, a one percent drop from the record set in 2000. Of these arrests, 88 percent were for possession—not for sale or manufacture. The Marijuana Policy Project reports that there are about 12,700 federal prisoners, 29,800 prisoners in state prisons, and 10,000 in local jails for marijuana offenses.[42]

Narcotics

Narcotics are opiates, either natural (codeine, morphine, and opium) or synthetic (heroin, meperidine [Demerol], and methadone). All have pain-killing properties and are very important to modern medicine. Before they realized the drugs' highly addictive qualities, physicians once indiscriminately prescribed morphine and later heroin, unintentionally creating patient **addiction**. Now doctors do not use heroin and only give extended prescriptions of morphine as a pain killer for terminally ill cancer patients. Methadone, a common treatment for heroin addicts, is itself addictive and has become a street drug as well. Codeine is normally found in prescription-only cough medicines, while morphine, heroin, and meperidine play important roles in medicine and surgery, because they relieve physical pain and psychological distress.

Dangers

Despite being highly addictive, narcotics are less deadly than alcohol, barbiturates, or tobacco, each of which directly or indirectly causes the deaths of thousands of people each year, compared to a few hundred deaths annually from heroin overdoses. Heroin withdrawal is less harsh than withdrawal from alcohol or barbiturate dependency, which can be fatal. Alcohol and tobacco are far more damaging physically, so a narcotics addict who avoids excess doses and maintains a steady supply of the drug can continue for decades without physical signs of ill effects or body deterioration. Sharing a needle, using an unsterile needle, or coming into contact with other contaminated paraphernalia, however, can cause infections or spread HIV. Liver damage from hepatitis is also common among heroin users.

Use

Heroin use remains a serious problem in the United States. A worldwide opium glut in the 1990s pushed heroin prices to an all-time low, and its purity levels on the street reached as high as 97 percent compared to 20 percent thirty years earlier.[43] Such high potency allows users to experience euphoria by snorting or smoking the drug, eliminating messy, HIV-carrying needles. As a result, heroin use is increasing in almost every part of the United States, among all age groups, including middle school-age children and high school teens. Unlike the crack-cocaine epidemic that continues to plague U.S. inner cities, heroin has infiltrated both city and suburb, affecting the lives of rich and poor alike.

Survey-based estimates of heroin use range from 456,000 past-year users (2002 NHSDA) to 980,000 addicts (National Institute on Drug Abuse). Some experts, however, estimate that as many as 3 million people in the United States use heroin recreationally. Certainly the number of heroin-related emergency room cases skyrocketed from 33,900 in 1990 to 93,000 in 2001.[44]

As with marijuana, heroin's resurgence coincided with greater visibility in the media and in modern rock culture. Young people have powerful role models in celebrities, from motion picture stars to popular musicians, who either portray themselves using it or actually do take the drug. "**Heroin chic**" became part of 1990s advertising (from Calvin Klein ads to Packard-Bell computer commercials), part of fashion photography (most notably in the work of David Sorrenti, dead in 1997 at age twenty of a heroin overdose), and of films. Part of the mystique that created heroin chic lies in Hollywood's fascination with it. Heroin as a theme appeared in *Requiem for a Dream* (2000), *Trainspotting* (1995), *The Basketball Diaries* (1995), *Pulp Fiction* (1994), *Killing Zoe* (1994), *My Own Private Idaho* (1993), and *Drugstore Cowboy* (1988).

For years, heroin afflicted the lives of young celebrities at the peak of their careers. The morbid fascination with the "celebrity drug" came to an unfathomable peak in the days immediately following the death of rocker Jonathan Melvoin from a heroin overdose, when people rushed to buy a particularly potent and lethal version of heroin, "Red Rum" (*murder* spelled backward). Recent heroin-related deaths of celebrities include Howie Epstein, 47, of Tom Petty and the Heartbreakers (2003); Brad Nowel, 28, of Sublime (1997); Jonathan Melvoin, 34, of Smashing Pumpkins (1996); Jerry Garcia, 53, of The Grateful Dead (1995); Kristen Pfaff, 27, of Hole (1994); River Phoenix, 23, of motion pictures; Stefanie Sargent, 24, of 7 Year Bitch (1993); Johnny Thunders, 38, of New York Dolls (1991); Andrew Wood, 24, of Mother Love Bone (1990); Hillel Slovak, 25, of Red Hot Chili Peppers (1988); and Will Shatter, late twenties, of Flipper (1987). This list does not include near-deaths from heroin overdoses of other rock stars nor the 1994 death of Kurt Cobain, twenty-seven, of Nirvana from a self-inflicted shotgun blast one week after nearly dying from a heroin overdose.

In recent years many college students learned about a drug called Rohypnol, which is not a narcotic, but a depressant. Also called "rope," "R-2," "Ruth," "roofies," or "roopies," it is a tasteless and odorless tranquilizer about ten times more powerful than the prescription drug Valium, and inexpensive at a street price of one to eight dollars a pill. Because numerous women were raped after an acquaintance secretly slipped the pill—ground into powder—into their drink, Rohypnol—and a similar drug, GHP—are known as the "date rape" drugs. They render women vulnerable by quickly producing a drunken state, lack of judgment, and amnesia for up to twenty-four hours. In 2001, emergency room admissions involving GHP totaled 3,340.[45]

Tobacco

Tobacco is probably the most physically harmful of all drugs Americans use. Smokers inhale nicotine, coal tars, nitrogen dioxide, formaldehyde, and other substances that continually assault their bodies. Chances of emphysema, bronchitis, and throat and lung cancer significantly increase, as do the probabilities of heart disease and stroke, especially among women using birth control pills. Cigarette smoking reduces life expectancy: a person who smokes less than half a pack a day has a four-year shorter life expectancy than a nonsmoker, while someone who smokes two or more packs a day has an eight-year shorter life expectancy. Pregnant women smokers double their likelihood of having a miscarriage or giving birth prematurely, and they are likely to have a low-birthweight child.

Tobacco causes one in every five deaths in this country. It causes nine out of every ten cases of lung cancer and nine out of every ten cases of chronic lung disease. It is one of the three leading causes of heart attacks. Overall, tobacco causes more than 440,000 deaths each year in the United States. In fact, tobacco-related deaths far outnumber the combined deaths related to AIDS, homicides, alcohol, illegal drugs, car accidents, fires, and suicides.[46]

In 2001, 35 percent of all Americans twelve and older smoked, compared to 42 percent in 1965. Each day about 4,000 people, mostly teenagers, begin smoking. The 3,000 of those who become regular smokers roughly balance out the people who die from smoking or who quit that same day. Most smokers were once between the ages of twenty-five and forty-four; but since the mid-1980s, the greatest rate of smoking has been in the eighteen-to-twenty-five age group.[47] With the rising number of women who smoke, lung cancer is now the leading cause of death among women.[48] Every year at least 140,000 women in the United States die from illnesses attributable to cigarettes.[49]

The World Health Organization estimates that one-third of the global population aged fifteen or older smokes and that smoking causes over 4 million deaths each year. Every ten seconds, somewhere in the world, tobacco kills another victim. The death toll is steadily increasing and, as mentioned earlier in this chapter, the figure will likely rise to 10 million deaths annually by the 2030, with 70 percent of those deaths occurring in developing countries.[50]

Why Smoke?

With all the information available about the physical damage caused by smoking, why do some people continue to smoke, and why do others start? Of the many possible answers to this question, two primary ones emerge: addiction and seduction.

Addiction

Smokers develop a tolerance for nicotine—a highly addictive drug—rather quickly, and so they tend to increase their daily consumption. Most smokers consume fifteen or more cigarettes a day, an average of at least one for every waking hour. Dozens of studies show nicotine to be at least as addictive as illegal drugs like cocaine and heroin, and smokers show all the physiological marks of the addict. Before the morning's first cigarette, for example, the smoker has all the signs of withdrawal, including hair-trigger reflexes, a lack of concentration, and altered brain waves.[51]

Dependence on tobacco becomes so strong that breaking the smoking habit is extremely difficult. Three out of four smokers say they are addicted and 88 percent say they wish they had never started smoking. Studies have shown that 70 percent of the people who make sincere efforts to stop smoking, even through special clinics, fail to do so.[52]

Seduction

Faced with first stagnant and then declining U.S. sales, the tobacco industry launched an advertising campaign to lure women and adolescents, two previously underrepresented smoker groups. The success of the "You've come a long way, baby" campaign for Virginia Slims prompted the introduction of other "women's" cigarettes and expensive advertising campaigns. For example, many Newport cigarette ads contained coded themes of sexual combat or attempts by females to eclipse dominant males, all buried in happy scenes of outdoorsy horseplay.

The cartoon character Joe Camel—part of a cigarette advertising campaign that deliberately targeted young people—served as an effective lure for adolescents, substantially increasing Camel sales. During the first three years of Joe Camel advertisements, Camel's share of the under-eighteen cigarette market jumped from 0.5% to 32.8%, representing a $476 million increase in annual sales for RJR Nabisco. After Joe Camel was introduced, the number of children who smoked Camels increased by a factor of 50. More than 90 percent of six-year-olds could match Joe Camel with a picture of a cigarette, making him as well-known among children that age as Mickey Mouse (by comparison, only 67 percent of adults recognized Joe Camel).[53] In 1997, after years of criticism, RJR Nabisco officially "retired" Joe Camel.

Another powerful seductive hook was RJR's Marlboro man, created in the 1950s when Philip Morris's research showed that young people searching for an identity often began smoking to declare their independence from their parents. The advertising concept was to harness this yearning for freedom and rebellion without making the message too antisocial. Marlboro's success (60 percent of young smokers pick Marlboro) lies not so much in its appeal to rugged masculinity, but in its offering both a sense of quiet rebellion against constraints and rules and a sense of belonging (to the tribe of Marlboro smokers). The once-secret RJR report, now available on the World Wide Web, says that "as social pressures tend to isolate younger adult smokers from their nonsmoking peers, they have an increased need to identify with their smoking peers, to smoke the 'belonging' brand."[54]

As John Leo states, the enormous past success of the cigarette companies in attracting youthful smokers lay in their "selling a sense of belonging and psychological self-control in a society in which nobody seems to belong anymore, except tribally by skin color or gender."[55] In 1994, then–Surgeon General Joycelyn Elders attacked the tobacco industry for exploiting adolescent insecurities and desires for independence from adults by attempting to convince them that by smoking, "they're slim, they're sexy, they're sociable, they're sophisticated, and successful."[56]

Still, many young people and adult women begin smoking, mostly because of peer pressure and the image successfully generated by the tobacco industry that smoking makes a person mature, sophisticated, and sexually attractive. Many females also smoke to control their weight and then hesitate to quit smoking, or quit only to relapse, because they fear the eleven-pound weight gain that often accompanies cessation.[57] Many people also hold a cavalier attitude that the health hazards are not immediate but distant, and that they can quit at any time.

Anti-Smoking Campaign

The history of smoking in the United States clearly illustrates shifting norms of drug use acceptability and nonacceptability. When the 1920s ushered in a period of cultural liberation, particularly from the sexually restrictive mores of the early twentieth century, cigarette smoking symbolized women's new sophistication. Films from the 1930s through 1950s offer abundant evidence of smoking as both normal and "cool"; nonsmokers were odd or "square."

Then, following the well-publicized reports on the harmful effects of cigarette smoking, the government mandated warnings on all cigarette packs beginning in 1964, and a ban of tobacco advertising on radio and television beginning in the 1970s. The 1986 report from then–Surgeon General C. Everett Koop labeled smoking the "chief, single, avoidable cause of death in our society and the most important public health issue of our time." Consequently, some states, such as California, instituted educational programs emphasizing the dangers of tobacco use, and they used increased taxes on cigarettes to finance the campaigns. Slowly, societal values changed, and what had been normal became deviant. First came the designation of nonsmoking areas in public places, followed by total smoking bans, requiring the smokers to go outside to indulge in their vice, now labeled addictive and self-destructive.

Second-Hand Smoke

Anti-smoking forces gathered more leverage with studies detailing the dangers to nonsmokers from environmental tobacco smoke (ETS, or second-hand smoke). A 1993 report by the Environmental Protection Agency classified **second-hand smoke** from tobacco as a Group A carcinogen—that is, as one of the most potent known cancer-causing agents. Analysis showed that it contains more than 4,000 different chemicals, including forty-three known carcinogens, such as cyanide and formaldehyde, and other hazardous substances, such as ammonia. Drawing on data from thirty epidemiological studies, the EPA estimates that second-hand smoke results in 3,000 U.S. deaths annually among nonsmokers, as well as approximately 300,000 respiratory infections, such as bronchitis and pneumonia in children.[58] Moreover, nearly nine out of ten nonsmoking Americans are exposed to second-hand smoke, according to a study conducted by the Centers for Disease Control and Prevention. Scientists reached this conclusion by measuring in the blood of more than 10,000 participants the presence of continine, a chemical the body metabolizes from nicotine.[59]

Tobacco Industry–Government Agreement

Faced with numerous lawsuits by federal and state governments, the tobacco industry—to avoid state-by-state litigation—made a strategic decision. In 1998, it reached agreement with forty-six states. In this Master Settlement Agreement, the states agreed to end all state litigation and to grant immunity to the companies from any future state lawsuits. In return, the companies agreed to (1) eliminate their famous logos (Joe Camel, the Marlboro Man); (2) stop sponsoring sporting events; (3) remove 50,000 cigarette billboards; and (4) pay the states $246 billion over a twenty-five-year-period, ostensibly to help cover government expenses to pay health costs of cigarette smoking through Medicaid, as well as to fund anti-smoking campaigns. In reality, most states have used the annual funds to plug their budget gaps instead. The tobacco companies actually benefited from the settlement, as the $246 billion is tax deductible, and they are shielded from lawsuits that had actually totaled over $516 billion.[60]

Yet, even though the agreement expressly forbid tobacco companies from taking "any action, directly or indirectly, to target Youth within any Settling State in the advertising, promotion or marketing of Tobacco Products, or take any action the primary purpose of which is to initiate, maintain or increase the incidence of youth smoking," they found loopholes to do so anyway. Researchers in 2002 reported all three major companies followed a new pattern. They eliminated tobacco advertisements in closely monitored publications (more than a 15 percent youth readership) and in those with less than a 10 percent readership, but increased by 60 percent their advertising in publications with a youth readership between 10 and 15 percent.[61]

The current picture, then, is mixed. Cigarette smoking is down in the United States, but 35 percent of Americans still smoke. The companies are still thriving, with world sales increasing, as they seek ways to improve their domestic market share among youth, while enjoying the protection against further lawsuits.

Social Consequences of Drug Use

At first glance the misuse of drugs might seem to be nothing more than an act of self-abuse or potential self-destruction. Actually, though, drug abuse creates many social and economic dysfunctions in a society, and both innocent victims and society as a whole suffer. Even though society's own norms may generate some of these social problems, the consequences of drug misuse and abuse can be devastating to the entire community. Some of these problems are obvious and quantifiable, but others lie hidden, and their cost to society is less easy to measure.

Crime

The popular belief that drug use causes crime is inaccurate, although a strong correlation exists between violent crime and certain drugs. Among violent offenders in state prisons, 51 percent admit having been under the influence of drugs or alcohol at the time of their offenses. People who drank alcohol immediately beforehand committed up to 80 percent of all murders and 75 percent of all rapes. Amphetamine users, reacting to the drug's powerful effects, disproportionately commit violent crimes, particularly assault and robbery. Significant evidence, in fact, shows that persons using alcohol, amphetamines, or barbiturates are far more likely to commit murder, rape, and assault than narcotics addicts.[62]

Crack addiction and heroin addiction correlate strongly with nonviolent crime, as addicts often steal, burglarize, sell drugs, or prostitute themselves to support their habit, which may cost

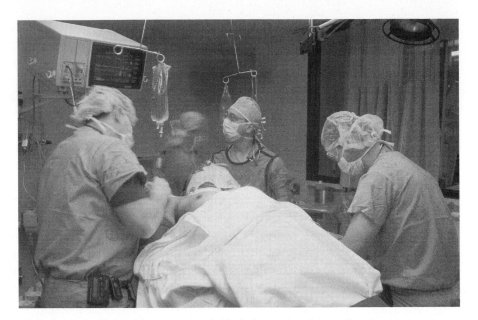

Emergency room personnel work feverishly to save the life of a drug overdose victim, an all-too-frequent occurrence among the nation's hospitals. Why do people take drugs? How do they become addicted? How does their addiction become a social problem?

them as much as $200 a day. Drug laws, though enacted to protect society from harmful drug use and crime, often have the reverse effect—and produce other unintended negative consequences. Because such laws drive up the price of illicit drugs, they force addicts to take desperate measures to feed their habit.[63] As a result, Americans continue to fear drug-related crime. Although violent crime is dropping, reports of gun battles on the city streets and of children and innocent bystanders hit by dealers' bullets still take place. Muggings occur and cars disappear, and desperate addicts still kill their grandmothers or someone else's for drug money.

In making certain drugs illegal, society creates a black market that organized crime finds enormously profitable. This underworld monopoly—combined with the risk of producing, transporting, or selling the illegal drugs—drives the price up far beyond its actual cost. Most addicts, unable to afford such high costs, resort in desperation to criminal activity, spending much of their time pursuing opportunities in this area instead of fulfilling any normally productive function within the society. Besides securing money for the drug at others' expense, these addict criminals endanger their own health and life by exposing themselves to the varying strengths and impurities of the available dope.

Evidently, then, narcotics addiction itself does not cause crime, but its illegality does. Because addiction is labeled an act of criminal deviance instead of a sickness, the punitive laws cost society millions of dollars each year in enforcement costs and severely strain our judicial and prison systems. Organized crime prospers from selling drugs; addicts commit crimes to buy drugs; and the laws designed to suppress drug abuse continue to produce crime and criminals.

Automobile Accidents

Automobile accidents involving drunk driving are the nation's most frequently committed violent crime. So extensive is this problem that about three of every ten Americans will be involved in an alcohol-related auto accident sometime in their lifetimes. In the past decade, four times as many Americans died in drunk-driving crashes than were killed in the Vietnam War. In 2002, alone, 17,970 persons—almost one-third of them under age twenty-five—died in U.S. alcohol-related traffic crashes, an average of one every thirty minutes. (Auto accidents involving drinking have long been the leading cause of death among persons aged fifteen to twenty-four.) In addition, alcohol use is responsible for more than a half-million serious personal injuries and many millions of dollars in property damage every year. Alcohol-related motor vehicle crashes cost the nation $51 billion annually in lost productivity, medical costs, property damage, and other direct expenditures; an additional $70 billion is lost in quality-of-life devaluation, since 30,000 people each year suffer permanent work-related disabilities. Although traffic fatalities involving alcohol-impaired drivers have declined in recent years, 26 percent of drivers involved in a fatal accident are driving under the influence of alcohol.[64]

Because of its widespread use, alcohol remains by far the most serious cause of auto accidents, particularly among drivers aged twenty-one to thirty-four. This age range is involved in 42 percent of all fatal traffic accidents. Drivers sixteen to twenty-one years old constitute 13 percent of the drinking drivers in fatal accidents.[65]

More people die in alcohol-related car crashes over Thanksgiving than on any other holiday, federal safety statistics show. Nationwide, drunk drivers killed 551 people on Thanksgiving four-day holidays in 2000 and 2001, compared with 454 on New Year's Eve holidays. The carnage increases on three-day holiday weekends, which helps to explain the special lethalness of Labor Day (532 deaths) and Memorial Day (539 deaths) in the same period. Experts say these two holidays are most dangerous holidays, weekend or not, because people are on the roads longer, often driving long distances to visit family or friends. Moreover, warmer weather makes downing some cold beers or mixed drinks more "fun," thus increasing the likelihood of alcohol-related fatal crashes.[66]

Health

Drug dependence exacts a heavy toll on the personal health and mental well-being of the users and quite often of their families as well. The death rate among alcoholics is about three times greater than that of the total population. Continuous heavy drinking also leads to malnutrition and weakened body resistance to infectious diseases, and contributes to many types of heart ailments and possibly to cancer. A third of all suicides each year are committed by alcoholics. Incidents of family violence and child and spouse abuse are fairly common among problem drinkers, as are above-average rates of emotional illness among family members, brought on by stress, the burden of coping with unpredictable behavior, and financial worries.

Alcohol is the third most frequent cause of birth defects in this country. About 1 in every 400 infants born have birth defects because their mothers drank alcohol during pregnancy.[67] Because a human fetus is unable to metabolize alcohol, its blood alcohol level becomes about ten times greater than that of the mother during an episode of drinking. Children born to alcoholic mothers are themselves addicted and are likely to exhibit **fetal alcohol syndrome,** which comprises many congenital problems including mental deficiency, heart problems, and deformities. Similarly, mothers who are addicted to narcotics have babies who are addicted at birth and suffer from the **fetal narcotic syndrome,** or withdrawal symptoms. Newborns whose mothers frequently took barbiturates or other sedatives also display these symptoms at birth; and all infants, regardless of the drug involved, gain weight with much difficulty. Addict mothers are at high-risk for HIV and can infect their unborn children with the virus and thereby condemn them to an early death. Between 1981 and 2000, nearly 7,000 children under age five contracted AIDS.[68]

Alcohol and drug abuse creates severe health problems, damaging organs and compromising the body's defense systems. Problems with accidental injury, poor blood circulation, chronic fatigue, and respiratory infections are frequent. Alcoholics thus use a disproportionate share of the nation's health resources, with one-fourth of all U.S. hospital beds occupied by persons whose health conditions represent complications of alcohol abuse and alcoholism.[69] Alcoholics and drug addicts also have far higher death rates from many illnesses than nonabusers. Alcoholics typically live ten to twelve years less than nonalcoholics, and the death rate for drug-induced deaths has been climbing steadily since 1980. Indeed, between 1980 and 2000, the numbers more than doubled from 6,900 to 19,700.[70]

Economic Losses

In workplaces ranging from airline hangers and construction sites to chemical plants and corporate offices, illegal drug use on the job is a serious problem for U.S. business. Of all illegal drug users eighteen and older, the vast majority are currently employed. That reality, coupled with the 13 percent of heavy drinkers who miss at least a day's work each month, imposes a staggering cost on the economy, about $125 billion each year.[71] The rate of work absenteeism among substance abusers is three times higher than among other workers, and abusers are more likely to injure themselves or someone else. Moreover, investigators have linked up to 40 percent of industrial fatalities and 47 percent of industrial injuries to alcohol consumption and alcoholism.[72]

Most workers who use drugs are not addicts. They may be secretaries or blue-collar workers who smoke a joint at lunchtime; high-tech employees or Wall Street traders who snort lines of coke at work; or night-shift workers who take amphetamines to keep up their energy level. Often, however, the drug use results in damaged or contaminated products, shoddy repairs, an increase in minor injuries and absenteeism, and a decrease in output.

Many U.S. businesses addressed the problem. Pre-employment drug testing became routine in corporate America in the aftermath of the 1980s cocaine boom and the "war on drugs," marked by passage of the 1988 Drug Free Workplace Act, which required federal contractors and grant recipients to provide drug-free workplaces. However, a tight labor market led to a decline in drug testing, falling from 81 percent in 1996 to 66 percent in 2000.[73] Numerous companies hire drug consultants to run educational seminars for management and staff. Another major step has been the proliferation of Employee Assistance Programs (EAPs) offering professional help to employees for drug and other personal problems. Virtually every Fortune 500 company has some type of EAP, but the smaller the company the less likely it is to have such a program. At present, 31 percent of all U.S. employees work for a company with an EAP.[74]

Drug Abuse in Sports

Drug and alcohol problems in sports draw public attention because of the prominence of the athletes involved. Illegal drug use affects almost all competitive fields of sports. In the 2000 Summer Olympics in Sydney, Australia, for example, officials took action against athletes from Belarus, Bulgaria, China, Latvia, Romania, and Russia for testing positive for banned stimulants.[75] Suspensions for illegal drug use hound professional sports, such as baseball (Dwight Gooden, Darryl Strawberry), basketball (Michael Ray Richardson), hockey (Craig MacTavish), and football (Lawrence Taylor, Dexter Manley).

Unlike the National Football League or college and Olympics sports, Major League baseball does not randomly test players for steroids and other performance-enhancing drugs. Perhaps it should. Many people in baseball suspect that the national pastime has become tainted with steroid abuse. One reporter's interviews with over twenty-five major league strength coaches, general managers, league officials, and players indicated a general view that steroid abuse has become a problem in baseball, perhaps even widespread, and that the sport must address it. One veteran outfielder said he believed as many as 40 percent of major leaguers use muscle-building drugs.[76]

Early deaths are even more shocking than the suspensions and banishments, such as the 1986 cocaine deaths of Boston Celtics top draft choice Len Bias and Cleveland Browns defensive back Don Rogers. More recent are the deaths of football stars Lyle Alzado (brain cancer, 1993) and Steve Corsen (damaged heart, 1994) caused by heavy use of anabolic steroids, and in basketball the death of Boston Celtics captain Reggie Lewis (cocaine, 1993) and Baltimore Orioles pitcher Steve Bechler (ephedra, 2003).

Addiction to painkillers is common in the National Football League. In a 1997 survey of players and league executives, consensus estimates indicated that as many as 10 percent of the league's 1,500 players were seriously addicted to painkillers, despite NFL rules against using such drugs. Some players spend weeks, even months, in the off season overcoming their dependency on medications and dealing with withdrawal symptoms. These can be as simple as a case of the shakes or as dangerous as seizures like the one suffered in 1996 by Brett Favre, quarterback of the Super Bowl champion Green Bay Packers, who before the 1996 season admitted his addiction to the painkiller Vicodin.[77]

The lifestyle of professional athletes—preferential treatment for much of their adolescent and adult lives, lots of money, long hours spent traveling and staying temporarily at many places, pressures to perform, and lack of job security—produce both temptations and inducements to use other drugs. Because anabolic steroids and other "enhancing" drugs improve athletes' strength and energy in the short term, many athletes are encouraged to take them despite the risks—often as early as in high school and in college as well.

Once athletes become hooked on drugs, their stamina and skills deteriorate, as numerous ex-athletes and their coaches confirm. The social consequences are not limited to shortened careers for the athletes. Questions of on-field performances undermine both the integrity and popularity of sports. The all-American image of our athletes—and the respect youngsters have for them—erodes. Even worse, these athletes offer improper role models for impressionable young people.

Social Control and Solution Attempts

The early 1900s marked a change in the social definition of drug addiction. The Harrison Narcotics Act of 1914 made the manufacture, sale, and use of cocaine and opiates federal offenses except in cases involving "legitimate medical uses." This law, which followed passage of state antinarcotics legislation, made using these drugs a criminal activity instead of a health problem. Identifying such drug use as a social problem and a crime was, as we discuss later, the result of its being associated with lower-class minorities and crime. Today, efforts at resolving the drug problem in the United States still focus primarily on repressive measures—arrest and punishment. Although the federal government established a few hospitals in the 1930s to treat addicts, only in recent decades—with the spread of illicit drug use to the middle and upper classes—have preventive and treatment programs increased along with corrective actions.

Preventive Programs

A formal drug education program for youth is a necessity. Otherwise, their only source of information will be their informal communication network, which is highly effective but often filled with inaccurate, sometimes dangerous, information about drug use. Two decades ago, school drug education programs were a dismal failure because they used alarmist tactics about the dire consequences of drug use. Such an approach contradicted the "facts" gained from firsthand experience or from friends. Moreover, this approach tended to arouse youthful curiosity and experimentation. Because many young people typically have a cavalier belief about their own invulnerability to risk and only know about the short-term positive aspects of drug taking, programs using emotional appeal or morality issues lost credibility and were unsuccessful.[78]

One controversial notion is the concept of a "gateway" drug that paves the way for "soft" drug users to become "hard" drug users. The Partnership for a Drug-Free America, in cooperation with the National Institute on Drug Abuse (NIDA) and the White House Office of Drug Control Policy, launched a still-continuing campaign targeting marijuana on the premise that reducing marijuana consumption was a practical strategy for reducing the use of more dangerous drugs. Fueling the debate was a 1994 highly criticized national study released by the Center on Addiction and Substance Abuse at Columbia University. It showed that children (twelve to seventeen years old) who use marijuana are eighty-five times more likely and adults who used marijuana as children are seventeen times more likely to use cocaine than nonmarijuana users.[79]

However, no causal relationship exists between marijuana use and subsequent heroin use, and very few marijuana users progress to hard drugs. The consistent disparity in the percentages using both types of drugs illustrates this point. On the other hand, frequent users of marijuana (such as twice weekly for a year) are far more likely to use cocaine than are nonusers.[80] But, to be consistent with the logic of outlawing marijuana because heroin addicts once used it, we would have to also outlaw aspirin, coffee, cigarettes, and antacids, since addicts used them, too.

Instead of such dubious claims that can undermine a sound drug education program, an approach using accurate information, effectively communicated, is necessary. This would require the inclusion of scientific studies with solid evidence of the effects of the various drugs. If some, such as alcohol, are beneficial in moderation, then that needs to be told along with their harmful effects if overused. Attempts to impose one's own values about any form of drug use on youth will be less effective than a balanced approach that objectively presents the scientific data. To be successful, a drug education program must focus on eliminating drug *abuse,* not drug *use.* Informed choice usually wins out over attempts at forced abstinence (recall the Prohibition era).

Through funded teacher preparation programs, curriculum guides, texts, and media materials aimed at various grade levels, American School Health Association drug prevention efforts are a popular approach. Programs focus on elementary schools as the first line of attack, since the average age of first use of drugs is now thirteen, down from the midteens of five years ago. Often it's even lower: the 2001 National Household Survey revealed that 356,000 youths aged twelve had used illicit drugs.

The General Accounting Office estimates that the nation's schools spend over $125 million on drug abuse prevention curricula each year.[81] Of forty-seven curricula available to schools, only ten (21 percent) have been evaluated in rigorous studies. At least eight programs were judged to be effective at reducing tobacco or drug use, in at least some studies. One program (Life Skills Training) showed lasting effects into young adulthood. Evaluations of Life Skills Training included measures of tobacco, alcohol, and marijuana use. Another six of the ten curricula (Alcohol Misuse Prevention Project, Growing Healthy, Know Your Body, Life Skills Training, Project Northland, and STAR) showed positive effects lasting for at least two years after the pretest. Two programs (Project Alert and DARE) did not appear to have any sustained effects on drug use, although they did have variable success at reducing substance use early on.[82]

Treatment Programs

Different methods have been developed for dealing with alcohol and drug abuse as a medical and psychological problem rather than as an act of criminal deviance. Through professional assistance in self-help addict communities or in health clinics, rehabilitation efforts have met with limited success. Some programs combine a detoxification effort with exercises aimed at building self-confidence and willpower to avoid a relapse into drug taking; others offer a substitute maintenance program or therapeutic sessions to combat the problems that foster drug dependency.

Alcoholics Anonymous (AA)

Founded in 1935 by two alcoholics to help themselves stop drinking, Alcoholics Anonymous (AA) has grown to more than 50,000 chapters in the United States, with over 2 million members. Companion groups are Al-Anon for the spouses of alcoholics and Alateen for the children of alcoholics.

Alcoholics Anonymous offers a mutual support system and a sense of security to its members. Instead of relying on trained therapists or treatment programs, AA uses small-group dynamics among alcoholics to share their drinking histories, confirm the need for total abstinence, take the challenge one day at a time, meet together frequently to reinforce their resolve, and call one another when the temptation to drink becomes strong. Emphasis on spiritual beliefs and help from God and positive reinforcement of self-image are important parts of this interdependent member effort.

A 1997 study substantiated other studies that have documented AA's status as the most effective of all drug addiction treatment programs. Most of the men and women in this study from the San Francisco area were severe alcoholics when they first joined AA. Three years later, 46 percent had not drunk at all in the previous six months nor had any alcohol-related problems (cravings or other physical symptoms, health problems, family quarrels, or arrests).[83] Still, even this "most effective" program against drug dependence only helped 46 percent; 54 percent lapsed back into alcohol use.

Methadone Clinics

A person who has been a heroin addict for at least one year and has failed in at least two other attempts at treatment may be accepted into a **methadone maintenance** program. Accepted volunteers first enter the clinic to become gradually stabilized on a regular dosage of methadone in place of heroin. Methadone is a synthetic narcotic, also addictive, that prevents withdrawal symptoms and satisfies physical cravings. Taken orally (usually mixed with fruit juice), it does not produce a high, allows a person to function normally, and lasts about twenty-four hours—four times longer than heroin. Once stabilized, the person is discharged but must return to the clinic each day for an additional dose.

Methadone maintenance simply substitutes a legal form of drug addiction for an illegal form. Its cost—about $3 a week compared to as much as $200 a day for heroin—makes it an acceptable alternative to many addicts, however. Unfortunately, methadone clinics meet considerable opposition from neighborhood residents who fear the presence of addicts in their community, even though methadone treatment dramatically lowers the crime rate, since addicts no longer need to steal or prostitute themselves to pay for their habit.[84] Of the estimated 1 milliion heroin addicts in this country, only 20 percent receive methadone treatment. A 2000 study showed that longer-term methadone maintenance therapy, combined with some psychosocial counseling, is far more effective than any short-term effort.[85]

Therapeutic Communities

Therapeutic community programs are a total immersion effort in which the addict voluntarily lives for up to a year in a treatment center where strict discipline, monitored daily routines, continuous antidrug indoctrination, and intensive encounter-group sessions dominate. Following the founding of Synanon in California in 1959, other **therapeutic communities**—including Phoenix House and Daytop Village—have come into existence and now number over four hundred. Staffed by both professionals and former addicts, these therapeutic communities together

Helping teenagers face their situation, a male drug counselor at a drug rehab meeting facilitates discussion to get them to strip away their masks and excuses. Rehabilitation groups for all ages often utilize the group process, finding more success in this method than in a one-on-one approach. Why is the group method more successful? What limitations might it have?

treat about 15,000 people. Their efforts to resocialize addicts have achieved only limited success. Over three-fourths of the addicts drop out, and many of those who complete the program still return to drug use.[86]

Still, some success is better than no success. For the past three decades, the National Institute for Drug Abuse conducted several large studies on the outcomes of treatment in various types of U.S. therapeutic community programs. These studies found that those who successfully completed treatment (one in four) had lower levels of cocaine, heroin, and alcohol use; criminal behavior; unemployment; and indicators of depression than they had before treatment.[87]

Antagonistic Drugs

Another approach to behavior modification involves negative reinforcement—using **antagonistic drugs** to negate any short-term euphoric or other benefit the addict might otherwise experience from renewed taking of the desired drug. For example, the drug Antabuse causes the body to react with violent nausea when the person subsequently drinks alcohol, creating a powerful motivation not to drink again. Two narcotic antagonists—Cyclazocine and Naloxone—each prevent the euphoria usually produced by heroin and other opiates. However, the success of these drugs rests on the addicts' taking them long enough to overcome psychological dependency on the problem drug. Not all addicts are willing to take the antagonistic drug regularly, and many lapse back into alcoholism or narcotics addiction a year or more later when they find themselves unable to cope with some personal crisis.

Corrective Efforts

The criminalization of drugs has not reduced the drug problem, nor have mandatory jail terms for selling or possessing illegal drugs. Just as the failure of Prohibition demonstrated that legislation and law-enforcement efforts cannot eliminate a drug problem, the failure of laws against cocaine, heroin, marijuana, and other drugs to reduce their use has shown the limitations of this punitive approach. On balance, the laws have fostered a drug subculture and even worse social problems by providing a lucrative source of income for organized crime. They have also increased individual acts of violence, theft, and prostitution by addicts who need money to pay for artificially expensive drugs.

Efforts to prevent drugs from reaching consumers have limited effect. Occasional drug busts and seizures of contraband command headlines, but law enforcement officials admit that these represent only the tip of the iceberg compared to what safely reaches dealers. Eliminating one source of supply simply generates another source, whether the target be a country (opium and marijuana grow in many locales) or a drug kingpin. Ex-drug czar, retired Army General Barry McCaffrey, admits that the United States "will not solve the drug problem by arrests." The long-term answer, say McCaffrey and others, lies in persuading people to stop using drugs.[88]

The Dutch Experiment

When drug use in the Netherlands rose significantly in the mid-1970s, the Dutch government formed a commission to investigate the matter. This commission concluded that attempting to eliminate drug use was unrealistic; it recommended instead that drugs be regulated according to the risk criterion of each drug. In its Opium Act of 1976, the Dutch government classified some amphetamines, cocaine, heroin, and LSD as dangerous and marijuana and hashish as less dangerous. Punishments for use of dangerous drugs increased and penalties for use of cannabis products ended.[89]

Currently, about 1,500 coffee shops in the Netherlands list high-quality marijuana and hashish on their menus, legally selling the substances to customers. Most also distribute literature about the dangers of both soft and hard drugs. Interestingly, the per capita regular use of marijuana and hashish is much lower in the Netherlands than in the United States, as is the heroin addiction rate. In fact, the European Union (EU) Monitoring Centre for Drugs and Drug Addiction found that the Dutch rate of "problem drug use" was lower than that of most other European countries.[90]

Although penalties for hard drug use are severe, the Dutch implemented a "harm reduction" program aimed at addicts who are unwilling or unable to kick their habit. Drug counselors also seek out addicts to offer free sterile needles (to combat HIV) and a free supply of methadone, which more than half of the 35,000 hard drug addicts receive. The pragmatic Dutch drug policy has been relatively successful and serves as one practical alternative to current U.S. drug policy and practice. (See the box on pp. 414–415 for other international examples.)

Sociological Perspectives

Drug use is so widespread in U.S. society that it has become part of the daily life of almost every person. From birth through life's ailments to death, drugs ease our pain and suffering. For many of us, drugs serve such utilitarian purposes as keeping us awake, helping us sleep, and easing our feelings of stress. For others, recreational drugs increase pleasure or sociability at festive or informal gatherings. We take other drugs routinely, without even thinking of them as drugs, as when we smoke cigarettes or drink caffeinated or alcoholic beverages.

Since psychoactive drugs alter mind, mood, and physical functioning, their varying social definitions and social significance are at least as important to our understanding as their physiological capabilities. Why are some drugs legal or respectable and others not? What causes value conflicts within society about certain drugs? What occasions hostile social reaction to certain drugs, in particular? Let us again seek insights into these questions by applying different theoretical perspectives as different lenses to view the same problem.

The Functionalist Viewpoint

Functionalist analysis focuses on the social norms and conditions that foster drug use in a society, rather than on the particular reasons why individuals use drugs. As you have seen, the use of some drugs is socially acceptable: for medical, recreational, or therapeutic purposes, society condones the moderate use of alcohol, amphetamines, caffeine, cocaine, depressants, marijuana, narcotics, and tobacco. Prescription drugs, in particular, are highly functional for medical practitioners and their patients. One notable example of this involves the precipitous drop in the number of patients confined to mental hospitals. The number has fallen by more than half, from about 560,000 in 1956 to less than 262,000 today, largely as a result of drug therapy—the use of mood-altering psychopharmaceuticals.[91] That some of these former mental patients have become homeless city dwellers lacking social competency is a dysfunction requiring corrective action.

Drugs are a multibillion-dollar industry in this country, providing a living for tens of thousands of people who help provide drugs through testing, growing, processing, manufacturing, distributing, or selling. The alcohol, pharmaceutical, and tobacco industries prosper, as does the highly profitable illegal drug market. Abuse and misuse of drugs also provide jobs for persons who enforce drug laws or help drug addicts.

Anomie

Rapid social change—high technology, shifts in occupational patterns, lack of urban jobs for low-skilled minorities concentrated in cities, and disappearing rural work opportunities—helps create social problems: poverty, alienation, and greater social class disparities. The outside pressures of school, work, and everyday life also increase the stress on individual and family well-being. For many people who feel confused because their societal role is threatened by occupational dislocation or changing traditions, drugs offer an escape from unpleasant or difficult situations. Prevailing social norms about drug use may have little influence over such individuals, who feel

The Globalization of Social Problems

Alcohol and Drug Abuse

Practices that are acceptable practices in one culture may not be permitted in another. Possession of marijuana continues to be a criminal offense in most of the United States, but it is acceptable across much of the Middle East and North Africa. Drinking is an institutionalized practice in the United States, but is forbidden by the Koran and is illegal in some Islamic countries. In India the national constitution prohibits alcohol consumption, but opium is openly sold in the marketplace. Cocaine use or possession draws severe penalties in a great many countries, but South American Indians, particularly those who live in the Andes mountains, use it—in its unrefined, more diluted form, which they ingest by chewing coca leaves—almost universally.

The social pressures that curbed drinking in the United States are not necessarily present elsewhere.

Although per capita alcohol consumption has declined in many of the countries listed in Table 13.3, people drank more in other countries, particularly in Europe. One of alcohol's side effects, liver diseases such as cirrhosis, strike unevenly, but their incidence tends to be higher in countries where more people either drink mostly hard spirits or else where they drink daily, even in moderate amounts, than where drinking is confined to weekends or special occasions.

The World Health Organization (WHO) estimates that approximately 15 million people worldwide put their health at risk by using psychoactive substances; at least 5 million of these users inject drugs. Use of cannabis, or marijuana, is increasingly widespread throughout the world; and in both developed and developing countries, intentional inhalation of volatile

Table 13.3   Per Capita Alcohol Consumption in 2001 and Cirrhosis Deaths by Year Indicated

	Liters of Alcohol	Deaths per 100,000		Liters of Alcohol	Deaths per 100,000
1. Luxembourg	17.0	22.7 (1997)	16. Austria	10.3	7.8 (1995)
2. Portugal	16.6	31.9 (1998)	17. New Zealand	9.8	3.9 (1996)
3. Ireland	15.8	3.1 (1996)	18. Finland	9.7	18.0 (1996)
4. Czech Republic	14.9	26.2 (1998)	19. United Kingdom	9.7	10.3 (1997)
5. France	13.1	23.2 (1996)	20. Belgium	9.6	11.8 (1995)
6. Slovenia	12.6	36.1 (1995)	21. Latvia	9.5	22.5 (1995)
7. Germany	12.5	30.9 (1997)	22. Netherlands	9.5	6.2 (1997)
8. Croatia	12.2	21.0 (1995)	23. Greece	9.2	8.3 (1997)
9. Slovakia	12.1	37.5 (1995)	24. Italy	9.2	29.2 (1995)
10. Austria	12.0	33.3 (1998)	25. United Sates	9.1	9.6 (2000)
11. Hungary	11.5	107.8 (1998)	26. Estonia	8.8	1.6 (1995)
12. Switzerland	11.5	13.4 (1996)	27. Belarus	8.3	7.7 (1995)
13. Denmark	11.3	19.1 (1996)	28. Poland	8.3	17.4 (1996)
14. Spain	11.2	25.0 (1995)	29. Bulgaria	7.7	33.3 (1998)
15. Russia	10.7	18.6 (1995)	30. Canada	7.6	8.8 (1997)

Sources: World Drink Trends and World Health Organization.

The Globalization of Social Problems (continued)

Other countries struggle with substance abuse and related criminal activities. Alcoholism is rampant in countries of the former Soviet Union, for example, and affect all segments of society, including even chief executives of government. What measures have been taken to address problems of alcohol and tobacco in the United States, and with what results?

solvents and other inhalants is an increasing problem, especially in such marginalized groups as street children and indigenous young people.

Tobacco use cuts across all cultural barriers. Worldwide, some 100,000 to 200,000 people die each year from drug abuse, but nearly 5 million die from the effects of tobacco. More Colombians die from American tobacco products than do Americans from cocaine, and more Thais die from our tobacco than do Americans from Southeast Asian heroin. WHO estimates that about 1.2 billion regular smokers inhabit the world today, about 300 million of them in the developed countries, and three times as many (900 million—750 million males and 150 million females) in developing countries. Half the men living in developing countries are smokers. If the current trend of rising cigarette consumption rates per capita in developing countries continues, WHO anticipates the death toll from tobacco to rise dramatically in developing countries in the 2030s to around 10 millions deaths per year. Absent some dramatic reversal in this trend, WHO reports, the chief uncertainty is not whether but when these deaths will occur.

The Russian Federation is but one example of the world tobacco epidemic, which kills 750 people every single day. Two-thirds of all men and one-third of all women smoke, and smoking rates among adolescents are increasing, especially among girls. Today, 55 percent of all deaths in Russia result from heart diseases, followed by cancers, which account for another 20 percent. Smoking causes between 25 and 30 percent of both groups of diseases. WHO reports that 32 percent of all male deaths and 5 percent of all female deaths are tobacco related.

Source: World Health Organization, Tobacco Free Initiative, 2003.

alienated from society or overwhelmed by the many social demands they face. The dysfunctions of alienation, confusion, rootlessness, stress, anxiety, and unattainable goals occasioned by the social system thus create in some individuals a sense of normlessness regarding drugs. Despite societal remonstrances, the refuge of drugs presents a tempting alternative for those caught in life's confusing demands.

Value Conflict

Our widespread diversity in occupations and specialization has created significant structural differentiation, as manifested in the existence of countless subgroups or subcultures. Consequently, achieving a value consensus about drug use is difficult. What is acceptable to one group often is not acceptable to another. The failure of Prohibition offers a notable illustration of a clash of values; in this case, widespread public deviance led to repeal of an unpopular law against alcohol that had originally enjoyed sufficient support to win approval from three-quarters of the nation's state governments.

Present-day value conflicts abound. Anti-smoking groups have succeeded in having laws enacted that restrict smoking in public areas and forbid television advertising; but the federal government continues to subsidize the tobacco industry, despite the surgeon general's warnings of the dangers inherent in tobacco use. Marijuana and cocaine enjoy widespread and growing use, often at socially fashionable gatherings; yet if caught, users face felony charges in most states. In the 1960s, marijuana use was a means for hippies to express rejection of middle-class values. Similarly, some young people today view illegal drug use as a way of asserting their independence from the older generation's values.

The Conflict Viewpoint

Conflict theorists also emphasize value conflicts in analyzing the drug problem, but they focus on how and why those with power and influence react to various forms of drug use. If a drug becomes identified with a group whose social characteristics are considered disreputable or threatening to the society, it is likely to be declared illegal. The powerful, in this view, act to protect themselves from a potential threat rather than responding to the health hazards posed by that form of drug use. A related point is that the dominant group attempts to impose its morality on others, especially if a subgroup has a "subversive" lifestyle (e.g., the hippie counterculture of smoking "grass" and advocating LSD, free love, communal living, and nonmaterialism).

Drugs and Social Class

History records numerous instances in which values change when previously legal drugs become associated with a low-status group. For example, excessive drinking has existed since Puritan times and was called an "addiction" as early as 1785 by Dr. Benjamin Rush, then–Surgeon General of the United States. However, not until native-born Americans associated alcohol with the swelling numbers of poor Irish Catholic immigrants did the all-out Prohibition movement begin. By 1855, at the height of Irish migration, thirteen of the thirty-one states had prohibition laws. Although most of them subsequently repealed or modified the laws over the next decade, the

Women's Christian Temperance Union (WCTU) spearheaded an anti-liquor campaign in the late nineteenth century directed primarily at Blacks and Catholic and Jewish immigrants living in poverty in the cities. During World War I, the Anti-Saloon League argued that the major beer breweries were all German-American owned and were destroying American character and productivity.[92] With anti-German feelings still high after the war, a constitutional amendment prohibiting alcoholic drinks nationwide was ratified in 1919.

Similarly, growing opium poppies and manufacturing and selling opiates were legal activities in the nineteenth century. People could buy opiates in pharmacies, groceries, and general stores, as well as by mail order, to treat teething pains, toothaches, coughs, diarrhea, dysentery, consumption, pain, "woman's trouble," and many other legitimate purposes. Hundreds of patent medicines containing opium or morphine were easily accessible. Only when anti-Chinese sentiment flared up in the 1870s, during economic hard times over cheap Chinese labor, did anti-opium laws pass. Even then, the laws targeted the Chinese coolies (in the form of prohibitions against the Chinese import of opium and against opium dens), not opium use itself.

Cocaine was a respectable drug until newspapers around the turn of the nineteenth century linked it with Blacks, criminals, and violence. Media sensationalism encouraged a public belief that "Blacks plus cocaine equals raped White women," and the drug became illegal in 1914.[93] Heroin receives greater attention than more widely used dangerous drugs because of its frequent association with poor non-Whites and criminals. Marijuana, as noted earlier, became synonymous with antiestablishment subcultures, but when many "normal" affluent Whites used it, eleven states liberalized their marijuana laws.

Interest Groups

Powerful corporate interests spend hundreds of millions of dollars each year to influence public opinion and legislators. Tobacco, for example, is a major cash crop in several states, generating income for manufacturers, wholesalers, transporters, advertising agencies, vending machine companies, and retailers. Through the industry's advocate, the Tobacco Institute, these commercial interests conducted intensive lobbying to fight and discredit the efforts of the American Cancer Society and citizens' groups to enact antismoking legislation. As it intensifies its lobbying efforts to fight increasingly strict domestic restrictions, it expands its international sales to compensate for declining U.S. sales.

The issue of drugs causes unlikely alliances of special-interest groups to band together. Religious groups seeking prohibition or severe restriction of drugs for moral reasons endear themselves to organized crime, for whom illegal substances offer enormous profits on the black market; law enforcement agencies, too, advocate a tougher drug policy since that will mean higher department budgets, better pay, more personnel, and job security. Meanwhile, civil libertarians seeking liberalization of drug laws find themselves bedded down with free marketeers, primary producers who hope to expand their sales volume, and (of course) addicts looking for cheap, high-quality drugs.

Perhaps the most notable example of how economic self-interest helps shape institutional views of a drug problem involves Harry J. Anslinger, head of the Narcotics Bureau from 1931 to 1962, who waged an effective propaganda campaign against marijuana during much of his tenure. After his budget and staff were cut back for four consecutive years from 1933 to 1936, Anslinger launched a media attack on marijuana, calling it an assassin of youth that led to heroin addiction. He offered the media questionable stories about "dope fiends" who committed "marijuana atrocities." In 1936, the bureau sponsored a sensationalist, commercial movie, *Reefer Madness*, that purported to document how hopelessly hooked marijuana users would stop at nothing to get the "killer weed." In response to Anslinger's crusade, Congress passed the Marijuana Tax Act of 1937, designed to eliminate use of the drug. Needless to say, the Narcotics Bureau received increased funding to fight this "evil."[94]

The Interactionist Viewpoint

Users may view drugs as an adventure, an escape, a necessity, or a religious experience. The same drug viewed as a patient aid to the medical profession can be evil to moralists if used nonmedically. The underworld finds it a lucrative trade, while law enforcement personnel see it as the center of criminal activity. In addition, from time to time society redefines drugs and their symbolic meaning as an evil, a social problem, or an acceptable practice. This fact provides the foundation on which interactionist theorists build their analyses.

Although some people have maladjusted personalities or other psychological characteristics that influence their drug experimentation, sociologists find such individualized explanations inadequate, since drug use does not occur in isolation from society. Interactionists interpret drug use as a behavior pattern learned through the socialization and resocialization that occur in group interaction. Because drinking alcohol is an acceptable social practice in the United States, for example, children grow up learning a favorable definition and attitude about its use; and as they grow older, they are more likely to drink, too. Similarly, an adult's habitual use of tobacco, caffeine, stimulants, or sedatives in the presence of a maturing individual can influence the younger person's actions.

Cultural Factors

The prevalence of norms among certain ethnic groups regarding alcohol consumption illustrates the differences in learned behavior patterns. Orthodox Jews restrict drinking to special occasions among relatives and close friends, consider excessive drinking a bad reflection on their culture, and associate drunkenness with the behavior of non-Jews. Having learned norms on moderation in childhood, even adult Jews who have drifted away from orthodoxy continue their restraint in drinking.[95] Italian-American children grow up in households where wine drinking is an integral part of eating; and again, moderate consumption is the norm. Neither Italians nor Jews tend to drink to relieve stress, since they have defined drinking not as an acceptable means of dealing with problems, but as a part of family life.[96] Irish Americans, on the other hand, have traditionally associated drinking with any social gathering, using it to create a good time. Traditional Irish values do not hold public drunkenness to be as disgraceful as it is according to Jewish and Italian values, unless it results in income or property loss. Consequently, excessive drinking at these gatherings is not uncommon. The rate of alcoholism among Irish-American men is relatively high, but alcoholism is rare among Italians and Jews.[97]

Drug Subcultures

Peer groups are the major agent of socialization for drug taking. Friends typically introduce new users to any drug—alcohol, amphetamines, cocaine, marijuana, or whatever else. If the dominant culture holds a negative attitude toward use of a particular drug, an individual is more likely to overcome societal disapproval and use it anyway in the presence of encouraging friends. Since drugs are most commonly taken within the social context of a group where peer reassurance makes drug use more desirable, the longer and more intense a person's association with a drug subculture is, the more likely that group's norms are to outweigh those of the dominant society.

Once an individual begins using illicit drugs, the shared experience draws that person closer to the group and its norms. For many, the camaraderie within the group is just as important as the effect of the drug, and they may continue using the drug to retain group acceptance. Others, often called "mellow dudes" within the subculture, devote their free time to a life of parties, music, and sex, augmented by marijuana, cocaine, and Quaaludes, with occasional use of amphetamines and hallucinogens. "Turning on" others is a common act of friendship, in their view.

Among drug addicts, a more intensive subculture exists. Labeled as deviants by society and its laws, drug addicts experience disapproval, rejection, and exclusion from conventional groups. Forced to interact with others who share their need for a regular drug supply, addicts develop a closer bond with their peers as they struggle to survive and find sources for drugs. Isolated from the rest of society, they gradually assume a deviant identity, and their behavior revolves around continued drug use, reinforced by the ideology they now share with the only group that does not condemn them.[98]

Thinking About the Future

We appear headed in two directions simultaneously concerning drugs. The government spends tens of millions of dollars on antismoking campaigns while spending tens of millions of dollars on tobacco subsidies. Some states have decriminalized individual marijuana use, while other states refuse to do so; meantime, the federal government launches such countermeasures as field burnings and sprayings, contraband seizures, arrests, and prosecution. Meanwhile, alcohol consumption is increasing among young people, as is the use of such other drugs as cocaine and marijuana, and abuse of other stimulants or depressants. We are a drug-taking society, but where are these somewhat contradictory trends taking us? How do you envision our future?

Will a new generation of Americans—exposed to alcohol, marijuana, cocaine, and other drugs at an early age (as many now are)—grow up and take a drug-friendly lifestyle into the workplace far beyond what now exists? Will coked-up, stoned, or strung-out employees cost U.S. industry billions of dollars in slowed productivity, absenteeism, tardiness, and irrational decisions, ultimately leading to high product costs and a poor delivery record that causes the United States to fall behind other industrialized nations in output? Moreover, will that drug-friendly lifestyle extend into many homes? Will a greater proportion of tomorrow's youth, influenced by a stronger drug-use model than their parents had when they were young, slip into alcohol and drug dependency? Are we witnesses to the beginning of a vicious cycle that will feed itself into a worst-case scenario?

How do we combat drug use? Do we need even tougher laws and mandatory sentences? Should we get tougher on sports figures and ban them for life from competition if they use drugs? Should we increase funding to law enforcement agencies for more crackdowns on suppliers and dealers? Should we engage in an all-out effort in the "drug war" and send our troops into countries growing massive quantities of opium and marijuana to destroy the crops, the land, and buildings of those involved, and bring them to justice before the World Court? Or is the reverse action better? Should we not only decriminalize, but also legalize, some or all drugs (as in the Netherlands) to take away the lure of the "forbidden," and remove criminal involvement in the manufacture, distribution, and sale of drugs? Should we have licensing, regulation, even taxation, of these drugs for greater control over them as legal instead of illegal drugs? What are the ramifications if we take this course of action?

Should our emphasis instead be on prevention and treatment? Should we mandate the full integration of drug education programs into the school curriculum at all levels? Should our schools, churches, and community organizations get the necessary training and funding for programs to enhance individual self-confidence, self-esteem, and life skills, to convey effectively the message that people who feel good about themselves do not abuse their bodies? How else do we promote a value orientation that the greater pleasure is not artificially induced but natural, that greater satisfaction comes from getting "high" on life, not drugs? And what of the many treatment programs? What more can we do with these to make them more available and more effective?

How do we address the use of alcohol and tobacco? We saw what happened during the Prohibition era when we outlawed alcohol, so declaring them to be illegal does not appear to be a solution. Several states' economies depend heavily on their tobacco crops, which receive government subsidies. Do we end the subsidies? How do we avoid the severe economic problems in those states if we do? Should we lessen the alcohol content in drinks to reduce the subsequent problems of intoxication (as is done on military bases)? What else can we do about the problems of alcohol and tobacco use, as well as other drugs?

SUMMARY

1. Alcohol and other drugs have been an institutionalized part of many different cultures throughout world history. Sociologists are interested not only in how cultural values about their acceptability vary from one society to another, but also in how social definitions of their use change within one society over a period of time. Drug abuse is a worldwide problem.

2. Psychoactive drugs are chemical substances that affect consciousness, mood, or perception. Some of the more harmful ones, such as alcohol, tobacco, and barbiturates, do not draw the same intensity of societal criticism as do less harmful drugs like marijuana. All, however, can produce harmful effects, including life endangerment, if used excessively.

3. Many serious problems result from drug use: a profitable black market for organized crime; personal health problems; ruined careers; severe economic losses to individuals and businesses; and the harsh reality of thousands of deaths, millions of serious personal injuries, and billions of dollars in property damage from drug-related accidents.

4. Drug dependence takes a heavy toll on our personal and mental health. Drug abuse shortens the abuser's life, causing various health problems and often—in the case of amphetamines and excessive drinking—violence. Newborns often suffer birth defects or physiological addiction because of the mother's use of alcohol or narcotics. Drug abuse has infiltrated professional sports (shortening players' careers), and American business (costing about $125 billion annually in economic losses and medical bills).

5. Attempts at solutions have included both preventive and treatment efforts. Rehabilitation efforts, whether by self-help therapeutic communities or health clinics, have achieved limited success. Employing antagonistic drugs or corrective efforts has not been very effective. The Dutch model of categorizing drugs as dangerous or less dangerous, decriminalizing the latter and taking harm reduction steps with hard drug users offers a viable alternative model of drug policy and practice.

6. Drug use is widespread in U.S. society, but our values treat some drugs as respectable and others as a social problem. Functionalist analysis examines the medical, recreational, and therapeutic benefits of moderate drug use, as well as the dysfunctions resulting from value conflicts and the waste of human potential. Conflict analysis examines the clash of dominant-versus-minority moral values and scrutinizes special interest groups with self-serving motivations. Interactionist analysis stresses socialization, resocialization, and peer-group norms.

KEY TERMS

Antagonistic drug	Methadone maintenance
Depressant	Narcotics
Fetal alcohol syndrome	Psychoactive drug
Fetal narcotic syndrome	Second-hand smoke
Gateway drug	Therapeutic communities
"Heroin chic"	

INTERNET RESOURCES

At this book's Web site with Allyn & Bacon, you will find numerous links pertaining to the problems of alcohol and drug abuse. To explore these resources, go first to the author's page (**http://www.ablongman.com/parrillo**). Next, select this edition of *Contemporary Social Problems* and then choose **Internet Readings and Exercises**. Then select **Chapter 13,** where you will find both a variety of sites to investigate and some questions that pertain to those sites.

SUGGESTED READINGS

Barrows, Susanna, and Robin Room (eds.). *Drinking Behavior and Belief in Modern History*. Berkeley: University of California Press, 1991. An informative anthology of articles on historical and cross-cultural drinking patterns, from Puritans to modern Irishmen, and on past and present efforts to regulate alcohol consumption.

Currie, Elliot. *Reckoning: Drugs, Cities, and the American Future*. New York: Hill & Wang, 1994. Draws upon three decades of research to explain why drug use has reached epidemic proportions in U.S. inner cities and why the federal war on drugs has failed.

Ettore, Elizabeth. *Women and Substance Abuse*. New Brunswick, N.J.: Rutgers University Press, 1992. Helpful analysis of women's use and abuse of alcohol, barbituates, cocaine, heroin, and tobacco.

Goode, Erich. *Drugs in American Society*, 5th ed. New York: McGraw-Hill, 1998. A definitive sociological introduction to the issues of drug use and abuse, including an Interactionist view of attitudes toward various drugs.

Inciardi, James A. *The War on Drugs III: The Continuing Saga of the Mysteries and Miseries of Intoxification, Addiction, Crime, and Public Policy*. Boston: Allyn & Bacon, 2001. A candid view of the issues, history, and abuse patterns of the major drugs.

Males, Mike A. *Smoked: Why Joe Camel Is Still Smiling*. Monroe; Maine: Common Courage Press, 1999. This small book gives a disturbing insight into how the tobacco industry undermines the anti-smoking lobby.

Royce, James E., and David Scratchley. *Alcoholism and Other Drug Problems,* 2d ed. New York: Free Press, 1996. Offers a balanced and comprehensive account of the nature, causes, prevention, and treatment of alcoholism and the impact that addition can have on special groups such as children, minorities, and the elderly.

Sandmaier, Marian. *The Invisible Alcoholics: Women and Alcohol*. 2nd ed. New York: Human Services Institue, 1992. Revealing portrait of an often-ignored dimension of alcoholism: problem drinking by women of all ages and backgrounds.

Streatfeild, Dominic. *Cocaine: An Unauthorized Biography*. New York: Picador, 2003. A fascinating, highly readable history of cocaine use and the current scene, with detail no other book can match.

Szasz, Thomas S. *Ceremonial Chemistry: The Ritual Persecution of Drugs, Addicts, and Pushers,* rev. ed. Syracuse: Syracuse University Press, 2003. An intriguing best seller in which the author examines the negative consequences of our nation's anti-drug crusades.

Wright, James D., and Joel A. Devine. *Drugs as a Social Problem*. New York: HarperCollins, 1994. Provides a detailed examination of substance abuse in the United States and the social and/or economic consequences in families, schools, the workplace, and society.

14

Sexual Behavior

Facts About Sexual Behavior

- By age sixteen almost half of all teenagers are no longer virgins.

- Seventy-five percent of husbands and 85 percent of wives maintain that they have never been unfaithful to their spouses.

- In 1994, 71 percent of men said it was difficult to have sex without emotional involvement, up from 59 percent in 1984.

- About one in five Americans carry some type of sexually transmitted disease, many without knowing it.

- Over 10,000 Web sites are devoted to various forms of pornography.

- About a half-million prostitutes ply their trade in the United States.

- From 11 to 38 percent of girls and from 3 to 17 percent of boys are victims of sexual abuse as children.

Sexual behavior varies greatly among human beings because cultural norms shape how members of a society may acceptably express their sex drive. In no society is the number or type of sex objects (people who can be "legitimately" desired) or the form of sexual activity left entirely up to the individual. All societies—either by strictly held mores or by law—forbid sexual contact with certain individuals, as well as some types of sexual behavior. However, some societies are sexually permissive, allowing a broad range of sexual expression and making getting a divorce easy, while other societies are sexually restrictive, exercising more control over acceptable patterns of sexual behavior and divorce.

Two of the most widely disapproved forms of sexual behavior anywhere are incest (sex between close family kin) and sex between an adult and a child (typically defined as abusive exploitation, even if the child is a prostitute). Yet despite almost universal condemnation, an estimated 300,000 child prostitutes sell their bodies in the United States, according to the United Nations Children's Fund (UNICEF), and globally about 1 million children enter the sex trade each year.[1] Moreover, cases of child molestation and sexual abuse seem to occur more frequently now than ever before. Adult prostitution, the "world's oldest profession," continues to draw moral outrage, yet it remains commonplace in the United States and has increased rapidly worldwide in recent years, particularly in Africa, Asia, Eastern Europe, and Latin America. Pornography remains a multibillion-dollar industry and continues to grow, thanks in part to the Internet and VCRs.

These forms of sexual behavior and others—casual sex, premarital and extramarital sex, unmarried couples living together—offer examples of changing social definitions or growing social problems that merit our attention. Without dwelling on the moral aspects of this subject (which falls outside the sociological discipline), we will examine its various social aspects.

The Cross-Cultural Context

As suggested in the first sentence of this chapter, norms governing acceptable sexual behavior vary enormously over time and place. What passes for conforming to social norms in one society may constitute deviant behavior in another. In Western civilization, for example, kissing and touching a woman's breasts are natural forms of sexual expression. In many other cultures, however, people feel no erotic attraction to breasts and view kissing them as disgusting.

Sexual norms in the United States can in part be traced back to the Old Testament, which placed severe restrictions on any sexual contact outside heterosexual marriage. At one point Westerners defined the only "normal" sexual position during intercourse as lying down face to face, with the man on top. In 1948, Alfred Kinsey's trailblazing study of sexual behavior revealed that 70 percent of Americans had never tried any other position.[2] People in many other societies found this practice strange, however: only 17 of 131 societies studied at that time used this position by custom or preference.[3] Nineteenth-century Pacific Islander women, after having sex with visiting U.S. missionaries, laughingly called it the "missionary position."

Past and Preliterate Societies

Even sexual acts that our society considers the most deviant have been viewed by people in other places and times as normal forms of sexual expression. In some societies, for example, rape was all women's first sexual experience.[4] Among the Yanomamo Indians, a woman from another tribe captured in battle was gang-raped, first by her captors and then by the men waiting in the village for the return of the war party.[5] No one considered these acts to be war crimes, nor did anyone define them as deviant acts of brutality.

Many ancient Western civilizations regarded incest, the most universally condemned of all sexual practices, as perfectly natural for their gods. Similarly, Japanese mythology tells the story of Izanagi and Izanami, a brother and sister who, as creators of the world, invented many things, including sexual intercourse.[6] Furthermore, among the ancient Egyptians and royal Hawaiians, brother married sister to secure rule over the people.

Social Control of Sexual Intercourse

In virtually all societies, marital intercourse accounts for most of the sexual activity adults engage in. Roughly two-fifths to one-half of all preliterate societies studied allowed females to have premarital sex. This percentage rises to about 70 percent if we include societies that do not consider premarital sex an important deviation. In almost all societies, men have more freedom than women in this area.[7] (See the box on the next page.)

In all societies, once a marriage takes place, different sanctions, or rules, apply. These may be so strict and so firmly enforced that sexual activity with anyone other than the spouse is punishable by execution, as in many Islamic countries. Other societies forbid extramarital intercourse in general but allow such intercourse at certain ceremonies or festivals. For example, wife lending among certain specified individuals may be included in the marriage ceremony. And among the Inuit peoples of central Alaska and the Bahimas of East Africa, a man was deemed a poor host if he did not share his wife with his overnight guest.[8]

Changing U.S. Patterns of Sexual Behavior

Until the 1960s, most Americans professed conservative views about sexual behavior. In reality, a sexual revolution began during the "Roaring Twenties" but remained unacknowledged by mainstream society for several decades. To be sure, all forms of sexual behavior—more so in cities, perhaps—took place in each generation, but the norm among most Americans was to have sex only within the confines of marriage and, even then, mostly (as Kinsey discovered) in one way.

In the United States in the mid-1960s, many youths and young adults began a pattern of experimenting with casual sex, taking their cue from the "free love" doctrine of the hippies. This pattern persisted for nearly twenty years until health concerns about AIDS and other social realities prompted its decline. Having many sexual partners ceased to be a mark of freedom and adventure. Not only did such behavior violate traditional values, which enjoyed a resurgence, but it also seemed foolish and dangerous. As a result, casual sex gave way to sexual caution and a linking of sex with commitment.[9]

For many people, the so-called sexual revolution led to feelings of humiliation. Sexual partners never "called back" and offered no real personal connection. For others, sheer boredom slowed their activities. In addition, as they neared forty, those who began the "revolution" felt more inclined to look for the rewards provided by stable careers and family life. Whether or not marriage was the goal, people wanted more commitment.

Women once placed more importance on the emotional aspects of sex than did men, but the situation has apparently changed. A 1994 major national study found that 86 percent of women

The Globalization of Social Problems

Genital Mutilation and Female Sexuality

Today, like most days, about 6,000 girls will spread their legs for a surgical operation (often not performed by a doctor). If they are lucky, only their clitoris will be cut off. If not, someone will remove all their visible genitals, then stitch the residue together, perhaps with thorn. And it will be their mothers, grandmothers, female neighbors, or friends who urge them to lie back and think of traditional culture as they undergo what is known as female circumcision, or, more truthfully, female genital mutilation (FGM). The procedure is commonly performed upon girls anywhere between the ages of four and twelve as a rite of passage. In some cultures, it is practiced as early as a few days after birth and as late as just before marriage or after the first pregnancy.

Female genital mutilation, practiced chiefly in countries with large Muslim populations, has damaged as many as 140 million women all over the world. Prevalence varies significantly from one country to another. For example, the prevalence rate is 98 percent in Somalia and 90 percent in Mali, compared to 20 percent in Senegal. The practice, usually done by female relatives, occurs in twenty-eight African countries, some Asian countries, and immigrant-receiving countries, including in North America, Europe, Australia, and New Zealand. Each year an estimated 2 million additional females are at risk of undergoing FGM.

According to a 1997 U.S. State Department report, FGM is generally performed without the aid of anesthesia, particularly in villages. Unsterilized razors, pieces of glass, knives, and sharp stones may be used on one girl after another, risking the transmission of infections, including AIDS. Girls who struggle violently have often had bones broken as others attempted to hold them still, the report said.

Although defended as a religious practice, FGM lacks Koranic or biblical backing and is not practiced in much of the Middle East and such Islamic countries as Bangladesh, Pakistan, Indonesia, and Malaysia. The tradition, which predates Islam and Christianity, is fundamentally a cultural method that men use to exert power over women's sexuality, to keep them chaste until marriage and faithful thereafter. Without some form of circumcision, argue its mostly African Muslim proponents, women will be wracked with sexual desire. So instead, they must risk infection, abscesses, gangrene, infertility, painful sex, difficult childbirth, even death from FGM.

Because tens of thousands of African immigrants come to the United States, FGM has come with them. The U.S. Department of Health and Human Services estimated in 1998 that 160,000 girls and women in the U.S. immigrant community have submitted to the procedure or are at risk of being subjected to it, although it cautioned that no field surveys had been done to confirm that statistic.

In 1996—responding to a celebrated case of a teenage girl from Togo seeking asylum in the United States to escape the genital mutilation rite—Congress outlawed the rite of female genital cutting in the United States. It directed federal authorities to inform new immigrants from countries where FGM is commonly practiced that parents who arrange for their children to be cut here, as well as people who perform the cutting, face up to five years in prison. The legislation also directs U.S. representatives to the World Bank—and to other international financial institutions that have lent billions of dollars to the twenty-eight African countries where the practice exists—to oppose loans to governments that have not carried out educational programs to prevent it.

The Globalization of Social Problems (continued)

In 2002, over 190 countries reached agreement on preventing female circumcision. Whether this action is strong enough to overcome the view in many traditional cultures that this is an essential rite of passage to womanhood, remains to be seen.

Source: World Health Organization, *Female Genital Mutilation,* Fact Sheet No. 241. Available at: http://www.who.int/inf-fs/en/fact241.html [July 13, 2003].

said it would be difficult to have sex without emotional involvement, a percentage that remained unchanged since 1984. The dramatic change appeared in men, among whom the percentage increased from 59 to 71 percent during the same period. Put differently, the percent of men *not* finding it difficult to have casual sex fell from 41 to 29 percent.[10]

Casual sex behavior in the United States, though, as measured by number of sex partners, exceeds that in Britain and France, but not Finland, according to a recent study shown in Table 14.1 on the next page. Of the four countries surveyed, France has the highest percentage of women who have had only one sex partner (46 percent), and Finland has the lowest (28 percent). The United States ranks second lowest with 31 percent. The United States is also closer to Finland at

What is the social construction of "love" in Western cultures? For example, what meanings does this kiss convey? How might this behavior be viewed in relation to the social norms in other countries? In what other ways might the public expression of affection or sexual interest vary over time and place?

Table 14.1   Sex Abroad: Lifetime Total Number of Sex Partners by Percent

	One Partner		Five or More Partners	
	Male	Female	Male	Female
Britain	21%	39%	44%	20%
France	21%	46%	45%	14%
Finland	12%	28%	60%	34%
United States	20%	31%	56%	30%

Source: Robert T. Michael, John H. Gagnon, Edward O. Laumann, and Gina Kolata, *Sex in America: A Definitive Survey* (Boston: Little, Brown, 1994).

the other extreme: 30 percent of American women have had five or more sex partners. In all four of the countries studied, the typical man had more sex partners than the typical woman. And contrary to the stereotype of the suave, libertine French male, Finland—not France—reported the highest percentage of men who have had five or more sex partners.

Premarital Sex

Prior to the 1960s, the topic of premarital sex drew attention as a form of deviant behavior to be explored and explained. Society defined sexual intimacy as appropriate behavior only within the marital union. Since then, sexual mores have changed so much that most people now have sex at an earlier age than their parents did, and premarital sex is the norm. Among ever-married women fifteen to forty-four years of age, 82 percent had first intercourse before they were married. The changing trend becomes more apparent when we compare those who married in 1965–1974 and those who married in the 1990s. Only 2 percent of those in the first group had their first intercourse five or more years before marriage compared to 56 percent of those in the second group.[11]

The increase in premarital sex includes adolescents. Despite a decline in teen pregnancies, at every stage of adolescence there is greater sexual activity than thirty years ago. Also, more teenagers have sex at an earlier age. Research shows that the average age of first sexual intercourse has dropped by a full year (from eighteen to seventeen for girls, from seventeen to sixteen for boys), and one-fifth of all fifteen-year-olds have had sex at least once.[12] One study showed that 31 percent of adolescents in the United States had intercourse by age fifteen in 1995, up from 25 percent in 1980, and the 2001 Youth Risk Behavior Survey, a national student poll by the Centers for Disease Control and Prevention, reported that 5 percent of high school students had intercourse before age thirteen.[13] Still another government study said that about 12 percent of males and 3 percent of females aged eighteen to twenty-one reported they had sexual intercourse by age twelve.[14]

Besides an earlier age for teen sexual activity, health professionals report another trend. An increasing number of girls in the sixth, seventh, and eighth grades admit to "hooking up" (the "in" term for oral sex and other intimate contact) at parties with people they often hardly know.

While some teens say they have pressure to do it and others are judgmental about their friends who do it, many openly admit that they had sex just for the experience. Specialists in adolescent medicine say that one reason that some young teenagers have oral sex is that they think of it as "safe" because it cannot lead to pregnancy nor spread sexually transmitted diseases (**STDs**). In fact, those diseases can be spread this way. Some teenagers also falsely assume that sexual experiences other than intercourse have little consequence emotionally, but experts say such activity does impact negatively on self-esteem and emotional development.[15]

The Center of Media and Public Affairs in Washington thinks the increase in sexual imagery in popular entertainment is a contributing factor to greater teen sexual activity. In a comprehensive 2000 study, it found that: (1) broadcast TV shows averaged a sex scene every four minutes, while cable TV shows averaged a sex scene every five minutes; (2) MTV's music videos averaged ninety-three sex scenes per hour; and (3) the popular teen movie, "There's Something About Mary," had fifty-three sex scenes. The Parents Television Council (PTC) also disclosed that TV references to sex proliferated between 1989 and 1999, from thirty-six references to sex in nearly 181 hours of programming to 342 references in nearly 236 hours of programming, including twenty references to oral sex, a previously taboo subject on television.[16]

When young people postpone sexual intimacy, their reasons are less likely to involve societal disapproval than other concerns. By age sixteen almost half of all teenagers are no longer vir-

The high percentage of sexual activity among teenagers and of sexually transmitted diseases and AIDS, has prompted many high schools to offer sex education classes. Some parents object, saying that schools are usurping their role to instill moral guidance and that safe sex instruction encourages promiscuity. Who do you think should assume responsibility for teaching about sex? Why?

gins. Among the 20 percent of nineteen-year-olds who are still virgins, 80 percent cited fear of contracting AIDS or a STD as a major factor in their abstinence. Less than 40 percent mentioned moral or religious reasons.[17] Teens, particularly girls, are also less likely to have sex than are less religious teens, largely because their religious views lead them to view the consequences of having sex negatively.[18]

Two factors appear to have encouraged the increase in premarital sex: first, inexpensive, effective contraception became legal and widely available; and second, the age at which people entered their first marriages rose dramatically. These two trends reinforced one another, further supported by the influence of increasingly daring movies and television programs.[19]

Because premarital sex was uncommon prior to the 1960s, society viewed it as an individual problem, not a social problem. Now that premarital sex is the norm, it remains undefined as a social problem in and of itself, except on moral grounds. Its potential after-effects, however—teenage pregnancies, abortions, unwed mothers, single-parent families, welfare costs, and disease—are indeed regarded as social problems.

Extramarital Sex

Adultery may be an even older vice than prostitution, for we find reports of its existence among many ancient civilizations. Today, we also find many records of its practice, often in divorce proceedings. Although many Americans believe that extramarital affairs are common, 80 percent of Americans believe it is always wrong and another 18 percent think it is often wrong.[20] Recent studies reveal that 75 percent of husbands and 85 percent of wives claim never to have been unfaithful to their spouses, and over 90 percent report having had sex only with their spouse in the previous year. The real world certainly differs from the soap-opera world![21]

George Sponaugle summarized the variables reported in various research studies involving instances where extramarital sex does occur.[22] Among the most common predictor variables for extramarital intercourse were approval of premarital sex, lower marital satisfaction, less religiosity, living in a larger community, endorsement of gender equality, perceived opportunity, less satisfaction with marital sex, sociopolitical liberalism, and childlessness.

Safe Sex

Safe sex is a relatively new term that broadly means physical sexual intimacy without any exchange of body fluids. This practice, a precaution against contracting HIV and other STDs, has entailed increased use of condoms in both the homosexual and heterosexual communities. Just a generation ago, the condom functioned as a "health device" to protect against the raging STDs of that time. When the two primary venereal diseases, syphilis and gonorrhea, became "curable," the definition of the condom as a health device faded. Today's advertising campaigns again stress that the condom is the only way to ensure "safe" sex. Perhaps the harshest reality about unsafe sex, given that the AIDS virus may not manifest itself for seven or more years, is that you are in effect sleeping with everyone your sex partner has slept with during those past years. A single sexual encounter can infect a person with as many as five different diseases (see the accompanying box).

Social Constructions of Social Problems

Sex Scourges: An Old Social Problem

About 3,000 years ago, the Hebrew soldiers returned home after defeating the Midianites and brought with them thousands of captive women. The rapid spread of sexually transmitted diseases (STDs) caused Moses to condemn "every woman that hath known man by lying with him," and to label the problem "a plague among the congregation." His solution was to impose a one-week quarantine.

Centuries passed and many other sex plagues occurred. Some scholars cite ancient and medieval sources as evidence for syphilis in Europe before Columbus, but none of the descriptions by Greek and Roman authors are specific enough to be certain. Returning crusaders brought "Saracen ointment" containing mercury for treating "lepers," an appropriate medication for syphilis but not for leprosy. Thirteenth- and fourteenth-century references to "venereal leprosy" may also indicate syphilis, because leprosy is not sexually transmitted. However, the first unambiguous descriptions of syphilis appeared around 1500. These may either reflect growing medical knowledge and ability to differentiate syphilis from other diseases or else signal its arrival from the New World. The truth still remains in dispute.

Some say Columbus's crew brought syphilis back from the Americas. Some say that it was already present in Europe, but that something happened to convert a benign infection into a highly virulent one by 1495. In that year, after the troops of Charles VIII of France were decimated by syphilis following the capture of Naples, many called it the Neapolitan disease. Prior to the defeat of Naples, Spanish mercenaries in the employ of Alphonso II occupied the city, and it is they who reportedly brought syphilis to Naples from Barcelona; thus the Italians called it the Spanish disease. Each country named it after the country from whence it came—the English called it the French pox, Poles called it the *mal*

des Allemands, and the Russians the *mal Polonais.* It reached Scotland in 1497, India (with Vasco da Gama) in 1498, and from there Chinese junks took it to Canton in 1505. Thus in ten years syphilis had circled the known world, as AIDS did later.

Popes, kings, and queens have suffered from STDs. City populations, armies, and navies have often become infected. Ivan IV, a seemingly enlightened ruler in sixteenth-century Russia, contracted syphilis and degenerated into the infamous Ivan the Terrible. Another despot, Adolf Hitler, also had the disease, as did the twentieth-century American gangster, Al Capone.

Over the years countless cures have been tried. In the fifteenth century, German men thought that frequent use of the public bathhouses would eliminate syphilis. However, nude women did the scrubbing, leading to sexual liaisons and the further spread of the disease. At the beginning of the twentieth century, Americans relied mostly on alcohol-based quack remedies, since physicians did not have any real cure for STDs. Many physicians, in fact, believed that treating sex diseases tacitly condoned sinful living, so they ignored the problem altogether.

Because of the close connection between war, sex, and venereal disease, military literature offers some interesting information about measures used for STD control. For example, in response to the alarming rate of STDs in the British army and navy, the Contagious Diseases Act of 1866 mandated the examination and treatment of suspected prostitutes in garrison and seaport towns. Thousands of women (including Florence Nightingale) then successfully campaigned for the repeal of the Act on the grounds that: (1) as the Queen's subjects, prostitutes had certain constitutional rights; and (2) public health would not be improved by making them alone, of all British subjects, liable to arbitrary

(continued)

Social Constructions of Social Problems (continued)

arrest, examination, and detention. Recent objections to the use of compulsory HIV testing are very reminiscent of this episode. Similarly, just as people viewed syphilis a few hundred years ago as a manifestation of the wrath of God, so, too, do many people today consider AIDS to be God's punishment for immoral sexual behavior, even though other causes (such as multiple needle use) exist.

In 1938, Congress appropriated funds to support state programs to control venereal disease (VD). Shortly thereafter, every state required a blood test to check for VD before issuing a marriage license. The 1940s saw a concerted effort to wipe out VD, aided greatly by the discovery of penicillin in 1944. Though effective, the campaign never completely succeeded, and STDs remain a problem. AIDS (or more accurately, HIV) is the newest STD in a 3,000-year history of sexual scourges.

Source: Partly based on remarks by Richard Travers, "Of Epidemics in General," in an introduction to an AIDS Exhibition at Monash University, Australia, on March 19, 1998, and various other sources.

The sexual scourge is a real problem. Each year an estimated 13 million Americans contract a sexually transmitted disease, with about one-fourth of the new cases occurring in teenagers (see Figure 14.1). Health experts estimate that about one in five Americans carries some type of sexually transmitted disease, many without knowing it. As a result, more than two-thirds of infections are spread by people who have no visible symptoms. One STD—HIV—is especially deadly; two others cause cancer; and four can cause infertility in women. Obviously, the health risks and widespread prevalence of STDs are ample cause for concern.[23]

STDs affect men and women of all backgrounds and economic levels, with almost two-thirds occurring in people under age twenty-five. A conservative estimate predicts that STDs will affect one in four sexually active Americans at some time. The most common STDs on college campuses include chlamydia, genital herpes, and genital warts. Unfortunately, some sexually transmitted diseases cause no symptoms. For example, it is estimated that 50 percent of the male population and 75 percent of the female population who are infected with chlamydia experience no symptoms but it can cause severe reproductive problems, including infertility. You can be infected and unknowingly transmit a disease.[24]

Figure 14.1   New U.S. Cases of Sexually Transmitted Diseases, 2002

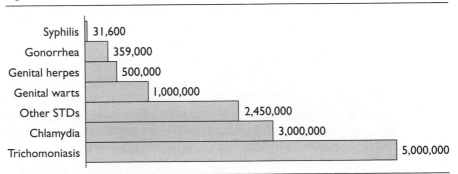

Source: Centers for Disease Control and Prevention.

STDs cause physical and emotional suffering to millions and are costly to individuals and to society as a whole. Sometimes people are too embarrassed or frightened to ask for help or information, even though most STDs are readily treated. The earlier a person seeks treatment and warns sex partners about the disease, the less likely the disease will be spread to others and/or do irreparable physical damage. The most obvious outcome of nontreatment for an STD is its transmission to one's sexual partner(s). Other consequences include continued uncomfortable symptoms, development of precancerous conditions, serious infection and possible damage of the reproductive organs, infertility, transmission of the disease to a baby during childbirth, heart disease, brain damage, blindness, and death.

Pornography

What, exactly, is pornography? As in many other areas identified as social problems, the definition varies according to time and place. Some observers would call any spoken, written, or visual presentation of sexual interaction or genitals pornographic, but artifacts from historic and prehistoric cultures depicting genitals or sexual interaction sometimes reveal a deeply religious basis celebrating life and fertility, as in the case of the bas-relief sculptures adorning many ancient temples. Such examples take us beyond conventional notions of moral and immoral subject matter, or conservative and liberal attitudes, to another insight into the importance of social definitions.

Even defining pornography in contemporary U.S. society is difficult, as presidential commissions, Supreme Court justices, and many others have discovered. Feminist Kate Millett suggests making a distinction between **eroticism** (the vivid depiction of sexual passion and love) and **pornography** (the depiction of brutal sexual behavior resulting in female or male dehumanization, degradation, and exploitation).[25] Even this distinction, however, can create a problem. For example, Arab culture has traditionally drawn a clear distinction between the erotic and the pornographic in literature, but not in the visual arts. Thus Arabs would consider the highly valued erotic poetry of Ka'b ibn Zuhayr and Hassan ibn Thabit pornographic if it were represented in the visual arts.[26]

Over the years, courts have repeatedly, without success, attempted to formulate an acceptable definition of pornography. U.S. Supreme Court responses ranged from vaguely defining obscenity (the legal term for pornography) as material that has "no redeeming social value" and is designed to appeal to "prurient" interests, to declining to define obscenity at all, and instead delegating the task to local communities. Even then, it needed to clarify in 1987 that judges and juries must determine the legality of sexually explicit material by assessing its social value from the viewpoint of a "reasonable person," thus indicating that extreme libertine or puritanical views cannot serve as valid criteria. But who or what is a reasonable person? Because that question is so difficult to answer, no agreement exists as to what constitutes pornography; and statutes and enforcement vary from place to place. One main argument against censoring pornography is that censorship violates the constitutional right to free speech. Critics argue that the whole purpose of the First Amendment is to protect unpopular ideas and forms of expression from suppression by an offended or antagonized majority.

The Victims of Pornography

Unlike erotica, pornography—in Millett's sense—is actually less about sex than about the degradation of women and children through sex.[27] By depersonalizing sex and objectifying women, most pornography depicts women sexually accessible, wanting to be taken and used, enjoying sex even if they first resist, and being bound, humiliated, raped, tortured, defiled, and dehumanized. Susan Brownmiller sums up the attitude of many women toward such pornography:

> The gut distaste that a majority of women feel when we look at pornography . . . comes, I think from the gut knowledge that we and our bodies are being stripped, exposed, and contorted for the purpose of ridicule to bolster that "masculine esteem" which gets its kicks and sense of power from viewing females as anonymous, panting playthings, adult toys, dehumanized objects to be used, abused, broken and discarded.[28]

With the advent of VCRs, the sale of sexually explicit materials skyrocketed, once the curious discovered they could watch erotica in the privacy of their home. Americans who rented 75 million hard-core videos in 1985, rented 686 million "adult" tapes in 1998. In 1990, 1,275 hard-core videos hit the U.S. retail market, but that number zoomed to 11,000 by 2003. Nearly 14 percent of all video transactions and more than one-fourth of all pay-per-view home viewings are pornographic. Americans now spend more than $10 billion a year on hard-core videos, peep shows, live sex acts, sexual devices, adult cable programming, computer porn, telephone

Found in urban locales and on highways throughout the country, sex shops offer a wide array of provocative lingerie, lotions, magazines, sexual paraphernalia, and adult videos. Mail order and Internet businesses trading in pornography continue to flourish as global moneymakers. In what ways is pornography a social problem? To what other social problems does pornography contribute?

sex, and sex magazines—more than they spend on Hollywood movies or on music recordings. Americans also now spend more money at strip clubs than at all Broadway, off-Broadway and regional, nonprofit theaters, as well as at opera, ballet, and jazz and classical music performances combined.[29]

A survey of readers of *Redbook*—a mainstream family magazine—may best illustrate the pervasiveness of pornography among Americans; almost half reported that they regularly watched pornographic movies in the privacy of their homes. Moreover, most of the businesses earning profits from porn today are not those typically associated with the sex industry; they are mom-and-pop video stores, long-distance telecommunications giants like AT&T, cable companies like TCI and Time-Warner, and hotel chains like Marriott, Hyatt, and Holiday Inn, which make millions of dollars each year supplying adult films to their guests.[30]

One area where the debate over pornography receives little argument about its wrongness is the use of children in the production of pornographic photo books, films, and videos. No one knows or can even estimate the number of children exploited this way. However, the prevalence of materials involving children in adult porn stores, or confiscated by police in raids on homes of pedophiles and members of child sex rings, gives some indication of the extent of this social problem. Although child pornography constitutes only a small portion of the pornography industry, it draws the strongest condemnation from the public.

Pornography and Violence

One major point of contention in the debate over pornography is whether pornography incites men to act violently toward women. In 1970, President Nixon's Commission on Obscenity and Pornography concluded that no causal relationship existed between exposure to pornography and subsequent sexual aggression against women.[31] In 1986, however, Attorney-General Edwin Meese's Commission on Pornography decided that violent pornography "bears a causal relationship to sexual violence."[32]

Edward Donnerstein and Daniel Linz, two social scientists quoted throughout the 1986 report, disassociated themselves from its conclusions, calling the report flawed because it failed to recognize that X-rated material is not alone in portraying women as enjoying men overpowering them. Indeed, society promotes this dangerous image in many ways. As Donnerstein and Linz put it, "The most clear and present danger, well documented by the social science literature is that all violent material in our society, whether sexually explicit or not, is what promotes violence against women."[33]

Why such different conclusions from two national commissions? Part of the answer may lie in the difficulty of defining what constitutes pornography. Differences in the membership of the two commissions and changes in pornographic materials during the fifteen-year interval offer other insights. Reagan-era conservatives and law enforcement officials dominated the second commission and took a more traditionalist, family values–oriented view of pornography and its effects than had the civil libertarians and liberals who dominated the first commission. Moreover, new technologies—providing fairly inexpensive home video cameras and VCRs—increased the ease of making and viewing pornographic features, in turn generating more hard-core materials.

Debate over the connection between pornography and violence continues. During hearings before passage of the Pornography Victims Compensation Act of 1992, members of the Senate Committee on the Judiciary heard testimony that research gathered over the past few decades demonstrates pornography contributes to sexual assault, including rape and the molestation of children.[34] In *Pornography: Women, Violence, and Civil Liberties* (1993), Catherine Itzin offered a comprehensive review of research to argue that pornography has a profound harmful effect on women *and* men, and provided an invaluable introduction to new Feminist thinking.[35] A 1998 study of U.S. abused women found a significant correlation between their partners' violence against them and the abusers' use of pornography.[36] In contrast, one research team found that attitudes toward pornography were unrelated to attitudes toward rape, while other researchers found increased rates of rape associated with a *decline* in pornography consumption.[37] Moreover, some Feminists defend pornography as one means out of many that women freely choose to enjoy sexual relations.[38]

Pornography and the Internet

The Internet has opened another avenue of easy access to pornographic materials, with over 4.2 million sites (12 percent) on the Internet devoted to various forms of pornography.[39] Alarmed that minors could access cybersmut from a home computer, parents, civic groups, and legislators united to urge passage of the Communications Decency Act (CDA). Enacted in 1996, the CDA forbade putting online, where children might see it, not just obscene or pornographic material, but any "indecent" word or image—a prohibition so vague that it might even criminalize an AIDS-awareness lesson.[40] Immediately, a coalition of Internet users, computer industry groups, and civil libertarians challenged the law's constitutionality on grounds that it restricted free speech in cyberspace.

By the time the U.S. Supreme Court ruled on the case in mid-1997, at least seventeen states had passed or were considering their own legislation to regulate the Net. The court unanimously declared the CDA unconstitutional and held that free speech on the Internet is entitled to the highest level of First Amendment protection, similar to that given to books and newspapers. Although the justices sympathized with the goal to protect children from pornographic material, they ruled that "encouraging freedom of expression in a democratic society" outweighed "any unproven benefit of censorship."[41]

As a result, parents must do the censoring, either by using the parental control options that on-line companies provide or by securing filter software such as Cyber Patrol, Surf Watch, or Net Shepherd that can block Web sites with explicit materials.

International Comparisons

The World Wide Web, of course, is just that, enabling anyone to access Web sites anywhere. In cyberspace no distance separates a Web site and the viewer. From Los Angeles, it takes just as long to look at a picture stored on a computer in Japan as to view one housed in New York or Amsterdam. People in any country can visit the same sexually explicit Web sites. The universality of cyberporn makes government restrictions almost impossible except as practiced by authoritarian governments like China, Singapore, and Vietnam, which control the physical infrastructure of local Internet connections to maintain access restrictions.[42]

Sexually explicit material is available in adults-only stores in the United States, most European countries, and Israel. Long-term follow-up studies of the effects of the legalization of sexually explicit film and print products have revealed no negative consequences and possibly even some positive consequences. For example, in Denmark the public appeared to lose interest in such materials once they became widely available.[43]

Prostitution

Prostitution is the act of selling sexual favors for money or goods. In existence since the beginning of recorded history, it continues to thrive almost everywhere. As many as 500,000 prostitutes ply their trade today in the United States, and millions more work throughout the world.[44] Most prostitutes (or sex workers, as many now call themselves) are female, but some are male; both genders serve a mostly male clientele.

In numerous ancient societies (Egyptian, Greek, Roman, Middle Eastern, and Far Eastern, to name a few), prostitutes enjoyed a highly respected status; they moved freely in artistic and political social circles and were part of religious rituals in the temples. Today, however, prostitutes hold

These young girls working in a brothel can be bought on the street and sexually abused or enslaved. Are they "sex workers" or victims? What makes prostitution a social problem on an international scale? Is the sexual abuse of children, even in their own homes, on the increase, and, if so, why? To what extent and in what ways does the Internet potentially contribute to social problems relating to sexual behavior?

a low social status in society, although high-priced call girls and call boys clearly enjoy a higher status than brothel prostitutes or streetwalkers.

Brothels are an old institution, as anyone knows who saw the musical about ancient Rome called *A Funny Thing Happened on the Way to the Forum.* Today, legal brothels exist in parts of Nevada, Europe, and Asia. Not only are such houses far from new, they have not been limited to heterosexuals. For example, during the eighteenth century, a male homosexual club called "Mollies" gathered to dress in women's clothes, drink, and party. Houses of homosexual prostitution thus became known as "molly houses." One of the most famous, located in a popular English resort, was run by Margaret Clap, known as Mother Clap.[45] Her name survives today in the slang term for a form of sexually transmitted disease.

The Sexual Career of a Prostitute

In the United States a small number of people, perhaps no more than 4 percent of all sex workers, are forced into prostitution.[46] Of interest to sociologists then, are two issues. What social factors motivate so many others to enter a trade that society deems degrading and unacceptable, and what social processes lead a person to become a professional prostitute? Although no causal relationship exists between any variable and individuals becoming prostitutes, several background commonalities exist among persons who sell their bodies.

Poverty

This is the single most important factor motivating women to become prostitutes, concluded Eleanor Miller after her field research on streetwalkers. Poor women are far more likely to enter this line of work than affluent women.[47] Similarly, T. M. Williams and William Kornblum found that teenage girls, living in impoverished communities in four U.S. cities where prostitutes were a visible presence, viewed part-time prostitution as a means to make money for clothes and entertainment.[48]

Experiencing Sexual Abuse as a Child

Early sexual abuse is a second commonly shared trait among prostitutes. Researchers have typically found that more than half their interviewees had been raped as children or otherwise sexually victimized. Such experiences may affect the victims' self-esteem, lessening their resistance to self-identification as a "saleable commodity."[49]

Dysfunctional Families

Another contributing factor linked with prostitution is family instability. Several researchers determined that female prostitutes frequently emerge from broken homes or dysfunctional families; experience alienation from parents or outright hostility toward fathers; and/or feel friendless, misunderstood, or unwanted.[50] Studies of male prostitutes reveal similar patterns. Many also experienced physical and/or sexual abuse in unstable or foster families. In addition, gay prostitutes are often runaways or "push-outs" from families where conflict over their sexual orientation became too much of a hassle.[51]

Juvenile Delinquency

This shows a high correlation with prostitution, too. Often, prostitutes reported to interviewers that, in their childhood, family and teachers viewed them as "bad" or "troublemakers." Involvement in juvenile gangs helped perpetuate this early negative labeling and led to further deviant behavior. In thirty in-depth interviews of prostitutes, Nanette Davis learned that, as adolescents, twenty-three of the women had spent time in correctional facilities for various delinquency charges. There they encountered prostitute inmates whose occupation seemed attractive and prestigious to these alienated girls, who were typically confused about their own identities and therefore susceptible to learning a new role.[52]

Differential Association

Social relationships oriented toward particular types of people—termed **differential association**—also play a role.[53] Potential recruits learn positive attitudes about prostitution as a way to make "easy money" from friends, relatives, other prostitutes, or pimps who convince them to "turn out" into a life of prostitution. These direct influences into a deviant lifestyle appear critical both in initiating recruits into the business and developing their clientele.[54]

Drug Use

Particularly among street prostitutes, drug use is fairly common. Not all prostitutes are drug addicts, but those who are sell their sexual favors to get money to buy drugs. One study found that almost two out of every three male prostitutes and nine out of every ten female prostitutes had used drugs other than alcohol and tobacco in the preceding year.[55] Even though some of these prostitutes may have been occasional, not regular, users, this high ratio suggests that a much more severe drug problem exists among them than in workers in most other occupational endeavors. Moreover, intravenous drug users are susceptible to the AIDS virus. In some U.S. cities, 20 to 40 percent of the prostitutes are HIV-positive, either from having taken drugs intravenously themselves with an infected needle or from having had unprotected sex with men who did. The dangers of their spreading the disease further are obvious.[56]

And what about the male clients? What motivates men to visit prostitutes instead of seeking a partner through socially approved means? Analysts suggest that the six most common reasons are as follows: sex without negotiation; involvement without commitment; sex for eroticism and variety; a form of socializing; sex when away from home; and sex without risk of rejection.[57]

The Process of Becoming a Prostitute

Becoming a professional prostitute involves more than just deciding to suspend morality and "do what comes naturally" for money. From interviews with imprisoned prostitutes, Nanette Davis identified a three-stage process through which the women progressed, from casual sex through a transitional stage to final professionalization as a prostitute.[58] The critical point in this evolution, Davis concluded, is the woman's self-definition as a person who is no longer bound by societal norms and values and who is thus free to behave accordingly.

The first stage involves drifting from casual sex to the first act of prostitution, a process that usually happens in a person's mid- to late teens, typically after several years of casual sex. "Pick-up" sex often initiates this stage, reinforced by peer group expectations about early sexuality as a way to get excitement and male attention. When the "kicks" from these experiences fade, the incentive shifts from adventure to making a profit.

During the second stage of transitional deviance, the individual usually engages in prostitution as a part-time activity, with economic need—and perhaps also loneliness or entrapment by the pimp—serving as motivation. Self-definition remains mostly in the conventional world, as the individual maintains social ties with the straight world, possibly including a job and marriage. During this transitional period the person finds out whether he or she can (1) accept fulfilling a broad range of client requests, including some that seem very odd; (2) learn to adapt to police surveillance and entrapment procedures; (3) handle clients who are unable to pay; and (4) substitute a business ethic for previous motivations. A person who cannot adjust to all these conditions is likely to remain an occasional or part-time prostitute.

The third and final stage is acceptance of one's identity as a professional prostitute. A small percentage of sex workers still insist that their activity is temporary, and a rare few may even retain a home with children and keep their two lives separate; but most adapt fully to the life of a prostitute.

Youth and physical attractiveness are a prostitute's greatest assets. Not surprisingly, the vast majority of prostitutes are between seventeen and twenty-four years old; the peak earning age is about twenty-two.[59] Downward mobility awaits a prostitute whose youthful beauty fades; and falling demand obliges the call boy or girl to solicit directly, the house prostitute to work the streets, and the streetwalker to charge less than others to attract clients.

Is Prostitution a Social Problem?

According to one social viewpoint, prostitution in no way constitutes a social problem; it is a private activity between two consenting adults and therefore no business of society or law enforcement. Indeed, as a "victimless crime," it should not even be illegal.[60] Arguments in favor of legalizing prostitution (as has been done in parts of Nevada as well as in Germany and the Netherlands) include claims that such action would actually reduce other social problems. For example, unlike in other parts of the country, where illegal prostitution causes the spread of STDs and AIDS, in Nevada the state's control over licensed brothels continually results in all the sex workers' testing negative, thereby ensuring protection against this health threat.[61] Moreover, where illegal prostitution flourishes, mercenary pimps and organized crime prosper; but Nevada has encountered no evidence of serious crime problems associated with legalized prostitution.

Counterarguments include the points that immorality should never be legalized, that illegal prostitution spreads crime and disease, and that all prostitution—legal and illegal—creates victims: the exploited children, teenagers, male and female adults used as sexual toys by male customers. From this viewpoint, prostitution is an oppressive system that uses power and control tactics to use people as sexual objects, degrading, dehumanizing, and defining them as mere instruments for the pleasure of others.

International Comparisons

Prostitution is so widespread globally that few places are free of its presence. Some people willingly choose to become prostitutes, but necessity forces many others into this life. In recent years, poverty-stricken East European women, numbering in the hundreds of thousands, have migrated to the West, desperate to sell their bodies in its fleshpots. In once prudish Eastern Europe, streetwalkers and whorehouses are now commonplace. Fleeing Russia, where female unemployment runs at 75 percent, thousands of "Natashas" (as they are called) prostitute themselves in Israel, Japan, and Turkey. Even in the Middle East, weekly charter flights bring Russian women on fourteen-day visas into such places as Dubai, where they ply their trade and then return home with money and gifts.[62]

Elsewhere less fortunate women live a life of forced or less glamorous prostitution:

In Nepal's Himalayan hill villages, some 7,000 adolescents are sold each year to slave traders for the sweat-drenched brothels of Bombay. In Brazil an estimated 25,000 girls have been forced into prostitution in remote Amazon mining camps. In Italy, Nigerian streetwalkers are flooding into Bologna, while in Belgium, the neon-bright windows of Antwerp's red-light district are filled with Ghanaians in lace underwear. Around Miami, massage parlors owned by Cuban immigrants import prostitutes from Colombia, Nicaragua and Canada.[63]

Eastern-bloc women are not the only ones enticed into Western Europe. Latin Americans, Asians, and Pacific Islanders also work in sex clubs and brothels, many of them duped by slave-trafficking sex rings into thinking they were going to find legitimate jobs and then forced to become prostitutes. Organized package sex tours take hundreds of thousands of Germans, Japanese, Koreans, and Taiwanese to Thailand's brothels each year, while Arab sex tourists flock to upscale brothels in Morocco or India.

How many of these women are victims of physical abuse and economic exploitation? Almost everywhere—from Japan, Pakistan, and Sri Lanka to Belgium, the Czech Republic, and Spain—authorities report numerous violent incidents by pimps and gangs against entrapped women. In 1991, a conference of Southeast Asian women's organizations estimated that 30 million women had been sold into sexual slavery since the mid-1970s. Experts agree that this figure is only an estimate and may be just the tip of the iceberg.

Several Western European countries have either taken steps to suppress sex trafficking or are debating in their parliaments whether and how to do so. Some activist groups hope that strengthening the United Nations guidelines will help eliminate the problem. Meanwhile, the boom in worldwide prostitution continues to debase and exploit several million children and women, often against their will.

Child Molestation

Besides the exploitation of children in prostitution, other sexual predators psychologically scar children by molesting them. **Child molestation** is the legal term for child sexual abuse, which occurs when an adult engages in sexual activity such as exposure of genitalia, fondling, intercourse, oral sex, or pornography (exposure to or involvement in) with a minor.

Child molestation is no longer an ignored or hidden form of abuse. It crosses all socioeconomic levels, although a disproportionate number of child molesters are White.[64] Sex offenders come in all shapes and sizes, from all parts of society, and with all sexual preferences. Many child molesters experienced sexual abuse during their own childhood, and most often the victim knows the offender.[65]

The Extent of Child Molestation

About 87,000 child molestation cases were reported in 2001 in the United States, but the number of unreported instances is far greater, because children are often afraid to tell anyone what happened.[66] A 1997 study of 10,000 Canadians aged fifteen and up revealed that approximately one in eight females reported that they had experienced some form of sexual abuse as children, most often by nonfamily members.[67] Psychologist Jim Hopper offers a higher estimate of one in three girls sexually abused before age eighteen, with one in four by age fourteen, and approximately one in six boys sexually abused before age sixteen.[68] Summarizing fourteen American and Canadian studies on the subject, Ann Salter reported incidence rates ranging from 11 to 38 percent for females and 3 to 11 percent for males.[69] Her figures for girls are comparable to the other sources mentioned, but fall below Hopper's almost 17 percent for boys.

Whatever the actual numbers, the prevalence of child molestation is high. In recent years, child molestation charges against coaches, teachers, babysitters, day-care workers, and clergy have rocked communities in Australia, Britain, Canada, Ireland, and the United States. Katherine Beckett—in a content analysis of *Time, Newsweek, U.S. News & World Report,* and *People Magazine*—determined that, from 1980 to 1984, 33 percent of all reported child sexual abuse incidents involved a babysitter or day-care worker, and 22 percent involved a family member. From 1985 to 1990, babysitter and day-care cases remained at the same level, but family member involvement rose dramatically to 55 percent. From 1991 to 1994, virtually no cases involved babysitters or day-care workers and cases involving family members dropped to 39 percent, but the clergy were prominent at 26 percent.[70]

Responding to the Problem

Clergy sexual abuse occurs in both Catholic and Protestant churches. Such cases are particularly upsetting because the perpetrators' actions completely violate the principles of their vocation. Although critics have charged that the church hierarchy often ignored the problem in the past, Hilary Kaiser notes that the United States now deals with the problem effectively through positive and transparent responses, as support groups put pressure on church leaders and find lawyers for victims.[71] The World Wide Web contains a great many sites run by activist and support groups dedicated to fighting this social problem and to aiding its victims. In 2002–2003, U.S. bishops adopted a "Charter" to remove offending clergy, reach out to victims, and work to restore public trust.

To protect themselves from perpetrators of sex crimes, people have demanded to be notified of the release of sex offenders and child molesters. A number of laws, such as Megan's Law, mandate this public notification, and many states have public sex-offender registries as a result. What issues are involved in balancing the rights of former convicts and the rights of potential victims of repeat offenders?

One controversial effort to reduce the problem of child molestation involves the passage of state laws requiring notification of local residents and police when a released sex offender still classified as dangerous moves into the neighborhood. First enacted in New Jersey, the notification statute is called Megan's Law—named after a seven-year-old New Jersey girl raped and killed in 1994 by a twice-convicted sex offender living across the street from her house. In 1996, President Clinton signed Megan's Law into federal law, obliging local law enforcement agencies in all fifty states to notify schools, day-care centers, and parents about the presence of dangerous offenders in their area. A federal appeals court upheld the constitutionality of the law in 1997. Rejecting claims that the notification law breached the rights of individuals who have paid their debt to society, the court ruled 2-1 that it merely enhanced "vigilance against possible re-abuse." In 1998, the U.S. Supreme Court refused to hear a challenge to that ruling.[72] The registration of all sex offenders and public notification about where those classified as dangerous are located continues, alerting law enforcement officials and neighbors. At present there are over 426,000 registered sex offenders.[73] In 2003, the court ruled that state governments cannot erase statutes of limitations retroactively. This decision prevents prosecution of sex crimes committed years ago.

Sociological Perspectives

Sociological analysis from the different perspectives often amounts to a continuation of earlier discussions in some of the preceding sections.

The Functionalist Viewpoint

For a century, the Functionalists studied sexuality primarily in the context of marriage, so they defined sexual expression as either premarital, marital, or extramarital. Social control of sexuality was necessary for preserving the family, which in turn was necessary for a stable society. This view sees deviation as a symptom of social disorganization and the breakdown of society's morals and social institutions. The family is the crucial source of appropriate or inappropriate sexual lessons to succeeding generations. Family disorganization leads to disrupted role relationships that in turn lead to deviant sexuality. For example, many instances of child sexual abuse in families occur in reconstituted families, where ambiguous roles and boundaries introduce such risks as stepfathers molesting their stepdaughters.

Kingsley Davis suggested that prostitution is functional because on the one hand it offers the prostitute a less tedious and better-paying alternative to other unskilled jobs, while on the other it meets the sexual needs of men who are away from home, are too old or unattractive to enjoy sex otherwise, or desire certain sex acts they cannot enjoy at home.[74] Ironically, even as society condemns prostitution as immoral and degrading, Davis says, its existence preserves the moral system by providing a sexual outlet that does not undermine the family system as would more emotionally invested extramarital relationships.

The Conflict Viewpoint

At the beginning of this chapter, we discussed how all societies set sexual behavior norms. From the Conflict perspective, the powerful impose their values on the less powerful, thereby institutionalizing behavioral standards of propriety and impropriety, morality and immorality, legality and illegality (as, for example, with homosexuality). Religion sets the moral guidelines and, together with the social institutions of family and education, socializes individuals into accepting these depictions and definitions as "normal." Another powerful social institution, the media, can strengthen or undermine these societal dictates. By holding nonconformists up to public censure, media exposure motivates others not to act similarly for fear of incurring like embarrassment and sanctions. Conversely, by promulgating sexually provocative stories, films, and television shows, the media can encourage behavior at odds with that advocated by the other social institutions.

Conflict theorists argue that prostitution reveals the power relationships in society. It is noteworthy, they contend, that so many women sell themselves to men while so few men prostitute themselves to women. Moreover, the men—the pimps and clients—continually benefit at the expense of the exploited women, whose value persists only as long as their youth, beauty, and health last. Moreover, most become prostitutes because their lower- or working-class backgrounds and limited education make their sexual availability one of their few economic resources. Conflict theorists also note that police crackdowns typically result in the arrest of the prostitutes, not of their "respectable" male clients—although in some locales males, too, now face charges.

According to Conflict theorists, prostitution is one of many societal illustrations of the economic and political inequality of the sexes. Until women gain equal power, we can expect prostitution as we know it to continue. This last part of Conflict analysis complements the Feminist orientation, as we will see next.

The Feminist Viewpoint

Past Feminists—such as essayist Mary Wollstonecraft, political activist Emma Goldman, suffragist Charlotte Perkins Gilman, and sociologist Victoria Woodhull—argued that recognizing the socially subordinate position of women was the keystone to understanding the existence of prostitution. Although a few Feminists today take a pro-prostitution stance, arguing that it is a "career choice" of sexual liberalism and a form of empowerment for women, most Feminists contend that prostitution epitomizes and perpetuates harmful patriarchal beliefs and principles that damage not just the women who sell sex, but all women in our society.[75]

Pornography (the word in Greek literally translates to "writing about prostitutes") draws even more intense condemnation than prostitution. Susan Brownmiller argues that hard-core pornography is "not a celebration of sexual freedom," but "a cynical exploitation of female sexual activity through the device of making all such activity and consequently all females 'dirty.' "[76] Feminist research on the subject of pornography often focuses on the processes in a social system whose underlying dynamic is the sexual objectification of women as a means to maintain male dominance and female submission. Catharine MacKinnon maintains that pornography is one way in which this occurs—that it both symbolizes and actualizes the distinctive social power of men over women. Pornography at least partly creates, defines, and reinforces the gender qualities we know as "male" and "female." Defining pornography as "explicit sexual material that subordinates women," she places the dehumanization of women within a continuum of female submission that starts with the visual appropriation of women in pornography, then moves on to physical appropriation in prostituted sex, then to forced sex in rape, and finally to sexual murder.[77] (Because rape is a crime of violence, and not a form of sexual expression, we discuss it in Chapter 9 on crime and violence.)

In her book, *Only Words* (1994), MacKinnon attacks what she calls the absolutist view that pornography is a form of speech protected by the First Amendment. Even if pornography is a form of speech—which MacKinnon doubts, suggesting instead that it communicates its ideas through "unconscious primitive conditioning"—it is nonetheless subject to government regulation, as are other kinds of invidious expression precisely because of their content. For example, saying "We serve only Whites here" or "If you sleep with me, I'll give you a promotion" can trigger legal sanctions because these examples of speech are recognized not as only words, but as acts of discrimination and harassment. Nobody claims that they merit First Amendment protection nor does anyone reasonably suggest that their prohibition brings us closer to the Orwellian nightmare of Big Brother totalitarianism. In these cases the clear social interest in eliminating racial discrimination and sexual harassment outweighs any concomitant limitation of the right to free speech.

The Interactionist Viewpoint

Because of its microsocial emphasis on everyday social interactions and not on the macrosocial forces affecting life, the Interactionist approach offers insights into how sexual "deviants" define themselves rather than how society views them. Two helpful focal points are sexual careers and self-definition.

Sexual Careers

Sociologists use the term **career** to mean any continuing role or activity in a person's life. This concept allows analysis of all forms of sexual behavior. If a young person engages in one homosexual act (and if we accept the findings of the 1994 national study, about 7 percent of all males and 4 percent of all females fall into this category), the act per se does not signal the beginning of a homosexual career. Indeed, the 1994 study found that only 3 percent of males and 1 percent of females had engaged in homosexual sex in the previous twelve months.

For such a sexual career to begin, the person committing the act must be labeled as a homosexual, thereby losing the reference group of straights and forcing a search for another reference group—in this case, the homosexual subculture. The labeling thus initiates a process that moves an individual who conforms to the dominant system of values in other respects from one random, isolated behavioral act to a persistent pattern of behavior with different social status and membership in a subculture with its own norms and patterns. Identifying with and eventually joining the homosexual subculture begins the sexual career.

Self-Definition

Within a sexual subculture, previously stigmatized individuals reject the negative views others hold of them, create a new in-group ethic that affirms their worth as equal members of society, and transforms their identity into a positive and viable self-conception. Prostitutes typically develop a set of values to enhance their own self-worth by holding "respectable" women in contempt as prostitutes in disguise and to justify their own activities as socially valuable. They see themselves as honest and respectable, their clients as hypocritical, and their work as helpful to marriages and to lonely, frustrated men.[78]

Sometimes this process partly reflects the changing times. For example, a content analysis of articles and stories published in *The Ladder,* a well-known lesbian publication, revealed just such an evolution. In its early years, *The Ladder* advocated an accommodative stance, urging lesbians to fit in as well as possible and to conceal any outward differences between themselves and straight women. *The Ladder* metamorphosed from a lesbian periodical to a Feminist magazine that openly supported lesbians, defining lesbianism as a sensible choice made by women in response to a sexist society. Lesbianism, it maintained, was a radical political statement, not a deviation for which a person was labeled and rejected.[79]

Thinking About the Future

Significant changes have occurred in the patterns of sexual behavior in the United States since the 1960s. From a period of "free love" and casual sex among many youths and young adults, we evolved into a period of sexual caution, a linking of sex with emotional involvement and commitment, but with a norm of premarital sex at an increasingly earlier average age. Sexual frankness in the media, concerns about sexually transmitted diseases, pornography, and prostitution, as well as child molestation worries, are parts of our lives. What future awaits us in these areas? Are we headed toward an improved or worsening world involving sex? What steps do you think we should take to combat the problems?

Many people worry about our moral fiber, that we are adrift in a "sea of sensuality," that our pursuit of pleasure comes at a high cost: our character, integrity, values, respect for individuals, and eventually the decline of our society itself, much like the Roman Empire mired in the excesses of carnal pleasure. Are the high activity levels of premarital sex a threat to our society? Moral issues aside, is this a social problem? Are there nonreligious concerns and negative societal consequences from the popularity of premarital sex? What of this new trend of "hooking up" among sixth, seventh, and eighth graders? Should we initiate any social policy or program to encourage young people to wait before having sex? How would you address this issue?

AIDS may be the worst fear, but other sexually transmitted diseases also spread easily and can have serious consequences. If one in four sexually active Americans get an STD at some time, we clearly face a contagious health problem that involves both oral sex and intercourse. How do we overcome this? Is it a matter of moral education or health education? Is it a matter of changing people's values, attitudes, and behavior? Where do you think the problem lies, and how do we solve it?

Technology and changing values have made pornography more accessible and popular than ever before. Does pornography harm women as some Feminists claim, or does it emancipate women as other Feminists claim? Does pornography enhance our sexual lives, or does it rob us of the eroticism and mutual sensual pleasure that romantic love brings? What of sexual violence depicted in some pornography? Is that simply fantasy escapism as proponents claim, or does it shape attitudes about women and set the stage for actual violence? Is all pornography protected by the First Amendment guaranteeing freedom of speech? How do we keep minors from accessing pornography on the Internet? Should we regulate, control, or ban pornography? What should society do differently from what it is presently doing?

Is prostitution a social problem? A victimless crime? Should it even be a crime? Some European countries regulate prostitution and require periodic health examinations. Should we? As with pornography, should we have morality laws and enforce them for the good of society, or should people have the freedom to choose what they want to do? If we enforce morality, we impose our values on others. If we allow others to do as they wish, how do we stop them from affecting the rest of us, including minors? Where do we draw the line? What do you suggest?

Most people would agree that child molestation is an abomination. Megan's Law is one approach to controlling repeat offenders. Is it enough? Should we have harsher punishments, such as mandatory castration, mandatory drug-taking to control behavior, or life imprisonment to keep such predators away from the rest of us? Are there other ways to protect our children?

SUMMARY

1. Cultural norms modify expressions of the human sex drive. Because these norms vary enormously over time and place, so does "acceptable" human sexual behavior.

2. U.S. sexual behavior was primarily conservative until the 1960s, when a two-decade experiment with casual sex began. Health fears and lack of personal fulfillment prompted another change. Although most people now have sex at an earlier age and premarital sex is the norm, not the exception, individuals mostly seek sex with commitment rather than casual relationships.

3. Most Americans do not have extramarital affairs. Recent studies reveal that 75 percent of husbands and 85 percent of wives claim never to have been unfaithful to their spouses. Moreover, over 90 percent said that they had only had sex with their spouse in the previous year.

4. Safe sex is a recent response to the threat of AIDS and other sexually transmitted diseases. Nevertheless, about one in five Americans carry some type of sexually transmitted disease, many without knowing it.

5. New technologies such as VCRs and the Internet have contributed to the dramatic increase in sexually explicit materials. Unlike erotica, pornography is actually less about sex than about the degradation of women and children through sex. One controversial issue is whether the violence found in much pornography leads to a predisposition among pornography consumers to commit violence against women.

6. Common background factors shared by prostitutes are poverty, early sexual abuse, social isolation, juvenile delinquency, social isolation, differential association, and (possibly) drug use. Becoming a prostitute involves both a transitional process and a "turned-out" learning process. Debate rages over whether prostitution is a social problem or a victimless crime; but worldwide, millions are forced into this life, some at an early age.

7. Most child molesters are White, but they come from all socioeconomic backgrounds and can be of any sexual preference. Many experienced sexual abuse during their own childhood; and most often, the victim knows the offender. Studies reveal that somewhere between 11 to 38 percent of all girls and 3 to 17 percent of all boys are victims of childhood sexual abuse.

8. Functionalists see deviant sexuality as a symptom of social disorganization and the breakdown of society's institutions. Conflict theorists state that power plays a key role in depicting and defining what constitutes "normal" sexual relations. Feminists view prostitution and pornography as rooted in the basic subjugation of women in our society. Interactionists suggest that the concepts of labeling theory, sexual careers, and self-definition offer helpful insights.

KEY TERMS

Career	Pornography
Child molestation	Prostitution
Differential association	Safe sex
Eroticism	STD

INTERNET RESOURCES

At this book's Web site with Allyn & Bacon, you will find numerous links related to the problems pertaining to sexual behavior. To explore these resources, go first to the author's page (**http://www.ablongman.com/parrillo**). Next, select this edition of *Contemporary Social*

Problems and then choose **Internet Readings and Exercises**. Then select **Chapter 14,** where you will find both a variety of sites to investigate and some questions that pertain to those sites.

SUGGESTED READINGS

Bart, Pauline B., and Eileen G. Morgan (eds.). *Violence Against Women: The Bloody Footprints.* Newbury Park, Calif.: Sage, 1993. Anthology about social structure supports of violence against women and institutional responses after the violence occurs.

Brownmiller, Susan. *Against Our Will: Men, Women, and Rape,* reprint ed. New York: Fawcett Books, 1993. Challenging presentation of the historical dimensions of sexual violence and rape, and their roots in the male-female relationship.

Chauncey, George. *Gay in New York: Gender, Urban Culture, and the Making of the Gay Male World: 1890–1940.* New York: Basic Books, 1995. A well-researched look at gay life in New York City before society built the closet.

Donnerstein, Edward; Daniel Linz; and Steven Penrod. *The Question of Pornography: Research Findings and Policy Implications.* New York: Free Press, 1987. A good summary of recent social science research on the relationship of pornography to attitudes and behavior.

Hyde, Janet S. *Understanding Human Sexuality,* 7th ed. New York: McGraw-Hill, 2000. A comprehensive interdisciplinary introduction to this field from a Feminist perspective.

Kimmel, Michael S. *Men Confront Pornography.* New York: Crown, 1991. An informative, insightful book that includes material about the negative effects of pornography on masculine identity and sexual fulfillment.

Laumann, Edward; Robert Michael; Stuart Michaels; and John Gagnon. *The Social Organization of Sexuality.* Chicago: University of Chicago Press, 2000. An extensive study of sexuality based on a probability sample.

Michael, Robert T.; John H. Gagnon; Edward O. Laumann; and Gina Kolata. *Sex in America: A Definitive Survey.* Boston: Little, Brown, 1995. A readable book on the most thorough national survey ever conducted of sexual practices in the United States.

Schwartz, Pepper, and Virginia E. Rutter. *The Gender of Sexuality: Sexual Possibilities.* Thousand Oaks, Calif.: Pine Forge Press, 1998. A fine, comprehensive book on all aspects of gender and sexuality, including sexual desire and behavior, everyday influences on committed sex, teenage sexuality, single life, marriage, divorce, and sexual violence.

Segal, Lynne, and Mary McIntosh (eds.). *Sex Exposed: Sexuality and the Pornography Debate.* New Brunswick, N.J.: Rutgers University Press, 1993. A collection of articles on the value of eroticism and the danger of pornography for men and women.

Strossen, Nadine. *Defending Pornography: Free Speech, Sex, and the Fight for Women's Rights.* New York: New York University Press, 2001. Written by the Feminist president of the ACLU, this book argues that censorship, not pornography, is the real enemy of women's equality and offers constructive approaches to reducing violence and discrimination against women.

Notes

Chapter 1

1. Peter Collier and David Horowitz, *The Rockefellers: An American Dynasty* (New York: Signet, 1976), pp. 62–63.
2. John P. Hewitt and Peter M. Hall, "Social Problems, Problematic Solutions, and Quasi-Theories," *American Sociological Review* 38 (1973): 367–374.
3. John Stimson and Ardyth Stimson, "Quasi-Theories and Research Origination, Part I: Quasi-Theories as Substitute Cures," *Sociological Practice* 2 (1977): 38–48.
4. D. C. Miller (ed.), *Handbook of Research Design and Social Measurement,* 4th ed. (New York: Longman, 1983), pp. 23–29.
5. Randall Collins, *Four Sociological Traditions* (New York: Oxford University Press, 1994), p. 181.
6. Robert K. Merton, *Social Theory and Social Structure* (Glencoe, Ill.: Free Press, 1957), pp. 132ff.
7. Randall Collins, *Four Sociological Traditions,* p. 198.
8. Ibid., p. 264.
9. Travis Hirschi, "Procedural Rules and the Study of Deviant Behavior," *Social Problems* 21 (1973): 159–173.
10. W. Lawrence Neuman, *Social Research Methods,* 2d ed. (Boston: Allyn & Bacon, 1994), p. 72.
11. Edward T. Cahill, "Sociologists as Planners," in A. B. Shostak (ed.), *Putting Sociologists to Work* (New York: David McKay, 1974).
12. Joe Bailey, *Social Theory for Planning* (Boston: Routledge & Kegan Paul, 1975), p. 142.
13. Willard Waller, "Social Problems and the Mores," *American Sociological Review* 1 (1936): 926ff.

Chapter 2

1. C. Wright Mills, *The Sociological Imagination* (New York: Oxford University Press, 1959).
2. Emile Durkheim, *Suicide* (1897), translated by John A. Spaulding and George Simpson (New York: Free Press, 1951).

3. Philip G. Zimbardo, *Shyness: What It Is, What To Do About It,* reissue ed. (New York: Perseus, 1990).

4. Robert Nisbet, *Sociology as an Art Form* (New York: Transaction Publishers, 2001), p. 120.

5. Robert MacIver, "The Great Emptiness," in Eric and Mary Josephson (eds.), *Man Alone: Alienation in Modern Society* (New York: Dell Laurel, 1962), p. 49.

6. Robert N. Bellah, Richard Madsen, William M. Sullivan, Ann Swidler, and Steven M. Tipton, *Habit of the Heart: Individualism and Commitment in American Life* (New York: Harper & Row, 1985), pp. 52, 153.

7. Ibid., pp. 72–73.

8. Jason Fields and Lynne M. Casper, "America's Families and Living Arrangements." *Current Population Reports,* Washington, D. C.: U. S. Government Printing Office, 2001, pp. 20–539.

9. U.S. Bureau of the Census, "Marriage, Divorce, and Remarriage in the 1990s," *Current Population Reports,* Washington, D.C.: U.S. Government Printing Office, 1992, pp. 23–180.

10. Robert Nisbet, *Sociology as an Art Form,* p. 123.

11. Emile Durkheim, "Anomic Suicide," in Kenneth Thompson and Jeremy Tunstall (eds.), *Sociological Perspectives, reprint ed.* (Baltimore: Penguin, 1989), p. 111.

12. William H. Swatos, Jr., "Revolution and Charisma in a Rationalized World: Weber Revisited and Extended," in Ronald M. Glassman and Vatro Murvar eds., *Max Weber's Political Sociology* (Westport, Conn.: Greenwood Press, 1984).

13. Anton C. Sijderveld, "Industrial Society Tends to Reduce Man to a De-humanized Functionary," p. 70, in George McKenna and Mirela Baroni-Harris eds., *Taking Sides: Clashing Views on Controversial Social Issues* (Guilford, Conn.: The Dushkin Group, 1980).

14. Andrezej Walicki, "Marx and Freedom," *The New York Review of Books* (November 24, 1983), p. 52.

15. Paul Goodman, *Growing Up Absurd* (New York: Random House, 1983).

16. Robert Blauner, *Alienation and Freedom: The Factory Worker and His Industry* (Chicago: University of Chicago Press, 1964), summarized by H. W. Smith, *Introduction to Social Psychology* (Englewood Cliffs, N.J.: Prentice-Hall, 1987), p. 117.

17. U.S. Bureau of the Census, *Statistical Abstract of the United States 2002,* Washington, D.C.: U.S. Government Printing Office, 2002, Table 601, p. 392.

18. Richard Sennett and J. Cobb, *The Hidden Injuries of Class,* reprint ed. (New York: W.W. Norton & Company, 1993), p. 179.

19. Virginia Hodgkinson, Murray Weltzman, and the Gallup Organization, *Giving and Volunteering in the United States: 1996 Edition.* (Washington, D.C.: Independent Sector, 1996.)

20. "Politics of Distrust," *PBS News Hour,* February 5, 1996.

21. Gary Langer, "Water's Edge: Greater Trust in Government Limited to National Security," *ABC News.* Available at http://abcnews.go.com/sections/politics/DailyNews/poll0120115.html. [April 26, 2003]

22. Virginia Hodgkinson, et al., *Giving and Volunteering in the United States.*

23. U.S. Bureau of the Census, *Statistical Abstract,* Table 396, p. 255.

24. Christopher Lasch, *Culture of Narcissism: American Life in an Age of Diminishing Expectations* (New York: W. W. Norton & Co., 1991), p. 137.

25. C. Wright Mills, "The Competitive Personality," in Lewis A. Coser (ed.), *The Pleasures of Sociology* (New York: Mentor, 1980), p. 270.

26. Ralph Keyes, "We the Lonely People," in Kurt Finsterbush and George McKenna (eds.), *Taking Sides* (Guilford, Conn.: Dushkin, 1982), p. 79.

27. Christopher Lasch, *Culture of Narcissism.*

28. Joseph Bensman and Robert Lielienfield, *Between Public and Private: Lost "Boundaries of the Self"* (New York: Free Press, 1979), pp. 12–13.

29. Elaine Walster, "Playing Hard to Get: Understanding as Elusive Phenomenon," in T. Blass (ed.), *Contemporary Social Psychology* (Itasca, Ill.: F. E. Peacock, 1976, pp. 94ff.

30. Walter R. Gove, M. Hughes, and M. R. Geerkin, "Playing Dumb: A Form of Impression Management with Undesirable Side Effects," *Social Psychology Quarterly* 43 (1980): 89–102.

31. Stanley Cohen and Laurie Taylor, *Escape Attempts: The Theory and Practice of Resistance in Everyday Life,* rev. ed. (New York: Routledge, 1992), p. 213.

32. Peter L. Berger, "Secularization and the Problem of Plausibility," in K. Thompson and J. Tunstall (eds.), *Sociological Perspectives,* p. 455.

33. Ibid., p. 447.

34. Institute for the Study of American Religion, "Flowering of Cults in the 20th Century." Available at http://www.americanreligion.org/cultwtch/20thcen.html [March 6, 2004].

35. Irving Louis Horowitz, "The New Fundamentalism," *Society* (November/December 1982), pp. *40–47.

36. Ibid.

37. "Flowering of Cults in the 20th Century," *op.cit.*

38. Edwin Schur, *The Awareness Trap* (New York: McGraw-Hill, 1977).

39. David A. Karp and William C. Yoels, *Symbols, Selves, and Society* (New York: J. B. Lippincott/Harper & Row, 1979), p. 199.

40. Mary Klages, "Postmodernism." Available at: http://www.colorado.edu/English/ENGL2012Klages pomo.html [April 27, 2003].

41. National Center for Health Statistics, cited by National Center for Injury Prevention and Control. Available at www.cdc.gov/ncipc/fact_book/26_Suicide.htm. [April 27, 2003].

42. National Center for Health Statistics, cited by National Center for Injury Prevention and Control. Available at: www.cdc.gov/ncipc/factsheets/suifacts.htm [April 27, 2003].

43. Ibid.

44. Alex Crosby, "The Romeo and Juliet Myth: Teenage Suicide Isn't Romantic." Available at: http://www.millville.org/School_Pages_html/Elem_Schools_F/CFCF_earlychild/early_whacked/suicide.html [March 6, 2004].

45. Karen R. Scheel and John S. Westefeld, "Heavy Metal Music and Adolescent Suicidality," *Adolescence* 34 (Summer 1999): 253–274.

46. Eno Lacourse, Michel Claes, and Martine Villeneuve, "Heavy Metal Music and Adolescent Suicidal Risk." Journal of Youth and Adolescence 30 (June 2001): 321–332.

Chapter 3

1. U.S. Census Bureau, "World Vital Events." Available at: http://blue.census.gov/egi-bin/ipe/pewe [April 28, 2003].

2. Ibid.

3. United Nations Population Division, *World Population Prospects: The 2002 Revision.* Available at: http://esa.un.org/unpp/p2kOdata.asp [July 14, 2003].

4. As told by Donnella Meadows in *The Limits to Growth*, quoted in *World Development Forum* (May 31, 1984), p. 2.

5. Robert L. Heilbroner, *The Worldly Philosophers,* 7th ed. (Carmichael, Calif. Touchstone Books, 1999). p.76.

6. Dennis H. Wrong, *Population and Society,* reprint ed. (New York: McGraw-Hill, 1990), p. 102.

7. See, for example, Paul R. Ehrlich, *The Population Bomb,* rev. ed. (Mattituck, N.Y.: Amereon Ltd., 1976). Paul R. Ehrlich and Anne H. Ehrlich, *The Population Explosion* (New York: Touchstone/Simon & Shuster, 1991); Lester R. Brown, "Reassessing the Earth's Population," *Society* 32 (1995): 7–10.

8. Paul Kennedy, *Preparing for the Twenty-First Century* (New York: Random House, 1993).

9. Jay A. Weinstein, *Demographic Transition and Social Change* (Morristown, N.J.: General Learning Press, 1976), pp. 57–79.

10. U.N. Population Division, *1998 Revision of the World Population Estimates and Projections.* Available at: http://www.popin.org pop1998 [July 8, 2000].

11. Laurent Belsie, "How Many People Does It Take to Change the World?" *The Christian Science Monitor* (June 22, 2000), p. 11.

12. U.N. Population Division, loc. cit.

13. Based on data at U.N. Population Division, loc. cit.

14. Ibid.

15. Nicholas Eberstadt, "World Population Implosion?" *Public Interest* 122 (Fall 1997): 3–22.

16. Mary Mederios Kent, "Shrinking Societies Favor Procreation," *Population Today* 27 (December 1999): 4–5.

17. U.S. Census Bureau, *World Population Profile: 1998—Highlights.* Available at: http://www.census.gov ipc/wlw/wp98.html [May 2, 2003].

18. David Pimentel and Marcia Pimentel, "Population Growth, Environmental Resources, and the Global Availability of Food," *Social Research* 66 (1998): 417–428.

19. William Bender and Margaret Smith, "Population, Food, and Nutrition," *Population Bulletin* 51 (February 1997): 10–11; U.N. Population Division, loc. cit.

20. Leon F. Bouvier and Lindsey Grant, *How Many Americans?* (San Francisco: Sierra Club Books, 1994), p. 54.

21. Ibid., p. 18.

22. 2002 World Summit on Sustainable Development, "Facts about . . . Consumption and Production Problems." Accessed at: www.johannesburgsummit.org/html/media_info/pressreleases_factsheets/wssd9_consumption.pdf [May 3, 2003].

23. Don Hinrichson, "Putting the Bite on Planet Earth," *International Wildlife* (September/October 1994). Available at: http: dieoff.org/page120.htm [May 3, 2003].

24. Facing the Future, "Modern Impacts: The Loss of Forests." Available at: http://www.popinfo.org/redbook/chap5_1.htm [May 3, 2003].

25. Don Hinrichson, "Putting the Bite on Planet Earth," loc. cit.

26. Facing the Future, "Modern Impacts: The Loss of Forests," loc. cit.

27. The Nature Conservancy, "Tropical Rain Forest." Available at: http://nature.org/tropical_rainforest.html [May 3, 2003].

28. Rainforest Action Network, "Facts About the Rainforests." Available at: http://www.ran.org/info_center/about_rainforests_html [May 3, 2003].

29. Ibid.

30. Hinrichson, "Putting the Bite on Planet Earth," loc. cit.

31. Werner Forno, president of Population Institute, "Gaining People, Losing Ground," address given at William Paterson University, Wayne, New Jersey, October 23, 1996.

32. Rainforest Action Network, "7 Things You Can Do to Save the Rainforests." Available at: http://www.ran.org/info_center/factsheets_01c.html [May 3, 2003].

33. Christopher N. Allo, *Rainforests Around the World* (Champaign: University of Illinois Press, 1996).

34. Rainforest Action Network, "About Rainforests." Available at: www.ran.org/info_center/about_rainforests.html; see also Norman Myers; *The Primary Source: Tropical Forests and our Future* (New York: W. W. Norton, 1984).

35. Norman Myers, "Biological Diversity and Global Security," in Herbert F. Bohrmann and Stephen R. Kellert (eds.), *Ecology, Economics, and Ethics: The Broken Circle* (New Haven, Conn.: Yale University Press, 1991), pp. 11–25.

36. Rainforest Action Network, "Species Extinction." Available at: www.ran.org/info_center/factsheets/o3b.html [May 3, 2003].

37. Bread for the World Institute, "Hunger Basics." Available at: http://www.bread.org/hungerbasics/index.html [May 3, 2003].

38. The Hunger Site. Available at: http://www.thehungersite.com/cgi-bin/WebObjects/CTDSites [May 3, 2003].

39. World Health Organization, "Combating Vitamin A Deficiency." Available at: http://who.int/nut/vad.htm [May 3, 2003].

40. "Undernourishment Around the World," *The State of Food Insecurity in the World: 2002.* (Rome: UN Food and Agriculture Organization, 2002). Available at: www.fao.org [May 4, 2002].

41. "International Facts on Hunger and Poverty," loc. cit.

42. Bender and Smith, "Population, Food, and Nutrition," p. 6.

43. "Undernourishment Around the World," Table 1.

44. Ibid.

45. David Pimentel and Marcia Pimentel, "Feeding the World's Population," *Bioscience* 50 (2000): 387–391.

46. "Domestic Hunger and Poverty Facts." Available at: http://www.bread.org/hungerbasics/domestic.html [May 4, 2003].

47. See Gary P. Nabhan, *Cultures of Habitat* (Boulder, Colo: Counterpoint Press, 1997).

48. World Watch Institute, "Information Economy Boom Obscuring Earth's Decline." Available at: http://www.worldwatch.org/alerts/000115.html [May 4, 2003].

49. Lester R. Brown "Crossing the Sustainability Threshold" in Lester R. Brown et al., *State of the World 2000* (New York: W. W. Norton, 2002), Chapter 1.

50. See Fred Pearce, "Dam Villagers Await the Apocalypse," *New Scientist* 153(March 1997):8.

51. Leslie Alan Horvitz, "More Precious Even Than Oil," *Insight on the News* 13 (March 17, 1997): pp. 42–43.

52. Environmental Protection Agency, "Global Warming—Climate." Available at: http://yosemite.epa.gov/oar/globalwarming/nsf/content/climate.html [May 4, 2004].

53. Lisa M. Pinsker, "Tales from a Warming Arctic," *Geotimes* 48 (January 2003): 11–12..

54. Sharon Begley, "Too Much Hot Air," *Newsweek* (October 27, 1997), p. 49.

55. Sierra Club, "Population and Global Warming," Available at www.sierraclub.org/population/reports/globalwarming.asp [May 4, 2003].

56. U.S. Environmental Protection Agency, "Global Warming: Climate," loc. cit.

57. Sierra Club, "Population and Global Warming," loc. cit.

58. Ibid.

59. Sharon Begley, "Too Much Hot Air," op. cit.

60. U.S. Environmental Protection Agency, "Acid Rain." Available at http://www.epa.gov/airmarkets/acidrain [May 4, 2003].

61. Ibid.

62. Ibid.

63. Norman Miller, "Rains of Terror," *Geographical* 75 (2000): 90–91.

64. Ibid.

65. Winnie Hu, "Mercury Levels Found Unsafe in Fish from 6 New Sites Upstate," *The New York Times* (June 15, 2000), p. B10.

66. "Inhaling China," *Christian Science Monitor* (January 25, 2000), p. 10.

67. United Nations Environment Programme, "Global Environment Outlook 2000." Available at http://www.unep.org/geo-text [May 4, 2003].

68. Leslie Roberts, "Acid Rain: Forgotten, Not Gone," *U.S. News & World Report* (November 1, 1999), p. 70. See also G. E. Likens, C. T. Driscoll, and D. C. Buso, "Long-term Effects of Acid Rain: Response and Recovery of a Forest Ecosystem," *Science* 272 (April 12, 1996): pp. 244–46; Jocelyn Kaiser, "Acid Rain's Dirty Business: Stealing Minerals from Soil, *Science* 272 (April 12, 1996): p. 198.

69. Sierra Club, "Population and Water." Available at http://www.sierraclub.org/population/reports/water.asp [May 4, 2003].

70. Population Reference Bureau, *U.S. in the World: Connecting People & Communities to Ensure a Healthy Planet* (Washington, D.C., 1998).

71. Population Reference Bureau, *World Population: More Than Just Numbers* (Washington, D.C., 1999).

72. Sandra L. Postel, "Dehydrating Conflict," *Foreign Policy* 126 (September–October 2001), 61.

73. Lester R. Brown and Brian Halweil, "China's Water Shortage Could Shake World Grain Markets." Worldwatch Institute. Available at http://www.worldwatch.org/alerts/pr980422.html [June 3, 2003].

74. Worldwatch Institute, "Information Economy Boom Obscuring Earth's Decline," Available at: www.worldwatch.org/alerts/000115.html [June 3, 2003].

75. Sierra Club, "Population and Water," loc. cit.

76. United Nations Population Fund, "Population and Sustainable Development." Available at http://www.unfpa.org/6billion/populationissues/development.htm [June 3, 2003].

77. See Paul Schneider, "Clear Progress: 25 Years of the Clean Water Act," *Audubon* 99 (September–October 1997): 36–49.

78. Tom Horton, "Bay Restoration Stalling, Experts Say," *Baltimore Sun* (March 12, 2003), p.1A.

79. Dan Whipple, "Blue Planet: A Hole in the Gulf of Mexico," United Press International (January 24, 2003).

80. Paul Ehrlich, *The Population Bomb*, p. 35.

81. PIRG, Executive Summary. Available at www.pirg.org/reports/enviro/home98/page1.htm [Accessed June 3, 2003].

82. Susan L. Cutter and Minhe Ji, "Trends in U.S. Hazardous Materials Transportation Spills," *The Professional Geographer* 49 (August 1997): 318–331.

83. *National Environmental Law Center Report* (Winter 1995): 5.

84. Michael Sachell, Michael Kovrig, and Karen Schmidt, "Death on the Danube," *U.S. News & World Report* (February 28, 2000): p. 42.

85. Michael H. Brown, *Laying Waste* (New York: Random House, 1983), p. 105.

86. See Gregory E. McAvoy, *Controlling Technocracy: Citizen Rationality and the Nimby Syndrome* (Washington, D.C.: Georgetown University Press, 1997).

87. Michael Satchell, "A Black and Green Issue Moves People: EPA Weighs Health Risks and Racial Politics," *U.S. News & World Report* (April 21, 1997), pp. 41–42.

88. Ernst F. Schumacher, *Small Is Beautiful,* 2nd ed. (Berkley, Calif.: Hostley & Marks, 1999).

89. Barry Commoner, "The Economic Meaning of Ecology," in Jerome H. Skolnick and Elliott Currie (eds.), *Crisis in American Institutions* 11th ed. (Boston: Allyn & Bacon, 2000), p. 263.

90. Michael H. Brown, *Laying Waste,* p. 292.

91. United Nations Population Fund, "Population and Sustainable Development," loc. cit.

92. Ibid.

93. Maria Mies and Vandana Shiva, *Ecofeminism,* Atlantic Highlands (N.J.: Zed Books, 1993); Carolyn Merchant, *Radical Ecology: The Search for a Livable World* (New York: Routledge, 1992).

94. United Nations Population Fund, "Population and Sustainable Development," loc. cit.

95. Margaret Mead, "Preface," in P. Reining and I. Tinker, *Population: Dynamics, Ethics and Policy* (Washington, D.C.: American Association for the Advancement of Science, 1975), pp. v–vi.

96. U.S. Census Bureau, *Statistical Abstract of the United States: 2002* (Washington D.C.: U.S. Government Printing Office, 2002), Table 1374, p. 803.

97. Worldwatch Institute, "Information Economy Boom Obscuring Earth's Decline," loc. cit.

98. Reported in Ines Capdevila, "Rising Population Faces Shrinking Water Supply," *Insight on the News* (May 1, 2000), p. 30.

Chapter 4

1. See Kenneth T. Jackson, *Crabgrass Frontier: The Suburbanization of the United States* (New York: Oxford University Press, 1987).

2. Truman A. Hartshorn and Peter O. Muller, *Suburban Business Centers: Employment Implications* (Washington, D.C.: U.S. Government Printing Office, 1987).

3. Joel Garreau, *Edge City: Life on the New Frontier* (New York: Doubleday, 1991).

4. William A. Caldwell (ed.), *How to Save Urban America* (New York: Signet, 1973), pp. 45–56.

5. Ibid., pp. 216–217.

6. Todd S. Purdum, "Suburban 'Sprawl' Takes Its Place on the Political Landscape," *The New York Times* (February 6, 1999), pp. A1, A12.

7. Sierra Club, "What Is Sprawl?" Available at http://www.sierraclub.org/sprawl/report98/ [June 3, 2003].

8. Anthony Downs, *Stuck in Traffic: Coping With Peak-Hour Traffic Congestion,* (Washington, D.C.: Brookings Institution Press, 1992). See also Michael Danielson and Julian Wolpert, "From Old to New Metropolis," *Research in Community Sociology* 4 (1994): 71–96.

9. Texas Transportation Institute, *Urban Mobility Study.* Available at http://mobility.tamu.edu/ums/study/issues_measures/congested_roads.stm [June 3, 2003].

10. Ibid.

11. "Free the Roads," *Wall Street Journal* editorial (April 21, 2000), p. A14.

12. U.S. Department of Transportation, *Commuting Alternatives in the United States: Recent Trends and a Look to the Future* (Washington, D.C.: U.S. Government Printing Office, 1994), No. DOT-T-95-11, Table 21.

13. Francis Bello, "The City and the Car," in A. N. Cowings and H. Nagpaul (eds.), *Urban Man and Society* (New York: Alfred A. Knopf, 1957).

14. U.S. Bureau of the Census, *Statistical Abstract of the United States 2002*, Table 1081, p. 684.

15. See Penny Loeb and Warren Cohen, "The New Redlining." *U.S. News & World Report* (April 17, 1995), pp. 51–57; Patricia Hanrahan and Katharine Rankin, "How Lawyers Can Help Provide Housing for the Neediest," *Human Rights* 17 (Summer 1990): 37–39.

16. Lori Mardock, *Predicting Housing Abandonment in Central: Creating an Early Warning System.* Available at http://www.ncpr.org/reports/ncpr1089/ncpr1089.html [June 4, 2003].

17. Morton J. Schussheim, "Housing in Perspective," *Public Interest* (Spring 1979).

18. Jeanne R. Lowe, *Cities in a Race with Time* (New York: Random House, 1967), Chapter 6.

19. Scott Greer, *Urban Renewal and American Cities* (Indianapolis: Bobbs-Merrill, 1965), p. 3.

20. Herbert Gans, *The Urban Villagers*, expanded ed. (New York: Free Press, 1983).

21. U.S. Bureau of the Census, *Statistical Abstract of the United States 2002*, Table 514, p. 342.

22. Steve Daniels, "Wards Site's Affordable Housing Deal," *Crain's Chicago Business* (September 3, 2001). p. 1.

23. James E. Rosenbaum, Linda K. Stroh, and Cathy A. Flynn, "Lake Parc Place: A Study of Mixed-Income Housing," *Housing Policy Debate* 9(1998), 703–40.

24. U.S. Bureau of the Census, *Statistical Abstract of the United States 2002*, Table 516, p. 344; and 1999 edition, Table 613, p. 389.

25. Martha S. Burt, "What Will It Take to End Homelessness?" Urban Institute. Available at www.urban.org [June 5, 2003].

26. U.S. Conference of Mayors. *A Status Report on Hunger and Homelessness in America's Cities:* 2002. Also available at http://www.usmayors.org/uscm/hungersurvey/2002/ [June 5, 2003].

27. Ibid.

28. "Why Are People Homeless?" National Coalition for the Homeless, 2002. Available at: www.nationalhomeless.org/causes.html [June 5, 2003]. See also Yvonne Vissing, *Out of Sight, Out of Mind: Homeless Children and Families in Small-Town America* (Lexington: University Press of Kentucky), 1996.

29. "What Does Homelessness Have to Do with Foster Care?" *Institute for Children and Poverty* 2 (August 1993): 1–2.

30. "Education: An Underlying Tenet in the Struggle Against Poverty," *Institute for Children and Poverty* 1 (January 1993): 1.

31. "What Does Homelessness Have to Do with Foster Care?" pp. 1–2.

32. U.S. Bureau of the Census, *Statistical Abstract of the United States 2002*, Table 33, pp. 36–38.

33. Ibid.

34. Ibid., Table 953, p. 608.

35. U.S. Federal Bureau of Investigation, *Crime in the United States 2001* (Washington, D.C.: U.S. Government Printing, 2002).

36. Jean Gottman, *Megalopolis: The Urbanized Northeast Seaboard of the United States* (Cambridge, Mass.: MIT Press, 1961).

37. U.S. Bureau of the Census, *Statistical Abstract of the United States 2002*, derived from Table 635, p. 420 and Table 18, p. 22.

38. U.S. Federal Deposit Insurance Corporation, *Statistics on Banking: 2001* (Washington, D.C.: U.S. Government Printing Office, 2002).

39. Rushworth M. Kidder, "The Northeast Rebounds," *Christian Science Monitor* (January 1983), pp. 1, 14.

40. H. Bauder and E. Perle, "Spatial and Skills Mismatch for Labor-Market Segments," *Environment and Planning* 31 (1999), 959–977.

41. David Rusk, *Cities Without Suburbs* (Baltimore: Woodrow Wilson Center Press, 1993).

42. Neal Peirce et al., *Citistates* (Washington, D.C.: Seven Locks Press, 1993).

43. United Nations Population Division, "World Urbanization Prospects: The 2001 Revision." Available at http://www.un.org/esa/population/publications/wup2001dh.pdf [July 14, 2003].

44. Martin Brockerhoff, "The Urban Demographic Revolution," *Population Today* 28 (August/September 2000): 1.

45. Manuel Castells, *The Urban Question: A Marxist Approach* (Cambridge, Mass: MIT Press, 1979); and *The City and Grass Roots* (Berkeley: University of California Press, 1983).

46. See Josef Gugler, *The Urban Transformation of the Developing World: Regional Trajectories* (New York: Oxford University Press, 1996).

47. Jacqueline Leavitt and Susan Saegert, "Women and Abandoned Buildings," *Social Policy* 15 (1984): 32–39.

48. Daphne Spain, *Gendered Spaces* (Chapel Hill: University of North Carolina Press, 1992); Judith A. Garber and Roby Turner (eds.), *Gender in Urban Research* (Thousand Oaks, Calif.: Sage, 1993).

49. Doreen Massey, *Space, Place, and Gender* (Minneapolis: University of Minnesota Press, 1996); Sheila Scraton and Beccy Watson, "Gendered Cities: Women and Public Leisure Space in the 'Postmodern City,'" *Leisure Studies* 17 (1998): 123–137.

50. Judith DeSena, "Gendered Space and Women's Community Work," *Research in Urban Sociology* 5 (2000): 275–297.

Chapter 5

1. Sara Nathan, "Oil Companies Subpoenaed in Price-Fixing Investigation," *USA Today* (July 28, 2000), p. B1.

2. Jayne O'Donnell, "Ongoing Price-Fixing Investigations," *USA Today* (July 10, 2000), p. 3B.

3. Sharon Bernstein, "Drug Maker to Settle Case for $135 Million," *Los Angeles Times* (July 13, 2000), p. 1.

4. "Carpet Makers Shaw, Mohawk Will Settle Price-Fixing Lawsuit," *Wall Street Journal* (August 14, 2000), p. B6.

5. Nicholas Stein, "Introduction to American Business," *Fortune*. Available at http: www.fortune.com fortune fortune500 giants.html [August 22, 2000].

6. "Fortune 5 Hundred: 2002. Available at http://www.fortune.com/fortune/fortune500 [June 9, 2003]; U.S. Bureau of the Census, *Statistical Abstract of the United States 2002* (Washington, D.C.: U.S. Government Printing Office, 2002), Table 637, p. 422, and Table 1320, p. 834.

7. Joel Millman, Nina Munk, Michael Schuman, and Neil Weinberg, "The World's Wealthiest People," *Forbes* 152 (1993): 66–69.

8. David Moberg, "Decline and Inequality After the Great U-Turn," *In These Times* (May 27–June 9, 1992), p. 7; See also "U.S. Wealth—2% Own 28%," *Parade Magazine* (December 9, 1984).

9. From Edward Wolff, "Shifting Fortunes: The Perils of the Growing Wealth Gap in America," *Socialism Today*. Available at http: www.netaxs.com/fightbak/editorial.html [August 22, 2000].

10. C. Wright Mills, *The Power Elite* (New York: Oxford University Press, 1956), p. 123.

11. Maureen Jung, Dean Purdy, and D. Stanley Eitzen, "The Corporate Inner Group," *Sociological Spectrum* 1 (1981): 317–33.

12. Mark S. Mizruchi, "What Do Interlocks Do? An Analysis, Critique, and Assessment of Research on Interlocking Directorates," *Annual Review of Sociology, 1996* 22 (1996): 271–98.

13. Mark S. Mizruchi, B. B. Potts, and D. W. Allison, "Interlocking Directorates and Business Transactions: New Evidence on an Old Question," paper presented at annual meeting, American Sociological Association, Miami Beach, August 1993.

14. U.S. Bureau of the Census, *Statistical Abstract of the United States 2002*, Tables 726 and 727, p. 487.

15. Karen Miller, "The Giants Stumble," *Newsweek* (July 8, 2002), p. 14.

16. Quoted in John S. DeMott, "White Knights and Black Eyes," *Time* (February 14, 1983), p. 56.

17. Charles V. Bagli, "Conditions Are Right for a Takeover Frenzy," *New York Times* (January 2, 1997), p. 81.

18. Ibid.; Miller, "The Giants Stumble," p.14.

19. John Kenneth Galbraith, *The New Industrial State*, 4th ed. (Boston: Houghton Mifflin, 1985), p. 71.

20. Leonard Silk and David Vogel, *Ethics and Profits* (New York: Simon & Schuster, 1978), p. 207.

21. Jean-Claude Bosch and E. Woodrow Eckard, Jr. "The Profitability of Price Fixing: Evidence from Stock Market Reactions to Federal Indictments," *Review of Economics and Statistics* 73 (1991): 309–317.

22. Edward Felsenthal, "Manufacturers Allowed to Cap Retail Prices," *Wall Street Journal* (November 5, 1997), p. A3.

23. David Barboza, "30 Firms to Pay $900 Million in Investor Suit," *New York Times* (December 25, 1997), p. 1.

24. John M. Broder, "Toys 'R' Us Led Price Collusion, Judge Rules in Upholding F.T.C.," *New York Times*, October 1, 1997.

25. Bradford Snell, "American Ground Transport," in Jerome H. Skolnick and Elliot Currie (eds.), *Crisis in American Institutions* (Boston: Little, Brown, 1985), pp. 319–342.

26. Alexander Liazos, *People First: An Introduction to Social Problems* (Boston: Allyn & Bacon, 1982).

27. Ibid.

28. Vance Packard, *The Hidden Persuaders* (New York: Pocket Books, 1958).

29. Wilson Bryan Key, *Subliminal Seduction* (New York: Signet, 1974).

30. Jules Henry, *Culture Against Man* (New York: Vintage, 1965).

31. President Dwight D. Eisenhower, *Farewell Radio and Television Address to the American People* (January 17, 1961), quoted in Seymour Melman, *Pentagon Capitalism: The Political Economy of War* (New York: McGraw-Hill, 1970), p. 235.

32. U.S. Bureau of the Census, *Statistical Abstract of the United States 2002*, Table 475, p. 321.

33. U.S. General Services Administration, *Inventory Report of Real Property Owned by the United States Throughout the World: 1992* (Washington, D.C.: U.S. Government Printing Office, 1992).

34. U.S. Bureau of the Census, *Statistical Abstract of the United States 2002*, Table 487, p. 327

35. Peter A. DeFazio, *More Pentagon Follies*. Available at http: www.taxpayer.net/TCS/Reports/PentagonFollies/washer.htm [July 14, 2003].

36. "Jet Fighter Should Be Grounded," Taxpayers for Common Sense. Available at: www.taxpayer.net/TCS/wastebasket/nationalsecurity [June 7, 2003].

37. Jonathan D. Salant, "Half of Top Clinton Aides Now Lobbyists Trying to Use Washington Influence," Associated Press Wire Service (March 30, 2003).

38. Steve Forbes, "Lobbyists: Their Gain Is Our Loss," *Forbes* (July 15, 1996), p. 23.

39. Daniel Bell, *The Coming of Post-Industrial Society* (New York: Basic Books, 1973, reissue edition, 1999).

40. Derived from U.S. Bureau of the Census, *Statistical Abstract of the United States 2002*, Table 588, p. 381–383.

41. See U.S. Bureau of the Census, *Statistical Abstract of the United States 2002*, Table 1099, p. 697.

42. See Alvin Toffler, *The Third Wave,* reissue ed. (New York: Morrow, 1989).

43. Ibid., p. 238.

44. U.S. Bureau of Labor Statistics, *Employment and Earnings 2002.* Available at www.bls.census.gov [June 7, 2003].

45. U.S. Bureau of the Census, *Statistical Abstract of the United States 2002*, Table 561, p. 367.

46. Ibid., Table 564, p. 369.

47. "Laying Off the American Dream," *America* 74 (March 23, 1996): p. 3.

48. For the human element in downsizing, see the seven-part series, "The Downsizing of America," *New York Times* (March 3–9, 1997), p. A1.

49. William Bridges, "The End of the Job," *Fortune* 130 (September 19, 1994), pp. 62–67.

50. U.S. Department of Labor, *Monthly Labor Review* (November 2001) Table 5.

51. See Philip Mattera, *Prosperity Lost* (Reading, Mass.: Addison-Wesley, 1991); Barry Jones, *Sleepers Awake! Technology and the Future of Work* (New York: Oxford University Press, 1991); Bennett Harrison and Barry Bluestone, *The Great U-Turn: Corporate Restructuring and the Polarizing of America* (New York: Basic Books, 1988).

52. Jeremy Rifkin, *The End of Work: The Decline of the Global Labor Force and the Dawn of the Post-Market Era* (New York: Putnam, 1995).

53. Bjorgulf Claussen, Arild Bjorndal, and Peter F. Hjort, "Health and Re-employment in a Two Year Follow Up of Long Term Unemployed," *Journal of Epidemiology & Community Health* 47 (1993): 14–18.

54. Sara Willott and Christine Griffin, "'Wham Bam, Am I a Man?' Unemployed Men Talk about Masculinities," *Feminism & Psychology* 7 (1997): 107–128.

55. See Marie-Luise Friedemann and Adele A. Webb, "Family Health and Mental Health Six Years After Economic Stress and Unemployment," *Issues in Mental Health Nursing* 16 (1995): 51–66.

56. See Amiram D. Vinokur, Yaacov Schul, Jukka Vuori, and Richard H. Price, "Two Years After a Job Loss: Long-term Impact of the JOBS Program on Reemployment and Mental Health," *Journal of Occupational Health Psychology* 5 (2000): 32–47.

57. M. E. J. Wadsworth, S. M. Montgomery, and M. J. Bartley, "The Persisting Effect of Unemployment on Health and Social Well-Being in Men Early in Working Life," *Social Science & Medicine* 48 (1999): 1491–1499.

58. Abraham Maslow, *Motivation and Personality* (New York: Harper & Row, 1954), pp. 35–47.

59. Frederick Herzberg, *Work and the Nature of Man* (New York: World, 1966).

60. Becca Mader, "What Do Job Seekers Want?" *The Business Journal* (January 14, 2002), p. 1.

61. U.S. Bureau of the Census, *Statistical Abstract of the United States 2002*, Table 579, p. 377.

62. Catherine Romano, "What's Your Flexibility Factor?" *Management Review* 83 (January 1994), 9.

63. See Christopher C. Sellers, *Hazards of the Job: From Industrial Disease to Environmental Health Science* (Chapel Hill: University of North Carolina Press, 1997).

64. U.S. Bureau of the Census, *Statistical Abstract of the United States 2002*, Table 622, p. 408.

65. "The Safety Challenge," *Government Executive* 31 (February 1999): 77–79.

66. Richard B. Elsberry, "OSHA's New Plan for the Millennium," *Electrical Apparatus* 52 (1999): 48–49.

67. Ibid.

68. Patti Bond, "Mohawk Fined $105,000 after Worker Killed," *The Atlanta Constitution* (August 17, 2000), p. E4.

69. Ken Wood Jr., "Metal Manufacturer Draws $288,000 Fine from OSHA," *Charleston Gazzette* (August 13, 2002): 1.

70. "Fines and Citations," *Occupational Health & Safety* 69 (June 2000): 20.

71. John E. Sacco, "Lukens to Pay $237,500 in OSHA Fines," *American Metal Market* 105 (April 22, 1997): 2.

72. Christopher Dinsmore, "OSHA Fines Virginia Shipbuilding Company in Employee Deaths," *Knight-Ridder/Tribune Business News* (October 9, 1997), p. 1.

73. Statistics for mining and other occupations discussed in this section are drawn from *U.S. Bureau of the Census, Statistical Abstract of the United States 2002*, Table 626, p. 410.

74. Joseph S. Stroud, "Black-Lung Cases Are Common, But Victories in Efforts to Get Federal Benefits Are Rare," *Knight-Ridder/Tribune News Service* (October 15, 1993), p. 1; "Agency Seeks to Reduce Black Lung Disease," *New York Times* (July 7, 2000), p. 15.

75. S. L. Smith, "Silicosis: A Dusting of Death," *Occupational Hazards* 56 (April 1994): 38–41.

76. "Operating Experience Summary," Office of the Environment, Safety and Health, U.S. Department of Energy, Summary 2002, 13 (July 1, 2002), p.1.

77. "NIOSH Issues Alert to Workers on Organic Dust Syndrome," *Feedstuffs* 66 (June 20, 1994), p. 21.

78. Kendal M. Thu, "The Health Consequences of Industrialized Agriculture for Farmers in the United States," *Human Organization* 57 (1998): 335–341.

79. See Russell Mokhiber, et al., *Corporate Predators*.

80. Mike Everley, "HSE Under Wraps?" *The Safety and Health Practitioner* 18 (January 2000): 1.

81. "Quarter of a Million Asbestos Deaths Predicted in Next 35 Years," *The Safety & Health Practicioner* 17 (March 1999): 4.

82. Ming-Tsang Wu, Karl T. Kelsey, I-Fang Mao, David Wypij, Hong-Wen Liu, and David C. Christiani, "Elevated Serum Liver Enzymes in Coke Oven and By-product Workers," *Journal of Occupational and Environmental Medicine* 39 (June 1997): 527–533; Farhang Akbar-Khanzadeh and Ruben D. Rivas, "Exposure to Isocyanates and Organic Solvents, and Pulmonary-function Changes in Workers in a Polyurethane Molding Process," *Journal of Occupational and Environmental Medicine* 38 (December 1996): 1205–1212; Rita Ouellett-Hellstrom and Jerry D. Rench, "Bladder Cancer Incidence in Arylamine Workers," *Journal of Occupational and Environmental Medicine* 38 (December 1996): 1239–1247; Gary M. Liss and Murray M. Finkelstein, "Mortality Among Workers Exposed to Carbon Disulfide," *Archives of Environmental Health* 51 (May–June 1996): 193–200; Frank D. Gilliland and Jack S. Mandel, "Mortality Among Employees of a Perfluorooctanoic Acid Production Plant," *Journal of Occupational Medicine* 35 (September 1993): 950–954.

83. See Gloria Borger, "Stupid Advertising Tricks," *U.S. News & World Report* (August 1, 1994), p. 66.

84. Michelle Murphy, "Toxicity in the Details: The History of the Women's Office Worker Movement and Occupational Health in the Late-Capitalist Office," *Labor History* 41 (May 2000): 189–213.

85. Ibid.

86. Michael Colligan, James Pennebaker, and Lawrence Murphy, eds., *Mass Psychogenic Illness* (Hillsdale, N.J.: Lawrence Erlbaum Associates, Inc., 1982); Neal Schmitt, Michael Colligan, and Michael

Fitzgerald, "Unexplained Physical Symptoms in Eight Organizations: Individual and Organizational Analyses," *Journal of Occupational Psychology,* 53 (1980): 305–317.

87. M. G. Smith, "Potential Health Hazards of Video Display Terminals" (Cincinnati: NIOSH, June, 1981).

88. See Keith Mulvihill, "Is Your Office Making You Sick?" *Working Mother* 23 (May 2000): 20–22; Donald J. Minnick, "Is Your Office Free of Health Hazards?" *The Office* 114 (October 1991): 67–68.

89. Peter L. Berger, "Some General Observations on the Problem of Work," in Peter L. Berger (ed.), *The Human Shape of Work* (New York: Macmillan, 1964), p. 215.

90. Ibid.

91. Two particularly helpful sites are www.wfs.org and www.futurist.org.

Chapter 6

1. Matthew 26:4.

2. Council of Economic Advisors, *1964 Economic Report to the President* (Washington, D.C.: U.S. Government Printing Office, 1964), pp. 69–70.

3. National Public Radio, Kaiser-Family Foundation, and Harvard University Kennedy School Poll on Poverty in America. Available at www.npr.org/programs/specials/poll/poverty/ [June 12, 2003].

4. Richard Herrnstein, *I.Q. in the Meritocracy* (New York: Allan Lane, 1973).

5. Richard J. Herrnstein and Charles Murray, *The Bell Curve: The Reshaping of American Life by Differences in Intelligence* (New York: Free Press, 1994).

6. See, for example, Vincent N. Parrillo, *Strangers to These Shores*, 7th ed. (Boston: Allyn & Bacon, 2003) pp. 186–191.

7. Robert Holman, *Poverty: Explanations of Social Deprivation* (New York: St. Martin's Press, 1978); Thomas Sowell, "New Light on Black I.Q.," *New York Times Magazine* (March 27, 1977): 57.

8. Oscar Lewis, "The Culture of Poverty," *Scientific American* 215 (October 1966): 19–25.

9. Edward Banfield, *The Unheavenly City Revisited* (Boston: Little, Brown, 1974).

10. William Ryan, *Blaming the Victim*, rev. ed. (New York: Vintage, 1976).

11. Charles A. Valentine, *Culture and Poverty: Critique and Counterproposals* (Chicago: University of Chicago Press, 1968).

12. U.S. Bureau of the Census, "Poverty in the United States: 2001,"*Current Population Reports, Series* P60-219 and unpublished data.

13. See Patricia Ruggles, *Drawing the Line: Alternative Poverty Measures and Their Implications for Public Policy* (Washington D.C.: Urban Institute, 1990).

14. David Caplovitz, *The Poor Pay More* (New York: Free Press, 1967).

15. David Whitman, "The Poor Aren't Poorer," *U.S. News & World Report* (July 25, 1994), pp. 33–38.

16. Susan Mayer and Christopher Jencks, "Trends in the Economic Well-Being of Children," reported in David Whitman, "The Poor Aren't Poorer."

17. Ibid.

18. See Edwin S. Mills and Han S. Lubuele, "Inner Cities," *Journal of Economic Literature* 35 (1997): 727–756.

19. Michael Harrington, *The Other America* (Baltimore: Penguin Books, 1969).

20. U.S. Bureau of the Census, "Poverty in the United States: 2002," *Current Population Reports,* series P60-222, Table 1, p.2.

21. U.S. Bureau of the Census, *Statistical Abstract of the United States 2002* (Washington, D.C.: U.S. Government Printing Office, 2002), Table 54, p. 51.

22. Ibid.

23. U.S. Bureau of the Census, "Income in the United States: 2002," *Current Population Reports* (September 2002), Series P-60, Table 3, p.4.

24. U.S. Bureau of the Census, *Statistical Abstract of the United States:* 2002, Table 51, p. 49.

25. U.S. Bureau of the Census, "Poverty in the United States: 2002," p.2.

26. Annie E. Casey Foundation and the Center for the Study of Social Policy, *1993 KIDS COUNT Data Book* (Washington, D.C.: Center for the Study of Social Policy, 1993), p. 13.

27. U.S. Bureau of the Census, "Poverty in the United States: 2001," Table POV01.

28. Ibid., Table 2, p. 6.

29. Ibid.

30. "Prematurity Associated with Inadequate Diet," *FDA Consumer* 27 (July–August 1993): 5.

31. Janet L. Peacock, J. Martin Bland, and H. Ross Anderson, "Preterm Delivery: Effects of Socioeconomic Factors, Psychological Stress, Smoking, Alcohol, and Caffeine," *British Medical Journal* 311 (August 26, 1995): 531–535.

32. U.S. National Center for Health Statistics, *National Vital Statistics Reports*, (August 28, 2002):1..

33. See National Center for Health Statistics, "Deaths: Final Data for 2000," *National Vital Statistics Reports* (September 16, 2002).

34. Susan E. Mayer, "Are there Economic Barriers to Visiting a Doctor?" JCPR Working Papers. Available at http://www.harrisschool.uchicago.edu/wp/author.html#mayer [June 10, 2003].

35. See Janice F. Madden, "The Changing Spatial Concentration of Income and Poverty among Suburbs of Large US Metropolitan Areas," *Urban Studies* 40 (2003): 481–503.

36. Ross Atkin, "Public Housing at a Crossroads," *Christian Science Monitor* (March 12, 2003), p.11.

37. U.S. Bureau of the Census, *American Housing Survey: 2001.* Available at http://www.census.gov/hhes/www.ahs.html. [June 11, 2003].

38. David Whitman, "What Keeps the Poor Poor?" *U.S. News & World Report* (October 21, 1991), pp. 42–44.

39. See William J. Wilson, *The Truly Disadvantaged: The Inner City, the Underclass, and Public Policy* (Chicago: University of Chicago Press, 1987).

40. U.S. Bureau of the Census, *Statistical Abstract of the United States 2002,* Table 675, p. 444.

41. William P. O'Hare, "A New Look at Poverty in America," *Population Bulletin* 51 (September 1996): 10.

42. Richard Kazis and Marc S. Miller (eds.), *Low-Wage Workers in the New Economy* (Washington, D.C.: Urban Institute Press, 2001).

43. William P. O'Hare, "A New Look at Poverty in America," p. 12.

44. U.S. Bureau of the Census, *Statistical Abstract of the United States 2002,* Table 442, p. 296.

45. U.S. Office of Management and Budget "A Citizen's Guide to the Federal Budget." Available at http://w3.access.gpo.gov/usbudget/fy1999/guide/guideoz.html [June 11, 2003].

46. Ibid., Table 534, p. 353.

47. Ibid., Table 516, p. 344.

48. Mary J. Corcoran, Greg J. Duncan, Gerald Gurin, and Patricia Gurin, "Myth and Reality: The Causes and Persistence of Poverty," *Journal of Policy Analysis and Management* 4 (1985): 516–36; see the PSID Web site available at www.isr.umich.edu/src/psid.

49. Harry Hampton, "America's War on Poverty," PBS Television Series, January 16–18, 1995; see also U.S. Bureau of the Census, *Current Population Reports,* 1990–1998.

50. Mary J. Corcoran et al., "Myth and Reality: The Causes and Persistence of Poverty," p. 524.

51. Joan R. Rodgers and John L. Rodgers, "Chronic Poverty in the United States," *Journal of Human Resources* 28 (Winter 1993): 25–54; Joel A. Devine, Mark Plunkett, and James D. Wright, "The Chronicity of Poverty: Evidence from the PSID, 1968–1987," Social Forces 70 (March 1992): 787–812.

52. Steven A. Holmes, "Income Disparity Between Poorest and Richest Rises," *New York Times* (June 20, 1996), p. A1.

53. U.S. Bureau of the Census, "Income in the United States: 2002," Table 7, p.15.

54. See Sheldon Danziger and Peter Gottschalk, "Do Rising Tides Lift All Boats? The Impact of Secular and Cyclical Changes on Poverty," *American Economic Review* (May 1986): 405–410.

55. See "America's Underclass: Doomed to Fail in the Land of Opportunity," *The Economist* (March 15, 1986), pp. 29–32.

56. Diana B. Henriques, "10 Years After Tax Overhaul, the Loopholes Expand," *New York Times* (December 19, 1996), p. E3.

57. Michael Harrington, "Introduction," in Louis A. Fernan, Joyce l. Kornbluh, and Alan Haber (eds.), *Poverty in America: A Book of Readings* (Ann Arbor: University of Michigan Press, 1965), pp. vii–xiv.

58. Charles Murray, *Losing Ground: American Social Policy, 1950–1980* (New York: Basic Books, 1984).

59. Daniel T. Lichter and Rukamalie Jayakody, "Welfare Reform: How do We Measure Success?" *Annual Review of Sociology* 28 (2002): 117–141.

60. Daniel T. Lichter and Martha L. Crowley, "Poverty in America: Beyond Welfare Reform," *Population Bulletin* 57 (June 2002): 6.

61. Douglas J. Besharov, "The Past and future of Welfare Reform," *The Public Interest* 150 (Winter 2003): 4–21.

62. Ibid.

63. Ibid. The remaining paragraphs in this section draw from Douglas Besharov's analysis.

64. Kingsley Davis and Wilbet E. Moore, "Some Principles of Stratification," *American Sociological Review* 10 (April 1945): 242–249; Charles Hurst, *The Anatomy of Social Inequality* (St. Louis: Mosby, 1979).

65. Herbert J. Gans, "The Uses of Poverty: The Poor Pay All," *Social Policy* 2 (July/August 1971): 20–24; see also Herbert J. Gans, "The Positive Functions of Poverty," *American Journal of Sociology* 78 (September 1972): 275–288.

66. Ralf Dahrendorf, *Class and Class Conflict in Industrial Society* (Stanford, Calif.: Stanford University Press, 1989); see also Ralf Dahrendorf, "Toward a Theory of Social Conflict," *Journal of Conflict Resolution* 11 (1958): 170–185.

67. Michael Harrington, "Why We Need Socialism in America," *Dissent* 76 (May/June 1970): 240–303.

68. Michael Harrington, *Decade of Decision* (New York: Simon & Schuster, 1982).

69. Michael Betz, "Riots and Welfare: Are They Related?" *Social Problems* 21 (1974): 345–355.

70. Frances Fox Piven and Richard A. Cloward, *Regulating the Poor* (New York: Vintage, 1993).

71. Frances Fox Piven and Richard A. Cloward, *The Politics of Turmoil* (New York: Pantheon, 1974); see also Francis Fox Piven and Richard A. Cloward, "Social Movements and Social Conditions: A Response to Roach and Roach," *Social Problems* 26 (1978): 172–178.

72. See Dorothy E. Smith, *Texts, Facts, and Femininity: Exploring the Relations of Ruling* (New York: Routledge, 1990); Mary E. Swigonski, "The Logic of Feminist Standpoint Theory for Social Work Research," *Social Work* 39 (1994): 387–393.

73. Patricia Hill Collins, Black Feminist Thought: Knowledge, Consciousness, and the Politics of Empowerment (New York: Routledge, 2000); D. Height, "Family and Community: Self-Help—a Black Tradition," *The Nation* 249 (July 1989): 136–138.

74. See Nancy Folbre, "How Does She Know? Feminist Theories of Gender Bias in Economics," *History of Political Economy* 25 (1993): 167–184.

75. Karen C. Holden and Pamela J. Smock, "The Economic Costs of Marital Dissolution: Why Do Women Bear a Disproportionate Cost?" *Annual Review of Sociology* 17 (1991): 51–78.

76. Children's Defense Fund, *The State of America's Children—Yearbook* (Washington, D.C.: 1997).

77. Rose M. Brewer, "Black Women in Poverty: Some Comments on Female-Headed Families," *Signs* 13 (1987): 331–339.

78. Elaine McGrate and Joan Smith, "When Work Doesn't Work: The Failure of Current Welfare Reform," *Gender and Society* 12 (1998): 61–80.

79. Howard S. Becker, *Outsiders: Studies in the Sociology of Deviance* (New York: Free Press, 1997).

80. Jonathan Kozol, *Savage Inequalities: Children in America's Schools* (New York: Crown, 1991); Ronald R. Edmonds, "Some Schools Work and More Can," *Social Policy* (March–April 1979): 28–32; Jonathan Kozol, *Death at an Early Age*, reissue ed. (New York: New American Library, 1990); Robert Rosenthal, *Pygmalion in the Classroom*, 2nd ed. (London: Crown House Publishing, 2003).

81. L. Richard Della Fave, "The Meek Shall Inherit the Earth," *American Sociological Review* 45 (December 1980): 955–71.

Chapter 7

1. Sandra L. Bem and Daryl J. Bem, "Training the Woman to Know Her Place: The Power of a Nonconscious Ideology," in Howard Robboy (ed.), *Social Interaction*, 5th ed. (New York: St. Martin's Press, 2000), p. 87.

2. Ann Douglas, *The Feminization of American Culture* (New York: Farrar Straus & Giroux, 1998).

3. Arno Karlen, *Sexuality and Homosexuality* (New York: W. W. Norton, 1971), p. 34.

4. Laud Humphries, *Tearoom Trade: Impersonal Sex in Public Places* rev. ed. (New York: Aldine de Gruyter, 1975), p. 121.

5. S. Krieger, "Lesbian Identity and Community: Recent Social Science Literature," *Signs* 8 (1982): 91–108.

6. See, for example, Traci, Watson, and Joseph P. Shapiro, "Is there a Gay Gene?" *U.S. News and World Report* (November 13, 1995), pp. 93–95.

7. Stephen Jay Gould, *The Mismeasure of Man* (New York: W. W. Norton, 1996), pp. 104–105.

8. Anne Moir, *Brain Sex: The Real Difference Between Men and Women* (New York: Carol Publishing Group, 1991).

9. Thomas G. Wynn, Forrest D. Tierson, and Craig T. Palmer, "Evolution of Sex Differences in Spatial Cognition," *Yearbook of Physical Anthropology* 39 (1996): 11–42.

10. Deborah Blum, *Sex on the Brain: The Biological Differences Between Men and Women* (New York: Viking, 1997).

11. Tabitha M. Powledge, "Ever Different: Brain Sex Differences, Research Update," *BioScience* 46 (June 1996): 394–395.

12. Ibid.

13. Nicholas Wade, "How Men and Women Think: Brain Sex and Intellectual Ability," *New York Times Magazine* (June 12, 1994), p. 32.

14. Margaret Mead, *Sex and Temperament in Three Primitive Societies* (New York: Dell, 1935); Herbert Barry, "A Cross-Cultural Survey of Some Sex Differences in Socialization," *Journal of Abnormal and Social Psychology* 55 (1957): 327–52; Roy G. D'Andrade, "Sex Differences and Cultural Institutions," in Eleanor E. Maccoby (ed.), *The Development of Sex Differences* (Palo Alto, Calif.: Stanford University Press, 1966); Ernestine Friedl, *Women and Men: An Anthropologist's View* (New York: Holt, Rinehart & Winston, 1975).

15. Lynne Brydon and Sylvia Chant, *Women in the Third World: Gender Issues in Rural and Urban Areas* (New Brunswick, N.J.: Rutgers University Press, 1989).

16. Carol Tavris, *The Mismeasure of Woman* (New York: Simon & Schuster, 1992).

17. Simon LeVay, "A Difference in Hypothalamic Structure between Heterosexual and Homosexual Men," *Science* 253 (1991): 1034–1037.

18. Laura S. Allen and Roger A. Gorski, "Sexual Orientation and the Size of the Anterior Commissure in the Human Brain," *Proceedings of the National Academy of Science* 8 (1992): 7199–7202.

19. Dean Hamer and Peter Copeland, *The Science of Desire: The Search for the Gay Gene and the Biology of Behavior* (New York: Simon & Schuster, 1994).

20. George Rice, Carol Anderson, Neil Risch, and George Ebers, "Male Homosexuality: Absence of Linkage to Microsatellite Markers at Xq28," *Science* 284 (1999): 665–667.

21. George Chauncey, *Gay in New York: Gender, Urban Culture, and the Making of the Gay Male World: 1890–1940* (New York: Basic Books, 1994).

22. Ibid., p. 9.

23. Eric Marcus, *Making History: The Struggle for Gay and Lesbian Equal Rights* (New York: HarperCollins, 1992).

24. Martin B. Duberman, *Stonewall* (New York: Dutton, 1993).

25. Gregory M. Herek and Kevin T. Berrill, *Hate Crimes: Confronting Violence Against Lesbians and Gay Men* (Newbury Park, Calif.: Sage, 1992); John Gagnon, Cathy Greenblat, and Michael Kimmel, *Human Sexualities* 2d ed. (Boston: Allyn & Bacon, 1995); W. R. Greer, "Violence Against Homosexuals Rising, Groups Seeking Wider Protection Say," *New York Times* (November 23, 1986): p. A36.

26. Valerie Jenness, "Social Movement Growth, Domain Expansion, and Framing Processes," *Social Problems* 42 (1995): 145–170.

27. Steven A. Holmes, "Gay Rights Advocates Brace for Ballot Fights," *New York Times* (January 12, 1994), p. A17.

28. Wilbur J. Scott and Sandra Carson Stanley (eds.), *Gays and Lesbians in the Military: Issues, Concerns, and Contrasts* (New York: Aldine de Gruyter, 1994).

29. Priscilla Painton, "The Shrinking Ten Percent," *Time* (April 26, 1993), pp. 27–29.

30. Robert T. Michael, John H. Gagnon, Edward O. Laumann, and Gina Kolata, *Sex in America: A Definitive Survey* (Boston: Little, Brown, 1994).

31. The Gallop Organization, May 15, 2003. Available at www.gallup.com/poll/releases/ [June 13, 2003].

32. "More Americans Support Gay Adoption," ABC News, (April 2, 2002). Available at http://abcnews.go.com/sections/us/DailyNews/gayadopt_poll020402.html [June 13, 2003].

33. See F. W. Bozett, "Gay Fatherhood," in P. Bronstein and C. P. Cowan (eds.), *Fatherhood Today: Men's Changing Role in the Family* (New York: John Wiley & Sons, 1988), pp. 214–235; D. Polman, "A Backlash Against Gays as Parents," *Philadelphia Inquirer* (July 21, 1985), pp. 1F, 6F.

34. "Straight Talk About Gays," *U.S. News & World Report* (July 5, 1993), p. 46.

35. NORC, *General Social Surveys, 1972–2001*.

36. K. MacDonald and R. D. Parke, "Parent-Child Physical Play: The Effects of Sex and Age on Children and Parents," *Sex Roles* 15 (1986): 367–378.

37. Susan D. Witt, "Parental Influence on Children's Socialization to Gender Roles," *Adolescence* 32 (1997): 253–259.

38. Hugh Lytton and David M. Romney, "Parents Differential Socialization of Boys and Girls: A Meta-analysis," *Psychological Bulletin* 109 (1991): 267–296; Andree Pomerleau, Daniel Bolduc, et al., "Pink or Blue: Environmental Gender Stereotypes in the First Two Years of Life," *Sex Roles* 22 (1990): 359–367.

39. Erving Goffman, *Gender Advertisements* (New York: Harper Colophon, 1979); Jean Kilbourne, *Can't Buy My Love: How Advertising Changes the Way We Think and Feel* (Carmichael, Calif.: Touchstone Books, 2000).

40. Anthony J. Cortese, *Provocateur: Images of Women and Minorities in Advertising* (Lanham, MD: Rowman & Littlefield, 1999).

41. Susan Douglas, *Where the Girls Are* (New York: Random House, 1994), pp. 297–299.

42. Ibid., p. 296.

43. Ibid., p. 303.

44. Lin Farley, quoted in Dale Spender, *Man Made Language,* 2d ed. (Boston: Routledge & Kegan Paul, 1985), pp. 184–85.

45. P. D. Horn and J. C. Horn, *Sex in the Office: Power and Passion in the Workplace* (Reading, Mass.: Addison-Wesley, 1982), pp. 62–63.

46. Susan P. Phillips and Margaret S. Schneider, "Sexual Harassment of Female Doctors by Patients," *New England Journal of Medicine* 329 (December 23, 1993): 1936–1939.

47. Patti A. Giuffre and Christine L. Williams, "Boundary Lines: Labeling Sexist Harassment in Restaurants," *Gender & Society* 8 (1994): 378–401.

48. Ibid., p. 70.

49. Michele Ingrassia, "Abused and Confused," *Newsweek* (October 25, 1993): 57.

50. Andrea Sachs, "9-Zip! I Love It!" *Time* (November 22, 1993): 44.

51. Belle R. Ragins and Terri A. Scandura, "Antecedents and Work-Related Correlates of Reported Sexual Harassment: An Empirical Investigation of Competing Hypotheses," *Sex Roles* 32 (1995): 429–455.

52. Cited in Feminist Majority Foundation, "What to Do If You or Someone You Know Is Sexually Harassed." Available at http: www.feminist.org 911 harasswhatdo.html#general [June 13, 2003].

53. Jackie K. Rogers, "Hey, Why Don't You Wear a Shorter Skirt?': Structured Vulnerability and the Organization of Sexual Harassment on Temporary Clerical Employment," *Gender & Society* 11 (1997): 215–237.

54. James E. Gruber, "The Impact of Male Work Environments and Organizational Policies on Women's Experiences of Sexual Harassment," *Gender & Society* 12 (1998): 301–320.

55. Andrew Hacker, *U/S: A Statistical Portrait of the American People* (New York: Viking Press/ Penguin Books, 1983), pp. 240–41.

56. Katia Hetter, "End of an All-Male Era," *U.S. News & World Report* (July 8, 1996), p. 50.

57. Lyn Nell Hancock and Claudia Kalb, "A Room of Their Own," *Newsweek* (June 24, 1996), p. 76.

58. See Kathleen Vail, "Same-Sex Schools," *The American School Board Journal* 189 (November 2002): 32–35; also "Same-Sex Schools May Still Get a Chance," *Education Digest* 68 (December 2002): 32–38.

59. Kristin S. Caplice, "The Case for Public Single-Sex Education," *Harvard Journal of Law & Public Policy* 18 (Fall 1994): 227–292.

60. Lyn Nell Hancock and Claudia Kalb, "A Room of Their Own."

61. Valerie E. Lee, Helen M. Marks, and Tina Byrd, " Sexism in Single-Sex and Coeducational Independent Secondary School Classrooms," *Sociology of Education* 67 (April 1994): 92–120.

62. Susan Black, "Boys and Girls Together," *American School Board Journal* 185 (December 1998): 30–33; "All-Girl Classes Aren't Necessarily Better," *American School Board Journal* 185 (May 1998):16.

63. U.S. Bureau of the Census, *Statistical Abstract of the United States 2002* (Washington, D.C.: U.S. Government Printing Office, 2002): Tables 258 and 276, pp. 166, 175.

64. Ibid., Table 279, p. 176.

65. Ibid., Table 564, p. 369.

66. Ibid. Table 569, p. 372.

67. Ibid., Table 570, p. 373.

68. Ibid., Table 588, pp. 381–383.

69. Ibid.

70. Leslie A. Zebrowitz, Daniel R. Tenenbaum, and Lori H. Goldstein, "The Impact of Job Applicants' Facial Maturity, Gender, and Academic Achievement on Hiring Recommendations," *Journal of Applied Social Psychology* 21 (1991): 525–548.

71. Myra Marx Ferree, "The Gender Division of Labor in Two-Earner Marriages: Dimensions of Variability and Change," *Journal of Family Issues* 12 (June 1991): 158–180.

72. Deborah L. Jacobs, "Back from the Mommy Track," *New York Times* (October 9, 1994), Section 3, p. 1.

73. David J. Maume, Jr., "Child-Care Expenditures and Women's Employment Turnover," *Social Forces* 70 (December 1991): 497–508.

74. Arlie Hochschild, *The Second Shift: Working Parents and the Revolution at Home* reissue ed.(New York: Penguin, 2003); Harriet B. Presser, "The Household Gender Gap," *Population Today* 21 (July–August 1995), p. 3.

75. Arlie Hochschild, *The Second Shift*, p. 238.

76. Patricia A. Ward, Peter F. Arazem, and Stefen W. Schmidt, "Women in Elite Pools and Elite Positions," *Social Science Quarterly* 73 (March 1992): 31–45; Joan Acker, "Thinking About Wages: The Gendered Wage Gap in Swedish Banks," *Gender & Society* 5 (1991): 390–417; Nicole Benokraitis and Joe Feagin, *Modern Sexism: Blatant, Subtle, and Overt Discrimination* (Englewood Cliffs, N.J.: Prentice-Hall, 1986).

77. Mathew Scott, "For Women, the Glass Ceiling Persists," *Black Enterprise* 32 (August 2001): 30.

78. Peter T. Kilborn, "For Many in Work Force, 'Glass Ceiling' Still Exists," *New York Times* (March 16, 1995), p. A22.

79. Elizabeth Larson, "Women Are on Track for Top Spots in Corporate America," Knight-Ridder News Service release, December 29, 1995.

80. David Leonhardt, "Wage Gap Between Men and Women Is Narrowest Ever," *New York Times* (February 17, 2003), p. A1.

81. U.S. Bureau of the Census, "Voting and Registration in the Election of November 2000," Current Population Reports (February 2002), Series P20-542, Table B, p. 6.

82. Center for American Women and Politics, "Women in Elected Office 2003." Available at http://www.rci.rutgers.edu/~cawp/facts/cawpfs.html [June 14, 2003].

83. Inter-Parliamentary Union, "Women in National Parliaments." Available at http://www.ipu.org/wmn-e/world.htm [June 14, 2003].

84. Center for American Women and Politics, loc. cit.

85. Gary Alan Fine, "The Dirty Play of Little Boys," *Society* (1986), pp. 63–67.

86. Herbert J. Freudenberger, "Today's Troubled Men," *Psychology Today* (December 1987), pp. 46–47.

87. Sebastian Kraemer, "The Fragility of Fatherhood," pp. 89–102 in Geoff Dench (ed.), *Rewriting the Sexual Contract* (New Brunswick, N.J.: Transaction, 1999).

88. Talcott Parsons, "The American Family: Its Relations to Personality and the Social Structure," in Talcott Parsons and Robert F. Bales (eds.), *Family Socialization and Interaction Process* (Glencoe, Ill.: Free Press, 1954), pp. 3–21.

89. Randall Collins, *Sociology of Marriage and the Family: Gender, Love, and Property,* 5th ed. (Belmont, Calif.: Wadsworth, 2000); Janet Saltzman Chafetz, *Sex and Advantage: A Comparative Macro-Structural Theory of Sex Stratification* (Totowa, N.J.: Rowman & Littlefield, 1984).

90. Arlie Hochschild, "A Review of Sex Role Research," in Joan Huber (ed.), *Changing Women in a Changing Society* (Chicago; University of Chicago Press, 1973), p. 258.

91. E. Goldfield, S. Munaker, and Naomi Weisstein, "A Woman Is a Sometime Thing," in Frank Lindenfeld (ed.), *Radical Perspectives of Social Problems,* 3rd ed. (New York: General Hall, 1986).

92. Arlie Hochschild, "A Review of Sex Role Research."

93. David A. Karp and William C. Yoels, *Symbols, Selves and Society* (New York: J. B. Lippincott/Harper & Row, 1979), p. 56.

94. J. Harrison, "Warning: The Male Sex Role May Be Dangerous to Your Health," *Journal of Social Sciences* 54 (1978): 65–86.

95. Susan Hekman, "Truth and Method: Feminist Standpoint Theory Revisited," *Signs* 22 (Winter 1997): 341–364.

96. Gail Lewis and Merl Storr, "Contesting Feminist Orthodoxies," *Feminist Review* (Autumn 1996): 1–2.

97. bell hooks, *Ain't I a Woman?: Black Women and Feminism* (Boston: South End Press, 1981), p. 13.

98. bell hooks, *Feminist Theory: From Margin to Center* (Boston: South End Press, 1984): p. 52.

99. Ibid.; bell hooks, *Talking Back: Thinking Feminist, Thinking Black* (Boston: South End Press, 1989).

100. Mary E. Swigonski, "The Logic of Feminist Standpoint Theory for Social Work Research," *Social Work* 39 (July 1994): 387–393.

101. Murray Forman, "Movin' Closer to an Independent Funk": Black Feminist Theory, Standpoint, and Women in Rap," *Women's Studies* 23 (January 1994): 35–55.

102. Mary E. Swigonski, "The Logic of Feminist Standpoint Theory for Social Work Research," p. 390.

103. Nancy Hartsock, *Money, Sex, and Power: Toward a Feminist Historical Materialism,* reprint ed. (Boston: Northeastern University Press, 1997).

104. Ibid., p. 232.

105. Sandra Harding, *Whose Science? Whose Knowledge? Thinking from Women's Lives* (Ithaca, N.Y.: Cornell University Press, 1991).

106. P. B. Walters, "Trend in U.S. Men's and Women's Sex-Role Attitudes: 1972–1978," *American Sociological Review* 46 (1981): 453–460.

107. David P. Aday, Jr., *Social Control at the Margins: Toward a General Understanding of Deviance* (Belmont, Calif.: Wadsworth, 1995), p. 25.

108. Michael Nava and Robert Dawidoff, *Created Equal: Why Gay Rights Matter to America* (New York: St. Martin's Press, 2002).

Chapter 8

1. Quoted in David Hatchett, "The Future of Civil Rights in the Twenty-first Century," in Richard C. Monk (ed.), *Taking Sides* (Guilford, Conn.: Dushkin Publishing Group, 1994), p. 181.

2. Rita J. Simon, "Old Minorities, New Immigrants: Aspirations, Hopes, and Fears," in Peter I. Rose (ed.), *Annals of the American Academy of Political and Social Science* 530 (1993), pp. 65–73.

3. National Center for Health Statistics, "Deaths: Final Data for 1998." *National Vital Statistics Reports* 50 (September 16, 2002); Table 34, p. 100.

4. Bureau of Justice Statistics, *Homicide Trends in the United States.* Available at www.ojp.usdoj.gov/bjs/homicide/homtrnd.htm [June 16, 2003].

5. See Vincent N. Parrillo, *Strangers to These Shores*, 7th ed. (Boston: Allyn & Bacon, 2003), pp. 328–329, 390–393.

6. Lewis Mumford Center, "Ethnic Diversity Grows, Neighborhood Integration Lags Behind. Available at www.albany.edu/mumford/census [June 16, 2003].

7. John Katsillis and J. Michael Armer, "Education and Mobility," in Edgar F. Borgatta and Marie L. Borgatta (eds.), *Encyclopedia of Sociology* (New York: Macmillan, 1992), pp. 541–544.

8. James S. Coleman, et al. *Equality of Educational Opportunity* (Washington, D.C.: U.S. Government Printing Office, 1966).

9. Erika Frankenberg and Chungmei Lee, "Race in American Public Schools: Rapidly Resegregating School Districts." Available at www.civilrightsproject.harvard.edu/research/deseg/reseg_schools02.php [June 16, 2003].

10. U.S. Bureau of the Census, *Current Population Survey,* March 2002, Table 22.

11. See Sol Stern, "The Catholic School Miracle," *New York Times* (September 25, 1996), p. A15; Kenneth L. Woodward "Catechism Lessons," *Newsweek* (September 23, 1996): 62.

12. Betsy Wagner and Stephen J. Hedges, "Education in Decay," *U.S. News & World Report* (September 12, 1994): 76–80.

13. Charles V. Willie, "The Future of School Desegregation," in J. E. Jacob (ed.), *The State of Black America* (New Brunswick, N.J.: Transaction Books, 1987), pp. 37–47.

14. W. D. Hawley and M. A. Smylie, "The Contribution of School Desegregation to Academic Achievement and Racial Integration," in Phyllis A. Katz and Dalmas A. Taylor (eds.), *Eliminating Racism* (New York: Plenum Press, 1988), pp. 281–297.

15. See, for example, Roslyn A. Mickelson, "Subverting Swann: First- and Second Generation Segregation in the Charlotte-Mecklenburg Schools." *American Educational Research Journal* 38 (Summer 2001): 21..

16. Roslyn A. Mickelson and Carol A. Ray, "Fear of Falling from Grace: The Middle Class, Downward Mobility, and School Desegregation," *Research in Sociology of Education and Socialization* 10 (1994): 207–238.

17. U.S. Bureau of the Census, *Statistical Abstract of the United States 2002* (Washington, D.C.: U.S. Government Printing Office, 2002), Table 598, p. 390.

18. U.S. Bureau of the Census, "Poverty in the United States: 2001" Current Population Reports, Series PBO-219 (September 2002), Table 1, p. 3.

19. Thomas Sowell, "Debate: Equal Opportunity or the Numbers Game?" *American Educator* (Fall 1978): 9–15.

20. John Leo, "Endgame for Affirmative Action," *U.S. News & World Report* (March 13, 1995), p. 18.

21. See Gertrude Ezorsky, *Racism and Justice: The Case for Affirmative Action* (Ithaca, N.Y.: Cornell University Press, 1991).

22. Michael Wines, "How Affirmative Action Got So Hard to Sell," *New York Times* (July 23, 1995), p. E3.

23. Paul Glastris, "The Thin White Line," *U.S. News & World Report* (August 15, 1994), pp. 53–54.

24. Mary Frances Berry, "How Percentage Plans Keep Minority Students Out of College," *The Chronicle of Higher Education* (August 4, 2000), p. A48.

25. Linda Greenhouse, "Justices Back Affirmative Action by 5 to 4, but Wider Vote Bans a Racial Point System," *New York Times* (June 24, 2003), p. A.

26. Steven Greenhouse and Jonathan D. Glater, "Companies See Law School Ruling as a Way to Help Keep Diversity Pipeline Open," *New York Times* (June 24, 2003), p. A25.

27. Jennifer Daskal, *In Search of Shelter: The Growing Shortage of Affordable Rental Housing* (Washington, D.C.: Center of Budget and Policy Priorities, 1998). Available at http://www.cbpp.org/615hous.pdf [June 20, 2003].

28. Ibid.

29. U.S. Bureau of the Census, "The Black Population in the United States: March 2002," *Current Population Reports,* Series P20-541, (April 2003), p.2.

30. John Jeter, "Black Suburb Jinxed by Lack of Commerce," *The Los Angeles Times* (April 19, 1998), p. 16.

31. David J. Dent, "The New Black Suburbs," *New York Times Magazine* (June 14, 1992), p. 20.

32. See, for example, Michael H. Tonry, *Sentencing Matters* (New York: Oxford University Press, 1996); Hiroshi Fukurai, Edgar W. Butler, and Richard Krooth. *Race and the Jury: Racial Disenfranchisement and the Search for Justice* (New York: Plenum Press, 1993); Pamela Irving Jackson, *Minority Group Threat, Crime, and Policing: Social Context and Social Control* (New York: Frederick Praeger, 1989); Christopher E. Smith, *Courts and the Poor* (Chicago: Nelson-Hall, 1991).

33. Ibid.

34. Michael J. Leiber and Jayne M. Stairs, "Race, Contexts, and the Use of Intake Diversion," *Journal of Research in Crime and Delinquency* 36 (1999): 56–86; Darrell Steffensmeier, "The Interaction of Race, Gender, and Age in Criminal Sentencing: The Punishment Cost of Being Young, Black and Male," *Criminology* 36 (1998): 763–797; Ed A. Munoz and David A. Stewart, "Misdemeanor Sentencing Decisions: The Cumulative Disadvantage Effect of "Gringo Justice'," *Hispanic Journal of Behavioral Sciences* 20 (1998): 298–319.

35. Doris M. Provine, "Too Many Black Men," *Law and Social Inquiry* 23 (1998): 56–86.

36. Allen J. Beck, "Prisoners in 1999," *Bureau of Justice Statistics Bulletin* (August 2000): NCJ183476.

37. See Ward Churchill, *Indians Are Us? Culture and Genocide in Native North America* (Monroe, Maine: Common Courage Press, 1994); Ronet Bachman, *Death and Violence on the Reservation: Homicide, Family Violence, and Suicide in American Indian Populations* (New York: Auburn House, 1992).

38. Gary Fuller, "A Snapshot Report on American Indian Youth and Families," *OCB Tracker.* Available at http://www.ocbtracker.com/0007/snapshot.html [July 14, 2003].

39. U.S. Bureau of the Census, *Statistical Abstract of the United States 2002,* Table 14, p. 16.

40. Ibid., Table 263, p. 169.

41. See R. Lin, "The Promises and Problems of the Native American Student: A Comparative Study of High School Students on the Reservation and Surrounding Areas," *Journal of American Indian*

Education 24 (1985): 6–15; Gerard E. Gipp, "Promoting Cultural Relevance in American Indian Education," *Education Digest* (November 1989): 58.

42. Gary Fuller, "A Snapshot Report on American Indian Youth and Families."

43. U.S. Bureau of the Census, Housing of American Indians on Reservations—Plumbing, April 1995, SB/95-9.

44. Thomas M. Becker et al., "Mortality from Infectious Disease Among New Mexico's American Indians, Hispanic Whites, and Other Whites, 1958–1987," *American Journal of Public Health* 80 (1990): 320–323.

45. U.S. Bureau of the Census, "The Black Population in the United States: March 2002."

46. National Center for Education Statistics, *Digest of Education Statistics, 2002.* Table 108.

47. U.S. Bureau of the Census, "The Black Population in the United States: March 2002."

48. U.S. Bureau of the Census, *Statistical Abstract of the United States 2002,* Table 255, p. 164.

49. Bureau of Justice Statistics, *Racial Composition of Offender and Victim for Homicide.* Available at http://www.ojp.usdoj.gov/bjs/homicide/ovrace.txt [March 6, 2004].

50. National Center for Health Statistics, "Deaths: Final Data for 1998," Table 8, p. 34.

51. U.S. Bureau of the Census, *Current Population Reports,* Series P25-1095 (Washington, D.C.: U.S. Government Printing Office, 1999).

52. U.S. Bureau of the Census, *Statistical Abstract of the United States 2002,* Table 251, p. 163.

53. U.S. Bureau of the Census, "The Hispanic Population in the United States 2002." *Current Population Reports,* Series P20-545 (June 2003), Table 7.2.

54. Ibid., Tables 9.3 and 14.1.

55. Ibid., Table 16.1.

56. U.S. Bureau of the Census, "The Asian and Pacific Islander Population in the United States: March 2002," *Current Population Reports,* Series P20-540 (May 2003), Tables 7 and 14.

57. See Lewis Mumford Center, "The New Ethnic Enclaves in America's Suburbs." Available at: http://mumfordl.dyndns.org/cen2000/report.html. Accessed June 21, 2003.

58. U.S. Immigration and Naturalization Service, *2001 Statistical Yearbook* (Washington D.C.: U.S. Government Printing Office, 2003), p. 239; August Gribbin, "8 Million Illegals Reported in U.S.," *Washington Times* (October 25, 2001), p. A3.

59. Larry Martz, et al., "Slamming the Golden Door," *Newsweek* (May 9, 1988), pp. 18–19; Matt S. Meier, "North from Mexico," pp. 309–311, in Carey McWilliams and Matt S. Meier (eds.), *North from Mexico* (New York: Praeger, 1990).

60. Edna Bonacich, "A Theory of Ethnic Antagonism: The Split Labor Market," *American Sociological Review* 3 (1972): 547–559.

61. W. Lloyd Warner and Leo Stole, *The Social System of American Ethnic Groups,* Yankee City Series, Vol. 3 (New Haven, Conn.: Yale University Press, 1945), pp. 285–286.

62. See, for example, Rodolfo de la Garza, *Latino Voices: Mexican, Puerto Rican, and Cuban Perspectives on American Politics* (Boulder, Colo: Westview Press, 1992).

Chapter 9

1. See Richard Quinney, *The Social Reality of Crime* (Somerset, N.J.: Transaction Publishers, 2001).

2. Miriam D. Sealock and Sally S. Simpson, "Unraveling Bias in Arrest Decisions: The Role of Juvenile Defender Type-Scripts," *Justice Quarterly* 15 (1998): 427–457; Mark Cooney, "Racial Discrimination in Arrest," *Virginia Review of Sociology* (1992): 99–119.

3. William Ryan, *Blaming the Victim* (New York: Vintage Books, 1976), p. 209.

4. Federal Bureau of Investigation, "Crime in the United States 2002" *Uniform Crime Reports* (Washington, D.C.: U.S. Government Printing Office, 2003), p. 14.

5. Federal Bureau of Investigation, "White Collar Crime." Available at http://jacksonville.fbi.gov/wcc.htm [June 21, 2003].

6. Bureau of Justice Statistics, "Criminal Victimization 2002," *National Crime Victimization Survey* (September 2003), Table 91.

7. Federal Bureau of Investigation, *Crime in the United States: 2001* (Washington, D.C.: U.S. Government Printing Office, 2002), p. 222.

8. Data throughout this section comes from the *National Crime Victimization Survey* cited in note 6.

9. Bureau of Justice Statistics, *Crime Characteristics*. Available at http://www.ojp.usdoj.gov/bjs/evict_c.htm violent [June 21, 2003].

10. Richard M. Brown, "The History of Extra-Legal Violence in Support of Community Values," in Thomas Rose (ed.), *Violence in America* (New York: Vintage Press, 1969), p. 87.

11. Ibid., p. 88.

12. Jason Vest, Warren Cohen, and Mike Tharp, "Road Rage," *U.S. News & World Report* (June 2, 1997): 24–30.

13. See Southern Poverty Law Center, *Intelligence Project*. Available at http://www.splcenter.org/intelligenceproject/ip_index.html.

14. Bureau of Justice Statistics, *Sourcebook of Criminal Justice Statistics,* Table 238. Available at www.albany.edu/sourcebook/1995/pdf/t238.pdf [June 22, 2003].

15. Wendy W. Simmons, "Half of Americans Still Say There Is More Crime in the Country Than a Year Ago," Available at www.gallup.com/poll/releases/pr000907.asp [June 22, 2003].

16. Lydia Saad, "Crime Tops List of Americans' Local Concerns." (June 21, 2000). Available at http://www.gallup.com/poll/releases/pr000621.asp [June 23, 2003].

17. Linda Heath and Kevin Gilbert, "Mass Media and Fear of Crime," *American Behavioral Scientist* 39 (February 1996): 378–385.

18. Cheryl Russell, "True Crime," *American Demographics* 17 (August 1995): 22–31.

19. Data for this section come from the sources cited in notes 6 and 14.

20. John M. Dawson and Patrick A. Langan, "Murder in Families," *U.S. Department of Justice Special Report* (July 1994), p. 1.

21. Eloise Salholz, "Short Lives, Bloody Deaths," *Newsweek* (December 17, 1990): 33.

22. Bureau of Justice Statistics, *Capital Punishment Statistics*. Available at http://www.ojp.usdoj.gov/bjs/cp.htm [June 22, 2003].

23. Shannon Brownlee, Dan McGraw, and Jason Vest, "The Place for Vengeance," *U.S. News & World Report* (June 16, 1997): 25–32.

24. See Ford Fessenden, "Deadly Statistics: A Survey of Crime and Punishment," *New York Times* (September 22, 2000), p. A23; Tom Kuntz, "The Rage to Kill Those Who Kill," *New York Times* (December 4, 1994), p. E1; Tom Kuntz, "Killings, Legal and Otherwise, Around the U.S.," *New York Times* (December 4, 1994), p. E3.

25. Shannon Brownlee, et al., "The Place for Vengeance," p. 27.

26. Bureau of Justice Statistics, "Sex Offenses and Offenders: An Analysis of Data on Rape and Sexual Assault" (February 1997), p. 3.

27. Data in this paragraph come from the sources cited in notes 6 and 14.

28. Bureau of Justice Statistics, *National Crime Victimization Survey 2001,* p. 7.

29. Ibid., p.10.

30. See Bonnie S. Fisher, Francis T. Cullen, and Michael G. Turner, "The Sexual Victimization of College Women" (Washington D.C.: U.S. Department of Justice, 2000).

31. Crystal S. Mills and Barbara J. Granoff, "Date and Acquaintance Rape Among a Sample of College Students," *Social Work* 37 (1992): 504–509.

32. Susan Estrich, "Balancing Act," *Newsweek* (October 25, 1993): 64.

33. Mary M. Fonow, Laurel Richardson, and Virginia A. Wemmerus, "Feminist Rape Education: Does It Work?" *Gender & Society* 6 (1992): 108–121.

34. Linda B. Bourque, *Defining Rape* (Durham, N.C.: Duke University Press, 1989).

35. Centre for International Crime Prevention, *Seventh United Nations Survey of Crime Trends and Operations of Criminal Justice Systems, 1998–2000,* pp. 62–64.

36. Calvin Sims, "Justice in Peru: Victim Gets Rapist for a Husband," *New York Times* (March 12, 1997), pp. A1, A12.

37. Skip Kaltenheuser, "Caveat Emptor," *World Trade* (May 1997): 40–41.

38. Edwin H. Sutherland, "White Collar Criminality," *American Sociological Review* 5 (1940): 1–12.

39. Richard C. Hollinger, *National Retail Security Survey* (November 2002). Available at http:web.soc.ufl.edu/SRP/finalreport_2002.pdf [June 24, 2003].

40. Based on data from U.S. Department of Justice, Federal Bureau of Investigation, *Crime in the United States, 2001* (Washington, D.C.: U.S. Government Printing Office, 2002), Table 41, p. 250

41. Grant Johnson, Tom Bird, and J. W. Little, *Delinquency Protection: Theories and Strategies* (Washington, D.C.: U.S. Department of Justice, LEAA, 1979), p. 19.

42. Ted H. Rubin, *Juvenile Justice,* 2nd ed. (New York: Random House, 1993), pp. 34–35.

43. See, for example, G. Roger Jarjoura and Ruth Triplett, "The Effects of Social Area Characteristics on the Relationship Between Social Class and Delinquency," *Journal of Criminal Justice* 25 (March–April 1997): 125–139; Nancy Jo Sales, "Teenage Gangland," *New York* (December 16, 1996), pp. 32–39.

44. See, for example, Margaret Farnworth, Terence P. Thornberry, Marvin D. Krohn, and Alan J. Lizotte, "Measurement in the Study of Class and Delinquency: Integrating Theory and Research," *Journal of Research in Crime and Delinquency* 31 (February 1994): 32–61.

45. G. Roger Jarjoura, "The Conditional Effect of Social Class on the Dropout-Delinquency Relationship," *Journal of Research in Crime and Delinquency* 33 (May 1996): 232–255.

46. Scott Cummings and Daniel J. Monti (eds.), *The Origins and Impact of Youth Gangs in the United States* (Albany: State University of New York Press, 1993), p. 30.

47. Ibid., p. 34.

48. Elijah Anderson, *Streetwise: Race, Class and Change in an Urban Community* (Chicago: University of Chicago Press, 1992); Scott Cummings and Daniel J. Monti, *The Origins and Impact of Youth Gangs,* p. 315.

49. Scott Cummings and Daniel J. Monti, *The Origins and Impact of Youth Gangs,* Table 10-4.

50. "What Is a Child?" *The Economist* 342 (April 19, 1997), pp. 29–30.

51. Ted Gest, "Crime Time Bomb," *U.S. News & World Report* (March 15, 1996), pp. 28–32.

52. Bureau of Justice Statistics, *Homocide Trends in the U.S.* Available at www.ojp.usdoj.gov/bjs/homocide/tables/oagetab.htm [June 24, 2003].

53. U.S. Department of Justice, *Juvenile Offenders and Victims: 1999 National Report* (Washington, D.C.: U.S. Government Printing Office, 1999), Chapter 4.

54. Margaret Talbot, "The Maximum Security Adolescent," *The New York Times Magazine* (September 10, 2000), p. 42.

55. "What Is a Child?"

56. Gwyn Smit Ingley, "Juvenile Justice News," *Corrections Today* 57 (December 1995): 174–175.

57. Bureau of Justice Statistics, *Law Enforcement Statistics*. Available at http://www.ojp.usdoj.gov/bjs/lawenf.htm [June 24, 2003].

58. "Drop in Random Killings Signals a Shift in Nature and Scope of New York Crime," *New York Times* (December 19, 1996), pp. L25, L28.

59. Paige M. Harrison and Allen J. Beck, "Prison and Jail Inmates at Midyear 2002," *Bureau of Justice Statistics Bulletin* (July 2003).

60. Ibid.

61. Ibid.

62. Melinda Beck, "Kicking the Prison Habit," *Newsweek* (June 14, 1993), p. 32.

63. Bureau of Justice Statistics, *Criminal Offenders Statistics*, Available at www.ojp.usdoj.gov/bjs/crimoff.htm [June 24, 2003].

64. Paige M. Harrison and Allen J. Beck, "Prison and Jail Inmates at Midyear 2002," p. 5.

65. "Prison Boot Camps May Not Help Inmates," *Christian Science Monitor* (September 4, 2001), p.4.

66. See Susan Turner and Joan Petersilia, "Work Release in Washington: Effects on Recidivism and Corrections Costs," *Prison Journal* 76 (June 1996): 138–164.

67. U.S. Department of Justice, *Intermediate Sanctions in Sentencing Guidelines*. Available at http://www.nejrs.org/txtfiles/165043.tx [June 24, 2003]..

68. Joan Petersilia, "Probation in the United States: Practices and Challenges," *National Institute of Justice Journal* 233 (September 1997): 4.

69. U.S. Department of State, *Patterns of Global Terrorism: 2002,* p. 1. Available at http://www.state.gov/documents/organization/20109.pdf [December 2003].

70. Ibid., p. 107.

71. Institute for Counter-Terrorism, *International Terrorism-Attack Data Base*. Available at http://www.ict.org.il [December 6, 2003].

72. U.S. Department of State, *Patterns of Global Terrorism: 2002,* p. xi.

73. Ted R. Gurr, *Why Men Rebel* (Princeton, N.J.: Princeton University Press, 1970), p. 212.

74. Robert K. Merton, *Social Theory and Social Structure* (New York: Free Press, 1968).

75. M. C. Wiatrowski, D. B. Grishold, and M. K. Probers, "Social Control Theory and Delinquency," *American Sociological Review* 6 (1981): 525.

76. Leslie W. Kennedy, *On the Borders of Crime: Conflict Management and Criminology* (New York: Longman, 1990); Richard Quinney, *Critique of Legal Order: Crime Control in Capitalist Society* (Somerset, N.J.: Transaction Publishers, 2001).

77. See Susan Caringella-Macdonald, "State Crises and the Crackdown on Crime Under Reagan," *Contemporary Crises* 14 (1990): 91–118; F. P. Williams III and M. D. McShane, *Criminological Theory* (Englewood Cliffs, N.J.: Prentice-Hall, 1988).

78. Myra Marx Ferree and Beth B. Hess, *Controversy and Coalition" The New Feminist Movement Across Three Decades of Change,* rev. ed. (New York: Twayne, 1997).

79. Edwin H. Sutherland, *Principles of Criminology* (Philadelphia: J. B. Lippincott, 1939).

80. Howard S. Becker, *Outsiders: Studies in the Sociology of Deviance* (New York: Free Press, 1963).

81. Edwin M. Lemert, *Human Deviance, Social Problems, and Social Control,* 2d ed. (Englewood Cliffs, N.J.: Prentice-Hall, 1972).

82. Raymond Paternoster and Lee Ann Iovanni, "The Labeling Perspective and Delinquency: An Elaboration of the Theory and Assessment of the Evidence," *Justice Quarterly* 6 (December 1989): 359–394.

Chapter 10

1. Stephanie Coontz, *The Way We Never Were: American Families and the Nostalgia Trap,* reprint ed. (New York: Basic Books, 2000).

2. Mark Baumgartner, "On the Daddy Track," *ABC News* (June 15, 2001); Geoffrey L. Grief, *The Daddy Track and the Single Father* (Lanham, MD: Lexington Books, 1990).

3. Arlie Hochschild, *The Second Shift,* reissue ed.(New York: Viking, 2003).

4. U.S. Bureau of the Census, *Statistical Abstract of the United States 2002* (Washington, D.C.: U.S. Government Printing Office, 2002): Table 49, p. 48.

5. National Center for Health Statistics, "Births, Marriages, Divorces, and Deaths," *National Vital Statistics Reports* 51 (June 17, 2003): Table 1, p. 1.

6. Michael Cohen, "Trying Second Marriage? Prenuptial Is Crucial," *Boston Globe* (August 20, 2000), p. G7. See also David Whitman, "The Divorce Dilemma," *U.S. News & World Report* (September 30, 1996), p. 58; Charles L. Jones, Lorne Tepperman, and Susannah Wilson. *The Futures of the Family* (Englewood Cliffs, N.J.: Prentice-Hall, 1995), p. 84.

7. Vijaya Krishman, "Premarital Cohabitation and Marital Disruption," *Journal of Divorce and Remarriage* 28 (1998): 157–170.

8. National Center for Health Statistics, "Cohabitation, Marriage, Divorce, and Remarriage in the United States," *Vital Health Statistics* 23 (July 2002): Table 21, p. 55.

9. J. Ross Eshleman, *The Family: An Introduction,* 10th ed. (Boston: Allyn & Bacon, 2002), p. 560.

10. Ann Swidler, *Talk of Love: How Culture Matters* (Chicago: University of Chicago Press, 2003).

11. Pamela J. Smock, Wendy D. Manning, and Sanjiv Gupta, "The Effect of Marriage and Divorce on Women's Economic Well-Being," *American Sociological Review* 64 (1999): 794–812; Karen C. Holden and Pamela J. Smock, "The Economic Costs of Marital Dissolution: Why Do Women Bear Disproportionate Cost?" *Annual Review of Sociology* 17 (1991): 51–78.

12. Nancy B. Miller, Virginia L. Smerglia, Scott D. Gaudet, and Gay C. Kitson, "Stressful Life Events, Social Support, and the Distress of Widowed and Divorced Women," *Journal of Family Issues* 19 (1998): 181–203; Debra Umberson and Christine L. Williams, "Divorced Fathers: Parental Role Strain and Psychological Distress," *Journal of Family Issues* 14 (1993): 378–400.

13. Paul Bohannan, *Divorce and After* (Garden City, N.Y.: Doubleday/Anchor Books, 1971).

14. Robert Weiss, *Marital Separation* (New York: Basic Books, 1983), pp. 48–56.

15. Charles L. Cole and Anna L. Cole, "Boundary Ambiguities That Bind Former Spouses Together," *Family Relations* 48 (July 1999): 271–272.

16. Frank F. Furstenberg, Jr., "Divorce and the American Family," *Annual Review of Sociology* 16 (1990): 383.

17. U.S. Bureau of the Census, "Children's Living Arrangements and Characteristics, March 2002," *Current Population Reports,* Series P20-547, Table C3.

18. Paul R. Amato and Bruce Keith, "Parental Divorce and the Well-Being of Children: A Meta-Analysis," *Psychological Bulletin* (1991): 26–46.

19. Frank F. Furstenberg, Jr., "Divorce and the American Family," p. 393.

20. J. Mauldon, "The Effect of Marital Disruption on Children's Health," *Demography* 27 (August 1990): 431–446.

21. Judith S. Wallerstein, Sandra Blakeslee, and Julia M. Lewis, *The Unexpected Legacy of Divorce: A 25-Year Landmark Study* (New York: Hyperion Books, 2001).

22. Frank F. Furstenberg, Jr., "Good Dads-Bad Dads: Two Faces of Fatherhood," in Andrew Cherlin (ed.), *The Changing American Family* (Washington, D.C.: Urban Institute, 1988), pp. 193–218.

23. U.S. Bureau of the Census, "Custodial Mothers and Fathers and Their Child Support," *Current Population Reports,* Series P60-217 (October 2002).

24. See, for example, Alex Liazos, "Grieving and Growing: Experiences of Divorced Fathers," *Humanity and Society* 21 (1997): 353–376; Joyce A. Arditti and Patricia Bickley, "Fathers' Involvement and Mothers' Parenting Stress Postdivorce," *Journal of Divorce and Remarriage* 26 (1996): 1–23; Jay D. Teachman, "Who Pays? Receipt of Child Support in the United States," *Journal of Marriage and the Family* 53 (1991): 759–772.

25. Frank F. Furstenberg, Jr., and Nancy Ten Kate, "The Future of Marriage," *American Demographics* 18 (June 1996): 34–40.

26. Chandler Arnold, *Children and Stepfamilies: A Snapshot,* Center for Law and Social Policy. Available at http://www.clasp.org/DMS/Documents/101188491724/children [June 27, 2003].

27. Andrew J. Cherlin, *Marriage, Divorce, Remarriage* (Cambridge, Mass.: Harvard University Press, 1992).

28. Chandler Arnold, *Children and Stepfamilies: A Snapshot,* loc. cit.

29. Mary Poulce, "Are Married Parents Really Better for Children?" Center for Law and Public Policy. Available at http://www.clasp.org/DMS/Documents/1052841451.72/marriage_Brief3.pdf [June 27, 2003].

30. U.S. Bureau of the Census, "Children's Living Arrangements and characteristics: March 2002," Table 8, p. 16.

31. U.S. Bureau of the Census, "Poverty in the United States: 2001," *Current Population Reports* (September 2002), Series P60-219, Table 1, p. 3.

32. Virginia E. Schein, *Working From the Margins: Voices of Mothers in Poverty* (Ithaca, N.J.: Cornell University Press, 1995); Carol Stack, *All Our Kin: Strategies for Survival in a Black Community* (New York: Harper & Row, 1974).

33. Donald J. Hernandez, "Poverty Trends," in Greg J. Duncan and Jeanne Brooks-Gunn (eds.), *Consequences of Growing Up Poor* (New York: Russell Sage Foundation, 1997), pp. 18–34; Donna L. Franklin, "Feminization of Poverty and African-American Families: Illusions and Realities," *School Social Service Administration* 7 (1992): 142–155; William J. Wilson, *The Truly Disadvantaged: The Inner City, the Underclass, and Public Policy* (Chicago: University of Chicago Press, 1987).

34. National Center for Health Statistics, "Births: Final Data for 2000," *National Vital Statistics Reports* (February 12, 2002), p. 10.

35. Ibid., p. 8.

36. Ibid., p. 9.

37. K. G. Mapanga, "The Perils of Adolescent Pregnancy," *World Health* 50 (March–April 1997): 16–17; D. Hollander, "Studies Suggest Inherent Risk of Poor Pregnancy Outcomes for Teenagers," *Family Planning Perspectives* 27 (November–December 1995): 262–263.

38. Sandra Arbetter, "Family Violence: When We Hurt the Ones We Love," *Current Health* 22 (November 1995): 6–12.

39. C. H. Kempe, "The Battered Child Syndrome," *Journal of the American Medical Association* 181 (1962): 17–24.

40. Federal Bureau of Investigation, "Incidents of Family Violence," Section V in *Crime in the United States: 1998* (Washington, D.C.: U.S. Government Printing Office, 1999).

41. Susan B. Sorenson, Dawn M. Upchurch, and Haikang Shen, "Violence and Injury in Marital Arguments: Risk Patterns and Gender Differences," *American Journal of Public Health* 86 (January 1996): 35–40.

42. Amy Holtzworth-Munroe, "Marital Violence," *Harvard Mental Health Letter* 12 (August 1995): 4–6.

43. Bureau of Justice Statistic, "Homicide Trends in the U.S." Available at www.ojp.usdoj.gov/bjs/homicide/intimates.htm [June 28, 2003].

44. Susan B. Sorenson et al. "Violence and Injury in Marital Arguments."

45. Judith Ivy Fiene, "Battered Women: Keeping the Secret," *Affilia Journal of Women and Social Work* 10 (Summer 1995): 179–193.

46. Betsy McAlister Groves, Barry Zuckerman, Steven Marans, and Donald J. Cohen, "Silent Victims: Children Who Witness Violence," *Journal of the American Medical Association* 269 (January 13, 1993): 262–264.

47. U.S. Department of Health and Human Services, Administration on Children, Youth and Families, *Child Maltreatment 2001* (Washington, D.C.: U.S. Government Printing Office, 2003) pp. 3–4.

48. Murray A. Straus and Carrie L. Yodanis, "Corporal Punishment in Adolescence and Physical Assaults on Spouses in Later Life: What Accounts for the Link?" *Journal of Marriage and the Family* 58 (November 1996): 825–841.

49. Jean Renvoize, *Web of Violence: A Study of Family Violence* (London: Routledge & Kegan Paul, 1978), pp. 113–127.

50. K. A. Pillemer and D. Findelhor, "The Prevalence of Elder Abuse: A Random Sample Survey," *The Gerontologist* 28 (1988): 51–57.

51. National Center on Elder Abuse, *The National Elder Abuse Incident Study: Final Report* (Washington, D.C.: Department of Health and Human Services, 1998).

52. Sandra Arbetter, "Family Violence."

53. National Center on Elder Abuse, "FAQ's About Elder Abuse." Available at www.elderabusecenter.org [June 28, 2003].

54. Richard J. Gelles and Donileen Loseke (eds.), *Current Controversies on Family Violence* (Newbury Park, Calif.: Sage Publications, 1993).

55. Murray A. Straus, "A Sociological Perspective on the Causes of Family Violence," in Maurice Green (ed.), *Violence and the Family* (Boulder, Colo.: Westview Press, 1981), p. 8.

56. Murray A. Straus and Christine Smith, "Family Patterns and Primary Prevention of Family Violence," in Murray A. Straus and Richard J. Gelles (eds.), *Physical Violence in American Families* (New Brunswick, N.J.: Transaction, 1995), pp. 508–509.

57. Cathy Young, "Complexities Cloud Marital Rape Case," *Insight on the News* 10 (August 1, 1994): 6–10.

58. Patricia Mahoney and Linda Williams, "Sexual Assault in Marriage: Prevalence, Consequences and Treatment of Wife Rape," in Jana L. Jasinski and Linda M. Williams (eds.), *Partner Violence: A Comprehensive Review of 20 Years of Research* (Thousand Oaks, Calif.: Sage, 1998), pp. 113–162.

59. Raquel Kennedy Bergen, *Marital Rape,* Violence Against Women Online Resources. Available at http://www.vaw.umn.edu/Vawnet/mrape.htm [June 28, 2003].

60. Candice M. Monson, Gary R. Byrd, and Jennifer Langhinrichsen-Rohling, "To Have and To Hold: Perceptions of Marital Rape," *Journal of Interpersonal Violence* 11 (September 1996): 410–424.

61. Lisa R. Eskow, "The Ultimate Weapon?: Demythologizing Spousal Rape and Reconceptualizing Its Prosecution," *Stanford Law Review* 48 (February 1996): 677–709.

62. See David Finkelhor, "The International Epidemiology of Child Sexual Abuse," *Child Abuse and Neglect* 18 (1994): 409–417.

63. David Finkelor, *Sexually Victimized Children* (New York: Free Press, 1981), pp. 71–72.

64. Judith L. Herman, *Trauma and Recovery,* reprint ed. (New York: Basic Books, 1997).

65. Noreen M. Glover, Timothy P. Janikowski, and John J. Benshoff, "Substance Abuse and Past Incest Contact: A National Perspective," *Journal of Substance Abuse Treatment* 13 (May–June 1996): 185–193; and "The Incidence of Incest Histories Among Clients Receiving Substance Abuse Treatment," *Journal of Counseling and Development* 73 (March–April 1995): 475–480.

66. Judith L. Herman, *Trauma and Recovery.*

67. Ibid.

68. Naomi A. Adler and Joseph Schutz, "Sibling Incest Offenders," *Child Abuse and Neglect* 19 (July 1995): 811–819; James R. Worling, "Adolescent Sibling-Incest Offenders: Differences in Family and Individual Functioning When Compared to Adolescent Nonsibling Sex Offenders," *Child Abuse and Neglect* 19 (May 1995): 633–643; see also David Finkelhor, *Sexually Victimized Children*, p. 130.

69. See Murray A. Straus and Richard J. Gelles, "How Violent are American Families? Estimates from the National Family Violence Resurvey and Other Studies," in Straus and Gelles, *Physical Violence in American Families* (New Brunswick, N.J.: Transaction Books, 1990). pp. 95–132.

70. William F. Ogburn, *On Culture and Social Change* (Chicago: University of Chicago Press, 1964).

71. Robert Nisbet, *The Quest for Community,* reprint ed.(Oakland, Calif.: Institute for Contemporay Studies, 1990), Chapter 3.

72. Judy R. Aulette, *Changing American Families* (Boston, Mass.: Allyn & Bacon, 2001).

73. Friedrich Engels, *The Origin of the Family, Private Property, and the State* (New York: International Publishing, 1942), originally published 1884.

74. Patricia S. Mann, *Micro-Politics: Agency in a Post-feminist Era* (Minneapolis, Minn.: University of Minnesota Press, 1994).

75. See, for example, Jane R. Wilkie, "Changes in U.S. Men's Attitudes Toward the Family Provider Role, 1972–1989," *Gender and Society* 7 (1993): 261–279.

76. See, for example, Jennifer A. Warren and Phyllis Johnson, "The Impact of Workplace Support on Work-Family Role Strain," *Family Relations* 44 (1995): 163–169.

77. Philippe Aries, *Centuries of Childhood: A Social History of Family Life* (New York: Random House, 1965).

78. Marie Winn, *Children Without Childhood* (New York: Pantheon Books, 1983).

Chapter 11

1. U.S. Bureau of the Census, *Statistical Abstract of the United States 2002* (Washington, D.C.: U.S. Government Printing Office, 2002): Table 113, p. 92.

2. United Nations, *The State of the World's Children 2003*, Table 1.

3. Ivan Illich, *Medical Nemesis: The Expropriation of Health,* reprint ed. (London, Marion Boyon, Ltd., 1998), pp. 32–36.

4. Ibid., pp. 40–41.

5. The Kaiser Commission on Medicaid and the Uninsured, *Uninsured in America: Key Facts* (March 2000), pp. 3–4.

6. Ibid. p. 6.

7. Ibid. p. 8.

8. Ibid. p. 9.

9. Arnold Birenbaum, *Putting Health Care on the National Agenda,* rev. ed. (Westport, Conn.: Praeger, 1995).

10. Erica Goode, "For Good Health, It Helps to Be Rich and Important," *New York Times* (June 1, 1999), p. F1; Holcomb B. Noble, "Health Care Systems in U.S. Called Separate and Unequal," *New York Times* (April 27, 1999), p. F8.

11. Katherine L. Kahn, Majorie L. Pearson, and Ellen R. Harrison, "Health Care for Black and Poor Hospitalized Medicare Patients," *Journal of the American Medical Association* 271 (April 20, 1994): 1169–1174.

12. John Biemer, "U.S. Black Caucus Seeks Better Care," *Chicago Tribune* (June 9, 2003), p. A1.

13. Peter T. Kilborn, "Foreign Doctors Flocking to Rescue Long-Shunned Areas of Dire Poverty," *New York Times* (November 2, 1991), p. 8.

14. U.S. Bureau of the Census, *Statistical Abstract of the United States 2002*, Table 150, p. 108.

15. Diane Seo, "Med Students Seek Cure for Debt," *The Los Angeles Times* (November 27, 1999), p. C1.

16. "Assessing the Appropriateness of Care," *RAND Research Highlights,* Document R8-4522, 1998.

17. National Center for Health Statistics, *National Hospital Discharge Survey: Annual Summary, 2000* (November 2002), Table 25, p. 35.

18. "Needless Surgery, Needless Drugs," *Consumer Reports on Health*, 10580832, 10 (March 1998).

19. Susan Brink, "C-sections Rise But May Not Be the Kindest Cut," *U.S. News & World Report* (September 4, 2000), p. 63.

20. See, for example, Edwin W. Brown, "50,000 Unnecessary Appendectomies a Year—and How to Prevent Them," *Medical Update* 20 (February 1997): 4; "Consumer Group Challenges C-section Rate," *Special Delivery* 17 (Summer 1994): 4.

21. "Wasted Health Care Dollars," *Consumer Reports* (July 1992): 440–441, 447.

22. James W. Coleman, *The Criminal Elite: The Sociology of White Collar Crime*, 3d ed. (New York: St. Martin's Press, 1994), pp. 113–114.

23. Jeffrey H. Reiman, *The Rich Get Richer and the Poor Get Prison: Ideology, Class, and Criminal Justice*, 6th ed. (Boston: Allyn & Bacon, 2000), p. 85–87.

24. "Most Hysterectomies Not Worth It," *Special Delivery* 16 (Spring 1993): 17.

25. See Julie Johnsson, "Columbia Still a Player: Inverstor-owned Hospitals Roll the Dice," *American Medical News* 40 (May 5, 1997): 3–5.

26. Vince Galloro, "Advantage: For Profits," *Modern Healthcare* 33 (March 17, 2003): 52–53, 55–58.

27. Health Forum, *Hospital Statistics 2000* (Chicago: American Hospital Association, 2000).

28. U.S. Health Care Financing Administration, *Health Care Financing Review* 21 (Winter 1999).

29. See Robert J. Samuelson, "Health Care: How We Got into This Mess," *Newsweek* (October 4, 1993), p. 35; Andrew Pollack, "Medical Technology 'Arms Race' Adds Billions to the Nation's Bills," *New York Times* (April 29, 1991), p. A1, B8.

30. Vince Galloro, "Advantage: For Profits"; U.S. Bureau of the Census, *Statistical Abstract of the United States: 2002,* Table 154, p. 110.

31. The Kaiser Commission, *Uninsured in America;* Robert Pear, "Number of Insured Americans Up for First Time Since '87," *New York Times* (September 29, 2000), p. A16; U.S. Census Bureau, *Who Goes Without Health Insurance?* (June 1999), P60-199, Table B.

32. John Colombotos, Corinne Kirchner, and Michael Millman, "Physicians View National Health Insurance: A National Study," *Medical Care* 13 (May 1975): 369–396.

33. "The New World of Health Care," *U.S. News & World Report* (April 14, 1986), pp. 60–63.

34. U.S. Bureau of the Census, *Statistical Abstract of the United States 2002,* Table 135, p. 101.

35. Chris Kelly, "Managed Care Woes," *Repertoire Magazine* 6 (February 1998). Available at http://www.medicaldistribution.com/rep/rep_1998 [July 1, 2003].

36. Susan Bink and Nancy Shute, "Are HMOs the Right Prescription?" *U.S. News & World Report* (October 13, 1997), p. 60.

37. Chris Kelly, "Managed Care Woes."

38. Daniel Q. Haney, "Nurses Hasten Death at Times," Associated Press (May 23, 1996); see also Katherine Bouton, "Painful Decisions: The Role of the Medical Ethicist," *New York Times Magazine* (August 5, 1990), pp. 22ff.

39. U.S. Bureau of the Census, *Statistical Abstract of the United States 2002,* Tables 88 and 89, p. 70.

40. David J. Garrow, "Abortion: Still Under Besiegement Abortion and the Future: Will the Nation Ever Find a Common Ground?" *Chicago Tribune* (January 21, 1998), p. 13.

41. Edd Doerr, "Priestly Politics," *The Humanist* (September/October 2000), p. 20.

42. "Final Request," *American Demographics* 23 (April 2001): 22

43. Centers for Disease Control and Prevention, *HIV/AIDS Fact Sheets*. Available at http://www.gov/hiv/pubs/facts.htm [July 1, 2003].

44. UNAIDS/WHO, *AIDS Epidemic Update 2002* Available at http://www.unaids.org/worldaidsday/2002/press/Epiupdate.html [July 1,2003].

45. Associated Press, "AIDS Care Costs Less Than Thought." (December 23, 1998). Available at http:/www.channel4000.com/sh/health/conditionsaz/news-health-981223-183853.html [December 8, 2003].

46. U.S. Department of Health and Human Services, *Mental Health: A Report of the Surgeon General—Executive Summary* (Rockville, MD: U.S. Department of Health and Human Services, 1999).

47. Robert E. L. Faris and H. Warren Dunham, *Mental Disorders in Urban Areas* (Chicago: University of Chicago Press, 1939).

48. August B. Hollingshead and Frederick C. Redlich, *Social Class and Mental Illness: A Community Study* (New York: John Wiley & Sons, 1958).

49. Leo Srole et al., *Mental Health in the Metropolis: The Midtown Manhattan Study*, rev. ed. (New York: Harper & Row, 1978).

50. David R. Williams, David T. Takeuchi, and Russell K. Adair, "Socioeconomic Status and Psychiatric Disorders among Blacks and Whites," *Social Forces* 71 (1992): 179–195.

51. Ibid.

52. National Institute of Mental Health, *Women Hold Up Half the Sky*. Available at http://www.nimh.nih.gov/publicat/womensoms.cfm [July 2, 2003]; See also Phyllis Chelser, *Women and Madness,* reprint ed. (New York: Four Walls Eight Windows, 1997).

53. See, for example, Jill Astbury, *Crazy for You: The Making of Women's Madness* (New York: Oxford University Press, 1996); Valerie Davis Raskin, *When Words Are Not Enough: The Women's Prescription for Depression and Anxiety* (New York: Broadway Books, 1997).

54. See David R. Williams, David T. Takeuchi, and Russell K. Adair, "Marital Status and Psychiatric Disorders among Blacks and Whites," *Journal of Health and Social Behavior* 33 (1992): 140–157; Ian M. Goodyer, "Family Relationships, Life Events, and Childhood Psychopathology," *Journal of Child Psychology and Psychiatry and Allied Disciplines* 31 (1990): 161–192.

55. Talcott Parson, *The Social System* (New York: Free Press, 1951), pp. 428–473.

56. See Christine A. Dietz, "Responding to Oppression and Abuse: A Feminist Challenge to Clinical Social Work," *Affilia* 15 (Fall 2000): 369–389.

57. Thomas Szasz, *The Myth of Mental Illness,* rev. ed. (New York : HarperCollins, 1984).

58. Erving Goffman, *Asylums: Essays on the Social Situation of Mental Patients and Other Inmates* (Garden City, N.Y.: Doubleday/Anchor, 1961), p. XII.

Chapter 12

1. Phillip Wambat, "Curbing Grade Inflation," *ASEE Prism* 12 (2002): 38; Jon Marcus, "Harvard Saves Face by Deflating Grades," *The Times Higher Education Supplement* (February 7, 2003), p. 11.

2. Jeffrey Mirel and David Angus, "High Standards for All? The Struggle for Equality in the American High School Curriculum, 1890–1990," *American Educator* 18 (Summer 1994): 4–9, 40.

3. Alvin Toffler, *Future Shock,* reissued. (New York: Bantam, 1999), p. 400.

4. See Jonathan Kozol, *Death at an Early Age,* reissued. (New York: New American Library, 1990).

5. Charles E. Silberman, *Crisis in the Classroom* (New York: Random House, 1971), p. 324.

6. Ibid.; see also John C. Holt, *How Children Fail,* rev. ed. (New York: Perseus Press, 1995).

7. Christopher Jencks, quoted in Charles E. Silberman, *Crisis in the Classroom*, p. 133.

8. Vincent N. Parrillo, *Strangers to These Shores*, 7th ed. (Boston: Allyn & Bacon, 2003), Chapter 6.

9. Robert Rosenthal and Lenore Jacobson, *Pygmalion in the Classroom*, 2d ed. (Carmarthen, England: Crown House Publishing, 2003; orig. ed. 1968).

10. Robert Rosenthal and Elisha Y. BaBad, "Pygmalion in the Gymnasium," *Educational Leadership* 43 (1985): 36–39; Carole C. Farrell, "Pygmalion in the Prison Classroom," *International Journal of Offender Therapy and Comparative Criminology* 30 (1986): 151–162. See also John W. Ritchie, "The Magic Feather: Education and the Power of Positive Thinking," *Teachers College Record* 78 (1977): 477–486; Janet D. Elashoff and Richard E. Snow, *"Pygmalion" Reconsidered* (Worthington, Ohio: Jones, 1971); William J. Gephart, "Will the Real Pygmalion Please Stand Up?" *American Education Research Journal* 7 (1970): 473–474.

11. See Eric M. Kramer and Lonnie Johnson, Jr., "A Brief Archeology of Intelligence," pp. 31–50, in Eric M. Kramer (ed.), *Postmodernism and Race* (Westport, Conn.: Praeger, 1997); Sarla Sharma, "Assessment Strategies for Minority Groups," *Journal of Black Studies* 17 (1986): 111–124.

12. Arthur R. Jensen, "How Much Can We Boost I.Q. and Scholastic Achievement?" *Harvard Educational Review* 39 (1969): 11–123.

13. In a later work, Jensen reaffirmed his position by arguing that the mean differences remain despite attempts to raise scores. See Arthur R. Jensen, *Bias in Mental Testing* (New York: Free Press, 1980).

14. Richard J. Herrnstein, "IQ," *Atlantic Monthly* 228 (September 1971): 43–64; Richard J. Herrnstein and Charles Murray, *The Bell Curve: The Reshaping of American Life by Differences in Intelligence* (New York: Free Press, 1994).

15. Lee J. Cronbach, "Heredity, Environment and Educational Policy," *Harvard Educational Review* 39 (1969): 338–347.

16. Philip Scrofani, Anatas Suziedelis, and Milton Shore, "Conceptual Ability in Black and White Children of Different Classes: An Experimental Test of Jensen's Hypotheses," *American Journal of Orthopsychiatry* 43 (1973): 541–543.

17. Thomas Sowell, "New Light on the Black I.Q. Controversy," *New York Times Magazine* (March 27, 1977): p. 57.

18. Constance Holden, "California Court Is Forum for Latest Round in IQ Debate," *Science* 201 (1978): 1106–1109.

19. National Center for Education Statistics, *Digest of Education Statistics 2002* (Washington, D.C.: U.S. Department of Education, 2003), Table 108, p. 164.

20. Will J. Jordon, Julia Lara, and James M. McPartland, "Exploring the Causes of Early Dropout among Race-Ethnic and Gender Groups," *Youth and Society* 28 (1996): 62–94.

21. National Center for Education Statistics, *The Digest of Education Statistics 2002,* loc, cit.
22. National Center for Education Statistics, *International Comparisons of Adult Literary.* Available at http://nces.ed.gov/pubs99/condition99/Indicator-8.html [July 2, 2003].
23. Ibid.; David A. Kaplan, "Dumber Than We Thought," *Newsweek* (September 20, 1993), pp. 44–45.
24. Ibid.
25. Jonathan Kozol, *Savage Inequities: Children in America's Schools,* reprint ed. (New York: Perennial, 1992).
26. National Commission on Excellence in Education, *A Nation at Risk: The Imperative for Educational Reform* (Washington, D.C.: U.S. Government Printing Office, 1983).
27. National Center for Education Statistics, *The Condition of Education 2003,* (Washington, D.C.: U.S. Government Printing Office, 2000), Indicator 10, Table 10-1.
28. Ibid., Indicator 9, Table 9-1.
29. Ibid., Indicator 13, Table 13-1.
30. National Center for Education Statistics, *Trends in Academic Progress: Three Decades of Student Performance* (Washington, D.C.: U.S. Government Printing Office, 2001), Indicator 10, Chart 1.
31. U.S. Bureau of the Census, *Statistical Abstract of the United States: 2002,* Table 244, p. 159.
32. John Cloud, "Who's Ready for College?" *Time* 160 (October 14, 2002): 60, 63.
33. Clifford Adelman, unpublished report to the National Commission on Excellence in Education, 1983.
34. National Commission on Excellence in Education, *A Nation at Risk.*
35. National Center for Education Statistics, *The Condition of Education 2003,* p. 43.
36. National Center for Education Statistics, *The Condition of Education 2003,* Section 1.
37. College Entrance Examination Board, *2002 College-Bound Seniors,* Table 4-1.
38. Robert J. Samuelson, "Merchants of Mediocrity," *Newsweek* (August 1, 1994), p. 44.
39. Lucia Solorzano, "What's Wrong with Our Teachers?" *U.S. News & World Report* (March 14, 1983), p. 38.
40. Edward B. Fiske, "Redesigning the American Teacher," *New York Times Education Supplement* (April 12, 1987), pp. 18–21.
41. Carnegie Corporation, *Report on Teaching as a Profession* (New York: Carnegie Corporation, 1986).
42. Daniel Gursky, "Recruiting Minority Teachers," *American Teacher* 86 (February 2002): 10–11, 19.
43. National Center for Education Statistics, "America's Teachers Ten Years After 'A Nation at Risk,'" no. 3 (May 1995), p. 2.
44. Jon Marcus, "Teachers Paid Less Than City Dustmen," *The Times Education Supplement* (March 10, 2000) p. 14.
45. NCES, *The Condition of Education 2003,* Indicator 59.
46. See, for example, Lucille Renwick, "Busing Rolls to a Stop," *The Nation* 269 (November 15, 1999): 17–18.
47. Ellen Goldring and Claire Smrekar, "Magnet Schools Reform and Race in Urban Education," *Clearing House* 76(September/October 2002).
48. Kimberly C. West, "A Desegregation Tool That Backfired: Magnet Schools and Classroom Segregation," *Yale Law Journal* 103 (June 1994): 2567–2592.
49. Adam Gamoran, "Do Magnet Schools Boost Achievement?" *Educational Leadership* 54 (October 1996): 42–46.
50. Thomas Toch, "Schools That Work." *U.S. News & World Report* (May 27, 1991), pp. 58–66
51. Allen Avery, "Do Magnet Schools Exacerbate Tracking?" *NEA Today* 13 (May 1995): 39.

52. See Martha M. McCarthy, "What Is the Verdict on School Vouchers?" *Phi Delta Kappan* 81 (January 2000): 371–378.

53. Paul E. Peterson, "Victory for Vouchers?" *Commentary* 114 (September 2002): 46–50.

54. Steve Forbes, "Ray of Education Sunshine," *Forbes* 160 (October 13, 1997), pp. 27–28.

55. Thomas Toch, "Liberal Vouching for City Schools," *U.S. News & World Report* (June 16, 1997), p. 40.

56. Lowell G. Rose and Alec M. Gallup, "The Public's Attitude Toward the Public Schools," *Phi Delta Kappan* 84 (September 2002): 41–56.

57. David A. Bositis, *2002 National Opinion Poll* (Washington, D.C.: Joint Center for Political and Economic Studies, 2002), Table 5, p. 7.

58. "Poll Finds 63% of Americans Favor School Choice," Center for Education Reform. Available at http://edreform.com/press/2002/choicepoll.htm [July 3, 2003].

59. Will Lester, "AP Poll: Public Mixed on Vouchers." Available at http://icrsurvey.com/icrinthenews/ap_vouchers_0802.html [July 3, 2003].

60. David Masci, "School Choice Debate: Are Tuition Vouchers the Answer to Bad Public Schools?" *CQ Researcher* 7 (July 18, 1997): 627–642.

61. National Center for Education Statistics, *The Condition of Education 2003,* Indicator 30.

62. National Center for Education Statistics, *Digest of Education Statistics 2002,* Table 95, p. 120.

63. Thomas Toch, "The New Education Bazaar," *U.S. News & World Report* (April 27, 1998), pp. 34–46.

64. National Center for Education Statistics and Bureau of Justice Statistics, *Indicators of School Crime and Safety: 2002.* NCES 2003-009/NCJ 196753, p. 24.

65. National Center for Education Statistics, *The Condition of Education 2003.* Indicator 15.

66. U.S. Department of Justice and U.S. Department of Education, *1999 Annual Report on School Safety,* p. 33.

67. See Sampson L. Blair, Marilou C. Blair, and Anna B. Madamba, "Racial/Ethnic Differences in High School Students' Academic Performance," *Journal of Comparative Family Studies* 30 (Summer 1999): 539–555.

68. Betty Levy, "The School's Role in the Sex-Role Stereotyping of Girls: A Feminist Review of the Literature," *Feminist Studies* 1 (1972): 5–23.

69. Myra Sadker and David Sadker, *Failing at Fairness: How America's Schools Cheat Girls* (New York: Scribner, 1994).

Chapter 13

1. Thomas S. Szasz, *Our Right to Drugs: The Case for a Free Market* (Syracuse, N.Y.: Syracuse University Press, 1996).

2. National Institute on Alcoholism and Alcohol Abuse, *Alcoholism: Getting the Facts.* Available at www.niaaa.nih.gov/publications/booklet [July 5, 2003].

3. National Council on Alcoholism and Drug Dependence. Available at http://www.ncadd.org/facts/numberoneprob.html/#3 [July 5, 2003].

4. J. McGinnis and W. Foege, "Actual Causes of Death in the United States," *Journal of the American Medical Association* 270 (18) (11/10/93): 2208.

5. Substance Abuse and Mental Health Services Administration. *2001 National Household Survey on Drug Abuse,* Washington, D.C.: U.S. Government Printing Office, 2002.

6. L.D. Johnston, D.M. O'Malley, and J.G. Bachman, *Monitoring the Future: National Results on Adolescent Drug Use* (Bethesda, MD: National Institute on Drug Abuse, 2003), pp. 30–31.

7. "Youth, Young Adults, and Alcohol: Key Facts and Prevention Strategies," American Medical Association. Available at http://www.ama-assn.org/ama/pub/article/3566-3641.html [July 6, 2003]; National Institute on Drug Abuse, *2002 Monitoring the Future Study,* Table 4-4b, p. 99.

8. The Scholastic/CNN Newsroom Survey of Student Attitudes About Drug and Substance Abuse, February 1990.

9. *The Weekly Reader, National Survey on Drugs and Alcohol* (Middletown, Conn.: Field Publications, Spring 1995).

10. "Rethinking Rites of Passage: Substance Abuse on America's Campuses." National Center on Addiction and Substance Abuse. Available at www.casacolumbia.org [July 6, 2003].

11. "Alcohol and Drugs on Virginia College Campuses," State Council of Higher Education for Virginia, March 1993, p. 11.

12. "Rethinking Rites of Passage," loc. cit.

13. H. Wesley Perkins, "Gender Patterns in Consequences of Collegiate Alcohol Abuse," *Journal of Studies on Alcohol* 53 (1992): 458–462.

14. NIDA, *2002 Monitoring the Future*, p. 25.

15. National Institute on Alcohol and Alcohol Abuse, *Ninth Special Report to U.S. Congress on Alcohol and Health,* U.S. Department of Health and Human Services, June 1997, p. 306.

16. B. Grant, et al., "Prevalence of DSM-W Alcohol Abuse and Dependence," *Alcohol Health & Research World,* 18 (1994): 257.

17. "Use of Alcohol and Other Drugs Among Women," National Council on Alcoholism and Drug Dependence. Available at www.ncadd.org/facts.html [July 6, 2003].

18. Alcoholics Anonymous Fact File. Available at http://www.alcoholics-anonymous.org [July 6, 2003].

19. B. A. Miller et al., "Interrelationships Between Victimization Experience and Women's Alcohol Use," *Journal of Studies on Alcohol,* Supp. 11 (1993): 107–117.

20. National Institute on Alcoholism and Alcohol Abuse, *Eighth Special Report,* p. 21.

21. U.S. Department of Education, *Raising More Voices Than Mugs* (Washington, D.C.: U.S. Government Printing Office, 1994).

22. D. Krahn et al., "The Relationship of Dieting Severity and Bulimic Behaviors to Alcohol and Other Drug Use in Young Women," *Journal of Substance Abuse* 4 (1992): 341.

23. Penny Booth Page, *Children of Alcoholics* (New York: Garland Publishing, 1991).

24. J. Collins and P. Messerschmidt, "Epidemiology of Alcohol-Related Violence," *Alcohol Health & Research World* 17 (1993): 95.

25. National Institute on Drug Abuse, *Crack and Cocaine.* Available at http://165.112.78.61/Infofax/Cocaine.html [July 6, 2003].

26. NIDA, *2002 Monitoring the Future*.

27. Ibid.

28. Laura Kann, Steven A. Kinchen, Barbara I. Williams, James G. Ross, et al., "Youth Risk Behavior Surveillance—United States, 1999," *The Journal of School Health* 70 (September 2000): 271–285.

29. National Institute on Drug Abuse, *Epidemiologic Trends in Drug Abuse* (Washington, D.C.: U.S. Government Printing Office, 1999).

30. Erich Goode, *Drug in American Society,* 5th ed. (New York: McGraw-Hill, 1998).

31. James A. Inciardi, *The War on Drugs III: The Continuing Saga of the Mysteries and Miseries of Intoxication, Addiction, Crime, and Public Policy* (Boston: Allyn & Bacon, 2001), Chapters 6–7.

32. Ted Gest, "New War Over Crack," *U.S. News & World Report* (November 6, 1995), pp. 81–82.

33. Ibid., p. 83.

34. National Institute on Drug Abuse, "Club Drugs," *NIDA Infofacts*. Available at http://www.nida.nih.gov/Infofax/Clubdrugs.html [July 12, 2003].

35. Alan I. Leshner, Testimony to the U.S. Senate Caucus on International Narcotics Control (July 25, 2000). Available at http://www.nida.nih.gov/Testimony/7-25-00Testimony.html [July 12, 2003].

36. Drug Abuse Warning Network, "Trends in Drug-Related Emergency Department Visits, 1994–2001 At a Glance," *The DAWN Report* (June 2003), p. 2.

37. Alan I. Leshner, Testimony to the Senate Subcommittee on Government Affairs (July 30, 2001). Available at http://www.nida.nih.gov/Testimony/7-30-01Testimony.html [July 12, 2003].

38. NIDA, *2002 Monitoring the Future*, Table 1.2B.

39. Bureau of Justice Statistics, *Sourcebook of Criminal Justice Statistics 2001* (Washington, D.C.: U.S. Government Printing Office, 2002), Table 2.84, p. 157.

40. National Institute on Drug Abuse, *Research Report Services: Marijuana Abuse* (Rockville, Md: U.S. Government Printing Office, 2002).

41. Ibid.

42. Chuck Thomas, *Marijuana Arrests and Incarceration in the United States:* June 1999, Marijuana Policy Project. Available at http: www.mpp.org/arrests/fas61699.html [July 7, 2003].

43. Reuters, "Purer, Cheaper, Snortable Heroin Floods U.S." Available at http://www.mapinc.org/drugnews/v98.n002.a01.html.

44. Drug Abuse Warning Network, "Trends in Drug-Related Emergency Department Visits, 1994–2001," *The DAWN Report* (June 2003), p. 2.

45. Ibid.

46. Centers for Disease Control and Prevention, "Targeting Tobacco Use: The Nation's Leading Cause of Death (March 2003), pp. 1–2.

47. U.S. Department of Health & Human Services, *2001 National Household Survey on Drug Abuse.*

48. The National Women's Health Information Center, "Lung Cancer." Available at http://www.4woman.gov/faq/lung.htm [July 14, 2003].

49. National Center on Addiction and Substance Abuse at Columbia University, *Substance Abuse and the American Woman* (June 1996).

50. World Health Organization, *The Tobacco Epidemic: A Global Overview* (August 31, 2000). Available at http://www.who.int/inf-fs/en/fact221.html [July 8, 2003].

51. See Erich Goode, *Drugs in American Society.*

52. Humphrey Taylor, "The Power of Tobacco Addiction." *Harris Poll #8.* (February 2, 2000). Available at http://www.harriszone.com/press/PowerOfTobacco.html [July 9, 2003].

53. Geoffrey Cowley, "I'd Toddle a Mile for a Camel," *Newsweek* (December 23, 1991), p. 70; see also www.wesleyan.edu/psyc/psyc260/joechemo.htm.

54. John Leo, "Boyz to (Marlboro) Men," *U.S. News & World Report* (June 2, 1997), p. 18.

55. Ibid.

56. Associated Press Wire Service, "Elders Rips Tobacco Ads, Calls Smoking an Addiction of Teens" (February 25, 1994).

57. National Center on Addiction and Substance Abuse at Columbia University, "Substance Abuse and the American Woman," June 1996, summarized at www.health.org/pressrel/casapr.htm.

58. Environmental Protection Agency "Secondhand Smoke Can Cause Lung Cancer in Nonsmokers." Available at www.epa.gov/iaq/pubs [July 9, 2003].

59. J. L. Pirkle, K. M. Flegal, J. T. Bernert, D. J. Brody, R. A. Etzel, K. R. Maurer, "Exposure of the U.S. Population to Environmental Tobacco Smoke: The Third National Health and Nutrition Examination Survey, 1988 to 1991." *Journal of the American Medical Association* 275 (1996): 1233–1240.

60. See "Master Settlement Agreement, 1998." Available at www.tobaccofree.com/msa [July 11, 2003].

61. "Cigarette Ads Target Youth, Violating 1998 Agreement," March 20, 2002. Available at www.tobaccofree.com/msa/articles/update_032002.html [July 11, 2003].

62. Bureau of Justice Statistics, *Drugs and Crime Facts: 2001* (Washington, D.C.: U.S. Government Printing Office, 2001).

63. See James A. Inciardi, *The War on Drugs II,* pp. 58–59.

64. National Highway Traffic Safety Administration, *Traffic Safety Facts 2001*, pp. 32–37, Mothers Against Drunk Driving. Available at: www.madd/org/stats [July 11, 2003].

65. Ibid.

66. Ibid.; also Matt Mossman, "The Most Dangerous of Days," Knight-Ridder New Service (July 2, 1997).

67. National Center for Health Statistics, *Monthly Vital Statistics Report* 50 (2002), Tables 24 and 25, pp. 55–56.

68. National Center for Health Statistics, *HIV/AIDS Surveillance Report,* Vol. 13, No. 2.

69. U.S. National Center for Health Statistics, "Exposure to Alcoholism in the Family: United States," *Advance Data* (Washington, D.C.: U.S. Government Printing Office, 1991).

70. U.S. National Center for Health Statistics, "Deaths: Final Data for 2000," *National Vital Statistics Reports* 50 (September 16, 2002), p. 10.

71. U.S. Department of Labor, "Alcohol and Drug Abuse in America Today." Available at www.dol.gov/asp/programs/drugs/workingpartners/screen15.htm [July 11, 2003].

72. *NCADD Fact Sheet: Alcohol and Other Drugs in the Workplace,* National Council on Alcoholism and Drug Dependence. Available at www.ncadd.org/facts/workplac.html [July 11, 2003].

73. P. J. Huffstutter and Robin Fields, "Drug Tests Are Multiple Choice at Tech Firms," *The Los Angeles Times* (October 2, 2000), p. 1.

74. Jamie Kieffer, "Employee Assistance Programs," *ESU Online Management Journal.* Available at www.emporia.edu/ibed/jour/jour11/jktp.htm [July 11, 2003].

75. Devon Gordon, and Sharon Begley, "Under the Shadow of Drugs," *Newsweek* (October 9, 2000), p. 56.

76. James C. McKinley, Jr., "Steroid Suspicions Abound in Major League Dugouts," *New York Times* (October 11, 2000), p. 1.

77. Mike Freeman, "Painkillers and Addiction Are Prevalent in N.F.L.," *New York Times* (April 13, 1997), p. S1.

78. See, for example, David J. Hanson, *Alcohol Education: What We Must Do* (New York: Praeger, 1996).

79. "National Study Shows 'Gateway' Drugs Lead to Cocaine Use," *Columbia University Record,* Vol. 20 (November 18, 1994).

80. Fernando A. Wagner and James C. Anthony, "Into the World of Illegal Drug Use." *American Journal of Epidemiology* 155 (May 2002): 918–925.

81. W. B. Hansen, L. A. Rose, J. C. Dryfoos, *Causal Factors, Interventions and Policy Considerations in School-Based Substance Abuse Prevention* (Washington, D.C.: U.S. Congress, Office of Technology Assessment; May 26, 1993).

82. Linda Dusenbury, Antonia Lake, and Mathea Falco, "A Review of the Evaluation of 47 Drug Abuse Prevention Curricula Available Nationally," *Journal of School Health* 67 (April 1997): 127–132.

83. Keith Humphreys and Rudolf H. Moos, "Saving Money with Alcoholics Anonymous," *Harvard Mental Health Letter* 13 (March 1997): 6–7.

84. See Richard Sadovsky, "Public Health Issue: Methadone Maintenance Therapy," *American Family Physician* 62 (July 15, 2000): 428–432.

85. National Institute on Drug Abuse, *New Study Underscores Effectiveness of Methadone Maintenance as Treatment for Heroin Addiction,* news release, March 7, 2000.

86. See James V. DeLong, "Dealing With Drug Abuse." Available at http://www.druglibrary.org/schaffer/Library/studies/dwda/staff3.htm [July 12, 2003].

87. National Institute on Drug Abuse, *Research Reports: Therapeutic Community* (Rockville, MD: U.S. Government Printing Office, 2002).

88. Gordon Witkin, "Why This Country Is Losing the Drug War," *U.S. News & World Report* (September 16, 1996), p. 60.

89. Robert J. MacCoun and Peter Reuter, "Does Europe Do It Better? Lessons from Holland, Britain, and Switzerland," *The Nation* 269 (September 30, 1999): 28–30.

90. Joseph A. Califano, Jr. and Joris Vos, "Dazed and Confused: Smoke and Mirrors Over Dutch Drug Policy," *Foreign Affairs* (November/December 1999), pp. 134–139.

91. *Statistical Abstract of the United States 2002,* Table 170, p. 117.

92. Peter H. Odegard, *Pressure Politics* (New York: Octagon Books, 1984).

93. Richard Ashley, *Cocaine: Its History, Uses, and Effects* (New York: St. Martin's Press, 1975).

94. Larry Sloman, *Reefer Madness: The History of Marijuana in America* (Torrance, Calif.: Griffin, 1998); Donald Dickson, "Bureaucracy and Morality: An Organization Perspective on a Moral Crusade," *Social Problems* 16 (1968): 146–156.

95. Barry Glasner and Bruce Berg, "How Jews Avoid Alcohol Problems," *American Sociological Review* 45 (1980): 647–664.

96. Giorgiio Lolli et al., *Alcohol in Italian Culture* (New Brunswick, N.J.; Rutgers Center on Alcohol, 1995.)

97. Richard Stivers, *A Hair of the Dog: Irish Drinking and the American Stereotype,* rev. ed. (New York: Continuum Publishing, 2000).

98. This concept of differential association was formulated by Edwin H. Sutherland in *Principles of Criminology* (Philadelphia: J. B. Lippincott, 1934).

Chapter 14

1. UNICEF, "UNICEF Hails Entry Into Force of Optional Protocol on the Sale of Children, Child Prostitution, and Child Pornography," October 23, 2001, press release.

2. Alfred C. Kinsey et al., *Sexual Behavior in the Human Male* (Philadelphia: W. B. Saunders, 1948).

3. Clyde Kluckhon, "As an Anthropologist Views It," in Albert Deutch (ed.), *Sex Habits of American Men* (New York: Prentice-Hall, 1948).

4. Marston Bates, *Gluttons and Libertines* (New York: Knopf, 1971), p. 80.

5. James M. Henslin (ed.), *The Sociology of Sex* rev. ed. (New York: Schocken, 1987), p. 14.

6. Marston Bates, *Gluttons and Libertines.*

7. Paul H. Gebhard, "Human Sexual Behavior," in Donald S. Marshall and Robert C. Suggs (eds.), *Human Sexual Behavior: Variations in the Ethnographic Spectrum* (Englewood Cliffs, N.J.: Prentice-Hall, 1971), pp. 21, 210.

8. Ibid.

9. See Michele Ingrassia, "Virgin Cool," *Newsweek* (October 17, 1994), pp. 59–69.

10. Edward G. Laumann, John H. Gagnon, Robert T. Michael, Stuart Michaels. *The Social Organization of Sexuality: Sexual Practices in the United States* (Chicago: University of Chicago Press, 1994).

11. National Center for Health Statistics, "Fertility, Family Planning, and Women's Health: New Data from the 1995 National Survey of Family Growth," *Vital and Health Statistics* (May 1997), Table 25, p. 45.

12. Liza Mundy, "Sex and Sensibility," The Washington Post (July 16, 2000), p. WMAG17.

13. Centers for Disease Control and Prevention, *Youth Risk Behaviors Surveillance: United States 2001* (Rockville, MD: U.S. Government Printing Office, 2002), Table 30.

14. Laurie L. Meschke, Suzanne Bartholomae, and Shannon R. Zentall, "Adolescent Sexuality and Parent-Adolescent Processes: Promoting Healthy Teen Choices," *Family Relations* 49 (April 2000): 143–154.

15. Ibid.

16. Cheryl Wetzstein, "Abstinence Makes the Heart Grow Fonder," *Insight of the News* (September 18, 2000), p. 31.

17. Edward G. Laumann, et al., *The Social Organization of Sexuality: Sexual Practice in the United States.*

18. National Institute of Child Health and Human Development, "Strong Religious Views Decrease Teens' Likelihood of Having Sex," April 2, 2003, News Release.

19. 2000 General Social Survey, National Opinion Research Center, "Trends in Attitudes toward Non-traditional Sexual Behavior." Available at www.cpsr.umich.edu:8080/GSS/homepage.htm [July 13, 2003].

20. Ibid.

21. Edward G. Laumann, John H. Gagnon, Robert T. Michael, and Stuart Michaels. *The Social Organization of Sexuality: Sexual Practices in the United States.* Chicago: University of Chicago Press, 1994; John O. Billy, Korey Tanfer, William R. Grady, and Daniel H. Klepinger, "The Sexual Behavior of Men in the United States," *Family Planning Perspectives* 25 (1993): 52–60; Kathryn Kost and Jacqueline D. Forrest, "American Women's Sexual Behavior and Exposure to Risk of Sexually Transmitted Diseases," *Family Planning Perspectives* 24 (1992): 244–254.

22. George Sponaugle, "Attitudes Toward Extra Marital Relations" in Kathleen McKinney and Susan Sprecher (eds.), *Human Sexuality: The Social and Interpersonal Context* (Norwood, N.J.: Ablex, 1990), p. 205.

23. National Institute of Allergy and Infectious Diseases, *An Introduction to Sexually Transmitted Diseases.* Available at http://www.niaid.nih.gov/factsheets/stdinfo.htm [July 13, 2003]. See also National Center for Health Statistics, *Health, United States: 2002,* Table 53.

24. Ibid.

25. Kate Millet, in *Not a Love Story* (National Film Board of Canada, 1983).

26. Adil Mustafa Ahmad, "The Erotic and Pornographic in Arab Culture," *British Journal of Aesthetics* 34 (July 1994): 278–284.

27. Gail Dines, Robert Jensen, and Ann Russo, *Pornography: The Production and Consumption of Inequality* (New York: Routledge, 1997). See also Gloria Steinem, "Erotica and Pornography: A Clear and Present Difference." *Ms.* (November 1978), pp. 53–54, 75–78.

28. Susan Brownmiller, *Against Our Will* reprint ed. (New York: Ballantine Books, 1993), pp. 442–443.

29. Joel Stein, "Porn Goes Mainstream," *Time* (September 7, 1998), p. 54; Anthony Flint, "Skin Trade Spreading Across U.S.," *Boston Sunday Globe* (December 1, 1996), p. A1.

30. Eric Schlosser, "The Business of Pornography, *U.S. News & World Report* (February 10, 1997), pp. 43–44.

31. "Patterns of Exposure to Erotic Material," *Report of the Commission on Obscenity and Pornography* (Washington, D.C.: U.S. Government Printing Office, 1970).

32. Attorney-General's Commission on Pornography, *Report to the Attorney General* (Washington, D.C.: U.S. Government Printing Office, 1986).

33. Edward L. Donnerstein and Daniel G. Linz, "The Question of Pornography," *Psychology Today* (December 1986), p. 59.

34. For a recent example, see Rachel K. Bergen and Kathleen A. Bogle, "Exploring the Connection Between Pornography and Sexual Violence," *Violence and Victims* 15 (Fall 2000): 227–234.

35. Catherine Itzin, *Pornography: Women, Violence, and Civil Liberties* (Oxford: Clarendon Press, 1993); see also Diana E. H. Russell (ed.), *Making Violence Sexy: Feminist Views on Pornography* (New York: Teachers College Press, 1993).

36. Elizabeth Cramer, et al., "Violent Pornography and Abuse of Women: Theory to Practice," *Violence and Victims* 13 (1998): 319–332.

37. Sandra L. Caron and D. Bruce Carter, "The Relationships among Sex Role Orientation, Egalitarianism, Attitudes toward Sexuality, and Attitudes toward Violence against Women," *Journal of Social Psychology* 137 (1997): 568–587; Michael S. Kimmel and Annulla Linders, "Does Censorship Make a Difference? An Aggregate Empirical Analysis of Pornography and Rape," *Journal of Psychology and Human Sexuality* 8 (1996): 1–20.

38. See Nadine Strossen, *Defending Pornography* (New York: New York University Press, 2000); Carol Avedon, *Nudes, Prudes, and Attitudes: Pornography and Censorship* (Cheltenham, England: New Clarion, 1994).

39. National Coalition for the Protection of Children and Families, "Harm Is Just a Mouse Click Away." Available at www.nationalcoalition.org [July 13, 2003].

40. Gary Chapman, "Not So Naughty," *New Republic* (July 31, 1995), p. 11.

41. Linda Greenhouse, "Court, 9-0, Protects Speech on Internet," *New York Times* (June 27, 1997), p. A1.

42. Amy Harmon, "Earthbound Laws vs. Cyberspace Sprawl," *Sunday Record* (March 23, 1997), p. RO1.

43. Edward L. Donnerstein and Daniel G. Linz, "Mass Media Sexual Violence and Mass Viewers," *American Behavior Scientist* 29 (1986): 601–618.

44. See Margaret Hornblower, "The Skin Trade," *Time* (June 21, 1993), pp. 44–51; Helen Reynolds, *The Economics of Prostitution* (Springfield, Ill.: Charles C. Thomas, 1986).

45. Arno Karlen, *Sexuality and Homosexuality,* (New York: W. W. Norton, 1971), p. 140.

46. Alex Thio, *Deviant Behavior,* 6th ed. (Boston: Allyn & Bacon, 1998).

47. Eleanor M. Miller, *Street Woman* (Philadelphia: Temple University Press, 1987).

48. T. M. Williams and William Kornblum, *Growing Up Poor* (Boston: Heath/Lexington Books, 1985).

49. Ronald L. Simons and Les B. Whitbeck, "Sexual Abuse as a Precursor to Prostitution and Victimization Among Adolescent and Adult Homeless Women," *Journal of Family Issues* 12 (September 1991): 361–379.

50. See D. Kelly Weisberg, *Children of the Night: A Study of Adolescent Prostitution* reprint ed. (Lexington, Mass.: Lexington Books, 1990); Nanette Davis, "The Prostitute: Developing a Deviant Subculture," in James H. Henslin (ed.), *Studies in the Sociology of Sex* (Englewood Cliffs, N.J.: Prentice-Hall, 1988).

51. See David F. Luckenbill, "Deviant Career Mobility: The Case of Male Prostitutes," in Delos H. Kelly (ed.), *Deviant Behavior,* 3d ed. (New York: St. Martin's Press, 1989), pp. 485–503; D. Kelly Weisberg,

Children of the Night; K. N. Ginzburg, "The 'Meat Rack': A Study of the Male Homosexual Prostitute," in C. D. Bryant (ed.), *Sexual Deviancy in Social Context* (New York: Human Sciences Press, 1982).

52. Nanette Davis, "The Prostitute."

53. Differential association theory was formulated by Edwin H. Sutherland, *Principles of Criminology* (Philadelphia: Lippincott, 1939).

54. See Charles H. McCaghy, Timothy A. Capron, and J. D. Jamieson, *Deviant Behavior,* 6th ed. (New York: Allyn & Bacon, 2002); Daniel S. Campagna and Donald L. Poffenberger, *The Sexual Trafficking in Children: An Investigation of the Child Sex Trade* (Dover, Mass.: Auburn House, 1988); Elaine Landau, *On the Streets: The Lives of Adolescent Prostitutes* (New York: J. Messner, 1987); D. Kelly Weisberg, *Children of the Night.*

55. N. Marshall and J. Hendclass, "Drugs and Prostitution," *Journal of Drug Issues* 2 (Spring 1986): 237–248.

56. James A. Inciardi et al., "Prostitution, IV Drug Use, and Sex-for-Crack Exchanges Among Serious Delinquents: Risks for HIV Infection," *Criminology* 29 (1991): 231–235; Carole A. Campbell, "Prostitution, AIDS, and Preventive Health Behavior," *Social Science and Medicine* 32 (1991): 1367–1378.

57. Edward Laumann, Robert Michael, Stuart Michaels, and John Gagnon, *The Social Organization of Sexuality* (Chicago: University of Chicago Press, 1994), p. 81.

58. Nanette Davis, "The Prostitute."

59. Robert F. Meier and Marshall B. Clinard, *Sociology of Deviant Behavior,* 11th ed. (Belmont, Calif.: Wadsworth, 2000).

60. Linda M. Rio, "Psychological and Sociological Research and the Decriminalization or Legalization of Prostitution," *Archives of Sexual Behavior* 20 (1991): 205–218.

61. Carole A. Campbell, "Prostitution, AIDS, and Preventive Health Behavior."

62. See Donna M. Hughes, "The Natasha Trade: The Transnational Shadow Market of Trafficking in Women," *Journal of International Affairs* 53 (Spring 2000): 625–651.

63. Margaret Hornblower, "The Skin Trade."

64. John West and Donald J. Templer, "Child Molestation, Rape, and Ethnicity," *Psychological Reports* 75 (December 1994): 1326.

65. See Elisa Romano and Rayleen V. DeLuca, "Exploring the Relationship Between Childhood Sexual Abuse and Adult Sexual Perpetration," *Journal of Family Violence* 12 (March 1997): 85–98.

66. U.S. Department of Health and Human Services, National Center on Child Abuse and Neglect, National Child Abuse and Neglect Data System, *Child Maltreatment, 2001,* Table 3-5.

67. "Disturbing New Figures About Child Abuse," *Maclean's* (July 21, 1997), p. 15.

68. Jim Hopper, *Child Abuse: Statistics, Research, and Resources.* Available at: www.jimhopper.com/abstats [July 13, 2003].

69. Anna Salter, *Treating Child Sex Offenders and Victims* (Newbury Park, Calif.: Sage, 1988).

70. Katherine Beckett, "Culture and the Politics of Signification: The Case of Child Sexual Abuse, *Social Problems* 43 (February 1996): 57–76.

71. Hilary Kaiser, "Clergy Sexual Abuse in U.S. Mainline Churches," *American Studies International* 34 (April 1996): 30–42.

72. Joan Biskupic, "High Court Upholds 'Megan's Law' in Controversial Decision," *The Washington Post* (February 24, 1998), p. 3.

73. Ashley Broughton, "Sex Offender Tracking Lags," *Salt Lake Tribune,* (February 24, 2003); Klaus Kids Foundation, *Megan's Law by State.* Available at www.meganslaw.com/ [December 8, 2003].

74. Kingsley Davis, "The Sociology of Prostitution," *American Sociological Review* 2 (1932): 744–755.

75. Laurie Shrage, *Moral Dilemmas of Feminism: Prostitution, Adultery, and Abortion* (New York: Routledge, 1994).

76. Susan Brownmiller, *Against Our Will,* pp. 442, 446.

77. Catharine A. MacKinnon, *Only Words,* reprint ed. (Cambridge, Mass.: Harvard University Press, 1996).

78. See Martha L. Shockey, "Class Dismissed? Doing the Life," in Jody O'Brien and Judith A. Howard (eds.), *Everyday Inequalities: Critical Inquiries* (Malden, Mass.: Blackwell Publishing, 1998), pp. 213–236.

79. Rose Weitz, "From Accommodation to Rebellion: Tertiary Deviance and the Radical Redefinition of Lesbianism," in Joseph W. Schneider and John I. Kitsuse (eds.), *Studies in the Sociology of Social problems* (Westport, Conn.: Ablex Publishing, 1984).

Glossary

Ability grouping Also known as tracking; placing students of comparable ability in the same class to maximize effective instruction.

Absolute deprivation A standard of living below the minimum necessary to secure the basic necessities of life.

Abuse Broadly, both physical and psychological harm, but narrowly the former alone as substantiated by the empirical evidence of police records.

Addiction A state of habitual drug use to such an extent that cessation causes severe physical and/or psychological trauma.

Affirmative action Antidiscriminatory policy to enhance the hiring of members of designated minority groups.

Alienation Disconnection from meaningful or authentic social participation resulting from loss of control of one's life or being forced to do senseless work.

Altruistic escape When the social group places more value on the group and its beliefs than on individual life, people more easily give up their individuality or even their lives when confronted with adversity.

Anomie A feeling of confusion and loss of direction resulting from rapid change or breakdown of social norms and values.

Antagonistic drug A counteractive drug causing either nausea from alcoholic drinking or prevention of euphoria if a narcotic is taken.

Anthropocentrism The belief that humans are the center and rightful rulers of the planet; the rejection of the idea we are only part of the ecosystem.

Aquifer Natural underground water storage, easily polluted by seepage from chemical dumps.

Ascribed status A label conferred on us at birth that determines how others define and treat us for our entire lives.

Assimilation The process by which members of racial or ethnic minorities are able to function within a society without indicating any marked cultural, social, or personal differences from the people of the majority group.

Biodiversity The variety of plant species and organic life found within a specific environment.

Bioethics The moral considerations in prolonging or aborting lives.

Blaming the victim Identifying the poor as responsible for their poverty and/or other problems instead of considering externally imposed conditions such as unemployment or lack of education.

Boomer city The most common type of edge city, usually situated at the intersection of two major highways, with a shopping center forming its urban core.

Business ethic   The belief that growth is always good and resulting pollution and shortage problems can be handled by new technologies.

Career   The chosen vocation of an individual, including such socially defined deviant paths as prostitution or drug dealing.

Charter schools   Innovative private schools that operate with less state regulation but higher accountability for achieving educational results.

Child molestation   The legal term for child sexual abuse, which occurs when an adult engages in sexual activity with a minor.

Citizens' militias   Paramilitary groups that cloak themselves in the Constitution even as they acknowledge no federal laws or authority.

Cohabitation   An arrangement where a man and a woman share a common dwelling without being legally married.

Commodity-self   When an individual evaluates herself/himself only in terms of what will be salable to others; what pleases society.

Community   A neighborhood or other group in which individuals feel emotionally connected and willing to support each other.

Community policing   A strategy that creates a strong working relationship between the police and the community to control crime.

Conflict orientation   A view of society that focuses on the social processes of tension, competition, and inequality.

Conglomerates   Large corporations owning businesses in greatly diversified fields.

Convenience sample   A nonobjective selection process that negates making generalizations about the results because of uncertainty that it represents a fair cross-section of the public.

Cost overruns   Expenditures allowed because of unforeseen production costs incurred in a multi-year project.

Crime index   The eight serious crimes tracked monthly by the FBI: murder, forcible rape, burglary, robbery, aggravated assault, larceny, motor vehicle theft, and arson.

Crime rate   The number of crimes permitted per 100,000 people, which allows for comparisons of crime in one city or region with another.

Criminal terrorism   Use of the tactics of terrorism for personal gain.

Culture of poverty   A controversial viewpoint arguing that the disorganization and pathology of lower-class culture is self-perpetuating through cultural transmission.

Date rape   Also known as acquaintance rape, it is forcible sexual activity by someone known to the victim.

Deductive hypothesis   The process of drawing a conclusion by reasoning about what is known or assumed.

Deinstitutionalization   The release of mental patients into the community.

Demographic transition theory   The theory that non-Western countries will follow the three-stage transition from high fertility and mortality to low fertility and mortality that occurred in Western countries.

Demography   The scientific study of the population, such as birth and death rates, migration, median age, and so on.

Depressant   A sedative-hypnotic drug intended to relieve stress or anxiety but often overused or abused.

Deviance   The violation of social norms beyond the allowed zone of tolerance.

Differential association   Social relationships oriented toward particular types of people.

Downsizing   The reduction in personnel in an organization to achieve greater efficiency and/or cost savings.

Ecofeminism   An approach that identifies the values and practices of patriarchal societies as the fundamental causes of environmental problems.

Ecosystem   The total interconnected, nondivisible environment; to understand one element requires studying the whole.

Edge city   An urban center that develops on the fringe of an older urban area.

Empirical referent   A definitive, observable form that can be accurately measured.

Eroticism   The vivid depiction of sexual passion and love.

Euthanasia   The putting to death, by a painless method, of terminally ill or seriously debilitated person; mercy killing.

Eutrophication   Fertilizer pollution of lakes and streams, stimulating heavy growth of algae that can kill the waterway by depleting its oxygen.

Exponential growth   Increases measured in their doubling capacity rather than in slow upwards progression.

Expressive leader   One who guides decision-making and task completion.

Extended family   A nuclear family extended to include the parental generations and also sometimes to include relatives such as aunts and uncles; two or more kinship families sharing economic and social responsibilities.

Extrinsic satisfaction   Factors enhancing job satisfaction, such as income, supervision, and working conditions.

False consciousness   A subjective understanding of one's situation that does not correspond to the objective fact(s).

False values   Dominant group emphasis, say conflict theorists, on competition-success that alienates people.

Fast track   When women delay child-bearing or forego motherhood entirely to give full commitment to the management to earn promotions over other candidates.

Feminist orientation   Viewpoint that incorporates subjective, empathetic advocacy of feminist value orientations.

Feminization of poverty   A term describing the rapid rise of female-headed households living in poverty.

Fetal alcohol syndrome   Addiction and congenital problems suffered by infants born to alcoholic mothers.

Fetal narcotic syndrome   Addiction and withdrawal symptoms suffered by infants born to narcotic addict mothers.

Flex time   An arrangement which allows workers, within predetermined limits, to set their own working hours.

Functionalist orientation   A macro view of society that examines the relationship between the parts and the whole of a social system.

Gateway drug   The unsubstantiated belief that use of a nonaddictive drug such as marijuana has a causal effect in leading to the use of other, more dangerous, drugs.

Gender identity   Culture-induced traits that males and females integrate into their personalities.

Gender inequality   When the distribution of power, prestige, and property are arbitrarily assigned on the basis of sex, not individual merit.

Gentrification   The buying and rehabilitation of buildings in decaying urban neighborhoods by middle- and high-income families.

Glass ceiling   A barrier preventing women from rising above middle management ranks.

Grade inflation   A liberal grading practice resulting in disproportionate numbers of high grades and distorting the picture of what really was learned.

Greenfield city   A planned edge city spread over thousands of acres.

Greenhouse effect   When the combustion of fossil fuels produces an accumulation of carbon dioxide to form a layer that reflects back the earth's heat instead of letting it radiate into the atmosphere.

Guaranteed annual income   Providing a minimum income through government-funded income maintenance programs for low-income families.

Health Maintenance Organizations (HMOs)   Groups that offer lower-cost preventive and corrective health care through prepaid group health plans.

"Heroin chic"   The depiction of heroin use in fashion photography, films, and art as having some sort of mystique.

Heterosexism   The attraction of people of the opposite sex to one another.

Hierarchy of needs   Abraham Maslow's concept that human needs exist in certain levels of priority.

Homelessness   An inability to maintain a permanent shelter for oneself and one's dependents, if any.

Homophobia   An irrational fear of gay people.

Hostile environment   As defined by the Supreme Court, any atmosphere so sexually tainted by abuse that it is too antagonistic for one to continue in it.

Hypothesis   A specific statement that predicts a relationship between variables.

Impression management   Conscious role behavior to elicit certain responses.

Incest   Sexual relations between close relatives in violation of societal norms.

Incidence   Measurement of the seriousness of a problem by the number of new cases within a given time period.

Inductive hypothesis   Drawing a general conclusion by reasoning from particular facts.

Infrastructure   A region's system of roads, bridges, water supply, and waste disposal to support its population.

Inner-ring suburbs   Older suburbs directly adjacent to a city.

Institution   An organized set of rules for doing things, centering on a particular societal activity, such as education, family, government, and so on.

Institutional discrimination   Differential and unequal treatment of a group or groups deeply pervading social customs and institutions, often subtly and informally.

Instrumental leader   One who holds the group together and guides their emotions.

Interactionist orientation   A micro view of society that examines how people influence, act toward, and respond to one another.

Interdependent functioning   A mutually supportive arrangement in which the actions of one person or element complements that of another for the benefit of both.

Interlocking directorates   Occur when executives or directors from one corporation sit on the board of directors of another corporation.

Intrinsic satisfaction   Factors enhancing job satisfaction, such as sense of personal achievement, responsibility, and challenge.

IQ test   Measurements of intellectual aptitudes in language, mathematical reasoning, and spatial and symbolic relationships.

Judicial discretion   When judges have flexibility to determine the severity of the sanctions imposed for the violation of the same rule.

Juvenile delinquency   A legal category for violations of law committed by a young person defined as a minor.

Juvenile Justice Code   The laws and court structure set up specifically to deal with persons under sixteen.

Labeling Theory   A theory explaining negative effects of societal labeling on concepts of self among poor people.

Labor racketeering   Infiltrating labor unions to gain access to pension funds and to extort money from management to avoid labor disputes.

Latent functions   The hidden, unexpected effects of a social change, not manifestly obvious when the change was planned.

Limbic system   The ring of structures that surround the brain stem and constitute the most primitive portions of the forebrain.

Literacy   The ability to read, write and comprehend.

Magnet schools   Urban schools offering special, exceptional programs to attract students from many districts in an effort to achieve integration.

Male anomie   A state of normlessness among men, resulting from an inability to define their masculine role in a sexually liberated society.

Manifest functions   Obvious and intended results of some element in a social system.

Master status   The most important position determining one's social identity and affecting most aspects of one's life.

Means-tested programs   Government assistance programs, where eligibility rests on income.

Medicaid   State-administered health payment program, partly federally funded, to assist the poor, blind, and disabled.

Medicare   Federally funded health payment program to assist those over sixty-five.

Megacities   Metropolitan areas with populations of 10 million or more.

Megalopolis   The interpenetration of previously separate metropolitan regions in commerce and communications.

Megamergers   The acquisitions of companies with assets valued at $1 billion or more by a multi- billion dollar company.

Methadone maintenance   A means of treating heroin addiction through stabilization by substituting daily dosages of methadone, a synthetic opiate.

Military-industrial complex   Term coined by President Eisenhower to describe military establishment and private firms doing business together.

Minimum-competency test (MCT)   A standardized test measuring knowledge of basic skills in reading, writing, and math, often a precondition to earning a high school diploma.

Mommy track   When women try to juggle both family and work, which often slows or halts their upward mobility within the company.

Moral entrepreneur   Howard Becker's term to describe any person who creates and enforces definitions of deviance.

Mores   Powerful norms with great moral significance whose violation prompts public outrage.

Motherhood mandate   The societal requirement that, to be complete, a woman must have children.

Multinational corporations   Large corporations operating across national boundaries, with plants and investments in many countries.

Narcissism   Excessive concentration on one's self, appearance, pleasure, and "scoring" in social competition.

Narcotics   Drugs having both a sedative and pain-relieving action, whether natural opiates (codeine, morphine, opium) or synthetic (heroin, methadone, meperidine, or Demerol).

National Crime Victimization Survey   An interview alternative to official statistics as reported in the UCR that reveals information about nonreported crimes and their victims.

Neuroses   Personality disorders including deep anxiety or depression, hypochondria, phobias, compulsive actions, and psychosomatic illness.

New value consensus   Proposal that industrialization values need replacement through voluntary simplicity and less economic complexity, conspicuous consumption, material wealth, and technical gadgetry now thought necessary for human survival.

New woman networks   Recent organizations of working women helping each other's professional progress, just as the "old boy" networks have helped men.

No-fault divorce   Dissolving a marriage by mutual consent, without blaming either party.

Normative integration   The mutual sharing of values and attitudes that allows people to live together equally and harmoniously.

Nuclear family   A unit consisting of a husband and wife and their children.

Occupational identity   Development of self-identification, self-respect, and prestige from one's work.

Oligopoly   When a few producers dominate an entire industry and thus control pricing in that market.

Operational definition   A definition that states a concept in terms that can be measured through research.

Overmedicalization   The view that the medical establishment has too much control over society and people's lives.

Patriarchal unit   A form of the family in which one male has dominance over the females.

Patriarchy   A social structure in which males dominate females.

Photosynthesis   When plants, aided by chlorophyll as a catalyst, use sunlight as a source of energy to absorb carbon dioxide and water.

Pink-collar jobs   Occupations stereotypically identified with women and therefore predominantly female.

Plea bargain   Pleading guilty to a lesser charge to resolve the matter quickly without a time-consuming trial.

Pluralism   A state in which minorities can maintain their distinctive subcultures and simultaneously interact with relative equality in the larger society.

Police discretion   When police flexibility in determining whether or not to make an arrest may reflect societal prejudices, leading to discriminatory behavior and/or preferential treatment.

Political fragmentation   The governance structure of numerous local municipalities in a metropolitan region, resulting in inability to adapt to regional needs.

Pornography   The graphic depiction of sexual behavior resulting in female or male dehumanization, degradation, and exploitation.

Postmodern orientation   A study of society breaking sharply with the past and emphasizing a bleaker, more complex world.

Price leadership   When a few producers dominate an industry and adopt coordinated pricing or parallel pricing to avoid price competition.

Prosecutorial discretion   When authorities decide how to apportion their resources to best serve their community.

Prostitution   The unemotional act of selling sexual favors for money or goods.

Psychoactive drug   Any chemical substance affecting consciousness, mood, or perception in an individual.

Psychoses   Severe personality disorders including paranoia, schizophrenia, manic depression, and melancholia.

Public housing   Government-built, owned and managed residences with subsidized rents and income limits for inhabitants.

Quality of life   Measuring and judging the worth of our lives not just by the quantity of things we have or produce but by our health and happiness.

Quasi-theory   A pseudo-scientific effort to define a problem in terms of its solution rather than defining its cause first and then finding the solution.

Quintile   One-fifth of a total group or population.

Random sample   An objective process that allows everyone the same chance of being selected.

Recidivism   A relapse into crime by those convicted of a previous crime.

Redistribution of wealth   A radical concept to eliminate the wide gulf between rich and poor by nationalizing large corporations, seizing large fortunes, and "soaking" the rich.

Redistricting   Redrawing boundary lines within a community to achieve a racial balance yet retain neighborhood schools.

Redlining   The designation of certain neighborhoods as "bad risk" areas for mortgages or home improvement loans.

Relative deprivation   A standard of living below that of most others in society, but not necessarily threatening to life or health.

Repressive terrorism   Use of the tactics of terrorism by the group in power.

Residential patterning   The type of settlement followed by a particular group of people.

Revolutionary terrorism   Use of the tactics of terrorism by a group hoping to gain power.

Revolving door   The continual interchange of administrative personnel between corporations and the government military.

Road rage   Aggressive driving by an impatient or angry driver trying to intimidate, injure, or even kill others after some type of traffic confrontation.

Role entrapment   The culturally defined need to be "feminine" that prevents many women from doing things that would help them achieve success and self-realization.

Safe sex   Physical sexual intimacy without any exchange of body fluids.

Scenario   An organized story about a possible future, exemplifying current trends and expectations and showing their impact on life in the future.

School voucher   When parents receive a payment guarantee from the state for education costs at the elementary or secondary school of their choice.

Second-hand smoke   Also known as environmental tobacco smoke (ETS), it is a potent carcinogen that poses health hazards to nonsmokers.

Section 8   A publicly-funded program which enables tenants to find private market housing and have the government pay two-thirds of the "fair rental value" directly.

Secularization   The long-term trend of the lessening power of established religion in social life, and the increasing power of science, technology, and rationality.

Sexism   Prejudicial attitudes and discriminatory behaviors based on gender.

Sexual harassment   Sexual advances or requests and sexual remarks or behaviors that are intimidating, hostile, or offensive in the working environment, especially if rejection of the advance is used as the basis of a future employment decision.

Sexual victimization   Sexual abuse because of age, naivete and relationship to the abuser, such as in father-daughter incest.

Single-parent families   Family units consisting of one parent and his or her children, the consequence of divorce, illegitimacy, or death of a spouse.

Situationality of sex differences   Environmental demands, not biological differences determining the responsibilities of males and females.

Social engineering   Use of the schools to correct the inequities in society and to fit individuals into adult occupational slots.

Social promotions   Moving children through grades with their age peers regardless of actual learning achievement.

Socioeconomic status One's position in society resulting from a combination of income, occupation, and education.

Sociological imagination An objective way of viewing what happens to individuals within the larger context of what is happening in society.

Skills mismatch The unavailability of jobs in a particular area that correspond to the qualifications of its residents.

Standpoint theory A framework for analysis grounded in concrete experience, not in abstract concepts, to formulate a distinctive—often feminist—perspective on reality.

Status offenses A wide range of activities once defined as crimes for those sixteen and under, such as running away, cutting school, or being uncontrollable.

Status position Position one holds in the social system.

STD Sexually transmitted disease.

Stewardess syndrome A ritualistic action of smiling warmly at strangers we have just met as if sharing some deep intimacy.

Strategic policing An aggressive tactic to reduce street crime through computer analysis of the most frequent crime locales, then directing increased patrols, decoys, and sting operations in those areas.

Structured observation An experimental comparison in the field or laboratory to gauge the effect of one variable upon another.

Survey research Data gathering through means of a structured questionnaire or interview.

Teacher expectations The positive or negative influence of an instructor on student achievement.

Technocrats Those with technical expertise, who provide the input and direction for corporate decisions affecting national policy and the quality of life.

Terrorism The use of intimidation, coercion, threats, and violent attacks to achieve the objectives of an individual or group.

Tertiary occupation A job providing services, such as banking, commerce, education, health care, and legal services.

Therapeutic communities A total immersion program in which the addict voluntarily lives for over a year in a treatment center in a structured environment.

Threshold The point at which the ecosystem reaches overload and can no longer detoxify the pollutants it encounters.

Total fertility rate The number of children a woman has in her lifetime.

Total institution A place of work or residence, such as a mental institution, where individuals are physically and socially insulated from the outside world.

Trickle-down economics Provide incentives in the private sector for expansion and greater employment that arguably create a period of prosperity that trickles down to the lowest strata so that all benefit.

Trigger effect When an action, even a relatively small human-made input, totally upsets the natural balance of nature with negative results.

Unconscious ideology A status requirement, such as motherhood, that is so deeply embedded in our cultue that it is taken for granted.

Underemployment When circumstances force people to take less challenging and financially rewarding jobs than their education and experience would seem to qualify them for.

Uniform Crime Report A common standard used by local, county, and state law enforcement agencies in defining and tabulating criminal offenses, and then reporting them to the Federal Bureau of Investigation (FBI).

Uptown city An edge city built on top of a pre-automobile city and becoming a new entity.

Urban homesteading A process whereby a city sells abandoned or foreclosed dwellings at a token price and buyers rehabilitate them within a time limit and also live there for a minimum number of years.

Urban renewal A publicly funded process of slum clearance and rebuilding.

Values Socially shared ideas about what is good, right, and desirable.

Vigilantism The use of violent force to protect community values, justified by saying no other way exists to preserve that way of life; many cruel and ugly acts against innocent people have been committed in the name of preserving community values.

Violence subculture   The concept of pervasive subculture that teaches proviolent values and attitudes, defining violence as an appropriate response to a perceived challenge or insult.

Water mining   The pumping of groundwater faster than it can be replenished.

Weberian paradox   The irony of scientific efficiency improving our lifestyle while simultaneously undermining our meaning systems and emotional security.

Welfare   Government economic assistance to societal members with incomes below an established minimum for securing basic necessities of life.

Western World View   The optomistic belief that humans have the right, even duty, to exploit nature and that all environmental problems have a technological solution.

White-collar crime   Law violations by persons of the upper socioeconomic class, committed as part of their normal business activity, not as part of some individual pathology.

Zero population growth (ZPG)   A stabilized population in which the number of annual births equals the number of annual deaths.

Index